TEACHER PREP

**MERRILL
PRENTICE HALL**

S0-AGD-722

Teacher Preparation Classroom

See a demo at
www.prenhall.com/teacherprep/demo

Your Class. Their Careers. Our Future. Will your students be prepared?

We invite you to explore our new, innovative and engaging website and all that it has to offer you, your course, and tomorrow's educators! Preview this site today at www.prenhall.com/teacherprep/demo. Just click on "go" on the login page to begin your exploration.

Organized around the major courses pre-service teachers take, the Teacher Preparation site provides media, student/teacher artifacts, strategies, research articles, and other resources to equip your students with the quality tools needed to excel in their courses and prepare them for their first classroom.

This ultimate online education resource will provide you and your students access to:

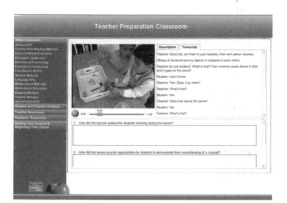

Online Video Library. More than 250 video clips—each tied to a course topic and framed by learning goals and Praxis-type questions—capture real teachers and students working in real classrooms.

Student and Teacher Artifacts. More than 200 student and teacher classroom artifacts—each tied to a course topic and framed by learning goals and application questions—provide a wealth of materials and experiences to help your students observe children's developmental learning.

Lesson Plan Builder. Step-by-step guidelines and lesson plan examples support students as they learn to build high-quality lesson plans.

Articles and Readings. Over 500 articles from ASCD's renowned journal *Educational Leadership* are available. The site also includes Research Navigator, a searchable database of additional educational journals.

Strategies and Lessons. Over 500 research-supported instructional strategies appropriate for a wide range of grade levels and content areas.

Licensure and Career Tools. Resources devoted to helping your students pass their licensure exam; learn standards, law, and public policies; plan a teaching portfolio; and succeed in their first year of teaching.

How to ORDER *Teacher Prep* for you and your students:

For students to receive a *Teacher Prep* Access Code with this text, instructors **must** provide a special value pack ISBN number on their textbook order form. To receive this special ISBN, please email **Merrill.marketing@pearsoned.com** and provide the following information:

- Name and Affiliation
- Author/Title/Edition of Merrill text

Upon ordering *Teacher Prep* for their students, instructors will be given a lifetime *Teacher Prep* Access Code.

Library of Congress Cataloging-in-Publication Data

Stichter, Janine P.

An introduction to students with high-incidence disabilities/Janine P. Stichter,
Maureen A. Conroy, James M. Kauffman.

p. cm.

Includes bibliographical references and index.

ISBN 0-13-117802-4 (alk. paper)

1. Special education–United States–Case studies.   2. Inclusive education–United States–
Case studies.   3. Children with disabilities–Education–United States–Case studies.
I. Conroy, Maureen A.   II. Kauffman, James M.   III. Title.

LC3981.P43 2008

371.9–dc22   2006037290

Vice President and Executive Publisher: Jeffery W. Johnston

Executive Editor: Ann Castel Davis

Editorial Assistant: Penny Burleson

Production Editor: Sheryl Glicker Langner

Production Coordination: Donna Leik, Techbooks

Design Coordinator: Diane C. Lorenzo

Cover Design: Jeff Vanik

Cover Image: Fotosearch

Photo Coordinator: Lori Whitley

Production Manager: Laura Messerly

Director of Marketing: David Gesell

Marketing Manager: Autumn Purdy

Marketing Coordinator: Brian Mounts

This book was set in Berkeley Book by Techbooks. It was printed and bound by
R. R. Donnelley & Sons Company. The cover was printed by R. R. Donnelley & Sons
Company.

Chapter Opening Photo Credits: Laura Bolesta/Merrill, p. 3; courtesy of the Library of
Congress, p. 23; GeoStock/Getty Images, Inc.—Photodisc, p. 43; Scott Cunningham/Merrill,
p. 75; David Young-Wolff/PhotoEdit Inc., p. 109; Liz Moore/Merrill, p. 139; Laura Bolesta/
Merrill, p. 165; Patrick White/Merrill, p. 196; Krista Greco/Merrill, p. 235; Ellen B. Senisi/
The Image Works, p. 261; Laura Bolesta/Merrill, p. 285, Hope Madden/Merrill, p. 315

Pearson Education Ltd.
Pearson Education Singapore Pte. Ltd.
Pearson Education Canada, Ltd.
Pearson Education–Japan

Pearson Education Australia Pty. Limited
Pearson Education North Asia Ltd.
Pearson Educación de Mexico, S.A. de C.V.
Pearson Education Malaysia Pte. Ltd.

10 9 8 7 6 5 4 3 2 1
ISBN-10: 0-13-117802-4
ISBN-13: 978-0-13-117802-1

This book is dedicated to the families and children who have taught us the value of evidence-based interventions, and to our fellow researchers who share the sense of responsibility to provide the evidence necessary to support the use of these practices.

Contents

Note: Every effort has been made to provide accurate and current Internet information in this book. However, the Internet and information posted on it are constantly changing, so it is inevitable that some of the Internet addresses listed in this textbook will change.

Historical Foundations of High-Incidence Disabilities

High-Incidence Disabilities: Definition and Prevalence

Devery R. Mock

Appalacian State University

URBAN LEGEND: *The most disabling thing about a disability is the label "disability."*

LEGENDARY THOUGHT: *Labels do not, and in most cases cannot, create disability.*

∷ LABELS AND CATEGORIES

Remember that labels are merely words that we use to designate specific things. Those who object to labeling object to using words. There is no way around it—labeling means using words to describe things. What should not be labeled? What labels should not be used? What are the advantages and disadvantages of labels? These are difficult questions to answer to everyone's satisfaction. But consider the relationship between labels and importance.

According to urban legend, the indigenous people of Alaska have up to 400 words (labels) for different kinds of snow (Pinker, 1994). The legend suggests that this plethora of synonyms reflects the great importance of snow in the lives of these northern-dwelling people. As listeners, we are led to believe that the more relevant something is to someone, the more names it should have. Thus, if something is truly important to us, we abandon specificity and clarity in favor of multiple, inter-changeable words. The opposite idea is that fewer, more precise terms reflect concepts or objects of lesser importance. In actuality, the urban legend is just that—a legend, a myth—false. The indigenous people of Alaska do *not* have 400 names for snow. Experts on the Eskimo language know that it contains as few as two synonyms for snow (Pinker, 1994). Does this mean that snow is less important to Eskimos than once believed? Of course not! Should we conclude that the indigenous people of Alaska do not actually live in a cold, snowy climate? No!

Using language is always tricky, and language pertaining to special education is perhaps the trickiest. Some disabilities have—or, at least, have had—multiple synonyms. For example, learning disabilities have also been known as mild exogenous mental retardation, minimal brain dysfunction, developmental aphasia, dyslexia, perceptual disabilities, perceptual impairment, hyperactivity, and slow learning (Hallahan, Lloyd, Kauffman, Weiss, & Martinez, 2005; Individuals with Disabilities Education Improvement Act of 2004 [IDEA], 2004) as well as neurodevelopmental dysfunction and learning differences (Levine, 2002). Is this variety of imprecise terminology a good thing? Is vague and nonspecific language more desirable than precise and descriptive language? We doubt that it is. As any science or craft develops, its terms expand in number because the subtleties of its knowledge and practice become more important. Labels become more specific.

Some special educators warn that labeling shapes teachers' expectations, exaggerates problems, and assigns blame to the individual who is labeled (Henley, Ramsey, & Algozzine, 2002) or that we have too many labels (Sailor & Roger, 2005). Some seem to believe that labeling is so powerful that it creates a disability by calling the disability into existence (Danforth & Rhodes, 1997; Gallagher, 1998). Following this line of reasoning, refusing to label a disability would somehow eradicate it

(Mostert, Kauffman, & Kavale, 2003). Some people seem to think that fewer, less specific labels are better than more differentiated and precise labels. We address both of these notions in depth in later sections of this text.

We believe it is important to recognize that language is inherently limited. In most cases, language alone cannot create or eradicate disability. Historically, special educators have attempted to increase the precision and specificity of the terms, or labels, that are used to identify and classify disabilities (Hallahan & Mercer, 2002; Kauffman, 2005a, 2006; Kauffman & Landrum, 2006; Kavale & Forness, 2000). We hope that the terminology we use in this book will facilitate the accurate identification and effective education of students with disabilities.

This book focuses on the characteristics of children in three disability categories: (a) **learning disabilities** (LD), (b) **emotional and behavioral disorders** (EBD), and (c) **mild mental retardation** (MMR). These disabilities now account for about 70% of all school-age students identified with disabilities (U.S. Department of Education, 2002). Together they constitute high-incidence disabilities, which occur more frequently than blindness, significant physical impairments, severe mental retardation or deaf-blindness—all of which are considered low-incidence disabilities. **Speech and language impairments** (SLI) and **attention deficit hyperactivity disorder** (ADHD) also occur with relatively high frequency among school-age children. In addition, **high-functioning autism** (HFA) and **traumatic brain injury** (TBI) are now being identified in school-age children with increased frequency and precision. However, students with HFA or TBI are not the topic of this book, except when these disabilities occur simultaneously with LD, EBD, or MMR.

Disability, Handicap, and Inability

The word *handicap* is often used as a synonym for *disability*. In this text, we make a distinction between these two labels. A **disability** is an atypical inability to perform a specific skill or a diminished capacity to perform a particular skill. It is often a lifelong condition that is present in a variety of settings. Although we never abandon hope for a cure, we recognize that at present, high-incidence disabilities such as LD, EBD, and MMR are likely to be lifelong conditions that may put individuals at risk for such things as school failure, poor peer acceptance, and diminished employment (Hallahan et al., 2005; Kauffman, 2005a; Kauffman & Hallahan, 2005b, 2006; Walker, Ramsey, & Gresham, 2004; Walker, Zeller, Close, Webber, & Gresham, 1999).

Another important point here is that although every disability involves an inability, not every inability is a disability. We have to look at ability or inability with reference to the age of the person as well as other contextual variables. Nobody expects a 5-year-old to be able to drive a car or the typical 25-year-old to be able to lift half a ton. We wouldn't expect most 85-year-olds to be able to run 10 miles. However, if a 10-year-old cannot read despite persistent, research-based reading interventions, then we see the inability to read as a disability (for further discussion, see Kauffman & Hallahan, 2005b). In short, a disability is merely an atypical inability to do something important.

A handicap is a disadvantage or inability *imposed* on an individual through an interaction with the demands of a particular environment. For example, a great number of individuals with and without disabilities experience handicaps in the game of golf. The game requires skills that are outside of the repertoire of many people's abilities; thus, most players receive a numerical handicap to compensate for their disadvantaged status. But consider the case of professional golfer Casey Martin. As a member of the Professional Golfers' Association, Martin is highly skilled at the game of golf. Few would argue that he experiences a handicap when driving, putting, or sinking a hole in one. However, when Martin is not allowed to use a golf cart and is required to walk the 18 holes in a standard golf game, he experiences a handicap. Martin was born with a rare circulatory disorder that has made his right leg extremely weak. When required to walk distances, Martin experiences a handicap. His disability is not a handicap in all situations; and more important, Martin's disability does not function as a handicap when he is provided appropriate accommodations.

In the same way, a tenth-grader with **dysgraphia,** a severe writing disability, will experience a handicap when he is required to handwrite an essay on an end-of-grade assessment. However, should this student receive the appropriate accommodation such as a keyboard to type his response, his disability would no longer be a handicap. Disabilities do not necessarily result in handicaps. They are made into handicaps by failure to make accommodations when such accommodations are possible.

:: HIGH-INCIDENCE DISABILITIES AND MILD DISABILITIES

Prevalence

Prevalence refers to the percentage of individuals manifesting a particular disability. In the term *high-incidence disabilities,* the terms *high* and *incidence* clearly suggest disabilities with a level of prevalence that is comparatively high. However, MMR and EBD each affect only about 1% of the school-age population (U.S. Department of Education, 2006). Although a disability affecting 1% of a population hardly seems to be high in incidence, MMR and EBD are considered high-incidence disabilities relative to the low-incidence disabilities of hearing impairments (about 0.1% of the school-age population), visual impairments (approximately 0.04%), deaf-blindness (a miniscule percentage), orthopedic impairments (about 0.1%), other health impairments (roughly 0.44%), autism (around 0.12%), traumatic brain injury (about 0.02%), or multiple disabilities (about 0.19%; U.S. Department of Education, 2002). Thus, even those categories identified in 1% of the population are identified 5 to 10 times as often as the low-incidence categories we named.

When combined with LD, a disability area that has tripled in size over the past three decades and now currently affects more than 4% of the school-age population (U.S. Department of Education, 2006), LD, EBD, and MMR constitute approximately 70% of all students identified with disabilities. In practice, the term *high-incidence* is somewhat misleading because it seems to suggest that MMR and EBD are identified at very high rates. In reality, most researchers contend that EBD is under-identified (Kauffman, 2005a, 2005b). This means that many school-age children and youth who suffer from EBD are not identified with this disability and therefore are ineligible for the protections and services provided through special education. In contrast, some researchers contend that LD is overidentified among school-age children and cite evidence of the rapid increase in prevalence of LD from 1975 to the present. Moreover, these researchers also suggest that the increasing prevalence of LD is causally related to the decreasing prevalence of MMR (Gresham, MacMillan, & Bocian, 1996). In other words, professionals and parents opt for the LD label over the MMR label because the former is ostensibly less stigmatizing than the latter. Not all researchers believe that LD is overidentified (Hallahan & Kauffman, 2006). Such individuals have argued that many of the risks prevalent in our society (e.g., poverty, malnutrition, exposure to prenatal toxins) leave children increasingly more vulnerable to LD. Many would have us believe that the problems of under- and overidentification are easily rectified. Unfortunately, this is not the case. Issues of identification are intricately tied to definitions of disability as well as federal- and state-level policies. As you will read in the remainder of this chapter and in Chapter 2, issues of definition and policy stir great controversy and remain difficult to resolve. Figure 1.1 provides a depiction of the hypothetical relationship of the incidence rates and overlap of LD, MMR and EBD.

Severity

The terms *high-incidence disabilities* and *mild disabilities* are often used synonymously to refer to LD, EBD, and MMR. In this text, we make a distinction between these two terms. We contend that *mild* is somewhat misleading. The term *mild disability* seems to suggest a disability that is not serious or severe. For example, a mild cold is generally considered to be one that is tolerable and does not cause too much discomfort. A mild day is one that is relatively temperate, and a mild-mannered person is one with an easy-going disposition. Unfortunately, LD, MMR, and EBD often have severe implications for the individual. For this reason, we have chosen to use the term *high-incidence disabilities*.

However, high-incidence disabilities, as well as low-incidence disabilities, *can* be severe as well as mild. For example, when reading ability is measured across a population of third graders, most students score at approximately the third-grade level; however, a few score on the early first-grade level, and a few score on the fifth-grade level. In the same way, the population of students with high-incidence

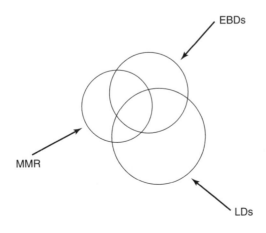

EBDs

MMR

LDs

Hypothetical relationship among the populations having mild mental retardation (MMR), emotional or behavioral disorders (EBDs) and learning disabilities (LDs)

disabilities demonstrate behaviors that vary in severity. Some students with LD achieve 1 to 2 years below grade level, whereas others might fail to progress beyond consonant-vowel-consonant words. Some students with EBD demonstrate noncompliance at persistent, low levels, which might be considered a mild disability. However, others will demonstrate aggressive behavior that puts them, their teachers, and other students at high risk, and such hyperaggression might be considered a severe disability. Some students with MMR might be able to dress and feed themselves by 5 years of age, whereas others might work on toileting issues throughout elementary school. We also see these variations in ability and achievement among individuals with other disabilities.

As we stated earlier, ADHD, autism, and TBI are increasingly recognized in school-age children. In each of these disability areas, severity varies. For example, some students with autism can function in regular classrooms with assistance. These students may be able to interact with peers and complete academic grade-appropriate assignments. Other students with autism may require specialized instructional settings (see Gliona, Gonzales, & Jacobson, 2005). They may need instruction and support in developing prosocial behaviors. For all of these reasons, the educational services that are provided to students with disabilities must also vary in levels of support.

The Importance of Labels

Whether we are speaking of specific categories of disabilities (LD, EBD, or MMR) or all high-incidence disabilities, the practice of classifying a disability or group of disabilities can be very controversial as well as scientifically difficult (Fletcher, Morris, & Lyon, 2003; Hallahan & Kauffman, 2006; Kauffman, 1999, 2002, 2003, 2005a; Kauffman & Hallahan, 2005a). Labels have the potential to stigmatize (Henley et al., 2002), but they are also essential if students with disabilities are to receive effective instructional interventions (Fletcher et al., 2002; Fletcher, Morris, & Lyon, 2003; Walker, Stiller, Severson, Feil, & Golly, 1998). We cannot talk about things without naming them—without labeling them something (Kauffman, 2003, 2006). Ideally, labels should communicate characteristics relevant for treatment.

Teachers and other school professionals must use labels so that students who need assistance are identified. Beyond the labels regularly assigned to students in public schools (e.g., "third grader," "bus rider," or even "student receiving free or reduced-cost lunch"), teachers must carefully and accurately identify those students whose disabilities put them at risk for school failure. In these cases, labels can determine eligibility for services, facilitate the appropriate individualized services and prevent later failure. When used correctly, labels allow educators to offer specific interventions based on individualized need. When used incorrectly, labels are demeaning ways of referring to children or their problems.

Keep this in mind too: We can use labels correctly, but this does not prevent others from misunderstanding or abusing them. Labels are not unique in this regard. You may be able to think of many examples to which this principle applies. Alcohol and other drugs (both therapeutic and recreational), airplanes, computers, and many other substances and devices can be abused. Labels are not the problem; misuse of labels is the problem.

Educational Services

The Individuals with Disabilities Education Improvement Act of 2004 (known as IDEIA or IDEA; first enacted under a different title in 1975) is the federal law that guarantees free and appropriate public education for students with disabilities. Pursuant to this law, students with identified disabilities are to be provided **individualized education programs** (IEPs) in the **least restrictive environment** (LRE) chosen from a **continuum of alternative placements** (CAP) (Hallahan & Kauffman, 2006, 2005a, Herr & Bateman, 2003). The **categorical provision** of special education services is clearly illegal (Bateman & Linden, 1998); this means that it is against the law to assign all students with a particular disability to the same educational program just because they fall into a given category. In other words, we cannot refer all students with MMR to the same classroom just because they all have MMR. This would be akin to an ophthalmologist recommending the same prescription lens for all near-sightedness or a physical therapist prescribing the same exercises for every leg injury. Such practices are, of course, unethical. Treatment must be matched to individual needs. In the same way, instruction must be in response to specific individual student needs. For this reason a decision is not categorically made to instruct all students with high-incidence disabilities in one particular setting. Instead, IDEA 2004 (and its federal predecessors) mandates that each student with an identified disability has a right to an individualized education plan designed to meet his or her specific needs.

Identification

The rights and protections afforded to individuals with disabilities under IDEA all hinge on the accurate identification of the disability. Precise terminology is especially important in the field of special education. Throughout history we have experienced successes and failures related to terminology, all accompanied by a strong measure of controversy. Labeling is essential if we are to communicate, but it is also an inherently dangerous act. Surely, labels can significantly alter a student's academic progress and life experience, especially if the student gets an inappropriate label or those responsible for him or her misunderstand the label's meaning. We cannot have labels for disabilities that have only positive meanings and bring only positive outcomes simply because disabilities are not something we consider desirable (we do not wish them for people, and we try to help people who have them). We cannot achieve positive outcomes in intervention without first identifying those students in need of assistance. Thus, disability must be identified with the utmost seriousness, diligently guarding against doing harm. If we are to employ labels, the benefits must outweigh the costs. To this end, labels should make use of language that minimizes stigma but promotes the delivery of effective intervention services. Stigma does not reside in a label, however, but in what people believe about the label (Kauffman, 2003).

In order to provide specific and appropriate educational services for individuals with high-incidence disabilities, students must be identified as having one of the disability categories stipulated in IDEA 2004:

a. Specific learning disabilities
b. Speech or language impairments
c. Mental retardation
d. Emotional disturbance
e. Multiple disabilities
f. Hearing impairments
g. Orthopedic impairments
h. Other health impairments
i. Visual impairments
j. Autism
k. Deaf-blindness
l. Traumatic brain injury
m. Developmental delay

:: DEFINITIONS AND TERMINOLOGY

Under the umbrella of disabilities recognized as high-incidence are, of course LD, EBD, and MMR. Each of these disabilities is defined within the federal law known as IDEA 2004 (although EBD is defined as emotionally disturbed, or ED). Because definitions and terminology are seldom uncomplicated issues in special education, each disability category has at least one additional definition, most often crafted by researchers or policy makers attempting to improve the specificity of the category. Sometimes these definitions overlap, and sometimes they do not. In each case, definitions are attempts by policy makers and researchers alike to both conceptualize problems and identify those intervention strategies considered appropriate in the treatment of specific disabilities (Hallahan et al., 2005; Kauffman, 2005a; Kauffman & Hallahan, 2005b). Definitions, especially those written into IDEA, communicate implications for policy makers, teachers, parents, students, and funding agencies. Thus, the definitions found in IDEA 2004 stipulate which students may be served under special education and how their special educations are to be funded. For these reasons, the definitions of LD, EBD, and MMR generate considerable controversy.

Emotional and Behavioral Disorders

The disability category that we have heretofore called EBD is actually termed *emotional disturbance* (ED) in IDEA (see Kauffman, 2005a, for a discussion of this difference in terminology). During the 2000–2001 school year, less that 1% (0.72%) of all school children ages 6 to 21 were identified as having emotional disturbance (U.S. Department of Education, 2002). In comparison, professionals have estimated that at least 3% to 6%—more likely 6% to 10%—of the student population currently experience some type of emotional or behavioral problems that warrant specialized educational services (Kauffman, 2005a; Walker et al., 2004). At the very least, more than two thirds of students who *should* be receiving services for EBD are not. One survey indicated that about half of all Americans will meet the criteria for mental illness of some type at some time in their lives and that the onset (when their disorder was first evident) most often was during childhood or adolescence (Kessler, Berglund, Demler, Jin, & Walters, 2005). Nevertheless, most of these children and adolescents with emotional or behavioral problems never received treatment or received treatment only after years had passed (Wang et al., 2005).

According to the interpretation found in federal laws that is used to determine eligibility for special education, **emotional disturbance** is defined as follows:

1. The term means a condition exhibiting one or more of the following characteristics over a long period of time and to a marked degree that adversely affects a child's educational performance:
   a. An inability to learn that cannot be explained by intellectual, sensory, or health factors.
   b. An inability to build or maintain satisfactory interpersonal relationships with peers and teachers.
   c. Inappropriate types of behavior or feelings under normal circumstances.
   d. A general pervasive mood of unhappiness or depression.
   e. A tendency to develop physical symptoms or fears associated with personal or school problems.
2. The term includes schizophrenia. The term does not apply to children who are socially maladjusted, unless it is determined that they have an emotional disturbance.

This definition, which has remained essentially unchanged since 1975 (originating from a definition from the 1950s) requires that students who are to be identified with emotional disturbance demonstrate one or more of the characteristics listed above over a "long period of time and to a marked degree." Neither "long period" nor "marked degree" are operationally defined within the definition; thus, the identification of students with emotional disturbance requires a significant degree of subjective judgment (see Kauffman, 2005a). In addition, the exclusion of students demonstrating social maladjustment seems at odds with the other components of the definition. Such students are likely to demonstrate the inappropriate types of behaviors that seem to be consistent with behavior disorders. This controversial aspect of the definition is addressed in greater detail in Chapter 5.

In response to objections to the federal definition of emotional disturbance, various professional and advocacy groups came together to select new terminology and craft a new definition (Forness, 1988; Forness & Knitzer, 1992). The definition proposed in the 1980s reads as follows:

1. The term *emotional* or *behavioral disorder* means a disability characterized by behavioral or emotional responses in school programs so different from appropriate age, cultural, or ethnic norms that they adversely affect educational

performance, including academic, social, vocational or personal skills, and which:

    a. is more than a temporary, expected response to stressful events in the environment;

    b. is consistently exhibited in two different settings, at least one of which is school-related; and

    c. persists despite individualized interventions within the education program, unless, in the judgment of the team, the child's or youth's history indicates that such interventions would not be effective. Emotional or behavioral disorders can coexist with other disabilities.

2. This category may include children or youth with schizophrenic disorders, affective disorders, anxiety disorders, or other sustained disturbances of conduct or adjustment when they adversely affect educational performance in accordance with section I. (Forness & Knitzer, 1992, p. 13)

Although this definition has yet to be adopted at a federal level, professionals in the field of behavioral disorders believe it to be a marked improvement over the definition currently included in IDEA 2004. Supporters are therefore advocating for the adoption of this definition at both state and federal levels. The debate over the definition of EBD illustrates the point made at the beginning of this chapter: language is a tricky business. Even when professionals agree on the necessity and utility of a certain label, consensual definition of that particular label can be very difficult to reach.

Students who have been identified as having EBD are at great risk for school and postschool failure. Over 40% of students with EBD who are 16 years old or older drop out of school. Within 3 years of leaving school, many of these students have been arrested at least once. Inside schools, students with EBD are strong candidates for both teacher and peer rejection. These students often demonstrate aggressive behavior, noncompliance, disruptive acts, and academic deficits that may make the school environment aversive to both teachers and students. Walker and Sprague (1999) described antisocial students labeled EBD as a violent population with what are often pathological problems and destructive outcomes (Steinberg & Knitzer, 1992; Walker & Spraque, 1999; Walker et al., 2004; Wehby, Symons, Canale, & Go, 1998).

Learning Disabilities

Students with LD (termed *specific learning disability*, or *SLD*, in IDEA) made up 4.36% of all school children ages 6 to 21 during the 2000–2001 school year (U.S. Department of Education, 2002). They represent about half of all students identified with disabilities. Since 1975, the rate at which students with LD are identified has tripled (Hallahan et al., 2005). For these reasons, LD has become a hotly debated disability category. The U.S. Office of Education has retained essentially the same definition of LD since 1975. This definition stipulates:

a. IN GENERAL—The term "specific learning disability" means a disorder in one or more of the basic psychological processes involved in understanding or in using language, spoken or written, which may manifest itself in an imperfect ability to listen, think, speak, read, write, spell, or do mathematical calculations.

b. DISORDERS INCLUDED—The term includes such conditions as perceptual disabilities, brain injury, minimal brain dysfunction, dyslexia, and developmental aphasia.

c. DISORDERS NOT INCLUDED—Such term does not include a learning problem that is primarily the result of visual, learning or motor disabilities, of mental retardation, of emotional disturbance, or of environmental, cultural, or economic disadvantage. (IDEA Amendments of 2004).

This definition, like the federal definition of ED, also requires that practitioners use a significant amount of subjective judgment when identifying students with LD. In identifying this disability, practitioners are asked to rule out several exclusionary criteria that could explain low achievement: (a) visual, learning, or motor disabilities; (b) mental retardation; (c) emotional disturbance; or (d) environmental, cultural, or economic disadvantage.

Not long after the Education for All Handicapped Children Act (the 1975 predecessor to IDEA) was ratified, the National Joint Committee on LD (NJCLD), a group formed by the merging of several professional organizations, proposed a second definition that omitted any reference to **psychological processing.** The NJCLD definition read:

> Learning disabilities is a generic term that refers to a heterogeneous group of disorders manifested by significant difficulties in the acquisition and use of listening, speaking, reading, writing, reasoning, or mathematical abilities. These disorders are intrinsic to the individual and presumed to be due to central nervous system dysfunction. Even though a learning disability may occur concomitantly with other handicapping conditions (e.g., sensory impairment, mental retardation, social and emotional disturbance) or environmental influences (e.g., cultural differences, insufficient-inappropriate instruction, psychogenic factors), it is not the direct result of those conditions or influences. (Hammill, Leigh, McNutt, & Larsen, 1981, p. 336)

Not all researchers agree with the role of central nervous system (CNS) dysfunction stipulated in this definition. In fact, this is one issue among many that seems to divide the field of LD. As a result of this division, the field has been widely criticized for its inability to coherently and consensually craft a specific definition of LD.

Note that neither the definition included in IDEA nor the one proposed by the NJCLD described a specific condition; instead, both attempted to outline a more generic concept. As such, learning disabilities are characterized by **heterogeneity,** probable CNS dysfunction, psychological process disorders, underachievement, manifestations in spoken language, academics or thinking, occurrence across the life span, and the exclusion of other causal conditions (Kavale & Forness, 2000).

In the case of LD, many researchers have asserted that it is difficult, if not impossible, to distinguish between the effects of the exclusionary criteria versus the effects of verifiable disorders in psychological processing. Thus, researchers have found it difficult to distinguish between students with LD and students with "garden variety" low achievement. Researchers have also questioned the reliability and validity of differentiating between students with LD and students with MMR. Many have argued that theses groups are more alike than different, and that the differences are not that important (Francis et al., 1996; Gottlieb et al., 1994; Lyon et al., 2001; Ysseldyke, Algozzine, Shinn, & McGue, 1982). These assertions have been rebutted (Fuchs et al., 2001; Kavale, 2001; Kavale & Forness, 2000; Kavale, Fuchs, & Scruggs, 1994) and countered with evidence suggesting that a particular type of LD—reading disability (RD)—has both a **neurobiological locus** (Filipek, 1996; Galaburda, Menard, & Rosen, 1994; Klingberg et al., 2000; Shaywitz et al., 2000; Zeffiro & Eden, 2000) and a significant degree of **heritability** (Olson, 1999). Nevertheless, questions about the validity of LD remain.

The lack of specificity within the disability category is thought to be a direct result of a flawed identification tool, the **discrepancy formula.** The discrepancy being referred to here is the difference (discrepancy) between IQ and achievement. A child's IQ gives us an idea about what to expect as far as his or her achievement is concerned. So *discrepancy* refers to the difference between what the IQ tells us to expect and the actual achievement of the child on a standardized test. Children with LD then show a big discrepancy—their achievement is way below what we would expect, given their IQ.

Between the enactment of the Education for All Handicapped Children Act (EAHCA) in 1975 and the most recent reauthorization of IDEA in 2004, the discrepancy formula was thought to be the *sine qua non* of learning disabilities (Frankenberger & Fronzaglio, 1991). This formula was originally conceived as a way to operationalize the concept of "unexpected underachievement" that is integral to the construct of learning disabilities. In practice, educators use a formula to calculate the discrepancy between a student's aptitude and his or her actual level of achievement. Discrepancy formulas are currently calculated in a variety of ways, including deviation from grade level, deviation from expectancy, and deviation from ability. Some discrepancy formulas attempt to control for correlation between IQ and achievement through a statistical approach called regression. Although regression-based formulas have successfully distinguished between impaired and unimpaired groups (Francis et al., 1996; Kavale & Forness, 2000), the overwhelming consensus is that the IQ-achievement discrepancy is a poor way to identify students with LD (Baldwin & Vaughn, 1989; Francis et al., 1996; Graham & Harris, 1989; Kavale & Forness, 2000; Keogh, 1987; Lyon, 1989; Norman & Zigmond, 1980; Shaywitz et al., 1992; Siegel, 1989; Vellutino, Scanlon, & Tanzman, 1998; Vellutino, Scanlon, & Lyon, 2000).

For this reason, new criteria for identifying LD have been included in IDEA 2004 and has thereby changed the way in which learning disabilities are identified and treated. The law reads:

a. In determining whether a child has a specific learning disability, a local educational agency may use a process that determines if a child responds to scientific, research-based intervention as a part of the evaluation procedures. [614(b)(2)(3)]

This amendment to IDEA carries serious implications for the identification and remediation of students with LD. This new identification procedure, as well as the discrepancy approach, are discussed in detail in Chapters 4 and 8.

Mild Mental Retardation

Students identified with any level of mental retardation (MR) comprised 0.93% of all school children ages 6 to 21 during the 2000–2001 school year (U.S. Department of Education, 2002). Unlike EBD or LD, MR is regularly divided into levels of severity. Traditionally, mild MR generally represents IQ scores ranging from 55 to 70, and moderate MR represents IQ scores ranging from 54 to 35. Together, these two levels of severity represent approximately 85% of all students identified with MR (Beirne-Smith, Ittenbach, & Patton, 2001). However, other classification schemes involving the level of support needed are additional ways of classifying MR (Hallahan & Kauffman, 2006). We use the IQ levels here for simplicity, although we acknowledge that there are different ways of referring to levels of mental retardation.

MMR is considered a high-incidence disability, whereas MR that is severe (IQ ranging from 34 to 20) or profound (IQ 20 and below) represents low-incidence disabilities. Although below-average intellectual functioning is a hallmark of MR, the definition of this disability includes other key criteria.

In federal laws, MR was defined as follows:

> Mental retardation means significantly subaverage general intellectual functioning, existing concurrently with deficits in adaptive behavior and manifested during the developmental period that adversely affects a child's educational performance.

Thus, students with mild mental retardation (MMR) demonstrate intellectual functioning ranging from 55 to 70 as well as a deficit in adaptive behavior. Adaptive behaviors are those skills or behaviors that allow an individual to adapt to and live, work, or play in a specific environment. These skills would include such things as personal hygiene, social skills, communication, and or functional academics.

In response to the definition of MR included in federal laws, the American Association on Mental Retardation (AAMR, 2002) proposed a definition of MR that is strikingly different from that written into federal laws. The AAMR definition reads as follows:

> Mental retardation is a disability characterized by significant limitations both in intellectual functioning and in adaptive behavior as expressed in conceptual, social, and practical adaptive skills. This disability originates before the age of 18. A complete and accurate understanding of mental retardation involves realizing that mental retardation refers to a particular state of functioning that begins in childhood, has many dimensions, and is affected positively by individualized supports. As a model of functioning, it includes the contexts and environment within which the person functions and interacts and requires a multidimensional and ecological approach that reflects the interaction of the individual with the environment, and the outcomes of that interaction with regards to independence, relationships, societal contributions, participation in school and community, and personal well-being. (p.1)

Like the definition included in IDEA, this definition identifies limitations in intellectual functioning and adaptive behaviors as markers of MR and states that such markers must be present in childhood. Unlike the definition included in the federal laws, the AAMR's definition stresses the importance of context when evaluating and understanding MR. This definition also suggests that MR is a disability that responds favorably to positive supports or interventions; moreover, this favorable response is identified as a characteristic of the disability itself.

:: OVERLAP AMONG HIGH-INCIDENCE DISABILITIES

High-incidence disabilities tend to overlap. As explained earlier, it is often difficult to distinguish between students with MMR and students with LD (Gottlieb et al., 1994; Gresham et al., 1996; Lyon et al., 2001). Moreover, researchers have observed an inverse correlation between the number of children that a state identifies as having MMR and the number of students identified as having LD (Gresham et al., 1996). Some researchers have even argued that there appear to be more similarities than differences between students with LD and MMR (Gresham et al., 1996). Research has shown that if students with EBD are identified for special education services, these services are most likely in response to academic deficits (Walker et al., 2004). From the definition included in IDEA 2004, we know that many students with EBD experience significant deficits in academics and adaptive behavior. In addition, there is substantial research with students having both EBD and MR (Barrett, 1986; Epstein, Cullinan, & Polloway, 1986; Lee et al., 2003; Menolascino, 1990).

Sometimes it is difficult to distinguish among EBD, LD, and MMR. Each disability involves some low-level academic achievement and a heightened risk for school and postschool failure. All three of these disabilities are associated with behaviors that may limit peer acceptance and teacher approval. These disabilities can look a lot alike, and at times we may find ourselves wondering about the point at which LD becomes MMR or MMR becomes EBD or EBD becomes LD. Of course, these disabilities are not mutually exclusive, either. Therefore a particular individual can have any combination of them. The distinctions among these categories can be subtle and are sometimes unclear to even the most trained eye; however, the distinctions are important and carry important implications for educational interventions. The important implications are highlighted later in this book.

Clearly high-incidence disabilities share a variety of characteristics. Unfortunately, those common characteristics are not the only things that make the identification of these disabilities difficult. Pure manifestations of disability are the exception and not the rule (Kauffman, 2005a; Tankersley & Landrum, 1997). Problem behaviors tend to change over time (Verhulst & Van der Ende, 1993), and more often than not, disabilities are co-occurring conditions.

We call the co-occurrence of disabilities *comorbidity*. Students with one disorder are often at risk for developing a second or **comorbid** disorder. This is true for disorders in a single category that we have discussed, such as EBD (Wang et al., 2005). It is also true when we consider the comorbidity of categories such as EBD and LD—students who have disorders defined by both categories.

Unfortunately, the combined effects of multiple disorders are not additive, but multiplicative (Tankersley & Landrum, 1997). That is, someone with a second, comorbid condition is not just twice as likely to have difficulties but many times more likely to have difficulties. Students with comorbid disabilities behave quite differently from students with single disabilities. In addition, students with comorbid disorders are likely to display these disorders over longer periods of time than are those with a single disorder (Verhulst & Van der Ende, 1993).

SUMMARY

Three high-incidence disability categories are EBD, LD, and MMR. Students with these disabilities account for the majority of students served by special education. These disabilities are lifelong conditions that may or may not prove to be handicapping, depending upon environmental demands or constraints.

High-incidence disabilities vary in prevalence and severity. Prevalence refers to the percentage of individuals manifesting a particular disability. Incidence refers to the frequency of occurrence. Together, high-incidence disabilities account for about 70% of all school-age students identified with disabilities. They range from behaviors requiring modest instructional support to behaviors requiring separate therapeutic settings.

To receive special education services, students must be identified as having one or more disabilities as defined in IDEA. The identification of these disabilities is controversial, with much data indicating underidentification, and some individuals making accusations of overidentification. These problems in identification result in part from the field's inability to agree on a definition for high-incidence disability categories. Each of these categories has a federal definition found in IDEA. In addition, each also has a definition constructed by advocates and professionals in each specific field. The divisions between the federal and professional definitions illustrate the controversies with which the field of special education currently wrestles. Identification of high-incidence disabilities is also complicated by the co-occurrence (comorbidity) of these disabilities.

COMPETENT TEACHING BOX   **B O X   1 . 1**

Knowing your students . . .

What we know about precision in the use of language and labels allows the field to better identify effective practices. How we label students for special education eligibility is NOT an automatic prescription for educational strategies or placement.

What you might want to remember about the use of labels for high-incidence disabilities:

- Many disability types have numerous labels. Therefore two children can have similar difficulties in reading, yet have varied labels. The same child can have many different labels, depending on whether he or she received them from an educational agency or medical doctor.
- LD, MMR, and EBD are considered high-incidence disabilities because they have a high prevalence rate in school-age children as compared to many other disability categories.

- LD, MMR, and EBD can occur by themselves, in conjunction with one another, or with other related disabilities. Therefore, regardless of label, each child will present with a unique set of educational needs.

Competent teachers . . .

- Competent teachers recognize that labels alone are not sufficiently powerful to create or eradicate disability status.
- Competent teachers understand the difference between a lifelong disability that places a student at risk for school failure and a handicap that is based on the interactions between skill and context.
- Competent teachers recognize that students with high-incidence disabilities can present mild to severe needs and will need to be educated accordingly.

We have stated that high-incidence disabilities overlap, are often comorbid, and are sometimes quite difficult to tell apart. We have also said that these disability categories are more alike than different, but their differences are important. With all of this similarity and overlap a final question remains: Why are the differences important?

To answer this question, consider the case of Marcus.

MARCUS

Marcus's teacher described him as being "hell on wheels." He was a 17-year-old sophomore who threw books, erasers, and chairs at anyone who disagreed with him. He refused to complete assignments or to participate in class activities. He bullied the boys in his classroom with open physical threats, and he bullied girls with more covert, sexually derogatory insults. He was a 6 feet 2 inch tall out-of-control adolescent.

On the first day of class, Marcus's teacher began by introducing herself. Marcus didn't miss a beat. He promptly announced to everyone in earshot that he heard that "they" had to make her teach this class. He accused the teacher of only liking "smart kids." He then proceeded to interrogate his teacher about every class she'd ever taught. His questions were punctuated by innuendo that skirted the edge of clearly inappropriate. As the year progressed, Marcus adopted other behaviors that were equally disruptive. He frequently ran out of the room in the middle of class. He came late and often left early. He argued with teacher directives and even locked his teacher out of the classroom on one specific occasion. On another occasion, a teacher in a neighboring classroom gave Marcus detention. Marcus then spent the better part of the next class banging his fists against the shared classroom wall and hurling insults through the drywall.

Early in his life, doctors had diagnosed Marcus with conduct disorder and attention deficit hyperactivity disorder (ADHD). Many of the behaviors consistent with conduct disorder, as well as those described above, would warrant special education services for EBD. However, Marcus was not identified with EBD. He was identified and received special education services for learning disabilities in reading and written expression.

At 17 years of age, Marcus read on the fourth-grade level and spelled on the third-grade level. In the area of writing, Marcus wrote only when forced to do so and used only those words he knew he could spell. Generally this took the shape of two to three simple sentences and contrasted dramatically with his expressive oral communication skills. The standard five-sentence paragraph was well beyond his reach. Also, Marcus demonstrated difficulty with basic academic behaviors. When asked to read silently, Marcus would provoke a neighbor or leave the classroom. He seldom completed homework or arrived at class with any school supplies. His test anxiety was so high that when his classroom teacher gave the first unit test, Marcus stood up, overturned his desk, and left the classroom.

Before landing in a classroom at an alternative high school, Marcus had transferred in and out of a series of five high schools. Clearly, this student was demonstrating academic deficits that were consistent with LD. He also demonstrated behaviors consistent with EBD, but was not identified as such. Instead, he received special education services that were primarily academic in nature. At the end of the school year, Marcus was expelled for violence on school grounds. We are left to wonder what would have happened had Marcus been identified with EBD.

1. Do you think it is important for eligibility labels (i.e., LD or EBD) to include all possible categories?
2. Should it matter which label is used for identification?

SARA

Sara was in Ms. Nick's Algebra 1 class. Basically, Sara was considered a rather unattractive girl. She wasn't from a poor home, yet she typically wore one of three pairs of baggy corduroys rolled up almost to her knees with mismatched colored socks and ill-fitting t-shirts. Her physical shape was not suited for typical teenager clothes of any type. She had a substantial pear shape, unusually disproportionate for a preadolescent; more like the shape of an older woman. Sara was also always late to class and was a very poor student academically. She was often the target of social jokes and sneers among her peers.

Ms. Nick's class was right after lunch, and Sara was consistently about 10 minutes late. Sara was typically slightly slow in speech, but would become very quick-tempered when asked about why she was late and was told to alter her behavior to become more timely. After several failed attempts at addressing the problem with Sara, her teacher discussed the issue with the school guidance counselor, who explained that last year Sara was caught using water from the toilet to brush her teeth after lunch (her mother had asked her to brush every day after lunch). It had caused such an uproar among the girls in the bathroom that the subsequent taunting had gotten out of control. To remedy the situation, Sara was allowed to brush after her peers were out of the bathroom once the class bell had rung. Sara had also been reminded to use only sink water. The counselor assumed Sara wanted to maintain this schedule for the year.

Ms. Nick went home and thought about her conversation with the school counselor. She also reflected on how socially inept Sara was, including her recent incident with some of the boys in her class who Ms. Nick caught sending Sara fake love notes asking her out. Sara had not faltered, saying yes right away without questioning why the most popular boy who always made fun of her would all of a sudden ask her out. Ms. Nick also thought about the slow speech, the poor academic performance, and unique perspective on personal hygiene.

1. Was there more to Sara's story than had been previously identified?
2. Would a label have potentially helped Sara? Why or why not?

REFERENCES

American Association on Mental Retardation. (2002). Ad Hoc Committee on Terminology and Classification. Washington, DC: Author.

Baldwin, R. S., & Vaughn, S. (1989). Why Siegel's arguments are irrelevant to the definition of learning disabilities. *Journal of Learning Disabilities, 22,* 513–520.

Barrett, R. P. (Ed.). (1986). *Severe behavior disorders in the mentally retarded.* New York: Plenum.

Bateman, B., & Linden, M. A. (1998). *Better IEPs.* Longmont, CO: Sopris West.

Beirne-Smith, M., Ittenbach, R., & Patton, J. (2001). *Mental retardation* (6th ed.). Upper Saddle River, NJ: Merrill/Prentice Hall.

Danforth, S., & Rhodes, W. C. (1997). Deconstructing disability: A philosophy for education. *Remedial and Special Education, 18,* 357–366.

Epstein, M. H., Cullinan, D., & Polloway, E. A. (1986). Patterns of maladjustment among the mentally retarded. *American Journal of Mental Deficiency, 91,* 127–134.

Filipek, P. (1996). Structural variations in measures in the developmental disorders. In R. Thatcher, G. Lyon, J. Rumsey, & N. Krasnegor (Eds.), *Developmental neuroimaging: Mapping the development of brain and behavior* (pp. 169–186). San Diego, CA: Academic Press.

Fletcher, J. M., Foorman, B. R., Boudousquie, A., Barnes, M. A., Schatschneider, C., & Francis, D. J. (2002). Assessment of reading and learning disabilities: A research-based intervention-oriented approach. *Journal of School Psychology, 40,* 27–63.

Fletcher, J. M., Morris, R. D., & Lyon, G. R. (2003). Classification and definition of learning disabilities: An integrative perspective. In H. L. Swanson, K. Harris, & S. Graham (Eds.), *Handbook of learning disabilities.* New York: Guilford.

Forness, S. R. (1988). Planning for the needs of children with serious emotional disturbance: The national special education and mental health coalition. *Behavioral Disorders, 13,* 127–133.

Forness, S. R., & Knitzer, J. (1992). A new proposed definition and terminology to replace "serious emotional disturbance" in Individuals with Disabilities Education Act. *School Psychology Review, 21,* 12–20.

Francis, D. J., Fletcher, J. M., Shaywitz, B. A., Shaywitz, S. E., & Rourke, B. P. (1996). Defining learning and language disabilities: Conceptual and psychometric issues with the use of IQ tests. *Language, Speech, and Hearing Services in Schools, 27,* 132–143.

Francis, D. J., Shaywitz, S. E., Stuebing, K. K., Shaywitz, B. A., & Fletcher, J. M. (1996). Developmental lag versus deficit models of reading disability: A longitudinal, individual growth curves analysis. *Journal of Educational Psychology, 88,* 3–17.

Frankenberger, W., & Fronzaglio, K. (1991). A review of states' criteria and procedures for identifying children with learning disabilities. *Journal of Learning Disabilities, 24,* 495–500.

Fuchs, D., Fuchs, L. S., Mathes, P. G. Lipsey, M. W., & Roberts, P. H. (2001, August). Is "Learning Disabilities" Just a Fancy Term for Low Achievement? A Meta-analysis of Reading Differences Between Low Achievers With and Without the Label. Paper presented at the LD Summit, Washington, DC: U.S. Department of Education.

Galaburda, A. M., Menard, M., & Rosen, G. (1994). Evidence for aberrant auditory anatomy in developmental dyslexia. *Proceedings for the National Academy of Science, 91,* 8010–8013.

Gallagher, D. J. (1998). The scientific knowledge base of special education: Do we know what we think we know? *Exceptional Children, 64,* 493–502.

Gliona, M. F., Gonzales, A. K., & Jacobson, E. S. (2005). Dedicated, not segregated: Suggested changes in thinking about instructional environments and in the language of special education. In J. M. Kauffman & D. P. Hallahan (Eds.), *The illusion of full inclusion: A comprehensive critique of a current special education bandwagon* (2nd ed., pp. 135–146). Austin, TX: PRO-ED.

Gottlieb, J., Alter, M., Gottlieb, B., & Wishner, J. (1994). Special education in urban America: It's not justifiable for many. *Journal of Special Education, 27,* 453–465.

Graham, S., & Harris, K. R. (1989). The relevance of IQ in the determination of learning disabilities: Abandoning scores as decision makers. *Journal of Learning Disabilities, 22,* 500–503.

Gresham, F. M., MacMillan, D. L., & Bocian, K. M. (1996). Learning disabilities, low achievement, and mild mental retardation: More alike than different? *Journal of Learning Disabilities, 29,* 570–581.

Hallahan, D. P., and Kauffman, J. M. (2006). *Exceptional learners: Introduction to special education* (10th ed.). Boston: Allyn & Bacon.

Hallahan, D. P., Lloyd, J. W., Kauffman, J. M., Weiss, M., & Martinez, E. (2005). *Learning disabilities: Foundations, characteristics, and effective teaching* (3rd ed.). Boston: Allyn & Bacon.

Hallahan, D. P., & Mercer, C. D. (2002). Learning Disabilities: A Historical Perspective. In R. Bradley, L. Danielson, & D. P. Hallahan (Eds.), *Identification of learning disabilities: Research to practice* (pp. 1–67). Mahwah, NJ: Erlbaum.

Hammill, D. D., Leigh, J. E., McNutt, G., & Larsen, S. C. (1981). A new definition of learning disabilities. *Learning Disability Quarterly, 4,* 336–342.

Henley, M., Ramsey, R. S., & Algozzine, R. F. (2002). Characteristics of and strategies for teaching students with mild disabilities (4th ed.). Boston: Allyn & Bacon.

Herr, C. M., & Bateman, B. D. (2003). Learning disabilities and the law. In H. L. Swanson, K. Harris, & S. Graham (Eds.), *Handbook of learning disabilities.* New York: Guilford.

Individuals with Disabilities Education Act of 1997. Public Law 105–17.

Individuals with Disabilities Education Improvement Act of 2004 (2004). Public Law 108–446.

Kauffman, J. M. (1999). Commentary: Today's special education and its messages for tomorrow. *Journal of Special Education, 32,* 244–254.

Kauffman, J. M. (2002). *Educational deform: Bright people sometimes say stupid things about education.* Lanham, MD: Scarecrow Press.

Kauffman, J. M. (2003). Appearances, stigma, and prevention. *Remedial and Special Education, 24,* 195–198.

Kauffman, J. M. (2005a). *Characteristics of emotional and behavioral disorders of children and youth* (8th ed.). Upper Saddle River, NJ: Merrill/Prentice Hall.

Kauffman, J. M. (2005b). How we prevent the prevention of emotional and behavioural difficulties in education. In P. Clough, P. Garner, J. T. Pardeck, & F. K. O. Yuen (Eds.), *Handbook of emotional and behavioural difficulties* (pp. 429–440). London: Sage.

Kauffman, J. M. (2006). Labels and the nature of special education: We need to face realities. *Learning Disabilities: A Multidisciplinary Journal.*

Kauffman, J. M., & Hallahan, D. P. (Eds.). (2005a). *The illusion of full inclusion: A comprehensive critique of a current special educational bandwagon* (2nd ed.). Austin, TX: PRO-ED.

Kauffman, J. M., & Hallahan, D. P. (2005b). *What special education is and why we need it.* Boston: Allyn & Bacon.

Kauffman, J. M., & Landrum, T. J. (2006). *Children and youth with emotional or behavioral disorders: A history of their education.* Austin, TX: PRO-ED.

Kavale, K. A. (2001, August). Discrepancy Models in the Identification of Learning Disabilities. Paper presented at the LD Summit. Washington, DC: U.S. Department of Education.

Kavale, K. A., & Forness, S. R. (2000). What definitions of learning disability say and don't say: A critical analysis. *Journal of Learning Disabilities, 33,* 239–256.

Kavale, K. A., Fuchs, D., & Scruggs, T. (1994). Setting the record straight on learning disability and low achievement: Implications for policymaking. *Learning Disabilities Research and Practice, 9*(2), 70–77.

Keogh, B. K. (1987). Learning disabilities: In defense of a construct. *Learning Disabilities Research, 3,* 4–9.

Kessler, R. C., Berglund, P., Demler, O., Jin, R., & Walters, E. E. (2005). Lifetime prevalence and age-of-onset distributions of DSM-IV disorders in the national comorbidity survey replication. *Archives of General Psychiatry, 62,* 593–602.

Klingberg, T., Hedehus, M., Temple, E., Salz, T., Gabrieli, J., Moseley, M., & Poldrack, R. (2000). Microstructure of temporo-parietal white matter as a basis for reading ability: Evidence from diffusion tenso magnetic resonance imaging, *Neuron, 25,* 493–500.

Lee, P., Moss, S., Friedlander, R., Donnelly, T., & Honer, W. (2003). Early-onset schizophrenia in children with mental retardation: Diagnostic reliability and stability of clinical features. *Journal of the American Academy of Child and Adolescent Psychiatry, 42,* 162–169.

Levine, M. (2002). A mind at a time: America's top learning expert shows how every child can succeed. New York: Simon & Schuster.

Lyon, G. R. (1989). IQ is irrelevant to the definition of learning disabilities: A position in search of logic and data. *Journal of Learning Disabilities, 22,* 504–512.

Lyon, G. R., Fletcher, J. M., Shaywitz, S. A., Shaywitz, B. A., Torgesen, J. K., Wood, F. B., Schulte, A., & Olson, R.

(2001). Rethinking learning disabilities. In C. E. Finn, A. J. Rotherham, & C. R. Hokanson (Eds.), *Rethinking special education for a new century* (pp. 259–287). Washington, DC: Thomas B. Fordham Foundation.

Menolascino, F. J. (1990). The nature and types of mental illness in the mentally retarded. In M. Lewis & S. M. Miller (Eds.), *Handbook of developmental psychopathology* (pp. 397–408). New York: Plenum.

Mostert, M. P., Kauffman, J. M., & Kavale, K. R. (2003). Truth and consequences. *Behavioral Disorders, 28,* 333–347.

Norman, C. A., & Zigmond, N. (1980). Characteristics of children labeled and served as learning disabled in school systems affiliated with child service demonstration centers. *Journal of Learning Disabilities, 13,* 16–21.

Olson, R. K. (1999). Genes, environment, and reading disabilities. In R. J. Sternberg and L. Spear-Swerling (Eds.), *Perspectives on learning disabilities* (pp. 3–22). New Haven: Westview Press.

Pinker, S. (1994). *The language instinct.* New York: Harper Perennial.

Sailor, W., & Roger, B. (2005). Rethinking inclusion: School-wide applications. *Phi Delta Kappan, 86,* 503–509.

Shaywitz, B., Fletcher, J., Holahan, J., & Shaywitz, S. (1992). Discrepancy compared to low achievement definitions of reading disability: Results from the Connecticut Longitudinal Study. *Journal of Learning Disabilities, 25,* 639–648.

Shaywitz, S. E., Pugh, K. R., Jenner, A. R., Fulbright, R. K., Fletcher, J. M., Gore, J. C., & Shaywitz, B. A. (2000). The neurobiology of reading and reading disability (dyslexia). In M. L. Kamil, P. B. Mosenthal, P. D. Pearson, & R. Barr (Eds.), *Handbook of reading research* (Vol. III, pp. 229–249). Mahwah, NJ: Erlbaum.

Siegel, L. S. (1989). IQ is irrelevant to the definition of learning disabilities. *Journal of Learning Disabilities, 22,* 469–486.

Steinberg, Z., & Knitzer, J. (1992). Classrooms for emotionally and behaviorally disturbed students: Facing the challenge. *Behavioral Disorders, 17,* 145–156.

Tankersley, M. & Landrum, T. J. (1997). Comorbidity of emotional and behavioral disorders. In J. W. Lloyd, E. J. Kameenui, & D. Chard (Eds.), *Issues in educating students with disabilities* (pp. 153–173). Mahwah, NJ: Erlbaum.

U.S. Department of Education (2002). *Twenty-fourth annual report to Congress on implementation of the Individuals with Disabilities Education Act.* Washington, DC: Author.

U.S. Department of Education (2006). *Twenty-sixth annual report to Congress on implementation of the Individuals with Disabilities Education Act.* Washington, DC: Author.

Van Riper, C., & Erickson, R. L. (1996) *Speech Correction: An Introduction to Speech Pathology and Audiology.* (9th ed.) Boston: Allyn & Bacon.

Vellutino, F. R., Scanlon, D. M., & Lyon, G. R. (2000). Differentiating between difficult-to-remediate and readily remediated poor readers: More evidence against the IQ-achievement discrepancy definition of reading disability. *Journal of Learning Disabilities, 33,* 223–238.

Vellutino, F. R., Scanlon, D. M., & Tanzman, M. S. (1998). The case for early intervention in diagnosing specific reading disability. *Journal of School Psychology, 36,* 367–397.

Verhulst, F. C., & Van der Ende, J. (1993). "Comorbidity" in an epidemiological sample: A longitudinal perspective. *Journal of Child Psychology and Psychiatry, 34,* 767–783.

Walker, H. M., Ramsey, E., & Gresham, F. M. (2004). *Antisocial behavior in school: Strategies and best practices* (2nd ed.). Pacific Grove, CA: Brooks/Cole.

Walker, H. M., & Sprague, J. R. (1999). The path to school failure, delinquency, and violence: Causal factors and some potential solutions. *Intervention in School and Clinic, 35*(2), 67–73.

Walker, H. M., Stiller, B., Severson, H. H., Feil, E. G., & Golly, A. (1998). First step to success: Intervening at the point of school entry to prevent antisocial behavior patterns. *Psychology in the Schools, 35,* 259–269.

Walker, H. M., Zeller, R. W., Close, D. W., Webber, J., & Gresham, F. (1999). The present unwrapped: Change and challenge in the field of behavioral disorders. *Behavioral Disorders, 24,* 293–304.

Wang, P. S., Berglund, P., Olfson, M., Pincus, H. A., Wells, K. B., & Kessler, R. C. (2005). Failure and delay in initial treatment contact after first onset of mental disorders in the national comorbidity survey replication. *Archives of General Psychiatry, 62,* 603–613.

Wehby, J. H., Symons, F. J., Canale, J. A., & Go, F. J. (1998). Teaching practices in classrooms for students with emotional and behavioral disorders: Discrepancies between recommendations and observations. *Behavioral Disorders, 24,* 51–56.

Ysseldyke, J., Algozzine, B., Shinn, M., & McGue, K. (1982). Similarities and differences between low achievers and students classified as learning disabled. *Journal of Special Education, 16,* 73–85.

Zeffiro, T. J., & Eden, G. (2000). The neural basis of developmental dyslexia. *Annals of Dyslexia, 50,* 1–30.

The History and Current Trends Surrounding High-Incidence Disabilities

Devery R. Mock

Appalacian State University

URBAN LEGEND: *History is destined to repeat.*

LEGENDARY THOUGHT: *When it comes to history, once is sometimes enough.*

The study of special education history is not simply a matter of rote memorization. We need only remember the Holocaust in Germany in the mid-20th century and then the more recent genocides in the former Yugoslavia, Rwanda, and Darfur to be reminded that history repeats itself. The study of the dates and places associated with these events does little to prevent the recurrence of appalling acts of violence. The savvy student of history understands the context in which these events occurred as well as their long-term effects. Likewise, students of special education history must learn the hows and whys of our rich history. Some events, such as the 1975 Education for All Handicapped Children Act, have advanced the field and improved the educational experiences of students with disabilities. As students of the history of special education, we are committed to continuing advances. Other events, such as the **eugenics** movement of the early 20th century, in which people tried to purge the nation of mental retardation by controlling human reproduction, were horrific and have left lasting stains on the field. In these circumstances we use knowledge to guard against history repeating itself. In the case of the eugenics movement, science tells us that mental retardation is not always genetically determined, and thus the forced sterilization of individuals with mental retardation was both unethical and based upon a flawed supposition. On May 2, 2002 the governor of the Commonwealth of Virginia made a public apology for all of the atrocities carried in the name of eugenics. In so doing, he reminded us that many of the mistakes of history need not happen again.

In 1975, President Gerald Ford signed Public Law 94-142, the **Education for All Handicapped Children Act** (EAHCA). This law marked the beginning of the mandatory public education of students with disabilities. Many individuals imagine that this event marked the birth of special education, but it did not. It was only the first *federal, mandatory* law governing special education. Although PL 94-142 was a watershed event, the EAHCA is just one incident in a centuries-long, rich history (Hallahan & Kauffman, 2006; Kauffman & Landrum, 2006; Mann, 1979). American society has always contained individuals with disabilities, and at least since the early 1800s it has also included educators working to ameliorate the lives of individuals with disabilities.

:: BEFORE THE EDUCATION FOR ALL HANDICAPPED CHILDREN ACT

Students with high-incidence disabilities, those we now say have emotional and behavioral disorders (EBD), learning disabilities (LD), and mild mental retardation (MMR), have been present throughout history (Hallahan, Lloyd, Kauffman, Weiss, & Martinez, 2005; Kauffman, 2005; Kauffman & Landrum, 2006; Kauffman & Smucker, 1995). One of the earliest and best-known written accounts of a child with disabilities is that of Victor, the "wild boy of Aveyron" described by Itard

(1962—not the original publication date). Victor's documented behaviors, recorded at the end of the 18th century, have been referred to "as a study of behavior disorder and as a **thesis** on mental retardation" (Kauffman, 1976, p. 338; see also Kauffman & Landrum, 2006). Itard, the physician who taught Victor, failed to teach this uncivilized adolescent how to speak. However, Itard's chronicle of his experiences provides evidence of some of the initial attempts at instructing students with disabilities.

In the 19th century physicians like Samuel Gridley Howe and Itard's student, Edouard Seguin, embarked on pioneering work in the education of individuals with mental retardation (Kauffman, 1981). Howe was responsible for dramatic advances in the education of students with blindness. He established schools for the blind in Ohio, Tennessee, Kentucky, and Virginia and developed an early form of **Braille.** After his seminal successes in this area, Howe established special schools for students with mental retardation (MR). In all of his work he pioneered a new philosophy for educating students with disabilities. He believed that students with disabilities could learn and progress. Seguin worked with Howe and developed specific techniques for educating students with MR. These practices ranged from sensory training to self-care instruction to **vocational training.** They served as some of the earliest attempts to offer appropriate instruction to students with MR.

The Early 19th Century

During the 19th century, residential care facilities became one of the most common settings for treatment of individuals with disabilities. Institutions were therefore created for specific disorders including: (a) **juvenile delinquency,** (b) **mental illness,** and (c) **mental retardation.** In these **facilities,** professionals attempted to remediate mental and behavioral deficits and send residents back to their home environments transformed into improved, productive citizens. Dorothea Dix was one of the best known advocates for the treatment of individuals with disabilities within institutional settings. In the mid-19th century, Dix became concerned with the quality of care offered in poor-houses and prisons. She launched a crusade advocating the humane treatment of individuals with disabilities, and advocated institutions as ideal settings that could both protect against abuses and offer effective interventions (Kauffman, 1976; Kauffman & Landrum, 2006). Criticism of this practice was widespread and eventually culminated more than a century later in the **deinstitutionalization** and **normalization** movements.

During the 19th century, the public's perception of institutional settings changed dramatically. Whereas institutions were at one time considered ideal settings for the treatment of disabling conditions, they later became symbols of both abuse and neglect. This transformation resulted from the increasingly prevalent perception that disabilities were incurable, and individuals with disabilities were best relegated to separate institutions for their own protection as well as that of the greater society (Kauffman, 1976, 1981). This transformation occurred gradually, but eventually resulted in institutions that were overcrowded and unable to provide anything resembling humane care and treatment. Therefore, institutions became synonymous with segregation. It is important to note that this change did not occur with the consent of special education professionals. Individuals like Howe, who had once considered institutions to be ideal settings for the treatment of individuals with disabilities, began seeking out and using alternative placements. Often Howe moved residents out of an institution and into the house of a family that agreed to accommodate an individual with a disability. Unfortunately, these alternative placements numbered far fewer than individuals needing treatment (Dorn, Fuchs, & Fuchs, 1996).

Middle to Late 19th Century

The 19th century was not all bad for the field of high-incidence disabilities. In the middle of the 19th century, detailed descriptions of deviant behavior began appearing regularly in journals and books (Kauffman, 1976; Kauffman, Brigham, & Mock, 2004; Kauffman & Landrum, 2006). During this period, Franz Joseph Gall explored the relationship between brain injury and mental impairment, and Pierre Paul Broca worked on localizing specific speech functions within the left frontal lobe. Carl Wernicke also studied the relationship between brain injury and language disorders. This early work, demonstrating the neurological locus of language disorders, served as the foundation for much of the research that was to be conducted in the field of learning disabilities (Hallahan & Cruickshank, 1973; Hallahan & Mock, 2003). In the later half of the 19th century, individuals such as Sir William Broadbent, Adolph Kussmaul, W. Pringle Morgan, and the French physician, John Hinshelwood, built upon the earlier work of Gall, Broca, and Wernicke, and began investigating the nature of reading disabilities. Remember, all of this occurred at least a century before EAHCA was enacted. *High-incidence disabilities are not new phenomena.*

In the late 19th and early 20th centuries, specialized care for children and youth began to take hold. This period marked the advent of juvenile courts, child welfare programs, foster homes, and child psychiatric hospitals (Kauffman & Landrum, 2006). This period also ushered in a change in philosophy that would later be reflected in the work that individuals like Newell Kephart, Samuel Orton, and Grace Fernald conducted during the first half of the 20th century. As society began to differentiate between the special needs of children versus those of adults, researchers began to focus attention on child development. G. Stanley Hall, a student of the eminent psychologist William James, founded the **child study movement.** In so doing, he integrated the disciplines of education and psychology as they pertained to child development and learning. He conceptualized development as a constant process that is replicated across generations. Sigmund Freud's influence was also important during this period. Freud's **psychodynamic** approach to **psychopathology** formed the basis for much of the treatment offered in psychiatric hospitals throughout the United States and for early programs for children with emotional disorders (Berkowitz & Rothman, 1960).

The 20th Century

Whereas the 19th and early 20th centuries carry the shame of institutionalization gone awry, the 20th century also carries the shame of the **eugenics** movement and deinstitutionalization. The eugenics movement asserted that intellectual deficiency (mental retardation) was an inherited and undesirable trait. Thus, proponents of this movement advocated the sexual sterilization of individuals with mental retardation. Despite this critical low point in social history, the early 20th century was also marked by advances. By 1918, all states had passed laws requiring **compulsory education** for children. This milestone marks the beginning of a period in which researchers began to translate theoretical foundations into remedial practices (Wiederholt, 1974). With the advent of public education, high-incidence disabilities became more evident. When required to teach all children to read, teachers became more aware of students who had difficulty achieving this benchmark, for reasons of intellect, behavior, or an apparent discrepancy between intellectual aptitude and actual achievement. During the 20th century, the field of special education also developed an agenda for both advocacy and research. In 1922, the **Council for Exceptional Children** was founded, and in 1951, the first institution for research on exceptional children opened at the University of Illinois.

In the 20th century the deinstitutionalization movement, which began in the 1960s, ran into serious trouble. Although community-based mental health and mental retardation services may be good alternatives to institutions for many individuals, they have not been found effective in all cases. Moreover, community-based services were poorly funded, if at all, in many locations. Thus, by the late 20th century prisons and the streets had become the primary abode of most individuals with mental illness or mental retardation, just as in the days of Dorothea Dix in the mid-19th century.

After the mid-20th century, experimentation, based on the model provided by behavioral psychology, became more and more prevalent in schools as well as in institutions (Kauffman, Brigham, & Mock, 2004). Researchers intentionally measured the effects that different **antecedents, consequences,** and environmental conditions had on the observable behaviors of students in classrooms. For example, beginning in the mid-20th century, professional journals began publishing articles describing the principles and techniques that had implications for the behavior of students with disabilities in educational settings (Whelan & Haring, 1966). During this period, **behavior modification** became part of the special education vernacular, and educators began explicitly manipulating conditions that increased appropriate behaviors and decreased inappropriate behaviors. The behavioral analyses conducted during this period are now considered critical advances in research within the field of special education (Kauffman, Brigham, & Mock, 2004; Kauffman & Landrum, 2006; Landrum & Kauffman, 2006).

:: 1975—EDUCATION FOR ALL HANDICAPPED CHILDREN ACT

In 1966, almost 10 years before the signing of the landmark special education law, Education for All Handicapped Children Act (EAHCA), the Education of the Handicapped Act was passed. This law provided funding to individual states to be used voluntarily for the education of students with disabilities (i.e., at first, federal law *permitted* but did not *mandate* special education).

Before 1966, advocacy groups were working to secure rights for students with learning disabilities (LD), who had previously been unrecognized by federal law. Although many parent and professional groups advocated for students with LD, the parents and advocates of children with mild mental retardation (MMR) were more influential and powerful. These parents were concerned that if students with LD received federal recognition, the already limited federal resources would be reallocated, and children with MMR would thereby end up short-changed. Opponents of the recognition of students with LD in special education law maintained that such children were already receiving services through compensatory education programs such as **Title I**. However, Title I allocates federal funds for the education and remediation of students from economically disadvantaged environments and does not specifically address the educational needs of students with LD. Nonetheless, the passage of the 1966 Education of the Handicapped Act did not extend federal assistance and protection to students with LD. This legislative controversy is just one example of how high-incidence disabilities tend to intersect and overlap. Controversy about LD continues and will likely redirect the future of services for students with high-incidence disabilities (Fuchs, Mock, Morgan, & Young, 2003; Lyon et al., 2001).

In 1975, the *Education for All Handicapped Children Act* (EAHCA; Public Law 94-142) became law. This law, which reached full implementation in 1977, did recognize and provide services for students with specific learning disabilities. It required school districts to provide free and appropriate education to all students with identified disabilities. It also guaranteed students with identified disabilities:

1. Free and appropriate education
2. Nondiscriminatory testing, evaluation, and placement
3. The right to due process
4. Education in the least restrictive environment

Beyond all of these rights and safeguards, every student with an identified disability was also to be ensured an **Individualized Education Program** (IEP). EAHCA mandated that students with identified disabilities receive IEPs, to be reviewed at least annually, that specified:

1. Relevant instructional goals and objectives
2. Appropriate length of school year
3. The criteria to be used in evaluation and measurement
4. The most appropriate educational placement

IEPs were to be safeguards, ensuring that students with disabilities received educational programs specific to their needs. In many cases, these programs were to be markedly different from those offered to students without disabilities. Paralleling the civil rights movement, EAHCA secured the right to a free and appropriate education for students who had not yet been recognized and protected by federal law (Bateman & Linden, 1998; Hallahan & Mercer, 2001; Hallahan & Mock, 2003; Huefner, 2000).

Additionally, EACHA allocated federal funds that were to be used for research in specific disability areas. In the years that followed enactment of EACHA, federally funded research on LD was supported and conducted at Columbia University (Connor, 1983), the University of Illinois at Chicago (T. Bryan, Pearl, Donahue, J. Bryan, & Pflaum, 1983), the University of Kansas (Schumaker, Deshler, Alley, &

Warner, 1983), the University of Minnesota (Ysseldyke et al., 1983), and the University of Virginia, (Hallahan et al., 1983). Across these university sites, researchers investigated topics ranging from attention to social competence to the identification of students with LD. A federally funded research institute was headed by Siegfried Engelmann and Wesley Becker. These individuals carried out research specific to the effectiveness of **Direct Instruction** (DI) (Engelmann, Becker, Hanner, & Johnson, 1978, 1988; Engelmann & Osborn, 1977). These research centers produced data that inform and direct much of the practices we now implement when instructing students with high-incidence disabilities.

Beyond establishing a legal mandate for the education of all students with disabilities and allocating federal funds to support research about disabilities, EAHCA required procedures and services to guarantee the rights of students with disabilities and their parents. All students with suspected disabilities were to receive nondiscriminatory testing, evaluation, and placement. This evaluation had to cover all areas related to the student's suspected disability (including hearing, vision, health, emotional health, intelligence, and academic achievement) and had to occur at no cost to parents. Placement was to be specific to the student's needs and never to be determined according to disability categories. All students with identified disabilities were afforded the right to **due process,** meaning that parents could request a legal hearing if they disagreed with the identification, evaluation, educational placement, or any other matter related to their child's free and appropriate education.

EAHCA required that every student with an identified disability receive a **free and appropriate education.** This free and appropriate public education (FAPE) was required to occur in the *least restrictive environment* (LRE). Originally, LRE was interpreted to be the "where" and not the "what" of education (Herr & Bateman, 2003). The courts later disagreed with this interpretation and stipulated that LRE referred to the general type of educational program in which a student was placed. In short, LRE was never operationally defined in EAHCA or any of the reauthorizations that followed, and consequently this term became one of the hotly debated concepts in special education legislation and practice (Gliona, Gonzales, & Jacobson, 2005). In its first incarnation, the debate about LRE took the shape of the **regular education initiative** (REI). Later, in a second incarnation, LRE became the central issue in the movement for **full inclusion movement** (FIM).

The EAHCA was amended and reauthorized in 1983 and 1986. The 1983 amendments included (a) the mandate to collect data on students with disabilities who exit educational systems; and (b) the allocation of federal incentives for states that provide services to infants and preschoolers with disabilities. In 1986, the EAHCA was further amended to encourage states to provide comprehensive services for infants and toddlers with disabilities and to expand special education services provided to preschool children (ages 3 to 5).

:: THE REGULAR EDUCATION INITIATIVE

The Regular Education Initiative (REI) seems to have roots in two articles published just before the enactment of EAHCA. Dunn (1968) and Deno (1970) called into question many of the practices that special educators used to address the needs of students with disabilities. Dunn (1968) criticized special education placements as morally and educationally wrong. He asserted that **homogeneous grouping** disadvantaged slow learners and damaged their self-esteem. He also called upon educators to stop "segregating" students through special programs. Deno (1970) echoed these concerns and argued against categorizing students in special education. She suggested that special education should try to "work itself out of business" (Deno, 1970, p. 233).

The REI has been described as a movement advocating cooperation between special and general education (Fuchs & Fuchs, 1994). The movement was led by advocates for students with high-incidence disabilities (Gersten & Woodward, 1990; Jenkins, Pious, & Peterson, 1988; Pugach & Lilly, 1984; Reynolds, 1988). It was based on the assumption that all students are very much the same for educational purposes. Separate special education was thus assumed to be unnecessary for many, if not most, students with high-incidence disabilities. Consequently, the responsibility for *many* or *most* students with disabilities should be reassigned to regular classroom teachers, according to the REI. Advocates of the REI interpreted the LRE to be, in essence, the general education classroom. As a result, the practice of mainstreaming, or integrating students with disabilities back into the regular classroom, became the *sine qua non* of the REI. However, neither rational analysis nor research supported the proposals known as the REI (Kauffman, 1989; Kauffman & Hallahan, 2005b; Singer, 1988).

:: THE FULL INCLUSION MOVEMENT

As illustrated by the institutionalized settings that proved controversial in the 19th century and REI of the 20th century, *placement* remains a hot topic in special education. Historically, educational settings have proved as controversial as religion, politics, or even inlaws. However, the controversy about placement did not end in the 1990s. Following REI, the Full Inclusion Movement (FIM) emerged and exemplified what was purported to be the most comprehensive of all special education reform movements (see Fuchs & Fuchs, 1994; Kauffman & Hallahan, 2005b; Mock & Kauffman, 2005). Advocates of the FIM argued that students were "more alike than different"; thus, practices of grouping for specialized instruction were deemed unnecessary (Lipsky & Gartner, 1987, 1996, 1998; Stainback & Stainback, 1992). Proponents of full inclusion maintained that the dual system of special and regular education harmed both students with and without disabilities. In fact, some suggested that special education violated the rights of students with disabilities (Lipsky & Gartner, 1998).

Arguments for full inclusion focused on the goals of equality, happiness, and human dignity, but neglected more pragmatic goals such as student achievement and effective instruction. Thus, proponents of full inclusion were criticized for their lack of clear definitions and logical arguments, as well as their failure to specify how every child with a disability was to be included and appropriately educated in the regular classroom (Kavale & Forness, 2000; MacMillan, Gresham, & Forness, 1996). Proponents of the FIM also argued that students learned appropriate behaviors and skills merely by observing and interacting with nondisabled peers (Stainback & Stainback, 1992).

Research did not support this assertion. Instead, researchers presented evidence suggesting that students *do not* consistently learn from peer models, and opportunities to apply new skills *do not* necessarily result in the acquisition of new skills (Hallenbeck & Kauffman, 1995; Kauffman & Pullen, 1996). Moreover, although existing research does not support the claims of the advocates of the REI or the FIM, research on the effects of place *per se* is virtually nonexistent and perhaps unobtainable. We may conclude that the claims of advocates of full inclusion are not practical, nor have their claims been supported by rigorous research (Kauffman & Hallahan, 2005a, 2005b; Mock & Kauffman, 2005; Singer, 1988).

:: REAUTHORIZATION OF EAHCA

The 1990 Reauthorization, Now IDEA

Fifteen years after its inception, EAHCA was amended and renamed the **Individuals with Disabilities Education Act** (IDEA). Although most of the basic components of this law remained the same, reauthorization involved a rather significant change in name. The new law included **person-first language** that replaced *handicapped student* with *student with disabilities*. This change in language reflected a supposedly more sophisticated understanding of the differences between handicaps and disabilities, as well as an increased sensitivity regarding the nature and locus of disability. For example, when a person has 20-20 vision, we do not say, "He *is* normal vision." Instead, we say, "He *has* normal vision," because vision is just a single aspect of this person. He is not defined by his vision—except perhaps metaphorically. In the same way, EAHCA became IDEA to reflect the assertion that disabilities are only aspects, or parts, of the people who experience them. In this way, a child is not a behavior disorder, a learning disability, or mental retardation. Instead, he or she is a child *with* a behavior disorder, *with* a learning disability, or *with* mental retardation.

In addition to a change in language, IDEA (1990) included three major additions to EAHCA. First, IDEA identified two new categories of students with low-incidence disabilities: **autism** (now often referred to as **autistic spectrum disorders** or ASD) and **traumatic brain injury** (TBI). Second, the new law mandated the implementation of **transition plans** and services, to be stipulated in IEPs, for students beginning at 16 years, and 14 years wherever appropriate. Transition plans were to be used to enable students with disabilities to successfully transition from school to postsecondary settings such as college, community living, employment, or vocational programs. Third, IDEA (1990) extended the services outlined in EAHCA to children as young as 3 years of age. Additionally, discretionary (i.e., voluntary, permitted but not required for states) assistance was made available for children with disabilities from birth to three years of age.

The 1997 Reauthorization

Seven years following the renaming of EAHCA to IDEA, the law was again reauthorized and strengthened to include additional provisions. First, students with disabilities had to be included in statewide and districtwide assessments. Prior to this amendment, many individuals expressed concern regarding the degree to which teachers and schools were held accountable for the progress of students with disabilities. Participation in statewide and districtwide assessment ensures that schools will regularly monitor the progress of students in special education programs. Second, the 1997 version of IDEA required that IEP goals and objectives be constructed in such a way that progress is measurable. In practice, these objectives usually stipulate what behavior will be demonstrated and by what date. Third, reauthorization required the inclusion of **proactive behavior plans** in IEPs. According to this third provision, all students with disabilities had to have specific plans related to behavioral needs whenever appropriate and regardless of disability category. Additionally, students with disabilities, who were brought up on school discipline charges, were to receive a **functional behavioral assessment** (FBA). The FBA requires that data be collected to determine the *purpose* or *function* of the unacceptable behavior and to plan interventions to prevent the behavior from recurring. The FBA also may or may not be part of a **manifestation determination**, which is a way of determining whether the misbehavior is or is not a manifestation of the student's disability. Finally, the new law stipulated that transition planning was to be reflected in a student's IEP by 14 years of age. In addition, if the student was to be transferred from infant or toddler programs to preschool, those services must also be planned.

The 2004 Reauthorization, NCLB, and Related Events

In December 2004, IDEA was reauthorized a third time. The name used in this reauthorization was the *Individuals with Disabilities Education Improvement Act* (or IDEIA, although it is regularly called more simply IDEA 2004). This reauthorization included changes specific to special education concerns and issues. Some of these changes were efforts to reduce the paperwork associated with special education rules and procedures and the provisional approval of 3-year IEPs for 15 states. The reauthorization also prioritized research to eliminate the overidentification of students with LD as well as disproportionate representation of minority students among students with disabilities.

Unlike the reauthorizations occurring in 1990 and 1997, IDEA 2004 made several changes that aligned special education law with a general education law, **No Child Left Behind** (NCLB). As a result, some of the basic safeguards and rights established by EAHCA and strengthened by IDEA were restated. Previously, in 1997, legislators had required students with disabilities to participate in statewide and districtwide testing in an effort to increase accountability for the progress of these students. Still, students with disabilities were sometimes excluded from statewide and districtwide testing. Consequently, parents and other concerned individuals could not determine whether students with disabilities had made progress. They had no way to hold teachers accountable for the progress of students with disabilities. Therefore, in the 1997 reauthorization of IDEA, students with disabilities were required to take the same tests as their nondisabled peers. NCLB reiterated the demand.

When students with disabilities attend the same schools as their nondisabled peers, access can become an issue. For example, students in wheelchairs would be unable to use stairs, and students with blindness would be unable to read text-books. Thus, if students with disabilities are to have access to the educational services provided in a school, that school must often provide special provisions that remove the barriers posed by disabilities. These special provisions are called **accommodations.** For example, if a student must use a wheelchair, the school must accommodate this disability and provide elevators and ramps so that the student can access the school building and therefore participate in the general education curriculum. In the same way, the blind student needs the accommodation of textbooks written in Braille, as well as instruction in reading and writing in Braille, if he or she is to have access to the general education curriculum. Accommodations attempt to remove obstacles posed by disabilities. Effective accommodations level the playing field but do not give the individual with a disability an undue advantage. For example, an effective accommodation for a student with a reading disability might be to have math, social studies, and science textbooks available on tape. That way the student's disability (i.e., reading) would not prevent her from accessing the information in each of these textbooks. However, if we were to excuse her from all textbook responsibilities and assignments, this would be an ineffective accommodation, as it would give her undue advantage over her peers and would fail to provide access to the general education curriculum in a fair way.

In order for a student with a disability to take the same test as his nondisabled peers, he may need accommodations to remove the barriers posed by his disability. For example, a deaf student would need all oral instructions provided in sign language. This accommodation would allow the student access to the content of the test but would not provide the student undue advantage over peers. If the student had a reading disability, she would need all her math, science, and social studies assessments read to her. She would even need written instructions on any or all tests read aloud to her. These are all effective accommodations that would allow her access to the content of each test. However, when it came to reading assessments, this same accommodation would no longer be appropriate or effective. If this student had her reading assessment read aloud, she would not have to engage in any reading. Her score on this assessment would then fail to reflect her reading achievement. In this way, she would be given undue advantage over her peers. Her reading score would not reflect her reading achievement, whereas the scores of her peers would.

When in 1997 the IDEA amendments mandated that students with disabilities participate in all statewide and districtwide assessments, many students with disabilities began participating in these assessments with accommodations. Some of the accommodations that were regularly provided were appropriate and effective. These accommodations provided access to the content of the test and did not provide an undue advantage. Other accommodations were akin to administering a reading assessment in which all passages were read aloud by someone other than the student taking the test. These accommodations *did not* provide access and *did* provide undue advantage.

Because of such issues surrounding the provision of effective testing accommodations, professionals, both within and outside of the field of special education, have questioned the appropriateness of some testing accommodations (Council for Exceptional Children, 2003; Kauffman, McGee, & Brigham, 2004; Kauffman &

Wiley, 2004). Some individuals argue that testing accommodations invalidate both the test and the measured progress of the student in question. This means that the test would no longer measure what it purports to measure, and thus the scores of students on this measure would fail to reflect actual progress.

NCLB increased the frequency and importance of mandated assessment of both regular and special education students as a measure of student performance and school accountability. Accordingly, students were to participate in statewide and districtwide assessments with greater frequency. In turn, the results from these assessments would be used to hold teachers and schools accountable for the progress of their students. In 2004, IDEA was amended and reauthorized to reflect the mandates in NCLB. According to NCLB, student progress toward acceptable performance was to be measured using yearly assessments. Federal rules also precluded the use of testing accommodations for 95% of the student population. Thus, the testing mandates and provisions established in IDEA (1997) have been reiterated in IDEA 2004. In addition, federal rules would require most students with disabilities to participate in statewide and districtwide assessment without the use of accommodations.

IDEA 2004 aligned special education and regular education in another way. Consistent with NCLB, IDEA 2004 required that all special educators be "highly qualified." To achieve this status, teachers must possess (a) a bachelor's degree, (b) full state certification or licensure, and (c) proof that they know each subject that they teach. In keeping with NCLB and IDEA, special educators providing instruction in core academic areas must demonstrate competency in each academic area that they teach. Competency can be demonstrated via several routes. The teacher may (a) complete a college-level major or equivalent credit hours in the specific academic area, (b) pass a state-developed test or competency evaluation, (c) earn an advanced certification from the state, or (d) complete a graduate degree. If the special educator is not providing direct instruction in a core academic area, IDEA 2004 requires that the educator hold at least a bachelor's degree as well as full state special education certification by the end of the 2005–2006 school year. These provisions are designed to terminate the temporary, emergency, or provisional certifications that many special educators hold. In addition, both laws implicitly suggest that effective instruction begins with qualified instructors.

:: NO CHILD LEFT BEHIND

The reauthorization of the federal Elementary and Secondary Education Act (ESEA)—also known as the No Child Left Behind (NCLB)—was signed by President George W. Bush in 2001. In addition to the provisions described above, NCLB required that states develop grade-level expectations, or benchmarks, in reading and math for all students in grades 3 through 8, as well as grade 11. However, some have questioned whether NCLB actually recognizes the nature of disability (e.g., Johns, 2003; Kauffman, 2005b) or the basic realities of educational assessment (e.g., Kauffman, 2003, 2006; Kauffman & Konold, in press).

In evaluating student progress toward these benchmarks, federal rules require 95% of all students to participate in yearly standardized assessments that measure adequate yearly progress (AYP). Of the remaining 5% of students, a few are eligible to take tests based on alternative achievement standards. These are likely to be students with severe cognitive limitations, students who would be unable to complete a grade-level assessment even with accommodations. Other students with disabilities are eligible to take the yearly standardized assessment with appropriate accommodations. Special education students currently account for approximately 10% of all school-age children, with LD representing about 5% and EBD and MMR each representing about 1% of the school-aged population. Thus, high-incidence disabilities currently represent approximately 7% of the school-age population. Some of these students will take the yearly standardized assessments required by NCLB with appropriate accommodations; however, 7% clearly exceeds the 5% cap stipulated in federal rules. For this reason, many students with high-incidence disabilities will be required to take the yearly assessment without testing accommodations that would ideally minimize the handicapping effects of their disabilities.

Based upon the proficiency demonstrated by students during these assessments, teachers and schools are to be evaluated relative to progress toward annual objectives. The performance of schools is then to be judged at a federal level. Should schools fail to reach achievement goals for two consecutive years, they will be labeled "in need of improvement." At this time, students will be given the option of transferring to higher-performing schools. After 3 years of not meeting improvement goals, the school must provide students with supplemental services. After 4 years, the school must replace staff and institute a new curriculum, and after 5 years, the school must reopen as a charter school. The issue for special education is that each subgroup in the school must be evaluated independently for AYP, including students receiving special education.

The effects of NCLB on students with disabilities are profound. This law dramatically changed expectations for both general and special education students. For example, many students with MMR, LD, and EBD will be required to demonstrate a year's progress toward grade-level benchmarks even though their disabilities preclude such progress (Kauffman, 2005b). NCLB has dramatically reframed the way in which schools and teachers are to be evaluated and funded, and in so doing, has set a precedent for how the progress of students with disabilities is to be measured and judged. In many ways, it represents a shift away from consideration of individuals and toward concern for groups (Johns, 2003).

It is difficult to predict what the future of special education will bring. Will students with high-incidence disabilities be relegated to instruction provided only in the general education classroom? If so, who will teach these students to read, to add, and to recognize numbers when benchmarks dictate fourth-, fifth-, or even seventh-grade standards? Reading and adding are not the content of most classrooms beyond the early-elementary grades; however, many students with high-incidence disabilities struggle with these skills well into high school. Additionally, how will general education teachers meet the behavioral needs of students with high-incidence disabilities, while also meeting the needs of the other students in the class? Appropriate behavior is seldom part of a regular education curriculum, and almost never a grade-level benchmark. How will special education students receive appropriate educations? Only one thing is certain: New laws, new rules and regulations, and new court decisions will change how students with disabilities are treated and what is required to address their needs in our schools.

Special education is a field with a rich history. This history can be used as a guide for progress, or it can be ignored. At present, it seems that special educators are in danger of ignoring the lessons of the past (MacMillan et al., 1996). Historically, special educators have been preoccupied with where appropriate instructional settings are to be found. The field has shifted from virtually no special education services to institutionalized services to deinstitutionalization. The field has entertained arguments based solely on morality and ethics, as well as those based on rational and scientific considerations. In the end, scientific thought and reason have proven to be the most effective tools for improving the educational experience of students with high-incidence disabilities. Science enabled the field of special education to develop *discriminative ability*, which enables one to detect the difference between the effective and the ineffective (Mostert, 1999–2000). Perhaps this tool, as well as a strong knowledge of history, will ultimately help to solve the inclusion debate, to resolve the controversy about NCLB, and provide the best response to impending legal issues.

SUMMARY

As we conclude this chapter on trends that have influenced the field of high-incidence disabilities, let us return to the place where we began. This book is focused on high-incidence disabilities. As subsequent chapters will show, the identification and treatment of high-incidence disabilities are difficult tasks. To execute these tasks, the field of special education has sometimes relied on practices based on unscientific thinking. Often these practices have had intuitive appeal, but scant support in the form of data. As you, the readers of this book, make instructional decisions for students with high-incidence disabilities, we urge you to consider how you will make your decisions. Will you make decisions based on the lessons of history? Will you use the tools of science, rationality, and careful consideration of the data to guide your thinking and your moral and ethical practice?

We restate some of the lessons of special education history and interpret them for teachers of students with high-incidence disabilities:

1. *Look at the data.* Argument without support by reliable scientific evidence is only propaganda (Sasso, 2001). The research evidence investigating full inclusion suggests caution (Kavale & Forness, 2000). Experimental data have failed to show that full inclusion facilitates the development of social skills (MacMillan et al., 1996), and arguments in support of full inclusion have not been based upon replicable or reliable research (Kavale & Forness, 2000).

2. *Acknowledge important historical events.* Remember that the belief that special places could cure disabilities drove both the crusade for bigger and better institutions as well as the deinstitutionalization movement. History demonstrates that the place in which students with disabilities are treated has not by itself provided a solution (Kauffman & Landrum, 2006; Kauffman & Lloyd, 1995; Kauffman & Smucker, 1995).

3. *Use the lessons of history to make decisions about the future.* In the 1980s and 1990s great concern was focused on the "where" of instruction, and not the "what" of instruction (Crockett & Kauffman, 1999; Kauffman & Smucker, 1995). Thus, the field of special education was lured into repeatedly adopting instructional practices that had little scientific support (Hockenbury, Kauffman, & Hallahan, 1999–2000; Mostert, 1999–2000; Mostert & Crockett, 1999–2000). Many mistakes were thus repeated.

4. *Remember that everything appears to have worked at least once, and nothing works all the time (Kauffman, 2002).* Writing about the history of special education, Mann noted, "yes, almost every intervention approach has its successes. . . . And so we repeat and repeat and again repeat the outworn, the discredited, the valueless" (Mann, 1979, pp. 541–542). The process we call science is still our best tool for finding out what is likely to work and what is not (Crockett, 2001).

Box 2.1 sets forth criteria for competent teaching.

COMPETENT TEACHING BOX
BOX 2.1

Knowing your students . . .

Knowing the history of special education and knowing our students helps us teach them more effectively. However, what we know about the historical underpinnings of special education and what we know about our students is NOT an automatic prescription for educational strategies or special education services.

What you want to remember about the historical underpinnings of high-incidence disabilities:

- High-incidence disabilities are not a new phenomenon. Historically, we have demonstrated that students with high-incidence disabilities can learn when provided with the evidenced-based instruction that meets their individualized needs.
- Although legal mandates have provided much of the impetus for the special education services in place for students with high-incidence disabilities today, we need to be careful when implementing these services; keeping in mind what is best for individual students.
- Special education services should be provided on an individualized basis for all students with high-incidence disabilities. Just because a student has a high-incidence disability does not mean that the student has the same needs as other students with high-incidence disabilities.
- Rather than basing services only on legal mandates, evaluating individual student outcomes following specialized instruction allows us to evaluate the efficacy of specific strategies and services for individual students.

Competent teachers . . .

- Competent teachers learn to use legal mandates to help them implement evidence-based special education services, rather than allowing legal mandates to drive services for their students.
- Competent teachers evaluate the data supporting historical and current trends prior to implementing these trends with their students.
- Competent teachers recognize when politics may be interfering with services for their students with high-incidence disabilities and advocate for their students' needs.
- Competent teachers only repeat history when history has been demonstrated to effectively help students with high-incidence disabilities.

▪▪ CASE STUDY

GREG

Greg is a 10-year-old fourth grader who has been identified by his school system having EBD. For the past 3 years, Greg has left his regular classroom, for two hours each day, to receive special education instruction in a resource-room setting. In addition to his persistent behavioral problems, Greg's academic achievement is very low. In his fourth-grade year, Greg is just beginning to recognize letter names and sounds consistently. He is also beginning to demonstrate some conceptual understanding of addition and subtraction. When presented with single-digit addition and subtraction problems, Greg uses a number line and his fingers in order to count out the answer. Although he can recognize the numbers 1 through 5 consistently, he must use a number line to identify numbers greater than 5. Greg can write his first name consistently, but he struggles with the spelling of his last name. In short, Greg struggles in all academic areas also due to his lack of reading and writing skills. Art and physical education (PE) seem to be the only subject areas in which he experiences any success.

During Greg's resource room time, instruction often takes the shape of the interaction described here:

Greg was seated next to his special education teacher at a kidney-shaped table. His teacher asked him to reread a very familiar book aloud to her (this was a book that Greg had actually memorized). When asked to read, Greg responded, "Ahh. . . . I hate reading," "This is too hard," "I hate this!" Greg's teacher deftly reassured him that he could do it, and she would certainly help him if he needed it. Greg eventually complied with his teacher's request. He was then asked to complete a worksheet while the teacher sat next to him and worked with the other student seated at the table. One student was on the teacher's left, and Greg was seated on her right. When Greg was asked to begin the worksheet, he argued, "I don't want to do this." His teacher responded that she would come back to him when he was ready to work. Greg eventually began the worksheet, but then used the worksheet itself to hide his face from the teacher. His work was sloppy. Greg's teacher asked him to redo several problems because of sloppiness. Greg then refused all help from the teacher. He sighed loudly, stopped speaking to the teacher, and refused to work. Greg's teacher responded that he would be late for his recess if he could not finish his work. Eventually, Greg began to work and requested his teacher's help. Greg was able to complete his work on time.

His teacher responded by rewarding Greg with a sticker for work well done. He was sent to recess on time.

Greg's school system uses a standardized assessment, aligned with the grade-level curriculum, to measure student achievement. Consistent with NCLB, the school system will now administer this assessment every year in grades 3 through 8 and grade 11, in both reading and mathematics. In grade four, the reading assessment evaluates the degree to which students can:

a. Understand stated information.
b. Determine the meaning of new words from their context.
c. Draw conclusions, make references, and deduce meaning.
d. Infer traits, feelings, and motives of character.
e. Interpret information in new contexts.
f. Interpret information without literal language.
g. Determine the main idea of a book.
h. Identify the author's views or purpose.
i. Analyze the style or structure of a book.

Likewise, the math assessment evaluates the degree to which students can:

a. Understand and apply mathematical concepts.
b. Solve word problems.
c. Understand and apply methods of estimation.
d. Interpret data from graphs and tables.

Because of NCLB, 95% of all students in Greg's school must participate in this yearly assessment. Of the remaining 5% of students, 1% can participate in an alternate assessment and 4% can participate with testing accommodations.

Greg receives his special education instruction in a resource room setting. This means that he is in his regular classroom for the majority of the school day. Other special education students in Greg's school who have more severe disabilities are served in special self-contained classrooms. Because Greg receives special education services that are judged less intensive than those students served in self-contained classrooms, the principal has determined that Greg is ineligible for the alternate assessment given to 1% of students. He will therefore need to take the fourth-grade standardized assessment described above. Greg's special education teacher has suggested that he be allowed to take this assessment using accommodations. She has asked that he be given the accommodations of:

a. Extended time
b. Separate setting
c. Math test read aloud
d. Directions in reading test read aloud
e. Test administered by resource teacher

The principal in Greg's school argues that Greg can partici-pate with these accommodations. However, Greg's special education teacher fears that even with these specific accom-modations, Greg will be unable to demonstrate the Adequate Yearly Progress (AYP) required by NCLB. This student is reading on the first-grade level and being evaluated on fourth-grade standards.

(Contributions to the Case Study by Amy Jones)

1. In what ways does Greg benefit from the rights and protections afforded him under IDEA?
2. How does NCLB affect Greg and his special education services?
3. In compliance with IDEA 2004 and NCLB, Greg will participate in a statewide assessment using fourth-grade benchmarks. What are the benefits of this? What are the problems?
4. Considering the requirements of NCLB and IDEA 2004, what should Greg's school do?

REFERENCES

Bateman, B., & Linden, M. A. (1998). *Better IEPs*. Longmont, CO: Sopris West.

Berkowitz, P. H., & Rothman, E. P. (1960). *The disturbed child: Recognition and psychoeducational therapy in the class-room*. New York: New York University Press.

Bryan, T., Pearl, R., Donahue, M., Bryan, J., & Pflaum, S. (1983). The Chicago Institute for the Study of Learning Disabilities. *Exceptional Education Quarterly, 4*(1), 1–22.

Connor, F. P. (1983). Improving school instruction for learn-ing disabled children: The Teachers College Institute. *Exceptional Education Quarterly, 4*(1), 23–44.

Council for Exceptional Children (2003, March 14). CEC's proposals to develop three year IEP's: Questions and an-swers. *Public Policy Update,* website: www.cec.org.

Crockett, J. B. (Ed.). (2001). The meaning of science and empirical rigor in the social sciences. *Behavioral Disor-ders, 27*(1) [special issue].

Crockett, J. B., & Kauffman, J. M. (1999). *The least restrictive environment: Its origins and interpretations in special educa-tion*. Mahwah, NJ: Erlbaum.

Deno, E. (1970). Special education as developmental capital. *Exceptional Children, 37,* 229–237.

Dorn, S., Fuchs, D., & Fuchs, L. S. (1996). A Historical Per-spective on Special Education Reform. *Theory into Prac-tice 35,* 12–19.

Dunn, L. (1968). Special education for the mildly retarded—is much of it justifiable? *Exceptional Children, 34,* 5–22.

Engelmann, S., & Osborn, J. (1977) *DISTAR Language*. Chicago: Science Research Associates.

Engelmann, S., Becker, W. C., Hanner, S., & Johnson, G. (1978). *Corrective reading program: Series guide*. Chicago: Science Research Associates.

Engelmann, S., Becker, W. C., Hanner, S., & Johnson, G. (1988). *Corrective reading program: Series guide* (rev. ed.). Chicago: Science Research Associates.

Fuchs, D.,& Fuchs, L. S. (1994). Inclusive schools move-ment and the radicalization of special education reform. *Exceptional Children, 60,* 294–309.

Fuchs, D., Mock, D. R., Morgan, P. L., & Young, C. L. (2003). Responsiveness-to-Intervention: Definitions, evidence, and implications for the learning disabilities construct. *Learning Disabilities Research and Practice, 18,* 151–171.

Gersten, R., & Woodward, J. (1990). Rethinking the regular education initiative: Focus on the classroom teacher. *Remedial and Special Education, 11,* 7–16.

Gliona, M. F., Gonzales, A. K., & Jacobson, E. S. (2005). Dedicated, not segregated: Suggested changes in thinking about instructional environments and in the language of special education. In J. M. Kauffman & D. P. Hallahan (Eds.), *The illusion of full inclusion: A comprehensive critique of a current special education bandwagon* (2nd ed., pp. 135–146). Austin, TX: PRO-ED.

Hallahan, D. P., & Mercer, C. D. (2001, August). *Learning dis-abilities: A historical perspective*. Paper presented at the LD Summit. Washington, DC: U.S. Department of Education.

Hallahan, D. P., & Mock, D. R. (2003). A brief history of the field of learning disabilities. In H. L. Swanson, K. Harris, & S. Graham (Eds.), *Handbook of learning disabilities*. New York: Guilford.

Hallahan, D. P., & Cruickshank, W. M. (1973). *Psychoe-ducational foundations of learning disabilities*. Upper Saddle River, NJ: Prentice Hall.

Hallahan, D. P., Hall, R. J., Ianna, S. O., Kneedler, R. D., Lloyd, J. W., Loper, A. B., & Reeve, R. E. (1983). Sum-mary of research findings at the University of Virginia Learning Disabilities Research Institute. *Exceptional Edu-cation Quarterly, 4*(1), 95–114.

Hallahan, D. P., & Kauffman, J. M. (2006). *Exceptional learn-ers: An introduction to special education* (10th ed.). Boston: Allyn & Bacon.

Hallahan, D. P., Lloyd, J. W., Kauffman, J. M., Weiss, M., & Martinez, E. (2005). *Introduction to learning disabilities* (3rd ed.). Boston: Allyn & Bacon.

Hallenbeck, B. A., & Kauffman, J. M. (1995). How does observational learning affect the behavior of students with emotional or behavioral disorders? A review of research. *Journal of Special Education, 29,* 45–71.

Herr, C. M., & Bateman, B. D. (2003). Learning disabilities and the law. In H. L. Swanson, K. Harris, & S. Graham (Eds.), *Handbook of learning disabilities.* New York: Guilford.

Hockenbury, J. C., Kauffman, J. M., & Hallahan, D. P., (1999–2000). What is right about special education. *Exceptionality, 8,* 3–11.

Huefner, D. S. (2000). *Getting comfortable with special education law: A framework for working with children with disabilities.* Norwood, MA: Christopher-Gordon.

Itard, J. M. G. (1962). *The wild boy of Aveyron* (George & Muriel Humphrey, Trans.). Englewood Cliffs, NJ: Prentice-Hall.

Jenkins, J. R., Pious, C. G., & Peterson, D. L. (1988). Categorical programs for remedial and handicapped students: Issues of validity. *Exceptional Children, 55,* 147–158.

Johns, B. H. (2003). NCLB and IDEA: Never the twain should meet. *Learning Disabilities: A Multidisciplinary Journal, 12*(3), 89–91.

Kauffman, J. M. (1976). Nineteenth century views of children's behavior disorders: Historical contributions and continuing issues. *Journal of Special Education, 10,* 335–349.

Kauffman, J. M. (1981). Historical trends and contemporary issues in special education in the United States. In J. M. Kauffman & D. P. Hallahan (Eds.), *Handbook of special education* (pp. 3–23). Upper Saddle River, NJ: Prentice Hall.

Kauffman, J. M. (1989). The regular education initiative as Reagan-Bush education policy: A trickle-down theory of education of the hard-to-teach. *Journal of Special Education, 23,* 256–278.

Kauffman, J. M. (2002). *Education deform: Bright people sometimes say stupid things about education.* Lanham, MD: Scarecrow Education.

Kauffman, J. M. (2003). Appearances, stigma, and prevention. *Remedial and Special Education, 24,* 195–198.

Kauffman, J. M. (2005a). *Characteristics of emotional and behavioral disorders of children and youth* (8th ed.). Upper Saddle River, NJ: Merrill/Prentice Hall.

Kauffman, J. M. (2005b). Waving to Ray Charles: Missing the meaning of disability. *Phi Delta Kappan, 86,* 520–521, 524.

Kauffman, J. M. (2006). Labels and the nature of special education: We need to face realities. *Learning Disabilities: A Multidisciplinary Journal.*

Kauffman, J. M., Brigham, F. J., & Mock, D. R. (2004). Historical to contemporary perspectives in the field of behavioral disorders. In R. B. Rutherford, M. M. Quinn, & S. R. Mathur (Eds.), *Handbook of research in emotional and behavioral disorders* (pp. 15–31) New York: Guilford.

Kauffman, J. M., & Hallahan, D. P. (2005a). *Special education: What it is and why we need it.* Boston: Allyn & Bacon.

Kauffman, J. M., & Hallahan, D. P. (2005b). *The illusion of full inclusion: A comprehensive critique of a current educational bandwagon* (2nd ed.). Austin, TX: PRO-ED.

Kauffman, J. M., & Konold, T. R. (2007). Making sense in education: Pretense (including NCLB) and realities in rhetoric about schools and schooling. *Exceptionality, 15.*

Kauffman, J. M., & Landrum, T. J. (2006). *Children and youth with emotional and behavioral disorders: A history of their education.* Austin, TX: PRO-ED.

Kauffman, J. M., & Lloyd, J. W. (1995). A sense of place: The importance of placement issues in contemporary special education. In J. M. Kauffman, J. W. Lloyd, D. P. Hallahan, & T. A. Astuto (Eds.), *Issues in educational placement: Students with emotional and behavioral disorders* (pp. 3–19). Hillsdale, NJ: Erlbaum.

Kauffman, J. M., McGee, K., & Brigham, M. (2004). Enabling or disabling? Observations on changes in the purposes and outcomes of special education. *Phi Delta Kappan, 85,* 613–620.

Kauffman, J. M., & Pullen, P. L. (1996). Eight myths about special education. *Focus on Exceptional Children, 28*(5), 1–12.

Kauffman, J. M., & Smucker, K. (1995). The legacies of placement: A brief history of placement options and issues with commentary on their evolution. In J. M. Kauffman, J. W. Lloyd, D. P. Hallahan, & T. A. Astuto (Eds.), *Issues in educational placement: Students with emotional and behavioral disorders* (pp. 21–44). Hillsdale, NJ: Erlbaum.

Kauffman, J. M., & Wiley, A. L. (2004). How the President's Commission on Excellence in Special Education (PCESE) devalues special education. *Learning Disabilities: A Multidisciplinary Journal, 13,* 3–6.

Kavale, K. A., & Forness, S. R. (2000). What definitions of learning disability say and don't say: A critical analysis. *Journal of Learning Disabilities, 33,* 239–256.

Landrum, T. J., & Kauffman, J. M. (2006). Behavioral approaches to classroom management. In C. M. Evertson & C. S. Weinstein (Eds.), *Handbook of classroom management: Research, practice, and contemporary issues* (pp. 47–71). Mahwah, NJ: Erlbaum.

Lipsky, D. K., & Gartner, A. (1987). Capable of achievement and worthy of respect: Education for handicapped students as if they were full-fledged human beings. *Exceptional Children, 54,* 69–74.

Lipsky, D. K., & Gartner, A. (1996). Inclusion, school restructuring and the remaking of American society. *Harvard Educational Review, 66*, 762–796.

Lipsky, D. K., & Gartner, A. (1998). Taking inclusion into the future. *Educational Leadership, 56*, 78–81.

Lyon, G. R., Fletcher, J. M., Shaywitz, S. A., Shaywitz, B. A., Torgesen, J. K., Wood, F. B., Schulte, A., & Olson, R. (2001). Rethinking learning disabilities. In C. E. Finn, A. J. Rothrham, & C. R. Hokanson (Eds.), *Rethinking special education for a new century* (pp. 259–287). Washington DC: Thomas B. Fordham Foundation.

MacMillan, D. L., Gresham, F. M., & Forness, S. R. (1996). Full inclusion: An empirical perspective. *Behavioral Disorders, 21*, 145–159.

Mann, L. (1979). *On the trail of process: A historical perspective on cognitive processes and their training.* New York: Grune & Stratton.

Mock, D. R., & Kauffman, J. M. (2005). The delusion of full inclusion. In J. W. Jacobson, R. M. Foxx, & J. A. Mulick (Eds.), *Controversial therapies for developmental disabilities: Fad, fashion, and science in professional practice* (pp. 113–128). Mahwah, NJ: Erlbaum.

Mostert, M. P. (1999–2000). A partial etiology and sequelae of discriminative disability: Bandwagons and beliefs. *Exceptionality, 8*, 117–132.

Mostert, M. P., & Crockett, J. C. (1999–2000). Reclaiming the history of special education for more effective practice. *Exceptionality, 8*, 133–143.

Pugach, M., & Lilly, S. M. (1984). Reconceptualizing support services for classroom teachers: Implications for teacher education. *Journal of Teacher Education, 35*, 48–55.

Reynolds, M. C. (1988). Reaction to the JLD special series on the Regular Education Initiative. *Journal of Learning Disabilities, 21*, 352–356.

Sasso, G. M. (2001). The retreat from inquiry and knowledge in special education. *The Journal of Special Education, 34*, 178–193.

Schumaker, J. B., Deshler, D. D., Alley, G. R., & Warner, M. M. (1983). Toward the development of an intervention model for learning disabled adolescents: The University of Kansas Institute. *Exceptional Education Quarterly, 4*(1), 45–74.

Singer, J. D. (1988). Should special education merge with regular education? *Educational Policy, 2*, 409–424.

Stainback, S., & Stainback, W. (1992). Including students with severe disabilities in the regular classroom curriculum. *Preventing School Failure, 37*, 26–30.

Whelan, R. J., & Haring, N. G. (1966). Modification and maintenance of behavior through systematic application of consequences. *Exceptional Children, 32*, 281–289.

Wiederholt, J.L. (1974). Historical perspectives on the education of the learning disabled. In L. Mann & D. Sabatino (Eds.), *The second review of special education* (pp. 103–152). Philadelphia: JSE Press.

Ysseldyke, J. E., Thurlow, M., Graden, J., Wesson, C., Algozzine, B., & Deno, S. L. (1983). Generalizations from five years of research on assessment and decision making: The University of Minnesota Institute. *Exceptional Education Quarterly, 4*(1), 75–93.

Understanding Causal Factors Related to High-Incidence Disabilities

URBAN LEGEND: *Finishing the genome project will eventually allow us to prevent disabilities.*

LEGENDARY THOUGHT: *One cause does not fit all.*

One cause does not fit all. In fact, we could say that one cause does not apply to:

- All disabilities,
- All individuals having disabilities, or
- All behaviors of any individual with disabilities.

Research in numerous disciplines has demonstrated that *combinations* of biological, psychological, social, and cultural factors affect the development and maturation of individuals from childhood through adulthood. A great deal remains to be learned about the many causes of high-incidence disabilities and how multiple causes interact to affect academic and social learning.

At-risk is commonly used to describe children having a greater-than-normal likelihood for specific, undesired outcomes, such as school failure or antisocial behavior. Something that increases someone's risk of a negative outcome is called a **risk factor.** Risk factors include such things as lack of early training, biological factors, and environmental circumstances (e.g., parents who seldom or never read to their children, genetics, an unsafe environment, malnutrition).

In education and related disciplines, risk factors underscore the need for early intervention and assist us in identifying specific learning needs of students. Risk factors do not act in isolation or always have the same effect. They function in concert with each other and with their opposites—resiliency factors—to produce inconsistent outcomes. A **resiliency factor** decreases the likelihood of someone having a negative outcome (or increases the chances of a positive outcome). Resiliency factors might include, for example, good parenting, an attentive teacher, **genetic** factors (factors influenced by genes; i.e., inherited factors) that we do not understand completely, or robust physical health.

Think for a moment of someone falling down a few steps. Such a fall can produce different outcomes, depending on the person's age, strength, and physical condition and the medical attention the person receives. The short- and long-term effects of a four-step fall may differ dramatically, depending on the characteristics of the person who falls and on the medical attention they receive. The outcome may be trivial bruises or death, depending on risk and resiliency factors. The elderly gentleman who rarely gets out of his home will respond to the fall quite differently from the middle-age woman who is active and works out 5 days a week but suffers from severe osteoporosis. The elderly person who falls and sustains serious injury may die, acquire a permanent disability, or have no lasting effect, depending on medical treatment. Both older and less physically fit people are likely to experience far more injury than the 25-year-old athlete whose parents were both Olympiads and continue to compete at 60 years of age. And if a child carries a genetic predisposition to brittle bones, the result may be severe injury.

For students with high-incidence disabilities, the interplay of risk factors with resiliency factors occurs across and within biological and environmental factors. We discuss particular biological and environmental factors. Remember, however, that it is the complex interaction of these factors that determines whether or not a child has a disability.

:: NORMAL (TYPICAL) DEVELOPMENT, ABNORMAL (ATYPICAL) DEVELOPMENT, AND RISK

Families, teachers, and physicians all recognize that *normal* (typical) development includes a lot of variation. Some normal children walk at 9 months, others not until 15 months. A typical child may have intelligible speech at 9 months, but some normal children don't talk so that strangers can understand them easily until they are several years old. Despite the tremendous variations in normal development, most children fall within the bounds of development that we judge to be typical. Their rate of development—the **trajectory** or path of development they are on—leads us to believe that they are likely to become well-functioning, productive adults. Similarly, abnormal (atypical) development includes a lot of variation in the age at which a child achieves particular milestones and the type of behavior a child exhibits under given circumstances.

Although we use specific diagnostic criteria in identifying disability categories, most of these categories do not have a single course or path of origin. *Educational* labels (as opposed to medical labels, for example) are defined by behaviors or learning characteristics, not causes. Therefore, no one can give certain or brief answers to questions such as these:

What causes mild mental retardation (MMR)?
What causes learning disabilities (LD)?
What causes emotional or behavioral disorders (EBD)?

Instead of describing what causes a disability, we describe risk factors and possible outcomes under given conditions. We can identify some of the major risk factors involved, especially those linked to disabilities. Although researchers from different disciplines are actively engaged in targeted research to better understand the origins of disabilities, it is essential to recognize that when assessing potential causes, one has to account for a host of potential influences such as brain development, heredity, **prenatal** (before birth) factors, **perinatal** (around the time of birth) events, **postnatal** (after birth) problems, and continuing environmental factors. Relatively few of these risk factors are unique to specific disabilities. Most risk factors can have a variety of outcomes. Some may contribute to a variety of disabilities.

Risk factors fall into two major categories: biological and environmental. However, an important concept is that biological and environmental risks are related. First, one can contribute to the other, as when an unsanitary environment contributes to illness. Second, the boundaries between them are not absolute, such that genetic factors (biological) and environmental factors (in which genetics are determined or altered) are not always possible to separate entirely (see Pinker, 2002). We discuss some of the major risk factors in the biological and environmental categories, but it is important to recognize that these are not mutually exclusive categories.

:: BIOLOGICAL RISK FACTORS

Biological risk factors are things that go wrong physically. They include such things as atypical development of the brain, injury to the brain (by physical trauma, poisoning, deprivation of oxygen, and so on), disease, genetic flaws, and inborn temperament or predispositions to behave in certain ways under given circumstances. The major thing to remember is that some disabilities are related to physical development and health of the body.

We discuss risk factors as they are most obviously related to particular disabilities. This does not mean that risk factors cannot contribute to the cause of more than one disability. However, our discussion is focused on particulars of risks and disabilities whenever possible.

Brain Development and Function

Emotional or Behavioral Disorders (EBD)

The definitions of mental retardation and learning disabilities typically include references to brain functioning. However, people may avoid mentioning brain development or other biological factors when discussing EBD. Compared to LD or MMR, we understand less about the relationship between brain impairment and personality development or social-interpersonal behavior and feelings. Because a variety of brain systems and their components regulate such things as emotion and affect, the effects of specific or global brain malfunctions or disorders can influence many facets of behavioral and emotional development.

The brain is an exceedingly complex organ, so we should not be surprised that we still know relatively little about how it affects emotions and behavior. Neither should we be surprised to find that we need much more research by experts in physiology to be able to figure out how the brain works. Nevertheless, recent research has reinforced the notion that some brain disorders seem to influence the development of specific facets of EBD such as anxiety, hyperactivity, depression, defiance, and aggression. For example, **neurotransmitters** (chemicals necessary for brain cells to send or receive electrical impulses) have been studied for quite a long time. Researchers have studied the effects of these brain chemicals on depression, self-esteem, social status, and a variety of other behaviors and behavioral dispositions (Sylvester, 1997). We know that neurotransmitters affect how the brain functions and that these chemicals have been linked to impulsive, reckless, violent, and suicidal behavior in some cases. Still, we do not know how much of which chemical produces particular behavior. Nor do we understand how behavior may contribute to the production of certain brain chemicals. In short, we know that there is some sort of relationship between brain chemicals and emotions or behavior, but we do not understand much about just how the relationship works.

Advances in the ability to measure and translate the effects of neurotransmitters on behavior (and vice versa) will likely help us test hypotheses about the link between brain disorders and various disabilities. For example, research indicates that individuals identified with **ADHD** (which may be identified with LD or EBD) tend to have a deficiency or imbalance in one or more neurotransmitters (see Hallahan, Lloyd, Kauffman, Weiss, & Martinez, 2005; Kauffman, 2005 for more discussion of ADHD and Chapter 7 of this book).

Chemical imbalances are thought to affect the ability to select and maintain goals, manage competing tasks, and adapt plans to meet demands. These abilities, as well as those linked with problem solving, judgment, self-monitoring, and critical thinking, are all associated with executive functioning. However, besides chemical imbalances, damage to the brain may also be implicated in disabilities. Damage to the **prefrontal lobe** of the brain (see Figure 3.1) has been linked to impairments in executive functioning and consequent disorders of emotion and behavior (Damasio, 1985; Welsch, 1994).

Progress in understanding the specific neurodevelopmental risk factors and developmental stages related to the origin of EBD has been slow. Progress has been slowed by the great variety of intra-individual differences (differences found within the same person at various times or under various circumstances) (Reiss & Denckla, 1996). (See Figure 3.1.)

FIGURE 3.1   **Important regions of the left hemisphere associated with reading and behavior deficits**

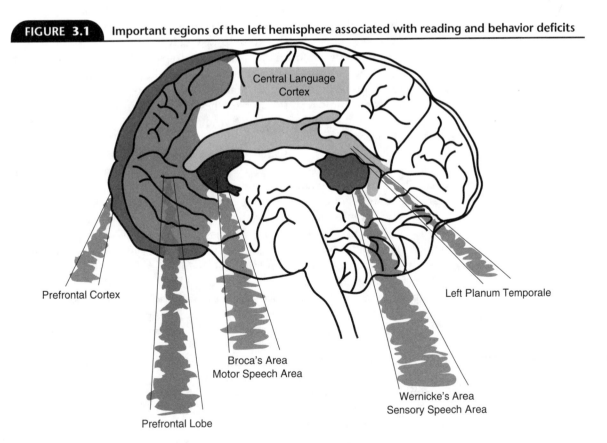

Behavioral neurogenetics attempts to link behavioral and cognitive problems with specific genetic effects on the brain (Baumgarten, Green, & Reiss, 1994). Researchers hope to improve their understanding of the role that genetically determined brain structure has on the development of disordered behavior. They also hope to develop interventions that are targeted more specifically and more efficient because they address these brain factors (Reiss & Denckla, 1996).

Neurological research in EBD is by no means conclusive. Additional research is necessary if we are to increase our understanding of differences in the neurological make-up of individuals with EBD (Kauffman, 2005).

Learning Disabilities (LD)

Central nervous system dysfunction (CNSD) is a presumed cause of LD (Evans, 2001; Hallahan et al., 2005). Researchers have suspected for over a century that LD reflects a neurological problem (e.g., Hinshelwood, 1900; Kussmaul, 1877; Morgan, 1896; see Chapter 2 and Hallahan et al., 2005, for more information). Early studies and hypotheses influenced later studies in cognitive and behavioral development relative to brain formation and function. Further inquiry identified the specific areas associated with central language areas of the brain. Specifically, researchers have been investigating asymmetry associated with the size of the **planum temporale** and the **frontal** and **central language cortex** (which includes **Wernicke's** area and the **arcuate fasciculus,** which serves as the connecting pathway between **Broca's** and Wernicke's regions) in the left **hemisphere** of the brain (see Figure 3.1). Damage to these areas affects the ability to learn to read and may result in other behavioral deficits associated with severe reading difficulties. **Neurobiological** research on the origins of learning disabilities have emphasized reading problems because reading disability is the most common problem in learning disabilities, involving up to 80% of all students with LD (Fiedorowicz et al., 2001). Researchers have hypothesized that if something goes wrong in the development of the language cortex, it *can* result in learning disabilities. This type of **maldevelopment** (development that is abnormal or deviant) can only occur during a specific time in development of the brain, namely the fifth and seventh month of pregnancy, which means in the second trimester (Hynd, & Hiementz, 1997). Some neurologists have focused on the planum temporale, specifically differences in the **symmetry** (or **asymmetry**) of brains or brain functions that distinguish individuals with and without learning disabilities. For example, an association has been found between individuals with larger right planum temporale and deficits in neurolinguistic processing, receptive language, and reading abilities, specifically comprehension (e.g., Kibby & Hynd, 2001). Research has also linked problems in various regions of the brain's cortex with difficulties in receptive and expressive language difficulties (e.g., Kral, Nielsen & Hynd, 1998). Related research on the correlation between brain functioning and learning disabilities, has used imaging to reveal **metabolic** (relating to the body's chemical processes) and blood flow differences across the two brain hemispheres between individuals with and without learning disabilities (Flowers, Wood, & Naylor, 1991). This research clearly has implications for other disability areas as well, given the co-occurrence of LD with EBD and related behavioral disabilities, such as ADHD (Filipek, 1999; see also Hallahan et al., 2005; Kauffman, 2005).

A significant body of research suggests anatomical discrepancies in specific brain regions between those with and without specific learning and behavioral difficulties (Kibby & Hynd, 2001). However, discrepancies across studies preclude us from reaching definitive conclusions. Such discrepancies include differing definitions of reading disabilities, differing tasks performed by participants, and differing measurement tools employed by investigators. Despite these discrepancies, researchers generally agree that localized, structural differences exist in the brains of individuals with and without LD. Additionally, these researchers hypothesize that LD may demonstrate some level of **comorbidity** (co-occurrence) with disorders like ADHD and other behavioral and cognitive disabilities. The biological basis of this comorbidity has yet to be isolated in research.

Mild Mental Retardation (MMR)

Given that even mild forms of mental retardation include cognitive delay, this disability is typically associated with some form of abnormal brain development. However, as we mentioned earlier, the brain is a very complex organ, and we understand little about the details of how it works. As in the area of EBD, the relationship between brain development and MMR is unclear, and we can say very little with certainty. Even though approximately 50% of diagnosed cases of severe MR can be linked to a known or suspected cause, for the majority of individuals diagnosed with MMR, the cause is unknown (Beirne-Smith, Ittenbach, & Patton, 2002). The traditional assumption is that there is a single biological cause for various severe disabilities (e.g., cerebral palsy) and a whole host of environmental risk factors contributing to milder forms of mental retardation (Beirne-Smith et al, 2002). However, we now recognize that biological factors may be partially responsible for many cases of MMR (McLaren & Bryson, 1987). In other words, biological risk factors such as brain development, most often linked to various syndromes associated with severe MR, may play a greater role in the occurrence of mild cognitive disabilities than previously assumed (such as brain structure abnormalities).

As discussed earlier, mild cognitive impairments co-occur with many other disorders of learning and behavior. Additionally, the combinations of characteristics exhibited by individuals identified as having MMR are vast and often associated with risk factors having to do with brain development and brain function.

Genes—Heredity

Heredity has been increasingly linked to altered neurological development and behavioral characteristics. Heredity refers to the transmission of genes from biological parents to their children. This genetic transmission occurs during fertilization of the egg by the sperm. We know that genes affect hair color, eye color, height, weight, and even traits such as personal preferences and tolerances. The **human genome project** has produced a complete a map of human DNA (Collins, 2003; Collins, Green, Guttmacher, & Guyer, 2003). Actually, maps of the gene sequence of many species have now been made. The map of human genes will allow scientists to identify variations within genetic makeup and thereby potentially identify the genetic basis of abnormal characteristics. This in turn could support targeted medical research aimed at preventing or eliminating some specific disorders. However, high-incidence disabilities such as LD, MMR, and EBD represent the complex interplay of many genes in addition to environmental factors, so the urban legend we mentioned at the beginning of this chapter stands as a legend: it is certainly *not* true that finishing the genome project will eventually allow us to prevent all disabilities, particularly not all of the disabilities we are discussing in this book. We know this because the map of the human genome has been completed, and no responsible scientist is even suggesting that it will eventually allow us to pinpoint the genes for all cases of LD, MMR, or EBD. Such a perspective would deny the importance of environmental influences on learning and development.

Mild Mental Retardation (MMR)

Even without a complete mapping of the specific **genes** that are located on the various **chromosomes,** researchers agree that when the structural arrangement (duplication and pairing) of chromosomes is interrupted or altered, the result *can* be an individual with some sort of disability. The majority of biological causes related to MMR are due to inherited traits and chromosomal abnormalities, which are then influenced by environmental variables. Notice that we did not say that MMR is merely biological or that it is merely inherited. It is far more complicated than that. Even though we know that genetic factors are among those contributing to MMR, it is important to remember this: bright parents can have children with MMR, and parents with MMR can have intellectually normal or gifted children. The genetics of mental ability are exceedingly complex, and it is not necessarily the case that children will inherit the mental abilities of their parents.

Some **syndromes** (a set of characteristics that together reflect a disorder) are typically associated with more severe forms of MR than are those we discuss in this book. Nevertheless, these syndromes associated with reproduction may help us understand the role of genetic factors in MR. **Fragile X syndrome,** for example, is the result of an abnormality in the X chromosome (specifically, a broken part at the bottom of the 23rd pair of chromosomes). Although this syndrome was originally discovered in 1943, a more complete understanding of it and its origin was not developed until the late 1970s and early 1980s. **Down syndrome** (so named after Dr. Down, who first identified it) is also related to genetics. It is sometimes called trisomy 21 because there are three rather than two copies of the 21st chromosome when cells start dividing (making 47 instead of the normal 46 chromosomes). Down syndrome is the most common form of MR recognizable at birth, and the cognitive disability associated with this syndrome can range from mild to severe. Fragile X is the most common type of MR that has a known genetic cause (Hallahan & Kauffman, 2006; Lachiewicz, Harrison, Spiridigliozzi, Callanan, & Livermore, 1988). **Phenylketonuria** (PKU) is an example of an inborn metabolic disorder in which individuals have difficulty breaking down and using (metabolizing) the amino acid phenylalanine. Both PKU and **Trisomy 18** (development of an extra chromosome 18) are also examples of genetically derived disorders that if not caught early can cause various forms of MR. These are just a few examples of genetic syndromes that can lead to various levels of MR, including MMR. Currently there are approximately over 350 inborn errors of metabolism that have been identified, most of which are associate with MR, with additional disorders identified annually (AAMR, 2002).

Although numerous other syndromes exist, some are extremely rare, and most are associated with more severe MR. Our understanding of genetics and MR continues to evolve. Furthermore, our knowledge of the implications of reproductive accidents like Down syndrome continues to evolve, too. For example, historically individuals with Down syndrome were assumed to function primarily in the moderate and severe ranges of MR, dying at a relatively young age. However, with better medical treatment and improved environmental conditions, including early educational intervention, individuals with Down syndrome have an increased life expectancy, live more productive lives, and may have MR that is considered mild (Hallahan & Kauffman, 2006).

Emotional and Behavioral Disorders (EBD)

As we indicated previously, there is no single gene that causes MMR. Similarly, no single gene causes EBD. This is not to suggest that genes are irrelevant to this high-incidence disability. To the contrary, inherited emotional and behavioral dispositions do factor into the development of EBD. The genes we obtain from our ancestors may give us a predisposition to certain psychological and physical responses to our environment. For example, an individual may inherit fair skin from one or both parents. This inherited characteristic does not in and of itself cause the person to have sunburn. However, the inherited pigmentation may provide that person with a predisposition to burn easily when exposed to direct sunlight. Another person may have inherited a more olive color of skin that burns only with much greater exposure to the sun, and yet another individual with fair skin who grows up in the Bahamas or has a slightly different combination of genes, may tan rather easily without burning.

In the same way, inherited traits may provide a predisposition to have EBD. An individual with these traits may inherit a predisposition to interact and react in certain ways to specific events and activities. We know, in fact, that some problems such as schizophrenia and depression have substantial genetic components, although we still do not know just how the genes work (Kauffman, 2005). We know that there is a genetic component in these disorders because of the way they are related to family trees and the fact that differences in environments cannot explain variations in behavior.

Learning Disabilities (LD)

Many children with learning disabilities have another family member who has or had similar learning difficulties. Research suggests that when one parent reports reading deficits, up to 55% of the sons also have similar problems. Increased risk also exists for daughters if there is a history of LD in the family. Furthermore, one twin is more likely to have LD if the other twin does (Defries et al., 1997; Fiedorowicz et al., 2001; Pennington et al., 1999).

Genetic factors have been identified that result in a predisposition to develop reading disabilities have been noted (Fiedorowicz et al., 2001; Grigorenko, Wood, & Meyer, 1997). However, a predisposition does not in and of itself cause a disability. A complex combination of genetics and environmental influences probably cause such disorders (Hallahan et al., 2005). Researchers focus on how specific predispositions combine with social learning to produce a disability. A combination of biological and environmental factors determines an individual's response to a set of experiences, which may then set the stage for the gradual or more immediate onset of certain illnesses or disorders. For this reason, researchers are interested in studying resiliency and the degree to which other factors can buffer individuals against emotional fragility or predispositions or stressors within the environment. In this way, researchers hope to better understand those environmental factors that best support typical development.

Temperament

Professionals use the term **temperament** to refer to a child's innate behavioral style (Chess & Thomas, 2003; Keogh, 2003). Interestingly, a child's temperament is present at birth and remains relatively stable through development. The temperament parents see in their three-year-old toddler is generally the same temperament they witness when that child enters adolescence (although, as we shall discuss, temperament can also be modified to some extent by parenting and teaching).

Psychologists have identified approximately nine different aspects of temperament. As described first by Thomas, Chess, and Birch (1968) and later by Thomas and Chess (1977), these aspects of temperament include:

- Activity level
- Adaptability
- Approach/withdrawal
- Attention span and persistence
- Distractibility
- Intensity of reaction
- Quality of mood
- Regularity
- Responsiveness

As you can imagine, various levels of each of these nine factors are more or less desirable and effective in specific environments. All children exhibit various degrees of these characteristics. Babies and children usually considered to have a difficult temperament are characterized by certain styles of behavior. Although many different behavioral styles or temperaments might be identified, difficult children usually exhibit high levels of distractibility, a tendency to withdraw from situations, and intense reactions to events. They often exhibit a low attention span and persistence as well as low levels of adaptability (flexibility), an unwillingness to approach other people and things, irregularity in behavior patterns, and they tend to be less responsive to their environment. Children with a difficult temperament are, unsurprisingly, at higher risk than those with an easy temperament for having disabilities.

We do not know exactly what genes determine someone's temperament. However, we do know that genes are involved and that there is individual variation in what is described as temperament from the moment of birth. The fact that we do not know what biological factors cause someone to have a particular temperament does not mean that we cannot identify temperamental characteristics or that temperament cannot be modified.

Emotional and Behavioral Disorders (EBD)

Many children with EBD are highly irritable. Their difficult temperament may put them at odds with the expectations of their parents, peers, and teachers. Often, these children exhibit hyperactivity and antisocial behavior. Some are extremely withdrawn, avoiding many situations that other children embrace and find exciting, and their mood is often sad or depressed. They may show unusually intense reactions to situations that other children take in stride. They are not easy to live with or to teach. Many, though not all, children with EBD are at high risk for disabilities from the beginning of their lives (see Kauffman, 2005 for further discussion).

Learning Disability (LD)

Children with LD often have little ability to sustain attention and focus on the things that are important, especially academic tasks. Distractibility and lack of persistence when they encounter failure is typical of these children. Some are hyperactive. With these temperamental characteristics, it is little wonder that they do not experience success in school. Children with LD tend to behave in ways that frustrate their parents from the time they are babies. They frustrate their teachers once they reach school age (see Hallahan et al., 2005 for further discussion).

Mild Mental Retardation (MMR)

Children with MMR tend not to be as adaptable, inquisitive, persistent, and responsive to situations as typical children. They are often slow to warm up, and they are slower than normal in reaching most important developmental milestones, such as walking and talking (see Hallahan & Kauffman, 2006 for further discussion).

Children with high-incidence disabilities, regardless of the particular category to which they are assigned (LD, EBD, or MMR), tend to be children with difficult temperaments. An important point here is that children assigned to one category (e.g., LD) may well exhibit the characteristics of those in another (e.g., EBD). In fact, many children with disabilities have multiple problems that make them candidates for identification in several categories.

Other Biological Risk Factors

We have already said that the brain is a complex organ. Even more complex is how the whole body works together. How people act, how they feel, and how they learn may be affected by nearly any of the body's organ systems. Diseases, faulty metabolism, poor nutrition, accidents, chronic illnesses, and so on affect behavior, emotions, and learning, but we can very, very seldom pinpoint the cause of a high-incidence disability as simply biological.

So, what ideas about biological factors should stick in your mind? We think you should remember at least these big ideas:

1. Biological risk factors are complex and interact with each other.
2. Brain function (including brain damage), genetics, and temperament are three major biological risk factors.
3. We can seldom pinpoint a biological cause for high-incidence disabilities.
4. Environmental factors are also in the picture and may interact in very complex ways with biological risk factors.

Implications of Biological Risk Factors

Many teachers and others are tempted to make false assumptions about biological risk factors. They may assume that all of these factors can be changed or that none of them can be changed or that the degree of change we can make in them is insignificant. True, some risk factors cannot be changed at all. For example, we cannot change the genes the child has received from his or her parents, and we cannot reverse time and undo damage to the brain. For some biological risk factors, we do not know what changes to make or how to make them. For example, gene replacement or gene therapy may be possible now or in the future for some chronic health conditions (e.g., **cystic fibrosis**), but it has very limited application, if any, to high-incidence disabilities.

So, what implications should teachers keep in mind? We suggest these:

1. Focus on changing what you can. If you cannot change everything, this is no excuse for failing to change what can be changed.
2. Nearly everything teachers can change is environmental—things that are not biological. However, teachers can often be effective in altering biological risk factors by
   a. teaching well, which may help compensate for biological risks, such as a difficult temperament, and
   b. urging the assessment and treatment of biological risk factors by professionals who are trained to do so.
3. Just because a biological risk factor cannot be changed completely or be completely reversed does not mean that no change is worthwhile. Sometimes, less than total reversal or elimination of a biological risk factor makes a substantial difference in life outcomes for a child (e.g., early educational intervention to address cognitive or emotional problems identified at an early age, even if we suspect they are primarily of biological origin).

:: ENVIRONMENTAL RISK FACTORS

Genes and chromosomes can be altered to some extent by what happens to children during the prenatal, perinatal, or postnatal stages of development (see Pinker, 2002). Thus the complete DNA map will never be able to tell the whole story. In order to understand and prevent the disabilities we can, we need especially to understand the environmental factors that seem to contribute to abnormal development.

Notice that some of the environmental risk factors we discuss have a biological basis such as the age of the parents, especially the mother or exposure to substances **in utero** (while in the mother's womb). There is not a perfectly clear line of demarcation between biological and environmental factors. This is true not only because biological and environmental factors affect each other but because some factors appear to have elements of both biology (e.g., age of parent or obesity of the mother) and environment (e.g., the developing **embryo** or **fetus,** which is affected by such factors as maternal nutrition or substances that are toxic to the fetus).

Prenatal Factors

Some risk factors, present prior to conception, have been associated with babies who at birth or shortly thereafter develop some form of learning, behavioral, or physical disability. Some of the most commonly cited "prebirth" risk factors surround the health of the mother, including poor medical care, poor nutrition, substance abuse (especially use of alcohol and other mind-altering drugs), extreme obesity, and a history of specific illnesses. A mother's age (whether she is a teenager or a woman older than 40) has been recognized as a potential risk factor, but the health and age of the father is also a potential risk factor (see Abroms & Bennett, 1980; Hallahan & Kauffman, 2006).

Once conception has occurred, the prenatal period begins and lasts until at least the seventh month of pregnancy. The first seven months of pregnancy are considered a critical period for brain development. During this period, risk factors include maternal malnutrition, maternal exposure to **teratogens** (things that may produce deformities) such as mercury, lead, metals, and infections, or x-rays. Infections contracted by the mother during the first **trimester** (first third) of pregnancy (e.g., measles, AIDS, venereal diseases) have been directly linked with central nervous system damage in the developing fetus. These infections, as well as incompatibility between components of the blood of the fetus and mother, are highly correlated with MR and other disabilities.

Although these risk factors are frequently cited in relation to intellectual, behavioral, and learning disabilities, factors such as maternal nutrition and exposure to toxins are difficult to study as separate risk or causal factors. This is due to the frequent co-occurrence of poor nutrition, inadequate prenatal care, and substandard housing. For example, lead poisoning is caused by a toxin found at disproportionately high levels in economically-depressed urban areas (Rhode Island KIDS COUNT, 2003). Lead in the body causes permanent and progressive damage to the brain. Lead poisoning has been directly linked to behavioral disorders, including aggressive behavior and attention deficits (Marlowe & Errera, 1982; Needleman,

Herbert, & Reiss, 1996) and it may contribute to LD, MMR, and other problems (e.g., irritability, drowsiness, seizures) that can place a child at risk for developmental delay (USDHHS, 1999; Minder, Das Samaal, & Orlebeke, 1998).

Drug use and abuse by the mother also increases the risk for long-term complications (U.S. Department of Health and Human Services, 1999). The effects of alcohol on an unborn child were not formally studied until the 1970s (Jones, Smith, Ulleland, & Streissguth, 1973) when the term **fetal alcohol syndrome** (FAS) was coined. FAS is the result of consistently heavy alcohol consumption by the mother while pregnant (Fiedorowicz et al., 2001). Approximately 5,000 children with FAS are born each year. This syndrome remains one of the leading nonhereditary causes of MMR (Ackerman, 1998; Hallahan & Kauffman, 2006; Warren & Bast, 1998).

Beyond alcohol, maternal smoking and other drug use pose numerous risks for the developing fetus. When mothers smoke or use substances recreationally, they place their unborn children at risk for a host of problems, including emotional, behavioral, and learning disabilities (Fergusson, Horwood, & Lynskey, 1993; Fried, Watkinson, & Gray, 1992; Olds, Henderson, & Tatelbaum, 1994). Drug exposure is difficult to study, partly because maternal drug abuse generally occurs in the presence of other risk factors such as mental illness, nutritional deficits, and other environmental dangers. Although these factors are difficult to isolate and measure, they remain very important, particularly in combination.

Perinatal Factors

Potential risks to the fetus can also occur throughout the perinatal period, the period from approximately 7 months gestation through about the first month after birth (*perinatal* refers to *around the time of* or near birth). In addition to the aforementioned risk factors, a fetus may also experience increased risk for complications when born with very low birth weight (less than 3 pounds). Although low-birth-weight babies are now more apt to survive and appear healthy due to advances in medicine and medical technology, studies have indicated that these babies have an increased risk for developmental problems in such areas as perceptual-motor and fine motor skills, expressive language, memory, hyperactivity, and academics (Saigal, Hoult, Streiner, Stoskopf, & Rosenbaum, 2000). Babies with low birth weight have a much higher than normal likelihood of developing learning disabilities, including problems in reading, arithmetic, attention, and perception (Fiedorowicz et al., 2001). Babies are also exposed to risk in the perinatal period when complications arise during their birth. Anoxia (significantly decreased supply of oxygen at birth), brain hemorrhaging, and exposure to sexually transmitted diseases carried by the mother have all been correlated with mental retardation and hyperactivity. Clearly the potential effects of all of these risks underscore the need for effective prenatal and perinatal care for all mothers.

Postnatal Factors

The postnatal period extends from birth through early childhood. Although this period begins after birth, exposure to risk factors such as malnutrition, lead, or abuse during this period still threatens the child's brain. Again, the degree of risk is not easily measured, and the exact cause of any disability is not easily pinpointed. As suggested in the opening of this chapter, one cause does not fit all. We hope that future research will provide more information about the specific interactive effects of these risk factors and the degree to which protective factors can lessen or buffer against disabling outcomes.

Family Factors

Any discussion of family influences must first begin with a *definition* of family. As compared to the 1980s or earlier, the composition of the typical American family has changed notably. Data show that children are often raised in single-parent households, not always consisting of a biological or adoptive parent. The effects of divorce, parental separation, family discord, hostility, and a chaotic environment are all identified risk factors for emotional, behavioral, and cognitive development. Additionally, educational level, socioeconomic status, parental age, and cultural isolation have been linked to learning, emotional, and cognitive deficits. These risk factors are proportionally higher for women and ethnic minorities (Larson et al., 2000; U.S. Department of Commerce, 1999). Moreover, as families have become more mobile, direct involvement with extended family members, particularly grandparents, has decreased. Irrespective of the exact family composition, different facets of family life have been studied to understand the effects of specific practices and experiences on the manifestation of various disabilities.

Developmental Nurturing

Early intervention is a key component of effective special education practices. Intervention occurring in the early years of a child's life or school experience can have a strong influence on a child's developmental trajectory. During this time, the role of the family is formative in assisting the child in making attachments, meeting behavior expectations, and acquiring the core skills needed to become a successful learner. By age four the majority of brain development, particularly nerve and cortical development, are complete. During this same time, infants and toddlers are the most dependent on the culture of adults and the experiences these key people play in socializing them (Hart & Risley, 1995). Recent research on the relation between vocabulary and reading fluency highlights the importance of initial language-based social experiences by children with the family (Torgeson, 2003; Weizman, & Snow, 2001). Data clearly show discrepancies between children exposed to specific environmental stimuli within the family structure and the development of language and related cognitive skills (Hart & Risley, 1995). The family serves as a fundamental link to the community, while simultaneously providing the support and nurturing necessary to promote cognitive and social skills. Without access to this type of developmental nurturing, children are at risk for environmental deprivation akin to the experiences of children studied in orphanages (Skeels, 1966; Skeels & Dye, 1939).

Why do some children thrive in the midst of severe environmental adversity? There is no simple answer to this question. Research on what makes a child more or less resilient or vulnerable to specific factors continues. We do know that multiple factors affect the outcome for children on an individual basis. In relation to families, several variables reliably emerge, including parenting styles and disruptions of family life.

Parenting styles are typically predicated on the temperament of the parent and child and how the parent(s) tends to respond to the child's behavior, emotional states, and achievement of expectations. In addition, research indicates that although temperament tendencies across family members may have a hereditary component, the social influences of the family also contribute to changes in children's temperament (Rende & Plomin, 1995). The degree to which a match is established between child and parent temperament may play a large role in the degree to which children develop appropriate attachments.

Attachment is defined as the interaction between an infant and the primary caregiver. Research indicates that attachment is directly linked to the child's emotional and behavioral development, the consequences of which reach into adulthood (Pianta, 1999). The implications of inappropriate attachment are most often directly linked to EBD (American Psychiatric Association, 1994). Appropriate attachment is directly linked to how a child responds to his or her environment. Environments rich in stimuli for young children are considered ideal for optimal cognitive development. This is why poverty or living conditions that promote isolation and little variation in stimuli are considered risk factors for various high-incidence disabilities.

Subsequent research also shows that overall inadequate attachment early in life has been linked to patterns of depression, defiance, aggression, and overall deviance

Nurturing interactions with caregivers facilitate learning and growth in children.
(Photo credit: Eddie Lawrence © Dorling Kindersley)

(Olson, Bates, Sandy, & Lanthier, 2000; Rutter, 1995). Whether it results in emotional and behavioral difficulties or learning and cognitive delays, the effect of ineffective parenting on child development is significant. Therefore, researchers maintain that certain parenting styles, specifically discipline styles, may be a better fit for certain types of child temperament. Although a continuum of parenting styles exists, researchers have predominantly identified two continua of discipline styles among parents, permitting/controlling and accepting/rejecting (Becker, 1964; Hetherington & Martin, 1986; Wicks-Nelson & Israel, 2003). Each dimension shown in Figure 3.2 demonstrates a range of parental behaviors that are employed by parents. The terms

FIGURE 3.2   A simple model of parental discipline styles

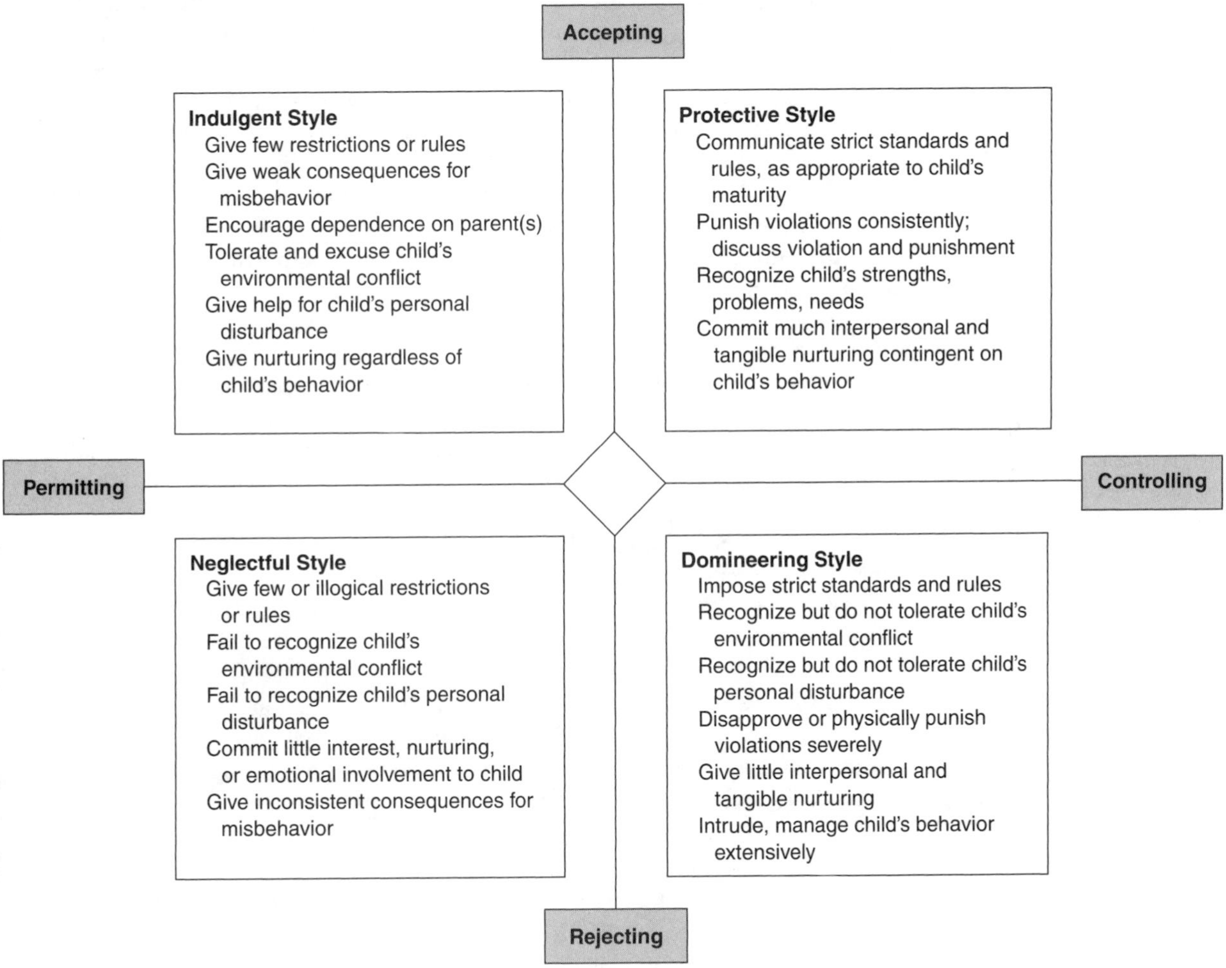

Accepting

Indulgent Style
Give few restrictions or rules
Give weak consequences for
   misbehavior
Encourage dependence on parent(s)
Tolerate and excuse child's
   environmental conflict
Give help for child's personal
   disturbance
Give nurturing regardless of
   child's behavior

Protective Style
Communicate strict standards and
   rules, as appropriate to child's
   maturity
Punish violations consistently;
   discuss violation and punishment
Recognize child's strengths,
   problems, needs
Commit much interpersonal and
   tangible nurturing contingent on
   child's behavior

Permitting

Controlling

Neglectful Style
Give few or illogical restrictions
   or rules
Fail to recognize child's
   environmental conflict
Fail to recognize child's personal
   disturbance
Commit little interest, nurturing,
   or emotional involvement to child
Give inconsistent consequences for
   misbehavior

Domineering Style
Impose strict standards and rules
Recognize but do not tolerate child's
   environmental conflict
Recognize but do not tolerate child's
   personal disturbance
Disapprove or physically punish
   violations severely
Give little interpersonal and
   tangible nurturing
Intrude, manage child's behavior
   extensively

Rejecting

Source: Cullinan, Douglas. *Students with Emotional and Behavior Disorders: An Introduction for Teachers and Other Helping Professionals,* 1st Edition. © 2002, p. 212. Adapted by permission of Pearson Education, Inc., Upper Saddle River, N.J.

identified with each continuum simply represent generalized types of discipline. Although there is not an absolute consensus on which combination type of parental discipline is optimal, certain trends have consistently emerged. Researchers generally agree that the authoritative style, encompassing consistent, firm, yet warm and responsive parenting, has been most closely associated with favorable child outcomes (Steinberg, Lamborn, Darling, Mounts, & Dornbusch, 1994). However, it is important to note that cultural values play an important role in family functioning. Much of the research conducted on optimal parenting styles and definitions of terms such as control were not done across different cultures. (See Figure 3.2.) Therefore, what might seem controlling in European-American culture may not translate as such within other cultures. Furthermore, issues such as safety and security in living environments may also dictate a need for more control by parents in certain communities (e.g., urban communities) as opposed to families living in other settings (e.g., rural communities).

Additionally, the temperament and developmental needs of the child (those with and without specifically identified learning, behavioral, or cognitive disabilities) may require a varied combination of parenting styles as compared to other children in the family or community. Understanding the different styles and individual tendencies can lead to developing a balance between the child's and parents' needs (McHugh, & Slaveny, 1998). Therefore, as with all of the risk and resiliency factors discussed thus far, parental discipline does not have a direct cause-and-effect relationship with child development. It simply serves as one potential factor in both risk and resiliency.

Disruptions to Family Life

As mentioned earlier, consistency in parenting is one of the prerequisites for achieving healthy child outcomes, irrespective of parenting style. However, not all children are raised in stable environments that support consistency, and for other families who aspire to an optimal balance, altered life circumstances can often adjust the parents' responses to their children. Circumstances such as divorce, removal of a parent from the home (e.g., by imprisonment), financial strain, emotional well-being of the parents, as well as degree of family support from outside sources can contribute to interruptions in optimal child rearing (Loeber et al, 2000; Forehand, Bigger, & Kotchick, 1998).

It is important to note that the risk factor of family break-up does not discriminate across socioeconomic classes (Emery, 1999; Grych & Finchman, 1999). Furthermore, other family-related risk factors, such as parental incarceration, parental institutionalization, and removal of children from the home due to neglect or abuse, place children at increased risk for behavior and learning disabilities as well as mental retardation (Evans, 2001).

The effects of various risk factors mentioned above can be time-limited or ongoing. Research has suggested that dramatic changes in family life may have destabilizing effects of approximately two years. However, for some children the risk factors are continuous, and family life never becomes stable or returns to stability. In situations where society has deemed the degree of disruption to be unmanageable or constitutes maltreatment, children are often removed from their homes. The definitional shift from unstable home to maltreatment is a rather subjective one at best. Despite a great deal of research and policy on the topic, maltreatment or abuse remains difficult to define operationally. Is spanking abusive? Is it simply unfortunate or abusive to require a 10-year-old to manage a household due to a parent suffering from depression? Traditional definitions of abuse identify physical neglect, physical abuse, and verbal abuse, encompassing various forms of sexual, mental, and physical injury to individuals prior to age 18. Furthermore, many communities and cultures define abuse and neglect differently, exacerbating the difficulty in identifying and preventing maltreatment of children.

Regardless of specific definition, the impact of maltreatment is significant. Significant child abuse can result in neurological damage as well as disorders of emotions and behavior (Trawick-Smith, 2000). Severe trauma to the head from physical assault or from being shaken can result in seizures, brain hemorrhaging, and varied levels of developmental retardation. In addition, for children with disabilities, abuse is even a greater risk due to their frequent inability to defend themselves adequately or seek assistance (Zantal-Weiner, 1987). In these cases, child abuse may increase the degree of the present disability or increase the likelihood of additional delays. Even for those children not physically abused, neglect and verbal abuse can significantly affect long-term neurological developmental as well as emotional growth. Issues of trust, lack of necessary and appropriate stimuli, and lack of sufficient supports are all risk factors that contribute to numerous disabilities.

When abuse happens in the home or is perpetrated by family members, the results extend far beyond the immediate environment. If abuse is confirmed, children may be removed from their homes. The effects of a non-nurturing environment can be an extremely powerful risk factor. A recent study by Evans underscores the impact of environmental deprivation and neglect on high-incidence disabilities (Evans, 2001; Rutter, 1998; Wyatt, Simms, & Horowitz, 1997). Evans (2001) compared children who were placed in foster care for reasons of parental neglect to those children placed in foster care for reasons other than parental neglect (e.g., death of parents). His findings indicated that students who entered foster care due to neglect or abuse had increased rates of learning disabilities compared to the control group. Although children adopted into nurturing homes may demonstrate gains, research suggests that the amount of gain may be related to the length of the abuse or neglect they experienced prior to adoption (O'Conner, Rutter, Beckett, Keaveney, & Kreppner, 2000). Additionally, as children enter school-age years, those gains are more difficult to achieve. This line of research is particularly informative for prevention efforts and in the areas of mental retardation and learning disabilities, where there is often a predisposition to assume a sole biological cause (Evans, 2001; Nasstrom & Koch, 1996).

Community Factors

Increased financial demands on single-parent households, as well as lack of extended family involvement, often result in less direct involvement and supervision of children by their families. Such families may rely more heavily on community involvement in their children's day-to-day lives. That is, if parents or extended family members are not available for child rearing, the children may be, in effect, reared in collaboration with the local community. This increases the potential influence of various community demographics on student development. Poverty, community and cultural differences, as well as problems with peer relations are among the multitude of risk factors associated with mild disabilities. For example, recent national data suggest that individuals with income levels below the poverty line are three times more likely than normal to have MR. The rate is greater for children than for adults (Larson et al., 2000). Furthermore, the rates are two to three times higher for black children than for white children.

As we discussed earlier, stimulating and nurturing environments are essential for proper cognitive and emotional development. Children living in poverty frequently lack nurturing. Poverty is frequently associated with exposure to violence (McCloskey & Walker, 2000). Poverty is also linked with single parenting, young children, young parents, malnutrition, multiple caregivers, and under-stimulating environments (Larson et al., 2000). There are, of course, exceptions, but poverty is generally correlated with many negative environmental conditions. Living in poverty can also induce greater levels of stress and anxiety for parents and children.

In addition, poverty typically restricts access to sufficient medical care. Children entering school with colds or allergies, hunger, and fatigue due to poor housing conditions are not ready to learn. Children may express this through acting out or withdrawing. Either way, they are often disciplined and are not able to accomplish their expected work. As a primary or secondary risk factor, conditions of poverty easily increase the discrepancy between these children and their peers in terms of learning. For this reason alone, educational agencies must actively partner with community agencies to ensure that adequate social services are available to reduce the effects or potential effects of poverty and its related risk factors.

Difficulties in learning, whether from environmental or biological causes, increase children's frustration in school. Some frustrated children may seek out environments in which they feel more successful and accepted. These environments may include peer groups consisting of others who also feel alienated in some way from educational settings. These peers may have similar difficulties or may be considered higher-status peers who take advantage of others who are less well connected in the community. Successful peer interactions are associated with self-esteem, collaboration, and the development of overall social skills essential for successful maturation and desirable adult outcomes (Boivin & Hymel, 1997; Cullinan, Evans, Epstein, & Ryser, 2003). However, the wrong peer group can contribute to many risk factors such as school failure, dropping out of school, poor grades, early sexual activity, and violence (Vitaro, Brendgen, & Tremblay, 2000).

School and Cultural Factors

Understanding and discussion about the impact of families and the communities in which they live on child development is clearly necessary and important. The primary focus of this book in on how this information is relevant for educators supporting students. Educational communities are typically considered places for learning and for remediation. However, it would be inappropriate to assume that educational environments do not pose risk factors. As a matter of fact, educational settings in combination with family and community factors can promote what has been termed **developmental retardation**—the culmination of identified environmental risk factors on school and postschool failure (Greenwood, Hart, Walker, & Risley, 1994). For example, Greenwood and colleagues have outlined the following model for progression of developmental retardation:

1. Parents of children in poverty tend to provide their infants and toddlers less-varied vocabulary and as a result, these children tend to have smaller vocabularies at age 36 months than same age children from higher SES (socioeconomic status) families.
2. These same children with lower vocabularies enter school at-risk for school failure due to poorer school readiness.
3. Research indicates these children do not receive differentiated instruction in school to close this gap.
4. The continuing developmental gap between low and high SES extends to adolescents, resulting in less engaged time within the school day. Therefore, based on the data, low-SES students would need to attend school an extra 1.6 years to attain the same educational experience as high-SES students.

This trajectory extends to adulthood for low-SES students. Although prevention needs to occur in early life to increase vocabulary growth, the data are clear that ineffective teaching as well as inadequate behavior management are factors that exacerbate learning deficits (Fiedorowicz et al., 2001; Kauffman, 2005; Walker et al., 2004). In addition, setting inappropriate expectations for these students can enhance self-fulfilling prophecies regarding expectation of school failure for students with high-incidence disabilities. According to the research, increased exposure to academic subject matter, and higher engagement in academic behaviors, such as increased writing, academic game play, reading aloud, silent reading, academic talk, and answering and asking questions encompass key activities providing higher levels of academic engagement for students who enter school at-risk for school failure (Greenwood et al., 1981; Greenwood et al., 1994). Environmental conditions such as poor organization or deteriorating physical environments and learning conditions such as large class size and unavailability of teachers to respond to students' needs have also been linked to inferior student outcomes (Slavin, Karweit, & Wasik, 1994).

School attendance is considered a protective factor against long-term antisocial behavior (Ripple & Luthar, 2000). Schools need to send the message that attendance is valued and required. The necessity of schools to be actively involved in the prevention of various mental health and learning disorders is clear (Forness et al., 2000; Kauffman, 1999, 2003, 2004, 2005). By reducing chaos within schools while simultaneously supporting individual learning, schools can reduce learning and behavioral problems (Walker, Ramsey, & Gresham, 2004).

Additional factors associated with school success promote the student's sense of assimilation within the school community. Students from culturally diverse backgrounds can be at greater risk for experiencing a disconnect between their natural environments and school (Allen, Harry, & MacLaughlin, 1995; Harry, Klinger, & Hart, 2005). Lack of effective communication between families of diverse cultures and lack of information about parenting practices of differing cultures can set the stage for misunderstanding and blame. Parents who do not feel accepted and understood, whether due to cultural differences or differing socioeconomic status, are not able to communicate well with their child's school or teachers. This can be to the detriment of the child.

:: INTERACTION OF BIOLOGICAL AND ENVIRONMENTAL FACTORS

We have discussed the roles that genetics and the gestational environment play in the development of the high-incidence disabilities EBD, LD, and MMR. Research has also identified the important interaction between biological makeup and environmental factors vis-á-vis the development of these disabilities.

A significant amount of research has examined the biological origins of high-incidence disabilities, including inherited problems. However, much less attention has been paid to environmental contributions to these disabilities (Evans, 2001). We do not know for certain the degree to which environmental factors cause high-incidence disabilities, but we do know that environmental conditions can ameliorate them. For example, current research of the effects of early intervention on reading for students with LD suggests that good teaching can remediate reading disabilities in many cases (Torgeson, 2003).

The achievement gap between those with and without learning disabilities can certainly be attributed in part to environmental factors (Hart & Risley, 1995). Irrespective of the term used to designate a disability, the potential effects of environmental factors on the long-term outcomes of having a high-incidence disability cannot be overemphasized. Teachers must understand that regardless of the causes of high-incidence disabilities, good teaching is critically important.

SUMMARY

An understanding of the biological and environmental risk factors contributing to high-incidence disabilities is essential if we are to dismiss common misperceptions about them (e.g., urban legends). Contrary to what the current education "culture" suggests, one cause does not fit all. Risk factors are multiple and complex, and we can seldom pin down the exact causes of disabilities. For parents, educators, and related professionals, a working knowledge of *potential* casual factors can be a powerful tool to assist in the identification and evaluation of individualized educational strategies and supports. Educators and the larger society must also focus on developing and promoting protective factors to increase resiliency and desired outcomes. Regardless of the cause of a disability, effective teaching is important.

COMPETENT TEACHING BOX

BOX 3.1

Knowing your students . . .

What we know about our students helps us teach them more effectively. What we know about our students is NOT an automatic prescription for educational strategies or placement.

What you might want to remember about the *causes* of high-incidence disabilities:

- Genetic and chromosomal syndromes tend to be more highly correlated with EBD for males than for females. Yet, peri- and postnatal causes are similar for both males and females.
- More boys than girls are identified with EBD and LD. Girls with EBD and LD tend to be underidentified.
- Children living in poverty associated with substandard housing, poor nutrition, inadequate supervision, and ongoing exposure to environmental teratogens are at increased risk for developing associated learning and behavior problems.

Competent teachers . . .

- Competent teachers recognize but do not automatically assume the presence of risk factors.
- Competent teachers make use of school- and community-based resources designed to assist in reducing risk, such as free and reduced breakfast and lunch programs, safe and structured before and after school programs, and community watch agencies designed to secure safe and appropriate housing by working with landlords and community leaders.
- Competent teachers discriminate between personal beliefs (such as an automatic assumption of malnourishment due to a unique diet driven by cultural or religious beliefs) from true risk factors.
- Competent teachers recognize the need for individualized academic and behavioral approaches for students who are at-risk or have specific needs.
- Competent teachers actively pursue effective and ongoing collaboration with *all* families and relevant caregivers to reduce risk.

:: CASE STUDIES

CHANDLER

When Chandler started second grade he had just turned 7 years old. He would get this huge grin on his face when you asked him his age and comment that he is definitely going to grow up to be one handsome guy. During school, Chandler seemed to enjoy hanging outside with his friends at recess, swapping stories with them about who is better at basketball and what he loved to eat. Beyond that, on most days at school Chandler looked pretty miserable and distracted.

Chandler lived in a small rural town mostly comprised of families who were farmers or those who found hourly work nearby. He had two older brothers, a 2-year-old younger sister, and lived with his mom in a single-wide trailer. His mother was very interested in everything Chandler did and had been raising him and his brothers to be kind and respectful boys. Unfortunately, the family was having serious financial difficulties. Chandler's mother was unemployed and did not have a car. The family struggled with basic resources such as food and had no medical coverage. Also, because of the tight living quarters they had difficulty maintaining a consistent schedule, and Chandler often missed his bus. Without a car, his mother had trouble getting him to school every day and on time. Nevertheless he did attend (typically late) almost every day.

Chandler seemed to view school as an opportunity to be with friends and get out of the close living quarters that his family shared. Even though he was a bit small for his age and was constantly moving and talking, he seemed to get along with his peers well. However, he was not interested in schoolwork and increasingly displayed frustration and poor work products. Reading was especially difficult for him, and his writing was incomprehensible in structure and content, if he even completed his work. He also often complained of headaches and seemed to be always hungry. His second-grade teacher had begun to suspect that he was also suffering from untreated allergies and noticed that he was receiving very poor dental care.

By the middle of second grade, Chandler was referred for a diagnostic battery to determine his need for special education services due to his increasing problems in reading and written work. His mom did not have a history of attending parent-teacher conferences or any other types of school-related activities. She had shared with the social worker a few years prior on a home visit to discuss the potential of exposure to lead paint that she had never really liked school because it was difficult for her and she had a hard time reading. Her

parents had been told that she had dyslexia and therefore would never be expected to read very well anyway. She said she didn't really know what to say to teachers. She assumed that they knew best, and she hoped that with their help her boys would turn out smarter than herself. Yet, Chandler's mom always returned all paperwork signed, usually on time. Chandler's assessments found him eligible for special education services, with an educational diagnosis of learning disability in the areas of reading and written expression and a notation that he should be further assessed for ADHD.

1. What environmental and/or biological risk factors did Chandler experience?
2. What kinds of family-based supports might Chandler benefit from to reduce his risk?
3. What types of changes could school personnel make?

Learn more about Chandler's story in Chapter 12.

RHIANNON

Everyone at Fleetwood Middle School knew that it was going to be a rough day with Rhiannon. Her seventh-grade home room teacher Mr. Buckingham was out sick, and there was a substitute teacher. Rhiannon's behavior was always considered unpredictable, yet you could generally count on the fact that she did not deal well with authority and really did not like changes in her day. Most of the time Rhiannon appeared fairly oblivious to her surroundings. When a teacher asked her questions or made requests of her, she would ignore them, say she didn't know the answer, or just stare off into space. However, this perceived passive defiance could quickly shift to very intense verbal threats or aggressive acts if Rhiannon felt that someone was "harassing her" or looking at her too long. The intensity of these reactions seemed to increase as a result of any schedule changes or novel requests given to her by her teachers or parents. Rhiannon was capable of grade-level general education work; however, her erratic behavior and strong reactions created several concerns for her ongoing placement in general education classrooms. Special and general educators worked to increase the structure of her environment and systematically provided her with supports to complete requested tasks. However, Rhiannon lived a very different life outside of school and was not convinced she needed to change her behavior on the few days she did attend school.

Home-school collaboration had not been particularly successful for many years in Rhiannon's case. Because Rhiannon did not attend any form of daycare or preschool, she was not identified as needing additional supports until she entered kindergarten. At that time it was clear that Rhiannon did not have age-appropriate peer interaction skills, or developmentally necessary attention skills to complete daily routines within the kindergarten classroom. Rhiannon did not enter kindergarten "ready to learn." The school social worker visited with the family to share some of the behavioral concerns and to determine whether these behaviors were seen at home as well (and, if so, the extent to which they had been occurring). Mother indicated that Rhiannon had always been "doing her own thing." She said that when Rhiannon was born it took her forever to cry, and since then she has never really "shut up." Rhiannon's mother further indicated that the father was tired of dealing with Rhiannon and left, probably because Rhiannon had the same bad temper that he did. She said she was just too busy to be worrying about whether her daughter had "good manners" at school. She said Rhiannon's grandmother doesn't take any flack from "no one," and when mom is working the grandmother is in charge. Rhiannon knows to stay in her room and be quiet. The social worker included in her report that during the interview the 5-year-old Rhiannon and her 4-year-old brother were sitting in the middle of a very dirty floor watching a "slasher movie." When asked if she had any concerns about the content of the movie for her children, the mother had commented, "They like it, and it keeps them quiet."

Through second grade Rhiannon received counseling and social worker services to help temper her behavior patterns. By the end of second grade she was found eligible for special education services under the label of emotional/behavioral disorder. The school had not been able to encourage either parent or the grandmother to attend parent teacher conferences or agree to another home visit since the initial visit when Rhiannon was 5. Additionally, it had become quite clear that Rhiannon was often left unsupervised and there had been suspicions that she was also often in charge of her younger brother. School personnel began to more aggressively seek out additional community supports to help address the multiple-faceted needs that Rhiannon's situation presented and that affected her ability to attend school with any regularity, limiting the benefit from educational services.

1. What type of risk factors is Rhiannon exposed to?
2. What risk factors can we change?

LINDSEY

Once again, Lindsey was rolling down the window and whistling at the sorority girls as he was driving down the road. This behavior was not that abnormal for a 17-year-old male.

His mom just wished he would do it when he was in the car with his brother and not her. Her hunch was just that most guys did not do that with their mom in the car. Yet she smiled, thinking about how normal this moment was and in that way so wonderful—considering how far they had all come.

Lindsey was adopted. The Taylors had had two healthy boys who were 7 and 9 when Mr. Taylor, the minister at the local church, received a call about a new mother who needed to give up her newborn baby boy. The reason they were calling him was because they were looking for a special home, because this boy would most likely have special needs. He had fetal alcohol syndrome, and mom had received no prenatal care during her pregnancy. The law allowed the mother to remain anonymous, and she had refused to provide any medical history about herself or the assumed father. The prognosis for this little boy was totally unknown. The Taylors agreed to take in little Lindsey until a good home was found. It had been an interesting 17 years.

Lindsey's early childhood years were a little different than they had been for his older brothers. He always seemed to get to the milestones like babbling, crawling, and social interactions about 6 months behind the rest of his same-age peers. When he was upset, his tantrums were much more pronounced, and he seemed to reach frustration quicker and take longer to calm down. Lindsey also looked slightly different. He had a noticeably larger head circumference than most boys his age, and his head also seemed to be very long, his chin very pronounced. The Taylors had become his parents and spared no resources to have him evaluated and assessed medically and educationally. By the time Lindsey was 5, the doctors thought he might have autism. This, they said, would explain his behavior problems and unique developmental patterns. Less was known about autism back then, and this diagnosis seemed to fit. However, no one could pinpoint cognitive delays, and when Lindsey entered elementary school his behavior worsened and his grades bottomed out. He was placed in a room for students with autism, which at that time emphasized behavior management. Yet the Taylors and even the teachers consistently noted that he seemed different from most of the children with autism that any of them had ever seen. He was definitely much more social than most children with autism, and he thought his peers in the room were "weird" because they did not talk.

By the time Lindsey was 15 years old he had become quite large and strong, and was interested in females. The Taylors were finding it challenging to maintain his and their safety at home as well as in the community. They made the very difficult choice to place him in a group home for adolescent boys with developmental disabilities at the age of 14. They had him home every weekend and stayed very involved in every aspect of his educational and residential life. One day a newer staff member at the home suggested to the Taylors that Lindsey seemed to have the characteristics of a syndrome called Fragile X. She indicated that researchers had recently developed a simple blood test for his syndrome. Lindsey was tested and indeed found to have this genetic disorder. Based on this new information, educational staff were educated about the disorder, and additional assessments and plans were created for Lindsey. The people who worked with Lindsey quickly realized that much of his challenging behavior and lack of success within his curriculum was due to an ongoing mismatch between educational and home supports and his needs and abilities. This included recognizing that he did not have autism, but in conjunction with Fragile X syndrome he had a mild cognitive disability. Following intervention to address these specific needs, marked improvements were realized for Lindsey within 6 months.

1. Why was proper diagnosis helpful for Lindsey?
2. What impact do you think being adopted by the Taylors made on Lindsey's overall life outcomes?

REFERENCES

Abroms, K. K., & Bennett, J. W. (1980). Current genetic and demographic findings in Down Syndrome: How are they represented in college textbooks on exceptionality? *Mental Retardation, 18,* 101–107.

Ackerman, M. E. (1998). Fetal alcohol syndrome: Implications for educators. (ERIC document reproduction Service No. Ed 426–560).

Allen, N., Harry, B., & McLaughlin, M. (1995). Communication vs. compliance: African- American parents' involvement in special education. *Exceptional Children, 61,* 364–377.

American Association on Mental Retardation (2002). *Mental retardation: Definitions, classifications, and systems of supports.* (10th ed), pp. 123-142. DC: Author.

American Psychiatric Association. (1994). *Diagnostic and statistical manual of mental disorders* (4th ed.). Washington, DC: Author.

Baumgardner, T. L., Green, K. E., & Reiss, A. L. (1994). A behavioral neurogenetics approach to developmental disabilities: Gene-brain-behavior associations. *Current Opinion in Neurology, 7,* 172–187.

Becker, W. C. (1964). Consequences of different kinds of parental discipline. In M. L. Hoffman & L. W. Hoffman (Eds.), *Review of child development research* (Vol. 1). New York: Russell Sage Foundation.

Beirne-Smith, M., Ittenbach, R. F., & Patton, J. R. (2002). *Mental retardation.* Upper Saddle River, NJ: Merrill/Prentice Hall.

Boivin, M., & Hymel, S. (1997). Peer experiences and social self-perception: A sequential model. *Developmental Psychology, 33,* 135–145.

Chess, S., & Thomas, A. T. (2003). Foreword. In B. K. Keogh, *Temperament in the classroom: Understanding individual differences.* Baltimore: Brookes.

Collins, F. (2003, April 22). A common thread. *The Washington Post,* A19.

Collins, F., Green, E. D., Guttmacher, A. E., & Guyer, E. S. (2003). A vision of the future of genomics research. *Nature, 422,* 835–847.

Cullinan, D. (2002). *Students with emotional and behavioral Disorders: An introduction for teachers and other helping professionals.* Upper Saddle River, NJ: Merrill/Prentice Hall.

Cullinan, D., Evans, C., Epstein, M., & Ryser, G. (2003). Characteristics of emotional disturbance of elementary school students. *Behavioral Disorders, 28,* 94–110.

Damasio, A. R. (1985). The frontal lobes. In M. K. Heilman & E. Valenstein (Eds.) *Clinical neuropsychology* (pp. 339–376). New York: Oxford University Press.

DeFries, J. C., Filipek, P. A., Fulker, D. W., Olson, R. K., Pennington, B. F., Smith, S. D., & Wise, B. W. (1997). Colorado learning disabilities research center. *Learning Disabilities, 8,* 7–19.

Emery, R. E. (1999). *Marriage, divorce and children's adjustment* (2nd ed). Thousands Oaks, CA: Sage.

Evans, L. D. (2001) Interactional models of learning disabilities: Evidence from students entering foster care. *Psychology in the Schools, 38,* 381–390.

Fergusson, D. M., Horwood, L. J., & Lynskey, M. T. (1993). Maternal smoking before and after pregnancy: Effects on behavioral outcomes in middle childhood. *Pediatrics, 92,* 815–822.

Fiedorowicz, C., Benezra, W., MacDonald, W., McElgunn, B., Wilson, A., & Kaplan, B. (2001). Neurobiological basis of learning disabilities: An update. *Learning Disabilities, 11,* 61–74.

Filipek, P. A. (1999). Neuroimaging in the developmental disorders: The state of the science. *Journal of Child Psychology and Child Psychiatry, 40,* 113–128.

Flowers, D. L., Wood, F. B., & Naylor, C. E. (1991). Regional cerebral blood flow correlates of language processes in reading disability. *Archives of Neurology, 48*(6), 637–643.

Forehand, A., Bigger, H., & Kotchick, B. A. (1998). Cumulative risk across family stressors: Short- and long-term effects for adolescents. *Journal of Abnormal Child Psychology, 26,* 119–128.

Forness, S. R., Serna, L. A., Nielsen, E., Lambros, K., Hale, M., & Kavale, K. (2000). A model for early detection and primary prevention of emotional or behavioral disorders. *Education and Treatment of Children, 23,* 325–345.

Fried, P. A., Watkinson, B., & Gray, R. (1992). A follow-up study of attentional behavior in 6-year old children exposed prenatally to marijuana, cigarettes, and alcohol. *Neurotoxicology and Teratology, 14,* 299–311.

Greenwood, C. R., Delquadri, J. C., Stanley, S. O., Sasso, G, Whorton, D. & Schulte, D. (1981, Summer). Allocating opportunity to learn as a basis for academic remediation: A developing model for teaching. *Monograph in Behavior Disorders, 22–23.*

Greenwood, C. R., Hart, B., Walker, D., & Risley, T. (1994). *The opportunity to respond and academic performance revisited: A behavioral theory of developmental retardation and its prevention.* In R. Gardner III, D. M. Sainato, J. O. Cooper, T. E. Heron, W. L. Heward, J. W. Eshleman, & T. A. Grossi, (Eds), *Behavior analysis in education: Focus on measurably superior instruction.* Pacific Grove, CA: Brooks/Cole.

Grigorenko, E. L., Wood, F. B., & Meyer, M. S. (1997). Susceptibility loci for distinct components of developmental dyslexia on chromosome 6 and 15. *American Journal of Human Genetics, 60,* 27–39.

Grych, J. H., & Finchman, F. D. (1999). Children of single parents and divorce. In W. K. Silverman & T. H. Ollendick (Eds.), *Developmental issues in the clinical treatment of children,* (pp. 321–357). Needham Heights, MA: Allyn & Bacon.

Hallahan, D. P., & Kauffman, J. M. (2006). *Exceptional learners: Introduction to special education* (10th ed.). Boston: Allyn & Bacon.

Hallahan, D. P., Lloyd, J. W., Kauffman, J. M., Weiss, M., & Martinez, E. (2005). *Introduction to learning disabilities* (3rd ed.). Boston: Allyn & Bacon.

Hammill, (1990). On defining learning disabilities: An emerging consensus. *Journal of Learning Disabilities. 23,* 74–84.

Harry, B., Klinger, J. K., & Hart, J. (2005). African American families under fire. *Remedial and Special Education, 26,* 101–112.

Hart, B., & Risley, T. (1995). *Meaningful differences in the everyday experience of young American children.* Baltimore: Paul H. Brooks.

Hetherington, E. M., & Martin, B. (1986). Family factors and psychopathology in children. In H. C. Quay & J. S. Werry (Eds.), *Psychopathological disorders of childhood* (3rd. ed., pp. 332–390). New York: Wiley.

Hinshelwood, J. (1900). Congenital word blindness. *The Lancet, 1,* 1506–1508.

Hynd, G. W., & Hiemenz, J. R. (1997). Dyslexia and gyral morphology variation. In C. Hulme & M. Snowling (Eds.), *Dyslexia: Biology, cognition and intervention* (pp. 38–58). London: Whurr Publishers, Ltd.

Jones, K. L., Smith, D. W., Ulleland, C. N., & Streissguth, A. P. (1973). Patterns of malformation in offspring of chronic alcoholic mothers. *The Lancet, 1,* 1267–1271.

Kauffman, J. M. (1999). How we prevent prevention of emotional and behavior disorders. *Exceptional Children, 65,* 448–468.

Kauffman, J. M. (2003). Appearances, stigma, and prevention. *Remedial and Special Education, 24,* 195–198.

Kauffman, J. M. (2004). Foreword. In H. M. Walker, E. Ramsey, & F. M. Gresham (Eds.), *Antisocial behavior in school: Strategies and best practices* (2nd ed.) (pp. xix–xxi). Belmont, CA: Wadsworth.

Kauffman, J. M. (2005). *Characteristics of emotional and behavioral disorders of children and youth* (8th ed.). Upper Saddle River, NJ: Merrill/Prentice Hall.

Kibby, M. Y., & Hynd, G. W. (2001). Neurobiological basis of learning disabilities. In D. P. Hallahan & B. K. Koegh (Eds), *Research and global perspectives in learning disabilities: Essays in honor of William Cruickshank,* (pp. 36–37). Mahwah, NJ: Erlbaum.

Keogh, B. K. (2003). *Temperament in the classroom: Understanding individual differences.* Baltimore, MD: Brookes.

Kral, M., Nielsen, K., & Hynd, G. W. (1998). Historical conceptualization of developmental dyslexia: Neurolinguistic contributions from the 19th and early 20th centuries. In R. Licht, A. Bouma, W. Slot, & W. Koops (Eds.), *Child neuropsychology* (pp. 1–16). Delft, The Netherlands: Eburon Publishers.

Kussmaul, A. (1877). Disturbances of speech. *Cyclopedia of the practice of medicine, 14,* 581, 875.

Lachiewicz, A., Harrison, C., Spiridigliozzi, G. A., Callanan, N. P., & Livermore, J. (1988). What is the Fragile X syndrome? *North Carolina Medical Journal, 49,* 203–208.

Larson, S. A., Lakin, K. C., Anderson, L., Kwak, N., Lee, J. H., & Anderson, D. (2000). Prevalence of mental retardations and /or developmental disabilities: Analysis of the 1994/1995 NHIS-D. *MR/DD Data Brief, 1*(2). Minneapolis: University of Minnesota, Institute on Community Integration, Research and Training Center on Community Living.

Loeber, R., Drinkwater, M., Yin, Y., Anderson, S. J., Schmidt, L. C., & Crawford, A. (2000). Stability from family interaction from ages 6 to 18. *Journal of Abnormal Psychology, 28,* 353–369.

Marlowe, M. (1986). Metal pollutant exposure and behavior disorders: Implications for school practices. *Journal of Special Education, 20,* 251–264.

Marlowe, M., & Errera, J. (1982). Low lead levels and behavior problems in children. *Behavioral Disorders, 7,* 163–172.

McClosky, L. A., & Walker, M. (2000). Posttraumatic stress in children exposed of family violence and single event trauma. *Journal of the American Academy of Child and Adolescent Psychiatry, 39,* 108–115.

McHugh, P. R., & Slavney, P. R. (1998). *The perspectives of psychiatry* (2nd ed.). Baltimore, MD: Johns Hopkins University Press.

McLaren, J., & Bryson, S. E. (1987). Review of recent epidemiological studies of mental retardation: Prevalence, associated disorders, and etiology. *American Journal of Mental Retardation, 92,* 243–254.

Minder, B., Das Samaal, E. A., & Orlebeke, J. F. (1998). Cognition of children does not suffer from very low lead exposure. *Journal of Learning Disabilities, 31,* 495–501.

Morgan, W. P. (1896). A case of congenital word-blindness. *British Medical Journal, 2,* 1378.

Nasstrom, K., & Koch, S. M. (1996, March). Addressing the needs of children in out-of-home care. *Paper presented at the 28th annual meeting of the National Association of School Psychologists,* Atlanta, GA.

Needleman, H. L., Herbert, L., & Riess, J. A.(1996) Bone lead levels and delinquent behavior. *Journal of the American Medical Association, 275,* 363–369.

O'Connor, T. G., Rutter, M., Beckett, C., Keaveney, L., & Kreppner, J. M. (2000). English and Romanian adoptees (ERA) Study Team. The effects of global severe deprivation on cognitive competence: Extension and longitudinal follow-up. *Child Development, 71,* 376–390.

Olds, D. L., Henderson, C. R., & Tatelbaum, R. (1994). Intellectual impairment in children of women who smoke cigarettes in pregnancy. *Pediatrics, 93*(2), 221–227.

Olson, S. L., Bates, J. E., Sandy, J. M., & Lanthier, R. (2000). Early developmental precursors of externalizing behavior in middle childhood and adolescence. *Journal of Abnormal Child Psychology, 28,* 119–133.

Pennington, B. F., Filipek, P. A., Lefly, D., Churchwell, J., Kennedy, D. N., Simon, J. H., Filley, C. M., Galaburda, A., Alarcon, M., & DeFries, J. C. (1999). Brain morphometry in reading-disabled twins. *Neurology, 53,* 723–729.

Pianta, R. C. (1999). Early childhood. In. W. K. Silverman & T. H. Ollendick (Eds.), *Developmental issues in the clinical treatment of children* (pp. 88–107). Needham Heights, MA: Allyn & Bacon.

Pinker, S. (2002). *The blank slate: The modern denial of human nature.* New York: Viking.

Reiss, A. L., & Denckla, M. B. (1996). The contribution of neuroimaging to behavioral neurogenetics research: Fragile X syndrome, Turner syndrome, and neurofibrmatosis. In G. R. Lyon & J. M. Rumsey (Eds.), *Neuroimaging: A Window to the Neurological Foundations of Learning and Behavior of Children,* (pp.147–148). Baltimore, MD: Paul H. Brookes.

Rende, R., & Plomin, R. (1995). Nature, nurture, and the development of psychopathology. In D. Cicchetti & D. J. Cohen (Eds.), *Developmental psychopathology: Vol. 1. Theory and methods* (pp. 291–314). New York: Wiley.

Rhode Island KIDS COUNT (2003). Childhood lead poisoning: Rhode Island KIDS COUNT Issue Brief. New York: Ford Foundation.

Ripple, C. H., & Luthar, S. S. (2000). Academic risk among inner city adolescents. The role of personal attributes. *The Journal of School Psychology, 38,* 277–298.

Rutter, M. (1995). Clinical implications of attachment concepts: Retrospect and prospect. *Journal of Child Psychology and Psychiatry, 36,* 549–571.

Rutter, M. (1998). Developmental catch-up, and deficit, following adoption after severe global early privation. English and Romanian adoptees (ERA) Study Team. *Journal of Child Psychology and Psychiatry and Allied Disciplines, 39,* 456–476.

Saigal, S., Hoult, L. A., Streiner, D. L., Stoskopf, B. L., & Rosenbaum, P. L. (2000). School difficulties at adolescents in a regional cohort of children who were extremely low birth weight. *Pediatrics, 105,* 325–331.

Skeels, H. M. (1966). Adult status of children with contrasting early life experiences. *Monographs of the Society for Research in Child Development, 31* Ser. No. 105.

Skeels, H. M., Dye, H. B. (1939). A study of the effects of differential stimulation on mentally retarded children. *American Journal of Mental Deficiency, 44,* 114–136.

Slavin, R. F., Karweit, N. L., & Wasik, B. A. (Eds.) (1994). *Preventing early school failure: Research, policy, and practice.* Boston: Allyn & Bacon.

Steinberg, L., Lamborn, S. D., Darling, N., Mounts, N. S., & Dornbusch, S. M. (1994). Over-time changes in adjustment and competence among adolescents form authoritative, authoritarian, indulgent and neglectful families. *Child Development, 65,* 754–770.

Sylvester, R. (1997). The neurobiology of self-esteem and aggression. *Educational Leadership, 54*(9), 74–77.

Thomas, A., & Chess, S. (1977). *Temperament and development.* New York: Brunner-Mazel.

Thomas, A., Chess, S., & Birch, H. (1968). *Temperament and behavior disorders in children.* New York: New York University Press.

Torgeson, J. K. (2003). *Longitudinal reading data.* Presentation at the 25th International Conference on Learning Disabilities, Seattle, WA.

Trawick-Smith, J. (2000). *Early child development: A multicultural perspective.* (4th ed.). Upper Saddle River, NJ: Merrill/Prentice Hall.

U.S. Department of Commerce. (1999). *Statistical abstract of the United States* (119th ed.). Washington, DC: U.S. Government Printing Office.

U.S. Department of Health and Human Services. (1999). *Mental Health: A report of the surgeon general.* Rockville, MD: U.S. Department of Health and Human Services, Substance Abuse and Mental Health Services Administration Center for Mental Health Services, National Institutes of Health, National Institute of Mental Health.

Vitaro, F., Brendgen, M., & Tremblay, R. E. (2000). Influence of deviant friends on delinquency: Searching for moderator variables. *Journal of Abnormal Psychology, 28,* 213–325.

Walker, H. M., Ramsey, E., & Gresham, F. M. (2004). *Antisocial behavior in school: Strategies and best practices* (2nd ed.). Pacific Grove, CA: Brooks/Cole.

Warren, K. R., & Bast, R. J. (1998). Alcohol related birth defects: An update. *Public Health Reports, 103,* 68–642.

Weizman, Z. O., & Snow, C. E. (2001, March). Lexical input as related to children's vocabulary acquisition: Effects of sophisticated exposure and support for meaning. *Developmental Psychology, 37*(2), 265–279.

Welsch, M.C. (1994). Executive functioning and the assessment of attention deficit hyperactivity disorder. In L.C. Wilkinson (Ed.), *Learning about learning disabilities* (pp. 21–42). New York: Guilford.

Wicks-Nelson, R., & Israel, A. C. (2003), *Behavior disorders of childhood* (5th ed.). Upper Saddle River, NJ: Prentice Hall.

Wyatt, D. T., Simms, M. D., & Horowitz, S. M. (1997). Widespread growth retardation and variable growth recovery in foster children in the first year after placement. *Archives of Pediatrics and Adolescent Medicine, 151,* 813–816.

Zantal-Wiener, K. (1987). *Disciplinary exclusion of special education students.* ERIC Digest #453. Washington, DC: Office of Educational Research and Improvement.

The Unique Characteristics and Learning Needs of Students with High-Incidence Disabilities

Characteristics of Students with Learning Disabilities

Kenneth A. Kavale

Regent University

URBAN LEGEND: *Anyone who is a slow learner might have a learning disability.*

LEGENDARY THOUGHT: *A special education category of "specific learning disability" really does exist.*

Contemporary society possesses an informal understanding of learning disabilities (LD) in the form of students experiencing school failure because of an inability to acquire, assimilate, or retain academic content. The difficulty is that these "learning disabilities" may not involve special education. The formal special education category of "specific learning disability" (SLD) is a legally defined entity that has its own history, characteristics, and methods. The clash between the formal and informal understandings (LD vs. SLD) has created controversies that remain unresolved but has not prevented SLD from becoming the largest category in special education.

:: HISTORY

The SLD category is relatively new. It was first recognized by the federal government in 1969. Consequently, an understanding of the history of SLD provides a context for understanding the many issues facing the field. The history of SLD has been well documented (e.g., Hallahan & Mercer, 2002; Wiederholt, 1974). These histories trace the origins of SLD from about 1800 and divide its development into different periods. The following summary of historical periods is documented in these histories. Learning disability grew out of unexplained failures to learn particular skills and out of research on brain injury.

Foundation Period

Language and Reading Disabilities

Over a century ago, Gall, Wernicke, and Broca studied the effect of brain pathology. Their research addressed this question: How does brain injury influence cognitive functioning? In studying **aphasia,** or difficulties in generating speech, Head (1926) showed that there was *no* generalized impairment of intellectual ability even with significant expressive and/or receptive language impairment. Broadbent (1872) reported cases of intelligent adults with no apparent disabilities other than an almost complete inability to read. Hinshelwood and Morgan found *word-blindness* in children and termed the condition *congenital word blindness.* Orton found congenital word-blindness in children, which he termed *strepthosymbolia* (Greek for twisted symbols)(Orton, 1925). While Hinshelwood believed word-blindness was associated with brain pathology (i.e., lack of development of the angular gyrus in the left hemisphere), Orton preferred an explanation based on mixed cerebral dominance, which would explain frequently observed symptoms such as letter reversals (b and d, p and q or b) confusion of palindromes (was and saw), and mirror reading and writing (Orton, 1937).

Orton's theoretical ideas have not been validated, but his ideas about remediation remain influential. Orton was critical of the "look-say" approach to reading and advocated "phonics instruction" delivered through a *multisensory method* (Orton, 1937). Orton's program is described in *Remedial Training for Reading, Spelling, and Penmanship* (Gillingham & Stillman, 1936) and is still widely used today. Similarly, Fernald (1943) emphasized a multisensory approach known as the visual-auditory-kinesthetic-tactile (VAKT) method. As opposed to Orton's phonics emphasis, Fernald stressed the necessity for reading and writing words as wholes.

Psychological Processing (Perceptual-Motor) Disabilities

Goldstein (1939) continued the study of brain pathology by examining soldiers who had head wounds during World War I. He found that brain injury causes a consistent set of symptoms, including perceptual impairment, most notably in figure-ground discrimination, distractibility, concrete thinking, rigidity, and perseveration (inability to cease repeating a verbal or motor behavior). Goldstein's research was continued in the United States by Werner and Strauss (1940) at the Wayne County Training School in Northville, Michigan, where they investigated whether children with brain damage resulting in their mental retardation resulted in the same symptoms found in adults with brain injury. Through a series of research studies, they found that the retarded children with brain damage exhibited the same behavioral characteristics as Goldstein's brain-injured adults. They described their findings in *Psychopathology and Education of the Brain-injured Child* (Strauss & Lehtinen, 1947).

Although behavioral differences between the brain-injured and non-brain-injured groups were established, Sarason (1949) criticized the means by which brain damage in mental retardation was diagnosed, especially the practice of making a diagnosis of actual brain injury solely on the basis of behavioral characteristics. Sarason suggested that such practice resulted in circular reasoning: "Some individuals with brain damage have certain behavioral characteristics, therefore individuals with these same behavioral characteristics must be presumed to be brain damaged" (p. 415).

Because Werner and Strauss studied only populations with mental retardation (MR), it was necessary to demonstrate that the set of behavioral symptoms associated with brain injury could be manifested independently of MR. William Cruichshank, a major figure in the study of LD, did this in investigations of children with cerebral palsy who possess indisputable diagnoses of brain injury (Cruickshank, Bice, & Wallen, 1957). Attention was then focused on the brain-injured child of average intelligence. Strauss and Kephart (1955), in *Psychopathology and Education of the Brain-injured Child: Progress in Theory and Clinic* (Vol. 2), viewed the brain-injured child not as a normal child of an earlier chronological age but rather as a child whose entire range of behavior had been adversely affected because of brain damage: "We cannot see what he sees, we cannot feel what he feels, and we cannot follow the processes which bring him to a certain end result. To us, his performance seems only bizarre" (p. 214).

By the mid-1950s, however, objection to the term *brain damage* emerged because it was viewed as a cause that does not describe a set of symptoms (Stevens & Birch, 1957). Birch (1964) suggested the need to differentiate the *fact* of brain injury, an anatomic alteration of the brain, from the *concept* of brain injury, a set of behaviors not necessarily descriptive of all children who are brain damaged.

With brain damage reduced to a subclinical level (i.e., no apparent anatomic alteration), the concept of *minimal brain dysfunction* (MBD) was introduced (Clements, 1966). The multitude of signs and symptoms associated with MDB, however, prevented it from being a *syndrome,* a cluster of symptoms characterizing a particular disorder, and led to the assertion that MBD is a myth: "The term MBD is simplistic, harmful, and overworked" (Schmitt, 1975, p. 1317).

One of the primary manifestations of minimal brain injury (or MBD) was a variety of perceptual-motor deficits. The deficits provided a cause-and-effect relationship between an etiology or cause (brain injury) and a direct consequence described as "central processing dysfunction" (Chalfant & Scheffelin, 1969). During the 1960s, several theoretical formulations were proposed that attempted to explain aspects of perceptual-motor functioning:

1. The *Illinois Test of Psycholinguistic Abilities* (Kirk, McCarthy, & Kirk, 1968), "was designed as a diagnostic test to delineate intra-individual variation in functioning" (Kirk & Kirk, 1971, p. 60).

2. Johnson and Myklebust's (1967) concept of "psychoneurological learning disability," in which the difficulty in learning is the "result of a dysfunction in the brain and the problem is one of altered processes, not of a generalized incapacity to learn" (p. 8).

3. Kephart's (1960) "perceptual-motor match" was necessary because "we cannot think of perceptual activities and motor activities as two different items; we must think of the hyphenated term perceptual-motor" (p. 63).

4. Getman's (1965) neuromotor complex of abilities merging into a total *visualization system* where *vision* (perception) is the primary processing system: "It is in this developmental level that overt performance can be transformed into covert behavior" (p. 71).

5. Frostig (1976) emphasized the role of visual perception and developed *The Marianne Frostig Developmental Test of Visual Perception* that assessed (a) eye-motor coordination, (b) figure-ground discrimination, (c) form constancy, (d) position in space, and (e) spatial relations (Frostig, Lefever, & Whittlesey, 1964).

6. Barsch (1967) developed the *Movigenic Curriculum*, which reflects "the origin and development of movement patterns leading to learning efficiency" (Barsch, 1967, p. 5).

7. Ayres (1968) postulated that learning was a function of the integration of visual and auditory input: "Certain types of learning disability may be interpreted partially in terms of dysfunction within the brain's integrative functions" (Ayres, 1968, p. 43).

Emergent Period

By 1963, the foundations of SLD had been established. The seminal event occurred in April 1963, when Samuel Kirk suggested "the term 'learning disabilities' to describe a group of children who have disorders in the development of language, speech, reading, and associated communication skills needed for social interaction" (Kirk, 1975, p. 9). The child described by Kirk is exemplified by the case of Robert.

Robert was a 9-year-old boy still in second grade because his academic performance was at the middle of first-grade level. His problems were most severe in reading with significant difficulties in word recognition, and, even when successful in recognizing words, he showed little understanding of what he had read. His writing was slow and laborious, and contained many spelling errors. His math calculations were slow but there was little difficulty with story problems when presented orally.

Robert's family situation was ideal. Both parents were professionals, and two older siblings experienced no difficulties in school. Robert's difficulties were a source of concern, and there was frustration about the family's inability to help him.

Robert's early history provided no hints of later difficulties. All developmental milestones were met or surpassed. His kindergarten experience was generally successful except for assessments of early reading which revealed a number of peaks and valleys in performance. Some concern was expressed but, because everyone agreed that Robert was a "bright" child, it was decided that he should enter first grade.

Robert's problems were considered to be related to immaturity which it was hoped would disappear over the course of first grade. The problems did not disappear, and Robert found it difficult to keep up with the class. After a routine vision screening, Robert was referred for a thorough eye examination which found minor vision problems easily corrected with glasses. Even with corrected vision, Robert's school problems continued.

By the middle of first grade, Robert's reading problems were pronounced, and his teacher asked for help. Robert was given an intelligence test and was found to have an IQ of 106. Because his siblings had IQs of about 125, Robert's parents expressed concern about the score and suggested it might be the source of his reading problems. The school explained that an IQ of 106 was actually above average and probably not the source of Robert's reading difficulties. In addition to the IQ test, Robert was asked to draw a human figure. The drawing showed some immaturity and some emotional indicators: dependency, impulsivity, and insecurity. These were not present to a significant degree and emotional disturbance was ruled out as a cause of Robert's reading difficulties.

During the second semester, the teacher asked for a conference with the parents. Besides continued reading failure, Robert was beginning to show attention problems and increased activity levels (ADHD). A neurological examination proved negative, and a diagnosis of minimal brain dysfunction (MBD) was made. Medication enhanced attention and decreased hyperactivity, but had little effect on Robert's learning difficulties.

Robert continued to experience severe reading difficulties, and it was questioned if he should proceed to third grade. Robert's parents were dismayed. Their child was not visually impaired, mentally retarded, emotionally disturbed, or brain injured, and had not been deprived of either a positive family environment or adequate learning opportunities.

The LD concept behind this case had been explained earlier by Kirk (1962) in the following definition:

> A learning disability refers to a retardation, disorder, or delayed development in one or more of the processes of speech, language, reading, writing, arithmetic, or other school subjects resulting from a psychological handicap caused by a possible cerebral dysfunction and/or emotional or behavioral disturbances. It is not the result of mental retardation, sensory deprivation, or cultural and instructional factors (p. 263).

Clearly, a new political and educational movement had been initiated. One of its first tasks was refining the above description to provide a more educationally focused definition (e.g., Bateman, 1965; Cruickshank, 1966; Kass & Myklehust, 1969). To bring order to the proliferation of SLD definitions, the *National Advisory Committee on Handicapped Children* (NACHC; 1968), headed by Samuel Kirk, was formed with the task of writing a definition of SLD that was to be the basis for Public Law 91-230 (Children with Specific Learning Disabilities Act). The definition, however, failed to provide a clear delineation of LD parameters (Hammill, 1974), but when Public Law 94-142, the *Education for All Handicapped Children Act,* was passed in 1975, SLD became an official category within the NACHC definition. With only minor wording changes, the NACHC definition was the one issued by the U.S. Office of Education (USOE). To this day it remains unchanged as the definition of SLD used by the federal government. The definition reads as follows:

> The term *specific learning disability* means a disorder in one or more of the psychological processes involved in understanding or in using language, spoken or written, which may manifest itself in an imperfect ability to listen, speak, read, write, spell, or to do mathematical calculations. The term includes such conditions as perceptual handicaps, brain injury, minimal brain dysfunction, dyslexia, and developmental aphasia. The term does not include children who have learning disabilities which are primarily the result of visual, hearing, or motor handicaps, or mental retardation, or emotional disturbance, or of environmental, cultural, or economic disadvantage (USOE, 1997, p. 65083).

The federal definition did not specify how states were to identify students as SLD. To remedy this situation the USOE issued regulations intended to provide criteria for determining eligibility. The regulations represent an *operational definition* of SLD and center on the presence of an ability-achievement discrepancy:

a. A team may determine that a child has a specific learning disability if:
   1. The child does not achieve commensurate with his or her age and ability levels in one or more of the areas listed in paragraph (a) (2) of this section, when provided with learning experiences appropriate for the child's age and ability levels; and
   2. The team finds that the child has a severe discrepancy between achievement and intellectual ability in one or more of the following areas: (i) Oral expression; (ii) Listening comprehension; (iii) Written expression; (iv) Basic reading skill; (v) Reading comprehension; (vi) Mathematical calculation; or (vii) Mathematical reasoning (USOE, 1997, p. 65083).

Discrepancy, or the difference between expected and actual achievement, represents an important criterion for the presence of SLD, and defines the concept of underachievement.

Although the federal definition of SLD is most often used, efforts to improve it continued (Kavale & Forness, 2000). The most prominent effort began in 1978 when major professional organizations interested in SLD united to address issues. The *National Joint Committee on Learning Disabilities* (NJCLD) developed the following definition:

> Learning disabilities is a generic term that refers to a heterogeneous group of disorders manifested by significant difficulties in the acquisition and use of listening, speaking, reading, writing, reasoning, or mathematical abilities. These disorders are intrinsic to the individual and presumed to be due to central nervous system dysfunction. Even though a learning disability may occur concurrently with other handicapping conditions (e.g., sensory impairment, mental retardation, social and emotional disturbance) or environmental influences (e.g., cultural differences, insufficient-inappropriate instruction, psychogenic factors), it is not the direct result of those conditions or influences (Hammill, Leigh, McNutt, & Larsen, 1981, p. 336).

The NJCLD definition included several significant changes:

- SLD is viewed as a generic (general) learning problem that is heterogeneous (can take many forms)
- LD is recognized as occurring in individuals of any age level
- The concept of psychological processes is excluded
- Analogous conditions (e.g., dyslexia, MBD) are excluded because of difficulties in defining these conditions
- The "exclusion clause" was modified to recognize that excluded conditions, although not a primary influence, could be secondary to and associated with LD.

Although the NJCLD definition was well received, it was not universally accepted. The ACLD (1986) did not approve the NJCLD definition and issued its own which emphasized the lifelong nature of (chronic) SLD, eliminated an exclusion clause, and made reference to adaptive behavior. The *Interagency Committee on Learning Disabilities* (ICLD, 1987), consisting of federal agencies, essentially endorsed the NJCLD definition with two modifications: (a) deficits in social skills were included as a primary disability, and (b) ADD was included as a comorbid (co-occurring) condition with LD. In response, the NJCLD (1988) issued a revised definition agreeing with the ACLD emphasis on the lifelong nature of SLD but disagreeing with the ICLD inclusion of social skills deficits as a primary SLD (Kavale & Forness, 1998). Several organizations contributed to the definition of SLD but had limited influence on the federal definition. In the 1977 reauthorization of IDEA, the SLD definition remained virtually unchanged since its first appearance in PL 94-142. Similarly, the 2004 reauthorization (*Individuals with Disabilities Education Improvement Act*) does not make any substantive change in the SLD definition. There are, however, major changes in the operational definition, that is, the way students with SLD are identified.

:: CHARACTERISTICS

Early Childhood

The SLD category is reserved for children who experience academic failure. But a variety of cognitive and behavioral characteristics place children at risk for academic failure. The problem is that these characteristics place the child at risk not only for SLD but also for a variety of other disabilities. For example, poverty, poor nutrition, and environmental hazards are risk factors for many disabilities. Because SLD includes multiple and complex causes that manifest themselves in a variety of conditions varying in type and severity, children under 6 years of age are often given a noncategorical designation such as *developmental delay*. The 1997 reauthorization of IDEA incorporated early childhood special education laws to ensure the same rights for younger children (ages 3–5).

Younger children may possess delays in one or more of the following areas: (a) physical development, (b) cognitive development, (c) communication development, or (d) adaptive development. Specifically, precursors of SLD may be found in the following areas: (a) gross motor skills, (b) fine motor skills, (c) auditory processing, (d) visual processing, (e) linguistic processing, or (f) attention problems. The following is typical of a child who acquires a SLD.

> Joseph is a 4-year-old boy considered high risk because of poor performance on screening tests assessing expressive language and social skills. A conference with his parents revealed that Joseph had been born 6 weeks early and weighed less than 5 pounds. From early on, Joseph suffered from frequent colds and flu, and between ages 2 and 3 1/2 ear infections became a serious problem. Physical development was normal, and Joseph sat up, crawled, and walked at the same time as his siblings. Language development, however, was slower than his peers. Although appearing to understand when spoken to, Joseph had great difficulty making himself understood. Language was delayed until about age 2, and communication is now short two- to three-word sentences with many wrong words. Joseph's inability to communicate often triggers temper tantrums.

Two areas provide the most reliable indicators of future problems. Kindergarten children at high risk for reading failure: (a) have limited phonemic ability (lack ability to add, delete, or substitute sounds in words); (b) cannot make letters of the alphabet and accompanying sounds; (c) lack fluency in naming letters (slow speed); and/or (d) cannot pronounce nonsense words (e.g., POV) (Speece, Mills, Richey, & Hillman, 2003). Kindergarten children are at high risk for social skill deficits (and school failure) if they: (a) do not demonstrate appropriate play, (b) do not experience appropriate friendships, (c) demonstrate aggressive or intimidating behavior, (d) do not respond to peer interactions, (e) make inappropriate social responses to adults, and/or (f) demonstrate inappropriate emotional responses (Vaughn et al., 2003).

The general term *developmental delay* is useful because children may be at risk for SLD, MR, or EBD. The goal is not to identify a specific disability but rather to provide early intervention to prevent future problems. As children approach school entry, reading deficits (e.g., phonemic awareness), often the central feature of SLD, assume more importance as specific indicators of future problems. Because children do not mature at the same rate, there is the possibility that developmental lags may disappear before formal schooling. Additionally, identification of developmental lags may create lower expectations and cause teachers to act differently toward identified children. By identifying children at age 3 or 4 as at risk, teachers may inadvertently reinforce learning and behavior problems.

Elementary Grades

The federal definition describes SLD as "a disorder in one or more of the basic psychological processes involved in understanding or in using language, spoken or written, which may manifest itself in an imperfect ability to listen, think, speak, read, write, spell, or to do mathematical calculations." A SLD is conceptualized as a deficit in one or more processes (e.g., listening, memory, perception, attention, etc.) assumed to be the underlying reason for academic difficulties.

Dyslexia is a particular SLD—severe difficulty in learning to read. It is primarily a medical term, but dyslexia is often used by educators to describe students with unexpected reading failure. Although possessing average or above-average intelligence, students with dyslexia have significant difficulties in reading, spelling, understanding language, and expressing themselves in speaking or writing. Even though there is disagreement about how dyslexia should be defined, there is agreement about the following (Hynd, 1992).

- Dyslexia has a biological basis and is caused by a different anatomical brain structure.
- Dyslexia persists in adolescence and adulthood.
- Dyslexia has linguistic, cognitive, and perceptual manifestations.

Reading

In a comprehensive review of the reading literature in 2000, the National Reading Panel determined that five areas in reading should receive primary instructional focus: phonemic awareness, phonics, fluency, vocabulary, and comprehension. These areas connect and build upon one another, leading to proficient reading. Unfortunately, for about 90% of students with SLD (Kavale & Forness, 2000) reading problems are a significant cause of low academic performance. The basic nature of the problem is found at the linguistic level of phonology (Liberman & Shankweiler, 1985), where a critical aspect of reading involves manipulating phonemes, the smallest sound unit of language (Liberman & Shankweiler, 1991). The most basic deficit of students with SLD is the lack of *phonemic awareness,* the understanding that spoken language is composed of individual phonemes (Brady, 1997; Rack, Snowling, & Olsen, 1992). Without a knowledge of the phonological structure of language, the student with SLD is likely to also lack **phonological awareness,** the ability to **blend** (connect sounds of individual phonemes into syllables and words), **segment** (dividing words into their individual phonemes), and **rhyme** (finding words that sound the same) (Blachman, 2001; Muter, 1998; Wagner & Torgesen, 1987).

TABLE 4.1	Phonological awareness tasks
Task	**Activity**
Phoneme segmentation	How many phonemes in *clap*?
Phoneme isolation	What is the first sound in *meat*?
Phoneme blending	What word is /c/-/a/-/t/?
Phoneme identity	What sound is the same in *boy, bike, bell*?
Phoneme categorization	Which word does not belong? run, sun, ton
Rhyming	What words rhyme with *heat*?
Phoneme deletion	Can you say *smile* without the *s*?

Table 4.1 shows phonological awareness tasks listed in order of difficulty (Coyne, Kame'enui, & Simmons, 2001).

The difficulties in phonemic and phonological awareness indicate that the reading deficits of students with SLD will be at the word rather than text level of processing (Ehri, 1998). The student with SLD cannot decode single words accurately, which creates difficulties in obtaining meaning from text.

The student with SLD may also manifest a second processing deficit termed **rapid naming-speed,** the inability to quickly retrieve the spoken referent for visual stimuli (Badian, 1997). Naming speed deficits adversely affect **orthographic processing,** establishing representations of letter sequences in memory (Bowers, Golden, Kennedy, & Young, 1994). The deficit in naming-speed that affects reading ability was identified independently from phonological processing (Wolf, 1997), and led to the **double-deficit** rapid theory (Wolf & Bowers, 1999). The effect of the double-deficit (naming-speed and phonological awareness) is to limit **automatization**—learning a skill so well that you use it automatically (Fawcett & Nicholson, 1994). Efficient decoding needs to be automatic, and, according to the theory of automaticity (LaBerge & Samuels, 1973), decoding that is not automatic requires a larger share of finite cognitive processing ability. This reduces the amount of cognitive resources that can be directed at understanding what is read.

Comprehension is the goal of reading. However, if the reader is forced to focus on recognizing single words, understanding the meaning of words is difficult because understanding text occurs at the sentence, paragraph, and story level. Because students with SLD do not decode automatically, they lack reading fluency. *Fluency* includes not only rate but also accuracy and expression. Besides decoding problems, problems in comprehension may be influenced by general language problems. Difficulties with **syntax** (grammatical structure of language) interfere with decoding (Lovett, 1987), comprehension (Resnick, 1970), and with **semantics** (intent and meaning of words) (Nation, Marshall, & Snowling, 2001). A limited vocabulary makes it difficult to associate printed words with their meaning (Roth, Speece, & Cooper, 2002). Additionally, comprehension problems experienced by students with SLD may be negatively influenced by poor early language experiences and insufficient background knowledge.

In summary, a student's initial difficulties in phonemic awareness lead to difficulty with phonological awareness, which leads to decoding that is less than automatic. When students do not develop automaticity in decoding, they have to decode word-by-word, which reduces fluency. This reduction in fluency translates into inadequate comprehension, as students are expending so much cognitive energy on decoding that they have little left for comprehending what they are reading.

Written Language

Students with a SLD perform poorly on written expression tasks, especially those involving vocabulary, grammar, punctuation, and spelling (Newcomer & Barenbaum, 1991). Students with SLD approach writing with minimal planning, effort, and strategic behavior (Thomas, Englert, & Gregg, 1987). The consequences are found in difficulties in text production, limited knowledge of the writing process (e.g., drafting and revising), poor idea generation and organization, and impoverished theme development (Graham, Harris, MacArthur, & Schwartz, 1991). The resulting written products are limited in comparison with average-achieving peers. Students with a SLD produce fewer words and sentences, fewer words with seven or more letters, and a greater number of spelling and capitalization errors (Houck & Billingsley, 1989).

Students with a SLD may also experience difficulties with the mechanics of writing (handwriting), as manifested in problems in letter formation and fluency. Extremely poor handwriting is sometimes termed **dysgraphia** (Denel, 1995).

Spelling is another written language deficit that may be experienced by students with a SLD. The inconsistent pattern of English caused by the lack of one-to-one phoneme-grapheme correspondence makes spelling difficult. Students with a SLD have difficulty segmenting words into phonemes and their conventional graphemes, and therefore spell fewer words correctly. Because spelling ability progresses through a series of developmental stages (Treiman & Bourassa, 2000), students with a SLD spell words in a manner similar to those of younger students. The reading and spelling deficits are primarily related to difficulties in phonemic awareness, suggesting that it is a language-based skill only modestly influenced by nonlinguistic factors (e.g., visual memory, auditory discrimination).

Mathematics

Students with a SLD may experience math difficulties related to numerical reasoning and calculation. Compared to average-achieving peers, students with a SLD perform more poorly in every aspect of arithmetic at every grade level (Cawley, Parmar, Foley, Salmon, & Roy, 2001). Notable are deficits in retrieving number facts and solving story problems (Geary, Hamson, & Hoard, 2000). Students with a SLD progress slowly in math, and many plateau by age 12 (Cawley, Parmar, Yan, & Miller, 1998).

Students with a SLD may experience only a deficit in math that is sometimes termed **dyscalculia** (Cohn, 1968) or problems in both math and reading (Robinson,

Menchetti, & Torgeson, 2002). When this combination of deficits is present, the math performance of students with a SLD likely demonstrates many errors (Miller & Milam, 1987).

Processes

Students with SLD demonstrate many processing deficits. In terms of cognitive styles (approaches to problem solving), students with SLD are generally more field dependent (i.e., influenced more by environment) and more impulsive (i.e., respond quickly with little reflection) (Blackman & Goldstein, 1982).

Memory difficulties often occur in students with a SLD. **Short-term memory** (ability to remember information immediately) tends to be more deficient in the auditory than in the visual realm (Hulme & Snowling, 1992). Reading and math problems appear to be more adversely influenced by deficits in **working memory** (ability to retain information while performing a mental operation) (Swanson & Ashbaker, 2000; Swanson & Sachse-Lee, 2001).

A major processing deficit in students with SLD involves **executive control** abilities (**metacognition**—thinking about one's thoughts) that include (a) recognition of the skills, strategies, and resources required to perform a task and (b) ability to monitor and regulate performance (Borkowski & Burke, 1996). Students with SLD may be deficient in a variety of metacognitive areas (e.g., **metamemory, metacomprehension**) resulting in such students becoming inactive or passive learners (Torgesen, 1977).

Motivation (activating, guiding, and maintaining behavior) is a problem area for students with SLD that results from three sources: (a) an external **locus of control** in which students with SLD wait for others to organize their behavior (Bryan & Pearl, 1979) and (b) negative **attributions** (beliefs about the causes of success and failure) in which students with SLD are often not proud of success, minimize accomplishments, and are more prone to accept responsibility for failure. Such negative attributions tend to lower belief in academic self-efficacy (Tabassam & Grainger, 2002), and (c) **learned helplessness** (belief that effort will not result in desired outcomes) which makes the students with SLD come to expect failure no matter how much effort they expend (Settle & Milich, 1999).

The presence of attention problems is an important component of SLD (Hallahan & Reeve, 1980). Attention problems were central to conceptualizations like the Strauss syndrome (Stevens & Birch, 1957) and (MBD) (Clements, 1966). These ideas ultimately resulted in attention-deficit hyperactivity disorder (ADHD), described in the American Psychiatric Association's (1994) *Diagnostic and Statistical Manual of Mental Disorders (DSM-IV)*. DSM-IV recognized several types of ADHD: (a) ADHD-inattentive type, (b) ADHD-Hyperactive-impulsive type, and (c) ADHD-combined type (see Table 4.2).

The ADHD syndrome is characterized by a primary deficit in **behavioral inhibition**, in which there is an inability to delay a response, to interrupt an ongoing response, and to protect a response from competing stimuli (Barkley, 1997). The difficulties in behavioral inhibition result in an impaired sense of time awareness and management, which causes problems in **executive functioning** (e.g., negative effects on working memory, inner speech, and self-regulation of emotions) (Barkley, 1998). The estimates of SLD in the ADHD population range from 9% to 80%, and

TABLE 4.2	ADHD Behaviors

Inattentive

- Easily distracted
- Ignores instructions
- Short attention span
- Limited attention to details
- Forgetful
- Lacks sustained attention
- Difficulty in organizing tasks
- Loses work materials
- Fails to finish activities

Hyperactive-Impulsive

- Fidgety
- Moves constantly
- Leaves seat unexpectedly
- Often "on the go"
- Often talks excessively
- Difficulty awaiting turn
- Often interrupts or intrudes
- Answers before question is completed

Combined

Any and all behavioral indicators under inattentive and hyperactive-impulsive.

ADHD prevalence rates for students with SLD range from 41% to 80% (Riccio, Gonzalez, & Hynd, 1994). Thus, there is overlap between SLD and ADHD, and they have come to be viewed as co-occurring (**comorbid**) conditions (Kotkin, Forness, & Kavale, 2001). There are similarities between students with ADHD (inattentive type) and students with SLD (Stanford & Hynd, 1994).

Behavior and Social Skills

Behavioral problems appear at a higher-than-expected rate among students with SLD (Kavale & Forness, 1998). McLeskey (1992) found that the percentage of students (15%) with behavioral problems remained consistent across grade levels (K–12). The cause-and-effect relationship between behavior problems and academic difficulties remains unclear. Additionally many students with SLD demonstrate no behavior problems.

Students with SLD are more likely to manifest social skill deficits. Kavale and Forness (1996) found that almost 75% of students with SLD exhibited deficits in social skills. Students with SLD appear to be less socially accepted because of difficulties in using language in social situations, in being sensitive to social cues, in correctly perceiving their social status, and in adapting to social situations (Sridhar & Vaughn, 2001). Poor social skills are associated with fewer positive interactions with teachers, difficulty in making friends, and loneliness (Haager & Vaughn, 1995). A fundamental problem in contributing to poor social skills may be an inability to perceive emotions in others, most particularly nonverbal affective expressions (Most & Greenbank, 2000).

Adolescence

The same academic and social problems found in children with SLD are likely to continue into adolescence and adulthood (Kavale, 1988). The following case is typical of the adolescent with SLD.

> John, now 14 years old, was identified in elementary school and received special education services. John improved his academic performance throughout elementary school and, at the beginning of eighth grade, was placed in regular content-area classes with no provisions for special education services. Although requiring significant effort, John received above-average grades and felt ready for high school.
>
> As a Jefferson High School freshman, John did not experience similar success. His first semester grades showed that he failed three subjects—English, algebra, and science, received a D in history, and a C in physical education. John feels that he cannot cope with the demands of the courses and struggles with the assignments. Reading textbooks is laborious, and taking notes in class is slow, which causes John to lose track about what is going on. He does particularly poorly on written tests. Generally, John feels overwhelmed, and knows he needs help.
>
> The school seems not overly concerned. In a conference with his parents, they were told that John should be doing better based on his school history and needs to try harder. John was discouraged and began to cut classes. Because of his embarrassment about grades, John has withdrawn from social interactions. John is increasingly frustrated and appears depressed enough to drop out of school.

In adolescents, SLD often manifests the following characteristics: (a) passive learning, (b) poor self-concept, (c) social and behavior problems, (d) attention problems, and (e) lack of motivation. Most important, adolescents with SLD demonstrate an increasing achievement gap related to the content area driven nature of secondary school for which the student with SLD lacks the requisite basic skills (Deshler et al., 2001). Students with SLD entering high school are lowest of the low achievers and usually perform below the 10th percentile in reading, written language, and math (Hock, Schumaker, & Deshler, 1999).

The cumulative deficits experienced by adolescents with SLD are likely associated with higher dropout rates, higher underemployment, and greater dependency on others (Blackorby & Wagner, 1996). Only about one-third of students with SLD graduate with a high school diploma. Significant differences in terms of employment and postschool adjustment exist between students with SLD who drop out and those who graduate (Thurlow, 2000).

:: IDENTIFICATION OF STUDENTS WITH SLD

Early Childhood

Haring et al. (1992) questioned the labeling of preschoolers as SLD because of lack of academic progress as a central notion to the SLD concept. Instead, generic labels such as *developmentally delayed* or *at-risk* are preferred because they do not create lowered expectations like specific categorical labels.

The goal is to predict potential learning problems and poor achievement. For example, early language development is highly predictive of later reading achievement (Snow, Burns, & Griffin, 1998). In particular, tests of phonological awareness are robust predictors of later reading achievement (Olofsson & Niedersoe, 1999). Other areas that are predictive include evaluation of cognitive, motor, social-emotional, and adaptive development. Also useful are teacher perceptions, especially when structured with the use of scales and checklists (Coleman & Dover, 1993; Mantzicopoulos & Morrison, 1994).

Elementary Grades

The IDEA definition outlines the concept of SLD and includes, implicitly or explicitly, ideas about achievement problems, inter- and intra-individual variation, etiology, and exclusions. For use in practice, however, the legal definition needs to be operationalized, as in the 1997 reauthorization of IDEA. In federal law, the criteria used to determine whether (a) the child does not achieve commensurate with his or her age and ability levels in one or more of the areas listed, if provided with learning experiences appropriate for the child's age and ability levels; (b) the team finds that a child has a *severe discrepancy* between achievement and intellectual ability in one or more of the following areas:

  i. Oral expression
 ii. Listening comprehension
iii. Written expression
 iv. Basic reading skill
  v. Reading comprehension
 vi. Mathematical calculation
vii. Mathematic reasoning

Finally, (c) the team may not identify a child as having a SLD if the severe discrepancy between ability and achievement is primarily the result of any of the following:

1. A visual, hearing, or motor impairment
2. Mental retardation
3. Emotional disturbance
4. Environmental, cultural, or economic disadvantage
   (U.S. Department of Education, 1999, p. 12457)

The most recent reauthorization of IDEA (2004) introduces a significantly different operational definition of SLD in which (a) the local education agency (school system) shall not be required to take into consideration whether a child has a severe discrepancy between achievement and intellectual ability, and (b) the local educational agency may use a process that determines whether a child responds to scientific, research-based interventions.

The proposed process is usually termed **response to intervention** (RTI), in which schools provide differing types and levels of instruction for low achieving students (usually in reading). The possible elimination of IQ-achievement discrepancy is predicated on the assumption that IQ tests are not needed to define SLD

(Fletcher et al., 2002). Kavale (2002) defended the use of the discrepancy criterion by suggesting that it is psychometrically sound and is the operational definition of underachievement, rather than LD. This means it should not be the sole criterion for SLD identification. MacMillan, Gresham, and Bocian (1998) showed that there was a "discrepancy" between definitions of SLD and school practice (i.e., how students were actually identified as SLD). The significant variability means that other factors (e.g., less stigma for SLD than MR, help for a student when special education is the only available option) may determine SLD status (MacMillan & Siperstein, 2002). Despite the presence of the RTI model in IDEA (2004), there has been debate regarding if and how the model should be implemented. Discussion will continue regarding the effectiveness of using a RTI model for purposes of eligibility diagnosis until data can be collected on the model's effectiveness.

The RTI model can be implemented in different ways that include variations in instructional interventions, levels of intervention before special education, and means by which students are deemed nonresponders (Fuchs, Mock, Morgan, & Young, 2003). The RTI model is seen as a means to address alleged shortcomings of the discrepancy model by focusing on risk factors and student outcomes rather than deficits (Vaughn & Fuchs, 2003). Kavale, Holdnack, and Mostert (2005) suggested that the RTI model is better suited for prevention rather than diagnosis. Is the lack of response due to SLD or EBD? What happens after a student does not respond and is deemed eligible for special education? Kavale et al. (2005) suggested that RTI is best viewed as an initial part of a psychometrically based identification procedure which provides for greater confidence in the validity of the SLD classification *and* information useful for designing an individualized academic program. A reasonable person might ask whether, if RTI is implemented only with much effort and controversy by researchers, it is a procedure than can be widely implemented with fidelity and success by teachers and others who have relatively little training and experience in using RTI.

Tests of cognitive ability provide information about a student's aptitude for learning and specific cognitive processing strengths and weaknesses. Commonly used tests include the WISC-IV (*Wechsler Intelligence Scale for Children—Fourth Edition*), Kaufman Assessment Battery for Children (*K-ABC*), *Stanford-Binet Intelligence Scale—Fourth Edition,* and *Woodcock Johnson III Complete Battery* (includes both tests of cognitive abilities and achievement). Actual achievement is usually assessed with comprehensive academic assessments like the *Metropolitan Achievement Test, Iowa Test of Basic Skills, Stanford Achievement Test,* and *Wide-Range Achievement Test—III.* When more in-depth information about achievement is desired, diagnostic test batteries may be administered. Examples include the *Kaufman Test of Educational Achievement, Peabody Individual Achievement Test-Revised, Brigance Diagnostic Comprehensive Inventory of Basic Skills-Revised,* and *Woodcock Johnson Psychoeducational Battery III—Achievement Tests.*

The RTI model is best viewed as a **prereferral** strategy in which instructional or organizational suggestions for enhanced achievement are provided before referral for special education evaluation (Graden, 1989). What happens after students proceed through the RTI process? Are they referred for a comprehensive evaluation? Answers to such questions are unclear. With perhaps 25% of students being involved in RTI procedures, it is difficult to see how fewer students will be referred for special education than is the case with the discrepancy model.

What is to be done with a student who does not respond? The student has been provided with scientifically, research-based interventions that did not enhance performance. What happens at this point? Besides determining eligibility, a comprehensive evaluation can also assist instructional planning. The goal of a comprehensive assessment is to compare student performance with average achieving students similar in age, gender, cultural group, intelligence, and opportunities to learn, *and* finding out what a particular student knows and does not know.

Standardized testing (a set procedures for administration, objective scoring criteria, and frames of reference for score interpretation) is the traditional way of evaluating students with SLD (Lopez-Reyna, Bay, & Patrikakou, 1996). For the student with SLD, standardized testing may be accompanied by **neuropsychological assessment** (linking psychological characteristics to brain functioning) (Hale & Fiorello, 2004), **curriculum-based assessment** (CBA) (frequent and systematic sampling of instructional sequences used for daily instruction in reading, math, or other curriculum areas) (Deno & Fuchs, 1987), **functional behavioral assessment** (FBA) (direct observation to analyze a student's behavior in relation to social and physical aspects of the environment) (Scott & Nelson, 1999). The FBA includes (a) identifying target problem behaviors, (b) developing hypotheses about conditions that may provoke the problem behavior, and (c) determining what maintains the problem behavior. Typically, an **ABC procedure** is used: **Antecedent** (What triggers the behavior?), **Behavior** (Precisely what does the student do?), and **Consequence** (What immediately follows the behavior?). IDEA requires a positive behavior support plan (a problem-solving focus that aids the prevention of problem behaviors and aids students in acquiring new social skills) that is based on a FBA for students whose behavior interferes with their own or other's learning.

Although IDEA does not specify particular assessments, there are requirements for evaluation procedures that include:

1. Using a variety of assessment tools and strategies to gather relevant functional, developmental, and academic information, including information provided by the parent;
2. Not using any single procedure, measure, or assessment as the sole criterion for determining whether a child has a disability or determining an appropriate educational program for the child; and
3. Using technically sound instruments to assess the relative contribution of cognitive and behavioral factors, in addition to physical or developmental factors (IDEA, S. 1248, 2003).

Adolescence

For adolescents with SLD, identification per se is usually not an issue. Rather, attention is focused on how to include students with SLD in statewide assessment programs. The 1997 reauthorization of IDEA mandates participation but also guarantees testing accommodations (alterations in testing procedures that minimize the effects of a disability in student performance) (Fuchs & Fuchs, 2001). Testing accommodations usually include extended-time, small-group administration, tests read aloud, and responses dictated to a scribe (Bielinski, Ysseldyke, Bolt, Friedbach, & Friedbach, 2001), but research evidence has failed to support one particular accommodation for all students with SLD.

For adolescents with SLD, the statewide standards (high-stakes) tests represent the perceived basic competency for success in society (Lanford & Cary, 2000; Manset & Washburn, 2000). For students with SLD, it is important that statewide testing programs:

- be validated for use with students with SLD.
- not measure the disability directly.
- be aligned with the curriculum.
- are not used for high-stakes decision making.

Although high school standards tests define competency at about an eighth-grade level, the adolescent with SLD may actually be achieving at the fifth- or sixth-grade level, making test accommodations essential if students are to succeed. Yet, the practice of allowing test accommodations has raised concerns about the validity of these modified assessments (Johnson, Kimball, Olson-Brown, & Anderson, 2001).

:: UNIQUE LEARNING NEEDS OF STUDENTS WITH SLD

Early Childhood

For preschool children (ages 3–5), IDEA provides the same rights as older children. If special services are required due to a disability, IDEA suggests a plan for working with the child's family termed **Individualized Family Service Plan** (IFSP) that is similar to an IEP required for school-age children.

For the early childhood student, three service models are commonly found: home-based, center-based, and combination. In the home-based model, the child's parent assumes the role of primary teacher in a natural setting, while the center-based model provides facility-based instruction several times a week for 3–5 hours per day. A combination model usually includes a center-based education program that focuses on all areas of development and includes substantial family involvement in all program features. When evaluated, combination models that offer a range of programming options are more effective than either home- or center-based services (Eiserman, Weber, & McCoun, 1995).

As a child enters kindergarten, a major focus should be on actively planning for the transition from home or center to school by helping children to become more self-directed and less dependent on adults (Rosenkoetter, Whaley, Hains, & Pierce, 2001). Nevertheless, there are difficulties surrounding the relationship between general and special early childhood education (Odom, 2000).

General early education is often guided by **developmentally appropriate practice** (DAP), which emphasizes child-initiated learning, exploratory play, and the child's interests (Bredenkamp & Copple, 1997). For the child with developmental delays, DAP guidelines may not be appropriate because of their need for direct intervention, structured learning experiences, and extrinsic motivation (i.e., rewards) (Carta, 1995). Consequently, if placed in a general early childhood class, students with developmental delays will require adaptations and modifications of the DAP curriculum

(Wolery, Werts, & Holcombe, 1994). Nevertheless, inclusive (i.e., general) classrooms for students with developmental delays may produce better outcomes than early childhood special classes, particularly for children with milder problems who attend full-day rather than half-day programs (Holahan & Costenbader, 2000).

Elementary

Beginning with Strauss and Lehtinen's (1947) suggestion that perceptual and conceptual deficits need to be remediated for enhanced learning, process (ability) training dominated special education for students with SLD and most usually included psycholinguistic training (Kirk & Kirk, 1971) or perceptual-motor training (e.g., Frostig & Horne, 1964; Kephart, 1960). With the recognition that process training did not usually enhance either process or academic outcomes (Kavale & Forness, 1999), attention shifted to remediating basic skill deficits and the **diagnostic-prescriptive model** became prominent. This model is predicated on the assumption that psychological processes (e.g., sound blending) and/or basic skill areas (e.g., reading) might be deficient as revealed by standardized testing and then addressed through prescribed remedial programs. The remediation of process deficits provides for more normal learning; the remediation of basic skill deficits improves academic achievement.

Over time, the diagnostic-prescriptive model began to focus solely on basic skill remediation, but then the remediation-only approach began to shift toward approaches that permitted more meaningful access to the core curriculum (Klingner & Vaughn, 1999). This shift reflected the recognition that students with SLD did not have process deficits *per se* but rather (a) difficulties in organizing information, (b) limited stores of background knowledge, and (c) difficulties in approaching learning tasks in an effective and efficient manner (Gersten, 1998).

Educational interventions for students with SLD took on a more dynamic character with elements like the principles of **effective design** to make curriculum and instruction more effective (see Table 4.3 and Kame'enui, Carnine, Dixon, Simmons, & Coyne, 2002). In terms of actual methods, *best practice* became embodied in

TABLE 4.3	Principles of effective instructional design

Big ideas—highly selected material that facilitates the broadest acquisition of knowledge

Conspicuous strategies—a full and clear explication of the sequence of teacher actions that outline steps in learning

Mediated scaffolding—support for learning new material that is faded over time

Strategic integration—sequencing of instruction that shows the commonalities and differences between old and new knowledge

Primed background knowledge—related knowledge required to learn new knowledge

Judicious review—opportunities to apply and to develop facility with new knowledge through review that is adequate, distributed, varied, and cumulative procedures like **explicit instruction** involving carefully designed materials and activities that provide structures and supports that aid students with SLD in organizing and assimilating new information. Gersten (1998) outlined principles for explicit instruction including:

- providing a wide range of examples to illustrate a concept or strategy
- providing models of proficient performance, including step-by-step strategies or generic questions that focus attention and initiate processing
- providing situations where students may explain how and why they made decisions
- providing frequent feedback about performance
- providing activities that are interesting and engaging as well as opportunities for practice

Many of the features of explicit instruction are found in **Direct Instruction** (DI) (Adams & Carnine, 2003), which stresses a systematic analysis of the concept to be taught through **task analysis.** The goal is to break down an academic task into its component parts so teachers are able to teach parts separately and then teach students to put the parts together to demonstrate acquisition of the larger skill.

Direct Instruction programs are available for reading, language, and math. Each DI program includes the following features:

- Curriculum structured around mastery learning
- Sequenced, scripted teacher-led lessons
- Small-group instruction (4–10 students)
- Lessons presented in small steps and at rapid pace
- Frequent teacher questioning and student response

With appropriate curricular modifications and supports, many students with learning disabilities can succeed in the general education classroom. (Photo credit: Valerie Schultz/Merrill)

- Emphasis in drill and practice
- Feedback, reinforcement, and correction
- Frequent assessments

Thus, DI takes a bottom-up approach where complex tasks are built from component skills. For students with SLD, DI has demonstrated substantial positive effects on academic learning (Adams & Engelmann, 1996).

In addition to explicit instruction, **cognitive training** is important for students with SLD because it aids in overcoming problem solving difficulties and motivational problems caused by learned helplessness and passive (inactive) learning. Over time, the focus on information processing has shifted to functions like memory and thinking rather than sensory functions like visual and auditory processing. For example, the idea that instruction could be adapted to modality preference (learning style) has received little empirical support (Kavale & Forness, 1987).

For memory, **mnemonic strategies** have been used with students with SLD to enhance memory and retrieval skills using visual and/or acoustic representations (Mastropieri & Scruggs, 1991). Strategies may include (a) *letter strategies* (teaching HOMES as the representation for the Great Lakes—Huron, Ontario, Michigan, Erie, and Superior); (b) *keyword* method (new word recoded into concrete word that is acoustically similar to target word and linked by a picture showing keyword and definition together); (c) *pegword* method (keyword method plus a rhyming proxy for numbers)—for example, to aid students in remembering the order of the U.S. presidents, Mastropieri, Scruggs, and Whedon (1997) used pictures with two elements—one for name and one for ranking; and (d) *reconstructive elaborations* for abstract concepts that are made more familiar, more meaningful, and more concrete. Being taught with mnemonic techniques produces substantial gains (Scruggs & Mastropieri, 2000).

In terms of thinking, the focus is on *metacognition* (thinking about thinking) which is reflected in

1. **Self-instruction** (verbalizing the steps in a task) that includes the following training sequence (Meichenbaum & Goodman, 1971)
   a. The teacher performs the task while verbalizing
      1. questions about the task.
      2. self-guiding instruction on how to perform the task.
      3. self-evaluation of performance.
   b. The child performs the task while the teacher instructs aloud.
   c. The child performs the task while verbalizing aloud.
   d. The child performs the task while verbalizing in a whisper.
   e. The child performs the task while verbalizing covertly.
   Self-instruction has been shown to be an effective technique for students with SLD (e.g. Case, Harris, & Graham, 1991; Montague, Warger, & Morgan, 2000; Smith, Dittmer, & Skinner, 2002).
2. **Self-monitoring** (students keeping track of their own behavior) through the processes of *self-evaluation* and *self-recording*. The self-monitoring can be successful in evaluating academic and behavioral performance (Harris, Graham, Reid, McElroy, & Hamby, 1994; Mathes & Bender, 1997).

3. **Scaffolded instruction** (assistance is provided for students during initial learning that is gradually reduced until task is completed independently) typically involves the teacher modeling specific behaviors. Scaffolded instruction is often linked to the concept of the **zone of proximal development** (Vygotsky, 1962), which refers to the difficulty level for effective learning: neither too hard nor too easy. Sexton, Harris, and Graham (1998) provided an example in a three-step strategy for writing that includes saying aloud:
   a. THINK, who will read this, and why am I writing it?
   b. PLAN, what to say using TREE procedure (i.e., topic sentence, reasons, examine, endings)
   c. Write and say more.

4. **Reciprocal teaching** (student gradually assumes the role of co-instructor) while the teacher models four strategies (a) predicting, (b) questioning, (c) summarizing, and (d) clarifying. In a manner similar to scaffolded instruction, reciprocal teaching involves an interactive dialogue between teacher and student similar to that of expert and apprentice (Palinscar & Brown, 1986).

5. **Cognitive strategies** (how to approach and complete learning tasks in an efficient and effective manner) teach students to reproduce the learning of expert learners (Ryan, Short, & Wend, 1986). The Strategic Instruction Model (Deshler, Ellis, & Lenz, 1996) suggests teachers include the following steps in teaching learning strategies: (a) pretest and make commitments, (b) describe, (c) model, (d) verbal practice, (e) controlled practice and feedback, (f) advanced practice and feedback, (g) posttest and commitment to generalize, and (h) generalization. The teaching sequence requires repeated instruction and practice, and should be embedded in the following instructional principles:
   - Teach requisite skills before strategy instruction
   - Teach strategies regularly and intensively
   - Emphasize individual effort
   - Require mastery of strategies
   - Integrate instruction with strategy learning
   - Emphasize covert processing
   - Emphasize generalization of strategies.

Learning strategies may be used to teach specific skills. For example, to improve reading content area texts, Grant (1993) developed the SCROL strategy:

- *S*—Survey headings and subheadings to determine what information is being presented.
- *C*—Connect the headings with key words that show how each relates to one another.
- *R*—Read each heading with attention to words and phrases that express information about the heading.
- *O*—Outline the major ideas and supporting details in headings without looking at the text.
- *L*—Look at headings to check outline for accuracy and make any necessary corrections.

For problems with motivation, **attribution training** (indicating when students do well and suggesting that it is due to hard work and not giving up) has been suggested as a means for keeping students actively involved in learning (Borkowski, Wehring, & Carr, 1988). Research on attribution training (e.g., Fulk, 1996; Johnson, Graham, & Harris, 1997) has shown equivocal results, suggesting that the elements associated with low motivation (learned helplessness, negative attributions, external loss of control) may be difficult to change in students with SLD. A major factor in eliminating these negative influences on motivation is to ensure that students with SLD experience academic success (Meltzer & Montague, 2001).

In evaluating best practice for students with SLD, both explicit instruction and cognitive training are necessary. Explicit instruction is necessary to teach skills and strategies directly, while cognitive training is necessary to reinforce and practice the learned skills and strategies (Swanson & Hoskyn, 1998; Vaughn, Gersten, & Chard, 2000).

Adolescence

Federal law requires that a transition plan be integrated into a student's IEP and must be individualized because of changing needs and aspirations (Shapiro & Rich, 1999). Although mandated, comprehensive transition planning has been inconsistent (Johnson, Stodden, Emanuel, Luecking, & Mack, 2002) primarily because (a) students are not actively involved in transition planning, (b) professionals do not fully understand the transition needs of students with SLD, and (c) students with SLD possess inadequate **self-advocacy** skills (Cummings, Madden, & Casey, 2000; Thompson, Fulk, & Piercy, 2000). *Self-advocacy* refers to students with SLD (a) demonstrating understanding of their disability, (b) being aware of their legal rights, and (c) demonstrating the ability to communicate understanding of their needs and rights to those in positions of authority (Skinner, 1998). Research has demonstrated that self-advocacy can be taught (Lock & Layton, 2001). A related concept is **self-determination** (making one's own decisions about important life events) which may also be inadequate in students with SLD. Self-determined behavior is achieved when (a) the individual acts autonomously, (b) behavior is self-regulated, (c) the individual responds in a psychologically empowered manner, and (d) the individual acts in a self-realizing manner (Wehmeyer, Agran, & Hughes, 1998). Research has demonstrated that self-determination can be taught (Durlak, Rose, & Bursuck, 1994; Malian & Nevin, 2002).

The various needs and differing aspirations of adolescents with SLD have fostered the development of different programming options (e.g., Deshler, Schumaker, Lenz, & Ellis, 1984; Johnson, 1984; Zigmond & Sansone, 1986):

1. *Consultation*—special education teacher advises general education teacher on ways to modify the general education curriculum.
2. *Co-teaching*—the general and special education teachers work together in general education classroom.
3. *Basic skills*—the special education teacher delivers instruction in reading, math, and writing in a separate setting for varying amounts of time.

4. *Tutorial*—the special education teacher tutors the student in various content areas for specified periods.
5. *Learning strategies*—to deal specifically with metacognitive deficits, the model developed by Deshler et al. (1996) is implemented by the special education teacher.
6. *Work-study*—provides supervised work experiences during the school day.
7. *Functional Skills*—concentrates on independent living skills necessary to adapt to the world outside of school, often combined with a work-study or basic skill approach.

Adolescents with SLD may have reading and language skills at the fourth- or fifth-grade level, making the lecture and assigned textbook readings format of high school particularly difficult. Consequently, strategies have been developed to aid such students in reading textbooks by directing their attention to such things as bold print, headings, and text structure (e.g., Englert & Mariage, 1991; Schumaker, Deshler, Alley, Warner, & Denton, 1984). **Content enhancement** is the term used to describe modifications that allow students with SLD to better organize, comprehend, and retain information and may include the use of advanced organizers, guided notes, graphic organizers, and visual displays (Hudson, Lignugaris-Kraft, & Miller, 1993). Transition is particularly important for adolescents with SLD because adults with SLD are likely to manifest persistent problems in learning, socializing, holding jobs, and living independently (Gerber & Reiff, 1991). Factors that lead to successful adjustment of adults with SLD are not exclusively related to IQ and achievement, but also to (a) significant ability to persevere, (b) ability to set realistic goals, (c) acceptance of weakness with an accompanying ability to build on strength, (d) access to a strong network of social support, (e) access to long-term educational interventions, and (f) an ability to take full control of one's life.

SUMMARY

The category of specific learning disability (SLD) developed from the study of brain pathology that causes specific types of language and reading disability. When Public Law 94-142, the *Education for All Handicapped Children Act* was passed in 1975, SLD became an official category with the NACHC definition. Students with SLD are likely to demonstrate inefficient processing that creates difficulties in acquiring and assimilating information. Students with SLD are characterized by unexpected learning failure, meaning that SLD is primarily a category of underachievement.

The definition of SLD has not changed since the inception of the term as a federal category in 1969 but has been interpreted differently over time. Since 1977, *discrepancy*, a significant difference between predicted and actual achievement, has been the primary identification criterion for SLD. The new IDEA indicates that the discrepancy criterion is no longer required and agencies may use a process that determines if a child responds to empirically validated interventions. The process is usually termed responsiveness to intervention (RTI).

Although reading difficulties can be found in approximately 90% of students with SLD, these children can also have other challenges separately or in combination in one or more of the following areas: oral expression; listening comprehension; written expression; basic reading skill; reading comprehension; mathematical calculation; or mathematical reasoning. Comprehensive evaluations can assist instructional planning when results provide information about a student's performance compared with average-achieving students similar in demographics and opportunities to learn, therefore specifically identifying what a particular student does and does not know. Comprehensive evaluations typically include standardized testing of students with SLD accompanied by a combination of other relevant assessments such as neuropsychological assessment, curriculum-based assessment, and functional behavioral assessment.

Students with SLD are likely to be inactive or passive learners caused by metacognitive deficits, especially executive control. Students with SLD may often manifest the comorbid condition of ADHD, especially the Inattentive type. Yet, SLD remains a heterogeneous condition whose manifestations differ significantly across students, requiring an individualized education plan implementing research–based intervention practices.

COMPETENT TEACHING BOX

BOX 4.1

Knowing your students . . .

What you might want to remember about specific learning disability (SLD):

- Students with SLD are not simply low achievers, but rather students with complex, neurologically based learning deficits.
- SLD is associated with average IQ levels. Students with SLD do not have mental retardation.
- Students with SLD are likely to demonstrate developmental delays prior to school entry, especially in language and behavior.
- Students with SLD are most likely to experience reading problems with difficulties in math and writing also likely.
- The most likely reading problem for students with SLD involves word recognition, most often related to fundamental difficulties in phonemic awareness and naming speed.
- Students with SLD often demonstrate writing problems related to producing written material, using proper grammar, and possibly the mechanics of writing.
- The problems with phonemic awareness may also cause spelling difficulties.
- Math difficulties of students with SLD are often related to numerical reasoning and calculation. Reading problems are likely to cause difficulties in solving story problems.
- Students with SLD are likely to manifest process deficits that include:
  - A field-dependent cognitive style
  - Greater impulsivity
  - Memory deficits (short-term and working)
  - Poor motivation cause by external locus of control, negative attributions, and learned helplessness
- Students with SLD may possess behavior problems but are more likely to manifest social skill deficits especially related to social problem solving.
- Adolescents with SLD reveal the same academic and social problems found in children.

Competent teachers understand that . . .

- Students with SLD are most likely to have reading difficulties, followed by math and writing problems.
- Students with SLD have learning strengths and weaknesses.
- Instructional decisions are based on analyses of student, curriculum, and environment.
- Instructional goals must be comprehensive and unified.
- Intervention needs to be based on a diagnostic-prescriptive approach that includes assessment, planning, implementation, evaluation, and modification as needed.
- Students with SLD require intense and sustained intervention activities.
- There is a need for active learning to overcome the inactive learning of students with SLD.
- "Best practice" is predicated on using research-supported materials.
- Students with SLD will likely require specialized methods for teaching basic skills.
- Content area instruction should be based on the use of learning strategies and study skills.
- There is a necessity for modifying the pace of instruction and providing organizational cues.
- There is a need for students with SLD to experience success.

:: CASE STUDIES

ELTON

Elton was so excited to finally start the first grade. He could hardly contain his exuberance entering Mrs. Benny's classroom. Elton made sure that he approached each of his new classmates and introduced himself to them and easily began joking and laughing with the group. Elton seemed to be quick with a joke and moved easily about the class talking to his classmates, but truth be told, he was also more comfortable watching television alone than interacting with his friends or mother (Elton's parents separated shortly after his third birthday). Elton was working hard in class to keep his classmates and Mrs. Benny from finding out that he did not know the names of the colors, the numbers, or even the days of the week.

It did not take long for Mrs. Benny to discover that Elton could not read even at the simplest level. He very often just stared at a page containing two different letters. Mrs. Benny also discovered that Elton would jump at the chance to be the helper during group activities, and as always, Elton would become the entertainer for the class, even to the point of bringing props and costumes to class in order to entertain his classmates. Yet, Elton still did not perform academic tasks when requested. On several occasions Mrs. Benny sent notes home to Elton's mother explaining to her the difficulties that Elton had in his schoolwork. The notes would always come back to school with a note saying that Elton tried to do his assignments and he and his mother sometimes worked together, but that Elton often seemed to get frustrated and upset at being forced to complete his homework. Elton was falling behind his classmates very quickly and Mrs. Benny felt that Elton could not begin the class project in the computer lab without learning some basic reading skills.

1. What suggestions would you give Mrs. Benny to find out why Elton is not learning basic skills at an appropriate rate?
2. Could a physical deficit be contributing to Elton's learning difficulties?
3. What could Mrs. Benny do in order to discover why Elton is not learning?
4. Should Elton be held in the first grade until he is able to perform at an appropriate level?

CARMEN

The bell rings for the start of third period and Carmen, a quiet sixth grader, is late in arriving at her most dreaded class, Communication Arts. Today, Carmen must take part in a group project that requires each student to read a part of a play that the class is studying. Carmen knows her speaking skills are not very good and also that she will constantly lose her place while reading the play. The pressure seems to cause Carmen distress.

On arriving in the class, Carmen approaches her teacher, Mr. Charles, and informs him that she does not feel well and wants to go to the school nurse. Mr. Charles is familiar with Carmen's routine and asks her to wait a few minutes and see if she feels better once she has taken her seat and rested for a moment. Soon the class is busy forming into groups, discussing their projects and awaiting their turn to show the class what they have done. Mrs. Windsor, Carmen's special education teacher, gave her suggestions for learning her lines, but Carmen did not complete the cue cards and did not rewrite her sentences so that she could recognize the words and structure of the play's dialog.

Carmen's group is called upon by Mr. Charles to stand in front of the class. Mr. Charles begins by asking questions regarding the part of the play that Carmen's group was assigned. Each member of the group was quick to respond to the questions, except for Carmen. Finally, Mr. Charles grew tired of Carmen's lack of response and called on her to answer the questions. Carmen could not even remember what Mr. Charles was asking as she was trying to remember what was being said in the earlier questions. Carmen again asked Mr. Charles to go to the nurse, and Mr. Charles agreed.

1. What are the benefits and the disadvantages of Carmen having Communication Arts in the regular classroom versus in the special education room?
2. What strategies could be taught to Carmen to help her with group work and performing academic tasks? Are there strategies that might address both tasks simultaneously?
3. What role does motivation have in Carmen's classroom performance?
4. Is Carmen ready to move into junior high school?

MATT

Matt is getting ready to start his Earth Science exam in the school's resource room. Even though Matt is in the 10th grade, he still needs help reading and comprehending all of his assignments in high school. Matt's girlfriend, Katie, tries to help him with his homework and other assignments, but they routinely get "caught" cheating on their assignments by

101

Mr. Riker, their algebra teacher. Detention has become Matt's second home in high school.

Matt has decided to try to get into the local vocational school so that he can begin to plan for his career as an electrician. Miss Carter, Matt's resource room teacher, is helping him prepare for the entrance tests that are required for admission into the electrician program. Matt's dad is an electrician and knows the ins and outs of the circuit board in his sleep, so Matt feels very confident that he will be able to do well and get into the program. Miss Carter begins by reviewing basic math concepts and immediately, Matt complains that he has trouble with math and "always will!" He has difficulty reading the sample tests that Miss Carter provides for practice, and becomes frustrated with the process. The testing day arrives and Matt knows that he can explain the process of electrical circuitry to anyone without a problem. But first, Matt must complete the written portion of the tests. Matt gives the test his best effort, but he just isn't able to complete the reading comprehension or the math sections of the test. When the time is over for the test, Matt has over half of the scoring sheet blank. Upset at the process, Matt gives up and leaves the testing site. He returns to school on Monday and informs Miss Carter that he is going to quit school and go to work for his father.

1. Was Matt's goal of entrance into a vocational school appropriate for his level of academic achievement?
2. What could have Miss Carter done differently to help Matt prepare for the tests?
3. Could there have been a way to have Matt work with other students to increase his comprehension of content materials?
4. What accommodations could have helped Matt during the entrance exam?
5. What do you think Matt's future will look like?

REFERENCES

Adams, G., & Carnine, D. W. (2003). Direct instruction. In H. L. Swanson, K. R. Harris, & S. Graham (Eds.), *Handbook of learning disabilities* (pp. 403–416). New York: Guilford.

Adams, G., & Engelmann, S. (1996). *Research on direct instruction: 25 years beyond DISTAR.* Seattle, WA: Educational Achievement Systems.

American Psychiatric Association. (1994). *Diagnostic and statistical manual of mental disorders* (4th ed.). Washington, DC: Author.

Ayres, A. J. (1968). Sensory integrative processes and neuropsychological learning disabilities. In J. Hellmuth (Ed.), *Learning disorders* (Vol. 3, pp. 43–58). Seattle, WA: Special Child Publications.

Badian, N. A. (1997). Dyslexia and the double deficit hypothesis. *Annals of Dyslexia, 47,* 69–87.

Barkley, R. A. (1997). Behavioral inhibition, sustained attention, and executive functions: Constructing a unifying theory of ADHD. *Psychological Bulletin, 121,* 65–94.

Barkley, R. A. (1998). *Attention-deficit hyperactivity disorder: A handbook for diagnosis and treatment.* New York: Guilford Press.

Barsch, R. H. (1967). Achieving perceptual-motor efficiency: A space-oriented approach to learning. Vol. 1 of a perceptual-motor curriculum. Seattle, WA: Special Child Publications.

Bateman, B. D. (1965). An educator's view of a diagnostic approach to learning disorders. In J. Hellmuth (Ed.), *Learning disorders* (Vol. 1, pp. 219–239). Seattle WA: Special Child Publications.

Bielinski, J., Ysseldyke, J. E., Bolt, S., Friedbach, M., & Friedbach, J. (2001). Prevalence of accommodations for students with disabilities participating in statewide testing programs. *Assessment for Effective Intervention, 26,* 21–28.

Birch, H. G. (1964). *Brain damage in children: The biological and social aspects.* Baltimore: Williams & Wilkins.

Blachman, B. A. (2001). Phonological awareness. In P. D. Pearson (Ed.), *Handbook of reading research* (pp. 483–502). Mahwah, NJ: Erlbaum.

Blackman, S., & Goldstein, K. M. (1982). Cognitive styles and learning disabilities. *Journal of Learning Disabilities, 15,* 106–115.

Blackorby, J., & Wagner, M. (1996). Longitudinal postschool outcomes of youth with disabilities: Findings from the National Longitudinal Transition Study. *Exceptional Children, 62,* 399–413.

Borkowski, J. G., & Burke, J. E. (1996). Theories, models, and measurements of executive functioning: An information processing perspective. In G. R. Lyon & N. A. Krasnegor (Eds.), *Attention, memory, and executive function* (pp. 235–262). Baltimore, MD: Brookes.

Borkowski, J. G., Wehring, R. S., & Carr, M. (1988). Effects of attributional retraining on strategy-based reading comprehension on learning disabled students. *Journal of Educational Psychology, 7,* 46–53.

Bowers, P., Golden, J., Kennedy, A., & Young, A. (1994). Limits upon orthographic knowledge due to processes indexed by naming speed. In V. W. Berninger (Ed.), *The varieties of orthographic knowledge: Theoretical and developmental issues* (Vol. I, pp. 173–218). Dordrecht, The Netherlands: Kluwer Academic.

Brady, S. A. (1997). Ability to encodes phonological representations: An underlying difficulty of poor readers. In B. A. Blachman (Ed.), *Foundations of reading acquisition and* dyslexia: Implications for early intervention (pp. 21–47). Mahwah, NJ: Erlbaum.

Bredenkamp, S., & Copple, C. (Eds.). (1997). Developmentally appropriate practice in early childhood programs. Washington, DC: National Association for the Education of Young Children.

Broadbent, W. H. (1872). On the cerebral mechanism of speech and thought. Proceedings of the Royal Medical and Surgical Society of London (pp. 25–29). London: Anonymous.

Bryan, T. (1991). Social problems and learning disabilities. In B. Y. L. Wong (Ed.), Learning about learning disabilities (pp. 195–229). San Diego: Academic Press.

Bryan, T. S., & Pearl, R. (1979). Self-concept and locus of control of learning disabled children. Journal of Clinical Child Psychology, 8, 223–226.

Carta, J. J. (1995). Developmentally appropriate practice: A critical analysis as applied to young children with disabilities. Focus on Exceptional Children, 20, 68–71.

Case, L. P., Harris, K. R., & Graham, S. (1991). Improving the mathematical problem-solving skills of students with learning disabilities: Self-regulated strategy training. Journal of Special Education, 26, 1–19.

Cawley, J. F., Parmar, R. S., Foley, T. E., Salmon, S., & Roy, S. (2001). Arithmetic performance of students: Implications for standards and programming. Exceptional Children, 67, 311–318.

Cawley, J. F., Parmar, R. S., Yan, W., & Miller, J. H. (1998). Arithmetic computation performance of students with learning disabilities: Implications for the curriculum. Learning Disabilities Research and Practice, 13, 68–74.

Chalfant, J. C., & Scheffelin, M. A. (1969). Central processing dysfunction in children: A review of research (NINDS Monograph No. 9). Washington, DC: U.S. Department of Health, Education, and Welfare.

Clements, S. D. (1966). Minimal brain dysfunction in children: Terminology and identification (NINDS Monograph No. 3, U.S. Public Health Service Publication No. 1415). Washington, DC: Department of Health, Education, and Welfare.

Cohn, R. (1968). Developmental dyscalculia. Pediatric Clinics of North America, 15, 651–668.

Coleman, J. M., & Dover, G. M. (1993). The RISK Screening Test: Using kindergarten teachers' ratings to predict placement in resource classrooms. Exceptional Children, 59, 468–477.

Coyne, M., Kame'enui, E., & Simmons, D. (2001). Prevention and intervention in beginning reading : Two complex systems. Learning Disabilities Research and Practice, 16, 62–73.

Cruickshank, W. D. (Ed.) (1966). The teacher of brain-injured children. Syracuse, NY: Syracuse University Press.

Cruickshank, W. M., Bice, H. V., & Wallen, N. E. (1957). Perception and cerebral palsy. Syracuse, NY: University Press.

Cummings, R., Madden, C. D., & Casey, J. (2000). Individualized transition planning for students with learning disabilities. Career Development Quarterly, 49, 60–72.

Denel, R. K. (1995). Developmental dysgraphia and motor skills disorders. Journal of Child Neurology, 10 (Suppl. I, pp. 56–58).

Deno, S. L., & Fuchs, L. S. (1987). Developing curriculum-based measurement systems for data-based special education problem solving. Focus on Exceptional Children, 19, 1–16.

Deshler, D. D., Ellis, E. S., & Lenz, B. K. (1996). Teaching adolescents with learning disabilities: Strategies and methods. Denver: Love.

Deshler, D. D. Schumaker, J. B., Lenz, B. K., Bulgren, J. A., Hock, M. F., Knights, J., et al. (2001). Ensuring content-area learning by secondary students with learning disabilities. Learning Disabilities Research and Practice, 16, 95–108.

Deshler, D. D., Schumaker, J. B., Lenz, B. K., & Ellis, E. (1984). Academic and cognitive interventions for LD adolescents: Part II. Journal of Learning Disabilities, 17, 170–179.

Durlak, C. M., Rose, E., & Bursuck, W. D. (1994). Preparing high school students with leaning disabilities for the transition to postsecondary education: Teaching the skills of self-determination. Journal of Learning Disabilities, 27, 51–59.

Ehri, L. C. (1998). Grapheme-phoneme knowledge is essential to learning to read words in English. In J. L. Mestala & L. C. Ehri (Eds.), Word recognition in beginning literacy (pp. 3–40). Mahwah, NJ: Erlbaum.

Eiserman, W. D., Weber, C., & McCoun, M. (1995). Parent and professional roles in early intervention: A longitudinal comparison of the effects of two intervention configurations. Journal of Special Education, 29, 20–44.

Englert, C. S., & Mariage, T. W. (1991). Making students partners in the comprehension process: Organizing the reading "POSSE." Learning Disability Quarterly, 14, 123–138.

Fawcett, A., & Nicholson, R. (1994). Naming speed in children with dyslexia. Journal of Learning Disabilities, 27, 641–646.

Fernald, G. M. (1943). Remedial techniques in basic school subjects. New York: McGraw-Hill.

Fletcher, J. M., Lyon, G. R., Barnes, M., Stuebing, K. K., Francis, D. J., Olson, R. K., Shaywitz, S. E., et al. (2002).

Classification of learning disabilities: An evidence-based evaluation. In R. Bradley, L. Danielson, & D. Hallahan (Eds.), *Identification of learning disabilities: Research to practice* (pp. 185–250). Mahwah, NJ: Erlbaum.

Frostig, M. (1976). In J. M. Kauffman & D. P. Hallahan (Eds.), *Teaching children with learning disabilities: Personal Perspectives* (pp. 164–190). Columbus, OH: Charles E. Merrill.

Frostig, M., & Horne, D. (1964). *The Frostig program for the development of visual perception: Teacher's guide.* Chicago, Follett.

Frostig, M., Lefever, W., & Whittlesey, J. R. (1964). *Developmental test of visual perception* (rev. ed.). Palo Alto, CA: Consulting Psychologists Press.

Fuchs, D., Mock, D., Morgan, P. L., & Young, C. L. (2003). Responsiveness-to-intervention: Definitions, evidence and implications for the learning disabilities construct. *Learning Disabilities Research and Practice, 18,* 157–171.

Fuchs, L. S., & Fuchs, D. (2001). Helping teachers formulate sound test accommodation decisions for students with learning disabilities. *Learning Disabilities Research and Practice, 16,* 174–181.

Fulk, B. M. (1996). The effects of combined strategy and attribution training in LD adolescents' spelling performance. *Exceptionality, 6,* 13–27.

Geary, D. C., Hamson, C. O., & Hoard, M.K. (2000). Numerical and arithmetic cognition: A longitudinal study of process and concept deficits in children with learning disabilities. *Journal of Experimental Child Psychology, 77,* 236–263.

Gerber, P. J., & Reiff, H. B. (1991). *Speaking for themselves: Ethnographic interviews with adults with learning disabilities.* Ann Arbor: University of Michigan Press.

Gersten, R. (1998). Recent advances in instructional research for students with learning disabilities: An overview. *Learning Disabilities Research and Practice, 13,* 162–170.

Getman, G. N. (1965). The visuomotor complex in the acquisition of learning skills. In J. Hellmuth (Ed.), *Learning disorders* (Vol. I, pp. 49–76). Seattle, WA: Special Child Publications.

Gillingham, A., & Stillman, B. W. (1936). *Remedial training for reading, spelling, and penmanship.* New York: Sachett & Wilhelms.

Goldstein, K. (1939). *The organism.* New York: American Book.

Graden, J. L. (1989). Redefining "prereferral" intervention as intervention assistance: Collaboration between general and special education. *Exceptional Children, 56,* 227–231.

Graham, S., Harris, K. R., MacArthur, C. A., & Schwartz, S. (1991). Writing and writing instruction for students with learning disabilities: Review of a research program. *Learning Disability Quarterly, 14,* 89–114.

Grant, R. (1993). Strategic training for using text headings to improve students processing of content. *Journal of Reading, 36,* 482–488.

Haager, D., & Vaughn, S. (1995). Parent, teacher, peer, and self-reports of the social competence of students with learning disabilities. *Journal of Learning Disabilities, 28,* 205–231.

Hale, J. B., & Fiorello, C. A. (2004). *School neuropsychology: A practitioner's handbook.* New York: Guilford Press.

Hallahan, D. P., & Mercer, C. D. (2002). Learning disabilities: Historical perspectives. In R. Bradley, L. Danielson, & D. P. Hallahan (Eds.), *Identification of learning disabilities: Research to practice* (pp. 1–67). Mahwah, NJ: Erlbaum.

Hallahan, D. P., & Reeve, R. E. (1980). Selective attention and distractibility. In B. K. Keogh (Ed.), *Advances in special education* (Vol. I, pp. 141–181). Greenwich, CT: JAI Press.

Hammill, D. D., (1974). Learning disabilities: A problem in definition. *Division for Children with Learning Disabilities Newsletter, 4,* 28–31.

Hammill, D. D., Leigh, J. E., McNutt, G., & Larsen, S. C. (1981). A new definition of learning disabilities. *Learning Disability Quarterly, 4,* 336–342.

Haring, K. A., Lorett, D. L., Haney, K. F., Algozzine, B., Smith, D. D., & Clarke, J. (1992). Labeling preschoolers as learning disabled: A cautionary position. *Topics in Early Childhood Special Education, 12,* 151–173.

Harris, K. R., Graham, S., Reid, R., McElroy, K., & Hamby, R. S. (1994). Self-monitoring of attention versus self-monitoring of performance: Replication and cross-task comparison studies. *Learning Disability Quarterly, 17,* 121–139.

Head, H. (1926). *Aphasia and kindred disorders of speech.* London: Cambridge University Press.

Hock, M. F., Schumaker, J. B., & Deshler, D. D. (1999). Closing the gap to success in secondary skills: A model for cognitive apprenticeship. In S. Graham, K. Harris, & M. Pressley (Series Eds.) and D. Deshler, K. Harris, & S. Graham (Vol. Eds.), *Advances in teaching and learning, teaching every child every day: Learning in diverse schools and classrooms* (pp. 1–52). Cambridge, MA: Brookline Books.

Holahan, A., & Costenbader, Y. (2000). A comparison of developmental gains for preschool children with disabilities in inclusive and self-contained classrooms. *Topics in Early Childhood Special Education, 20,* 224–235.

Houck, C. K., & Billingsley, B. S. (1989). Written expression of students with and without learning disabilities: Differences across the grades. *Journal of Learning Disabilities, 22,* 561–567, 572.

Hudson, P., Lignugaris-Kraft, B., & Miller, T. (1993). Using content enhancements to improve the performance of adolescents with learning disabilities in content classes. *Learning Disabilities Research and Practice, 8,* 106–126.

Hulme, C., & Snowling, M. (1992). Phonological deficit in dyslexia: A "sound" reappraisal of the verbal deficit hypothesis. In N. Singh & I. Beale (Eds.), *Learning disabilities: Nature, theory, and treatment* (pp. 270–301). New York: Springer-Verlag.

Hynd, G. (1992). Neurological aspects of dyslexia: Comments on the balance model. *Journal of Learning Disabilities, 25,* 110–113.

Individuals with disabilities education improvement act (IDEA) (2003). Senate Bill 1248.

Interagency Committee on Learning Disabilities. (1987). *Learning disabilities—A report to the U.S. Congress.* Washington, DC: U.S. Department of Health and Human Services.

Johnson, C. L. (1984). The learning disabled adolescent and young adult: An overview and critique of current practice. *Journal of Learning Disabilities, 17,* 386–391.

Johnson, D. J., & Myklebust, H. R. (1967). *Learning disabilities: Educational principles and practices.* New York: Grune & Stratton.

Johnson, D. R., Stodden, R. A., Emanuel, E. J., Luecking, R. L., & Mack, M. (2002). Current challenges facing secondary education and transition services: What research tells us. *Exceptional Children, 68,* 519–531.

Johnson, E., Kimball, K., Olson-Brown, S., & Anderson, D. (2001). Statewide review of use of accommodations in large-scale, high-stakes assessments. *Exceptional Children, 67,* 251–264.

Johnson, L., Graham, S., & Harris, K. R. (1997). The effects of goal setting and self-instruction on learning a reading comprehension strategy: A study of students with learning disabilities. *Journal of Learning Disabilities, 30,* 80–91.

Kame'enui, E. J., Carnine, D. W., Dixon, R. C., Simmons, D. C., & Coyne, M. D. (Eds.). (2002). *Effective teaching strategies that accommodate diverse learners* (2nd ed.). Upper Saddle River, NJ: Merrill/Prentice-Hall.

Kass, C. E., & Myklebust, H. R. (1969). Learning disability: An educational definition. *Journal of Learning Disabilities, 2,* 377–379.

Kavale, K. A. (1988). The long-term consequences of learning disabilities. In M. C. Wang, M. C. Reynolds, & H. J. Walberg (Eds.), *Handbook of special education: Research and practice* (Vol. 2: Mildly handicapping conditions). New York: Pergamon.

Kavale, K. A. (2002). Discrepancy models in the identification of learning disability. In R. Bradley, L. Danielson, & D. Hallahan (Eds.), *Identification of learning disabilities: Research to practice* (pp. 369–426). Mahwah, NJ: Erlbaum.

Kavale, K. A., & Forness, S. R. (1987). Substance over style: A quantitative synthesis assessing the efficacy of modality testing and teaching. *Exceptional Children, 54,* 228–234.

Kavale, K. A., & Forness, S. R. (1996). Social skill deficits and learning disabilities: A meta-analysis. *Journal of Learning Disabilities, 29,* 226–237.

Kavale, K. A., & Forness, S. R. (1998). Covariance in learning disabilities and behavior disorders: An examination of classification and placement. In T. Scruggs & M. Mastropieri (Eds.), *Advances in learning and behavioral disabilities* (Vol. 12, pp. 1–14). Greenwich, CT: JAI Press.

Kavale, K. A., & Forness, S. R. (1999). *Efficacy of special education and related services.* Washington, DC: American Association of Mental Retardation.

Kavale, K. A., & Forness, S. R. (2000). What definitions of learning disability say and don't say: A critical analysis. *Journal of Learning Disabilities, 33,* 239–256.

Kavale, K. A., Holdnack, J. A., & Mostert, M. P. (2005). Responsiveness to intervention and the identification of specific learning disability: A critique and alternative proposal. *Learning Disability Quarterly, 28,* 2–16.

Kephart, N. C. (1960). *The slow learner in the classroom.* Columbus, OH: Merrill.

Kirk, S. A. (1962). *Educating exceptional children.* Boston: Houghton-Mifflin.

Kirk, S. A. (1975). Behavioral diagnosis and remediation of learning disabilities. In S. Kirk & J. McCarthy (Eds.), *Learning disabilities: Selected ACLD papers* (pp. 7–10). Boston: Houghton-Mifflin.

Kirk, S. A., & Kirk, W. D. (1971). *Psycholinguistic learning disabilities: Diagnosis and remediation.* Urbana, IL: University of Illinois Press.

Kirk, S. A., McCarthy, J. J., & Kirk, W. D. (1968). *Illinois Test of Psycholinguistic Abilities* (rev. ed.). Urbana, IL: University of Illinois Press.

Klingner, J. K., & Vaughn, S. (1999). Student's perceptions of instruction in inclusion classrooms: Implications for students with learning disabilities. *Exceptional Children, 66,* 23–37.

Kotkin, R. A., Forness, S. R., & Kavale, K. A. (2001). Comorbid ADHD and learning disabilities: Diagnosis, special education, and intervention. In D. Hallahan & B. Keogh (Eds.), *Research and global perspectives in learning disabilities* (pp. 43–63). Mahwah, NJ: Erlbaum.

LaBerge, D., & Samuels, S. J. (1973). Toward a theory of automatic information processing in reading. *Cognitive Psychology, 6,* 293–333.

Lanford, A. U., & Cary, L. G. (2000). Graduation requirements for students with disabilities: Legal and practice considerations. *Remedial and Special Education, 21,* 152–161.

Liberman, I. Y., & Shankweiler, D. (1985). Phonology and the problems of learning to read and write. *Remedial and Special Education, 6,* 8–17.

Liberman, I. Y., & Shankweiler, D. (1991). Phonology and beginning reading: A tutorial. In L. Reibent & C. A. Perfetti (Eds.), *Learning to read: Basic research and its implications* (pp. 3–17). Hillsdale, NJ: Erlbaum.

Lock, R. H., & Layton, C. A. (2001). Succeeding in postsecondary education through self-advocacy. *Teaching Exceptional Children, 34,* 66–71.

Lopez-Reyna, N. A., Bay, M., & Patrikakou, E. N. (1996). Use of assessment procedures: Learning disabilities teachers' perspectives. *Diagnostique, 21,* 35–49.

Lovett, M. W. (1987). A developmental approach to reading disability: Accuracy and speed criteria of normal and deficient reading skill. *Child Development, 58,* 234–260.

MacMillan, D. L., & Gresham, F. M., & Bocian, K. M. (1998). Discrepancy between definitions of learning disabilities and school practices: An empirical investigation. *Journal of Learning Disabilities, 31,* 314–326.

MacMillan, D. L., & Siperstein, G. N. (2002). Learning disabilities as operationally defined by schools. In R. Bradley, L. Danielson, & D. Hallahan (Eds.), *Identification of learning disabilities: Research to practice* (pp. 287–333). Mahwah, NJ: Erlbaum.

Malian, L., & Nevin, A. (2002). A review of self-determination literature. *Remedial and Special Education, 23,* 68–75.

Manset, G., & Washburn, S. J. (2000). Equity through accountability? Mandating minimum competency exit examinations for secondary students with learning disabilities. *Learning Disabilities Research and Practice, 15,* 160–167.

Mantzicopoulos, P. Y., & Morrison, D. (1994). Early prediction of reading achievement: Exploring the relationship of cognitive and noncognitive measures in accurate classifications of at-risk status. *Remedial and Special Education, 15,* 244–251.

Mastropieri, M. A., & Scruggs, T. E. (1991). *Teaching students ways to remember: Strategies for learning mnemonically.* Cambridge, MA: Brookline.

Mastropieri, M. A., Scruggs, T. E., & Whedon, C. (1997). Using mnemonic strategies to teach information about U.S. presidents: A classroom-based investigation. *Learning Disability Quarterly, 20,* 13–21.

Mathes, M. Y., & Bender, W. N. (1997). The effects of self-monitoring on children with attention-deficit/hyperactivity disorder. *Remedial and Special Education, 18,* 121–128.

McLeskey, J. (1992). Students with learning disabilities at primary, intermediate, and secondary grade levels: Identification and characteristics. *Learning Disability Quarterly, 15,* 13–19.

Meichenbaum, D., & Goodman, J. (1971). Training impulsive children to talk to themselves: A means of developing self-control. *Journal of Abnormal Psychology, 77,* 115–126.

Meltzer, L., & Montague, M. (2001). Strategic learning in students with learning disabilities: What have we learned? In D. Hallahau & B. Keogh (Eds.), *Research and global perspectives in learning disabilities* (pp. 111–130). Mahwah, NJ: Erlbaum.

Miller, J. H., & Milam, C. P. (1987). Multiplication and division errors committed by learning disabled students. *Learning Disabilities Research, 2,* 119–122.

Montague, M., Warger, C., & Morgan, T. H. (2000). Solve it! Strategy instruction to improve mathematical problem solving. *Learning Disabilities Research and Practice, 15,* 110–116.

Most, T., & Greenbank, A. (2000). Auditory, visual, and auditory-visual perception of emotions by adolescents with and without learning disabilities and their relationship to social skills. *Learning Disabilities Research and Practice, 15,* 171–178.

Muter, V. (1998). Phonological awareness: Its nature and its influence over early literacy development. In C. Hulme & R. M. Joshi (Eds.), *Reading and spelling: Development and disorders* (pp. 113–125). Mahwah, NJ: Erlbaum.

Nation, K., Marshall, C. M., & Snowling, M. J. (2001). Phonological and semantic contributions to children's picture naming skill: Evidence from children with developmental reading disorders. *Language and Cognitive Processes, 16,* 241–259.

National Advisory Committee on Handicapped Children. (1968). *First annual report to Congress on special education for handicapped children.* Washington, DC: Department of Health, Education, and Welfare.

National Joint Committee on Learning Disabilities. (1988). ACLD definition: Specific learning disabilities. *ACLD Newsbriefs,* 15–16.

National Reading Panel (2000). *Teaching children to read: An evidence-based assessment of the scientific research literature on reading and its implications for reading instruction.* Washington, D.C.: National Institute of Child Health and Human Development.

Newcomer, P. L., & Barenbaum, E. M. (1991). The written composing ability of children with learning disabilities: A review of the literature from 1980 to 1990. *Journal of Learning Disabilities, 24,* 578–593.

Odom, S. L. (2000). Preschool inclusion: What we know and where do we go from here. *Topics in Early Childhood Special Education, 20,* 20–27.

Olofsson, A., & Niedersoe, J. (1999). Early language development and kindergarten phonological awareness as predictors of reading problems: From 3 to 11 years of age. *Journal of Learning Disabilities, 32,* 464–472.

Orton, S. T. (1925). "Word-blindness" in school children. *Archives of Neurology and Psychiatry, 14,* 581–615.

Orton, S. T. (1937). *Reading, writing, and speech problems in children.* New York: Norton.

Palinscar, A. S., & Brown, D. A. (1986). Interactive teaching to promote independent learning from text. *The Reading Teacher, 39,* 771–777.

Rack, J. P., Snowling, M. J., & Olson, R. K. (1992). The nonword reading deficit in developmental dyslexia: A review. *Reading Research Quarterly, 27,* 28–53.

Resnick, L. B. (1970). Relations between perceptual and syntactic control in oral reading. *Journal of Educational Psychology, 61,* 382–385.

Riccio, C. A., Gonzalez, J. J., & Hynd, G. W. (1994). Attention-deficit hyperactivity disorder (ADHD) and learning disabilities. *Learning Disability Quarterly, 17,* 311–322.

Robinson, C. S., Menchetti, B. M., & Torgesen, J. K. (2002). Toward a two-factor theory of one type of mathematics disabilities. *Learning Disabilities Research and Practice, 17,* 81–89.

Rosenkoetter, S. E., Whaley, K. T., Hains, A. H., & Pierce, L. (2001). The evolution of transition policy for young children with special needs and their families: Past, present, and future. *Topics in Early Childhood Special Education, 21,* 3–15.

Roth, F. P., Speece, D. L., & Cooper, D. H. (2002). A longitudinal analysis of the connection between oral language and early reading. *Journal of Educational Psychology Research, 95,* 259–272.

Ryan, E. B., Short, E. J., & Wend, K. A. (1986). The role of cognitive strategy training in improving the academic performance of learning disabled children. *Journal of Learning Disabilities, 19,* 521–529.

Sarason, S. B. (1949). *Psychological problems in mental deficiency.* New York: Harper.

Schmitt, B. D. (1975). The minimal brain dysfunction myth. *American Journal of Diseases of Children, 129,* 1313–1318.

Schumaker, J. B., Deschler, D. D., Alley, G., Warner, M., & Denton, P. (1984). Multipass: A learning strategy for improving reading comprehension. *Learning Disability Quarterly, 5,* 295–304.

Scott, T. M., & Nelson, C. M. (1999). Using functional behavioral assessment to develop effective intervention plans: Practical classroom applications. *Journal of Positive Behavioral Interventions, 1,* 242–251.

Scruggs, T. E., & Mastropieri, M. A., (2000). The effectiveness of mnemonic instruction for students with learning and behavior problems: An update and research synthesis. *Journal of Behavioral Education, 10,* 163–173.

Settle, S. A., & Milich, R. (1999). Social persistence following failure in boys and girls with LD. *Journal of Learning Disabilities, 32,* 201–212.

Sexton, M., Harris, K. R., & Graham, S. (1998). Self-regulated strategy development and the writing process: Effects on essay writing and attributions. *Exceptional Children, 64,* 295–311.

Shapiro, J., & Rich, R. (1999). *Facing learning disabilities in the adult years.* New York: Oxford University Press.

Skinner, M. E. (1998). Promoting self-advocacy among college students with learning disabilities. *Intervention in School and Clinic, 33,* 278–283.

Smith, T. J., Dittmer, K. L., & Skinner, C. H. (2002). Enhancing science performance in students with learning disabilities using cover, copy, and compare: A student shows the way. *Psychology in the Schools, 39,* 417–427.

Snow, C., Burns, M., & Griffin, P. (1998). *Preventing reading difficulties in young children.* Washington, DC: National Academy Press.

Speece, D. L., Mills, C., Richey, K. D., & Hillman, E. (2003). Initial evidence that letter fluency tasks are valid indicators of early reading skill. *Journal of Special Education, 36,* 223–233.

Sridhar, D., & Vaughn, S. (2001). Social functioning of students with learning disabilities. In D. Hallahan & B. Keogh (Eds.), *Research and global perspectives in learning disabilities* (pp. 65–91). Mahwah, NJ: Erlbaum.

Stanford, L. D., & Hynd, G. W. (1994). Congruence of behavioral symptomatology in children with ADD/H, ADD/WO, and learning disabilities. *Journal of Learning Disabilities, 27,* 243–253.

Stevens, G. D., & Birch, J. W. (1957). A proposal for clarification of the terminology used to describe brain-injured children. *Exceptional Children, 23,* 346–349.

Strauss, A. A., & Kephart, N. C. (1955). *Psychopathology and education of the brain-injured child. Vol. II: Progress in theory and clinic.* New York: Grune & Stratton.

Strauss, A. A., & Lehtinen, L. E. (1947). *Psychopathology and education of the brain-injured child.* New York: Grune & Stratton.

Swanson, H. L., & Ashbaker, M. H. (2000). Working memory, short-term memory, speech rate, word recognition, and reading comprehension in learning disabled readers: Does the executive system have a role? *Intelligence, 28,* 1–30.

Swanson, H. L., & Hoskyn, M. (1998). Experimental intervention research on students with learning disabilities: A meta-analysis of treatment outcomes. *Review of Educational Research, 68,* 277–321.

Swanson, H. L., & Sachse-Lee, C. (2001). Mathematical problem solving and working memory in children with learning disabilities: Both executive and phonological processes are important. *Journal of Experimental Child Psychology, 79,* 294–321.

Tabassam, W., & Grainger, J. (2002). Self-concept, attributional style and self-efficacy beliefs of students with learning disabilities with and without attention deficit hyperactivity disorder. *Learning Disability Quarterly, 25,* 141–151.

Thomas, C. C., Englert, C. S., & Gregg, S. (1987). An analysis of errors and strategies in the expository writing of learning disabled students. *Remedial and Special Education, 8,* 21–30, 46.

Thompson, J. R., Fulk, B. M., & Piercy, S. W. (2000). Do individualized transition plans match the postschool projections of students with learning disabilities and their parents? *Career Development for Exceptional Individuals, 23,* 3–25.

Thurlow, M. (2000). Standards-based reform and students with disabilities: Reflections on a decade of change. *Focus on Exceptional Children, 33,* 1–16.

Torgesen, J. K. (1997). The role of nonspecific factors in the task performance of learning disabled children: A theoretical assessment. *Journal of Learning Disabilities, 10,* 27–34.

Treiman, R., & Bourassa, D. C. (2000). The development of spelling skills. *Topics in Language Disorders, 20,* 1–18.

U.S. Department of Education. (1999, March 12). Assistance to states for the education of children with disabilities and the early intervention programs for infants and toddlers with disabilities. Final regulations. *Federal Register, 64,* 12406–12672.

U.S. Office of Education. (1997). Assistance to states for education of handicapped children: Procedures for evaluating specific learning disabilities. *Federal Register, 42,* 65082–65085.

Vaughn, S, & Fuchs, L. S. (2003). Redefining learning disabilities as inadequate response to instruction: The promise and potential pitfalls. *Learning Disabilities Research and Practice, 18,* 137–146.

Vaughn, S., Gersten, R., & Chard, D. (2000). The underlying message in LD intervention research: Findings from research syntheses. *Exceptional Children, 67,* 99–114.

Vaughn, S., Kim, A., Sloan, C. V. M., Hughes, M. T., Elbaum, B., Sridhar, D. (2003). Social skills interventions for young children with disabilities: A synthesis of group design studies. *Remedial Special Education, 24,* 2–15.

Vygotsky, L. S. (1962). *Thought and language.* Cambridge, MA: MIT Press.

Wagner, R. K., & Torgesen, J. K. (1987). The nature of phonological processing and its causal role in the acquisition of reading skills. *Psychological Bulletin, 101,* 192–212.

Wehmeyer, M. L., Agran, M., & Hughes, C. (1998). *Teaching self-determination to students with disabilities.* Baltimore: Brookes.

Werner, H., & Strauss, A. A. (1940). Causal factors in low performance. *American Journal of Mental Deficiency, 45,* 213–218.

Wiederholt, J. L. (1974). Historical perspectives on the education of the learning disabled. In L. Mann & D. Sabatino (Eds.), *The second review of special education* (pp. 103–152). Philadelphia: JSE Press.

Wolery, M., Werts, M. G., & Holcombe, A. (1994). Current practices with young children who have disabilities: Placement, assessment, and instructional issues. *Focus on Exceptional Children, 20,* 68–71.

Wolf, M. (1997). A provisional, integrative account of phonological and naming-speed deficits in dyslexia: Implications for diagnosis and intervention. In B. A. Blachman (Ed.), *Foundations of reading acquisition and dyslexia: Implications for early intervention* (pp. 67–92). Mahwah, NJ: Erlbaum.

Wolf, M., & Bowers, P. G. (1999). The double-deficit hypothesis for the developmental dyslexias. *Journal of Educational Psychology, 91,* 415–438.

Zigmond, N., & Sansone, J. (1986). Designing a program for the learning disabled adolescent. *Remedial and Special Education, 7,* 13–17.

Characteristics of Students with Emotional and Behavioral Disorders

URBAN LEGEND: *Most students with emotional and behavioral disorders (EBD) are identified by the third grade.*

LEGENDARY THOUGHT: *Many students with EBD are never identified or treated for this disorder. The U.S. Department of Health and Human Services estimated that at least 5% of children and youth have serious mental health needs; yet only one in five of these children receive any services for their disability. Surveys indicate that although most mental health problems start in childhood or adolescence, they are typically not treated for years, if at all.*

What exactly do we mean by **emotional and behavioral disorders** (EBD)? Where does EBD come from? Are individuals born with EBD, or is this a disability that children and youth acquire? How do we treat EBD? Can we cure EBD? Is EBD preventable? Unfortunately these questions are not easily answered, although they have a long history (Kauffman & Landrum, 2006). EBD is one of the most difficult types of disability to identify and treat. No single litmus test exists that can help us identify individuals with EBD, nor is there a single characteristic demonstrated by the individuals who have this disorder. As discussed in Chapter 2, the existing research suggests that the causes of EBD are multiple and complex. Therefore, the identification and treatment of EBD should be multifaceted. In this chapter we begin by examining the characteristics of students with EBD. Next, we explore strategies for identifying students with EBD. Finally, we discuss the unique learning needs of these students. After reading this chapter, we hope you will have a better awareness of the characteristics and needs of children and youth with EBD.

:: CHARACTERISTICS AND IDENTIFICATION OF STUDENTS WITH EMOTIONAL AND BEHAVIORAL DISORDERS

As suggested by Kauffman (2005) one of the most difficult questions about EBD is: How do we know when a child has this disability? With some children and youth the distinction may be very clear; yet with others it is far less easy to judge. For example, consider the following.

> Tony, a fifth grade student in elementary school, frequently engages in behavior that is aggressive and disruptive toward his teachers. These behaviors also interfere with his development of peer-related friendships. Tony is often sent to the principal's office by his teacher for disruptive behavior and being verbally aggressive in the classroom. Tony frequently has to attend in-school suspension and has been suspended from school on eight different occasions for explosive behavior. Tony's behavior is affecting his ability to learn, and he is falling further and further behind in his studies. The classroom teacher, guidance counselor, and Tony's mother have all agreed that Tony's behavior and adjustment to school has been problematic since he was in kindergarten.

Most people would agree that Tony has some form of EBD. His behaviors are severe and chronic, they negatively influence his academic and social abilities, and they are abnormal for the environment that he is in. A student like Tony is not necessarily difficult to identify. However, in contrast, consider the following scenario.

> Carla is a ninth-grade student who has been described as having mild academic difficulties, few friends, and as extremely withdrawn in her school and the community. Carla completes her assignments during class, although much of her work is incomplete or incorrect. She usually is quiet during instructional times, calling very little attention to herself in the classroom. In fact, her teacher indicates that she is hardly noticeable. Her teachers and her parents are concerned because, although Carla has always been a shy child, she is becoming more and more reclusive. In addition to being withdrawn at school, Carla has been given a recent diagnosis of having depression and a chronic, significant eating disorder. Does Carla have an EBD for special education purposes? The distinction for Carla is far less clear. Perhaps she does. Perhaps she is just going through a difficult time during her adolescent years. A child like Carla is much more difficult to identify for special education.

When identifying some disabilities, standardized tests often yield cut-off scores indicating that the student has a particular disability (e.g., an IQ score that suggests mental retardation). However, the field of EBD has no such standardized scale or score that can be used to identify children and youth with EBD. Cullinan (2004) suggests that "EBD is a collection of problems involving behaviors, emotions, and thoughts that all people experience to some extent. Those who experience the problems to an extreme extent (unusual frequency, duration, intensity, or other aspects) are more likely to have an EBD" (p. 34). Although several rating scales *assist* in identification, the identification of EBD strongly depends on the judgment of adults involved in the process. One factor that contributes to the difficulty of defining and identifying EBD is that measuring internal states or personality constructs is difficult (Kauffman, 2005). Existing assessment tools, such as behavior rating scales and personality inventories, provide some information to help distinguish individuals with EBD (Epstein & Cullinan, 1998). However, we also need to measure the behaviors of individuals within specific contexts to judge their appropriateness. Given the difficulty in identifying EBD, it is important to examine the definitions that have been developed.

Defining Emotional and Behavioral Disorders

Terminology and Characteristics

Various terms refer to students with emotional and behavioral disorders including: **emotionally handicapped, behaviorally impaired, emotionally disturbed,** and **socially maladjusted.** The federal definition and regulations of the **Individuals with Disabilities Education Improvement Act** (IDEA, 2004) uses the term *emotionally disturbed* to refer to this population of students. However, the most widely accepted and preferred term in the field is *emotional* or *behavioral disorders*. Although not adopted into the federal law, the term emotional or behavioral disorders was adopted by the **National Mental Health and Special Education Coalition** (for a discussion, see Forness & Knitzer, 1992; Forness, 1988). This term was chosen because it clearly includes children and youth with emotional disorders or behavioral disorders or both and avoids arguments about whether the difficulty of the student is emotional or behavioral.

Regardless of terminology used, emotional and behavioral disorders are displayed through varying characteristics. Typically EBD is described across two dimensions: **externalizing disorders** (students who have acting out behaviors, such as Tony) and **internalizing disorders** (students who are withdrawn, such as Carla). Most often, children and young people diagnosed with EBD demonstrate either externalizing disorders or internalizing disorders, but they can demonstrate both. That is, a student may be acting out aggressively, but also have clinical depression that is demonstrated by social withdrawal. Regardless of which of these two dimensions they exhibit, most students with EBD have lower than average IQ. However, by definition EBD does not exclude students because of their intelligence, even if they score in the **gifted** range.

Rather than categorizing a student as having a particular type of EBD, we suggest that professionals examine the behaviors demonstrated by the student, the circumstances surrounding and contributing to the behavior, and provide intervention to change his or her behavior directly. As suggested by Kauffman (2005), it may, at first, seem that the student can control the **aberrant behaviors** (behaviors that deviate from what is desirable and normal). In actuality, the child or youth may have little control over his or her behavior. The good news is that with quality intervention, children and young people with EBD can learn appropriate behaviors, lessening the life-long implications of this disorder (e.g., Webster-Stratton, 1997). The bad news is that without quality intervention, we know that the difficulties encountered by students with EBD are very likely to worsen (Del'Homme, Kasari, Forness, & Bagley, 1996; Patterson, Reid, & Dishion, 1992; Wang et al., 2005). Unfortunately, many children and youth with EBD never receive intervention for their disability. So why don't we identify and provide services for all the children with this disorder? In the next section, we discuss some issues that affect identification.

The Difficulties of Defining EBD

"An emotional and behavior disorder is whatever behavior a culture's chosen authority figures designate as intolerable" (Kauffman, 2005, p. 11). Since EBD is determined by individuals in a society and the identification of EBD includes judgment by persons in that society, there is clearly a potential for conflicting impressions of an individual's behavior. This makes identification problematic. In addition, since the characteristics of EBD are so diverse and context-specific, one must evaluate the contexts within which the behaviors indicating EBD are occurring and determine the appropriateness or inappropriateness of the behavior based on the context. Consider the following example.

Americans spend a good portion of our time driving. It is not uncommon to see a driver yell at or even make an obscene gesture toward another driver who has just cut in front of him or her. In our society, we refer to this behavior as "road rage." Although many of us may not like road rage, we tolerate it and even accept it to a certain degree as part of being a driver. We suspect that most people have probably at one time or another engaged in some form of road rage. Society therefore tolerates some level of this behavior, even though the behavior is essentially aggressive. However, if an individual engages in road rage that is more severe and potentially harmful to others (e.g., threatening to run a driver off the road), we, as a society, are far less tolerant. Understanding and realizing that EBD is a social process can help us to identify and treat this disorder (Kavale & Mostert, 2003).

Federal Definition of EBD

The federal definition of EBD was based on the work of Bower (1981) (for a discussion, see Kauffman, 2005). According to Bower (1981), it is important to consider not only the form of the behavior (that is, what the behavior looks like), but the impact and severity of the behavior (how long the behavior has been occurring, how extreme the behavior is, and the effects of the behavior on others). Currently, the Individual with Disabilities Education Improvement Act (IDEA, 2004) uses the following criteria to define "emotional disturbance."

1. The term means a condition exhibiting one or more of the following characteristics over a long period of time and to a marked degree that adversely affects a child's educational performance;
   a. An inability to learn that cannot be explained by intellectual, sensory, or health factors
   b. An inability to build or maintain satisfactory interpersonal relationships with peers and teachers
   c. Inappropriate types of behavior or feelings under normal circumstances
   d. A general pervasive mood of unhappiness or depression
   e. A tendency to develop physical symptoms or fears associated with personal or school problems
2. The term includes schizophrenia. The term does not apply to children who are socially maladjusted, unless it is determined that they have an emotional disturbance.

Clearly, the federal definition has many factors that are problematic in the identification of EBD. The important features of the definition are vague and are somewhat illogically self-contradictory or redundant. In addition, the qualifying characteristics appear to be arbitrarily chosen and lack a scientific research base (Bower, 1982; Forness & Kavale, 2000). One factor added to the federal definition that was not a part of Bower's (1981) original definition is the exclusion of children and youth who are **socially maladjusted** unless it is determined that the individual also has an emotional disturbance. Another factor that may hinder the identification of children and youth with EBD is the phrase *adversely effects educational performance*. In other words, the federal definition indicates that if a student has any of the difficulties outlined in the definition, but these problems are not negatively influencing his or her academic performance, under the federal definition the student could not be identified as emotionally disturbed or receive any additional services.

Improving the Current Definition of EBD

Even though defining the characteristics of children and youth with EBD can be difficult, developing an accurate definition is critical. It is important for us to have a consistent way to communicate and organize information with others when we refer to individuals with EBD. In addition, having a definition helps us to establish a logical basis for providing services (Cullinan, 2004). When we are able to identify children and youth with EBD, we are able to provide them the appropriate, effective interventions needed (Kauffman, 2005). However, we must proceed cautiously when developing and using definitions, because the definition we use influences the type of services a student receives (Forness & Kavale, 1997; Kauffman, 1986, 1999; Morse, 1985; Smith, Wood, & Grimes, 1988).

Over the past 10 years, the National Mental Health and Special Education Coalition, made up of leaders in the field of EBD, has developed a more accurate and sensitive definition of EBD:

1. The term emotional or behavior disorder means a disability characterized by behavioral or emotional responses to school programs so different from appropriate age, cultural, and ethnic norms that they adversely affect educational performance, including academic, social, vocational or personal skills, and which:
    a. is more than a temporary, expected response to stressful events in the environment;
    b. is consistently exhibited in two different settings, at least one of which is school-related; and
    c. persists despite individualized interventions within the education program unless, in the judgment of the team, the child or youth's history indicates that such interventions would not be effective.
    Emotional or behavioral disorders can co-exist with other disabilities.
2. This category may include children or youth with schizophrenic disorders, affective disorders, anxiety disorders, or other sustained disturbance of conduct or adjustment when they adversely affect educational performance in accordance with section I. (Forness & Knitzer, 1992, p. 13)

This definition was developed to address some of the issues that have evolved by use of the federal definition. Specifically this definition (a) includes terminology that reflects current professional preference and concern that minimizes the stigma of EBD, (b) includes both disorders of emotions and behavior, (c) focuses on behaviors that occur within the school, while acknowledging that behavior disorders occur outside of school as well, (d) includes language that is sensitive to cultural and ethnic differences, (e) excludes individuals who demonstrate only minor or temporary problems or responses that are typical in particular stressful situations, (f) acknowledges that preferral interventions are important, (g) acknowledges that students with EBD may also have other disabilities, and (h) includes for a full range of emotional or behavioral disorders without arbitrarily excluding specific disorders (such as social maladjustment) (Forness & Knitzer, 1992).

The definition developed by the National Mental Health and Special Education Coalition has some of the same problems as the federal definition, in that judgment plays a considerable role in the identification process and the terminology is still vague. Terms such as "consistently exhibited in two different settings" and "is unresponsive to direct intervention in general education" are difficult to define precisely and measure (for a discussion, see Cullinan, 2004). However, this proposed definition has many strengths. One important factor is the inclusion of students with all types of emotional and behavioral disorders. The federal definition has been criticized and legally challenged for the exclusion of socially maladjusted children and youth, which contributes to the under-identification and exclusion of services for many needy children (Bower, 1982; Forness & Kavale, 2000). Advocates and professionals in the field of EBD have petitioned Congress to substitute this new definition for the existing one (Forness & Kavale, 2000); however, at this time there are no plans for changes to the current federal definition.

Identification of Students with EBD

Given the issues discussed regarding the definition of EBD, how do we know which children actually have EBD and which children do not? How do we decide which children to refer for services? The best approach for determining that a child or youth has or does not have EBD is to conduct a **nondiscriminatory assessment** by a **multidisciplinary team,** using multiple measures, sources of information, and direct observations. To meet eligibility for EBD under the federal definition, once the child study team or multidisciplinary team has referred the student for further testing, the following process is conducted.

An intelligence test, an achievement test, and a behavior checklist or rating scale are administered. These tools are used to help determine whether the child's intelligence, achievement, and behaviors are within the normal range or deviate significantly from his or her peers. Behavior checklists and rating scales are standardized instruments designed to measure an individual's behavior as objectively as possible. Typically, these identification tools are completed by individuals who have frequent contact with the child or young person across different contexts, such as a parent and a teacher. Fortunately, several valid and reliable behavior checklists and rating scales can be used to help make the identification process more objective (e.g., see the *Child Behavior Checklist* (CBCL; Achenbach 1991, 1997), *Scale of Assessing Emotional Disturbance* (SAED; Epstein & Cullinan, 1998; Epstein, Cullinan, Ryser, & Pearson, 2002); *Social Skills Rating Scale* (SSRS; Gresham & Elliot, 1990); *Systematic Screening of Behavior Disorders* (SSBD; Walker & Severson, 1990); *Social-Emotional Dimension Scale* (2nd ed.) (*SEDS-2;* Hutton & Roberts, 2004). In addition to these behavioral assessments, **anecdotal records, direct observation** by a school psychologist, and **curriculum-based assessment** (for a discussion, see Hyatt & Howell, 2004) may also be beneficial in helping to identify these children. Recently, the concept of **response to intervention** (i.e., the ongoing collection of data to determine how a child is progressing toward a desired goal or outcome) has been incorporated into the identification process implemented for determining EBD (Stoiber & Kratochwill, 2001). Examining a student's response to intervention can be a critical component in determining instructional needs and whether the target student has a disability (Reschly, Tilly, & Grimes, 1999).

The identification assessment process should collect nonbiased information about the student for the purpose of making an eligibility decision and intervention plan (Salvia & Ysseldyke, 1991). However, caution should be taken when using these tools because, as discussed earlier, the identification of EBD is dependent on societal views of behavior. We need to use caution when evaluating these students' learning and academic skills as well as their social environment and interactions with others, taking into consideration the severity and longevity of their problem behavior and possible bias of the measurement tools. The measurement and instrumentation tools available may be used subjectively and can be unreliable (for a discussion see Brigham, Tocheterman, & Brigham, 2000; Landrum, 2000). In addition, as discussed by Forness (2003), the standardized tools available for measuring EBD in children and youth are lacking. Therefore, the professional's role and responsibility in the decision making process is of utmost importance (for a discussion see, Bateman & Linden, 1998; Merrell, 1994; Taylor, 1997; Yell, 1998). Kauffman (2005) suggests using the following procedures to help minimize biases during the identification process:

- Use a multidisciplinary team with multiple sources of data that are relevant.
- Use prereferral strategies, involving the parent, teacher, and student (if appropriate).
- Document the characteristics of EBD that the student is demonstrating.

One issue professionals need to consider is the risks that may result from identifying the student as having EBD in comparison to not identifying a student as having EBD when that student is demonstrating seriously problematic behavior. Although labeling a student with EBD needs to be done with caution (see Chapter 2 for a discussion on labeling), accurately diagnosing a student with EBD can help to ensure that the student will receive and benefit from the appropriate services. Nevertheless, professionals need to be aware of and remain sensitive to the possibility of evaluator bias (Kauffman, 2005). The purpose of educational diagnostic assessment for EBD should be the identification of a disability (if one exists) in order to assist the student in obtaining instruction to help teach new skills and behaviors, replacing other less appropriate behaviors.

Changing Characteristics and Identification of EBD Across Age Levels

The characteristics of EBD and identification process may change across different age levels. In addition, students with EBD may have similar characteristics to students with other high-incidence disabilities, such as mild/moderate mental retardation, learning disabilities, and attention deficit disorders (Hallahan & Kauffman, 1977).

So what makes children and young people with EBD different from other children? At times, as discussed above, everyone engages in problem behaviors, but the behavior of individuals with EBD are so severe and occur for such extended periods of time that these individuals stand out from the rest of the crowd for an extended period of time.

As discussed earlier in this chapter, these students are generally classified into two broad categories: externalizing disorders or internalizing disorders. Externalizing disorders are "acting out" behaviors, such as verbal and physical aggression, noncompliance or disobedience, disruption, and impulsivity. (For a thorough review of externalizing disorders, refer to Furlong, Morrison, & Jimerson, 2004). Internalizing disorders are most often described as behaviors such as social withdrawal, depression, and anxiety (Walker & Bullis, 1991). (For a thorough review of internalizing disorders, see Gresham and Kern, 2004). Although externalizing and internalizing behaviors in students with EBD are chronic, occurring over an extended period of time, students with EBD may also demonstrate **behavioral earthquakes** (behaviors that are low in frequency but of high intensity), such as violent eruptions in schools that destroy property, setting fires, injuring animals, and so forth (Walker & Severson, 1990). Although students are often categorized as having either externalizing or internalizing behavior disorders, many of them have multiple types of problems that vary according to severity (Tankersley & Landrum, 1997). That is, many students may demonstrate aggression and noncompliance in one situation, but be socially withdrawn in another situation. It is important to remember that EBD is not a discrete disability; rather, the student's behavior is based on an acceptable standard or norm and is judged by others to be seriously deviant and unacceptable.

In addition to these behavioral characteristics, many students with EBD demonstrate academic deficits. Typically, they have lower than average intelligence; some may even have mild to moderate mental retardation. Additionally, they demonstrate unacceptable behaviors related to academics, including off-task behavior, underachievement, and language deficits (Colvin, Greenberg, & Sherman, 1993; Foley & Epstein, 1992). Frequently, students with EBD have cormorbid disorders (i.e., disorders occurring together), including attention deficit disorder and learning disabilities (Forness, 2003; Kessler, Chiu, Demler, & Walters, 2005). In fact, research indicates that 30–40% of students with EBD also have a **learning disability** (LD) (Fessler, Rosenberg, & Rosenberg, 1991). However, students with EBD are more likely to be mislabled, often due to the comorbidity of EBD with other disorders (Forness & Kavale, 2000). Table 5.1 presents an overview of the characteristics of internalizing and externalizing behaviors across various ages.

Early Childhood

The early childhood years are the best time to identify children who show signs of emotional and behavioral disorders. Research offers us solid evidence that behavioral disorders demonstrated by school-age children and adolescents originate from behavior patterns established during the early childhood years (e.g., see Campbell & Ewing, 1990; Patterson, Capaldi, & Bank, 1989; Webster-Stratton,

TABLE 5.1	Characteristics of internalizing and externalizing behaviors across ages	
Age Level	**Internalizing**	**Externalizing**
Early childhood	• Exhibits behaviors including: withdrawal, avoidance of social situations • Engages in repetitive behaviors that appear to have no purpose • Cries frequently • Demonstrates atypical affect for the situation • Has a low activity level	• Engages in repetitive aggressive behavior • Engages in high rates of noncompliance • Exhibits persistent tantrums • Exhibits a lack of social control and acting out behaviors • Has difficulty with interpersonal relationships
Elementary	• Has difficulty staying on task • Engages in repetitive behaviors that appear to have no purpose • Demonstrates atypical affect for the situation • Complains of physical symptoms as a result of fear or anxiety • Is uninterested in activities that were previously interesting • Has a low activity level • Demonstrates signs of physical, emotional, or sexual abuse • Exhibits behaviors including: withdrawal, avoidance of social situations, lack of personal care • Acts sad or unhappy for an extended period of time	• Engages in chronic aggressive behavior • Excessively argues with adults and/or peers • Is physically or verbally abusive to others • Engages in high rates of noncompliance • Exhibits persistent tantrums, lying, and/or stealing • Exhibits a lack of social control and acting out behaviors • Exhibits other specific behaviors that intrude on others • Has difficulty with interpersonal relationships
Adolesence	• Has difficulty staying on task • Engages in repetitive behaviors that appear to have no purpose • Demonstrates atypical affect for the situation • Complains of physical symptoms as a result of fear or anxiety • Reports suicidal thoughts • Is uninterested in activities that were previously interesting • Has a low activity level • Demonstrates signs of physical, emotional, or sexual abuse • Exhibits behaviors including: withdrawal, avoidance of social situations, lack of personal care • Acts sad or unhappy over an extended period of time	• Engages in chronic aggressive behavior • Excessively argues with adults and/or peers • Is physically or verbally abusive to others • Engages in high rates of noncompliance • Exhibits persistent tantrums, lying, and/or stealing • Exhibits a lack of social control and acting out behaviors • Exhibits other specific behaviors that intrude on others • Has difficulty with interpersonal relationships

Adapted from the University of Kentucky, Behavior Home Page [On-line]. Available at: http://www.state.ky.us/agencies/behave/homepage.html. Reprinted by permission. Retrieved September 11, 2006.

2000). Common sense tells us that if we identify young children with (or at risk) for the development of emotional and behavioral disorders, we are more likely to prevent further development of this disorder and lessen the long-term implications. Unfortunately, we often fail to identify EBD in young children. Although counterintuitive to what we consider recommended practice, the current strategies for identification are reactive. That is, we often wait to evaluate and identify children and youth for EBD until the behaviors become chronic and severe (typically around second to fourth grades). However, we should be proactive, which means evaluating and identifying young children with (or at risk for) EBD once we see the first risk factor appear. With the increasing prevalence of young children who demonstrate problem behaviors (Kaiser, Cai, Hancock, & Foster, 2002), early identification and treatment of these problem behaviors in young children is essential for the prevention and remediation of problems that may potentially lead to EBD (Conroy, Hendrickson, & Hester, 2004).

There are a number of factors that make identification of young children with EBD difficult. First, what are the characteristics of EBD in young children? Consider the toddler that often says "no" following a parental request or cries when a parent removes his favorite play item. Is this toddler at-risk for EBD? Most of us would agree that these are typical behaviors for a 2-year-old. As we know, saying "no" to adult requests (or crying) are how most 2-year-olds communicate with their parents. But what happens if this same child continues to refuse to comply with adult requests and engages in severe temper tantrums at age 4, 5, or 6? These may be warning signs indicating that the child is at risk for the development of EBD. Knowing when the behavior is developmentally appropriate for the child's age level versus inappropriate can be difficult, but such knowledge is an important part of the identification process, and this is one of the reasons teachers need to study normal child development. Determining whether a child's behavior is deviant at such a young age is problematic because young children can make rapid changes. Besides, behavioral deviance is a social construct—a reality related to societal expectations (Achenbach & Edelbrock, 1981; Campbell, 1995).

Furthermore, *where* do we identify young children with EBD? Most young children are either at home with a care provider (parent, grandparent, or babysitter) or attend a childcare center. Who are these children and how do we identify them? Consider the following scenario.

> Louie is 3 years old and attends a neighborhood childcare center. Louie's parents receive reports daily from the center staff that Louie is pinching and biting the other children in his class throughout the day, but especially during center time activities and free play time. This time, however, Louie's parents receive a phone call and are asked to come pick Louie up, because he pushed another child in the class. Unfortunately, the child fell down against a desk and has a severe gash on her forehead. When Louie's dad arrives to pick him up at the childcare center, the staff explained that Louie could not stay at the center any longer. They are concerned about Louie, but are also concerned about the safety of the other children in the class. Although not formally referred to as "expulsion," Louie was, in essence, expelled from the childcare center.

The above scenario is not uncommon for young children who have serious emotional and behavioral disorders. Currently, the policies and procedures for identification of these young children are severely lacking (Conroy, Hendrickson, & Hester, 2004; Smith & Fox, 2003). They often bounce from childcare facility to childcare facility until they reach kindergarten, or the parents end up keeping them at home. Either way, they end up falling through the cracks since they are not identified early as having characteristics associated with EBD or provided appropriate early intervention services. Although a few instruments are available that can assist in the early identification of EBD in young children, such as the *Early Screening Profile* (ESP; Walker, Severson, & Feil, 1994) and the *Child Behavior Checklist* (CBCL: Achenbach, 1991), these instruments are not widely used in a systematic manner within childcare centers or schools; therefore, early identification is less likely to occur. Alternatively, these children are more likely to come to the attention of various non-school-based services, such as outpatient clinics and therapeutic mental health facilities that provide clinic based or **itinerant services.** These children may eventually be given a label such as **conduct disorder, oppositional-defiant disorder,** or **schizophrenia** from the current edition of the American Psychiatric Association's *Diagnostic and Statistical Manual of Mental Disorders* (DSM) by a mental health professional (American Psychiatric Association, 2000 and subsequent revisions). Although these labels indicate a significant problem behavior, they do not necessarily qualify children for public early intervention services. Often, the public service delivery systems that treat these children have stringent eligibility criteria that actually end up limiting access to preventative services of young children at risk for EBD.

Finally, the federal definition previously discussed in this chapter lacks sensitivity to the characteristics of young children who are at risk for or have emotional and behavioral disorders. As a result, access to services in the public schools may be limited. The federal definition applies to all children and youth (ages 3–22 years) who meet eligibility criteria; however, the characteristics listed in the definition are not appropriate for children ages 3–5 years old. For example, given their age and developmental level, it is difficult to determine whether a young child's behavior is chronic. It is also difficult to determine whether he or she demonstrates an "inability to learn." Children may demonstrate risk factors or indicators suggesting they have EBD, but due to the constraints of the federal definition it may be difficult to identify them as having EBD and provide services to them under this label.

As a profession, we have a need to develop a *proactive,* universal, systematic, comprehensive screening program to assist in the identification of these young children. Targeting young children at heightened risk due to childhood or environmental factors is essential for the early identification and prevention or further development of EBD. Systematic screening and intervention efforts should bridge across the public schools, community-based childcare centers, and mental health facilities with the goal of identifying all young children at an early age in order to prevent problems in elementary school, adolescence, and adulthood. With early intervention services, the effects of EBD can be minimized or even prevented (Serna, Nielsen, Lambros, & Forness, 2002).

Elementary Grades

The goal is to identify children with (or at risk for) EBD at an early age prior to the development of emotional or behavioral disorders. As discussed in Chapter 12, this is referred to as **primary prevention.** However, as discussed above, primary identification and intervention do not always occur. Often, these children are not identified or provided services until an emotional or behavioral disorder has developed or they are misidentified (Walker et al., 2004; Wang et al., 2005). For instance, many children with EBD may originally be identified as having a learning disability (LD) (Forness & Kavale, 2001). This would not be unusual given the comorbidity between EBD and LD. However, if identified, these children are most likely to be identified during their elementary grades or later. Once identified, our job as professionals is to provide **secondary or tertiary prevention and intervention.** That is, we need to accurately identify their learning and behavioral needs and provide services that can ameliorate the child's difficulties, preventing their exacerbation and their interference with the child's development and life. Consider the following scenario.

> Raul entered second grade with a reputation. Everyone in the school knew who Raul was, because his first-grade teacher often had to discipline him. In fact, Raul was once suspended for hitting and kicking his first-grade teacher. However, Raul's behavioral problems did not begin in first grade. Even in kindergarten, he was noncompliant, disruptive, and difficult to manage. Raul's first-grade teacher reported him to the school's **child study team** (see Chapter 11 for a discussion of child study teams). The team worked with his teacher to implement several **preferral activities,** including providing positive attention or **reinforcement** for appropriate behavior and a **self-management program.** Initially, the preferral activities appeared to help decrease Raul's problem behaviors. However, over time, Raul's behaviors continued. By the end of the year, nothing seemed to work. Although Raul demonstrated chronic problem behaviors that were persistent over time, these behaviors were not significantly interfering with his ability to master the first-grade curriculum content. Therefore, a referral to special education seemed inappropriate at the time. Thus, Raul was promoted to second grade. During the first several weeks of second grade, the teacher noticed that Raul's behavior had become severe. He often bullied his peers, was noncompliant, and was severely disruptive during class time. Raul's behaviors began to interfere with his class work and academic skills and by December, he was lagging significantly behind his peers in most academic areas. His second-grade teacher put in another referral to the child study team after the first grading period of the year, and an evaluation for special education services began. At this point, Raul's problem behaviors and academic deficits had become so severe that he now met the criteria under the diagnostic category of *emotional disturbance*. At this point, the school staff needed to be proactive and design an intervention program that addressed both Raul's behavioral and academic deficits to prevent them from worsening. With specific intervention and supports that can address his learning and behavioral needs, Raul could develop the adaptive skills he needed to be successful in school.

As discussed throughout this chapter, the above scenario is common. In fact, it would be even more common for a child such as Raul not to be identified until third or fourth grade or even later. However, as a child's emotional and behavioral problems become more severe and persist over a longer time, his or her ability to be successful academically in school is diminished.

At this point, you may be asking yourself questions such as these: Didn't the school staff see Raul's problems earlier? Why didn't they do something sooner? What tools and strategies could the teachers have used to more proactively address a child, such as Raul's needs? Similar to the identification techniques discussed above in the early childhood section, several tools are available to assist in the identification process, such as the *Systematic Screening for Behavior Disorders* (SSBD; Walker & Severson, 1990), the *Behavior Assessment System for Children* (BASC; Reynolds & Kamphaus, 1992), and the *Child Behavior Checklist* (CBCL; Achenbach, 1991, 1997). Again, such issues as ambiguous definitions, terminology, eligibility criteria, and characteristics make identification and intervention during the elementary years problematic as well. For a variety of reasons, children with EBD very often are not identified at all or are not identified for years after their problems are first noticed (Kauffman, 1999; Wang et al., 2005).

One school-wide strategy targeted toward prevention of emotional and behavioral disorders is **Positive Behavior Support** (PBS) (see Chapter 12 for a comprehensive discussion of PBS). PBS is a school-wide system targeted toward prevention and remediation of school-age children who are at risk for or who demonstrate problem behaviors, including students with EBD. Since schools that implement a PBS system have a systematic structure in place that target children who are at risk for behavioral disorders, these schools are probably more likely to identify and provide intervention at an earlier stage. In addition to PBS, elementary schools have **wraparound services,** such as counseling, case management, and parent-advocacy services (Eber, Nelson, & Miles, 1997). Wraparound services are intended to help maintain children with EBD in their neighborhood schools and communities. In addition, wraparound services that can provide support for the families of these children may also be available through community agencies (e.g., mental health services and respite services).

Elementary school is a critical time for identifying and intervening regarding the emotional and behavioral needs of children. Although some children are identified during their elementary years, many children continue to fall through the cracks—they are not identified with EBD or mental disorders and do not receive the help they need. Systematic ways to identify these children are at the crux of this problem. Systemwide identification and prevention strategies, such as PBS, are promising practices that may help provide targeted children the services that they need. As professionals, teachers need to be aware of the early signals indicating the potential development of an emotional or behavioral disorders. Once a teacher first becomes aware of the at-risk signals in a child, it is the teacher's professional responsibility to assist in helping the child gain the necessary support and services to remediate and minimize the child's emotional and behavioral difficulties. With the necessary support, the effects of these children's emotional and behavioral deficits will be diminished.

Adolescence

If children who are preschool- and elementary-aged are not identified and provided intervention services, by the time they reach adolescence their emotional and behavioral problems become evident. Adolescents with EBD typically show extreme forms of externalizing and or internalizing behaviors. As their emotional and behavioral deficits become increasingly disabling, their success in school decreases. Even with identification and intervention at an earlier age, many of these children will continue to have difficulty into their adolescent and adult years. Often these students are frequently suspended or even expelled from school and eventually end up dropping out of school. In addition, they may be more likely to engage in acts of violence and criminal behavior (e.g., theft, drug-related behaviors, and so forth) and may get additional labels such as "juvenile delinquent" (see Walker, Ramsey, & Gresham, 2004; Wang et al., 2005). Consider the following scenario.

Jackson is an eighth grader who receives special education services under the label of *emotional disturbance*. Currently, Jackson attends a resource room to receive instruction in academic activities, but otherwise he has been included in other eighth grades classes, including homeroom, art, music, and physical education. Jackson's behavior has become increasingly problematic for his teachers. In his homeroom classroom, he refuses to comply with any of his teacher's requests. In addition, he often talks back to the teacher and receives a great deal of attention from his peers. Recently, he has begun leaving the school grounds without permission and returning hours later. His teachers believe that he is probably using drugs during this time. Jackson's most recent infraction was bullying another male student on the school grounds after school. Following the bullying, Jackson and one of his peers destroyed the inside of the boys' locker room by writing racial obscenities all over the walls, flooding the floors with water, and throwing toilet paper everywhere. These activities were reported to his homeroom and special education teachers by another student in the school. This was the "final straw" for Jackson. Prior to this incident, the school staff had implemented a **functional behavioral assessment** and **behavioral intervention plan.** However, even with the implementation of this plan, Jackson had been suspended a total of nine times. Following this incident, the school-based team met to discuss removing Jackson from his current educational placement at his neighborhood school and placing him in an **interim alternative education settings** (IAES). They were concerned that although Jackson was making progress on his academic skills, his increasing behavioral needs were not being met by his current school placement.

Adolescence is a difficult time for all children. It is not unusual for most adolescents to engage in some of the behaviors that Jackson displayed. However, as can be seen in the case of Jackson, behaviors that are indicative of EBD can be exacerbated, becoming even worse during this age period. Whether an adolescent with EBD is provided special education services in a **self-contained special education classroom, resource room,** or an IAES, one critical strategy to remember when working with these students is that teachers need to provide the education and support they need to transition into adulthood—that is, we need to teach them to become productive members of society. Most of these students will drop out of school or graduate and not go onto college or technical school (Turnbull, Turnbull, Shank, & Leal, 1999). They typically experience a high rate of unemployment or

Learning to cooperate and interact with their peers is an important part of instruction for students with emotional/behavioral disorders. (Photo credit: Silver Burdett Ginn)

problematic employment (frequent job turnover or low-paying jobs) (Walker et al., 2004).

Adolescence is a critical time when teachers can have a significant positive influence on these children and their behaviors (Kauffman, 2005). Adolescents with EBD often need intensive instruction and comprehensive wraparound services to help them learn alternative behaviors. Such intervention services may include **behavioral and mental health counseling, social skills instruction, conflict resolution strategies,** and **cognitive behavior therapy.** Targeting these students' social and behavioral skills for instruction and academic skills that are likely to enable them to be successful in the future is imperative. In addition, identifying these students' strengths and interests and then matching instruction to their strengths can facilitate their success. Work-related and social/behavioral skill instruction should begin early and continue throughout adolescence, thus making the transition from school into adulthood and work environments more successful.

:: UNIQUE LEARNING NEEDS AND EVIDENCE-BASED PRACTICES

What evidence-based practices are available for preventing and remediating EBD in children and youth? How can we help these children and young people learn adaptive behaviors so that they are more successful in school and their community? What types of practices can we employ with at-risk young children to prevent further development of EBD? How can we help adolescents with EBD transition into adulthood? What types of related services are needed to ameliorate internalizing and externalizing behaviors? As discussed earlier in this chapter, the characteristics and needs of children and youth with EBD are multiple and complex. Some students demonstrate internalizing disorders, others demonstrate externalizing disorders, and some students demonstrate both. Obviously, the way teachers approach intervention with these students may differ depending on the individual needs of these students. Therefore it is not surprising that no one single intervention practice can address the unique needs of all students with EBD. Similar to other students with disabilities such as mental retardation and learning disabilities, intervention strategies need to be individualized to address the specific areas of the student's need. Thankfully, some intervention approaches (with varying levels of evidence) have been used successfully with students with EBD that address their unique learning needs. Unfortunately, the field of EBD is still relatively new and there is much we do not know. Research on EBD has focused on identifying the characteristics of and techniques for diagnosing EBD, whereas research on widespread intervention approaches has taken a secondary role (Nelson, 2004). This is not to say that there are no evidence-based practices for intervening on the unique characteristics of EBD; indeed, much progress has been made, but the research is in the early stages (Landrum & Kauffman, 2006). The remainder of this chapter highlights evidence-based intervention practices that have been found to successfully address the unique characteristics of students with EBD.

Applied Behavior Analysis

As discussed throughout this chapter, one of the defining features of EBD is problem behavior. **Applied behavior analysis** (ABA) is one evidence-based approach that has considerable research supporting its use to decrease children and young people's problem behaviors and increase adaptive behaviors. When examining school-based intervention approaches with these students, these studies are primarily dominated by applied behavior analysis (ABA) techniques (Forness, 2003). ABA is founded on the belief that behavior occurs in response to various events that occur in the environment. These events are referred to as **antecedents** and **consequences.** Therefore, to change a behavior, one only need manipulate or change the appropriate environmental events. For instance, if the teacher provides attention in the form of a verbal reprimand to a student with EBD in his or her class every time he or she is disruptive, an ABA approach toward intervening with this behavior would suggest that the teacher's attention may be maintaining or controlling the student's disruptive behavior. Therefore, the teacher would need to change *his or her behavior* by providing attention to the student only when the student is engaged in appropriate behaviors and stop responding to the disruptive behavior by ignoring them. Effective ABA strategies have been documented in the research literature to effectively address students' behavior, such as noncompliance, disruption, aggression, off-task, and so forth. ABA strategies, such as the use of **positive reinforcement, negative reinforcement, positive** and **negative punishment,** manipulation of **antecedent events, establishing operations,** and **setting events,** typically include precise measurement of both problem behaviors and adaptive behaviors that replace the problem behavior, changes in the events that occur prior to the behaviors (the antecedents), and changes in the events following the problem behaviors (the consequences). These changes occur until predictable and durable changes occur in the targeted behaviors. (A review of ABA strategies and the supporting research literature is beyond the scope of this book; however, the reader is referred to the works by Alberto & Troutman, 2003; Kerr & Nelson, 2002; and Walker et al., 2004 for reviews).

One of the strengths of using an ABA approach to changing problem behaviors demonstrated by students with EBD is that "it takes the problem away from the child." Specifically, since behavior is a function of the student's environment, the problem becomes the student's behavior *and* the environment, rather than the student alone (Kauffman, 2005). However, this also means that the teacher is responsible for changing the environmental events related to the behavior. Perhaps one of the most common intervention approaches based on principles of applied behavior analysis seen in schools today is **Positive Behavior Support** (for a discussion, see Chapter 12). Positive behavior support, based on principles of ABA, helps teachers and schools arrange antecedent and consequence events in the school environment to promote adaptive behaviors and decrease or diminish maladaptive or problem behaviors (e.g., school-wide rules, arrangement of staff to supervise, and so forth).

Social Competence Interventions

Children and young people with EBD obviously have problems in the area of social competence. In fact, the federal definition of emotional disturbance states that these children have "an inability to build or maintain satisfactory interpersonal relationships with peers and teachers." Whether identified at an early age in preschool or later during middle or high school, students with EBD have problems relating socially to adults and often with their nondeviant peers as well. If they do have friends and imitate others, they tend to affiliate with other deviant peers, not the well-behaved members of their group. Obviously, they have had the opportunity to observe and imitate their better-behaved peers but have not done so (Hallenbeck & Kauffman, 1995; Rhode, Jenson, & Reavis, 1992).

Specifically, students with EBD may have difficulty with authority figures, such as teachers and parents; relating to their peers; and solving social problems in a positive manner (Kauffman, 2005). Their difficulties in the area of social competence significantly influence their educational as well as their social and psychological adjustment to school, resulting in such problems as low self-concept, peer rejection, loneliness, and problematic social relationships (Webster-Stratton, 1997). Furthermore, these are precisely the problems that may lead to further negative outcomes as these individuals become adults (Kavale, Mathur, & Mostert, 2004).

Fortunately, a number of evidence-based social competence interventions have been developed to address deficits in this area. The purpose of many of these interventions is to help teach these students to develop and maintain positive social interactions, friendships, social support networks with their peers, and learn coping or conflict resolution strategies for responding to social situations in their environment (Kauffman, 2005). For example, several social skills curricula are designed to teach children and youth interpersonal skills, including *Skillstreaming* (McGinnis & Goldstein, 2005) and *ACCEPTS* (Walker, McConnell, Holmes, Todis, Walker, & Golden, 1983). Typically, these curricula include small-group activities to teach specific strategies to students, followed by modeling, and guided practice. In addition to social competence curricula, a number of specific social skill intervention strategies have been investigated and found effective in teaching students to initiate and maintain positive interactions with their peers or respond to conflict more adaptively. Although a considerable number of research studies have been conducted validating the effectiveness of various approaches for teaching social skills, some researchers suggest the efficacy of these approaches in fostering long-term outcomes for children and youth with EBD is questionable (Kavale et al., 2004). (For a critical review of the social competence intervention literature, the reader is referred to Kavale et al., 2004.)

As stated by Kauffman (2005), "at the heart of social skills is the ability to communicate verbally and nonverbally—to use language competently" (p. 211). Often, children and youth with EBD have deficits in the area of language (Rogers-Adkinson & Griffith, 1999) and therefore will have social or communication skill deficits that interfere with their ability to engage in appropriate social behaviors (i.e., the student is unable to demonstrate the appropriate skill because it is not in his or her repertoire). In addition to skill deficits, some students have perform-ance deficits (i.e., the student has the appropriate skill, but chooses not to demon-strate it). Therefore, social competence interventions need to either *teach* these skills to the student or design an intervention to *encourage* the student to use these skills. Kauffman (2005) suggests the following critical social skills necessary for success in school: listening to others, taking turns in conversations, greeting others, joining in ongoing activities, giving compliments, expressing anger in an acceptable manner, assisting others, focusing on work-related tasks, and following societal rules.

The development of social competence in children and young people with EBD is essential, yet often one of the most difficult areas for teachers to address. Unfor-tunately, with the national emphasis on academic outcomes, there is very little time available during the school day to work on increasing children's social competence behaviors. It seems that schools are often much more focused on developing academic areas of development, such as reading, language arts, mathematics, and science and give little attention to teaching social competence skills. Although those areas are important to target for instruction, social competence is just as an impor-tant area to target for instruction, especially for students with EBD. Given that a deficit in social competence is one of the critical defining features of EBD, develop-ing the social competence of these students is a necessary goal.

Wraparound and Systems of Care

Given the complexity of characteristics and unique needs demonstrated by children and youth with EBD, these students and their families often have additional sup-ports from services outside of the school setting, such as mental health centers, juvenile justice services, child welfare programs, counseling, case management, respite services, and parent-advocacy. In addition, wraparound services also include services that can address the basic needs of the family and school. When working with these students, there is a need to link the supports provided through these multiple agencies and provide additional support that may increase the effectiveness of educational intervention provided in the school. The development of a comprehensive network to link these wraparound services or "systems of care" is often seen when working with students with EBD, especially adolescents. However, developing a coordinated, comprehensive system of care may be easier said than done.

In 1982, Knitzer proposed a "seamless system of care" when working with students with severe emotional disturbance. The primary goal of a system of care is to increase collaboration between, and accessibility to, an array of community-based services that can help ameliorate deficits in the area of EBD (Eber & Keenan, 2004). Over the past 20 years, states have received federal funding to help develop such services. In addition, one of the core features of IDEA (2004) is collaboration with families and related services (see Chapters 2 and 11 for a discussion of IDEA [2004] components and collaboration, respectively).

Although not defined by law, Eber and Keenan (2004) suggest that wraparound services and systems of care should include the following components:

1. Community-based
2. Individualized and strength-based
3. Culturally competent
4. Families as full and active partners
5. Team-based process involving family, child, natural supports, agencies, and community supports
6. Flexible approach and funding
7. Balance of formal and informal community and family resources
8. Unconditional commitment
9. Development and implementation of an individualized service/support plan based on a community/neighborhood, interagency, collaborative process
10. Outcomes determined and measured through the team process (p. 507).

Implementing systems of care and wraparound services can be difficult, because it requires cross collaboration, time, and resources. Some states have developed collaborative training programs to assist in the process. However, it still requires a mechanism for structuring communication among stakeholders, collaboration in problem-solving solutions for students, and sharing information across agencies—not to mention time. Although an important conceptual approach toward meeting the needs of students with EBD, there is limited evidence of the outcomes or effectiveness of a "systems of care" or "wraparound services" approach. Program evaluation research has been conducted that suggests a systems of care approach helps students to remain in schools in their communities, rather than going to more restrictive educational and community settings, such as residential placements. In addition, early findings suggest that parents and children are satisfied and functioning levels of students are increased at home, school, and in the community when a systems of care approach is taken (see Burns & Hoagwood, 2002). Even though the research may be in the early stages, approaching the complex needs of students with EBD using a systems of care or wrap-around service approach is promising and should be considered, when appropriate. In spite of the rhetoric about prevention and comprehensive services, most children and youth with EBD never receive mental health services or special education or get them only after years of delay (U.S. Department of Health and Human Services, 2001; Wang et al., 2005). Although this is true today, it has always been the case (Kauffman & Landrum, 2006).

Psychopharmacology Interventions

As stated earlier in this chapter, children and youth with EBD have complex characteristics and can be challenging to teach. Although they all demonstrate chronic behaviors that interfere with their functioning in school and community, the causes of their problems may be different. As discussed in the section on applied behavior analysis, above, the environment might be an important causal factor for the behavior. However, some children and youth may also have a biological basis for their behaviors. Medications (psychopharmacology) may provide an additional intervention strategy for dealing productively with behavioral deficits whether the problem is known to have originated in the individual's physiology or not.

In comparison to the other intervention approaches, such as applied behavior analysis, in the past psychopharmacology has been less likely to be a part of the special education services provided under IDEA (Konopasek & Forness, 2004). However, recent evidence suggests that psychopharmacological interventions can be a critical part of these students intervention programs and should be considered, if appropriate (MTA Cooperative Group, 1999). The application of psychopharmacology interventions with students with EBD focuses on examining the use of psychiatric medications with children and youth to treat various psychiatric disorders.

Although in the past this approach was avoided or used infrequently, psychopharmacology is rapidly gaining attention as an effective intervention tool, given the major advances in this field (Forness, Kavale, Sweeney, & Crenshaw, 1999). For example, researchers have found that different stimulants, antidepressants, and related medications can be helpful for children and youth with **attention deficit hyperactive disorder** (ADHD). In addition, antidepressants and mood stabilizers have been found to be useful when treating symptoms of **depression** and **mood disorders,** such as **dysthymia** and **bipolar disorder,** in children and adolescents. Additionally, different medications have been found effective in treating **anxiety disorders, schizophrenia,** and **psychotic disorders.** A review of various types of medications to treat different psychiatric disorders is beyond the scope of this chapter; therefore, the reader is referred to Konopasek & Forness (2004) for a comprehensive review of psychopharmacological treatments.

Even though recent research has established the appropriateness and usefulness of a pharmacological approach toward the treatment of various disorders in children and youth with (or at risk for) EBD, this approach needs to be implemented collaboratively with input from the special education staff, the family, and the medical community (Konopasek & Forness, 2004). Forness and Kavale (2001) suggest a series of steps to follow when evaluating students for EBD.

Step 1: Screen for psychiatric diagnosis when problems are resistant to other interventions or when the behaviors are indicative of psychiatric disorders.

Step 2: Screen for secondary diagnoses that may be present to determine the need for a referral to a specialist, such as a psychiatrist that specializes in children and youth.

Step 3: Provide parents information regarding the possibility of psychiatric disorders and assist them in obtaining an evaluation from a qualified physician.

Step 4: Provide the physician with diagnostic information gathered by the school.

Step 5: Provide classroom based intervention information and data to the physician to assist in tracking the effectiveness of pharmacological interventions (if indicated).

Step 6: Provide ongoing support and monitoring of behavioral changes, assisting the physician in monitoring the appropriate type and dose of medication prescribed.

Close collaboration between the school, family, and medical community is essential if psychopharmacological interventions are going to be monitored for effectiveness. The classroom teacher plays a critical role in assisting in this process. Therefore, teachers working with these students need to be trained and aware of the role these medications can play in designing an effective intervention program to address the behaviors of these students.

SUMMARY

This chapter reviewed the characteristics, defining features, and identification process for students with EBD. As discussed earlier, children and youth with EBD are a diverse group of individuals. This term is used to represent children and young people who demonstrate a wide variety of internalizing and externalizing behaviors. As a result, identification of this disorder is difficult at best. One common theme of these students is that they all demonstrate chronic problem behaviors that are interfering with their abilities to learn and adapt to the school.

Many different terms have been used and several definitions have been developed to assist in the identification of students with EBD. Typically, these students are referred to under IDEA (2004) as children and youth with *emotional disturbance.* However, the term *emotional or behavioral disorders* has been proposed as a more descriptive and accurate term.

One factor that makes identification of these students difficult is that diagnosis is based in part by individual judgment of behavior. Although there are behavior rating scales and standardized assessment measures to assist in the identification, no single assessment tool exists to diagnose children and youth with EBD. Most children and young people are identified through the IDEA (2004) definition, which excludes students who are socially maladjusted. Due to the difficulties in the identification process, many of these needy children are never identified and thus receive no specific intervention services. The lack of identification and services at an early age negatively affects the outlook for their future.

Like students with other disabilities (i.e., learning disabilities, mental retardation), these students have academic difficulties. In addition to their academic needs, they also have characteristics that are unique (e.g., social and behavioral needs). Given the unique needs of these students, researchers and practitioners have developed a number of specific interventions including the use of applied behavior analysis strategies, psychopharmacological interventions, social competence curricula, and wraparound services.

Unfortunately, as stated by Kauffman (1999):

> Prevention of emotional and behavioral disorders seems to be everyone's rhetorical darling, but I have come to the sad conclusion that most of our talk about prevention is of little substance. We often find ways to avoid taking primary or secondary preventive action, regardless of our acknowledgment that such prevention is a good idea. Other concerns take precedence, and as a result we are most successful in preventing prevention itself (p. 448).

In order to meet the unique characteristics and learning needs of these students, educators need to take charge and proactively identify and treat these individuals at an early age. If early identification and intervention are accomplished, the negative affects of EBD can be ameliorated and the trajectory of these students' development is far more promising.

COMPETENT TEACHING BOX

BOX 5.1

Knowing your students . . .

Working with students with EBD can be challenging. These children and young people have a number of complex characteristics. It can be difficult for the classroom teacher to meet all the needs of these children. When you work with children and young people with EBD, remember the following:

- Factors related to the development of EBD include poverty, family history, drug and substance abuse, and poor parenting skills. Even though there are environmental factors that are related to EBD, children and young people who have this disorder come in all shapes and sizes. Therefore, schools need to identify these children proactively as soon as early warning signs indicating EBD occur. Through early identification and intervention efforts, teachers can make a significant impact on these children's future development.

- The identification of EBD is difficult; therefore, as required by law identification should occur through a multidisciplinary process that evaluates the characteristics of the child across different situations, times, and people. Some of these children and young people will need to be evaluated for pharmacological interventions that can assist the teacher in meeting their educational needs.

- Although these children and young people engage in problem behaviors that are directed toward adults or other children, many of them lack the necessary skills to demonstrate adaptive behaviors and/or interact with their peers successfully. Therefore, teachers need to develop interventions that can help them learn these adaptive skills.

- Children and young people with EBD are served across a variety of educational settings. They may be served in general education classrooms, resource rooms, self-contained classes, special schools, or residential placements. Often these students are difficult to include in classrooms with their nondisabled peers due to their intensive behavioral needs. Therefore, schools need to consider the least restrictive placement when determining the most appropriate educational setting for these students.

Competent teachers . . .

- Target all of their students' problem behaviors for intervention.
- Design their classrooms to minimize the occurrence of problematic behaviors.
- Advocate for the early identification and prevention of EBD.
- Use a variety of interventions to meet the needs of students who engage in problematic internalizing and externalizing behaviors.
- Work with other members of the multidisciplinary team, including physicians (when appropriate) in order to provide the most comprehensive services to their students.

DEAN

They called him "Mean Dean." Everyone at the Rainbow Childcare Center knew when Dean had arrived for the day. As soon as he came to school, an "episode" would ensue. On this particular day, Dean was acting particularly difficult, and even punched one of his peers during breakfast. Later, on the playground he pushed a little girl down on the jungle gym—unfortunately, she fell and cut her face. The childcare director felt that she could no longer control Dean's behavior. She phoned Dean's mother and explained that she was sorry, but Dean could no longer attend the Rainbow Childcare Center. The director suggested that Dean's mother contact the local public schools and inquire about the possibility of early intervention services for her son. Later in the week, Dean's mother explained to the Child Find Specialist at the school district that he had previously been "kicked-out" of two other childcare centers due to his problem behaviors.

Clearly, Dean's mother was at her wit's end. She knew that he could be a handful, but she did not have any other place to leave him when she went to work. She had tried to control his behavior at home, but he was difficult for her to deal with, and she couldn't find any babysitters who wanted to watch him. In fact, she admitted that she was scared to leave him at home with his other siblings, because he would become explosive at times. She described her concern about Dean's behavior and frustration when she tried to discipline Dean. He wasn't like her other children—he just refused to comply and was often aggressive with her as well. In addition, he often engaged in tantrums—screaming, falling on the floor, and kicking when he didn't get his way. The Child Find Specialist suggested that they conduct a multidisciplinary evaluation examining Dean's development and behavior. A school psychologist specializing in young children assessed Dean's abilities using a behavior rating scale, a developmental inventory, and an adaptive behavior scale. In addition, she observed Dean at home and at his third childcare center. A speech-language pathologist also evaluated Dean's speech and language skills. After the assessment, the school psychologist, speech-language pathologist, and Child Find Specialist explained to Dean's mother that although he was demonstrating slight delays in the areas of cognitive and language skills, his social-emotional and behavioral skills were considerably atypical for a 3-year-old. They suggested that he needed intensive intervention to address his behavioral

needs. In addition, they suggested he receive speech-language therapy to help remediate his communication skills.

Fortunately, for Dean and his mother, they lived near an innovative early intervention program that included specific services targeting young children with or at risk for emotional and behavioral disorders. The program provided a center-based program with teachers who had expertise in early intervention strategies for addressing young children with challenging behaviors. In addition, the center provided related services, such as speech-language therapy. Their program used a behavioral approach to intervention by helping to identify the environmental factors that influenced the occurrence of children's problem behaviors. They conducted **functional behavioral assessments** on all the children enrolled in the program and developed individualized behavioral intervention strategies that modified the environmental events influencing the behavior. In addition, the early intervention program provided a parent-training program that taught parents how to change their children's problem behaviors. In fact, all parents were required to attend the parent-training program during the first month their child was enrolled in the early intervention program. Following completion of the parent-training component of the program, parents were required to volunteer and teach new parents entering the program the skills they had learned.

Dean began attending the early intervention program immediately. Within a month, Dean's problem behaviors were considerably better at school and at home. Dean had learned that he could gain his teacher's and mother's attention by engaging in more positive and adaptive behaviors. In addition, Dean had learned how to interact with his peers in a more positive manner. Finally, Dean had learned that when he engaged in his problem behaviors, they no longer served a purpose for him.

Dean and his mother spent 4 months attending the early intervention program. After this time, Dean was transferred back into a childcare center with itinerant support services from the early intervention center. Once a week, a teacher followed up on Dean with the childcare staff, which provided assistance as necessary. Dean is now in kindergarten. So far, his teacher reports that he is "getting along well with his peers" and reports having no problems.

1. Do you think Dean has or had EBD?
2. What do you think would have happened to Dean if he hadn't received early intervention that addressed his problem behaviors?

3. Do you think it is important to teach Dean's mother to work with his challenging behaviors? Why or why not?

4. Why do you think that not all school districts provide a comprehensive early intervention program targeted for young children with problem behaviors?

LARISSA

Eight-year-old Larissa was referred by her third-grade teacher to the Child Study Team for a comprehensive evaluation for special education. Larissa was oppositional, verbally threatening to her teacher, noncompliant, and lagged severely behind her peers in academics, particularly math and reading. In addition, Larissa often left the classroom during instructional times without permission. Larissa had a number of discipline referrals in second grade as well, so the problem behaviors seen by the third-grade teacher were nothing new. Larissa had been referred for special education services in second grade, and after a thorough assessment the Child Study Team had concluded that she did not qualify. Although Larissa demonstrated significant learning and behavioral problems, the evaluation results did not qualify her for receiving special education services under learning disabilities or emotional disturbance.

This year, in third grade, the teacher has met several times with Larissa's parents. Her parents expressed that Larissa was difficult for them to manage at home. When they tried to get her to do her homework, she frequently refused. If prodded to do her work, she would scream and yell and lock herself in her bedroom. They were concerned that Larissa was falling further and further behind and might end up needing to repeat third grade. The Child Study Team met, and once again, discussed Larissa's case. Everyone expressed concern about Larissa's behavior problems, but they also were concerned about her abilities to complete her academic work. Larissa seemed to engage in problem behaviors primarily during instructional times. Socially, she was well liked by peers and had some friends. Once again, they conducted a comprehensive evaluation of Larissa's abilities, including intelligence, achievement, speech-language, and behavior (including ratings and direct observations of her in her classroom). Following this evaluation, they found that Larissa's IQ was in the low-normal range. Her achievement in the area of math was within the low-normal range, but in the area of reading she scored significantly below normal. Her adaptive behavior and speech-language test results also indicated scores below normal. The largest change in the evaluation results from the previous year, however, were in the outcomes of the behavior rating scale. Whereas last year she

did not score within the "clinical" range, this year her score was different from the norm. In addition, when the school psychologist and the behavior specialist observed Larissa in her classroom, she was extremely disruptive and noncompliant in comparison to her peers. This time, Larissa's evaluation results qualified her for special education services under the label of emotionally disturbed. The Child Study Team and Larissa's parents agreed that the best educational placement would be to remain in her third-grade class, but receive special education services in a resource room for part of the day. In the resource room, Larissa received intensive instruction for her academic activities. In addition, a **self-management program** was implemented to help her learn how to monitor and change her behavior during academic activities. Finally, Larissa received social skills instruction in a small group setting, specifically working on anger-management and explosive behavior.

Larissa continued to be a member of her third-grade class for other times during the day, such as lunch, special activities, and so forth. Although her academic skills and behavior improved over the year, at the end of third grade the Child Study Team met with Larissa's parents to discuss her progress. They all agreed that Larissa had made some gains but that she continued to need the specialized services she was receiving in order to progress.

1. Which do you think came first—Larissa's learning deficits or behavioral problems?

2. Does Larissa have EBD or LD?

3. Would the special education services change depending on her label?

4. Could anyone have identified Larissa's disabilities earlier? If so, would this have prevented her problem behaviors?

5. Are there other services that Larissa needs that she is not getting? If so, what other services would you recommend

TOMMY

Tommy is the oldest child, living with his mother, three brothers, and one sister in a small three-bedroom apartment. His mother's only income is from welfare. She has had a history of drug and alcohol abuse over the years and has difficulty holding down a job. Tommy and his siblings are basically "raising themselves." Since sixth grade, Tommy has been receiving special education services under the category of emotional disturbance. At that time, he was placed in a self-contained class for students with behavioral disorders. However, due to his continued problem behavior, when Tommy was in ninth grade he was placed in the district's alternative school for students with emotional and behavioral disorders. At 18, Tommy has been in and out of trouble with the law for minor offenses (e.g., petty theft) and suspended from school a number of times for offenses such as smoking marijuana in the boy's bathroom, cursing at the principal, and fighting with other students. Academically, he barely reads on a fourth-grade level and has only basic math skills. The staff at the school has taught Tommy different self-management and conflict resolution strategies for dealing with his aggression. However, none of these seems to be very successful. In addition, teachers have continued to work on his academic and social skills.

The problem now is that Tommy hates coming to school. In fact, there are many days that he skips school and hangs out with his uncle who works at the Midas Automobile Service Center. His uncle has been at the Midas Automobile Service Center, working on cars, for over 10 years and is one of their more experienced service people. Recently, Tommy's uncle has been teaching him more and more about the "tricks of the trade." As it turns out, Tommy is fairly good with cars. Although Tommy skips school to be at the Midas Automobile Service Center, when he is in school his social and behavioral skills appear to be more typical. One day, the manager of the Midas Automobile Service Center offers Tommy a job as an assistant. The pay is low, but if he is successful, there may eventually be an opportunity for him to be hired as a mechanic. Tommy decides to drop out of school and go to work at the Midas Automobile Service Center. It has only been a year, but Tommy is doing very well in his new job. His uncle continues to mentor him. However, in order to become a mechanic, he will need a high school degree and must take classes at the community college. Presently, he is working on his GED.

1. What family factors may have contributed to Tommy's learning and behavior problems?
2. Was Tommy's decision to drop out of school a smart choice?
3. Do you think he would have better employment opportunities if he had remained in the alternative school until he was 22 years old?
4. Do you think Tommy will be able to continue in a positive direction? What obstacles might he encounter?

REFERENCES

Achenbach, T. M. (1991). *Manual for the child behavior checklist/4-18 and 1991 profile.* Burlington: University of Vermont, Department of Psychiatry.

Achenbach, T. M. (1997). *Guide for the caregiver-teacher report form for ages 2-5.* Burlington: University of Vermont, Department of Psychiatry.

Achenbach, T. M., & Edelbrock, C. S. (1981). Behavior problems and competencies reported by parents of normal and disturbed children aged four through sixteen. *Monographs of the Society for Research in Child Development, 46*(1, Serial No. 188).

Alberto, P. A., & Troutman, A. C. (2003). *Applied behavior analysis for teachers* (6th ed.). Columbus, OH: Merrill/ Prentice Hall.

American Psychiatric Association. (2000). *Diagnostic and statistical manual of mental disorders.* (4th text rev. ed.). Washington, DC: American Psychiatric Publishing.

Bateman, B. D., & Linden, M. A. (1998). *Better IEPs: How to develop legally correct and educationally useful programs* (3rd ed.). Longmont, CO: Sopris West.

Bower, E. M. (1981). *Early identification of emotionally handicapped children in school* (3rd ed.). Springfield, IL: Thomas.

Bower, E. M. (1982). Defining emotional disturbance: Public policy and research. *Psychology in the Schools, 19,* 55–60.

Brigham, F. J., Tochterman, S., & Brigham, M. S. P. (2000). Students with emotional and behavioral disorders and their teachers in test-linked systems of accountability. *Assessment for Effective Intervention, 26*(1), 19–27.

Burns, B. J., & Hoagwood, K. (Eds.). (2002). *Community treatment for youth: Evidence-based interventions for severe emotional and behavioral disorders.* New York: Oxford University Press.

Campbell, S. B. (1995). Behavior problems in preschool children: A review of recent research. *Journal of Child Psychology and Psychiatry, 36,* 113–149.

Campbell, S. B., & Ewing, L. J. (1990). Follow-up of hard-to-manage preschoolers: Adjustment at age 9 and predictors of continuing symptoms. *Journal of Child Psychology and Psychiatry and Applied Disciplines, 31,* 871–889.

Colvin, G., Greenberg, S., & Sherman, R. (1993). The forgotten variable: Improving academic skills for students with serious emotional disturbance. *Effective School Practices, 12*(1), 20–25.

Conroy, M. A., Hendrickson, J. M., & Hester, P. P. (2004). *Early identification and prevention of emotional and behavioral disorders. Handbook of research in emotional and behavioral disorders* (pp. 199–215). New York: Guildford Press.

Cullinan, D. (2004). Classification and definition of emotional and behavioral disorders. In R. B. Rutherford, Jr., M. M. Quinn, & S. R. Mathur (Eds.) *Handbook of research in emotional and behavioral disorders* (pp. 32–53). New York: Guilford.

Del'Homme, M. A., Kasari, C., Forness, S. R., & Bagley, R. (1996). Prereferral intervention and children at risk for emotional or behavioral disorders. *Education and Treatment of Children*, 19, 272–285.

Eber, L., & Keenan, S. (2004). Collaboration with other agencies: Wraparound and systems of care and alternative educational placements for children and youth with EBD. In R. B. Rutherford, M. M. Quinn, & S. R. Mathur (Eds.), *Handbook of research in emotional and behavioral disorders* (pp. 502–515). New York: Guilford.

Eber, L., Nelson, C. M., & Miles, P. (1997). School-based wraparound for students with emotional and behavioral challenges. *Exceptional Children*, 63, 539–555.

Epstein, M. H., & Cullinan, D. (1998). *Scale for assessing emotional disturbance*. Austin, TX: PRO-ED.

Epstein, M. H., Cullinan, D., Ryser, G., & Pearson, N. (2002). Development of a scale to assess emotional disturbance. *Behavioral Disorders*, 28, 5–22.

Fessler, M. A., Rosenberg, M. S., & Rosenberg, L. A., (1991). Concomitant learning disabilities and learning problems among students with behavioral/emotional disorders. *Behavioral Disorders*, 16(2), 97–106.

Foley, R. M., & Epstein, M. H. (1992). Correlates of the academic achievement of adolescents with behavioral disorders. *Behavioral Disorders*, 18(1), 9–17.

Forness, S. R. (1988). Planning for the needs of children with serious emotional disturbance: The national special education and mental health coalition. *Behavioral Disorders*, 13, 127–133.

Forness, S. R. (2003). Parting reflections on education of children with emotional or behavioral disorders. *Behavioral Disorders*, 28, 198–201.

Forness, S. R., & Kavale, K. A. (1997). Defining emotional or behavioral disorders in school and related services. In J. W. Lloyd, E. J. Kame'enui, & D. Chard (Eds.), *Issues in Educating Students with Disabilities* (pp. 45–61). Mahwah, NJ, Erlbaum.

Forness, S. R., & Kavale, K. A. (2000). Emotional or behavioral disorders: Background and current status of the E/BD terminology and definition. *Behavioral Disorders*, 25, 264–269.

Forness, S. R., & Kavale, K. A. (2001). Ignoring the odds: Hazards of not adding the new medical model to special education of prevention. *Behavioral Disorders*, 26, 269–281.

Forness, S. R., Kavale, K. A., Sweeney, D. P., & Crenshaw, T. M. (1999). The future of research and practice in behavioral disorders: Psychopharmacology and its school implications. *Behavioral Disorders*, 24, 305–318.

Forness, S. R., & Knitzer, J. (1992). A new proposed definition and terminology to replace "serious emotional disturbance" in Individuals with Disabilities Education Act. *School Psychology Review*, 21, 12–20.

Furlong, M. J., Morrison, G. M., & Jimerson, S. (2004). Externalizing behaviors of aggression and violence. In R. B. Rutherford, M. N Quinn, & S. R. Mathur (Eds.). *Handbook of Research in Emotional and Behavioral Disorders* (pp. 243–261). New York: Guilford.

Gresham, F. M., & Elliot, S. N. (1990). *Social skills rating system*. Circle Pines, MN: American Guidance Service.

Gresham, F. M., & Kern, L. (2004). Internalizing behavior problems in children and adolescents. In R. B. Rutherford, M. M. Quinn, & S. R. Mathur (Eds.), *Handbook of research in emotional and behavioral disorders* (pp. 262–281). New York: Guilford.

Hallahan, D. P., & Kauffman, J. M. (1977). Categories, labels, behavioral characteristics: ED, LD, and EMR reconsidered. *Journal of Special Education*, 11, 139–149.

Hallenbeck, B. A., & Kauffman, J. M. (1995). How does observational learning affect the behavior of students with emotional or behavioral disorders? A review of research. *Journal of Special Education*, 29, 45–71.

Hutton, J. B., & Roberts, T. G. (2004). *Social-emotional dimension scale* (2nd ed.). Austin: PRO-ED.

Hyatt, K. J., & Howell, K. W. (2004). Curriculum-based measurement of students with emotional and behavioral disorders: Assessment for data-based decision making. In R. B. Rutherford, M. M. Quinn, & S. R. Mathur (Eds.), *Handbook of research in emotional and behavioral disorders* (pp. 181–198). New York: Guilford.

Individuals with Disabilities Education Improvement Act (2004). 20 USC 1400. Public Law 108–446.

Kaiser, A. P., Cai, X., Hancock, T. B., & Foster, E. M. (2002). Teacher-reported behavior problems and language delays in boys and girls enrolled in Head Start. *Behavioral Disorders*, 28, 23–29.

Kauffman, J. M. (1986). Educating children with behavior disorders. In R. J. Morris & B. Blatt (Eds.), *Special education: Research and trends* (pp. 249–271). New York: Pergamon.

Kauffman, J. M. (1999). How we prevent the prevention of emotional and behavioral disorders. *Exceptional Children*, 65, 448–468.

Kauffman, J. M. (2005). *Characteristics of emotional and behavioral disorders of children and youth* (8th ed.). Upper Saddle River, NJ: Prentice Hall.

Kauffman, J. M., & Landrum, T. J. (2006). *Children and youth with emotional and behavioral disorders: A history of their education*. Austin, TX: PRO-ED.

Kavale, K. A., Mathur, S. R., & Mostert, M. P. (2004). Social skills training and teaching social behavior. In R. B. Rutherford, M. M. Quinn, & S. R. Mathur (Eds.). *Handbook of research in emotional and behavioral disorders* (pp. 446–461). New York: Guilford.

Kavale, K. A., & Mostert, M. P. (2003). River of ideology, islands of evidence. *Exceptionality, 11,* 191–208.

Kerr, M. M., & Nelson, C. M. (2002). *Strategies for addressing behavior problems in the classroom* (4th ed.) Upper Saddle River, NJ: Merrill/Prentice Hall.

Kessler, R. C., Berglund, P., Demler, O., Jin, R., & Walters, E. E. (2005). Lifetime prevalence and age-of-onset distributions of DSM-IV disorders in the national comorbidity survey replication. *Archives of General Psychiatry, 62,* 593–602.

Kessler, R. C., Chiu, W. T., Demler, O., & Walters, E. E. (2005). Prevalence, severity, and comorbidity of 12-month DSM-IV disorders in the national comorbidity survey replication. *Archives of General Psychiatry, 62,* 617–627.

Knitzer, J. (1982). *Unclaimed children: The failure of public responsibility to children and adolescents in need of mental health services.* Washington, DC: Children's Defense Fund.

Konopasek, D., & Forness, S. R. (2004). Research regarding the use of psychopharmacology in the treatment of emotional and behavior disorders. In R. B. Rutherford, M. M. Quinn, & S. R. Mathur (Eds.), *Handbook of research in emotional and behavioral disorders* (pp. 352–368). New York: Guilford.

Landrum, T. J. (2000). Assessment for eligibility: Issues in identifying students with emotional or behavioral disorders. *Assessment for Effective Intervention, 26*(1), 41–49.

Landrum, T. J., & Kauffman, J. M. (2006). Behavioral approaches to classroom management. In C. M. Evertson & C. S. Weinstein (Eds.), *Handbook of classroom management: Research, practice, and contemporary issues.* Mahwah, NJ: Erlbaum.

McGinnis, E., & Goldstein, A. P. (2005). *Skills-streaming: Teaching prosocial skills to the elementary-school child.* Champaign, IL: Research Press.

Merrell, K. W. (1994). *Assessment of behavioral, social, and emotional problems: Direct and objective methods for use with children and adolescents.* New York: Longman.

Morse, W. C. (1985). *The education and treatment of socioemotionally impaired children and youth.* Syracuse, NY: Syracuse University Press.

MTA Cooperative Group. (1999). A 14-month randomized clinical trial of treatment strategies for attention-deficit/hyperactivity disorder. *Archives of General Psychiatry, 56,* 1073–1086.

Nelson, C. M. (2004). Intervention and treatment research: Introduction. In R. B. Rutherford, M. M. Quinn, & S. R. Mathur (Eds.), *Handbook of research in emotional and behavioral disorders* (pp. 321–326). New York: Guilford.

Patterson, G. R., Capaldi, D., & Bank, L. (1989). An early starter model for predicting delinquency. In D. J. Pepler &

K. H. Rubin (Eds.), *The development and treatment of childhood aggression* (pp. 139–168). Hillsdale, NJ: Erlbaum.

Patterson, G. R., Reid, J. B., & Dishion, T.J. (1992). *Antisocial boys.* Eugene, OR: Castalia.

Reschly, D. J., Tilly, W. D., & Grimes, J. P. (Eds.). (1999). *Special education in transition: Functional assessment and noncategorical programming.* Longmont, CO: Sopris West.

Reynolds, C. R., & Kamphaus, R. W. (1992). *Behavioral assessment system for children.* Circle Pines, MN: American Guidance Service.

Rhode, G., Jenson, W. R., & Reavis, H. K. (1992). *The tough kid book: Practical classroom management strategies.* Longmont, CA: Sopris West.

Rogers-Adkinson, D., & Griffith, P. (Eds.). (1999). *Communication disorders and children with psychiatric and behavioral disorders.* San Diego: Singular.

Salvia, J., & Ysseldyke, J. E. (1991). *Assessment in special and remedial education* (5th ed.). Boston: Houghton Mifflin.

Serna, L., Nielson, E., Lambros, K., & Forness, S. (2002). Primary prevention with children at risk for emotional or behavioral disorders: Data on a universal intervention for Head Start classrooms. *Behavioral Disorders, 26,* 70–84.

Smith, B. J., & Fox, L. (2003). *Systems of service delivery: A synthesis of evidence relevant to young children at risk of or who have challenging behavior.* Denver, CO: Center for Evidence-based Practice: Young Children with Challenging Behaviors.

Smith, C. R., Wood, F. H., & Grimes, J. (1988). Issues in the identification and placement of behaviorally disordered students. In M. C. Wang, M. C. Reynolds, & H. J. Walberg (Eds.), *Handbook of special education: Research and practice* (Vol. 2, pp. 95–124). New York: Pergamon.

Stoiber, K. C., & Kratochwill, T. R. (2001). *Outcomes PME: Planning, monitoring, and evaluating.* San Antonio, TX: Psychological Corporation.

Tankersley, M., & Landrum, T. L. (1997). Comorbidity of emotional and behavioral disorders. In J. W Lloyd, E. J. Kame'enui, & D. Chard (Eds.), *Issues in educating students with disabilities* (pp. 153–173). Mahwah, NJ,: Erlbaum.

Taylor, R. L. (1997). *Assessment of exceptional students: Educational and psychological procedures* (4th ed.). Boston: Allyn & Bacon.

Turnbull, A., Turnbull, R., Shank, M., & Leal, D. (1999). *Exceptional lives: Special education in today's schools* (2nd ed.). Upper Saddle River, NJ: Merrill/Prentice Hall.

U.S. Department of Health and Human Services (2001). *Report of the Surgeon General's conference on children's mental health: A national action agenda.* Washington, DC: Author.

University of Kentucky, Behavior home page. http://www.state.ky.us/agencies/behave/hhomepage.html. Retrieved September 11, 2006.

Walker, H. M., & Bullis, M. (1991). Behavior disorders and the social context of regular class integration: A conceptual dilemma? In J. K. Lloyd, N. N. Singh, & A. C. Repp (Eds.), *The regular education initiative: Alternative perspectives on concepts, issues, and models* (pp. 75–93). Sycamore, IL: Sycamore.

Walker, H. M., McConnell, C., Holmes, D., Todis, B., Walker, J., & Golden, N. (1983). *The Walker social skills curriculum: The ACCEPTS program.* Austin, TX: PRO-ED.

Walker, H. M., Ramsey, E., & Gresham, F. M. (2004). *Antisocial behavior in school: Strategies and best practices* (2nd ed.). Pacific Grove, CA: Brooks/Cole.

Walker, H. M., & Severson, H. H. (1990). *Systematic Screening for Behavior Disorders (SSBD): A multiple gating procedure.* Longmont, CO: Sopris West.

Walker, H. M., Severson, H. H., & Feil, E. G. (1994). *The Early Screening Project: A proven child-find process.* Longmont, CO: Sopris West.

Wang, P. S., Berglund, P., Olfson, M., Pincus, H. A., Wells, K. B., & Kessler, R. C. (2005). Failure and delay in initial treatment contact after first onset of mental disorders in the national comorbidity survey replication. *Archives of General Psychiatry, 62,* 603–613.

Webster-Stratton, C. (1997). Early intervention for families of preschool children with conduct problems. In M. J. Gurlanick (Ed.), *The effectiveness of early intervention* (pp. 429–454). Baltimore: Brookes.

Webster-Stratton, C. (2000). Oppositional-defiant and conduct-disordered children. In M. Hersen & R. T. Ammerman (Eds.), *Advanced abnormal child psychology* (2nd ed., pp. 387–412). Mahwah, NJ: Erlbaum.

Yell, M. L. (1998). *The law and special education.* Upper Saddle River, NJ: Merrill/Prentice Hall.

Characteristics of Students with Mild Mental Retardation

URBAN LEGEND: *Individuals with mental retardation will never be contributing members of society.*

LEGENDARY THOUGHT: *With accurate identification, intervention, and the appropriate services and supports, individuals with mental retardation have the opportunity to become contributing members of society.*

◆

Mental retardation, regardless of its degree of severity, can have a devastating effect on a child's development. Although there are many causes of mental retardation, children who have mental retardation experience deficits not only in thinking but in most other areas of development as well. Besides cognition (thinking), mental retardation may affect communication and social abilities. So what is meant by *mild* mental retardation? Is any mental retardation really *mild*? What are the causes? How do we ameliorate the effects of mental retardation to help individuals become contributing members of society? Is **mild mental retardation** (MMR) preventable? Is it curable? Although we know a great deal about MMR, including its causes and characteristics, many questions remain to be answered. In Chapter 3, we provided an initial overview of students with mild mental retardation (MMR). In this chapter, we further examine the characteristics of students with MMR. We also explore strategies for identifying students with MMR and discuss their unique learning needs. Our goal is to provide a better awareness of the characteristics and needs of children and young people with MMR.

∷ CHARACTERISTICS AND IDENTIFICATION OF STUDENTS WITH MILD MENTAL RETARDATION (MMR)

The terms *retarded* or *retard* are used in a derogatory way to describe behaviors that connote a substandard or atypical level of functioning. For example, many of us have heard a child say, "Hey retard," to a peer who has made a mistake or done something embarrassing. Although sometimes said jokingly, when the term *retard* is used to describe an individual's mistake or embarrassing behavior, this helps to develop and sustain the notion that individuals with mental retardation are dumb, stupid, or incapable. Using the term *retarded* in a disparaging way fosters the belief that individuals with mental retardation are incapable of ever learning or becoming contributing members of society. True, by definition those with mental retardation have cognitive abilities significantly lower than average for the general population. However, individuals with all levels of mental retardation have many capabilities. Individuals with *mild* mental retardation have a greater capacity to develop independent abilities than those with more severe deficits. The challenge for teachers, parents, and advocates is to help individuals in our society understand the strengths and assets of individuals with MR, changing our views of the term **mental retardation** from a deprecating perspective to a compassionate and accepting perspective. This is the first step to helping them develop the skills

Vocational training for persons with mental retardation should begin in early adolescence to facilitate successful independence in adulthood. (Photo credit: Anthony Magnacca/Merrill)

needed to function in our society. And changing one's view of mental retardation need not be humorless, as the movie *The Ringer* featuring the Special Olympics illustrates (see http://www2.foxsearchlight.com/theringer [Accessed Sept. 14, 2006]).

A few parents know long before the professionals tell them that their child has mental retardation. However, if their child has mild mental retardation, most parents do not know this until they hear it from psychologists and teachers who have worked with their child. Learning, whether through observation or the work of others, that your child has mental retardation is not easy. Learning that your child has mental retardation is a disappointment and a great cause of concern, as many others have noted. Parents may with good reason find that acceptance of their child's mental retardation is easier to accept *if* effective special education and related services are provided (Kauffman, Mostert, Trent, & Pullen, 2006; Pullen, 2005). Parents may also find parent support groups helpful in dealing with their disappointment and concern for the future.

The term *mental retardation* has a long history and is used today to describe individuals who demonstrate deficits in intelligence and adaptive behavior occurring during the developmental period. However, the term **mild mental retardation** (MMR) is a more specific term with defining characteristics and represents the majority of the children and young people who have mental retardation. Consider the following illustration.

Emma

Emma was born with a *congenital disorder—microcephally* (unusually small head and brain). By 1 year of age, Emma's parents knew that her development was delayed. She was barely sitting up by herself and showed no indication of walking or talking. After a number of medical tests, they received the diagnosis of microcephally. Since microcephally is associated with mental retardation, Emma's parents knew that their child would always encounter cognitive and adaptive behavior deficits. As Emma progressed, her cognitive, language and communication, adaptive behavior, and motor skills continued to lag behind her peers'. Intelligence tests estimated her IQ to be below 50. At age 12, Emma's ability level resembles that of a preschooler. Although she is able to walk, her cognitive and communication skills are significantly delayed. She is beginning to learn basic concepts and has a receptive and expressive vocabulary of approximately 50 words. In addition, she still needs assistance taking care of basic needs, such as toileting and dressing. Emma receives many different types of special education services, including intensive, individualized instruction in functional academics and prevocational skills. In addition, she receives speech and language therapy services to help with her language and communication abilities. Emma also receives physical and occupational therapy skills to help her develop her fine and gross motor skills. It is obvious that Emma has mental retardation, most likely in the severe range. Her ability levels are significantly below her same age peers, with severe delays in the areas of cognition and adaptive behaviors.

Shemika

Shemika is a seventh-grade student who is receiving special education services under the category of mild mental retardation. Academically, she is a beginning reader, reading on a second-grade level. Her math abilities and other academic areas are comparable. Shemika has some difficulty forming friendships and socializing with her peers at school; they often make fun of her being "slow." Shemika was first diagnosed with mild mental retardation on entering first grade. Although she entered kindergarten with developmental delays, these delays did not become apparent until she received academic instruction in reading, writing, and mathematics. At that time, her teacher became concerned with her lack of progress and referred her to the **Child Study Team** at the school (see Chapter 11). Shemika demonstrates difficulty across most areas of development (i.e., academics, language, social skills), but also displays many learning strengths. For example, she is completely independent in self-help skills. Additionally, although Shemika has difficulty establishing peer-related friendships, at home, she is well accepted by her family and the other children in her neighborhood. Mainly, Shemika's needs are most obvious when she is at school.

As you can see from the examples of Emma and Shemika, mental retardation is a disability along a continuum, from severe to mild. Children and youth who demonstrate characteristics in the severe range of mental retardation demonstrate more obvious learning and behavioral characteristics, whereas the characteristics of those in the mild range of mental retardation are less obvious at first, becoming more apparent when they enter school. Both Emma and Shemika have mental retardation, but they are at different points on the continuum of cognitive ability. Therefore, the characteristics they display have similarities and differences. They are similar in that they both have cognitive and adaptive behavior delays, but they are also different—Shemika demonstrates a number of strengths that will likely enable her to be more independent than Emma.

Unlike some other disabilities, such as **emotional and behavioral disorders** (EBD) or **learning disabilities** (LD), mental retardation may be easier to identify, because, over the years, established criteria have been developed to define the disability. Along with the defining criteria, standardized tests are available for use to assist in the identification of individuals with mental retardation. These standardized tests yield cutoff scores, helping to indicate a person's level of mental retardation—mild, moderate, severe, or profound. In the next section, we discuss the evolution of the definition of MR, outlining the current standardized criteria for identification.

Defining Mild Mental Retardation (MMR)

Terminology and Characteristics

Similar to other disabilities, professionals and advocacy organizations have debated various definitions of the term *mental retardation*. Several definitions have been most prevalent: the American Association on Mental Retardation (AAMR) 1992 definition, the Diagnostic and Statistical Manual (DSM) definition of the American Psychiatric Association (2000), and the American Psychological Association (APA) 1996 definition. Of these, the **American Association on Intellectual and Developmental Disabilities** (formerly known as the American Association on Mental Retardation, [AAMR]) has played a leading role in the United States not only in defining mental retardation, but also suggesting intervention and prevention strategies for ameliorating the effects of this disability. The definition developed by the AAMR in the early 1970s served as a guideline for the classification criteria outlined in the **Individuals with Disabilities Education Act** (IDEA) for identifying students with mental retardation. This definition required that individuals diagnosed with mental retardation meet the following criteria:

1. Subaverage intellectual functioning,
2. Deficits in adaptive behavior resulting from intellectual functioning, and
3. Manifestation of intellectual and adaptive behavior deficits during the developmental period (Grossman, 1983).

IDEA adapted this definition and added a fourth component—to be classified as having mental retardation under IDEA, a student's educational performance must be adversely affected. In its 1982 definition, the AAMR classified subaverage intellectual functioning into the following four levels based on standardized scores on an intelligence test:

1. Mild mental retardation (IQ = 70/75–50/55)
2. Moderate mental retardation (IQ = 50/55–40/35)
3. Severe mental retardation (IQ = 40/35–25/20)
4. Profound mental retardation (IQ = below 25/20) (Grossman, 1983).

According to this definition, an individual must score at least two or more standard deviations below the mean (average) on an intelligence test to be considered to have significant subaverage intelligence, indicating mental retardation. However, in addition to subaverage intelligence, a deficit in adaptive behavior, as evaluated by a standardized test, must also be present. Although a major part of the diagnosis of mental retardation is often based on a deficit in intelligence, evaluation of an individual's adaptive behavior skills is an essential part of defining and identifying persons with mental retardation. Evaluation of adaptive behavior skills is important to determine if and how the person's intellectual disabilities limit the individual's abilities to engage in age and culturally-relevant social, learning, and independent abilities.

Following the adoption and inclusion of the AAMR definition within IDEA, many states developed classifications that separated students into three service delivery categories: **educable mentally retarded** (EMR), **trainable mentally retarded** (TMR), or **severely/profoundly mentally retarded** (SMR or PMR). Students categorized as EMR would most likely be comparable with students identified as having mild mental retardation, with an IQ between 50 or 55 and 70 or 75. Students categorized as TMR would most likely represent those individuals identified as having moderate mental retardation, with an IQ between 35 or 40 and 50 or 55. Students with an IQ below 35 or 40 would be considered to have severe or profound mental retardation. Although these terms are archaic, they continue to be used in many school districts and clinical settings today. To lessen the effects of labeling, other states and school districts use cross-categorical labels, such as mild disabilities, moderate disabilities, severe disabilities, and profound disabilities.

Current Definitions and Trends

The AAMR's 1982 definition of mental retardation served a guiding role in developing a definition and criteria for identification of children and young people with mental retardation in our schools; however, this definition is becoming outdated as societal views of mental retardation are progressing. Once seen as a deficit solely within the individual, an emerging view is that mental retardation is influenced by the environment.

The AAMR's definition was updated in the early 1990s to reflect a more progressive view of mental retardation. Rather than considering mental retardation a permanent condition that endures over time, the revised definition views mental retardation as a term describing a person's present level of functioning and the services and supports needed to help him or her progress. Specifically, mental retardation is defined as

> substantial limitations in present functioning . . . characterized by significantly subaverage intellectual functioning, existing concurrently with related limitations in two or more adaptive skills areas: communication, self-care, home living, social skills, community use, self-direction, health and safety, functional academics, leisure, and work. Mental retardation manifests itself before age 18. (AAMR Ad Hoc Committee on Terminology and Classification, 1992, p. 5)

The current AAMR definition is conceptualized with the following assumptions or beliefs:

1. The individual's present functioning level must be examined in relation to the cultural context in which the person lives, including community settings with peers;
2. The individual's communication, sensory, motor, and behavioral abilities must be evaluated using valid assessments that are culturally and linguistically sensitive;
3. The individual's strengths and needs must be identified;

4. The individual's needs are examined in relation to specific supports that can help address those needs;
5. The individual with mental retardation will progress over time when provided with these individualized supports (AAMR, 2002; Luckasson et al., 2002).

A major change between AAMR's 1982 definition and the 2002 definition is the emphasis on classification according to *levels of supports* as opposed to identifying an individual with mental retardation based on the results of an intelligence test. Individuals with severe mental retardation will need life-long support to help them function within all aspects of society, including school and community settings. With this more recent definition, the AAMR outlines four levels of supports: (a) intermittent (i.e., episodic need); (b) limited (i.e., needed for specific periods of time); (c) extensive (i.e., needed for an extended period of time); and (d) pervasive (i.e., lifelong, intensive needs) (for a thorough description of these levels, see Table 6.1 and AAMR, 2002). Typically, children and young people with mild mental retardation need intermittent to limited supports, whereas individuals with moderate to severe and profound mental retardation require extensive and pervasive supports. *Intermittent supports* are services provided either short-term or from time to time during various life transitions (e.g., transitioning from school to employment and independent living). *Limited supports* are services provided consistently over time, but that are not

TABLE 6.1	Intensities of supports for individuals with mental retardation
Intermittent	Supports are provided on an as-needed basis Characteristics of supports: Episodic Short-term during life span transitions Intermittent (high or low intensity)
Limited	Supports are provided on a consistent basis Characteristics of supports: Time limited, but not intermittent Requires fewer staff Costs less than more intensive supports
Extensive	Supports are provided on a regular basis Characteristics of supports: Provided in one or more environments Not time limited
Pervasive	Supports are high intensity and provided on a continual basis Characteristics of Supports: Provided across most environments Involve many staff members Are needed for survival May be intrusive

Adapted from American Association on Mental Retardation (AAMR). (1992). *Mental retardation: Definition, classification, and systems of support* (9th ed., p. 26). Washington, DC: Author. Reprinted with permission.

intensive. For example, job coaching or assistance to maintain a checking account would be considered limited supports. Occasionally, some individuals with MMR may even need extensive supports, which are considered long-term supports provided on a regular basis (e.g., daily assistance in personal care or a job). Again, the emphasis is on classification according to the level of support needed to progress and not on intellectual functioning (Luckasson & Reeve, 2001).

The provision of supports often occurs along a continuum, depending on the situation and environment. For example, an individual with MMR may be able to function independently at a job, but may need the support of parents or family members to live in the community. Therefore, the level and type of supports needed should be considered across contexts and situations. Recently developed, the *Supports Intensity Scale* (Thompson et al., 2002) is an assessment tool that can assist in planning and designing meaningful supports for persons with mild mental retardation (AAMR, 2004). The SIS measures the necessary types of supports across various daily living activities and medical areas with a focus on the types of supports needed to increase the individual's independence.

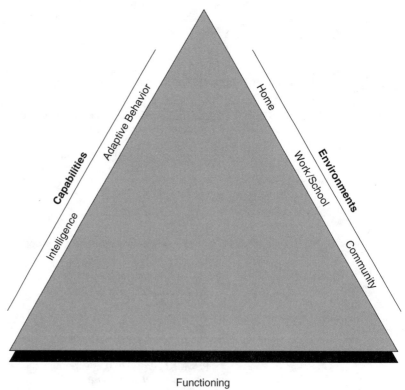

FIGURE 6.1

Structural definition of mental retardation

Source: Adapted from American Association on Mental Retardation (AAMR). (1992). *Mental retardation: Definition, classification, and systems of support* (p. 10). Washington, DC: Author. Reprinted with permission.

The level and type(s) of supports needed by an individual are determined by a **multidisciplinary team.** The AAMR (1992) illustrated this conceptualization of mental retardation and the identification of necessary levels of support based on the person's environment in Figure 6.1. In Figure 6.1, mental retardation is viewed as an interactive trait that is influenced by a person's different environments and demands of those environments, which are constantly changing. Therefore, the types of supports that a person with MR needs are always changing. Currently, the AAMR's level of support definitional system for identifying and classifying individuals with mental retardation is not as widely used as the previous identification system based on IQ scores (Conyers, Martin, Martin, & Yu, 2002).

The increasing emphasis on adaptive behavior and levels of supports, rather than reliance primarily on an IQ score, stems from a report developed by the **President's Committee on Mental Retardation** (1970) called *The Six-Hour Retarded Child*. This report suggested that a number of students from low socioeconomic and cultural and ethnic backgrounds were more likely to be diagnosed with mental retardation than students not from underrepresented groups. The committee members and report called for a refocusing of the criteria used to diagnosis mental retardation, away from primarily using IQ test scores, with an emphasis on *how* the student functions in a variety of environments, such as home and school.

Federal Definition of MMR

Although, the AAMR reconceptualized mental retardation, this conceptualization has had little impact on the current systems used to serve students with mental retardation in our schools (Conyers et al., 2002; Heward, 2003). The Individuals with Disabilities Education Improvement Act (IDEA, 2004) defines mental retardation as:

> significantly subaverage general intellectual functioning, existing concurrently with deficits in adaptive behavior and manifested during the developmental period, that adversely affects a child's educational performance. [34 Code of Federal Regulations §300.7(c)(6)]

Most states are continuing to use the categorical classifications based on intellectual functioning (i.e., mild, moderate, severe or profound mental retardation) or noncategorical classification based on levels of functioning (i.e., mild disabilities, moderate disabilities, or severe disabilities), rather than changing state guidelines to align with the AAMR definition (Denning, Chamberlain, & Polloway, 2000). Prior to making significant changes in the federal guidelines, the implications of the AAMR's definition need further consideration and evaluation, according to Smith (1994).

Since the majority of the students identified with mental retardation are classified in the mild range under federal and state guidelines, they are individuals who would score between 50 or 55 and 70 or 75 on a standardized IQ test and who demonstrate adaptive behavior deficits, with both these characteristics identified prior to age 18. So, how do we identify these children and young people? How do we distinguish them from students with learning disabilities or emotional or behavioral disorders? Do we overidentify or underidentify students with MMR?

Identification of Students with MMR

Identification of students with MMR for educational services entails using clear criteria and guidelines; however, obtaining a **nondiscriminatory evaluation** to assist in diagnosing an individual with MMR requires careful consideration of the evaluation tools and assessment methods used to obtain standardized scores. Both the student's intelligence and adaptive behaviors should be evaluated through the use of standardized measures. In addition, other sources, such as parent and teacher observations reporting how the student functions, should be considered. Finally, the results of all aspects of the evaluation process should be reviewed in relation to the student's environmental and cultural contexts by members of the multidisciplinary team prior to making a diagnosis. Typically, if mental retardation is suspected and the student demonstrates cognitive delays, the initial step is to administer an intelligence test to establish an IQ.

Intelligence Testing (IQ)

Intelligence testing is one of the first steps in the evaluation process of identifying a student with mild mental retardation. IQ tests are standardized tests designed to measure a person's intelligence in comparison to same-age peers. Theoretically, IQ scores are distributed along a normal curve with a 100 being an average IQ score. By definition, students with mild mental retardation would fall between two to three standard deviations below the mean, with estimated IQs between 50 and 70, depending on the standardized test used. Two of the most commonly used IQ tests are the *Wechsler Intelligence Scale for Children—Third Edition* (WISC-III) (Wechsler, 1991) and the *Stanford-Binet IV* (Thorndike, Hagen, & Sattler, 1986). Although an IQ test must be administered by a **licensed psychologist** to be valid, the test score should be considered by the entire multidisciplinary team and accompanied by additional information or test scores to verify the outcome (AAMR Ad Hoc Committee, 1992). IQ tests provide a reliable means for identifying a student's overall performance deficit and are a valid predictor of success in school (Heward, 2003). However, although IQ tests can be a valid predictor of a student's intellectual ability, they also have limitations. Heward (2003) suggested that IQ tests are lacking because they: (a) only measure how a child performs on a single test at a single point in time and the results can be influenced by a number of variables including administrator bias, location and time of the assessment, and a student's motivation and health-related issues, (b) may have cultural bias, (c) may produce different outcomes over time, and (d) provide limited information for designing interventions. These restrictions are especially applicable when using IQ tests to identify children and young people within the mild range of mental retardation. Since a number of factors can influence the outcomes of IQ tests, professionals involved in the diagnosis of MMR must be particularly cautious and should use additional assessment instruments to verify the outcomes.

Adaptive Behavior Testing

In addition to an IQ test, a nonbiased assessment of a student's **adaptive behavior** should be conducted when considering a diagnosis of mild mental retardation. Areas of adaptive behavior included in the assessment are: (a) conceptual (i.e., receptive and expressive language, ability to read and write, money concepts, self-direction), (b) interpersonal skills, responsibility, naïveté, gullibility, victimization, and following rules and (c) practical skills (e.g., self-care skills, daily living activities, maintaining a safe environment, occupational/employment skills) (AAMR, 2002). Assessing an individual's adaptive behavior goes far beyond obtaining test results to identify the student for eligibility under the category of mild mental retardation. In fact, a comprehensive assessment of adaptive behavior skills should provide information about the types of supports the student will need to develop independence (Rush & Francis, 2000; Schalock, 1999).

Several standardized adaptive behavior scales are commonly used when identifying children and youth with MMR, including the *Vineland Adaptive Behavior Scales* (Sparrow, Balla, & Cicchetti, 1984, 1985) and the *AAMR Adaptive Behavior Scale-School* (ABS-S) (Lambert, Nihira, & Leland, 1993). To be considered for a diagnosis of MMR, a person must score at least two standard deviations below the average (mean) for the general population. Generally, adaptive behavior scales are structured interviews that are completed by a parent, caregiver, or teacher who knows the person well. They allow the multidisciplinary team to determine whether the student needs assistance, the student's need for self-care and interactions in the community, and what type of help is needed.

Similar to the identification of **learning disabilities** (LD) and **emotional or behavioral disorders** (EBD), the identification of mild mental retardation should be based on nonbiased assessments and information about the student for the purpose of making an eligibility decision and developing an intervention plan (Salvia & Ysseldyke, 2001). However, as with all diagnoses, one must make certain that the information through the assessment process is valid and reliable. Depending on the tools used in the assessment process, an individual's score may vary considerably, thus influencing a diagnosis of MMR that is based on IQ. For example, if an IQ of 70 is used as the cutoff score for mild mental retardation, the specific norms and assessment instruments used are particularly important (Raymond, 2000). The AAMR (1992) definitions allow for flexibility on the upper limit of the IQ, with the suggestion of using a score between 70 and 75, depending on the instrument and standard deviation. In addition, Wodrich and Barry (1991) note that psychologists assessing culturally, linguistically, or economically diverse students, may apply alternative norms to decrease biases. Although both a deficit in IQ and adaptive behavior should be noted according to federal guidelines, unfortunately some states do not adhere to these criteria (Utley, Lowitzer, & Baumeister, 1987), resulting in a much more subjective diagnosis of MMR.

AAMR's Diagnostic, Classification, and Systems of Support Process

AAMR suggests a three-step process for determining eligibility, classification, and intervention supports for a person with mental retardation. The first step is diagnosing whether an individual has mental retardation—that is, to determine whether he or she is eligible for services under the category of mental retardation. As stated earlier, a diagnosis of mental retardation can be made if the student meets three criteria: (a) intellectual functioning—approximately 70 to 75 IQ or below; (b) significant deficit in at least two adaptive skills areas; and (c) age of onset prior to age 18. The second step in the process is identifying the person's strengths, needs, and crucial supports, that is; identifying, the person's intellectual and adaptive behavior strengths and needs. In addition, the presumed causes of the person's mental retardation and health-related conditions are described. Finally, the person's current environments are identified and future environments are targeted that will facilitate development and advancement. This third step focuses on the identification of needed supports according to the following four dimensions:

1. Intellectual abilities and adaptive behavior skills,
2. Psychological/emotional characteristics,
3. Physical health/etiology factors, and
4. Environmental aspects (AAMR, 1992).

Once these supports are identified, the multidisciplinary team intervention planning and implementation of intervention can begin.

Changing Characteristics and Identification of MMR Across Age Levels

The characteristics of persons with MMR are different from those of people with other degrees of mental retardation. However, they are similar to all levels of mental retardation, in that the characteristics and identification process change across different age levels. Overall, individuals who have MMR are not as likely to have an identifiable cause for their intellectual and adaptive behavior deficits as are persons with more severe retardation. Rather, their learning capabilities (as demonstrated by an overall IQ level) lag behind those of other people who are functioning within what is considered the normal range. Students with MMR often demonstrate cognitive deficits in memory, attention, and language development that may not be obvious until they enter school. As they progress through school, their delays often become more and more apparent because their same age peers progress at a faster rate. Although many of these individuals will live independently after school, all of them will need lifelong support. In the following sections, we will examine the characteristics and identification of MMR across various age ranges.

Early Childhood

As discussed in Chapter 3, various types of genetic anomalies and toxins can cause mental retardation, resulting in characteristics that become apparent and easily diagnosed during early childhood. However, many professionals are reluctant to diagnose a young child with mental retardation until later—providing an opportunity for the child to catch up with age peers. In fact, most young children with mental retardation do not actually receive an educational diagnosis of mental retardation (under IDEA) until after their ninth birthday. In order to avoid labeling these children with a MR classification, federal laws adopted the term *developmental delay* to be used with young children (nine years and under) who demonstrate delays in various developmental domains including cognition, communication, social, motor, and self-help skills. As a result, most young children who experience intellectual and adaptive behavior deficits are more often initially diagnosed as having a developmental delay rather than having mental retardation. **Early interventionists** agree that the term *developmental delay* is a more accurate way of characterizing and identifying young children who may have mild mental retardation due to instability in their intellectual traits and learning. Consider the case of Mia.

Mia

Mia was born with no observable deficits or delays. Her mother had a normal delivery, and the family was grateful for a healthy child. However, within the first few years, Mia's parents began to notice several things that concerned them about Mia's development. First, she wasn't as active as her older brother had been, and her skills were not developing as rapidly. He walked at 10 months; Mia didn't begin walking until 13 months. He was very talkative by age 15 months; Mia, on the other hand, was quiet. Although she had begun to talk, her vocabulary was not very extensive, and she didn't initiate conversations frequently.

At her second year checkup, Mia's parents discussed their concerns with her pediatrician. The pediatrician had been monitoring Mia's development and felt that, although she was not as advanced as some children of the same age, her development was at the low end of the normal range. The pediatrician suggested that the parents relax, but continue to monitor Mia's development.

Over the next year, Mia's parents became even more concerned. Her language skills continued to be a little slow, and she wasn't catching on to many of the concepts that her older brother had known at the same age. Right before Mia's third birthday, her parents contacted her pediatrician and expressed their concerns again. They were referred to the local **Child Find** office for a developmental screening. The **Child Find Specialist** administered a **developmental screening.** After failing the screening, Mia was referred to the early childhood **transdisciplinary team** for a comprehensive **developmental evaluation.**

Following the evaluation, the team met with Mia's parents and discussed the results. Mia showed mild delays across all areas of development including cognition, language, social skills, and self-help skills. Her motor skills were mildly delayed as well, but she scored a little bit higher on motor skills than she did in the other areas of development. At this meeting, Mia received a diagnosis of *developmentally delayed* and was found eligible for special education services under IDEA.

As one would imagine, Mia's parents were devastated, wondering why their child had delays. Later on, genetic and neurological testing was conducted, but none of the tests revealed any anomalies. However, it was clear from the developmental evaluation that Mia needed **early intervention services** to help support her development. The transdisciplinary team and the Child Find Specialist helped connect Mia's parents with the local school district, and Mia began attending an **inclusive early childhood program** at the neighborhood school her brother attended. Prior to this experience, Mia's parents didn't even know the program existed. Fortunately for them and Mia, the program had been in existence for over 10 years, serving a number of young children with special needs.

Early identification and intervention for young children with mild mental retardation can help to provide a "head start" for these children, ameliorating and possibly preventing further delays. Research suggests that if young children receive appropriate intervention early on, the effects of their disability are likely to be less severe (Reynolds, Temple, Robertson, & Mann, 2001). However, as with other types of mild disabilities, identification of young children can often be problematic, since the severity of their symptoms may not be as apparent in the early years as later. A child's **development milestones** evolve across a range of ages. As in the case of Mia, a child with mild mental retardation may only demonstrate subtle signs for several years, making identification during early childhood difficult.

Because children engage in rapid developmental changes during early childhood and traits such as intelligence at a young age may not be stable, determining whether the young child's development is impaired can be problematic. However, several early warning signs may help to alert parents and professionals. For example, young children with mental retardation may demonstrate delays in **mastery motivation** and **task persistence** as they encounter learning tasks. In addition, they may demonstrate difficulty grasping abstract concepts as their language develops and have problems regulating their behavior (Sternberg & Spear, 1985). As discussed earlier, these children will most likely demonstrate language delays.

As discussed in Chapter 2, labeling a child as mentally retarded has a number of significant implications; therefore, professionals are less likely to apply this label without feeling that their assessment and diagnosis is a valid indicator of that child's current and future potential for development. Children with MMR are more often identified when they enter school and their learning deficits become more apparent.

Although early identification of children with MMR may be difficult, the provision of **free appropriate public education** (FAPE) at a young age should occur. As discussed earlier, warning signs may not always be as clear at a young age, but several screening and assessment tools exist that can help identify a young child with mild mental retardation. For example, the *Bayley Scales of Infant and Toddler Development— Third Edition* (Bayley–III) (Bayley, 2005) can measure IQ for infants and toddlers. In addition, the *Vineland Adaptive Behavior Scale—Second Edition* (Vineland–II) (Sparrow, Balla, & Cicchetti, 1984) has an expanded interview version that can assess a child's adaptive behavior from birth.

Professionals should use caution when diagnosing a young child with mental retardation, but valid instruments exist that can help with a diagnosis if needed. Comprehensive screening programs, such as Child Find, assist in the identification of young children with developmental delays that may indicate mental retardation. However, special educators and other professionals (e.g., school psychologists) need to be more vigilant about teaching parents the early warning signs, so that identification and services can occur as early as possible. Targeting young children who have mental retardation at an early age may help to lessen the effects of this disability. Systematic screening, identification, and early intervention will help these children develop the learning skills they need entering school.

Elementary Age

Although our goal is to identify all children with mental retardation at an early age, sometimes the characteristics of children with MMR are not obvious until children enter school and their academic skill levels are challenged. For instance, some young children may show early signs of MMR by the early onset of mild language and cognitive delays; however, these delays do not become significant until they are enrolled in school and the academic demands and gaps between these children and their peers are clearer. Students with MMR present a different profile than students with EBD or LD. Students with MMR typically have global delays across areas of development related to IQ (e.g., reading, math) and adaptive behaviors (e.g., social and communication skills). Consider the following account.

Patrick

It is the end of the school year at Sullivan Elementary School and Patrick, who has repeated kindergarten, is still demonstrating serious developmental delays. After repeating kindergarten once, Patrick's teacher reported that he continued to lag significantly behind the rest of the children in the class, and now the gap between Patrick's skill level and the other children in the class is becoming more and more apparent.

Patrick is a quiet boy who just seems lost at times. He can identify all the letters of the alphabet and knows the numbers, but is having trouble with beginning reading and basic math skills. In addition, the teacher has noticed that he has difficulty problem-solving, and his attention span is shorter than one would expect for a first-grader. The teacher also notices that Patrick's language and social skills are immature. His vocabulary is below his peers. He also doesn't have many friends and usually plays by himself. On the playground, he often acts more like a preschooler. In response to his immaturity, some of the other children are starting to take on a "helping role" with Patrick.

Concerns about Patrick's development were discussed with his mom after his first year in kindergarten. At that time, the teacher thought that another year in kindergarten might help him to acquire some of the skills needed to be successful in first grade. Unfortunately, after another year in kindergarten, Patrick's skills deficits did not improve, but only became clearer. When his kindergarten teacher discussed Patrick's lack of progress with the Child Study Team, the team expressed concern. As a result, Patrick's teacher, mother, and the Child Study Team decided that Patrick should have further testing to help identify his learning needs and services to help address those needs.

The **school psychologist** on the Child Study Team conducted a comprehensive evaluation of Patrick's abilities. First, the school psychologist met with Patrick's mother to obtain a **developmental history.** The WISC-III (Wechsler, 1991), an IQ test, and the *Wide Range Acheivement Test–4 (WRAT 4;* Glutting & Wilkinson, 2005), an **academic achievement test,** were both administered. The *AAMR Adaptive Behavior Scale-School* (ABS-S) (Lambert, Nihira, & Leland, 1993) was conducted as well. In addition, the school psychologist observed Patrick in his classroom and met with his classroom teacher to obtain additional information about Patrick's functioning in the classroom. Also, a speech-language pathologist evaluated Patrick's communication abilities.

The evaluations indicated no known biological or environmental cause of Patrick's delays. However, Patrick's IQ was 65. His adaptive behavior was 62, and his overall achievement score was 63. He also demonstrated a mild global delay in language with isolated **articulation** deficits. Basically, the results of Patrick's educational diagnostic testing made him eligible under the categories of mild mental retardation and speech-language delays according to the school district's criteria.

The Child Study Team, along with Patrick's mother, developed an **individual educational plan** (IEP) to help provide him with the supports needed to be successful in school. The team decided that Patrick should be promoted to first grade. However, the team also decided that he should be given additional instructional support from a special education teacher in reading, math, and handwriting. To receive this support, Patrick would attend **a special education resource room** for 2 hours per day. In addition, he received articulation therapy twice a week for 30 minutes from a speech-language pathologist. The remainder of the time, Patrick would remain in the first grade classroom. However, while in the first grade classroom, the special education teacher agreed to conduct a weekly **social skills training** program to encourage friendships between Patrick and his peers.

Due to his disability, Patrick will always face challenges. However, with these continued supports provided at an early age, Patrick will have the opportunity to learn the basic academic and vocational skills needed to become an independent and contributing member of society.

Unfortunately, not all elementary school-aged children with MMR are diagnosed as early as Patrick. With the appropriate services needed to succeed in school, Patrick is receiving a solid beginning designed to help him develop critical skills leading to independence. Early diagnosis in elementary school may be difficult, because many of these children do not present obvious problems to the classroom teacher, and identification of their special learning needs may not become apparent until later in elementary school. In addition, because in about 75% of cases of MMR there is no identifiable biological cause, the assumption is that the environment may play a substantial and contributing role in their disability (Zigler & Hodapp, 1986). For example, if children's basic needs are not met, such as adequate stimulation, health care, nutrition, and so forth, this may contribute to delays in development. Consider the effects on development for a child who lacks the nutrition needed for adequate development growth at an early age. Similarly, consider the effects on development of a child who lives in a setting lacking adequate sanitation to promote health.

Questions remain, however: Can adverse environmental factors cause MMR, and can the deficits associated with MMR be remediated through environmental changes? The answers to these questions are complex. It certainly appears that the environment plays a critical role in a child's development, and environmental changes can help to foster children's development. However, the exact contribution of the environment as compared to that of genetics in mental retardation continues to be debated. It is clear that accurate diagnosis and identification of these children's needs and the provision of appropriate support services to address those needs early in elementary school are critical for their continued success.

Adolescence

By the time a child with mild mental retardation is an adolescent, unfortunately, the signs of delayed development are clear. Adolescents with MMR typically demonstrate delays across many areas of development including **functional academic skills** (including reading, writing, and mathematics), **prevocational and vocational preparation skills,** social skills, and **independent living skills.** The emphasis at this age is on identifying the skills needed to help these children become independent when they transition into adulthood. Consider the following example.

Ricky

Ricky is 21 years old. He was diagnosed with developmental delays at age 4, but this was changed to a label of mild mental retardation at age 9. Ricky has been fortunate to receive special education services that address his learning needs, beginning in early childhood and continuing throughout his education. Because students identified as having disabilities are eligible to receive services until age 22, Ricky will be graduating from high school this year.

Ricky lives in a small rural community in Tennessee where everyone knows everyone else. Ricky's family has worked hard over the years to make sure that he has been fully included in all aspects of the community. Ricky attended his local elementary school with his two sisters and neighborhood children. Additionally, in the past, Ricky has participated in organized intramural sports and the boy scouts.

Over the past 8 years, Ricky has had several jobs. First, he volunteered at the local Humane Society, helping clean out cages and care for the animals. When he turned 16, he was hired as a dishwasher at a local restaurant. Two years ago, with the help of a job coach, Ricky began work in a boot factory on the assembly line. Although he only works part-time in the boot factory and attends school the other part of his day, Ricky is learning the vocational skills needed to be independent.

Since Ricky was 14 years old, the school staff and his family have focused heavily on teaching Ricky the skills he needs for being on his own. Prevocational and vocational skills have been heavily emphasized as well as functional academics, and personal independence skills (e.g., money skills, personal hygiene, cooking, grocery shopping, etc.). Although the school has been instrumental in helping Ricky learn the skills he needs to be independent, his parents have been extremely involved. Their goal is to help Ricky lead as full a life as possible. Therefore, they have increasingly provided him with opportunities to learn these skills and become independent. Since Ricky is graduating in a few months, they enrolled Ricky in services with the local ARC (formerly known as the **Association for Retarded Citizens**). The ARC provides a variety of services for individuals with developmental disabilities.

After graduation, Ricky will work in the factory full-time. In addition, he will move into his own apartment with several other men his age. The ARC will provide support services—a support coordinator will help Ricky and his roommates manage their money, grocery shop, prepare meals, and use public transportation to get to and from work and other community-based activities. In addition, Ricky's parents are close by and will continue to help as needed. Ricky will likely always need ongoing supports to live independently. At certain times, he may need more supports than at other times (e.g., during a medical crisis). However, given the appropriate supports, Ricky has the potential to live an active and full life–to become a contributing member of society.

Adolescence is an important time for students with MMR to learn the functional skills they will need in the future. Adolescents with MMR often need an alternative curriculum than is provided only by participating in the **general education curriculum.** Although some components of the general education curriculum are appropriate, these students will need additional emphasis on learning independent living skills and vocational skills. Targeting these skills and functional academic skills for instruction are likely to enable these adolescents to be successful as they enter adulthood.

:: UNIQUE LEARNING NEEDS AND EVIDENCE-BASED PRACTICES

What are the unique learning needs of students with MMR? What evidence-based practices exist to support these students to learn the skills needed to become independent? How can we help them learn the functional academics needed to perform daily living activities in adulthood? How can we help adolescents with MMR transition from high school into independent living and work? Children and youth with MMR have many different learning needs. To respond to these needs, a number of interventions are available. Although different intervention strategies may be warranted depending on the individual's age and ability level, these students need intervention to help them learn the basic academic and adaptive behavior skills to be successful later in life. The unique learning characteristics of these children and evidence-based practices to address these characteristics are highlighted in the remainder of this chapter.

Unique Learning Characteristics

Children and young people with mild mental retardation not only learn at a slower rate than other children who are typically developing, but often have cognitive processing problems that are demonstrated through deficits in memory, attention, and motivation. As discussed earlier, they also have adaptive behavior deficits. Together, their cognitive processing and adaptive behavior deficits make learning for these children challenging.

Memory Deficits

Deficits in memory are one of the most challenging difficulties students with mild mental retardation demonstrate. Although their **long-term memory** does not appear to be as impacted (Ellis, 1963), *short-term memory* deficits are common (Bray, Fletcher, & Turner, 1997). Often times, they may have difficulty remembering directions to a task or information that was recently communicated to them. Even if they remember this information, recalling it can be slower than normal or remembering large amounts of information may be more difficult (Merrill, 1990). Deficits in memory certainly impact all areas of development including academics, language, and social-adaptive behavior. For example, at times we all forget a person's name following an introduction or forget a phone number. Although, we may be embarrassed, if need be, we apologetically ask for the information again, most likely storing it in our short-term memory. People with mental retardation, however, must compensate for a deficit in this skill and learn alternative strategies for remembering information.

Attention Deficits

Difficulty attending to relevant features of activities and tasks and paying attention for extended periods of time are also characteristic of students with MMR (Zeaman & House, 1979). Deficits in attention span can affect their learning across all areas of development. For example, they may have difficulty learning to read letters or words on sight, because they have difficulty attending to relevant aspects of the letters or words. Numbers and mathematical concepts may be difficult for them to understand because they may be distracted by irrelevant stimuli. Attention deficits can also impact social skills and the ability to attend to social cues and the **pragmatics** of language. Acquisition of vocational skills is another critical area that can be affected by attention deficits. For example, attending to a vocational task for a long period of time may be difficult. Even household activities, such as cooking, require attention skills. We use our attention skills for a wide variety of tasks and activities; therefore, deficits in this area significantly affect an individual's ability to function.

Motivation and Task Persistence

Since problem solving is difficult for persons with MMR (Switzkey, 1997), they often have impaired motivational abilities. Whereas many of us find challenging tasks somewhat enjoyable, persons with MMR may not even attempt these tasks, since they lack the interest to try. Their lack of motivation and task persistence can become cyclic, resulting in a characteristic called **learned helplessness** (Heward, 2003). Motivation to engage in learning and persistence at difficult tasks are both critical skills for development. Consider the toddler learning to walk—although she may fall a number of times, getting up and trying again is important for the development of this early motor skill. We all face difficult tasks or situations at times; having the motivation to persist in these situations is critical for development of skills. Since persons with MMR lack motivation and task persistence, we need to target this characteristic as we design instructional strategies to help them learn.

Adaptive Behaviors

Delays in adaptive behaviors become evident across a number of areas of development. For example, social interactions are often difficult for persons with MMR. They may have difficulty developing and sustaining friendships. Their limitation in social skills is also affected by deficits in other areas of development, such as language and cognition. Additionally, persons with MMR may also demonstrate problematic behaviors that interfere with their learning. Similar to other students with mild disabilities, they may engage in problem behaviors when demands are placed on them (e.g., noncompliance, disruption, tantrums); however, this is not their primary deficit, as it is with students with emotional and behavioral disorders (EBD). Finally, adaptive behaviors in daily living skills, including self-help skills, are common. These students may have difficulty at an early age dressing themselves, eating independently, and so forth. Later, their personal hygiene may be poor, and as mentioned earlier, skills needed for independent living may be absent. Deficits in adaptive behavior are extremely important to address when providing intervention. After all, our social relationships and independent living skills are foundations for success later in life.

Even though students with MMR have many areas of need, they also have many areas of strength. With the right services and supports, they can learn cognitive and adaptive behaviors to facilitate their growth across all areas of development. In addition, they are all unique individuals, even though they have many common learning needs (Smith & Mitchell, 2001). If their individual strengths are highlighted as these learning needs are addressed through evidence-based practices, the likelihood of success increases.

Evidence-Based Practices for Students with MMR

Using evidence-based practices to address the learning characteristics of persons with MMR is the first step toward ameliorating the impact of this lifelong disability. Fortunately, a number of evidence-based approaches are effective in teaching these students the skills they need to become contributing members of society.

Applied Behavior Analysis and Direct Instruction

Applied behavior analysis (ABA) is one of the most effective scientifically based approaches available for instructing individuals with mental retardation. ABA is comprised of a number of different behavioral strategies, such as use of **positive reinforcement, shaping,** and **chaining,** which have been found to be successful when teaching learners new skills (for a review, see Alberto & Troutman, 2003). Instruction using ABA principles includes identifying and task-analyzing new skills for instruction, arranging the learning environment to provide opportunities for skill acquisition, and designing consequences that help to establish and maintain those skills. Instruction that helps students with MMR learn in different environments and maintain their skills over time is particularly important in ABA. These aspects of instruction are often called **generalization** and **maintenance** of skills learned.

ABA strategies can help with the students' motivation and task-persistence difficulties discussed earlier. For example, use of positive reinforcement can provide the consequences needed to encourage a student to engage in a difficult task. In addition, ABA strategies such as **stimulus cueing** can also help with attention deficits. Task analysis is also a particularly useful strategy for learning different adaptive behaviors, such as self-help and vocational skills.

Along with ABA, direct instruction is also an effective teaching practice for students with mild mental retardation. Providing direct instruction, including the use of modeling techniques, graduated guidance, and errorless learning, facilitates skill acquisition and maintenance. Children and young people with MMR need explicit instruction that helps them to learn relevant skills needed for independence and success in school and community.

Functional Curriculum for Learning Academic and Life Skills

A functional curriculum emphasizes "real world" skills that facilitate a student's independence at home, school, work, and in the community (Heward, 2003). Functional curriculum highlights functional skills, which are relevant to the person's learning environment. For example, a student with MMR who lives in Puerto Rico or southern Florida may not need to learn how to dress for snow. However, for a student who lives in the far north, this is a critical survival skill. An important part of a functional curriculum is learning **functional academic skills** (basic reading, writing, and arithmetic skills).

The functional academic skills that will help the student obtain the life skills needed to live independently in future environments should be targeted for instruction at an early age. Developing a functional curriculum for individuals with MMR requires conducting inventories of the different environments in which the individual functions. For example, teachers and parents, along with the student, need to identify the skills that are required for the person to function independently and successfully in this and future environments.

What types of skills are needed for a person with MMR to attend his or her local high school independently? The student would likely need to be able to get to and from school, negotiate traffic in hallways, and locate his or her subject classrooms. In addition, the student would need to be able to interact socially with peers, attend to instruction, complete assignments, and possibly acquire the skills needed for extracurricular activities. All of these are functional life skills that can be assessed and taught based on individualized assessment and instructional planning.

SUMMARY

This chapter reviewed the characteristics, defining features, and the process needed to identify students with MMR. Individuals with MMR have many common features, but are also a diverse group with individual strengths. Many students with mild mental retardation can learn the skills needed to be independent and contributing members of society. One of the initial steps for helping them learn the skills they need is appropriate diagnostic and educational assessment.

There are several approaches for diagnosing individuals with mental retardation. One important aspect of the diagnostic process, particularly for individuals with mild mental retardation, is to examine their developmental needs in relation to the environments in which they live. However, as required by IDEA, individuals must show significant delays on measures of IQ and adaptive behavior to be diagnosed as mentally retarded and obtain educational services. Because in many cases there is no known case of mild mental retardation, diagnosis and identification during the early childhood years may not oc-cur. Many times, these students are not identified until they are challenged academically in our schools.

The outlook for persons with MMR to become contributing members of society is promising. However, they need to have appropriate supports and instruction that target remediation of their deficits. The AAMR (1992) proposed different levels of supports based on intensity (i.e., intermittent, limited, extensive, and pervasive).

Like students with other disabilities, students with MMR have a variety of unique learning needs and characteristics. By definition, some of their cognitive processes are impaired (e.g., memory, attention span, motivation). In addition, they have delays in areas of adaptive behavior skills (e.g., communication/language, self-help). Researchers and practitioners have used evidence-based interventions, including applied behavior analysis strategies, to remediate these students learning deficits and delays. Fortunately, if implemented at an early age systematically, these strategies can help students with MMR learn needed skills, improving their prospects for living independent lives.

COMPETENT TEACHING BOX　　　　B O X   6 . 1

Knowing your students . . .

Working with students with MMR is rewarding. When children and young people with MMR are given appropriate instruction and supports to be successful, developmental growth occurs. Through the acquisition of functional skills, their independence increases. When you work with children and young people with MMR, remember the following:

- Most individuals diagnosed with mental retardation function in the mild range. Persons with MMR have many assets, but for them to lead independent and successful lives, they need to have the appropriate supports to learn. These supports include individualized instruction in the least restrictive environment using evidence-based practices. To gain independence, they must learn the skills needed to function in different learning contexts, including home, school, and the community.
- Identifying students with MMR may be difficult during the early childhood years, because skill deficits may not show up until they reach school and begin academic instruction. Once MMR is suspected, a nondiscriminatory assessment, including an evaluation of the person's intelligence and adaptive behavior, should be performed by a multidisciplinary team. This evaluation should not only focus on skill deficits, but also on identifying the types of services and supports needed to help the person learn.
- Many of these students will acquire academic skills, but self-help, socialization, and vocational skills are also an important part of the curriculum for students with MMR.
- Depending on their instructional goals and needs children and young people with MMR are typically educated in the general education classroom or in a resource room. As their skills progress, instruction may occur in the community, such as vocational training. Often the most appropriate placement may be with these students' nondisabled peers who can serve as learning models. Educating these children in the least restrictive environment is important to facilitate their successful integration into the school and community.

Competent teachers . . .

- Identify the student's strengths and needs and provide the appropriate services for facilitating independence.
- Design their instruction to facilitate learning both cognitive and adaptive behavior skills that facilitate independence.
- Target identification at an early age to minimize the effects of mental retardation on development.
- Include students with MMR in their least restrictive environment, often with their same-age peers who can serve as learning models.
- Use applied behavior analysis strategies to strengthen a student's motivation, attention, and memory to support learning.

:: CASE STUDIES

CARRIE

Carrie was prenatally exposed to drugs and alcohol. At birth, she presented symptoms indicating an infant that may be going through drug withdrawal. After an investigation, Carrie was removed from her mother's care and placed in a foster home. Due to her high-risk circumstances, Carrie's development was carefully monitored. Within her first 6 months, developmental indicators suggested that Carrie lagged behind other babies her age. She was often fussy and difficult to comfort. Her receptive language and early cognition skills appeared slightly delayed and her fine and gross motor skills were more like those of a 4-month-old. Luckily, by the time Carrie was 1 year old, she was enrolled in an early intervention program funded through **IDEA Part C.**

Although Carrie was labeled as having a developmental delay during her first year of life, standardized assessment indicated that she had early signs of mental retardation. Today, Carrie is in her first year of kindergarten. Her development continues to show slight delays; however, due to the intense early intervention services she received, she acts and functions much like a kindergartener. Carrie is learning early math and reading skills, such as names of numbers and letters. She also has acquired a number of independent self-help skills including dressing and toileting.

Although Carrie has developed a number of skills, one of the main areas she needs help in is attention and problem solving. To help her acquire these skills, Carrie's teacher has modified her assignments by making them shorter and giving her extra time to complete them. The teacher also breaks new skills into smaller, more manageable tasks that help Carrie to be successful.

Carrie's language skills continue to need support, particularly her articulation; therefore, the speech-language pathologist works with Carrie several times a week. Finally, Carrie receives **occupational therapy** services to help her develop the fine motor skills she needs to improve her handwriting skills. Although Carrie continues to need support, her developmental skills have continued to evolve, lagging only slightly behind those of her age peers. She has friends in her kindergarten classroom, although she tends to have more in common with the younger children in the class. With continued appropriate instruction and support, Carrie's skills will continue to grow at a strong rate.

1. What would have happened to Carrie if she hadn't received early intervention?
2. How may her prenatal environment have contributed to her mental retardation?
3. Should Carrie continue to attend a general education classroom when she is promoted to first grade? Why or why not?
4. Do all states have early intervention services for children with mental retardation who are younger than 3 years old?

EVAN

Evan is a third grader with Down syndrome. Although all children with Down syndrome have mental retardation, the degree and severity can be highly variable. Evan is fortunate because, from birth, he and his family received early intervention services. By the time Evan entered kindergarten, his developmental abilities were within the normal range, with the exception of his speech-language skills. Therefore, the only special education services he was eligible to receive in kindergarten were speech and language services. His development was monitored very closely.

As the year advanced, although Evan's development progressed, delays in several areas became evident, especially in comparison to his peers. At the end of kindergarten, Evan was evaluated and found eligible for services under the category of mild disabilities (which included mild mental retardation). He entered first grade with his peers from kindergarten, but also began receiving special education services to foster his skills across all academic areas. Beginning with first grade, Evan became part of a multiage classroom that uses a **co-teaching teaching model** (see Chapter 12). In Evan's classroom, a general and special education teacher work collaboratively to teach children with disabilities and typically developing children.

In the co-teaching classroom, all the children in the classroom are given the supports they need to become successful and acquire the skills needed to learn. Although Evan continues to progress, his skill level is within the mild mental retardation range and his rate of learning is behind that of his peers. Outside of school, his parents provide him with many extracurricular activities that augment his participation at school. He receives tutoring for academic subjects, takes gymnastics lessons, and participates in a therapeutic horseback riding program. As he grows older, his parents worry

161

that the gap between him and his peers will widen. They know that he will always need support, but are taking his education and development one step at a time. They are working hard and advocating for the services and supports he needs now to help him gain independence in the future.

1. Why do you think Evan's developmental delays became more obvious as he progressed in school?
2. What does the future hold for Evan?
3. Will Evan ever live independently? Will he always need support?
4. How will Evan's mild mental retardation impact his life in middle and high school?
5. Why wasn't Evan provided special education services in kindergarten?

DAVID

David is 20 years old. Although David attends his local high school for a portion of the day, his main education occurs after school and on the weekends. After school, David goes to work in the afternoons and works full-time on the weekends with a landscaping company. His job entails mainly manual labor—assisting in planting and maintaining the landscaping. He also works in the company's nursery. David has an unusual living situation for a high school student. He lives in an apartment with two other men his age and works almost full time. How did David get this job? Why does he live in an apartment rather than at home?

David and his family began preparing for life after school, starting with the development of a **transition plan.** When David turned 14. Transition planning, which is a part of the Individualized Education Program (IEP) process, is an important part of preparing students with mild mental retardation for life after school and for becoming independent. In his transition plan, David, his family members, and his school staff targeted vocational, functional academic, and life skills that David would need to be able to support himself after school. The transition team identified landscaping as an interest area for David. He is physically strong and likes to work outdoors. Early on, the school's **job coach** helped David get a part-time job with a lawn maintenance company, where he learned basic lawn care skills and how to use power tools, including a lawnmover. Over time, David developed many new skills, and the job coach helped David get hired as a worker for a landscaping company. During the transition from working for the lawn maintenance company to working for the landscaping company, David's job coach provided assistance and support to help David learn the necessary job skills.

At age 18, as his fellow high school students were graduating, David wanted to move from his parents' home to his own place. David and his parents contacted their state developmental services office, which provides support services for individuals with developmental disabilities. David was assigned a **support coordinator** who helped enroll David in services to facilitate his transition from living at home to having his own apartment. The support coordinator, along with David's IEP team, identified skills David needed to learn to become independent.

At school, David takes classes that help him further develop his functional reading, writing, and math skills. The support coordinator provides intermittent support to David and his fellow roommates, helping them learn the "ins and outs" of living in their own apartment. Although David is saving his money to buy a pool table, in his spare time he also enjoys hanging out with his friends at the video arcade.

1. What factors may have contributed to David's success?
2. Where would David be today if a transition plan was not developed early on?
3. Is David a contributing member of society?
4. Do you think David will be able to continue in a positive direction? What obstacles might he have?

REFERENCES

Alberto, P., & Troutman, A. (2003). *Applied behavior analysis for teachers* (6th ed.).Upper Saddle River, NJ: Prentice Hall.

American Association on Mental Retardation (2004). *Supports intensity scale information.* Washington, DC: American Association on Mental Retardation.

American Association on Mental Retardation. (2002). *Mental retardation: Definition, classification, and systems of supports* (10th ed.). Washington, DC: Author.

American Association on Mental Retardation Ad Hoc Committee on Terminology and Classification. (1992). *Classification in mental retardation* (9th ed.). Washington, DC: American Association on Mental Retardation.

American Psychiatric Association. (2000). *Diagnostic and statistical manual of mental disorders* (4th text rev. ed.). Washington, DC: American Psychiatric Publishing.

Bayley, N. (2005). *Bayley scales of infant development: Second edition.* San Antonio, TX: The Psychological Corporation.

Bray, N. W., Fletcher, K. L., & Turner, L. A. (1997). Cognitive competencies and strategy use in individuals with mental retardation. In W. W. MacLean, Jr. (Ed.), *Ellis' handbook of mental deficiency, psychological theory, and research* (3rd ed.) (pp. 197–217). Mahwah, NJ: Erlbaum.

Conyers, C., Martin, T.L., Martin, G.L., & Yu, D. (2002). The 1983 AAMR Manual, the 1992 AAMR Manual, or the Developmental Disabilities Act: Which do researchers use? *Education and Training in Mental Retardation and Developmental Disabilities, 37,* 310–316.

Denning, C. B., Chamberlain, J. A., & Polloway, E. A. (2000). An evaluation of state guidelines for mental retardation: Focus on definition and classification practices. *Education and Training in Mental Retardation and Developmental Disabilities, 35*, 226–232.

Ellis, N. R. (1963). The stimulus trace and behavior inadequacy. In N. R. Ellis (Ed.), *Handbook of mental deficiency* (pp. 134–158). New York: McGraw-Hill.

Glutting, J. J., & Wilkinson, G. S. (2005). *Manual for the WRAT 4: Wide range achievement test* (4th ed.). Austin, TX: PRO-ED.

Grossman, H. (Ed.). (1983). *Classification in mental retardation*. Washington, DC: American Association on Mental Deficiency.

Heward, W.L. (2003). *Exceptional children: An introduction to special education* (7th Ed.). Columbus, OH: Merrill/Prentice Hall.

Individuals with Disabilities Education Improvement Act (2004). 20 USC 1400.

Kauffman, J. M., Mostert, M. P., Trent, S. C., & Pullen, P. L. (2006). *Managing classroom behavior: A reflective case-based approach* (4th ed.). Boston: Allyn & Bacon.

Lambert, N., Nihira, K., & Leland, H. (1993). *Adaptive behavior scale—School* (2nd ed.). Austin, TX: PRO-ED.

Luckasson, R., Borthwick-Duffy, S., Buntix, W. H. E., Coulter, D. L., Craig, E. M., Reeve, A., Schalock, R. L., Snell, M. E., Spitalnik, D. M., Spreat, S., & Tasse, M. J. (2002). *Mental retardation: Definition, classification, and systems of supports* (10th ed.). Washington DC: American Association on Mental Retardation.

Luckasson, R., & Reeve, A. (2001). Naming, defining, and classifying mental retardation. *Mental Retardation, 39*, 47–52.

Merrill, E. C. (1990). Attentional resource allocation and mental retardation. In N.W. Bray (Ed.), *International review of research in mental retardation*, Vol. 16 (pp. 51–88). Sam Diego: Academic Press.

President's Committee on Mental Retardation (PCMR). (1970). *The six-hour retarded child*. Washington, DC: U.S. Government Printing Office.

Pullen, P. L. (2005). *Brighter beginnings for teachers*. Lanham, MD: Rowman & Littlefield Education.

Raymond, E. B. (2000). *Learners with mild disabilities: A characteristics approach*. Needham Heights: Allyn & Bacon.

Reynolds, A. J., Temple, J. A., Robertson, D. L., & Mann, E. A. (2001). Long-term effects of an early childhood intervention on educational achievement and juvenile arrest. *Journal of the American Medical Association, 285*, 2339–2346.

Rush, A. J., & Francis, A. (Eds.). (2000). Expert consensus guideline series: Treatment of psychiatric and behavioral problems in mental retardation. *American Journal of Mental Retardation, 105*, 159–228.

Salvia, J. & Ysseldyke, J. (2001). Assessment in special and remedial education (8th ed.). Boston: Houghton Mifflin.

Schalock, R. L. (Ed.). (1999). *Adaptive behavior and its measurement: Implications for the field of mental retardation*. Washington, DC: American Association on Mental Retardation.

Smith, J. D. (1994). The revised AAMR definition of mental retardation: The MRDD position. *Education and Training in Mental Retardation, 29*, 179–183.

Smith, J.D., & Mitchell, A.L. (2001). "Me? I'm not a drooler. I'm the assistant": Is it time to abandon mental retardation as a classification? *Mental Retardation, 39*, 144–146.

Sparrow, S. S., Balla, D. A., & Cicchetti, D. V. (1985). *Vineland adaptive behavior scales: Classroom edition form*. Circle Pines, MN: American Guidance Service.

Sparrow, S. S., Balla, D. A., & Cicchetti, D. V. (1984). *Vineland adaptive behavior scales: Interview edition, expanded form*. Circle Pines, MN: American Guidance Service.

Sternberg, R.J., & Spear, I.C. (1985). A triarchic theory of mental retardation. In N. R. Ellis (Ed.), *International review of research in mental retardation* (Vol. 13, pp. 301–326). New York: Academic Press.

Switzkey, H.N. (1997). Mental retardation and the neglected construct of motivation. *Education and Training in Mental Retardation and Developmental Disabilities, 32*, 194–196.

Thompson, J. R., Bryant, B., Campbell, E. M., Craig, E. M., Hughes, C., Rotholz, D. A., Schalock, R. L., Silverman, W., & Tass'e, M. J. (2002). *Supports intensity scale*. Unpublished assessment scale. Washington, DC: American Association on Mental Retardation.

Thorndike, R. L., Hagen, E. P., & Sattler, J. M. (1986). *Technical manual, the Stanford-Binet intelligence scale: Fourth edition*. Chicago: Riverside.

Utley, C.A., Lowitzer, A.C., & Baumeister, A.A. (1987). A comparison of the AAMD's definition, eligibility criteria, and classification schemes with state departments of education guidelines. *Education and Training in Mental Retardation, 22*, 35–43.

Wechsler, D. (1991). *Wechsler intelligence scale for children—3rd edition*. San Antonio, TX: The Psychological Corporation.

Wodrich, D.J., & Barry, C.T. (1991). A survey of school psychologists' practices for identifying mentally retarded students. *Psychology in the Schools, 28*, 165–171.

Zeaman, D., & House, B.J. (1979). A review of attention theory. In N. R. Ellis (Ed.), *Handbook of mental deficiency: Psychological theory and research* (2nd ed., pp. 63–120). Hillside, NJ: Erlbaum.

Zigler, E., & Hodapp, R.M. (1986). *Understanding mental retardation*. Cambridge, England: Cambridge University Press.

Characteristics of Students with Other High-Incidence Disabilities

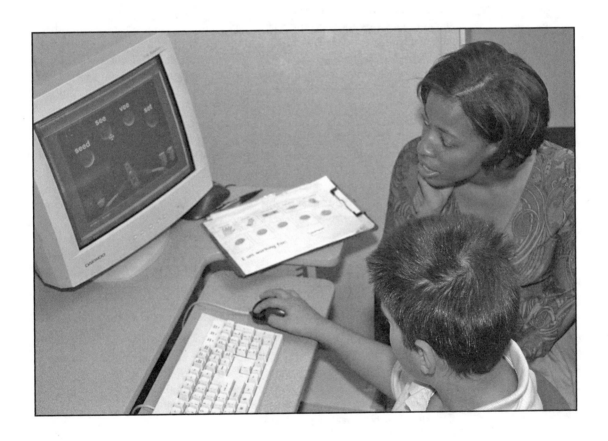

URBAN LEGEND: *Children and youth with high-incidence disabilities are a homogenous group of students, with similar characteristics and, therefore, the same services are appropriate across all students.*

LEGENDARY THOUGHT: *Children and youth with high-incidence disabilities are a heterogeneous group with diverse characteristics and learning needs. Services and interventions should be based on the individual student's particular characteristics and learning needs—one size does not necessarily fit all!*

Some students with high-incidence disabilities are not easily classified into the more commonly known IDEA (2004) diagnostic categories of **learning disabilities, emotional or behavioral disorders,** or **mental retardation.** Due to various factors, including causes and learning characteristics that distinguish them from the other disability categories listed in IDEA, novel, possibly more relevant classifications have been developed. In this chapter, we highlight three additional categories of students with high-incidence disabilities: (1) **Attention Deficit Hyperactivity Disorder (ADHD)**; (2) **Traumatic Brain Injury (TBI)**; and (3) **High-Functioning Autism (HFA).** Just how common are these other types of high-incidence disabilities? What characteristics make them unique? How are these students different from students identified with other disabilities? Do these children have similar learning needs, or do they require different types of instruction? We discuss the characteristics of students with ADHD, TBI, and HFA in the following sections. Additionally, we explore strategies for identifying students with these diagnostic labels and discuss their special learning needs. Our goal in this chapter is to provide you with a better awareness of the characteristics and needs of these unusual students.

:: CHARACTERISTICS AND IDENTIFICATION OF STUDENTS WITH ATTENTION DEFICIT HYPERACTIVITY DISORDER (ADHD)

The National Institute of Mental Health (2005) estimates that between 3% and 5% of children have ADHD; therefore, in almost every classroom in the United States, it is likely that a teacher will have at least one child with this disability. Given the alarming incidence of ADHD, teachers need to be familiar with the characteristics of these children and how to address their special learning needs. Since 1845, when Dr. Heinrich Hoffman, a physician who specialized in psychiatry, first identified ADHD in his young son, the characteristics, identification, and treatment of what is now known as ADHD has evolved.

ADHD has received a great deal of attention in the medical and educational literature, and current research efforts help us better understand the characteristics and treatment of this disorder. Over the past several decades, a professional debate has existed about whether ADHD is truly a separate disability or whether the characteristics of ADHD are similar to other disabilities, such as learning disabilities (LD). Some professionals suggest that ADHD is a fad, and that children who have these characteristics do not have distinguishing characteristics. However, the National Institutes of Health developed a consensus statement with professionals across a variety of disciplines including special education, medicine, and psychology, indicating that ADHD is a separate disorder and establishing criteria for identification based on cross-national studies, familial aggregation, and heritability (for a discussion, see http://consensus.nih.gov/1998/1998AttentionDeficitHyperactivityDisorder110html.htm). In the next section, we examine the unique characteristics of ADHD and how professionals diagnose and identify children and youth with this disorder.

Characteristics of ADHD

Charles

Charles's first-grade teacher, Ms. Cantucci, is meeting with the school's Child Study Team. She begins by saying, "I am concerned about Charles. He just can't sit still. He is always squirming in his seat and never seems to be able to just sit down and do his work. Every time he begins an assignment, I see him start to fidget—fussing with his pencil, pulling at his clothes, bothering the child next to him. I know he is able to do the work, but he just can't seem to stay on task long enough to complete anything. He also is always blurting out answers loudly during group lessons. He can't wait his turn. He reminds me of another student I have who has ADHD."

Ms. Cantucci is describing a child who is **hyperactive, inattentive,** and **impulsive**—all common characteristics of children with ADHD. Although, ADHD is present throughout a child's life, the characteristics of ADHD are typically more obvious when he or she enters school and is engaged in academic instruction (i.e., times when the context requires a child to be quiet, engage in and persist at a task, and attend to instruction).

One of the things that can make ADHD difficult to diagnose is that all young children at times are inattentive, hyperactive, and impulsive, so how can you tell when these symptoms are characteristic of ADHD, or are merely representative of typical development? Critics of the frequent diagnosis of ADHD may claim that the child is simply exhibiting ordinary behavior that is typical of gender or ethnicity and that teachers are at fault for not recognizing that the child's behavior is developmentally or culturally normative. However, when these symptoms (hyperactivity, inattention, impulsivity) appear over time and affect a child's school progress, there is a high probability that the child has ADHD. Further examination of these core characteristics may help clarify how they relate to a diagnosis of ADHD.

Hyperactivity

Most people who have been around a student with ADHD have said something like this: "He is always on the go." This is another way of describing hyperactivity. Hyperactivity is usually manifested by constant talking, excessive movement, and fidgeting. Children who are hyperactive have significantly more difficulty than most in staying in their seat. If they do remain in their seats, they usually fidget, moving around a lot more than their peers. Other symptoms may include (for a younger student) running around the room when the expectation is to be seated or difficulty waiting for a turn or turn-taking (NIMH, 2005). Older students with ADHD may also demonstrate behaviors that indicate they are "restless." For example, they may attend to many different things at once or constantly move body parts (e.g., moving their foot) (NIMH, 2005).

Impulsivity

All of us at times "act before we think," but students with ADHD appear to have tremendous inability to curtail their impulsivity. For example, even though a teacher asks a student to raise his hand, the student with ADHD consistently fails to do this, blurting out the answer. This characteristic can be extremely difficult for the classroom teacher, and teachers often report that these children's impulsivity seems almost uncontrollable. Impulsivity not only occurs during instructional times, but may also occur in social situations. For example, young children may hit other children or grab play materials without intending any harm to others (NIMH, 2005). Older students may have difficulty waiting their turn or waiting in line (NIMH, 2005).

Inattention

Inattention to important details and information can seriously affect a student's learning. Students with ADHD often have a difficult time attending to a task, especially when it is new or difficult. They often forget important details and become easily distracted by environmental sights and sounds. Their inattentiveness affects their ability to follow instructions. These children are often described as "spacey" or even lethargic. They often don't respond as quickly to the teacher and make more mistakes when they respond compared to their peers (NIMH, 2005; Tsal, Shalev, & Mevorach, 2005).

Additional Characteristics

Although hyperactivity, impulsivity, and inattentiveness are characteristics of ADHD, Barkley (1997, 1998) suggested that all these characteristics fall under a larger descriptive umbrella called **behavioral inhibition.** Behavioral inhibition is defined as the ability to stall or withhold a response that has been initiated or planned, such as refraining from saying something that will interrupt a conversation, or ignoring distractions (Tripp & Alsop, 2001). In other words, recent descriptions of ADHD suggest that this disorder is displayed by a lack of self-control that leads to a number of other symptoms and characteristics (Mather & Goldstein, 2001).

Organizational deficits are another common characteristic of students with ADHD (Barkley, 1990; Stormont-Spurgin, 1997). These organizational deficits interfere with activities within a classroom, such as task completion (Zentall, Harper, & Stormont-Spurgin, 1993). For example, as reported by Zentall et al. (1993), students with ADHD often report having more difficulty with organizational tasks, such as keeping track of school-related items (e.g., homework, books) and completing projects.

Identification of ADHD

Identification of ADHD is typically made by professionals using the American Psychiatric Association's (APA) *Diagnostic and Statistical Manual of Mental Disorders* (*DSM-IV—Text Revision*; APA, 2000) criteria (see Table 7.1).

To meet the eligibility criteria for a diagnosis of ADHD, the child must display six (or more) of the symptoms over a minimum period of 6 months. An additional part of the APA (2000) diagnosis of ADHD includes two dimensions: inattention and hyperactivity-impulsivity. APA (2000) distinguishes ADHD further into the following subtypes:

1. ADHD, Predominantly Inattentive Type;
2. ADHD, Predominantly Hyperactive-Impulsive Type; and
3. ADHD, Combined Type

Lahey et al. (1994, 2005) suggest that half of the children with ADHD fall in the third category—combined type, with the remaining children falling in either the inattentive or hyperactive-impulsive types.

Since ADHD is often diagnosed by a child's physician, the American Academy of Pediatrics (2000) developed clinical guidelines to assist physicians in the evaluation and diagnosis process. These guidelines recommend the following:

- The *Diagnostic and Statistical Manual of Mental Disorders–IV* (APA, 2000) should be used as the basis for a diagnosis of ADHD;
- Evaluation for ADHD should occur for children, ages 6–12 years old, who engage in inattention, hyperactivity, impulsivity, academic underachievement, or behavior problems;
- The assessment should include obtaining information from caregivers and family members with ongoing contact with the child in different settings about the child's age of onset and duration of symptoms and the amount of impairment caused by the behaviors;
- The assessment should include information from the child's teachers and school personnel regarding the duration of symptoms, the amount of impairment caused by the behaviors, and any conditions that may be associated with the symptoms;
- The assessment should include an evaluation for any co-morbid disorders, and diagnostic testing may be required to determine their presence (APA, 2000).

A number of different professionals are qualified to diagnose a child with ADHD, including psychologists, psychiatrists, pediatricians, neurologists and clinical social workers. Ideally, the specialist obtains information about the child's behavior and learning from the family members, school staff, and medical records. Direct observation of the child in an educational setting is recommended, along with the completion of various rating scales that compare the child's behavior to peers' behavior. Frequently, additional testing, such as IQ and achievement testing are conducted. Further diagnostic guidelines indicate that symptoms must be "pervasive," occur across two or more settings, be atypical for the child's age and level of development, and exist for at least 6 months (Rowland, Lesesne, & Abramowitz, 2002). Assessment of students with ADHD may be difficult due to their attention and behavioral deficits.

Additionally, a number of co-morbid disorders occur in children with ADHD, including learning disabilities, emotional or behavioral disorders, oppositional

TABLE 7.1	**Diagnostic criteria for attention deficit hyperactivity disorder**

A. Either (1) or (2)

1. Six (or more) of the following symptoms of inattention have persisted for at least 6 months to a degree that is maladaptive and inconsistent with developmental level:

   a. Often fails to give close attention to details or makes careless mistakes in schoolwork, work, or other activities
   b. Often has difficulty sustaining attention in tasks or play activities
   c. Often does not seem to listen when spoken to directly
   d. Often does not follow through on instructions and fails to finish schoolwork, chores, or duties in the workplace (not due to oppositional behavior or failure to understand instructions)
   e. Often has difficulty organizing tasks and activities
   f. Often avoids, dislikes, or is reluctant to engage in tasks that require sustained mental effort (such as schoolwork or homework)
   g. Often loses things necessary for tasks or activities (e.g., toys, school assignments, pencils, books, or tools)
   h. Is often easily distracted by extraneous stimuli
   i. Is often forgetful in daily activities

2. Six (or more) of the following symptoms of hyperactivity-impulsivity have persisted for at least 6 months to a degree that is maladaptive and inconsistent with developmental level:

   Hyperactivity

   a. Often fidgets with hands or feet or squirms in seat
   b. Often leaves seat in classroom or in other situations in which remaining seated is expected
   c. Often runs about or climbs excessively in situations in which it is inappropriate (in adolescents or adults, may be limited to subjective feelings of restlessness)
   d. Often has difficulty playing or engaging in leisure activities quietly
   e. Is often "on the go" or often acts as if "driven by a motor"
   f. Often talks excessively

defiant disorder, conduct disorder, Tourette syndrome, depression, anxiety disorders, and bipolar disorders (Rowland et al., 2002). That is, just because an individual has ADHD does not mean that he or she has no other disorders. Often, ADHD is seen first, followed by other problems and multiple diagnoses. However, it would also be a mistake to assume that because someone has ADHD he or she has other diagnosable disorders as well. Our point is simply that ADHD is often but not always accompanied or followed by other disorders.

Tsal and colleagues found that students with ADHD often perform poorly in academic areas, such as reading and math, in comparison to their peers (Tsal, Shalev, & Mevorach, 2005). Unfortunately, the quality and quantity of these students' work (affected by their inattentiveness and impulsivity) is not usually reflective of their abilities (Harris, Friedlander, Saddler, Frizzelle, & Graham, 2005). Similar to other high-incidence disabilities, the prevalence of ADHD in boys is much higher than in girls. The estimated ratio of boys to girls is from 2.5:1 to 5:1 (Barkley, 1998). This

Impulsivity

    g. Often blurts out answers before questions have been completed

    h. Often has difficulty awaiting turn

    i. Often interrupts or intrudes on others (e.g., butts into conversations or games)

B. Some hyperactive-impulsive or inattentive symptoms that caused impairment were present before age 7 years.

C. Some impairment from the symptoms is present in two or more settings (e.g., at school [or work] or at home).

D. There must be clear evidence of clinically significant impairment in social, academic, or occupational functioning.

E. The symptoms do not occur exclusively during the course of a Pervasive Developmental Disorder, Schizophrenia, or other Psychotic Disorder and are not better accounted for by another mental disorder (e.g., Mood Disorder, Anxiety Disorder, Dissociative Disorder, or a Personality Disorder).

Code Based on Type

314.01   Attention-Deficit/Hyperactivity Disorder, Combined Type: if both Criteria A1 and A2 are met for the past 6 months

314.00   Attention-Deficit/Hyperactivity Disorder, Predominantly Inattentive Type: if Criterion A1 is met but Criterion A2 is not met for the past 6 months

314.01   Attention-Deficit/Hyperactivity Disorder, Predominantly Hyperactive-Impulsive Type: if Criterion A2 is met but Criterion A1 is not met for the past 6 months.

Reprinted with permission from the *Diagnostic and Statistical Manual of Mental Disorders*, Fourth Edition, text revision, pp. 92–93. Copyright 2000 American Psychiatric Association.

does not mean that ADHD does not exist in girls. Indeed many females experience difficulties from the effects of this disorder.

Unique Learning Needs and Evidence-Based Practices (ADHD)

As indicated in our legendary thought, students with ADHD have learning needs that are unique to their characteristics. Therefore, teachers need to be aware of evidence-based strategies that can be used to adapt instruction to meet their learning needs. Since students with ADHD are easily distracted, Brown (2000) suggested that providing a classroom environment that addresses impulsivity and inattentiveness is the first place to begin. Classroom teachers can use simple strategies, such as changing the pace or presentation style of instruction to match the student's needs. Additionally, teachers may want to consider seating students with ADHD in areas of the classroom that may be further from typical distractions (Cooper & O'Regan, 2001). For example, if the student was highly distractible, the teacher would want to seat the student away from areas such as the classroom entrance, bathroom/sink area, and so forth. A critical part of effective instruction for students with ADHD is to be certain that the instructional content is both developmentally appropriate and engaging. Again, since students with ADHD are highly distractible, have difficulty attending, and are often hyperactive, it is logical that instruction that is appropriate for the student's ability level and is interesting and motivating to the student will be more successful. When explaining complex or challenging tasks, teachers will want to present instruction using short, concise steps, such as a **task analysis** (Cooper & O'Regan, 2001). Another strategy that can facilitate task completion and retention of instructions is to have the student repeat the directions orally (Cooper & O'Regan, 2001). Additionally, Stormont-Spurgin (1997) suggested the following strategies for assisting students with their organizational skill deficits:

- **cooperative homework teams** (O'Melia & Rosenberg, 1994),
- **positive reinforcement** and **contracts** (Patton, 1994),
- routines and lists (Lerner, Lowenthal, & Lerner, 1995),
- assignment folders and daily planners (McCrory & Gregg, 1995), and
- collaboration (McCrory & Gregg, 1995).

Finally, the use of **self-monitoring procedures** can be implemented to increase on-task behavior (Harris et al., 2005). Although implementing evidence-based teaching practices should always be a part of instructing students with ADHD, the use of medication is often one of the first types of interventions used. In fact, between 1 and 3 million school-age children use psychostimulant medications, such as Ritalin (Castellanos, et al., 2002). As discussed by Whalen (2001), research has suggested that using a combination of medication and behavioral treatments was more effective in controlling symptoms of ADHD in comparison to more traditional instructional practices, such as social skills training.

:: CHARACTERISTICS AND IDENTIFICATION OF STUDENTS WITH TRAUMATIC BRAIN INJURY (TBI)

Carla

Carla was a typical teenager. She liked to hang out with her friends, listening to music. She was a good student, typically receiving As and Bs in her courses. Although she was only 16, Carla and her parents had begun to discuss her future goals, which included going to college to study business. One evening, while driving around, Carla and her friends were in a serious car accident. Unfortunately, Carla sustained a **traumatic brain injury** (TBI) that left her significantly impaired. Immediately, she went from being a solid student, successfully progressing through high school, to a student with intensive learning needs. Carla sustained a number of orthopedic and medical injuries. However, the most disabling was her traumatic brain injury. This injury significantly impaired Carla's cognitive and language abilities. It also affected Carla's motor skills, such as her ability to move independently. Following the TBI, Carla went from being an independent individual to a person that was dependent on others for most of her basic needs (i.e., mobility, eating, toileting, etc.). Once Carla's medical conditions became stable, she began receiving **homebound special education services** to help her learn adaptive skills until she was able to return full-time to her school.

TBI is defined as "damage to brain tissue caused by an external mechanical force, as evidenced by loss of consciousness due to brain trauma, posttraumatic amnesia (PTA), skull fracture, or objective neurological findings that can be reasonably attributed to TBI on physical examination or mental status examination" (Rosenthal & Ricker, 2000, p. 49). Simply put, traumatic brain injury (TBI) is defined by a trauma that occurs, damaging the brain (National Institute of Neurological Disorders and Strokes, 2005). Typically, the trauma is a result of an object (e.g., a gunshot wound) piercing brain tissue and the skull (open head injury) or fiercely hitting or jolting the head (closed head injury) (National Institute of Neurological Disorders and Stroke [NINDS], 2005). One key defining feature in the IDEA definition is that TBI is differentiated from other conditions, such as anoxia or congenital birth defects (Cramer, 2002). Although TBI is a medical condition, the resulting impact on an individual's ability to function makes it an educational disability as well. Depending on the type and severity of the injury, TBI symptoms range from mild to severe. As suggested by the name, traumatic brain injury (TBI) is an extremely difficult and upsetting disability. Children and young people who acquire a TBI are often plagued by a number of complex problems (many that may not become apparent for several months following the injury) that require distinct instructional strategies.

Characteristics of TBI

Students with TBI have many different characteristics, making instruction of these students challenging for teachers. It is not uncommon for students with TBI to experience effects on their cognition, language, physical, social, and behavioral characteristics. For example, a TBI may affect a student's speech, sight, hearing, and other senses (Cramer, 2002). Such students may experience paralysis, muscle spasms, and seizures, all influencing their ability to function and learn (Cramer, 2002). Additional characteristics include "thinking problems"—that is, problems concentrating, focusing attention, sequencing, and remembering (Cramer, 2002). Social, behavioral, and emotional difficulties are also common. Changes in their personality often occur (Cramer, 2002). For example, they may experience depression, mood swings, and anxiety (National Dissemination Center for Children with Disabilities [NICHCY], 2004).

Hallahan and Kauffman (2003) outlined the following educational problems that may be displayed by students with TBI:

- Problems remembering things
- Problems learning new information
- Speech and/or language problems
- Difficulty sequencing things
- Difficulty in processing information (making sense of things)
- Extremely uneven abilities or performance (able to do some things but not others)
- Extremely uneven progress (quick gains sometimes, no gains other times)
- Inappropriate manners or mannerisms
- Failure to understand humor or social situations
- Becoming easily tired, frustrated, or angered
- Unreasonable fear or anxiety

- Irritability
- Sudden, exaggerated swings of mood
- Depression
- Aggression
- Perseveration (persistent repetition of one thought or behavior) (p. 385).

Obviously, a student with TBI would not demonstrate all of these characteristics. In fact, at first sight, the student with a TBI may appear to be "just like everyone else." However, once a teacher becomes more familiar with the student, individual needs will become more apparent.

Identification of TBI

Although not an identified disability in IDEA prior to 1990, to be identified under IDEA today, a student must meet the following eligibility criteria:

> . . . an acquired injury to the brain caused by an external physical force, resulting in total or partial functional disability or psychosocial impairment, or both, that adversely affects a child's educational performance. The term applies to open or closed head injuries resulting in impairments in one or more areas, such as cognition; language; memory; attention; reasoning; abstract thinking; judgment; problem-solving; sensory, perceptual, and motor abilities; psycho-social behavior; physical functions; information processing; and speech. The term does not apply to the brain injuries that are congenital or degenerative, or to brain injuries induced by birth trauma. (34 Code of Federal Regulations δ300.7 (c) [12]).

As suggested in the definition, TBI is different than other types of disabilities that may cause brain damage (e.g., cerebral palsy), because it is an injury that has been acquired after birth.

As discussed earlier, TBI is a neurological impairment that affects a student's ability to function normally within a classroom setting. Since different areas of the brain control different types of functioning, the impact and extent of the damage on the individual's functioning abilities should be evaluated by a **multidisciplinary team.** The person's learning needs across all developmental areas should be a part of the assessment, with special consideration given to cognitive processes (e.g., memory, problem solving) (Cramer, 2002). As noted by the Council for Exceptional Children (2001), the student's learning needs may change quickly depending on the TBI and the recovery process; therefore, identification of the person's learning needs should be reflected in short-term goals that can be accomplished within approximately 6 weeks and reevaluated frequently.

Unique Learning Needs and Evidence-Based Practices (TBI)

The learning needs of students with TBI are very likely to be distinct from students with other types of disabilities. Therefore, it is important for educators, medical personnel, and family members to collaborate to address the change in the student's educational needs (Dell Orto & Power, 2000). Since the student with a TBI is often in a hospital or rehabilitation center prior to returning to school, a transition plan should be developed to assist the student in returning to the school setting. This plan can help teachers be prepared to meet the new needs of the student (Stuart & Goodsitt, 1996). As suggested by Tyler and Mira (1999), the school staff should be trained in the implications of the TBI to assist in facilitating the transition. Part of the transition plan should be the development of an **individualized educational plan** (IEP) to address the student's areas of need.

Once the student is transitioned to school, the focus on developing new skills and relearning old skills can begin. As seen in the case of Carla, teachers may need to focus on skills such as mobility, communication, and daily living tasks. It is common for students with TBI to need related services, such as **physical therapy, occupational therapy,** or **speech-language services.** They may also need **assistive technology** in order to increase their independence. Of utmost importance is helping the student re-obtain cognitive functioning that may have been lost, such as problem solving, sustaining attention, and engaging in appropriate social behavior (Tyler & Mira, 1999).

Many of the difficulties encountered by students with TBI may also be psychological—that is, coming to terms with the changes that have occurred. TBI may negatively influence a student's sense of self, requiring a long recovery period (Dell Orto & Power, 2000).

Bowen (2005) suggested that teachers consider the following strategies to help re-assimilate the student with TBI into the classroom:

- Create a quiet classroom environment. Teachers should control the classroom environment and noise levels to help the student attend. Factors that may be distracting or annoying to the student should be decreased (e.g., noise, light). In addition, tasks should be divided into manageable components.
- Implement direct instruction. **Direct instruction** can assist the student by providing feedback and reinforcement that facilitates engagement.
- Teach the student to use **self-monitoring** and management. Training students to monitor and manage their own behaviors can help students learn coping strategies and be responsible for changing their own behaviors.

Additionally, teachers may want to provide the student with more time to complete work, provide directions in written form, use routines to help communicate expectations, use an assignment book and daily schedule, allow the student to rest if tired, and be patient (NICHCY, 2004).

:: CHARACTERISTICS AND IDENTIFICATION OF STUDENTS WITH HIGH-FUNCTIONING AUTISM (HFA)

Autism has been a separate disability category under IDEA since 1990 and is defined as

> a developmental disability affecting verbal and nonverbal communication and social interaction, generally evident before age 2, that affects a child's performance. Other characteristics often associated with autism are engagement in repetitive activities and stereotyped movements, resistance to environmental change or change in daily routines,

and unusual responses to sensory experiences. The term does not apply if a child's educational performance is adversely affected primarily because the child has a serious emotional disturbance. (34 C.F. R., Part 300, 300.7 [b][1])

The term **autism spectrum disorder** (ASD) is often used to refer to a child who displays characteristics commonly associated with autism. Included within the umbrella term ASD are **autism, Asperger syndrome** (AS), **Rett's disorder, childhood disintegrative disorder,** and **pervasive developmental disorder not otherwise specified** (PDD-NOS) (National Research Council, 2001). The National Research Council (2001) suggests that **autism** is

> a spectrum of disorders that vary in severity of symptoms, age of onset, and associations with other disorders (e.g., mental retardation, specific language delay, epilepsy). The manifestations of autism vary considerably across children and within an individual child over time. (p. 9)

Children and youth who display high-incidence characteristics associated with autism are often referred to as having **High-Functioning Autism** (HFA) or Asperger syndrome (AS). Individuals with HFA typically display the characteristics that are common under the diagnosis of autism, with the exception that their intelligence is within the normal range and their initial language deficits eventually disappear (Ozonoff, Dawson, & McPartland, 2002). Students with AS display characteristics that are similar to HFA, but do not demonstrate the initial difficulties in language acquisition and often do not have as many symptoms (Ozonoff et al., 2002). Although HFA and AS have distinct features from each other, these two diagnoses have many commonalities, and much of the current research is applicable to both conditions (Ozonoff et al., 2002). Therefore, in this section of the chapter, we will refer to both conditions under the HFA label. In the next section, we examine the unique characteristics of HFA.

Characteristics of HFA

Mark

Mark, a third grader, is captain of the chess team at his elementary school. His teacher is impressed with his academic abilities—he is often the first to know the answer to her questions, reads above his grade level, is excellent in math, and has an exceptional memory. But, both his teacher and his parents are concerned that Mark displays many unusual and problematic behaviors and lacks the appropriate social skills for interacting with his peers. Mark has difficulty making friends and knowing what to say to his classmates, and during recess he often ends up playing alone. Although Mark's language is well within the normal range (in fact, he has an advanced vocabulary for his age), he speaks very formally using a flat tone and usually ends up dominating most of the conversations he has with others. He also takes what others say quite literally. For example, when asked by other boys at school about the last time he took a bath, Mark responded by saying "I have never taken a bath." Although the boys thought that was humorous, Mark was just communicating that he literally never has taken a bath. What Mark failed to communicate to the boys was that he takes a daily shower. Although Mark's parents are grateful that his academic skills are strong, they are deeply concerned about their son's social and behavioral difficulties. One of their concerns is Mark's obsession with reptiles. Mark will obsessively talk about reptiles, using elaborate scientific terminology, which drives the other children (and many adults) away. Mark's obsession isolates him from others. Additionally, they are concerned about his problem behavior. Mark can become extremely stubborn, and when he is not given his way he will have a "meltdown." His behavior problems often happen on the way to school or when a change is made to his schedule. Once he has a meltdown, it is difficult for him to calm down enough to join the classroom activities. Frequently, Mark ends up leaving school early on these days, because his behavior interferes with the classroom activities.

Mark has high-functioning autism (HFA), which is affecting his ability to function and his participation in his third-grade class. Although Mark has many strengths, he clearly has a number of unique needs.

As stated earlier, students with HFA have many characteristics in common with those identified as autistic with the exception of their intelligence (Ghaziuddin & Mountain-Kimchi, 2004). That is, they often demonstrate communication difficulties and engage in unusual or **restricted interests** or have behavioral difficulties. However, researchers suggest that the core disabling feature of children and youth with HFA is their inability to socially interact (Ozonoff et al., 2002). Let's take a closer look at each of these features.

Social Interaction Problems

Students with HFA are often referred to as "odd." Their problems with social interactions are different depending on the child. Many children with HFA do not initiate social interactions. That is, they would not likely start a conversation; however, they would be more likely to respond if a person asks them a question. Other children with HFA actually do engage in social interactions, but due to the awkwardness of their interactions, these social relationships are not typically sustaining (Ozonoff et al., 2002). That is, they lack **pragmatic** language skills and social etiquette during conversations. Additionally, students with HFA may lack the ability to relate to other's feelings and responding appropriately to other's emotions. For example, they may not notice or show any concern for another child who is crying. Peer-related social relationships appear to be the most problematic for these children, but relationships with adults, such as their parents, may be forthcoming (Ozonoff et al., 2002). Unfortunately, as these children grow older, they become more and more aware of their social awkwardness, causing low self-confidence in social situations and leading to further social isolation (Ozonoff et al., 2002).

Communication Problems

Although children and young people with HFA have fluent language, the manner in which they use language is different than their peers (Ozonoff et al., 2002). For example, at times they will often use **delayed echolalia,** memorizing what they have heard on television or what has been said by others and then incorporating that phrase into their sentences. Additionally, they may have advanced on vocabulary at a young age, which impresses their parents and others. Finally, their speech has an unusual tone—that is, they may speak loudly or softly or their speech has an unusual pattern of tone, inflections, and pauses (Ozonoff et al., 2002). In general, their speech may be fluent and understandable, but the topics they choose to discuss, odd word choices, and abnormal speech conventions make communication difficult (Minshew, Goldstein, & Siegel, 1995). All of these irregular communication patterns make their language substantially different from their same-age peers.

Obsessions and Problem Behaviors

Children and youth with HFA demonstrate obsessions with narrow interests (Ozonoff et al., 2002). They often engage in the same activity or behavior for extended periods of time. For example, Mark was obsessed with reptiles and constantly talked and read about them. These obsessions may change over time and many times include video games and computers. Children with HFA are often resistant or reluctant to stop engaging in these obsessions when asked, which can lead to problematic behaviors. Unfortunately, these obsessions can lead to social isolation as well.

Identification of HFA

Similar to ADHD, the American Psychiatric Association's (APA) *Diagnostic and Statistical Manual of Mental Disorders* (*DSM-IV— Text Revision;* APA, 2000) is used to diagnose HFA (see Table 7.2). To be classified under autism, children must display at least six of the symptoms listed in the DSM-IV. However, in order to receive a diagnosis of HFA, the child must meet the criteria for autism, but demonstrate language and intellectual skills within the normal range (Ozonoff et al., 2002). As suggested earlier, the degree and severity of symptoms varies considerably (NRC, 2001), even with students who qualify under the high-incidence range.

Although the DSM-IV (APA, 2000) criteria are often used for diagnosing children with HFA, other diagnostic tools exist that can assist in the identification process, such as the *Asperger Syndrome Diagnostic Scale* (Myles, Bock, & Simpson, 2000), *Gilliam Asperger Disorder Scale* (Gilliam, 2001), and *Autism Diagnostic Interview—Revised* (ADI-R; Lord, Rutter, & LeCouteur, 1994). Researchers have suggested that if children meet the DSM-IV (APA, 2000) criteria for autism, have a cutoff score with the clinical range on the ADI-R, and have a full-scale IQ of at least 70, then they can be considered in the category of HFA (Ghaziuddin & Mountain-Kimchi, 2004).

Diagnosis for children with HFA can be difficult because they do not present all of the symptoms that are typical of many children who meet the more traditional diagnostic criteria of autism (Ozonoff et al., 2002). As a result, they may be misdiagnosed early on. For example, it is not uncommon for children with HFA to be misdiagnosed, since many of the symptoms may overlap with other types of disabilities (e.g., obsessive-compulsive disorder, ADHD).

Most often, psychologists or physicians diagnose children with HFA; however, individuals who have training in various diagnostic assessment tools and procedures may be qualified as well. Often a **multidisciplinary team** is involved in the diagnostic process, assisting in identifying the child's learning and behavioral needs. Regardless, the person evaluating the child's characteristics should have specific training and expertise in diagnosing individuals with autism, including HFA. To obtain a comprehensive diagnosis, the following information should be obtained: a developmental

TABLE 7.2	Diagnostic criteria—autistic disorder
DSM-IV Symptoms	**Examples**

Deficits in Reciprocal Social Interaction

1. a. Difficulty using nonverbal behaviors to regulate social interaction	• Trouble looking others in the eye • Little use of gestures while speaking • Few or unusual facial expressions* • Trouble knowing how close to stand to others* • Unusual intonation or voice quality*
1. b. Failure to develop age-appropriate peer relationships	• Few or no friends* • Relationships only with those much older or younger than the child or with family members* • Relationships based primarily on special interests* • Trouble interacting in groups and following cooperative rules of games*
1. c. Little sharing of pleasure, achievements, or interests with others	• Enjoys favorite activities, television shows, toys alone, without trying to involve other people* • Does not try to call others' attention to activities, interests, or accomplishments • Little interest in or reaction to praise
1.d. Lack of social or emotional reciprocity	• Does not respond to others; "appears deaf" • Not aware of others; "oblivious" to their existence • Strongly prefers solitary activities • Does not notice when others are hurt or upset; does not offer comfort*

Deficits in Communication

2.a. Delay in or total lack of development of language	• No use of words to communicate by age 2 • No simple phrases (e.g., "more mild") by age 3 • After speech develops, immature grammar or repeated errors*
2.b. Difficulty holding conversations	• Has trouble knowing how to start, keep going, and/or end of conversation* • Little back-and-forth; may talk on and on in a monologue* • Fails to respond to the comments of others; responds only to direct questions* • Difficulty talking about topics not of special interest*
2.c. Usual or repetitive language	• Repeating what others say to them (echolalia) • Repeating from videos, books, or commercials at inappropriate times or out of context • Using words or phrases that the child has made up or that have special meaning only to him or her* • Overly formal, pedantic style of speaking (sounds like "a little professor")*

(Continued)

TABLE 7.2	*(Continued)*
DSM-IV Symptoms	**Examples**
2.d. Play that is not appropriate for developmental level	• Little acting-out scenarios with toys. Rarely pretends an object is something else (e.g., a banana is a telephone) • Prefers to use toys in a concrete manner (e.g., building with blocks, arranging dollhouse furniture) rather than pretending with them* • When young, little interest in social games like peek-a-boo, ring-around–the-rosie, and the like
Restricted, Repetitive Behaviors, Interests or Activities	
3.a. Interests that are narrow in focus, overly intense, and/or unusual	• Very strong focus on particular topics to the exclusion of other topics* • Difficulty "letting go" of special topics or activities* • Interference with other activities (e.g., delays eating or toileting due to focus on activity) • Interest in topics that are unusual for age (sprinkler systems, movie ratings, astrophysics, radio station call letters)* • Excellent memory for details of special interests*
3.b. Unreasonable insistence on sameness and following familiar routines	• Wants to perform certain activities in an exact order (e.g., close car doors in specific order) • Easily upset by minor changes in routine (e.g., taking a different route home from school) • Need for advanced warning of any changes • Becomes highly anxious and upset if routines or rituals not followed
3.c. Repetitive motor mannerisms	• Flapping hands when excited or upset • Flicking fingers in front of eyes • Odd hand postures or other hand movements • Spinning or rocking for long periods of time • Walking and/or running on tiptoe
3.d. Preoccupation with parts of objects	• Uses objects in unusual ways (e.g., flicks doll's eyes, repeatedly opens and closes doors on toy car), rather than as intended • Interest in sensory qualities of objects (e.g., likes to sniff objects or look at them closely) • Likes objects that move (e.g., fans, running water, spinning wheels) • Attachment to unusual objects (orange peel, string)

*Indicates characteristics particularly applicable to HFA-AS.
Adapted from Ozonoff, S., Dawson, G., & McPartland, J. (2002). *A parent's guide to Asperger syndrome and high-functioning autism: How to meet the challenges and help your child thrive* (pp. 27–28). New York: Guilford.

history, direct observation of the child's characteristics and behavior, and a review of medical records. Frequently, additional testing, such as IQ and achievement testing, are also conducted and may be helpful in the diagnostic process. Once a diagnosis is made, it is critical for early intervention to occur to teach the child the skills needed to be independent and successful. In the next section, we will highlight the unique learning needs and practices for teaching these children and young people.

Unique Learning Needs and Evidence-Based Practices (HFA)

As indicated by the characteristics described above, students with HFA present a unique challenge for teachers. However, one of the biggest challenges is determining what interventions should be used to address these student's needs. For example, there are over 16 million references related to autism on the Internet (many related to intervention), so, how does a teacher determine which is the most effective practice? Fortunately, practices have been scientifically validated that can help teachers instruct students with autism; the communication, social, and behavioral skills they need to be successful. Many of these include practices within the field of applied behavior analysis (ABA) (see earlier discussion) including using visual instructional strategies, teaching executive functions, behavioral interventions, implementing social stories, and peer-related social skills training.

Visual Instructional Strategies

Students with HFA learn more effectively when material is presented visually rather than verbally. Therefore, structuring their environment visually can assist them in learning needed skills (Ozonoff et al., 2002). For example, teachers can provide written instructions for students with HFA, rather than presenting these instructions verbally. In addition, addressing directions directly to the child, rather than the entire class, can help communicate expectations. The Treatment and Education of Autistic and Related Communication-handicapped Children (TEACCH) program in North Carolina emphasizes the use of visual structure and organization of the environment to teach these students language, social, and cognitive skills (Schopler, Mesibov, Shigley, & Bashford, 1984).

Executive Function Assistance

The term **executive functioning** is used to describe the skills needed for organization and planning. Since students with HFA have organizational problems, strategies for assisting them in organizing their environment will also help them gain needed skills. Executive functioning is a type of skill that teachers can help with. For example, teachers may create homework logs, assignment checklists, or day planners to help the child organize (Ozonoff et al., 2002). "To do" lists can also help the child plan. One common characteristic of students with HFA is that many of them enjoy routines. Therefore, structuring tasks that become part of the student's routine can facilitate completion of these tasks.

Behavioral Interventions

Many students with HFA have behavior problems at school that can interfere with their learning and participation. As in the case of Mark, his resistance to change often produced problem behaviors that interfered with his ability to attend school.

It is likely that at different points in time, students with HFA will need a **functional behavior assessment** and **behavioral intervention plan** to help manage their behaviors. In addition, self-management instruction may help students learn to manage their own behavior.

Social Stories

Social stories, developed by Gray (1998), provide students with HFA a written (and illustrated) description of the critical events that occur in a social situation. In some ways, this technique resembles a **task analysis** in that the social story provides a step-by-step description of what will occur in the social situation. Gray (1998) suggests that social stories should focus more on informing the student about the social cues of the social situation and less on telling the student exactly "what to do."

Peer-Related Social Skills Training

A great deal of research has been conducted on peer-related social skills training. Of course, depending on the age level of the student, the type of skills and training may differ. For young children, a number of teacher and peer-mediated interventions have been found to be effective in helping to develop social skills (for a review, see Brown & Conroy, 2002). For example, environmental arrangement, such as incorporating toys that are a part of the child's **restricted interests** into social situations, has been found to be effective in increasing children's peer-related social skills (Boyd, Conroy, Mancil, Nakao, & Alter, in press). Additionally, altering social contingencies, such as prompting students to interact and providing praise following social interactions, may facilitate peer-related social interactions (Odom & Strain, 1986).

For older students, teachers may want to implement peer-network strategies (Garrison-Harrell, Kamps, & Kravits, 1997) or peer tutoring (Kamps, Kravits, & Ross, 2002). When using peer networks, a group of peers and the target child are provided training in social interaction skills with peers, followed by reinforcement of these skills through arrangement of specific peer-related activities. Additionally, peer tutoring recruits peers who are taught to assist the target child during needed instructional times. Since students with HFA are often bright, they can also provide assistance to other students in the class.

The ability to successfully interact with peers is a critical skill for success. Although students with HFA may never be the most social students in the room, they can learn skills to improve their social performance. In fact, many students with Asperger syndrome state that they want friendships, but do not know how to approach others.

SUMMARY

This chapter reviewed the characteristics, identification process, and evidence-based practices for students with ADHD, TBI, and HFA. As discussed earlier, individuals with these disabilities have unique characteristics and needs. As the urban legend suggests, one size does not necessarily fit all. One common characteristic of all of these students is that they have many strengths and when capitalized on, these strengths can help such students learn the critical skills needed to be successful. The place to start in

Students identified with other high-incidence disabilities have their own unique learning and require appropriate assessment and educational interventions to optimize their learning. (Photo credit: Valerie Schultz/Merrill)

fostering their learning and development is to obtain an appropriate diagnostic and educational assessment that identifies their unique learning characteristics and needs. Not only should their academic ability levels be assessed, but, also a critical area of assessment and intervention for all of these students is in the area of peer-related social interaction skills.

The outcome for persons with ADHD, TBI, and HFA to be successful in school is promising. However, appropriate instruction and supports that target learning and behavioral deficits need to be provided. These supports may include simple services such as instructional and task modifications, to more complex services, such as the provision of related services, and intensive instruction.

There are a number of evidence-based practices available to use with these students to help them meet their learning goals. ABA strategies are one set of practices that researchers have identified as particularly effective with all of these students. However, students may also need other instructional strategies to meet their unique learning needs (e.g., technological adaptations, etc.). Fortunately, if interventions are provided at an early age and consistently provided, the prospect for these students' future success and independence is hopeful.

COMPETENT TEACHING BOX   BOX 7.1

Knowing your students . . .

Working with students with ADHD, TBI, or HFA can be perplexing and challenging for teachers. However, when teachers provide these students with the appropriate instruction and supports to be successful, these students will gain critical skills. All of the students with these types of disabilities have strengths, and when these strengths are capitalized on, their skills will develop. When you work with children and youth with ADHD, TBI, or HFA, remember the following:

- Most individuals diagnosed with these disabilities have many different needs. Therefore, individualized assessment and interventions are critical for helping them learn. The assessment should focus on identifying the student's strengths and needs, including peer-related social skills training. Instruction for these students should occur in the least restrictive environment, many times the general education classroom.
- Identification of students with ADHD, TBI, and HFA should be conducted by a multidisciplinary team to assist identifying their needs across all developmental domains. Some of these students experience additional disabilities, including depression, mood swings, and obsessive-compulsive disorders. A comprehensive evaluation that is conducted by all the necessary professionals is a critical part of developing appropriate interventions.
- Although the general education classroom is often the least restrictive placement for these students, they may need many different types of special education services. For example, students with HFA may require services from an occupational therapist. Students with TBI may require hospital/homebound services or services from a physical therapist. Often times these related services, such as speech-language therapy and physical therapy may be provided within the general education classroom. Similar to students with other disabilities, these students will require transition services. Transition services may including transitioning across school settings or from school into the community. Regardless of the setting, instructional planning to facilitate peer-related social skills is a critical part of their intervention.

Competent teachers . . .

- Competent teachers conduct individualized assessments of their students' strengths and needs and provide the appropriate services for facilitating their learning.
- Competent teachers of students with ADHD, TBI, and HFA should focus on teaching peer-related social skills in addition to academic skills, knowing that social skills are the foundation for success in adulthood.
- Competent teachers target identification of students with ADHD and HFA at an early age to minimize the effects of these disabilities on development. With students who have a TBI, intervention should begin as soon as the child is medically stable and capable of participating.
- Competent teachers include students with ADHD, TBI, and HFA in their least restrictive placement; often with their same age peers where they can develop friendships.
- Competent teachers use evidence-based practices including applied behavior analysis strategies to strengthen a student's behavior to support learning.

:: CASE STUDIES

SAMANTHA

Samantha (Sam is her nickname) is in 5th grade. In first grade, Sam was diagnosed with ADHD. Sam was not particularly impulsive or hyperactive, but it was extremely difficult for her to concentrate and attend during instructional times. Sam and her parents were fortunate, because her first-grade teacher observed Sam across different types of instructional activities (group, independent seatwork, and so forth). She also observed her in social and other nonacademic times. After a period of time, it was clear to her that Sam may have a form of ADHD called ADHD—Predominantly Inattentive Type. The teacher met with Sam's mother and discussed her concerns. Sam's mother had noticed that Sam had a difficult time concentrating as well and that she didn't complete things she had started. However, Sam's mother and her father were going through a difficult divorce and she had attributed her daughter's inattentiveness to this life change. Following the parent-teacher meeting, Sam's teacher met with the Child Study Team to discuss pursing further evaluation of Sam's academic abilities. The school psychologist on the team observed Sam across several situations and completed an ADHD checklist. He found that Sam did demonstrate some of the common characteristics of ADHD, but did not demonstrate others. However, everyone noticed and was concerned about her inability to concentrate and attend. Unfortunately, Sam's academic progress was being affected by her inability to attend. Sam was falling significantly behind her peers in all academic areas and was demonstrating skills below her ability levels. To obtain a comprehensive and thorough evaluation of her learning needs, the Child Study Team decided to refer Sam to a specialty diagnostic assessment team that was located at the local university's College of Education. This team, called the Multidisciplinary Training Team, was comprised of a developmental pediatrician, licensed psychologist, speech-language pathologist, and classroom diagnosticians. Fortunately, Sam was given a thorough diagnostic assessment. The Multidisciplinary Training Team conducted IQ testing, achievement testing, and a complete medical assessment. The diagnosis was indeed ADHD—Predominant Inattentive Type with Learning Disabilities in reading, writing, and math. A placement meeting was held with Sam's school staff (general education teacher, special education teacher, and guidance counselor), her parents, and the university-based Multidisciplinary Training Team. The team decided that Sam needed extra assistance and instruction in her reading, math, and handwriting. Therefore, Sam was enrolled in special education services under the category of Learning Disability (LD). Additionally, the developmental pediatrician recommended medication to help increase Sam's attentiveness. It is now several years later and Sam is doing much better. She continues to need special education services to help her learn alternative strategies to accommodate for her learning disabilities. She also continues to use medication while she is at school to help increase her attention span. Additionally, Sam has been taught self-management strategies to help her focus her attention and concentration. Sam's teachers have also implemented strategies such as **cooperative learning groups** while Sam is in the general education classroom to help her follow through with task activities and instruction. Finally, Sam's mother and teacher are meeting this spring to discuss her transition to middle school next year and help plan for the appropriate supports needed for her to be successful.

1. What would have happened to Sam if her ADHD and LD were not discovered in her early elementary school years?
2. Do you think Sam needed medication to help her attention span? Why or why not?
3. What other types of interventions were useful in helping Sam's attention and skill development?

RACHAEL

Rachael and her brother lived in the country and were racing their bikes down a steep hill on a gravel road. The next thing Rachael knew, she woke up in the hospital with a head injury. Apparently, Rachael hit a crevasse in the road and went over the handlebars of her bicycle, landing on her head. Although she was wearing a helmet (which saved her life), her brain was injured by the fall. Rachael's brother immediately went for help and Rachael was rushed to the hospital unconscious. Once at the hospital, Rachael was immediately transferred by helicopter to a specialty hospital dealing with head injuries. Rachael was fortunate that she got help immediately. Her brain was badly bruised and jolted and she remained unconscious for 48 hours. The doctors were unsure if Rachael would ever gain consciousness again. When Rachael gained consciousness, her entire family was quite relieved—that was the best news! However, they quickly began to realize that Rachael had a tough journey ahead of her. Rachael had lost many cognitive abilities, including her short-term memory skills, receptive and expressive language abilities (e.g., articulation, understanding language), and most of her motor and self-help abilities. Basically, Rachael needed to learn to walk, talk, eat, and think again. Each day was a challenge. Fortunately, Rachael and her family had exceptional medical services available and Rachael was resilient. She spent approximately 4 months in the rehabilitation hospital, working hard every day to relearn the skills she had lost. Following her time in the rehabilitation center, she went home, received homebound instruction, which included special instructional services, as well as speech, occupational, and physical therapy. With this help, Rachael continued to gain skills on a daily basis. That was 2 years ago and Rachael is doing remarkably well. Although she is behind several years in school due to the injury, Rachael is back in the general education program fulltime, but receives itinerant special education services. She continues to have minor cognitive processing difficulties (including short-term memory deficits and problem solving deficits) as well as some speech difficulties, but her motor skills have fully recovered. Although Rachael does not really demonstrate any particular behavior problems or mood swings, her family has noticed that she is still having a time socially adjusting. Many of her friends prior to the accident have moved on and Rachael is older than the other students in her class. Additionally, she is often tired and needs frequent rest periods. The itinerant special education teacher has taught Rachael adaptive strategies for coping with her memory and problem solving difficulties. Additionally, she continues to strengthen her language deficits through speech-language services.

Rachael is one of the lucky ones. She received assistance immediately and after several years has been able to regain most of her skills. Rachael and her family are hopeful that things will soon be back to normal.

1. Why do you think Rachael has been able to recover many of her skills?
2. Should Rachael have been placed in the same grade level she was in prior to the accident or moved ahead with her same-age peers? What would be the positives about moving Rachael forward? What might be the negatives about retaining her?
3. Will Rachael ever be the same again? Can she lead a normal life?
4. Why did Rachael sustain such a traumatic injury when she was wearing a helmet? Could anything have prevented the injury?

JT

JT is in middle school. For years, his parents had been concerned about his learning and behavioral skills. Although, he was extremely bright and capable, he had many unusual behaviors and was very set in his ways. In elementary school, JT showed signs of inattentiveness and impulsivity and was diagnosed by his pediatrician with ADHD. These behaviors began to affect his performance at school. Since he was not eligible under IDEA for special education services, he began receiving additional supports through a **Section 504 plan.** Throughout elementary school, he had a great deal of difficulty in school and was very awkward in social situations with his peers. He wanted friends, but was not very successful at making them. As he progressed through school, his social difficulties became more and more apparent as well as his odd behaviors. Most recently, JT acted as if he was depressed and often told his parents he did not want to go to school. He said he would rather stay home and work on his computer, researching his favorite topic—dinosaurs. In fact, JT knew just about everything there was to know about dinosaurs—almost too much. He was planning on becoming a paleontologist after college.

JT's parents read a recent article in a national magazine about Asperser syndrome and High-Functioning Autism. Once they read the article, they knew that this described their son. JT's parents researched everything they could on the Internet and contacted a local advocacy organization to find out more information about AS and HFA. As they found out additional information and spoke with other parents, they became more and more convinced that JT had been misdiagnosed with ADHD; what he really had was AS. JT's parents were referred to a local psychiatrist who had experience and expertise in autism. After a comprehensive medical and diagnostic assessment, at age 14, JT was diagnosed with Asperger syndrome. The psychiatrist conducted direct observations of JT and completed several autism checklists. He believed that JT definitely met the DSM-IV (2000) criteria for AS. Following the diagnosis, JT was staffed into special education services to help with his learning and social problems. The main concern was his inability to interact socially with his peers; however, his obsessive-compulsive behaviors also required a **functional behavioral assessment** and **behavioral intervention plan.** Finally, JT needed additional instruction in learning readiness skills, such as completing assignments and following directions. JT's parents felt it was best to discuss with JT his diagnosis and the characteristics that accompany Asperger syndrome. JT wants to learn how to socially interact with his peers and become more integrated into his school, but he knows that this does not come naturally to him. JT's parents are glad that due to an appropriate diagnosis, he appears to be on a better path. But his parents are wondering how JT will learn the social skills he needs to hold down a job as an adult and become a member of society. From all the information they have read and the other parents they have met with, they know there is a long road ahead.

1. Why do you think JT doesn't have many friends?
2. How could JT have received a more accurate diagnosis at an earlier age? Did it harm him to not have an accurate diagnosis?
3. Is the general education classroom the least restrictive environment for JT?
4. What does JT's future hold?

REFERENCES

American Academy of Pediatrics, Committee on Quality Improvement, Subcommittee on Attention-Deficit/Hyperactivity Disorder. (2000). *Pediatrics, 105,* 1158.

American Psychiatric Association (2000). *Diagnostic and statistical manual of mental disorders, text revision: DSM-IV-TR* (4th ed.). Washington, DC: Author.

Barkley, R. (1990). *Attention deficit hyperactivity disorder: A handbook for diagnosis and treatment.* New York: Guilford.

Barkley, R. A. (1997). Behavioral inhibition, sustained attention, and executive functions: Constructing a unifying theory of ADHD. *Psychological Bulletin, 121,* 65–94.

Barkley, R. A. (1998). *Attention deficit hyperactivity disorder: A handbook for diagnosis and treatment* (2nd ed.). New York: Guilford.

Bowen, J. M. (2005). Classroom interventions for students with traumatic brain injuries. *Preventing School Failure, 49*(4), 34–41.

Boyd, B. A., Conroy, M. A., Mancil, G. R., Nakao, T., & Alter, P. J. (in press). Effects of circumscribed interests on the social behaviors of children with autism spectrum disorders: Use of structural analysis analogues. *Journal of Autism and Developmental Disorders.*

Brown, M. B. (2000). Diagnosis and treatment of children and adolescents with Attention-Deficit/Hyperactivity Disorder. *Journal of Counseling and Development, 78,* 195–203.

Brown, W. H., & Conroy, M. A. (2002). Promoting peer-related social-communicative competence in preschool children. In H. Goldstein, L. A. Kaczmarek, & K. M. English (Eds.) *Promoting social communication: Children with developmental disabilities from birth to adolescence* (pp. 173–211). Baltimore: Brookes.

Castellanos, F. X., Lee, P. P., Sharp, W., Jeffries, N. O., Greenstein, D. K., Clusen, L. S., et al. (2002). Developmental trajectories of brain volume abnormalities in children and adolescents with attention-deficit/hyperactivity disorder. *Journal of the American Medical Association, 288*(14), 1740–1748.

Cooper, P., and O'Regan, F. J. (2001). Educating children with AD/HD: A teacher's manual. London, England: Routledge Falmer.

Council for Exceptional Children. (2001). Traumatic brain injury—The silent epidemic. *CEC Today, 7*(7), 1, 5, 15.

Cramer, M. M. (2002). *Instructor's manual to accompany Exceptional Lives: Special Education in Today's Schools.* Upper Saddle River, NJ: Merrill/Prentice Hall.

Dell Orto, A. E., & Power, P. W. (2000). Brain injury and the family: A life and living perspective (2nd ed.). Washington, DC: CRC Press.

Garrison-Harrell, L., Kamps, D., & Kravits, T. (1997). The effects of peer networks on social-communicative behaviors for students with autism. *Focus on Autism and Other Developmental Disabilities, 12,* 241–257.

Ghaziuddin, M., & Mountain-Kimchi, K. (2004). Defining the intellectual profile of Asperger syndrome: Comparison with high-functioning autism. *Journal of Autism and Developmental Disorders, 34*(3), 279–284.

Gilliam, J. E. (2001). *Gilliam Asperger disorder scale.* Austin, TX: PRO-ED.

Gray, C. A. (1998). Social stories: Improving responses of students with autism with accurate social information. *Focus on Autistic Behavior, 8,* 1–10.

Hallahan, D. P., & Kauffman, J. M. (2003). *Exceptional learners: Introduction to special education* (9th ed.). Boston, Allyn and Bacon.

Harris, K. R., Friedlander, B. D., Saddler, B., Frizzelle, R., & Graham, S. (2005). Self-monitoring of attention versus self-monitoring of academic performance: Effects among students with ADHD in the general education classroom. *The Journal of Special Education, 39*(3), 145–156.

Individuals with Disabilities Education Improvement Act. (2004). 20 USC 1400.

Kamps, D. M., Kravits, T., & Ross, M. (2002). Social communicative strategies for school-aged children. In H. Goldstein, L. A. Kaczmarek, & K. M. English (Eds.) *Promoting social communication: Children with developmental disabilities from birth to adolescence* (pp. 239–277). Baltimore: Brookes.

Lahey, B. B., Applegate, B., McBurnett, K., Biederman, J., Reenhill, L., Hynd, G. W., Barkley, R. A., Newcorn, J., Jensen, P., Richters, J., Garfinkel, B., Kerdyk, L., Frick, P. J., Ollendick, T., Perez, D., Hart, E. L., Waldman, I., & Shaffer, D. (1994). DSM-IV field trials for attention deficit hyperactivity disorder in children and adolescents. *American Journal of Psychiatry, 151,* 1673–1685.

Lahey, B. B., Pelham, W. E., Loney, J., Lee, S. S., & Willcutt, E. (2005). Instability of the DSM-IV subtypes of ADHD from preschool through elementary school. *Archives of General Psychiatry, 62,* 896–902.

Lerner, J. W., Lowenthal, B., & Lerner, S. R. (1995). *Attention deficit disorders: Assessment and teaching*. Pacific Grove, CA: Brooks/Cole.

Lord, C., Rutter, M., & LeCouteur, A. (1994). The autism diagnostic interview—revised. *Journal of Autism and Developmental Disorders, 24,* 659–685.

Mather, N. & Goldstein, S. (2001). *Learning disabilities and challenging behaviors*. Baltimore: Brookes.

McCrory, J. C., & Gregg, S. (1995). ADHD: Instructional strategies that work. *The Link, 14,* 1–3.

Minshew, N. J., Goldstein, G., & Siegel, D. J. (1995). Speech and language in high-functioning autistic individuals. *Neuropsychology, 9*(2), 255–261.

Myles, B. S., Bock, S. J., & Simpson, R. L. (2000). *Asperger syndrome diagnostic scale*. Austin, TX: PRO-ED.

National Dissemination Center for Children with Disabilities (NICHCY). (2004). *Traumatic brain injury*. Retrieved December 8, 2005 from http://www.nichcy.org/pubs/factshe/fs18txt.htm

National Institute of Health. (1998). *ADHD Consensus Development Conference Statement*. Retrieved January 5, 2006 from http://consensus.nih.gov/1998/1998AttentionDeficit HyperactivityDisorder110html.htm

National Institute of Mental Health. (2005). Attention Deficit Hyperactivity Disorder. Retrieved July 15, 2005 from http://www.nimh.nih.gov/publicat/adhd.cfm?Output=Prin

National Institute of Neurological Disorders and Stroke (NINDS). (2005). *NINDS: Traumatic Brain Injury Information Page*. Retrieved December 8, 2005 from http://www.ninds.nih.gov/disorders/tbi/tbi.htm

National Research Council. (2001). *Educating children with autism*. Washington, DC: National Academy Press.

Odom, S. L. & Strain, P. S. (1986). A comparison of peer initiation and teacher-antecedent interventions for promoting reciprocal social interaction of autistic preschoolers. *Journal of Applied Behavior Analysis, 19,* 59–72.

O'Melia, M. C., & Rosenberg, M. (1994). Effects of cooperative homework teams on the acquisition of mathematics skills by secondary students with mild disabilities. *Exceptional Children, 60,* 538–548.

Ozonoff, S., Dawson, G., & McPartland, J. (2002). *A parent's guide to Asperger syndrome and high-functioning autism*. New York: Guilford.

Patton, J. R. (1994). Practical recommendations for using homework with students with learning disabilities. *Journal of Learning Disabilities, 27,* 570–578.

Rosenthal, M., & Ricker, J. (2000). Traumatic brain injury. In R. G. Frank, & T. R. Elliott (Eds.), *Handbook of rehabilitation psychology* (pp. 49–74). Washington, DC: American Psychological Association.

Rowland, A. S., Lesesne, C. A., & Abramowitz, A. J. (2002). The epidemiology of Attention-Deficit/Hyperactivity Disorder (ADHD): A public health view. *Mental Retardation and Developmental Disabilities, 8,* 162–170.

Schopler, E., Mesibov, G. B., Shigley, R. H., & Bashford, A. (1984). Helping autistic children through their parents: The TEACCH model. In E. Schopler, & G. B. Mesibov (Eds.), *The effects of autism on the family* (pp. 65–81). New York: Plenum Press.

Stormont-Spurgin, M. (1997). I lost my homework: Strategies for improving organization in students with ADHD. *Intervention in School and Clinic, 32*(5), 270–275.

Stuart, J. L., & Goodsitt, J. L. (1996, Winter). From hospital to school: How transition liaison can help. *Teaching Exceptional Children, 28*(2), 58–62.

Tripp, G., & Alsop, B. (2001). Sensitivity to reward delay in children with Attention Deficit Hyperactivity Disorder (ADHD). *Journal of Child Psychology and Psychiatry, 42,* 691–698.

Tsal, Y., Shalev, L., & Mevorach, C. (2005). The diversity of attention deficits in ADHD: The prevalence of four cognitive factors in ADHD versus controls. *Journal of Learning Disabilities, 38*(2), 142–157.

Tyler, J. S., & Mira, M. P. (1999). Educational modifications for students with head injuries. *Teaching Exceptional Children, 25*(3), 24–27.

Whalen, C. K. (2001). ADHD treatment in the 21st century: Pushing the envelope. *Journal of Clinical Child Psychology, 30,* 136–140.

Zentall, S. S., Harper, G. W., Stormont-Spurgin, M. (1993). Children with hyperactivity and their organization deficits. *The Journal of Educational Research, 97,* 112–117.

Educational Instruction

Assessment for Academic Instruction

Holly B. Lane
University of Florida

URBAN LEGEND: *It is important to use the best single assessment instrument.*

LEGENDARY THOUGHT: *There is no one best assessment instrument. Selection of an assessment instrument or method should be based on the purpose of the assessment, the domains to be assessed, and the characteristics of the student to be assessed. The most effective assessments occur when data are collected from multiple sources and analyzed carefully to make instructional decisions.*

◆

Assessment is a critical element of the instructional cycle, as shown in Figure 8.1. Assessment is used to plan instruction and to determine its effectiveness. Assessment provides the information necessary to make sound instructional decisions. Special education relies heavily on assessment data to identify students' needs and to ensure that appropriate and effective services are provided to students with disabilities. The many uses of assessment or testing are listed in Box 8.1.

:: PURPOSE AND BENEFITS OF ASSESSMENT

Assessment plays a critical role in the education of students with high-incidence disabilities. Sound educational decision-making must be based on data, and it is through assessment that these data are collected. Assessment can take the form of a formal standardized test, an informal teacher-made test, or a teacher's observation of a student's classroom academic performance or behavior.

The selection of an assessment method and instrument should be made only after considering the purpose of the assessment. The most common purposes for assessment include screening, diagnosis, progress monitoring, and outcome measurement (Kame'enui, 2002). Basic principles underlying all assessment are listed in Box 8.2, pages 195–196.

Screening

A window screen serves as a filter to let some things through and keep other things out. Screening assessment does just that. A screening assessment can be thought of

FIGURE 8.1

The instructional cycle

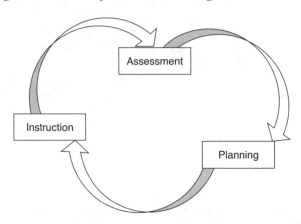

BOX 8.1 INSTRUCTIONAL USES OF TESTING

Rudman (1989) generated a list of useful purposes for assessment in education. Testing can be used for . . .

1. Gaining an overview of what students know at the beginning of the school year.
2. Making decisions about grouping students in the class.
3. Diagnosing what students know.
4. Determining the pace of classroom instruction.
5. Making promotion and retention decisions.
6. Sharing information with boards of education, parents, and the general public through the media.
7. Measuring the effectiveness of instruction and learning.

---

as the filter that separates typically achieving students from those who are most likely to need extra help. It screens out students who don't need help and lets through those who might need help. Typically, screening is conducted with all students at the beginning of each school year and as new students enter a school throughout the year.

Screening assessments are usually brief measures that give teachers a general idea about students' abilities. Teachers conduct screening assessments to determine which students in a group have met specific benchmarks of academic or behavioral performance and which have not. Using a screening measure, a teacher can identify those students who are most likely to experience difficulty. Screening assessments do not provide sufficient detail about a student's level to plan intervention. Further assessment is needed.

Diagnosis

Once a student has been identified as likely to need extra help through the use of a screening measure, additional information about the nature of the student's needs is collected using diagnostic assessment. Diagnosis is a process through which the assessor conducts a detailed examination of a student's performance on academic or behavioral skills. This in-depth analysis of a student's strengths and weaknesses is used to plan intervention.

Diagnostic assessment is used to make placement decisions in special education. States have specific criteria that must be met for a student to qualify for special education services, and diagnostic assessment is used to determine whether the student has met these criteria.

Diagnostic assessment requires a knowledgeable and skilled assessor, because the diagnostic process typically requires interpretation of test results from several sources. The ability to synthesize data from different tests is essential. Usually, a school psychologist or other professional conducts the diagnostic assessments used for special education placement, but a classroom teacher can conduct diagnostic assessments for planning instruction. Once diagnostic assessment data are collected and analyzed, planning for intervention can take place.

Progress Monitoring

Once instruction or intervention begins, frequent ongoing assessment can provide the teacher with information about the effectiveness of the intervention. This progress monitoring assessment may be conducted daily, weekly, monthly, or quarterly, using equivalent measures so that comparisons may be drawn over time. Teachers may also use informal observation of a student's learning to measure progress within a lesson.

According to the report of the Reading First assessment committee (Kame'enui, 2002), progress monitoring assessment may be used to (a) estimate rates of improvement; (b) identify children who are not making adequate progress and, therefore, require additional or different forms of instruction; and (c) compare the efficacy of different forms of instruction. Continual progress monitoring assessment may be used to design more effective instruction.

Teachers may assess a student's learning during a lesson and use the information to decide what to do next. If a teacher finds that a student is not learning as expected, the teacher may decide to reteach the lesson, review a concept, or choose a different instructional method to ensure the student learns. The best teachers understand that something has not been taught until the student has learned it. Only through assessment can the teacher be certain that the student has learned.

Outcome Measurement

Outcome assessment is used to determine whether students have achieved expected levels of performance after a given period of time. These assessments are usually conducted once each year to measure mastery of grade-level objectives. Classrooms, schools, districts, and states are compared using the results of outcome assessments.

Outcome measurement is sometimes used to make decisions such as whether a student should be promoted to the next grade or whether enough of a school's students are making adequate progress. When decisions such as students' grade-level promotion or school funding are tied to students' performance on an assessment, it is considered "high-stakes" testing.

:: TYPES OF ASSESSMENT

All assessment can be classified into two categories: formative and summative. Formative assessments are used to make decisions. According to Airasian (1997), formative assessment involves "collecting, synthesizing, and interpreting data for the purpose of improving learning or teaching" (p. 402). Summative assessments are used to evaluate the effectiveness of those decisions. Summative assessment

BOX 8.2 PRINCIPLES OF ASSESSMENT

Assessment involves professional judgment. As objective as we may attempt to be in our assessment practices, there will always be underlying values and assumptions that guide our thinking. Recognizing this fact will allow us to make better use of our assessment results.

Assessment requires understanding of measurement and evaluation. Conceptual understanding of statistics and statistical procedures is necessary to take part in and communicate about meaningful assessment.

Assessment decision-making is influenced by a variety of factors. Assessment methods that will provide the most thorough and useful information are not always feasible to use in educational settings. The methods that are often used in schools do not always provide the most useful information. Selection of the most appropriate assessment requires consideration of both the information needed and the constraints of administration.

Assessment influences students' learning and motivation. Knowledge of a forthcoming assessment may create an external motivation for learning, but the type of assessment selected may also affect how students learn. Students study differently based on what they know about the upcoming test, and preparation for a multiple-choice test may require less engagement than preparation for a problem-solving assessment.

Assessment contains error. Teachers and administrators must understand that there is error in all classroom and standardized testing. This understanding is particularly important in the age of high-stakes testing.

Assessment can enhance instruction. Good assessment allows teachers to continually improve instruction. Ongoing informal assessment tells the teacher when to move on, when to review a concept, and when and for whom to provide extra help.

Assessment should be valid. There is little point in conducting assessments that are not valid. A valid assessment measures what it purports to measure, and an invalid measure does not. Understanding validity is crucial to effective design, selection, or administration of assessments.

Assessment should be fair and ethical. Fairness in testing includes absence of bias, equitable treatment, and equality in outcomes and opportunities. Ethical considerations include what students should know about learning expectations and about the test itself, uses of test data, and confidentiality of test results.

Assessment should use multiple methods. Fair and valid decisions should be made only after a series of measures using multiple methods.

(Continued)

Given the amount of error in most forms of testing, educators should feel obliged to use multiple data sources to make important decisions. Making decisions about such issues as student promotion or retention should never be made using only one form of assessment.

Assessment should be efficient and feasible. The time and methods used for assessments should be reasonable when compared with the time allotted for teaching. Time is one of the most valuable resources in schools, and testing should only take the time necessary for it to be fair and useful.

Adapted from McMillan, James H. (2000). Fundamental assessment principles for teachers and school administrators. Practical Assessment, Research & Evaluation, 7(8). Retrieved July 17, 2005 from http://PAREonline.net/getvn.asp?v=7&n=8

involves "collecting, synthesizing, and interpreting information for the purpose of determining pupil learning and assigning grades" (p. 404).

Formal Assessments

Formal assessments are preplanned, structured assessments developed for evaluative purposes. Formal assessments are constructed to measure learning outcomes and student achievement and to assign student grades. Few formal assessments provide information that assists teachers in instructional decision-making. Most formal assessments are administered only once and do not provide the repeated measures necessary to analyze the effects of various factors on students' academic and social performance (Mercer & Mercer, 2005). Nevertheless, formal assessments play an important role in the education of students with high-incidence disabilities. Formal assessments are used to make placement decisions, diagnose disabilities, make instructional recommendations, measure achievement outcomes, and evaluate special education programs.

Standardized Tests of Intelligence

Standardized tests of intelligence are used to measure an individual's intellectual abilities. Although there is no consensus among professionals on the definition of intelligence, the assessment of intellectual ability is mandated by law for special education placement.

The most widely accepted tests of intelligence used in schools yield an intelligence quotient or score (IQ), but each measures and reports this score in a slightly different fashion (see Table 8.1 for a summary of such tests). The most common approach is to measure both verbal and nonverbal intelligence. Verbal intelligence refers to the ability to use and comprehend language. Nonverbal intelligence includes visual organization, spatial reasoning, and other abilities not based in language.

In educational settings, these and other measures of intelligence are used to determine an individual's capacity for learning. Most IQ tests have a **mean** or average

TABLE 8.1	Commonly used tests of intelligence (IQ)
Assessment Instrument	**Focus of Assessment**
Kaufman Assessment Battery for Children-II (KABC-II)	The KABC-II yields separate scores for Simultaneous Processing and Sequential Processing.
Stanford-Binet Intelligence Scales (SBS)	The Stanford-Binet provides a Verbal IQ, a Nonverbal IQ, and a Full-Scale IQ.
Weschler Intelligence Scale for Children-IV (WISC-IV)	The WISC-IV yields index scores for Verbal Comprehension, Perceptual Reasoning, Working Memory, and Processing Speed. A Full-Scale IQ score is derived from these indices.
Woodcock-Johnson III Tests of Cognitive Abilities (W-J III)	The W-J III reports scores to represent Verbal Ability, Thinking Ability, and Cognitive Efficiency, as well as General Intellectual Ability.

score of 100, with a **standard deviation** of 15. This means that scores that fall within one standard deviation of the mean (i.e., 85–115) are thought to be within the average range. Scores above 115 are considered above average, and scores below 85 are considered below average. Scores that are two or more standard deviations above or below the mean are considered exceptional. An IQ of 130 or above is generally considered to be in the gifted range, and a score of 70 or below is generally considered to indicate a cognitive disability.

Intelligence testing is also often used to identify the presence of a learning disability. The most commonly used criterion for identifying learning disabilities is a significant discrepancy between IQ and achievement (Müller & Markowitz, 2004). That is, a student's actual academic achievement must be significantly below the level of performance that would be expected for someone with his or her IQ. To determine whether such a discrepancy exists, both intelligence tests and standardized tests of achievement must be administered. In most states, the discrepancy between IQ and achievement must be at least one standard deviation. That is, to qualify for a specific learning disabilities program, a student with an IQ of 100 must score more than one standard deviation below average on a test of achievement.

Standardized Tests of Achievement

Standardized tests of achievement are used to measure a student's performance in a given area in a way that can be considered both reliable and valid. **Reliability** refers to the consistency or stability of scores from a given test (Airasian, 1997). **Validity** is the extent to which an assessment measures what it is intended to measure (Lefrancois, 1999). Standardized measures have uniform methods for administration and scoring.

Standardized tests may be **norm-referenced** or **criterion-referenced**. Norm-referenced assessments compare an individual's score to a normative group of the same age or grade level. Criterion-referenced assessments compare an individual student's performance to a criterion or benchmark. Norm-referenced tests typically yield a standard score or percentile rank, while criterion-referenced tests classify a student based on how close the student's score is to the established benchmark.

Teachers can use norm-referenced tests for general planning purposes, for identifying areas of student strength and weakness, and for grouping students for instruction. Criterion-referenced tests are generally more useful for daily instructional decision-making. Knowing how close a student is to a given benchmark will help the teacher pick the most appropriate method for teaching that student.

A number of commercially available assessments are packaged as batteries to assess student performance in a broad range of subject areas with just one test (see Table 8.2 for a summary of selected achievement batteries). These instruments

TABLE 8.2	Achievement test batteries	
Assessment Instrument	**Target Age/Grade**	**Focus of Assessment**
Brigance Comprehensive Inventory of Basic Skills—Revised (CIBS-R)	PreK-9	The *Brigance* is a criterion-referenced assessment of pre-academic and academic skills that includes subtests of reading, math, spelling, and motor skills.
Kaufman Test of Educational Achievement-II (K-TEA-II)	K-12	The K-TEA-II is used to assess academic skills in reading, math, written language, and oral language.
Peabody Individual Achievement Test—Revised (PIAT-R)	K-12	The PIAT-R is an individual measure of academic achievement in reading, math, and spelling. Its multiple-choice format makes the PIAT-R appropriate for assessing individuals with limited expressive abilities.
Wechsler Individual Achievement Test II (WIAT-II)	PreK-12	The WIAT-II is a brief assessment of oral language and academic knowledge.
Woodcock Johnson III Tests of Achievement-III (WJ-III)	PreK-adult	The WJ-III achievement battery can be used to identify academic strengths and weaknesses, measure performance levels, contribute to the detection of discrepancies between ability and achievement, assist in educational decision-making, and assess academic progress.

usually address reading and math, and some include sections on written expression, social studies, science, or reasoning, as well. Other assessments focus on one subject area or even specific skills within that subject area. Subject area assessments are addressed later in this chapter.

Informal Assessments

Most teachers rely far more on informal assessment than formal assessment to make day-to-day instructional decisions. To individualize instruction in special education, a teacher must also often individualize assessment procedures and materials. Understanding the features of effective informal assessment is therefore critical.

Criterion-Based Methods

Selection of assessment materials and procedures must begin with consideration of long-term goals for the student. From the long-term goals, the teacher determines the appropriate scope and sequence of instruction. The Individualized Education Program (IEP) should guide this process. In the development of the IEP, specific criteria for mastery are established. Measurement of progress toward mastery can be accomplished with **criterion-based assessments**, which determine how close a student's performance is to an established benchmark. For example, a student's IEP may include a goal that the student is able to say the name of each letter of the alphabet, with a criterion for mastery set at 85%. To measure progress toward that IEP goal, the teacher may provide a list of the letters of the alphabet in a random sequence. When the student can name 22 of the 26 letters, mastery of the goal has been reached.

Curriculum-Based Methods

One especially effective way of measuring individual students' progress is through **curriculum-based measurement** (CBM). CBM, initially developed by Stan Deno and his colleagues at the University of Minnesota in the late 1970s, helps teachers establish student goals and assess progress toward them. The focus of CBM is to monitor the effectiveness of instruction. If a teacher determines through CBM that a student is not making progress, the next step would be to examine the instruction to determine what alteration may be made to promote better student learning.

Most CBM assessment is conducted using repeated timed samples, or **probes**, of student learning. The teacher selects a representative sample of the curriculum with which to conduct the CBM and creates a probe. For example, the teacher may select a passage from a textbook and conduct a one-minute **timing** to determine how many correct words per minute (CWPM) the student can read. Or, the teacher can select math facts from the curriculum and compile a single page of these facts with which to conduct a timing. In each case, the teacher would record the student's data on a chart. Daily results using the same probe would be charted and analyzed to determine whether the student is making sufficient progress. If sufficient progress is being made, then the teacher continues on the current course of instruction. If the student's progress is inadequate, then the teacher reexamines the instructional methods being used and makes appropriate changes.

CBM assesses a student's fluency with a particular skill, which is thought to be the best representation of proficiency. That is, if one is proficient in a skill, then one can perform that skill effortlessly and automatically. Many schools and districts have developed local norms or expectations using CBM methods. With local norms, teachers know what students of similar backgrounds can be expected to accomplish in the local curricula.

The term curriculum-based measurement is often used interchangeably with **curriculum-based assessment** (CBA). These were, at least originally, different methods. The term CBA was first used by Edward Gickling in 1977 (Coulter, 1988). It was intended to represent an approach of determining students' instructional needs by assessing the percentage of items known. In contrast, CBM refers to a systematic set of measurement procedures to gather data for instructional decision-making (Deno, 1985).

CBA was conceived to answer five questions: What does the student know? What can the student do? How does the student think? How does the student approach what he or she is unsure of? As a teacher, now what do I do? (Gravois & Gickling, 2002). The underlying assumption of CBA is that the student should be compared only to himself and not to the academic development of classmates or other norms. The focus of this model is closing the gap between what the student knows or can do and what the task demands. In CBA, instruction drives measurement, and in CBM, measurement drives instruction (Burns, MacQuarrie, & Campbell, 1999).

Teacher-Made Tools

In many instances a teacher may find it more appropriate to design an assessment tool to address a specific need. Designing carefully to ensure validity is important (i.e., it is important to make sure you are measuring what you think you are). For example, if a teacher wants information about a student's knowledge of the alphabet, the nature of the assessment could determine how well the student performs. If the teacher asks the student to recite the alphabet, the student may be able to say every letter name in order. If the teacher asks the student to identify letters randomly ordered on a page, the student may only be able to name half the letters. If the teacher asks the student to write all the letters, the student may only be able to write the letters in her name. Although all these methods could be considered ways to assess a student's alphabet knowledge, the methods would yield quite different results.

Most teachers construct tests to assess students' content knowledge. Tests may take the form of open-ended essay questions, multiple-choice questions, short answer questions, oral responses, task performance, or some combination of these and other methods. The method of assessment should match both the purpose for assessment and the constraints of the setting. For example, although the most useful information about students' knowledge may be gathered through extensive written assignments, the time it takes students to write and teachers to read lengthy papers limits the utility of this approach. Rather than assign daily papers, a teacher may assign only one or two lengthy written assignments per school term. Assessment in the interim must take other forms. In addition to traditional tests, teachers make checklists, rubrics, and charts to record evidence of student learning.

Teacher Observation

Systematic observation of student performance can be one of the most useful and powerful forms of assessment. **Performance assessment** can be conducted at any time that the student is performing the task. To make observation of student performance more systematic, a **checklist** or **rubric** can be useful (see Box 8.3, page 203). A teacher might use a checklist to record when a particular student has demonstrated a particular skill in a skill set. If there are varying degrees of skill mastery possible, then a rubric can help the teacher systematically identify and record a particular student's degree of mastery. A rubric is a scoring method to evaluate the quality of students' work (see Figure 8.2 for a sample rubric). Rudner and Schafer (2002) identified two advantages to using a rubric: it supports evaluation of the extent to which criteria have been reached, and it provides feedback to students about how they can improve.

A teacher may also keep **anecdotal records** of a student's performance. This involves writing a narrative account of the student's performance for either immediate or subsequent evaluation. Anecdotal records, while primarily used for assessment of behavior, can be used to assess academic performance, such as oral reading or demonstrations in mathematics.

Teacher Questions

Perhaps the most common method of assessment in any classroom is the question from the teacher. Effective teachers ask a lot of questions. They also ask effective questions. Extensive research has been conducted to determine what makes an effective question. Although higher-order questions promote student thinking, lower-level, or literal, questions also promote student learning. More important is how questions are posed. Wilen and Clegg (1986) suggest that teachers (a) phrase questions clearly; (b) ask questions with an academic rather than procedural focus; (c) allow sufficient wait time after asking a question before requesting a response; (d) encourage all students to respond in some way to every question; (e) elicit a high percentage of correct responses; (f) probe after a student response to encourage clarification and expansion of ideas; and (g) acknowledge correct responses, but use specific and discriminating praise.

Portfolios

Collecting and analyzing authentic examples of student work as a form of assessment has gained enormous popularity in recent years. This approach is known as **portfolio assessment.** Although there are many portfolio-related resources available, there is little consensus about how to compile a portfolio or how to evaluate it. Most portfolios include a collection of artifacts of student work highlighting the learning goal of the activity. The teacher can develop a rubric to score each item in a

FIGURE 8.2	Sample rubric for scoring an expository writing sample		
Writing Component	**Needs Improvement**	**Adequate**	**Meets Expectations**
1. Complete and correct content	• Content is inaccurate • Lack of supporting evidence • Necessary information is omitted	• Content is mostly accurate with some errors • Some supporting evidence is provided, but it is insufficient • Some information is provided to support conclusions	• Content is accurate • Ideas are presented with sufficient supporting evidence • All necessary information is included to support conclusions
2. Coherent writing	• Inadequate transitions • Rambling format • Irrelevant information is included	• Basic transitions are used • A structured format is used • Some explanation of complex ideas is provided	• Effective transitions used throughout • Structured format is is used, including appropriate headings and subheadings • Thorough explanations are provided as needed
3. Sound mechanics	• Numerous distractions including: • Grammatical errors • Spelling errors • Punctuation errors • Sloppy appearance	• Few distractions related to: • Grammar • Spelling • Punctuation • Generally neat appearance	• Appropriate grammar, spelling, and punctuation used throughout • Professional appearance

portfolio or to evaluate the portfolio as a whole. Ideally, the student selects work representative of his or her best efforts. Portfolios offer a holistic option for evaluating student performance, but they are difficult to use for daily instructional decision-making because they are seldom sensitive to growth over a short period of time.

BOX 8.3 STEPS IN DEVELOPING A SCORING RUBRIC

1. Identify qualities necessary for highest score.
2. Develop a scoring scheme for each factor.
3. Define criteria for lowest level.
4. Contrast lowest and highest for middle level, including finer distinctions, if appropriate.

Adapted from Rudner, L. & Schafer, W. (2002). What Teachers Need to Know about Assessment. Washington, DC: National Education Association.

:: CONTENT OF ASSESSMENT

In addition to knowing *how* to conduct assessments, a competent teacher must have a strong understanding of *what* to assess (see Kauffman & Hallahan, 2005). Most states and school districts have standards that all students are expected to meet. Many also dictate specific curricular goals and objectives to be met and, sometimes, even the instructional materials that must be used. In special education, the teacher is mandated to individualize instruction, but the goal should always be to maximize special education students' access to the general education curriculum. One of the best ways to ensure access is to conduct frequent assessment of progress. This allows the special educator to see what instruction is working and what needs improvement. Each subject area has critical skills that must be mastered, without regard to the local curricular goals. Understanding these critical skills and using appropriate means of assessment helps the teacher prepare students for success.

Assessing Oral Language

Language forms the foundation for much of our learning. Difficulties in mastering language can affect learning in nearly every aspect of life and school. Many learning disabilities are based on language deficits. Understanding the nature of a child's language difficulties is essential for the teacher to remediate those difficulties and to make accommodations in instruction (Justice, 2006).

Spoken language consists of five key elements: phonology, morphology, syntax, semantics, and pragmatics (see Hallahan & Kauffman, 2006; Hallahan, Lloyd, Kauffman, Weiss, & Martinez, 2005). **Phonology** refers to the sound system of spoken language. **Morphology** refers to how words are formed and understanding the meanings of word parts. **Syntax** refers to the rules of phrase and sentence formation. **Semantics** refers to the meaning system of language and includes both word meaning and sentence meaning. **Pragmatics** refers to the rules of language use in various situations. Bloom and Lahey (1978) categorize these elements according to form (phonology, morphology, and syntax), content (semantics), and use (pragmatics). Language difficulties can be based in

TABLE 8.3	Commonly used assessments of oral language	
Assessment Instrument	Target Age/Grade	Focus of Assessment
Clinical Evaluation of Language Fundamentals—4 (CELF-4)	5–21	The CELF-4 is designed to help determine the nature of a language disorder, evaluate the student's receptive and expressive language strengths and weaknesses, and assess language structure, language content, and working memory.
Comprehensive Assessment of Spoken Language (CASL)	3–21	The CASL measures language processing skills—comprehension, expression, and retrieval—in four language structure categories: lexical/semantic, syntactic, supralinguistic, and pragmatic.
Expressive One-Word Picture Vocabulary Test—Revised (EOWPVT-R)		The EOWPVT-R is an individually administered, norm-referenced assessment of expressive vocabulary.
Peabody Picture Vocabulary Test—III (PPVT-III)	2.5–90+	The PPVT-III is a measure of receptive vocabulary and a screening test of verbal ability. It is an individually administered, norm-referenced instrument commonly used to screen young children for early receptive language difficulties. This test of vocabulary knowledge is highly correlated with verbal IQ measures (Dunn & Dunn, 1997).
Test of Language Development (TOLD)	4–8 (primary) 8–13 (intermediate)	The TOLD has both primary and intermediate versions designed to assess picture vocabulary, oral vocabulary, grammatic understanding, sentence imitation, grammatic completion, word discrimination, and word articulation.
Test of Early Language Development-3 (TELD—3)	2–7	The TELD-3 is a screening and/or diagnostic tool to assess receptive and expressive language development in young children.
Test of Word Knowledge (TOWK)	5–17	The TOWK is designed to assess a student's skill in reception and expression of semantics on three levels: ability to match spoken words with referents; knowledge of word definitions, opposites, and synonyms; and metalinguistic aspects of word knowledge.

any one of these elements of language or in any combination of elements. There are many standardized tests of language (see Table 8.3 for a summary).

Assessing Phonology

Phonology assessment focuses on the way a student processes the sounds of both expressive and receptive language. Assessment of phonological awareness, which is one component of phonology, is addressed in the section on reading assessment. Other aspects of phonology, especially articulation difficulties, are typically assessed by a speech and language clinician.

Assessing Morphology

Morphological difficulties typically manifest themselves in the way children combine **morphemes,** or meaningful word parts, such as roots, prefixes, or plural endings. For example, a young child may say, "I goed to the store" instead of "I went to the store." This is a typical phase of language development. If an older child uses this form, however, it may be indicative of a difficulty with morphology. Understanding how morphemes change in form and pronunciation when combined with other morphemes (e.g., nature → natural; heal → health) is a critical element of **morphological awareness.** Morphological awareness, or the knowledge of morphological structures of language, is closely tied to other linguistic abilities and plays an important role in a child's ability to understand complex words (Justice, 2006). Morphological awareness can be assessed informally through observation of children's language use and by asking children to perform tasks that require morphological knowledge. For example, a teacher might ask the child to make regular and irregular plurals, such as "I had one dog, but another came along, so now I have two ___?" and "I had one mouse . . ." Another method for assessing morphology is to measure the **mean length of utterance** (MLU). The MLU is computed by collecting a sample of a child's spoken language, counting the number of utterances, and then dividing by the total number of morphemes in the sample. The MLU is thought to represent the morphological complexity of language use in young children.

Assessing Syntax

Syntactic development occurs in phases, beginning with one-word utterances and moving to utterances of two or more words, simple sentences, and complex sentences. As children develop their ability to formulate ideas in spoken language according to the rules of our syntax, they may encounter difficulties. Some of the most common difficulties include problems with such syntactic structures as interrogatives and negatives. They may also lack the length and complexity of sentences that would be expected of children their age. Syntactic abilities are most often assessed by the speech and language clinician, but the classroom teacher can assess these abilities informally. The teacher's observation of the child's natural language use can be an effective tool. Through simple observation, the teacher can notice how the child asks questions or expresses ideas in the past tense. The teacher may also ask the child to repeat increasingly complex sentences. The ability to repeat spoken language is limited by the child's level of syntactic development.

Assessing Semantics

Semantics includes understanding of the meaning of words (lexical semantics) as well as the meaning produced by combining words in various ways (sentential semantics). In the classroom, semantic knowledge is measured most often through vocabulary assessment. There are many standardized assessments of both **receptive** and **expressive** vocabulary, but informal measures provide the teacher with more useful information for planning instruction. To assess students' vocabulary, the teacher provides a sentence stem that uses the target word but leaves the meaning ambiguous. The student's role is to complete the sentence. A good sentence stem requires the completion to reveal the student's understanding of the word. For example, the teacher might provide the following sentence stem: "Everyone said that Mark was *arrogant,* because. . . " The completion of this stem would reveal the student's knowledge of the word meaning. Completions such as ". . . they like him" or ". . . he liked to fly in airplanes" would reveal little to no understanding of the word. A completion such as ". . . he wasn't very nice to people" would reveal some word understanding. A completion such as ". . . he always acted stuck up and thought he was better than everyone else" would reveal deep understanding of the word. This kind of assessment can be conducted orally or, for older students, in writing.

Assessing Pragmatics

Pragmatic language difficulties occur most often when language is used in nonliteral ways. Mature users of the language understand implied meaning, but children with pragmatic difficulties may not. Questions such as "Do you have to talk so loud?" (where the implied meaning is "Please talk more quietly") would be misinterpreted by the student with a pragmatic deficit. Idioms, metaphors, and figures of speech pose particular difficulty for such students. A statement such as "he kicked the bucket" or "I was steaming" may be confusing when interpreted literally. Again, other than language assessments conducted by a speech and language clinician, the best source of information about difficulties with pragmatics is teacher observation. Posing questions about what is really meant by a figure of speech will provide insight into a child's pragmatic skills.

Assessing Written Language

Although the earliest uses of language are oral, school-aged students are also expected to use written language. Written language involves all of the same processes as oral language plus the mechanics of getting words on paper, such as spelling and handwriting. Assessment of written expression, spelling, and handwriting can be conducted through analysis of students' written products in any subject area, through teacher observation, or through formal assessment. There are numerous standardized assessments of written language available (see Table 8.4 for a summary).

Assessing Handwriting

Recently, handwriting instruction has been neglected because many teachers see it as unimportant or even obsolete, given the prevalence of word processing. Because

TABLE 8.4	Assessments of written language	
Assessment Instrument	**Target Age/Grade**	**Focus of Assessment**
Developmental Spelling Assessment (DSA)	K–5	The DSA is designed to assess students' spelling and word recognition strengths and weaknesses and to identify each student's stage of spelling development.
Test of Early Written Language-2 (TEWL–2)	4–11	The TEWL-2 is designed as a diagnostic assessment of written language for young children. It yields three writing scores: Global Writing Quotient, Basic Writing Quotient, and Contextual Writing Quotient.
Test of Written Expression (TOWE)	6.5–15	The TOWE is a comprehensive, norm-referenced assessment of writing achievement in which students respond to a prepared writing prompt and to items that tap into specific writing skills.
Test of Written Language—3rd Edition (TOWL-3)	7.5–18	The TOWL assesses students' writing abilities in both spontaneous and contrived writing tasks. The spontaneous writing assessment measures skills in contextual conventions (capitalization, punctuation, and spelling), contextual language (vocabulary, syntax, and grammar), and story costruction (plot, character development, and general composition). The contrived writing assessment measures vocabulary, spelling, style, logical sentence writing, and sentence combining (syntax).
Writing Process Test (WPT)	8–19	The WPT measures students' ability to plan, write, and revise an original composition. The WPT assesses both written product and writing process and includes a measure of fluency.
Written Expression Scale (WES)	5–22	The WES measures students' use of conventions (handwriting, spelling, punctuation), use of syntactical forms (modifiers, phrases, sentence structures), and ability to communicate meaningfully (relevance, cohesiveness, organization).

of the many and increasing demands on classroom time, it is one of the easiest subject areas for teachers to let go. This is unfortunate because learning to write letters and words to a level of automaticity or fluency can support early reading development. Learning to write letters strengthens letter knowledge and learning to write words strengthens word recognition (Ehri, 1998). There is mounting evidence that handwriting difficulties, long thought to be simply attributable to motor problems, are actually also related to language and memory deficits (Berninger & Graham, 1998). Studies of handwriting fluency, or the speed with which students can write legibly, have demonstrated that the written composition of students who are more fluent in handwriting tends to be longer and of overall higher quality (Graham, Harris, & Fink, 2000; Jones & Christensen, 1999).

Proper letter formation is essential for handwriting fluency; therefore, handwriting instruction should focus on letter formation rather than on penmanship. Children who learn to write letters without instruction do so by copying models of the letters. This method can result in inefficient letter formation habits, frequently including beginning all letters at the baseline. Handwriting assessment must involve observation of the process, not just evaluation of the product. Knowing where to begin to form a letter, which direction to move the pencil, and where to finish the letter are more important than what the written letter looks like. Although it may provide information about skills such as spacing, observing the finished product of handwriting practice tells the teacher nothing about the way the student formed the letter.

Assessing Spelling

Assessing spelling requires an understanding of spelling development, spelling rules, and common spelling error patterns. According to Ehri (1991, 1998), learning to spell and learning to read words follow similar, usually simultaneous paths. Assessment of a student's spelling abilities can provide insight into a child's decoding skills and into his or her understanding of the **alphabetic principle.**

Children learning to spell begin by attempting scribbles on a page. Soon, they begin to notice initial letter-sound correspondences and represent these in their spelling practice, most often with the first letter of a word. Before long, they learn to represent all the sounds in the word with letters that make those sounds. Spelling during this phonetic phase is often referred to as **invented spelling.** Examination of a child's invented spellings of words can reveal quite a bit about the child's command of letters and sounds. Children move from these invented or phonetic spellings into a transitional phase in which attempts are made to apply conventional spelling rules (e.g., *flote* for *float*). Eventually children learn to spell words correctly by applying spelling rules and becoming familiar with **orthographic patterns** within words. The most common form of spelling assessment, the weekly spelling test, does little to measure a child's true spelling abilities and is even less likely to promote learning. Spelling assessment is more effectively carried out through observation of students' actual spelling during written expression or during decoding and spelling instruction (Fresch & Wheaton, 1997).

To analyze a student's spelling, the teacher should look for spelling error patterns. Taylor and Kidder (1988) found the most common spelling error in first through eighth grade is deleting letters that are difficult to detect by sound in words. Hitchcock (1989) identified common error patterns for different phases of spelling development (see Table 8.5). Examination of spellings for these patterns can inform the teacher about the type of spelling instruction that would be appropriate.

TABLE 8.5		Most common spelling errors		
Phase	**Type of Error**	**What Is This?**		**Examples**
Letter name	Letter names for sounds	Student uses letter names in place of letter sounds		yt for white lfnt for elephant
Prephonetic	Phonetic spelling	Student uses one or more letters chosen phonetically to represent the sounds in a word		site for city
Phonetic	Omission of pronounced letter	Student omits a letter that is pronounced		bown for brown
	Homonym	Student uses wrong homonym for the meaning intended		see for sea
	Insertion of a letter	Student inserts a letter that is not needed		moste for most
	Pronunciation	Student shortens or lengthens words, substitutes graphemes, or shortens suffixes		prolly for probably workin for working
	Reversal of a letter	Student reverses letters in words		framer for farmer
	Vowel pattern rule	Student spells the word as it sounds, without regard for vowel digraphs or using the wrong vowel digraph		bred for bread rayn for rain
	Vowel substitution	Student substitutes one vowel for another, uses incorrect vowel to represent the schwa sound, or substitutes a vowel for a consonant		luser for loser happin for happen
Transitional	Affixes	Student uses the wrong prefix or suffix		unpossible
	Compounding	Student separates compound words or combines words that are not compound words		butter fly for butterfly noone for no one
	Consonant substitution	Student substitutes one consonant for another or substitutes a consonant for a vowel		agust for adjust

(Continued)

TABLE **8.5**	(Continued)		
Phase	**Type of Error**	**What Is This?**	**Examples**
	Double Consonants	Student doubles a consonant when it is not needed or fails to double a consonant when it is needed	untill for until runing for running
	Omission of a silent letter	Student omits silent letters that are not heard in the pronunciation of the word	dum, nock lissen for listen
	Plurals, possessives, and contractions	Student omits an apostrophe in possessives and contractions or adds an apostrophe in plurals	the students pencil's

Assessing Written Expression

Writing is a complex task that involves multiple, coordinated processes, including planning, organizing, generating content, transcribing, revising, and editing (Berninger, 1999; Berninger, Abbott, Whitaker, Sylvester, & Nolen, 1995). Assessing written expression can be challenging.

Many writing assessment methods require students to respond to a **writing prompt,** a topic sentence or story starter designed to elicit ideas from students. This can be problematic because different students respond in different ways to different types of prompts and different modes of prompt presentation (Hudson, Lane, & Pullen, 2005). For instance, some students respond better to a prompt that is dictated versus a prompt that they copy from the board. Whether the prompt is discussed before writing begins can also make a difference. If the teacher is aware of these potential differences, measures can be taken to account for them during the scoring process.

There are three main approaches to writing assessment that use writing prompts to assess writing quality: **holistic, analytical,** and **primary trait** (Espin, Weissenburger, & Benson, 2004). Each of these methods has advantages and disadvantages.

Holistic scoring requires the teacher to make an overall judgment of the writing sample and to assign a value according to a rating scale. Judgments are made by comparing writing samples of a group, establishing a range from best to worst, and assigning other samples values within this range. Although it is quick and efficient, there are many disadvantages to holistic scoring. It is not sensitive to student growth over time, does not provide diagnostic information, and focuses only on products, not the writing process.

Analytical scoring uses preestablished criteria to judge student writing, including idea expression (soundness, clarity, relevance), language usage (sentence structure, spelling, punctuation), organization, word choice, and style or flavor of writing. Samples are scored on each of these dimensions. This method provides more structure to the assessor than holistic scoring, but also has disadvantages. Scores from one dimension may influence scores from another (e.g., numerous problems with spelling and sentence structure may influence the assessor's interpretation of idea clarity). Perhaps the biggest disadvantage of analytical scoring is that it is time consuming, which also limits its utility.

Primary trait scoring is based on the notion that all writing must be purposeful and directed. Scoring therefore focuses on the audience of the writing, and on its purpose. First, the trait must be identified. Is the purpose of the writing to inform, persuade, or express an idea? Once the purpose is defined, a scale is developed to rate the writing samples. For example, if the primary trait is character development, a scale might range from "multiple well-developed characters with rich detail regarding appearance, personality, and motives" to "flat characters with minimal relevant details provided." Primary trait scoring provides more structure than holistic scoring and is less cumbersome than analytical scoring. The main disadvantage of this approach is that, because the traits and the rating system are predetermined, it does not allow for unanticipated features of a paper.

Other writing assessment methods focus on more objective measures of writing, such as fluency, syntax, and vocabulary. Fluency-based writing assessment focuses on quantity rather than quality. To assess fluency, the teacher counts the number of words written during a given time period. The syntax of a student's writing can be measured using average **T-unit** length. T-units are phrases that can stand alone, such as an independent clause with several dependent clauses attached to it. A complete sentence may have one or more T-units. T-unit length is calculated by counting the total number of words written and dividing it by the number of T-units. A greater T-unit length represents greater syntactic complexity. Vocabulary can be objectively measured by counting the number of mature words used correctly in a selection or by calculating the **type-token ratio,** which is the proportion of unique words in a writing sample. To calculate the type-token ratio, first count the total number of words written, and then count the number of words that are written only once in the passage—the unique words. Divide the number of unique words by the total number of words to arrive at the type-token ratio for the selection.

Assessing Reading

There are more tests of reading than any other subject area. This is probably because at least 80% of students with learning disabilities have difficulty in reading (Hallahan et al., 2005; Lerner, 1989; Lyon, 1995), and diagnosing problems in reading can be a complex process. Because 75% of children who are poor readers in third grade remain poor readers in ninth grade (Francis, Shaywitz, Stuebing, Shaywitz, & Fletcher, 1996), much of the emphasis in reading assessment and instruction is aimed at preventing reading problems in the early grades. Students with disabilities are most likely to get behind in reading and to stay behind.

Individual reading assessments can provide information about specific skills and abilities that a student must have to read proficiently. These include phonological awareness, decoding, sight word recognition, reading fluency, and text comprehension. Some tests focus on one skill area, and some tests address several skill areas within the same battery. Some tests are group-administered, and others must be administered individually. Selecting the appropriate measure and method for assessment requires consideration of the skill area(s) of interest and the amount of time available for assessment. Several standardized tests are available to assess reading (see Table 8.6 for a summary).

Assessing Phonological Awareness

Phonological awareness, or the conscious awareness of the sound structure of language, is a critical skill underlying proficient reading. To understand text, a reader must be able to read the words accurately and automatically. Reading words is accomplished most efficiently through skilled decoding. To be able to decode words, a reader must have phonological awareness. Developmental levels of phonological awareness are: word, syllable, onset-rhyme, and phoneme (Lane & Pullen, 2004). The word level of phonological awareness refers to the ability to isolate and distinguish among individual words within the speech flow. Syllable level awareness is the ability to detect syllables within words. Onset-rhyme awareness refers to the ability to recognize units within the syllable: the onset, which is the part of a syllable that comes before the vowel, and the rhyme, which is the vowel and anything that follows the vowel in a syllable. The ability to manipulate the individual phonemes (i.e., the smallest units of sound in language) within words is called phonemic awareness.

For a day-to-day gauge of student growth in phonological skill, a teacher can observe students' performance on tasks during instruction. The tasks that are most important for later decoding development are phonemic segmentation and blending. To assess phonological awareness, a teacher can simply ask a student to perform tasks using these skills and record the student's performance. For example, the teacher could say to the student, "What word do these sounds make: /s/ - /u/ - /n/?" If the student is able to successfully demonstrate this blending task, the teacher could ask a more challenging question, such as "What word do these sounds make: /b/ - /e/ - /s/ - /t/?" This questioning would continue until the teacher finds what tasks the student cannot perform successfully. This information would then guide subsequent instruction.

Assessing Decoding Skills

Written language is an alphabetic code, and the ability to **decode** a word accurately and automatically is essential for proficient reading (Adams, 1990). Ehri's theory of word reading development (Ehri, 1991; Ehri & Snowling, 2004) is useful for guiding decoding assessment. According to Ehri's theory, word recognition develops in phases. The first phase is known as the pre-alphabetic phase, during which

TABLE **8.6**   Standardized reading assessments

Assessment Instrument	Target Age/Grade	Focus of Assessment
California Diagnostic Reading Tests (CDRT)	Grades 1–12	The CDRT is an individually administered diagnostic measure of word analysis, vocabulary, and comprehension.
Comprehensive Test of Phonological Processing (CTOPP)	K–adult	The CTOPP is an individually administered assessment of phonological processing. It includes assessments of phonological awareness, phonological memory, and rapid naming.
Degrees of Reading Power	Grades 1–2	DRP is an individually administered measure of comprehension that is both norm-referenced and criterion-referenced. Reading comprehension of graded passages is measured using a modified cloze technique.
Durrell Analysis of Reading Difficulty	1–12	The Durrell is a comprehensive, norm-referenced reading assessment battery with 17 subtests: oral reading accuracy, rate and comprehension; silent reading rate and comprehension; listening comprehension; word recognition; word analysis; listening vocabulary; sounds in isolation; spelling; phonic spelling; visual memory of words; identifying sounds in words; prereading phonics abilities; syntax matching; identifying letter names in spoken words; phoneme awareness; letter names and letter writing; and copying.
Dynamic Indicators of Basic Early Literacy Skills (DIBELS)	K–3	DIBELS is a series of brief (1-minute) measures designed to assess fluency on a variety of reading skills, including letter naming, initial sounds, phonemic segmentation, nonword decoding, word use, and oral reading fluency. DIBELS is designed to be used as both a screening tool and a progress monitoring measure.
Early Reading Diagnostic Assessment (ERDA)	K–1	The ERDA is an individually administered, norm-referenced assessment designed to measure phonological awareness, concepts about print, letter knowledge, language, oral reading, listening comprehension, and reading comprehension.

(Continued)

TABLE 8.6	(Continued)	
Assessment Instrument	Target Age/Grade	Focus of Assessment
Fox in a Box	K–2	*Fox in a Box* is a criterion-referenced assessment of early literacy skills that can be either individually or group-administered. It includes measures of phonemic awareness, phonics, decoding, word recognition, listening comprehension, and reading comprehension.
Gates MacGinitie Reading Test (GMRT)	K–12	The GMRT is used as a group-administered screening tool to identify students' strengths and weaknesses in decoding and comprehension.
Gray Oral Reading Test, 4th Edition (GORT-4)	Grades 2 and higher	The GORT-4 is a test of oral reading fluency and comprehension. More specifically, it measures decoding skill, reading accuracy, reading rate, and reading comprehension.
Gray Oral Reading Test—Diagnostic (GORT-D)	Ages 6–14	The GORT-D is a norm-referenced diagnostic test that includes paragraph reading, decoding, word attack, word identification, morpheme analysis, contextual analysis, and word ordering.
Group Reading Assessment and Diagnostic Evaluation (GRADE)	PreK–adult	The GRADE is a comprehensive, norm-referenced assessment of early literacy designed to measure visual skills, verbal concepts, phonological awareness, print awareness, letter recognition, phoneme-grapheme correspondence, listening comprehension, word reading, word meaning/vocabulary, and passage comprehension. The GRADE can be either individually or group-administered.
Lindamood Auditory Conceptualization Test (LAC)	K–adult	The LAC is a comprehensive, individually administered, norm-referenced assessment of phonological awareness.
Metropolitan Achievement Tests, Reading Diagnostic Tests, 7th Edition (MAT-7)	K-12	The MAT-7 is a norm-referenced, group-administered assessment of auditory discrimination, phoneme-grapheme relationships, decoding, vocabulary, listening comprehension, word recognition, reading vocabulary, reading comprehension, and spelling.
Phonological Awareness Literacy Screening (PALS)	K–1	PALS is an individually administered, criterion-referenced assessment of early literacy skills, including phonological awareness, alphabet knowledge, and word reading.

Assessment Instrument	Target Age/Grade	Focus of Assessment
Slingerland Pre-Reading Screening—Revised	K–1	The Slingerland is a criterion-referenced, group-administered assessment of early literacy skills, including sound discrimination, phonemic awareness, letter knowledge, and listening comprehension.
Slosson Oral Reading Test—Revised (SORT-R)	PreK–adult	The SORT-R is an individually administered measure of decoding and word recognition.
Slosson Test of Reading Readiness (STRR)	K–1	The STRR is an individually administered assessment of letter knowledge, phonological awareness, sequencing, and visual discrimination.
Stanford 9 Open-Ended Reading Assessment	K–adult	The Stanford 9 is an individually administered, norm-referenced assessment of reading comprehension. It includes narrative passages with open-ended questions addressing three levels of comprehension (initial understanding, relationships in text and real-life, and critical analysis).
Stanford Diagnostic Reading Test (SDRT)	Grades 1–12	The SDRT is a group-administered diagnostic measure of phonetic analysis, reading and listening vocabulary, and reading comprehension that is both norm-referenced and criterion-referenced. Specific skills and levels can be selected for administration.
STAR Reading	Grades 1–12	STAR is a computer-based, individually administered, norm-referenced reading assessment that focuses on vocabulary and comprehension.
TerraNova Reading	K–12	TerraNova is a norm-referenced reading assessment that may be individually or group-administered. It is designed to assess decoding, word recognition, vocabulary, and comprehension.
Test of Early Reading Ability, 3rd Edition (TERA-3)	PreK–3	The TERA-3 is an individually administered, norm-referenced assessment of early reading skills, including alphabet knowledge, vocabulary, conventions of print, and comprehension.
Test of Phonological Awareness (TOPA)	K–2	The TOPA is a group-administered, norm-referenced assessment of phonological awareness.

(Continued)

TABLE 8.6 *(Continued)*		
Assessment Instrument	**Target Age/Grade**	**Focus of Assessment**
Test of Word Reading Efficiency (TOWRE)	Ages 6–25	The TOWRE is an individually administered, norm-referenced assessment of word reading. The test includes two brief sections: sight word efficiency and phonemic decoding efficiency.
Texas Primary Reading Inventory (TPRI)	K–2	The TPRI is an individually administered, criterion-referenced assessment designed to measure early reading skills, including phonemic awareness, alphabet knowledge, print awareness, listening comprehension, and reading comprehension.
Woodcock Diagnostic Reading Battery (WDRB)	K–adult	The WDRB is a compilation of the reading-related subtests of the Woodcock-Johnson achievement and cognitive batteries. It is individually administered and norm-referenced. It includes assessments of phonological awareness, decoding, word recognition, vocabulary, and comprehension.
Woodcock Reading Mastery Tests—Revised (WRMT-R)	K–adult	The WRMT-R assesses reading readiness, basic reading skills, and reading comprehension. The test is used to identify specific students' strengths and weaknesses in reading skills to determine appropriate instructional strategies.

children recognize logos or guess words from pictures with no attention to the letters in the word or the sounds those letters represent. In the second phase, the partial alphabetic phase, children attend to some of the letters in the word. Children in this phase tend to overgeneralize their knowledge of letter sounds and may, for instance, recognize any word that begins with "p" as "puppy." As children become more familiar with letters and sounds, they begin to decode by using every letter in the word. This phase is known as the full alphabetic phase. With extensive practice decoding, children begin to notice frequently occurring patterns or chunks within words. Children who can recognize chunks within words are in the consolidated alphabetic phase. Eventually, a reader reaches a phase where decoding is extremely rapid and effortless, so much so that they may not be consciously aware of their decoding process. This is known as the automatic phase.

To assess a student's decoding skills, the teacher first determines which phase the student has reached. The purpose of decoding instruction is to first get children to notice and use letters and their sounds (partial alphabetic phase), then to build proficiency at letter-by-letter decoding (full alphabetic phase), and finally, to call attention to the patterns within words (consolidated alphabetic phase). Movement into the automatic phase is promoted more through extensive reading practice than through decoding instruction. A child who focuses on the first couple of letters in an unknown word will need practice reading and spelling words sound by sound. A child who can read a word sound by sound but does so laboriously will need instruction directing attention to the chunks within words.

It is also important to consider the relative difficulty of various words when assessing decoding skills. For example a "VC" word such as "at" or "it," which consists of a vowel (V) followed by a consonant (C), may be the simplest combination of sounds to decode. Words that follow a CVC pattern, such as "fun," "sat," or "lip" are somewhat more challenging. Words that have consonant clusters, such as "last" (CVCC) or "flip" (CCVC), and words with more than one syllable are more difficult.

Assessing Word Recognition

High-frequency words, such as "was," "said" and "because," which do not closely follow decodable patterns, are called **sight words.** A proficient reader reads these words on sight, without stopping to decode. Lists of high-frequency words, such as the Dolch (1936) list, provide a good place to start for making a sight word test. Recognition of common words should be automatic and effortless, so timed tests are appropriate to assess sight word knowledge.

Words can be presented in a list or on cards. To use the list format, the teacher can either time the student's reading of the entire list, time the student's reading of the words to determine CWPM (correct words per minute), or uncover the words on the list one at a time, leaving each word exposed for only a limited amount of time (approximately 2 seconds to assess automatic recognition). In the card format, the teacher shows each card for a limited amount of time. Again, the focus of sight word assessment should be both accuracy and automaticity. Word recognition is usually included as a subtest in reading assessment batteries.

Assessing Reading Fluency

Passage reading **fluency** is highly correlated with text comprehension. Text read slowly and laboriously is seldom well understood because too much mental effort is devoted to figuring out words and too little is left to figuring out the author's message. Fluency can be defined as **accuracy, rate,** and **prosody** (Hudson, Lane, & Pullen, 2005). Accuracy is simply reading the words correctly, whether by decoding or by recognition of high frequency sight words. Rate can be considered on two levels: word reading automaticity and text reading rate. Prosody refers to the way oral reading sounds, including the expression and inflection of the reader's voice and the placing of pauses between phrases.

Measures of oral reading fluency most often assess only accuracy and rate. The most common assessment is a timed oral reading of connected text. Oral reading fluency (ORF) is usually recorded in CWPM. If the readability level of text is known, a teacher can make a sound judgment about a student's ORF by comparing the student's reading to established benchmarks. For example, according to oral reading fluency norms established by Hasbrouck and Tindal (2006), the average first grader reads grade-level passages at 53 CWPM by the end of the school year, and the average fourth grader reads at 123 CWPM. A fourth grader who reads only 65 CWPM in a grade-level passage would be considered significantly below average and in need of fluency intervention.

One tool used to assess accuracy of oral reading is the **running record** (Clay, 1985; Denton, Ciancio, & Fletcher, 2006). In this approach, the teacher listens to a student's oral reading and records marks on a page to indicate how the student read each word. In addition to noting each word read correctly, the teacher notes specific error types, including substitutions, omissions, insertions, repetitions, and hesitations. Analysis of the type of errors and patterns of errors can guide instruction.

The National Assessment of Educational Progress (NAEP) (Pinnell, Pikulski, Wixson, Campbell, Gough, & Beatty, 1995) evaluation of reading fluency focused on students' prosody. The researchers developed a scale for evaluating students' reading based on their phrasing and expression. This scale may be found in Table 8.7.

Assessing Comprehension

The RAND Reading Study Group (2002) defined reading comprehension as "the process of simultaneously extracting and constructing meaning through interaction and involvement with written language" (p. 11). Most group-administered reading assessments focus on text comprehension, because this is one of the few reading skills that can be assessed this way. Unfortunately, most group-administered assessments of reading comprehension also rely on multiple-choice formats that impose significant limits on the

TABLE 8.7	National Assessment of Educational Progress (NAEP) rubric for assessing oral reading fluency
Level	**Characteristics of Oral Reading**
4	Reads primarily in larger, meaningful phrase groups. Although some regressions, repetitions, and deviations from text may be present, these do not appear to detract from the overall structure of the story. Preservation of the author's syntax is consistent. Some or most of the story is read with expressive interpretation.
3	Reads primarily in three- or four-word phrase groups. Some smaller groupings may be present. However, the majority of phrasing seems appropriate and preserves the syntax of the author. Little or no expressive interpretation is present.
2	Reads primarily in two-word phrases with some three- or four-word groupings. Some word-by-word reading may be present. Word groupings may seem awkward and unrelated to larger context of sentence or passage.
1	Reads primarily word-by-word. Occasional two-word or three-word phrases may occur, but these are infrequent and/or they do not preserve meaningful syntax.

Source: U.S. Department of Education, Institute of Educational Sciences, National Center for Education Statistics. (1995). *Listening to Children Read Aloud, 15.* Washington, DC.

types of information that can be gathered. Little information about the depth or extent of the meaning constructed can be gathered through multiple-choice assessments.

An **informal reading inventory** (IRI) can provide more in-depth information about a student's reading comprehension. An IRI can be teacher-constructed, but many IRIs are available commercially (see Table 8.8). Most IRIs provide graded

TABLE 8.8	Commercial informal reading inventories (IRIs)	
Assessment Instrument	**Target Age/Grade**	**Focus of Assessment**
Qualitative Reading Inventory, 3rd Edition (QRI-III)	Grades 1–12	The QRI-III is a comprehensive IRI that includes assessment of decoding, word recognition, listening comprehension, and reading comprehension. Both narrative and expository passages are included, as well as a background knowledge assessment component.
Ekwall/Shanker Reading Inventory, 3rd Edition (ESRI-3)	Grades 1–8	The ESRI-3 is a comprehensive IRI designed to assess letter knowledge, decoding, word recognition, listening comprehension, and reading comprehension.
Woods and Moe Analytical Reading Inventory—6th Edition	Grades K–6	The Woods and Moe Analytical Reading Inventory is designed to assess decoding, oral reading comprehension, silent reading comprehension, and listening comprehension. This measure includes both narrative and expository passages.
Burns/Roe Informal Reading Inventory	1–12	The Burns/Roe IRI includes graded word lists and graded reading passages to assess reading accuracy and reading comprehension. Comprehension questions target main idea, detail, inference, sequence, cause-and-effect, and vocabulary.
Developmental Reading Assessment (DRA)	K–3	The DRA is a bit different from other IRIs because it uses leveled books rather than isolated graded passages.
Flynt-Cooter Reading Inventory for the Classroom	1–12	The Flynt-Cooter is designed to assess silent reading comprehension, oral reading miscues, and listening comprehension.
Stieglitz Informal Reading Inventory	1–12	The Stieglitz is designed to assess decoding, word recognition, and reading comprehension.

passages for students to read aloud and questions for the teacher to ask. Some IRIs distinguish between the type of passage (e.g., expository or narrative) and the type of questions (e.g., literal, inferential, application, evaluation) to provide more detailed information about the student's strengths and weaknesses. Some IRIs also include an option for the student to retell the story in as much detail as possible. The teacher then counts the number of idea units the student includes in the retelling. If the student reads the passage orally, the teacher can also assess decoding skills and reading fluency. Some IRIs even include components such as graded word lists to assess other aspects of the student's reading.

The **cloze procedure** provides an alternative method for assessing comprehension. In the cloze procedure, the teacher removes words from a passage and asks the student to fill in the blanks. To construct a cloze passage, begin with a 200–400 word selection of text. Keep the first sentence intact, but remove every nth word (usually every 5th, 6th, 7th, or 8th word) from the rest of the passage. The student's job is to figure out what word belongs in the blank. The **maze procedure** is a modification of the cloze method in which the student is provided choices for each blank.

For older students, summary writing can be an effective method of assessing comprehension. Instruction in note-taking methods and compilation of an adequate summary is usually necessary. Once students understand how to write a good summary, their summaries become valuable tools to reveal what they took from the passage.

Assessing Math

Like reading assessment, individual math assessment can provide detailed information about a student's skills and abilities. Several key elements of mathematics provide the basis for assessment. These include number sense, computation, problem solving, and real-life application. Although there are standardized tests of math achievement (see Table 8.9 for a summary), much can be learned from informal methods of math assessment.

Assessing Number Sense

Just as phonemic awareness is fundamental to developing later reading skills, **number sense** is fundamental to developing later math skills (Gersten & Chard, 1999). Number sense, although difficult to define, can be thought of as the awareness of numbers in everyday life and how they can be compared and manipulated. A child with strong number sense can count and compare quantities. Assessing number sense can be most effectively accomplished through teacher questioning and classroom observation. For example, asking a child to identify which of two numbers is bigger or to demonstrate one-to-one correspondence provides some insight into that child's number sense.

For older students, number sense takes on new meaning. It includes understanding of the meanings of various operations, knowing, for example, that adding two numbers will result in a larger number. Number sense also encompasses the

TABLE 8.9   Standardized math assessments

Assessment Instrument	Target Age/Grade	Focus of Assessment
California Diagnostic Math Test (CDMT)	Grades 1–12	The CDMT is a group-administered, criterion-referenced, diagnostic assessment of math skills. It includes measures of number sense, computation, and applications.
Comprehensive Mathematical Abilities Test	2–12	This individually administered, norm-referenced assessment is designed to measure skills in computation, math reasoning, and real-world application.
Group Mathematics Assessment and Diagnostic Evaluation (G-MADE)	K–12	The G-MADE is a group-administered, norm-referenced assessment designed to measure number sense, computation, and applications.
Key Math—Revised	K–12	The Key Math is an individually administered, norm-referenced, diagnostic battery of math assessments. It includes measures of basic math concepts, computation, and application.
Stanford Diagnostic Mathematics Test, 4th Edition (SDMT-4)	Grade 1–adult	The SDMT-4 is a group-administered, norm-referenced, diagnostic battery of math assessments. It includes measures of basic math concepts, computation, and application.
Test of Early Mathematics Ability-3 (TEMA-3)	Ages 3–9	The TEMA-3 is an individually administered, norm-referenced assessment designed to measure number sense, basic computation, and math concepts.
Test of Mathematical Abilities-3 (TOMA-3)	Grades 3–12	The TOMA is a norm-referenced assessment of broad math skills, designed for use as both a diagnostic and progress monitoring tool. It measures math vocabulary, computation, and applications.

understanding of whole numbers versus decimals and fractions and positive versus negative numbers. A student who understands these concepts knows, for example, that 2/5 is smaller than 4 and that .68 is smaller than 23.

Assessing Computation

Mathematical computations are easy to assess in terms of whether an answer is right or wrong. An effective teacher, however, will want to know more about a student's responses, such as the depth of the student's understanding of the operation and its underlying properties. Just as children move through different phases of word reading, they also move through phases of computation development: acquisition, fluency building, mastery, and generalization. As they develop understanding of math facts, they move through three levels: **concrete, representational,** and **abstract** (Mercer & Miller, 1992).

Early understanding of computation concepts is at the concrete level. A child at this level can demonstrate math facts by moving objects. For example, a child can show that two crayons combined with three more crayons results in a total of five crayons. Without manipulative objects, this child would not be able to explain the concept of addition. Once a child has a strong understanding of concrete operations, learning at the representational level can take place. A child at the representational level can demonstrate math operations with pictures or tally marks on paper. Without actually manipulating objects, the child can demonstrate computation of an equation using these written representations. A child at the abstract level can compute without the support of manipulative objects or any pictorial representation at all. Using only numbers, a child at the abstract level can explain an operation.

As children reach an abstract level of understanding, they move from the acquisition phase into the fluency-building phase. Fluency with math facts refers to the ability to compute with both accuracy and automaticity. As students become fluent with math facts, more of their attention can be devoted to problem solving. Many problems with complex math operations can be traced to dysfluency with basic math facts.

To assess the accuracy of students who are building math computation fluency, a teacher can check the answers as correct or incorrect. This will tell the teacher whether the skill has been mastered, but it will communicate little about the nature of any difficulties the student may be experiencing. To further understand such difficulties, the teacher can use **error analysis** to examine patterns of mistakes. In computation, errors typically are the result of one of four problems: random response, basic fact error, wrong operation, or defective algorithm (Mercer & Mercer, 2005). After determining which of these is the cause of the errors, the teacher can design more effective instruction to address the student's confusion.

Assessing Problem Solving

In problem solving, mathematical problems are expressed within a social context, in which the information needed must be identified and then used to solve the problem. Problem solving in mathematics instruction typically takes the form of word problems. Unfortunately, many students with learning disabilities have difficulty with word problems (Jitendra, DiPipi, & Perron-Jones, 2002). Such problems may be due to difficulty in reading, in processing language, in working memory, or in computation, or a combination of these.

Problem solving is best assessed in terms of problem components. That is, instead of simply checking the answer, the teacher should examine each component of the problem. This means that a student who completes a portion of the problem correctly will get partial credit, and the student who happens accidentally on the correct answer will also get just partial credit. Most importantly, analyzing problems one component at a time allows the teacher to notice exactly what kind of difficulty a student is having and design instruction to address this difficulty. The problem-solving components that are usually present are (a) reads the problem correctly, (b) correctly identifies the relevant information, (c) correctly converts the problem into a computation, and (d) correctly calculates the answer (Tindal & Marston, 1990).

Assessing the Instructional Environment

Learning is most likely to take place in an instructional environment that supports the learning process. The instructional environment includes the classroom's social climate, the interaction style of the teacher, the physical arrangement of the classroom, the instructional grouping arrangement, the instructional and supplemental materials, and the academic supports offered.

A classroom's social climate is constructed by the teacher and students together. A positive and encouraging climate contributes to student learning. In a positive climate, students are more likely to ask questions, more willing to take risks, and more likely to put forth their best effort. The interaction style of the teacher is an important element of the classroom climate. Teachers who are upbeat and positive are more likely to have positive and upbeat students than teachers who are negative or pessimistic. Communicating high expectations leads to better student performance. A teacher can assess the classroom climate either formally through checklists or student surveys or informally through observation.

The physical arrangement of the classroom can contribute to student achievement, as well. Classrooms in which the layout is functional and organized are likely to have fewer distractions related to movement or routines. The teacher can assess the physical arrangement of the classroom by asking a few key questions: Are high-traffic areas away from group instruction locations? Are all supplies in a logical place and easy to access? Can I see all students at all times and can they see me? Are students' desks arranged to facilitate classroom activities? Are students who are most likely to struggle seated near where I spend most of my time?

An appropriate instructional grouping arrangement can make the class function much more smoothly. Grouping decisions should be based on student needs in relation to the content being taught. Groups that are flexible and respond to specific needs tend to be most effective. Through regular, curriculum-based measurement, the teacher can determine whether each student in a group has made sufficient progress.

The instructional materials in the classroom can affect student learning. To ensure that the effects are positive, the teacher can assess the match of materials to students' academic needs. Struggling readers, for example, need access to a plentiful supply of books they can read (Allington, 2001). The teacher should examine the classroom library to determine how many books are available that are appropriate for the struggling readers in the class. Further, the teacher can examine those books to determine whether they are engaging enough to get those struggling students reading more. The quality of books is at least as important, if not more so, than the quantity.

The academic supports provided in a classroom can range from a bookmark that reminds a student to use a particular strategy to a paraprofessional sitting with a struggling student to provide additional explanation during instruction. The quality and effectiveness of academic supports can be measured by examining student growth. If the academic support provided requires time or funding, then evaluating its effectiveness is even more important. Periodic progress monitoring assessments or daily probes of skill development can be used to determine whether a support has made a difference.

:: ASSESSMENT PROCESS FOR HIGH-INCIDENCE DISABILITIES

Since its inception in 1975 as PL 94-142, special education law has required that the process for special education placement be clearly defined. The placement process has always involved assessment for identification of a disability, for planning an Individualized Educational Program (IEP), for measuring progress toward IEP goals, and for reevaluation. PL 94-142 became the Individuals with Disabilities Education Act (IDEA), and refinements continue to be added. Assessment continues to play a vital role in the identification and placement of students in special education programs and for the ongoing implementation and evaluation of these programs.

Screening, Referral, and Evaluation

Federal law mandates that school systems implement ongoing **screening** procedures to identify children who might have a disability. These screening procedures may involve a variety of formal and informal assessments, including standardized tests, skill checklists, and observations. Through these screening procedures or through the recommendation of a teacher or parent, a child is referred for evaluation and possible special education placement.

Before a referral can go forward, the school must demonstrate evidence of **prereferral intervention.** Prereferral intervention typically consists of at least 6 weeks of efforts to address the difficulties that preceded the referral. A team of school professionals generates the recommendations for prereferral intervention, and the classroom teacher is responsible for ensuring that the intervention is carried out. Parents must be notified and consent to each step in the process. The preferral process is designed to reduce the number of inappropriate referrals to special education.

If the prereferral intervention efforts do not bring about the desired changes in learning or behavior, a referral for formal evaluation for special education services is made. General requirements for special education eligibility are published in the

Prior to referring a student for evaluation for potential special education placement, educators must demonstrate prereferral intervention efforts to address the identified difficulties.

(Photo credit: Hope Madden/Merrill)

Federal Register, but how these eligibility requirements will be addressed in each state is determined by the individual **state education agency** (SEA). The **local education agency** (LEA) is responsible for ensuring that a comprehensive evaluation is carried out in a timely manner. In most states, a school psychologist or other assessment professional conducts the initial evaluation. Testing should be conducted one-on-one and in the child's native language. A battery of tests is administered to assess each suspected or potential area of academic or behavior difficulties. In addition to the formal assessments conducted by the school psychologist, the evaluation will typically include classroom observations and results from teacher-administered assessments.

A relatively recent development in the prereferral process is **response to intervention** (RTI), as we discussed in Chapter 4. The RTI approach assumes that students should first have an opportunity to respond to good instruction in general education before they are identified as having a disability. If a student is receiving good instruction in the general education classroom but is not responding to it (i.e., is not learning as expected), then he or she should be referred for possible placement in special education.

Placement and IEP Development

Once the evaluation is complete, the IEP team meets to determine if the student meets the eligibility criteria for special education services. The team consists of the child's parent or guardian, the child's teacher, a representative of the LEA who is qualified to provide or supervise special education, a professional qualified to explain the results of testing, and the child, if appropriate. To be eligible, a student must require special education intervention to receive benefits from schooling. The first step in special education placement is classification. Classifications include such labels as specific learning disability, emotional disturbance, speech impairment, and mental retardation.

Once the team determines that a student is eligible for special education services, they work together to develop an IEP. The IEP must include (a) a statement of the student's present level of educational performance, which should describe how the student's disability affects school performance; (b) a statement of annual goals and short-term objectives, which describe what the student is expected to accomplish during the next 12 months; (c) a statement of the special education and related services to be provided and the extent to which the student will participate in general education; and (d) the projected date for initiation of services. The services must be provided in the **least restrictive environment** possible.

Progress Monitoring

The IEP identifies the annual goals and the short-term objectives for the student. It also outlines a plan for ongoing assessment of progress toward these goals and objectives and the criteria for their mastery. An IEP may specify exactly what kind of assessment is conducted and how often, or it can outline a more general plan for ensuring progress. Whatever the plan for progress monitoring, it is the special education teacher's responsibility for ensuring these assessments are conducted on schedule and that the data gathered are used to make revisions to the IEP as needed. If a student meets a goal before the target date, the IEP may be revised to add new goals and objectives. If a student is not making adequate progress toward IEP goals, the data gathered can be used to generate recommendations for changes to instruction. Any changes to the IEP require a meeting with parents.

Reevaluation

Federal guidelines call for reevaluation of students placed in special education programs to determine whether continued placement is in the student's best interest. The National Association of School Psychologists (NASP, 2004) has identified three main purposes for reevaluation: accountability, planning, and qualification. The reevaluation ensures accountability by analyzing the effectiveness of the IEP. The reevaluation is used for planning modifications to the student's special education services and planning for the student's future needs. The reevaluation ensures continued qualification for services and the continued appropriateness of the initial disability classification.

:: TESTING ACCOMMODATIONS

As part of the IEP's statement of services to be provided, any necessary and reasonable testing accommodations are identified. A student with a disability may be entitled to specific accommodations on tests if the nature of the disability warrants. Accommodations may include extended testing time, alternative testing schedule (e.g., a test may be broken into small segments and administered over several sittings), or alternative testing format (e.g., items may be read aloud to the student, the student may respond orally, a scribe may record the student's answers). These accommodations apply to all testing situations, with reasonable restrictions. For example, the student may not have a reading comprehension test read aloud, because it would render the test invalid.

Accommodations are seen as essential to enable some students with disabilities to demonstrate their knowledge and skill (Thurlow, 2001). Decisions about accommodations should be made by the IEP team and are usually, but not always, aligned with accommodations the student receives during instruction. Policies vary widely from state to state regarding what accommodations are allowed.

:: CURRENT ISSUES IN THE ASSESSMENT OF STUDENTS WITH HIGH-INCIDENCE DISABILITIES

In January 2002, President George W. Bush signed into law the **No Child Left Behind** (NCLB) Act of 2001, reauthorizing the Elementary and Secondary Education Act. This law ushered in a new era of heightened accountability for schools. The most significant effect for students with disabilities is that NCLB requires that all students, including those with disabilities, participate in their state's high-stakes testing. The fact that the difference between the achievement of students with disabilities and those without disabilities can never be eliminated by any legitimate means does not seem to be recognized in the law (Kauffman, 2004, 2005).

Other current issues include how grade-level promotion decisions are made and the increased standards that students must meet. There are benefits for students, as well. With the increased emphasis on high-quality early reading instruction, it is thought that the fewer students will require special education services. Whether this is actually the case remains to be demonstrated. NCLB also requires that teachers be better prepared (Gelman, Pullen, & Kauffman, 2005). It is still too soon to know for certain how NCLB will affect students with disabilities in the long term.

Another hot topic that affects students with high incidence disabilities is the proposed changes to the identification procedures for students with learning disabilities. The problems with the currently prevalent discrepancy model have been well documented (Fletcher et al., 1994; Foorman, Francis, Fletcher, & Lynn, 1996; Stuebing et al., 2002). Most importantly, the discrepancy model is a wait to fail approach (Fuchs, Mock, Morgan, & Young, 2003; Vaughn & Fuchs, 2003). That is, failure cannot be identified until after test scores show a discrepancy between estimated potential and achievement. The President's Commission on Excellence in Special Education recommended that the student's response to intervention (RTI) be used as an alternative or replacement of the IQ-achievement discrepancy approach (Gresham, 2002). Implementation of an RTI model could result in sweeping changes in special education identification and placement procedures.

According to the report of the National Joint Committee on Learning Disabilities (NJCLD, 2005), "core concepts of an RTI approach are the systematic (1) application of scientific, research-based interventions in general education; (2) measurement of a student's response to these interventions; and (3) use of the RTI data to inform instruction" (p. 2; see also Chapter 4). The Learning Disabilities Roundtable (2005) addressed the issue of RTI. The LD Roundtable's key recommendations were that RTI should incorporate (a) high-quality, research-based instruction and behavioral supports in general education; (b) scientific, research-based interventions focused specifically on individual student difficulties and delivered with appropriate intensity; (c) a collaborative approach by school staff for development, implementation, and monitoring of the intervention process; and (d) data-based documentation reflecting continuous monitoring of student performance and progress during interventions.

SUMMARY

Assessment is at the heart of special education. Assessment determines which students may need extra help and determines the presence of a disability. Assessment helps select appropriate IEP goals and measures the effectiveness of those goals. Assessment enables us to make sound educational decisions in the classroom.

Special education assessment can take the form of formal, standardized assessment or informal, teacher-made tools. It can tell us about a student's skills, abilities, performance, or growth in language, reading, or math. Competent special education teachers value the critical role of assessment in their work. They understand its importance and they understand the importance of doing it well.

COMPETENT TEACHING BOX   BOX 8.4

Knowing your students . . .

Assessment is all about knowing your students, but there's more to it than just looking at test scores. Important factors to consider when conducting assessment and interpreting assessment data include:

- Assessment should be conducted in the student's native language. If the student's native language is not English, every effort must be made to find a qualified assessor who speaks the student's native language.
- Academic assessments may include directions that use language that is confusing to some students. Directions for standardized tests typically must be given exactly as presented. Therefore, because you cannot alter the directions, the results may not demonstrate your student's best performance. If you believe this to be the case, it is important to note this observation.

- Students with learning disabilities, attention deficit disorders, or emotional/-behavior disorders may need alternative test administration. To find out what your students can really do, you may need to break the testing session into short periods of time or find a testing location with no distracting noises.
- Just as it is important to know your students, when it comes to sharing assessment data, it is important to know your students' parents. If English is not their native language, they may need an interpreter present at meetings. Educators tend to use much educational jargon, especially when discussing test results, programs, and placement issues. Watch your language for jargon, and check parents' understanding frequently. Try to make them feel comfortable asking questions.

Competent teachers . . .

- Rely on asessment to determine what to teach, what students have learned, and whether an intervention is working.
- Use different assessment methods for different purposes: screening, diagnosis, progress monitoring, and measuring achievement outcomes.
- Recognize the importance of the validity and reliability of their assessments.
- Use assessment to measure students' progress toward IEP goals.

:: CASE STUDIES

BEYONCÉ

Beyoncé is in the middle of first grade at Walters Elementary School. Like her classmates, she started first grade eager to learn to read. Unlike her classmates, Beyoncé hasn't learned to read yet this year. Throughout the year, reading time has felt like a chore. She is starting to hate reading, even though she loves being read to.

Beyoncé is very bright and has a fairly large speaking vocabulary. Despite this, Beyoncé has never understood what her teacher, Ms. Lentz, meant when she said "sound it out" or prompted her to blend the sounds together. Because she is clever, however, she has learned to memorize the way some words look and to listen carefully when someone else reads from a book. Beyoncé will memorize the words she hears and pretend to read the book herself. She has memorized enough words to make this charade convincing. She is also very good at using the pictures to figure out what is happening in a story and at using the context to guess words she doesn't have memorized.

Unfortunately, Ms. Lentz has been fooled by Beyoncé's performances. She doesn't recognize that Beyoncé has significant difficulty reading, but she has noticed a change in Beyoncé's attitude during reading class and toward reading in general.

1. How could Ms. Lentz have known more about Beyoncé's reading abilities? What assessment routines might have helped?
2. What aspects of Beyoncé's reading should Ms. Lentz assess?
3. What instruments or methods would be appropriate for conducting the assessment?

RAPHAEL

Raphael is in the seventh grade at Cunningham Creek Middle School. He has been identified as having a learning disability, with deficits in processing speed and language, since the third grade. Although he has always struggled in reading and writing, math has always been an area of relative strength for Raphael. This year, however, he has started to experience a great deal of difficulty in math class. The demands of his math class are much different this year. Unlike his previous math instruction, in which mastery of computational skills was emphasized, now the math he is expected to do now requires him to apply what he knows in real-life situations.

Mr. Parker, Raphael's math teacher, has noticed that, although Raphael is able to perform the computations required, he computes very slowly. He is usually the last one to finish an assignment, and he often fails to finish at all. He also is unsure about what operations are necessary to solve a particular problem. When extra information is included in a word problem, Raphael is unlikely to notice that this information is unnecessary to solve the problem, and he will get bogged down in trying to figure out how it fits.

1. Where should Mr. Parker begin to determine the nature of Raphael's difficulty in math?
2. What aspects of Raphael's math performance should Mr. Parker assess?
3. What instruments or methods would be appropriate for conducting the assessment?

HEATHER

Heather is a 10th-grade student at Englewood High School. She has been in the EBD program since fourth grade. Despite her difficulties with social skills, Heather's academic performance has always been average to above average in most subject areas. Her least favorite subject has always been language arts. In particular, she hates writing. She avoids writing whenever she can.

Mr. Bermudez, her English teacher this year, is particularly concerned about Heather's writing for two reasons. First, he knows that writing becomes more and more important in 11th and 12th grade and that it may be Heather's main obstacle to attending college. Second, he believes that if Heather had better writing skills, she might be inclined to use writing as an outlet for some of her emotional difficulties.

Mr. Bermudez is determined to get to the bottom of Heather's problems in writing. He is sure that Heather dislikes writing because she finds it difficult. Her writing samples tend to be very short with many misspellings. Her grammar is strong, but although she has an excellent speaking vocabulary, her writing tends to include mostly simple words. Despite all this, Heather's writing content is rich. It's as though she has plenty to say, but she does not have the skills to say it.

1. Where should Mr. Bermudez begin to determine the nature of Heather's difficulty in writing?
2. What aspects of Heather's writing performance should Mr. Bermudez assess?
3. What instruments or methods would be appropriate for conducting the assessment?

REFERENCES

Adams, M. J. (1990). *Beginning to read: Thinking and learning about print*. Cambridge, MA: MIT Press.

Airasian, P. (1997). *Classroom assessment* (3rd ed.). New York: Macmillan.

Allington, R. L. (2001). *What really matters for struggling readers*. Boston: Allyn & Bacon.

Berninger, V. (1999). Coordinating transcription and text generation in working memory during composing: Automatized and constructive processes. *Learning Disability Quarterly, 22*, 99–112.

Berninger, V., Abbott, R., Whitaker, D., Sylvester, L., & Nolen, S. (1995). Integrating low-level skills and high-level skills in treatment protocols for writing disabilities. *Learning Disability Quarterly, 18*, 293–309.

Berninger, V., & Graham, S. (1998). Language by hand: A synthesis of a decade of research on handwriting. *Handwriting Review, 12*, 11–25.

Bloom, L., & Lahey, M. (1978). *Language development and language disorders*. New York: Wiley.

Burns, M. K., MacQuarrie, L. L., & Campbell, D. T. (1999). The difference between curriculum-based assessment and curriculum-based measurement: A focus on purpose and result, *Communiqué, 27*(6), 18–19.

Clay, M. M. (1985). *The early detection of reading difficulties: A diagnostic survey with recovery procedures* (3rd ed.). Auckland: Heinemann.

Coulter, W. A. (1988, November). Curriculum-based assessment: What's in a name? *Communiqué, 18*(3), 13.

Deno, S. L. (1985). Curriculum-based measurement: The emerging alternative. *Exceptional Children, 52*, 219–232.

Denton, C. A., Ciancio, D. J., & Fletcher, J. M. (2006). Validity, reliability, and utility of the Observation Survey of Early Literacy Achievement. *Reading Research Quarterly, 41*, 8–34.

Dolch, E. W. (1936). A basic sight vocabulary. *Elementary School Journal, 36*, 456–460.

Dunn, L. M., & Dunn, L. M. (1997). *Product development publication summary report*. Circle Pines, MN: AGS.

Ehri, L. C. (1991). Learning to read and spell words. In L. Rieben & C. A. Perfetti (Eds.), *Learning to read: Basic research and its implications* (pp. 57–73). Hillsdale, NJ: Erlbaum.

Ehri, L. C. (1998). Research on learning to read and spell: A personal-historical perspective. *Scientific Studies in Reading, 2*, 97–114.

Ehri, L.,C., & Snowling, M. (2004). Developmental variation in word recognition. In C. A. Stone, E. Silliman, B. Ehren, & K. Apel (Eds.), *Handbook of language and literacy development and disorders* (pp. 433–461). New York: Guilford.

Espin, C. A., Weissenburger, J. W., & Benson, B. J. (2004). Assessing the writing performance of students in special education. *Exceptionality, 12*, 55–66.

Fletcher, J. M., Shaywitz, S. E., Shankweiler, D. P., Katz, L., Liberman, I. Y., Stuebing, K. K., Francis, D. J., Fowler, A. E., & Shaywitz, B. A. (1994). Cognitive profiles of reading disability: Comparisons of discrepancy and low achievement definitions. *Journal of Educational Psychology, 86*, 1–18.

Foorman, B. R., Francis, D. J., Fletcher, J. M., & Lynn, A. (1996). Relation of phonological and orthographic processing to early reading: Comparing two approaches to regression-based, reading-level-match designs. *Journal of Educational Psychology, 88*, 619–652.

Francis, D. J., Shaywitz, S. E., Stuebing, K. K., Shaywitz, B. A., & Fletcher, J. M. (1996). Developmental lag versus deficit models of reading disability: A longitudinal, individual growth curves analysis. *Journal of Educational Psychology, 88*, 3–17.

Fresch, M., & Wheaton, A. (1997). Sort, search, and discover: Spelling in the child-centered classroom. *The Reading Teacher, 51*, 20–31.

Fuchs, D., Mock, D., Morgan, P., & Young, C. (2003). Responsiveness-to-intervention: Definitions, evidence, and implications for the learning disabilities construct. *Learning Disabilities: Research and Practice, 18*, 157–171.

Gelman, J. A., Pullen, P. L., & Kauffman, J. M. (2005). The meaning of highly qualified and a clear roadmap to accomplishment. *Exceptionality, 12*, 195–207.

Gersten, R., & Chard, D. (1999). Number sense: Rethinking arithmetic instruction for students with mathematical disabilities. *Journal of Special Education, 44*, 18–28.

Graham, S., Harris, K. R., & Fink, B. (2000). Is handwriting causally related to learning to write? Treatment of handwriting problems in beginning writers. *Journal of Educational Psychology, 92*, 620–633.

Gravois, T., & Gickling, E. (2002). Best practices in curriculum-based assessment. In A. Thomas & J. Grimes (Eds.), *Best practices in school psychology* (Vol. IV, pp. 1–13). Washington, DC: National Association of School Psychologists.

Gresham, F. M. (2002). Responsiveness to intervention: An alternative approach to the identification of learning disabilities. In R. Bradley, L. Danielson, & D. P. Hallahan (Eds.), *Identification of learning disabilities: Research to practice* (pp. 467–519). Mahwah, NJ: Erlbaum.

Hallahan, D. P., & Kauffman, J. M. (2006). *Exceptional learners: Introduction to special education* (10th ed.). Boston: Allyn & Bacon.

Hallahan, D. P., Lloyd, J. W., Kauffman, J. M., Weiss, M. P., & Martinez, E. A. (2005). *Learning disabilities: Foundations, characteristics, and effective teaching* (3rd ed.). Boston: Allyn & Bacon.

Hasbrouck, J., & Tindal, G. A. (2006). Oral reading fluency norms: A valuable assessment tool for reading teachers. *The Reading Teacher, 59,* 636–644.

Hitchcock, M.E. (1989). *Elementary students' invented spelling at the correct stage of spelling development.* Unpublished doctoral dissertation. Norman: University of Oklahoma.

Hudson, R. F., Lane, H. B., & Pullen, P. C. (2005). Reading fluency assessment and instruction: What, why, and how? *The Reading Teacher, 58,* 702–714.

Jitendra, A. K., DiPipi, C. M., & Perron-Jones, N., (2002). An exploratory study of word problem-solving instruction for middle school students with learning disabilities: An emphasis on conceptual and procedural understanding. *Journal of Special Education, 36*(1), 23–38.

Jones, D., & Christensen, C. (1999). The relationship between automaticity in handwriting and students' ability to generate written text. *Journal of Educational Psychology, 91,* 44–49.

Justice, L. M. (2006). *Communication sciences and disorders: An introduction.* Upper Saddle River, NJ: Prentice Hall.

Kame'enui, E. J. (2002). *Final report: An analysis of reading assessment instruments for K-3.* Retrieved Sept. 24, 2006 from http://reading.uoregon.edu/assessment/analysis.php.

Kauffman, J. M. (2004). The president's commission and the devaluation of special education. *Education and Treatment of Children, 27,* 307–324.

Kauffman, J. M. (2005). Waving to Ray Charles: Missing the meaning of disability. *Phi Delta Kappan, 86,* 520–521, 524.

Kauffman, J. M., & Hallahan, D. P. (2005). *Special education: What it is and why we need it.* Boston: Allyn & Bacon.

Lane, H. B., & Pullen, P. C. (2004). *Phonological awareness assessment and instruction: A sound beginning.* Boston: Allyn & Bacon.

Learning Disabilities Roundtable. (2004, February). *Comments and recommendations on regulatory issues under the Individuals with Disabilities Education Improvement Act of 2004, Public Law 108-446.* Retrieved Sept. 24, 2006 from http://www.nasponline.org/advocacy/04LDRoundtableRefMat.pdf.

Lefrancois, G. (1999). *Psychology applied to teaching* (10th ed.). Belmont, CA: Wadsworth.

Lerner, J. (1989). Educational interventions in learning disabilities. *Journal of the American Academy of Child and Adolescent Psychiatry, 28,* 326–331.

Lyon, G. R. (1995). Toward a definition of dyslexia. *Annals of Dyslexia, 45,* 3–27.

McMillan, James H. (2000). Fundamental assessment principles for teachers and school administrators. *Practical Assessment, Research & Evaluation, 7*(8). Retrieved July 17, 2005 from http://PAREonline.net/getvn.asp?v=7&n=8.

Mercer, C. D., & Mercer, A. R. (2005). *Teaching students with learning problems* (7th ed.). Upper Saddle River, NJ: Merrill/Prentice Hall.

Mercer, C. D., & Miller, S. P. (1992). Teaching students with learning problems in math to acquire, understand, and apply basic math facts. *Remedial and Special Education, 13*(3), 19–35, 61.

Müller, E., & Markowitz, J. (2004). *Disability categories: State terminology, definitions & eligibility criteria.* Alexandria, VA: National Association of State Directors of Special Education (NASDSE).

National Association of School Psychologist. (2004). *Position statement on periodic reevaluations for students with disabilities.* Retrieved July 17, 2005 from http://www.nasponline.org/about_nasp/pospaper_tye.aspx.

National Joint Committee on Learning Disabilities. (2005, June). *Responsiveness to intervention and learning disabilities.* Retrieved Sept. 24, 2006 from http://www.ldonline.org/njcld/index.html.

Pinnell, G. S., Pikulski, J. J., Wixson, K. K., Campbell, J. R., Gough, P. B., & Beatty, A. S. (1995). *Listening to children read aloud.* Washington, DC: U.S. Department of Education, National Center for Educational Statistics.

RAND Reading Study Group. (2002). *Reading for Understanding: Toward an R & D Program in Reading Comprehension.* Washington, DC: RAND Corporation.

Rudman, H. C. (1989). Integrating testing with teaching. *Practical Assessment, Research & Evaluation, 1*(6). Retrieved July 17, 2005 from http://PAREonline.net/getvn.asp?v=1&n=6.

Rudner, L., & Schafer, W. (2002). *What teachers need to know about assessment.* Washington, DC: National Education Association.

Stuebing, K. K., Fletcher, J. M., LeDoux, J. M., Lyon, G. R., Shaywitz, S. E., & Shaywitz, B. A. (2002). Validity of IQ discrepancy classifications of reading difficulties: A meta-analysis. *American Educational Research Journal, 39,* 469–518.

Taylor, K. K., & Kidder, E. B. (1988). The development of spelling skills: From first grade through eighth grade. *Written Communication, 5,* 222–244.

Thurlow, M. (2001). *Use of accommodations in state assessments: What databases tell us about differential levels of use and how to document the use of accommodations* (Technical Report 30). Minneapolis, MN: University of Minnesota, National Center on Educational Outcomes. Retrieved July 17, 2005 from http://education.umn.edu/NCEO/OnlinePubs/Technical30.htm.

Tindal, G. A., & Marston, D. B. (1990). *Classroom-based assessment: Evaluating instructional outcomes.* New York: Merrill/Macmillan.

Vaughn, S., & Fuchs, L. (2003). Redefining learning disabilities as inadequate response to intervention: The promise and potential problems. *Learning Disabilities: Research and Practice, 18*, 137–146.

Wilen, W., & Clegg, A. (1986). Effective questions and questioning: A research review. *Theory and Research in Social Education, 14*, 153–161.

Evaluation for Social Instruction

URBAN LEGEND: *Children should come to school "ready to learn."*

LEGENDARY THOUGHT: *"Ready to learn" is defined by most schools as the equivalent of appropriate social and interpersonal skills. These are skills learned in context and throughout life. Some children don't just learn social skills. Often, these skills need to be directly taught to students with high-incidence disabilities.*

Maladaptive social behavior is an ongoing concern of any society. A large number of individuals living and working together within a community framework must have expectations for appropriate behavior. Deviations from these expectations are cause for concern, as they can significantly disrupt the comfort and productivity of others. Typically, those engaged in social behaviors that deviate from the standard are considered less successful than their peers and are either involuntarily or by default isolated from mainstream society.

Students with high-incidence disabilities like learning disabilities (LD), emotional and behavioral disorders (EBD), mild mental retardation (MMR) and even attention deficit hyperactivity disorders (ADHD) often exhibit difficulties in planning and organizing their thoughts, solving problems, controlling their impulses, and directing and sustaining attention to tasks (maintaining on-task behavior). Mastering all of these behaviors is associated with being considered "ready to learn." The *absence* of difficulties with all these behaviors is considered necessary for school success and social adaptation (Charlebois, Normandeau, Vitaro, & Bernache, 1999). Moreover, these same difficulties in organizing thoughts, solving problems, controlling impulses, and directing and sustaining attention are among the defining characteristics of all high-incidence disabilities. Problems in social skills are essentially the same in their characteristics and consequences regardless of the student's disability category. Therefore, we do not discuss EBD, LD, MMR, or any other category of high-incidence disability separately in this chapter.

In recent years, maladaptive social behavior within schools has come to the forefront of public concern, given the increased reports of bullying, shootings, and weapons offenses reported in schools, as well as the increasing numbers of adolescents and preteens being adjudicated (Bullis, Walker, & Sprague, 2001). Students identified with high-incidence disabilities are disproportionately among those who are in trouble with the law, drop out of school, are underemployed, or not otherwise successfully transitioning into adulthood (Bullis et al., 2001; Gresham, 1986). For example, for students with EBD longitudinal data have shown arrest rates during high school (or drop-outs of high school age) of 50%–73%. For those completing high school, 59% of individuals identified as EBD and 41% of those identified as LD were unemployed (Valdes, Williamson, & Wagner, 1990a, 1990b, 1990c; Wagner, 1991; Wagner & Shaver, 1989).

For students with high-incidence disabilities like those discussed in this text, the causes of poor or maladaptive social behavior are varied. Research typically points to the origins of social behavior deficits as stemming from one or more of the following: developmental issues (see Chapter 3 for a discussion on variations in communicative abilities, temperament, and learning characteristics); ineffective parenting practices; inadequate schooling and academic failure; peer rejection; association with others who also lack prosocial behavior (see Chapter 3 on the influence of environments); and drug use (Bullis et al., 2001; Patterson, Reid, & Dishion, 1992). Some students have difficulty learning appropriate social skills due to developmental delays or to a specific syndrome that hinders the ability to decode social contexts or interactions correctly and acquire the needed skills. For other individuals, maladaptive social behavior may be related to social deficits stemming from temperament or environmental factors such as poverty, poor parenting, peer rejection, and poor role models. In these cases there is a tendency to engage repeatedly and inaccurately in what is called **situational analysis** (Eisenberg & Miller, 1987). This is the process by which the student interprets the context of an interaction to determine the appropriate response. A student with a history of repeated academic failure or peer rejection and negative or harsh social experiences is likely to **decode** social situations incorrectly and therefore respond in a nonfunctional manner to social interactions. The result all too often is an unintended consequence, or minimally, one inappropriate for the context. Once again, one cause does not fit all. The causes of poor, absent, or maladaptive social behaviors are most often a combination of developmental and environmental factors that result in social challenges that, if unaddressed, can have long-lasting effects on school success and, consequently, lifelong outcomes. Research clearly indicates that deficits in **social competence** can affect academic success, peer interactions, and intimate relationships, as well as the ability to enter the work force and maintain employment (Kavale, Mathur, & Mostert, 2004).

:: DEFINING SOCIAL COMPETENCE

Despite the fact that poor or maladaptive social behavior is a top concern among educators and the public, social skills training has not been integrated into school-based curricula. Such integration is necessary to support students at-risk for deficits in social competence. Social competence is defined as a student's ability to perform a set of contextually appropriate behaviors that elicit desirable and socially valid outcomes (Gresham, 1998; McFall, 1982; Stichter & Conroy, 2005). Just as fluency in literacy is not solely defined by adequate reading skills, but a combination of reading and writing competencies, social competence is not simply mastering a set of social skills. Rather, it is a combination of competencies across both **adaptive behavior** and specific social skills. For example, most students identified with high-incidence disabilities can request, in one form or another, a turn with their peer's hand-held video game. However, all too often they may provide that request in the form of a demand (i.e., "Give me that!") or pair a physical gesture with the request, such as grabbing the device while saying, "I want a turn!". In other instances the student may ask appropriately and the peer may say that he or she is not willing to share. The initiating student, however, may not accept this and may respond inappropriately to the rejection of the request, demonstrating weaknesses in adaptive behavior (Gresham, 1985). In either instance, teachers or peers would not consider the outcome socially acceptable (i.e., they would be wanting positive interaction regarding the use of the hand-held game). A socially acceptable outcome here is important because although the socially inept student may have gotten his turn with the video game he may have interrupted his peer's game or annoyed him. The student with the social skills problem may have achieved some level of personal satisfaction, but his way of doing so was socially inappropriate. Therefore, a socially acceptable or socially valid outcome is defined as one that is viewed by other people important to the individual and environment as both successful and appropriate (Gresham, 1998).

Social Skills

Social skills are specific behaviors that, when successfully executed within an appropriate context, can lead to socially valid outcomes—to social competence. In the previous example regarding the hand-held game, asking for a turn with the video game appropriately would be an example of a specific social skill. In some contexts, this may be defined as appropriate initiations, or turn-taking skills; in other contexts with older students it may be related to goals associated with impulse control or behavior regulation when being rejected (e.g., not becoming verbally abusive when a peer declines a request).

How social skills are targeted and defined are often highly related to:

- Age of the student
- Developmental curriculum (e.g., preschool versus secondary)
- Social expectations of the environment
- Language abilities and cultural experiences in and outside of school

Social skill development is a lifelong process by which individuals learn a set of core social behaviors early on and spend the remainder of their lives learning to adapt those core skills across people, situations, and environments. For students with high-incidence disabilities the ability to constantly conduct situational analysis, decode interactions, and adjust their behavior can present the greatest challenges. Therefore, it is particularly important for teachers to target specific social skills that are relevant to school survival and yet have the most applicability to contexts and situations outside the classroom as well. For example, the practice of responding to adults with "yes sir" or "yes ma'am" may be considered desirable or even be demanded—a culturally normative way to show respect to adults in authority—in some regions of the nation. However, for a student with MMR who responds to adult requests with "ok" or "yes," it may be more important to spend the time and effort on practicing and reinforcing him or her for saying "excuse me" when appropriate and waiting for others to move over as opposed to brushing into them. In school and future work and living environments, avoiding inappropriate physical contact with others is essential for socially valid outcomes.

Table 9.1 provides a list of commonly targeted social skills for school contexts separated into social behavior categories. This list is not exhaustive, nor does it preclude the need for individualized assessment of both social skills as an adaptive behavior to determine the priorities for instruction. However, this list highlights the social skills relevant for social competence within school settings and can serve as a reminder that

TABLE **9.1**	Social skills

Interpersonal Behaviors
  Accepting authority
  Conversation skills
    Greeting
    Commenting
    Maintaining conversations
    Repeating what others say
    Clarifying a peer's comments
    Establishing eye contact
  Cooperative behaviors
    Helping, showing affection, or comforting
    Requesting information or assistance from peers/adults
    Dispensing information to peers
    Providing complimentary statements to peers
  Play behaviors
    Turn taking
    Sharing
    Organizing a social activity
    Responding to peers' initiations
Self-related Behaviors
  Expressing feelings
    Identify concerns
    Acknowledge ability to seek solutions
  Ethical behavior
    Honesty
    Trustworthiness
  Positive attitude toward self
Task-related Behaviors
  Paying attention
  Completing tasks
  Following directions
  Completing independent work

Adapted from Gresham, F. M., & Reshley, D. J. (1986). Social skill deficits and low peer acceptance of mainstreamed learning disabled children. *Learning Disability Quarterly, 9,* 23–33.

many students may already have some or most of these skills. Gaps in one or a few specific skills or an inability to incorporate these skills into appropriate contexts can result in significant challenges for socially valid outcomes, including school success.

Adaptive Behavior

The term **adaptive behavior** typically refers to an individual's ability to adapt to the expectations of the environment(s) in which he or she is expected to function. It is a measure of the personal independence an individual achieves relative to his or her age, cultural group, and environmental expectations (Grossman, 1983). For example, behaviors thought to demonstrate the appropriate independence of a young child at the dinner table are quite different from those anticipated for an adolescent. Likewise, although we might expect eating in a restaurant to challenge a young child's display of independence, we would expect an adolescent to adapt to a restaurant environment, exhibiting perhaps an increase in appropriate manners. The concept of adaptive behavior has probably most fully been explored by professionals and advocates associated with mental retardation. Over the last half century, several prominent definitions of mental retardation have emerged, describing the types and levels of adaptive behavior necessary for operational definition (see Chapter 6 for a full discussion) (AAMR, 1992; Grossman, 1983; Heber, 1959, 1961). The need for this level of clarification is due to the realization that an individual may experience deficiencies in one area of adaptive behavior at one time during his or her life, yet may seem to possess strong or sufficient adaptive behaviors in other areas or environments or at later points in time. Grossman (1973) suggested the following adaptive behavior domains:

> *During infancy and early childhood:*
>> Sensory-motor skills development
>> Communication skills
>> Self-help skills
>> Socialization
>
> *During childhood and early adolescence:*
>> Application of basic academics in daily life activities
>> Application of appropriate reasoning and judgment in mastery of the environment
>> Social skills
>
> *During late adolescence and adult life:*
>> Vocational and social responsibilities and performances

As is evident by the aforementioned areas of adaptive behavior, abilities related to social competence is a consistent theme. This is, of course, why the notion of socially valid outcomes is paramount when assessing social competence. What may appear as a mastered skill or ability in one environment may in reality not be realized in another context based on contextual expectations within that environment. For example, when looking at the above list for childhood and early adolescence, most educators who have worked with students with high-incidence disabilities can think of a student who seemed to have mastered the application of appropriate reasoning and judgment in mastery of the environment when on the playground with peers. However, when this same student is asked to work cooperatively in small groups on an academic project with peers or interact appropriately with adults, he or she may be unable or unwilling to execute the contextually appropriate judgment and reasoning required for appropriate social skills. Most likely, this very child would have had different scores on assessment of adaptive behavior across these two areas. All too frequently, such a student is considered noncompliant, aberrant, and is otherwise considered to exhibit maladaptive behavior. Some students seem to do sufficiently well academically and can articulate appropriate social skills, yet repeatedly do not execute them consistently or appropriately. Assessment of social competence therefore requires measurement of both social skills and adaptive behavior across contexts and time to ensure a true picture of the student's personal independence and social responsibility as compared to expectations relevant to his age, cultural group, current and probable future environments (Gresham,1986; Grossman, 1973).

:: ASSESSMENT

Many curricula, manuals, and other published materials are available to teach social skills. Yet very little is available on how to determine what to teach. Therefore, there is often a mismatch between the skill that needs to be targeted and the appropriateness of the chosen intervention to address that need (Gresham, 1998). This mismatch contributes to the unimpressive conclusions about the overall effects of social skills training reported in the literature (Kavale et al., 2004). As with academic subject areas, effective instruction in social competence requires careful planning and strong assessment-based instruction. These assessments typically serve four distinct purposes: (a) to screen the overall social competence of a student or group of students; (b) to identify the specific nature of a student's deficits in social competence; (c) to assist in matching appropriate interventions and skills training curricula to specific deficit areas; and (d) to allow for ongoing monitoring and evaluation of student progress over time and contexts (Sugai & Lewis, 1996). Therefore it is essential to employ measures that accurately assess the various social skills of interest and to measure these skills across contexts and over time, including those related to improving peer acceptance, which will require short- as well as long-term measures across a combination of skills.

Measures

Social competence and its components have been measured in the research literature in many ways, depending on the context, purpose of the assessment, and student characteristics (i.e., age and defining disabilities) (Guralnick, 1992; Odom & McConnell, 1985; Sugai & Lewis, 2004). As a result, several different types of assessment tools for use by educators have emerged. Appropriate assessment of social competence requires measurement processes that sample as many relevant contexts as possible, provide information over time, and adequately capture the **antecedents** (i.e., what occurs just before the target behavior) and the **consequences** (i.e., what happens immediately after the target behavior) (Gresham, 1986; LeBlanc, Sautter, & Dore, 2006). Depending on the social skill or level of social competence the student already exhibits, it is typically almost impossible to find a measure that captures all of these to the level of specificity desirable at each stage of instruction. Therefore, educators may employ a combination of the following types of measures at various times for given students. Understanding each type of measure, including its general purpose and the specific type of information that can be gathered from it, is necessary to avoid wasting time and risking poorly matched instruction as a result of misapplied assessment tools. The following sections provide an overview of global assessments, targeted assessments, and sociometric assessments, including examples of each. Table 9.2 provides an overview of these and two additional types of assessments.

Global Assessments

Some measures are designed to be all inclusive and to capture an overview of most if not all of the pertinent contexts and variables. These measures often tend to be interviews or rating scales. Most rely on some form of judgment by people important

TABLE 9.2	Types of social skills assessment	
Assessment Type	**Description**	**Example**
Global assessments	• Rating scales and interviews: Perceptions, judgment, and reports, etc. by teachers, parent, peers, or student about relative and general status of student social skill competence (indirect method)	• Teacher, parents, and others rate student's ability to converse with others • Teacher, parents, and others report the concerns they have about the child's ability to maintain friendships
Targeted assessments	• Direct observation measures: Direct observation of behavioral events (frequency, durations, intensity) and the contexts (triggering and maintaining events, people, activities, etc.) in which they occur	• Counts in the classroom the number of times anger is managed appropriately and inappropriately • Functional behavior assessments (antecedents, behavior, and consequences) to determine why student uses inappropriate skills
Sociometrics	• Rating scales: Perceptions, judgments measured by nominations and rankings of student as compares to peers (indirect method)	• Teacher lists students from most to least on their ability to perform a task • Students indicate who they would most/least like to play with
Role plays and situation problem solving	• Situational scenarios in which students demonstrate how they might behave (indirect method)	• You and your friends are in a situation in which _____. Show how you would solve this problem
Archival review	• Review of student's behavior history, previous social skills instruction attempts, or prior assessment information (indirect methods)	• Office discipline referral data patterns • Behavior intervention plan and individual education plans

Sugai, G., & Lewis, T. J., "Social skills Instruction in the classroom," in C. B. Darch, & E. J. Kame'enui, (Eds.), *Instructional classroom management: A proactive approach to behavior management,* 2nd ed., 2004, p. 160. Adapted by permission of Pearson Education, Inc., Upper Saddle River, NJ.

in the student's environment of interest (e.g., school, home). The end result is typically an overall rating or perception about the student's general ability to function under certain social demands, circumstances, and expectations. Some of the more popular versions of these rating scales provide global indices of a student's overall social performance as compared to a normal range of appropriate and inappropriate levels (see Chapter 8 for a discussion of norm-referenced assessment). These measures are most useful when comparing overall progress over extended time periods (e.g., comparing the student's social skills in the beginning of the year to the social skills at the end of the year) or when comparing the benefits of a specific social skills program that has been implemented over time across a group of students. For example, one such measure, the *Social Skills Rating Systems* (SSRS) (Gresham & Elliot, 1990), might be used to assess a group of 20 students with high-incidence disabilities taking part in a weekly social skills group over a 12-week period. The SSRS provides a standard measure of social competence through a multirater (i.e., teachers, student) assessment of the student's social behavior. National norms were compiled on a diverse sample of more than 4,000 children. Using either an elementary or secondary version, three behavioral domains can be assessed using this tool: social skills, problem behavior, and academic competence. The social skills scale contains 30 items describing pro-social behaviors, which are rated using a **Likert scale,** according to their frequency of occurrence as never, sometimes, and very often. The problem behavior domain consists of 18 items that assess **externalizing, internalizing,** and **hyperactivity** problems. Again, a Likert scale is used to indicate the frequency of occurrence of the behaviors. Last, the student's academic functioning is assessed through the use of the academic competence subscale. This subscale contains nine items, rated according to placement in the class (e.g., lowest 10%). In the previous example of the social skills group intervention, the SSRS might be given prior to initiation of the program and then again after the completion of the program as a type of standardized measure of pre- and post-skill growth for each student which can then be tallied across students to look at growth across the entire group. For this example, we are presuming that the SSRS is assessing measures related to the intervention implemented, something that would need to be secured before using this tool. The SSRS is also often used as a measure of the type of social skills concerns the student exhibits most (e.g., externalizing problems) and the degree to which he or she exhibits social problems as compared to a normal range.

The *Matson Evaluation of Socials Skills with Youngsters,* 2nd ed. (MESSY: Matson, 1994) is another rating scale designed for children and youth from 8 to 18 years of age. The MESSY is designed to identify children and youth with social and emotional skills deficits as well as respond to related interventions through 64-item scales completed by the teacher and child. The MESSY is used by practitioners and researchers. The *Social Behavior Assessment Inventory* (SBAI: Stephens & Arnold, 1992) is designed to be used with the *Social Skills in the Classroom* curriculum. This tool can be used as a screening instrument or as a targeted assessment (discussed in a later section) and is comprised of 136 social behaviors organized and rated for observability on a four-point scale across four scales. *Preschool and Kindergarten Behavior Scale-2* (PKBS-2: Merrill, 2002a) is used to screen young children across three subscales who are at-risk for severe social, behavioral, and emotional problems. It can additionally be used according to the author for effective intervention planning. *School Social Behavior Scales-2* (SSBS-2: Merrill, 2002b) is a school-based version of the PKBS-2 designed to screen children needing social skills intervention. The *Social Competence and Behavior Evaluation—Preschool Edition* (SCBE-PE: LaFreniere & Dumas, 1995) assesses social competence in preschool age children 30–78 months. Three subscales are used: emotional expression, social interaction, and teacher-child relations. The previous assessment scales are just a sample of several such measures available to educators. However, educators typically derive increased direct benefit from targeted assessments, which are more specific to daily curricular and intervention decisions.

Targeted Assessments

Specific or targeted assessments may be what are typically considered more *behavioral* or *discrete* in nature. These measurement systems focus on a single or set of specific social skills (e.g., greetings, taking turns, problem solving difficult situations). Typically, these tools are variations of direct observation systems by which the educator can specifically measure the amount, length, and steps, as well as contextual factors related to a specific social interaction or skill. These tools can usually be individualized, allowing an educator to monitor daily progress of specific skills across multiple contexts. Given this potential for specificity, these types of assessments are very beneficial for monitoring IEP objectives, for use with reinforcement systems, and for quickly identifying areas in need of error correction. Therefore, they are often employed for **skill deficits** (i.e., the student does not have or is missing a step in performing a social skill sequence) or to monitor improvements in **performance deficits** (i.e., the student has the skill, but may not know when to use it, may use it too slowly, or may be unable to modify the skill in different situations) (Gresham, 1998). One such assessment tool is the *Snapshot Assessment Tool* (SAT), which captures a picture of a student's use of social skills across various contexts (for a description, see Conroy & Brown, 2002 and Stichter & Conroy, 2005). The SAT, originally designed for younger children, allows the user to efficiently document the antecedents and consequences surrounding a child's social behavior. In addition, the SAT helps to identify the functional outcomes of the child's social interactions. Figure 9.1 shares an example of the SAT used with a younger student. In this example, the target student, Sean, engages in social initiations and responses under different contexts for different purposes. In the first observation, Sean does not respond to a peer's initiations requesting play materials, but moves away from the peer. The outcome of this social interaction sequence is obtaining the play materials and escaping the peer's attention. In the next scenario, Sean initiates to the peer, requesting the peer's attention, and successfully obtains this outcome. In the final observation, Sean responds to the peer's initiation and successfully receives the tangible outcomes. As you can see, the SAT allows the observer not only to examine the outcomes or perceived goals of the social interaction exchanges, but the contexts in which they occur, the appropriateness, and reciprocity of the exchange.

Figure 9.2 demonstrates the use of an *instructional matrix* to assess specific social behaviors related to IEP objectives across the daily class schedule for an older student. In this example the student has identified needs both related to appropriate responses to adult initiations as well as initiations with peers. Because the definition of what is perceived as "appropriately initiating" conversation with adults can vary substantially across school environments, particularly as a student enters secondary

FIGURE 9.1 Example of completed SAT

Type and Form of Behavior	Context and Appropriateness of Behavior	Reciprocity of Exchange	Perceived Goal of Behavior	Actual Outcome
• Peer initiated to Sean • Peer said, "Sean, give me some legos." • Sean moved all of the legos away from the peer	• Two children were playing in manipulative area of classroom • Sean's behavior was not socially or age appropriate	• Yes, there was social reciprocity because Sean did respond • Peer initiation did not lead to a social interaction	• To maintain access to tangible items (i.e., legos) • To escape peer attention	• Sean was successful in maintaining access to the legos and escaping peer attention, because the peer left the manipulative area and began playing with another child.
• Sean initiated to peer • Sean said, "Swing." • Peer began running with Sean to the swing set	• Outside play • Sean's behavior was socially appropriate	• Yes, there was social reciprocity • Peer began running with Sean to the swing set, and it led to a social interaction	• To obtain peer attention	• Sean was successful in obtaining peer attention because Sean and the peer started running together to the swing set.
• Peer initiated to Sean • Peer said, "Do you want juice?" • Sean looked at peer and smiled	• During snack time in the classroom • Sean's behavior was socially appropriate	• Yes, there was social reciprocity • Sean smiled at peer and the peer gave Sean juice	• To obtain tangible food item (i.e., juice)	• Sean was successful in obtaining tangible food item because the peer gave Sean juice.

Adapted by permission from H. Goldstein, L. A. Kaczmarek, & K. M. English (Eds.) (2002). *Promoting social communication: Children with developmental disabilities from birth to adolescence* (p. 26). Baltimore: Paul H. Brookes Publishing.

grades, the team has taken the time to identify what those appropriate skills would look like in each environment through the student's day.

One frequent challenge that educators articulate when collecting direct observation data during the social skills assessment phase is the concern that when student errors are made, teaching is not to occur. Although there are definite benefits to obtaining true observational data, in some cases it's not feasible and is highly impractical. Concerns surrounding appropriate initiations and responses might be one of them. It may not be feasible to allow a student to respond inappropriately to an adult initiation in the middle of class, depending on the form that response takes (e.g., aggression). Also, if the adult with whom the student is to engage in appropriate interactions is the same adult who is taking the data, it is not beneficial to alter the behavior patterns that would typically occur. The adult is part of the actual social interaction. Therefore, if the typical pattern includes a correction through a verbal prompt or cue to use an existing self-management program (see codes 1 and 2 in the key of Figure 9.2), then this is an integral part of the assessment data. It would be very informative to know if the student received the same type and levels of prompts from all adults and how well the student responds to those prompts across environments. This leads to additional information about which **stage of learning,** (acquisition, fluency, generalization, maintenance, and adaptation) in which the student is currently functioning (Haring & White, 1980; Sugai & Lewis, 2004). We discuss these stages in more depth in a subsequent section of this chapter.

The instructional matrix allows multiple observers to be consistent in what they are looking for, and in how they record the result. This provides a clearer understanding of the antecedents and consequences under which the behavior occurs. If Jamie is consistently exhibiting the appropriate behavior independently in homeroom and lunch but seems to need constant prompts to engage in the self-management system to respond appropriately in academic subjects, this provides the IEP team with valuable information. The information may concern potential triggers for prosocial behavior (e.g., it tends to occur in less structured and less demanding settings). It may reveal those environments in which the student is having great difficulty generalizing the behavior and may need increased instructional or varied support. The instructional matrix can be used over time and across contexts. An additional use of this form is its adaptability for ongoing assessment during instructional practices. Yet, because the instructional matrix, the SAT and other systems like them are direct observation tools, they are rarely sufficient to fully define whether gains in specific behaviors are resulting in overall improvements in socially valid outcomes.

Sociometrics

Checks of social validity are occasionally built into more global measures, as is the case with the previously mentioned SSRS or in limited form through some targeted assessments such as the SAT. However, typically the measures of social validity serve as companion measures to both the global and targeted behavioral assessments, often in the form of **sociometrics,** behavior checklists, and direct observation (Pepler & Craig, 1998). Regardless of form, the goal is to ensure that once the

FIGURE 9.2 Instructional matrix

Child's Name: _____ Date: _____
Recorder: _____

DAILY CLASSROOM SCHEDULE

Objective	Home-room	Special Class	Math	Reading	Lunch	Recess	Science	Handwriting/ Power writing
Social Skills: Appropriately response to adult initiations	Acknowledges adults with appropriate facial expression and looks towards them when spoken to	Participates with peers in class activity	Interacting with teacher by asking questions, offering ideas or other appropriate communication	Interacting with teacher by reading when asked, offering ideas or other appropriate communication	Will return greeting by principal when entering lunch room	When prompted, will engage in appropriate conflict resolution	Will follow small group procedures by interacting with peers, asking questions, offering ideas or other appropriate communication	Will share work when asked, will respond to questions, will offer ideas or other appropriate communication
Data code								
Appropriately initiates conversation with peers	Greets peers at assigned table with a hello or a smile	Participates in classroom discussion when called upon	Interacting with peers in small groups by asking questions, offering ideas or other appropriate communication	Interacting with peers in small groups by asking questions, offering ideas or other appropriate communication	Initiates conversation with peers, joins conversation when peers interact with him	Initiates conversation with peers, joins conversation when peers interact with him	Interacting with peers in small groups by asking questions, offering ideas or other appropriate communication	Interacting with peers in small groups by asking questions, offering ideas or other appropriate communication
Data code								

Social Skills Recording Key

3 = Independent

2 = Verbal prompt

1 = Visual prompt (self-management cue card)

Note: Observer enters code (1, 2, or 3) about every 30 seconds.

Evaluating the social validity, or quality, of the social interaction is in many situations as important as the actual execution of the skills.
(Photo credit: David Mendelsohn/Masterfile USA Corporation)

student has successfully executed the skill the end result is considered in terms of the context and a successful outcome. For example, one middle schooler's goal might be to successfully secure a seat at a lunch table with some peers from her class. Therefore, she may have been provided instruction and coaching on the importance of using an appropriate greeting and asking whether there is room for her to sit down. Upon observation she gets her lunch and then asks her peers, "Ummm. . . is it OK if I ummm sit here? If not I can ummm go away. I ummm was just wondering." Technically she has asked an appropriate question. However, the end result is very likely to be mocking by her peers, given her nervous body language and excessive "ummms." She ends up once again sitting by herself. Contextually and based on her peers' response, the executed social skill does not result in a socially successful outcome.

Behavior checklists and direct observation are familiar forms of assessment to professionals. Sociometrics serve a specific purpose and are not as widely used, but can be invaluable when assessing social competence. Sociometrics assess the target social behavior's value and execution as perceived by significant social agents in the relevant context (Sugai & Lewis, 2004). For students with high-incidence disabilities within school settings these assessments typically involve rating scales filled out by teachers, parents, peers and even the students themselves, depending on the skill and context. Collectively, behavior checklists, sociometrics, and direct observation procedures serve two purposes in these situations. First, they ensure that targeted skills are appropriate priorities for current and future environments. Although a parent may have become accustomed to her daughter tapping her on the shoulder whenever she wants her attention, teachers and peers may identify that behavior of a fifth grader as unacceptable and expect an appropriate verbal initiation. However, both peers and the student may feel that a verbal initiation chosen by a teacher or parent (e.g., "excuse me") is "dorky." Therefore, using "excuse me" could exacerbate the student's likelihood of peer rejection and low self-esteem. The second purpose is to confirm the occurrence of the behavior and its significance. To continue the above scenario, peers may also confirm the teacher's data that appropriate verbal initiations to get attention have increased and physical contact has decreased (the desired effect). Yet, both teacher and peer ratings confirm that the frequency of physical contact has not declined sufficiently because the target student was not provided the full set of social tools to employ when the teacher or peer does not respond right away. Hence, the target student reverts to physical contact to obtain their attention. Clearly, information about the social validity of the targeted skill through a variety of sources and measures provides a wealth of information to secure meaningful long-term progress toward social competence.

Peer Sociometrics. Developmentally, direct observations by adults (teachers) and behavior checklists typically serve as the most sophisticated judge of young children's specific social abilities and the functional outcomes of their relations with peers and adults. Parents and teachers can provide a wealth of information across a number of contexts. Assessments by adults tend to be more time-efficient than peer assessments (Ladd & Profilet, 1996). However, adult informants run the risk of relationship bias when they review and report behavior. For example, an itinerant teacher may view a child's problem with turn taking as more frequent and problematic because it occurs each time she meets with the student in a small group. However, the regular teacher may view the problem with turn taking in terms of occurrences throughout the day, which proportionally may be calculated as significantly less, when opportunities for turn taking are not factored in. Nevertheless, turn taking at a young age is highly correlated with peer acceptance. Therefore, peer sociometrics are useful because they can provide gold standard information about the impact of poor turn taking skills on the target child's social status, reciprocal friendships, and friendship qualities—all variables related to peer acceptance and potential predictors for future peer rejection such as victimization from bullying (LeBlanc et al., 2006).

Peer assessments become increasingly important in older children. As children develop they are expected to display social competence across increasingly varied and complex environments. For students with high-incidence disabilities, who by definition experience challenges related to social competence when they enter middle and secondary school, these social deficits are increasingly associated with poor academic performance, drop-out rates, mental health issues, and externalizing behavior problems (Kauffman, 2005). The impact of peer rejection on outcomes at this age cannot be underscored (Kupersmidt & Dodge, 2004; McDougall, Hymel, Vaillancourt, & Mercer, 2001). During the preteen and adolescent years, peers spend increased time with each other, including target students with high-incidence disabilities, without adult supervision. This means that peers will be experts of social norms and defining characteristics of social competence in many contexts. These data should be incorporated with other adult rating and direct observation data as well as ongoing global measures.

Stages of Learning

Effective assessment of various social skills across multiple contexts results in a wealth of information regarding if, when, and how the social skill is used and if the social skill results in socially valid outcomes for the student within current and future environments in which he or she needs to function. Although having a lot of data can be valuable, it can also be overwhelming when trying to decide what intervention to use and how to address the social competence needs of students with high-incidence disabilities. One of the first and most important ways to organize assessment data in relation to social competence is to determine in which stage of learning the student is engaged relative to the specific skill. Haring and White (1980) describe these as acquisition, fluency, generalization, maintenance, and adaptation. Like academic learning, social skills development proceeds through a logical sequence of understanding the specific purposes, features, and accurate execution of the actual social behaviors involved with the social skill (acquisition). Then comes consistent and accurate application of the skill at an appropriate pace (fluency). Next, the goal becomes the student's demonstration of the skill across contexts and situations (generalization). Finally, the goal is ongoing levels of accuracy across contexts without direct instruction (maintenance).

Social competence is demonstrated when the student is able to vary the skill (e.g., asking for assistance in a variety of appropriate ways) in settings that have not been taught (e.g., a boss in a work setting) but are important (adaptation). Table 9.3 provides an expanded definition of each stage as well as key distinctions associated with each stage associated with instructional practices.

A condensed version of these stages can be described as assessing whether a student is displaying a social skill deficit or a performance deficit. In other words, it is essential to determine whether the assessment indicates that the targeted social deficits are a result of an acquisition problem or a performance or fluency problem. Some students lack the skills needed to execute appropriately the set of behaviors desired. Again, this lack of skills may be due to developmental differences, environmental background, or cultural language differences. In any case, common social expectations may be a hidden curriculum for many children, particularly those with high-incidence disabilities. For example, a hidden curriculum for many new kindergarteners includes the expectation that they will sit still, use appropriate voice levels, respond appropriately to authority, wait their turn, complete tasks independently and so forth. Telling children to be appropriate assumes that they have mastered the necessary skills; their failure to exhibit appropriate behavior may be seen as either a performance deficit or intentional deviance. Yet many of these children truly do not yet have the skills to understand exactly what responding appropriately to adults in schools looks like. They may not even realize that "appropriate" looks different from how they behave. In other cases or for other students, the specific skills are understood but the student is displaying a performance deficit. These are the students that often most frustrate educators because when asked, "What were you suppose to do?" the students can readily and accurately state the specific behaviors they should have displayed. Yet, these students do not consistently perform these behaviors at the right time or the right place.

A child may have a skill deficit in one area of interaction or context (e.g., how he or she solicits assistance) and a performance deficit in another (e.g., how he or she interjects a comment into someone else's conversation). Figure 9.3 provides an example of one direct observation tool that can be employed to assist in discerning which type of deficit a student may be exhibiting. In this example, a middle school

TABLE 9.3	Stages of learning	
Phase	**Description**	**Instructional Emphasis**
Acquisition	Accurate performance (shape, order, content, etc.) of the social skill behaviors.	1. Show, tell, model, and describe the behavior. 2. Guide, lead, and coach the student through the behaviors. 3. Give high rates of positive reinforcement for correct displays of behaviors. 4. Give informative correction when errors occur.
Fluency	Accurate, smooth, even performance of social skill at situation-appropriate rates or speeds.	1. Provide multiple opportunities to practice (e.g., role play). 2. Give high rates of positive reinforcement for fluent performance.
Generalization	Accurate and fluent performance of the social skill beyond the classroom or instructional setting.	1. Teach with multiple representative examples from the universe of situations in which the skill will and will not be required. 2. Teach in the settings in which the social skill will be required. 3. Incorporate relevant features from the required settings as instructional prompts (e.g., people, material, activities). 4. Use forms of positive reinforcement found in noninstructional settings.
Maintenance	Continued performance of the social skill when instruction has been discontinued in the instructional setting.	1. Use systematic fading or removal of instructional prompts or assists. 2. Decrease amounts and rates of instructional positive reinforcement. 3. Increase use of naturally occurring types and rates of positive reinforcement.
Adaptation	Use of social skill variations that have not been taught but are required in noninstructional and/or novel situations.	1. Teach representative multiple variations of the social skill behaviors. 2. Teach and link behavior variations to the defining features of the required setting.

Source: Haring, N., & White, O. (1980). *Exceptional teaching.* Columbus, OH: Merrill.

FIGURE 9.3	Discrepancy analysis

Student Name: _____
Environment: Social studies cooperative learning group
Social Skill: Soliciting assistance from peer in group
Desired Socially Valid Outcome: Working with peer in a mutually beneficial manner

DISCREPANCY ANALYSIS

Contextual Expectations	Summative Inventory of Target Student	Identified potential skill or performance deficits to be further assessed and or targeted for instruction
1. Works through tasks that can be done alone first	1. Comments that work looks easy and begins task	1. Within range of typical middle school behavior, not a priority
2. Indicates to peer that he will need assistance when peer is done with her solo tasks	2. Tells peer it's time for her to do her part so he can move on	2. Requires further assessment in other context to assess if he can ask politely for assistance and adopt appropriate vocal tone (perhaps changing from gym class to current setting) or is missing key steps in appropriate requesting skill
3. Occupies time with related tasks while waiting for peer	3. Begins tapping pencil and repeatedly says in a loud whisper "Hurry up" once every 30 seconds	3. Appears to be a skill deficit in appropriate wait behaviors
4. When prompted by peer, will verbally communicate necessary or desired supports	4. When prompted by peer, says, "Just fix this, just do your thing"	4. Requires data from other contexts if he has ever exhibited this skill
5. Allows peer to provide support by leading on their designated task	5. Looks out the window, taps pencil and begins an off task conversation	5. Most likely lacks specific skills
6. Asks clarifying questions of peer at appropriate times throughout	6. Waits until the very end and asks, "OK, so what am I suppose to do now?"	6. Most likely a performance deficit, understands need for clarification, and requests it, poor execution
7. Thanks peer for help or compliments peer on job	7. Tells peer that since she is so good at it, she should just do the whole thing	7. Again most likely a performance deficit, perhaps due to few opportunities to practice

student with a high-incidence disability is having difficulties successfully working in a cooperative learning group. Although his educational team feels he is appropriately matched for the academic tasks targeted for the group, the interactive nature of the group goals are consistently posing problems between the student and his peers. His peers have expressed that he is annoying and not acting like a team player in the group, and it would just be easier to work without his disrupting them. A traditional perspective is to view the target student as exhibiting behavior problems and perhaps not yet appropriate enough for this type of learning group. However, breaking down the contextual expectations of the group task shows that a number of core social skills are required that this student either does not have or has not yet learned to generalize appropriately. This tool highlights specific skills that should be targeted for direct skills training because they seem to remain in the acquisition stage, and others that involve generalization or adaptation. Other skills may not be perfect, yet are sufficiently within the typical range and not necessarily a priority. Some skills warrant similar assessment data from other contexts. In these cases, direct observation or archival information searches, interviews, or rating scales can be employed to assist in gathering sufficient information without excessive data collection time.

The discrepancy analysis in Figure 9.3 is a compilation of several days worth of observations during the same task and time. It can also be used during a single day to monitor ongoing progress. Once the type of deficit is identified, the type and level of training can be best matched. The goal for educators in partnership with families is to teach and promote social competence, not just social skills. Therefore, understanding the stage of learning in relation to the social skill is essential to best identify appropriate interventions that will not only teach specific skills but also develop them in such a way that they are considered adaptive in nature and socially valid in outcome.

SUMMARY

Learning social skills should be compared to learning to read. Children learn to read in part through a well-focused reading curriculum typically delivered daily for an hour or two during elementary school years. However, targeted instruction is insufficient to develop fluent literacy skills. Instead, literacy instruction and related practice must be infused throughout the day as students explore mathematical concepts, read directions for their science and art projects, the lunch menu, and field trip details. In other words it is inconceivable that children would learn to read functionally without the combination of direct instruction, guided practice, and multiple opportunities for generalization. We would certainly never assume that students would learn to read by placing them into a school setting and surrounding them by others who can read. However, practices related to developing social competency within school-based curriculum often function this way.

Despite a national realization that poor outcomes associated with a lack of social competence are on the rise, students continue to be expected to enter school and quickly learn and easily assimilate these somewhat hidden contextual norms and expectations for social behavior. Students who are not quickly successful experience punitive consequences, and then occasionally are targeted for a standard remedial social skills training. By prioritizing social competence as an integral part of the educational curriculum, educators can employ comprehensive and ongoing assessment strategies to identify the nature as well as the specific type of deficit(s) experienced by students. In doing so appropriate social skills training interventions can be best matched to deficit areas, increasing the success of these strategies. Acquisition of social competence is linked with successful interpersonal relationships as well as increased post school outcomes. Social competence improves the trajectory for many students with high-incidence disabilities. Without social competence, they are more likely to experience consistent underemployment, require extensive mental health supports, or become institutionalized or involved with the legal and justice systems throughout adolescence and adulthood (Kavale, Mathur, & Mostert, 2004).

COMPETENT TEACHING BOX

BOX 9.1

Knowing your students . . .

What we know about our students helps us teach them more effectively. Understanding how challenges associated with social competence can manifest at different developmental levels can assist teachers in planning for present and future needs.

What you might want to remember about social competence deficits:

- Very young children may display particular difficulty with behaviors associated with play, such as turn taking and sharing, as well as impulse control, such as keeping their hands to themselves, or initiating interactions or responding to others.
- Elementary age students often present established patterns of behavior, such as aggression, defiance, or disruption. They may be among a growing number of children entering schools deemed "not ready to learn." As they progress through elementary school without effective social skills training, these children are considered at risk of school failure due to their maladaptive social behaviors.
- Middle school students with social competence deficits demonstrate increased problems with self-management processes at this age. The ability to assess and apply moderation within the normal boundaries of risk-taking behavior typical for this age group, anger management, rule-governed behavior, and responding appropriately to increased academic demands become increasingly challenging for these students.
- High school students are increasingly required to generalize their behaviors to community settings. Those with deficits in social competence increasingly do not complete high school, are underemployed, or are adjudicated by the courts during or after high school. This is particularly true for those with high-incidence disabilities, such as LD and EBD. For students with these disabilities, we already know a lot about post-school outcomes.

Competent teachers . . .

- View the assessment of social competence with equal regard to academic assessments.
- Use an appropriate assessment protocol to prioritize socially valid target behaviors for their students.
- Use an appropriate assessment protocol to accurately measure the rate and quality of targeted socially valid behaviors.
- Systematically assess to discriminate between skill deficits and performance deficits.
- Recognize the need for short- and long-term assessment of specific types of social competence behaviors.

:: CASE STUDIES

STEVIE

Stevie is a 10-year-old boy in Mr. Nick's fourth-grade class. He is considered quiet and was consistently performing one to two grade levels below his fourth-grade peers academically. He receives resource support in reading and math from Mr. Mac, the special education teacher, in his classroom, an hour a day. He enjoys hands-on activities but seems to prefer to work alone. In small group activities, he seems quiet and unwilling to work.

Stevie's favorite independent activity is playing on the class computer. He does this whenever he has a chance. Whenever his classmates come over to either join in on a two-person game, or ask for a turn, the interaction does not seem to go well, and the peers return upset. Stevie likes to go out for recess, but spends all of his time either on the swings or waiting for the swings. Peers report that he stares at them while they are on the swings, constantly asking when they will be off. They report that he will not move back from the swings while they are trying to swing on them, and ignores them if they suggest he join them in other activities. Stevie is considered the least desirable classmate with whom to eat lunch by his peers. They report that he scarfs down his food, tries to steal their food, and picks his nose at lunch. Stevie usually returns from the after-lunch recess with food still on his face, hands, and clothes. When encouraged to interact with Stevie, peers report that he does not seem to care about anything they like. When he does get excited, he jumps up and down like a little kid, and it's embarrassing.

1. What specific social skills does it appear that Stevie needs support to work on? Why would these skills be an important part of social competence for a student his age?
2. What type of assessment does it seem was the basis for most of the information provided in this case study?
3. What other assessments should be employed to develop the most appropriate and comprehensive plan for social competence intervention?

RHIANNON

Rhiannon thought Ms. McVee was OK, as far as counselors go, and she knew many. Ms. McVee got her out of earth science once a week, and anyone who could do that was OK. There really could not have been a more boring class, in Rhiannon' opinion. To pass the time in that class, she had tried to explain to her teacher that if they would have made those "plates" out of some decent stoneware we would not have all these cracks and, therefore shifting, and then earthquakes. All of the other seventh graders, except the students she called the *brown-nosers* who sit up front in class, thought that was pretty funny. Rhiannon received detention, and Ms. McVee decided this incident was a great opportunity to role play some of the social skills they had been working on for interactions with adults. This, of course, was the day Rhiannon told Ms. McVee that she had become very uncool.

Ms. McVee and Rhiannon used the lesson on the earth's plates to reenact the scenario with Rhiannon showing Ms. McVee, now playing her Earth Sciences teacher, some of her newly learned social skills. Instead of the comment about how they need to be made of stoneware, Rhiannon blurted out that she did not understand how the earth which was so strong, could deal with the hot sun and not explode, could have such wimpy plates that made earthquakes. It did not make sense to her. Ms. McVee, as the teacher, praised Rhiannon for posing a good question and then reminded her to raise her hand first next time. After the role play, Ms. McVee pointed out to Rhiannon that she did that well and it would have saved her a detention if she would use those skills in more environments. She suggested that Rhiannon might join an after school acting club that was just formed. Rhiannon responded that it did not matter because her Earth Science teacher would come up with a boring answer that was dumb and made no sense, and at least the stoneware answer was funny. Ms. McVee explained to Rhiannon that teachers are the experts on these topics and that she needed to remember to be respectful.

1. What specific social skill was Ms. McVee targeting? What stage of learning was Rhiannon in for that skill?
2. Based on the stages of learning, was Rhiannon ready for the next phase Ms. McVee suggested for her? Why or why not?
3. Did any additional skills needing targeting related to Rhiannon's difficulties in earth science class?

NICK

Nick was thrilled—OK, maybe not thrilled, but relieved. It was his senior year in high school, and he was finally done with the reading-writing stuff. He had always struggled with reading, had special tutors, special teachers, and extra homework since he was in forth grade. Everyone had always been on him to get better at reading. He understood things pretty well when he was read to, and he certainly could read basic things on walls, instructions, and day-to-day items.

However, those large social studies books or chapter books where he was supposed to read the story, then write a paper, were the worst. Although he was average in math, he had never been considered a good student, and once he got into high school Nick took the most basic classes to earn his credits and tried to take as much hands-on course work as possible. Finally, this year he was allowed to enroll in a new school-to-work program that the school offered.

The school-to-work program would allow Nick to earn the rest of his high school credits off-site at a job instead of at a desk, struggling through all of the reading and writing. The work experience they had found for him was at a large warehouse for a chain store that sold household goods. Nick would get to use his math skills there by keeping track of inventory, learning how to identify when items get low, and to enter this information in the hand-held and desktop computers. Nick, his Individualized Education Program (IEP) team, and especially his parents were very pleased with this placement. Computers and math were Nick's strengths, and these work experiences would certainly assist Nick after school. The first month of the job went very well. Nick came home very confident and positive about his work ability and looked forward to going every day. However, one day his supervisor explained that they were changing database systems and handed Nick a 30-page manual on the new database systems and required him to read and memorize it by the end of the week, so that when the consultant came he could ask any clarifying questions. His supervisor knew that Nick had a history of learning problems, but he was not aware of the exact nature of these problems. So he simply asked if this was OK with Nick and whether Nick felt it was something he could handle. Nick indicated that he thought it was unreasonable to ask someone to read that much and re-member everything. He assumed that it was his boss's job to teach people how to use the computer so they didn't have to sit at home all night reading a bunch of boring stuff.

Nick's supervisor indicated that he needed to learn to con-trol his temper and change his attitude if he wanted to keep this work experience. He told Nick to go home early and to change his attitude. He also mentioned that since they were talking about changing things, he was going to wait until the 8-week review, but this seemed like a good time to bring up that Nick needed to work on presenting himself more neatly at work. He indicted that Nick's clothes seemed tattered, his shirt was only partly tucked in, his pants were ill-fitting, and his hair rarely seemed combed. Nick left quickly and quietly.

That night at home, Nick was very depressed. He indi-cated to his parents that the job was not going to work out and that he was too dumb to do anything.

1. Reflect on the full definition of social competence. Where does Nick seem to need the most help and why?
2. Given what you know about skill deficits and perfor-mance deficits, reflect on Nick's exchange with his

supervisor. What kind of deficits would emerge if you did a discrepancy analysis on that exchange?
3. What are the implications for Nick's post-school outcomes if the above issues are not fully addressed?

REFERENCES

American Association on Mental Retardation (1992). *Mental retardation: Definition, classification, and systems of supports* (9th ed.). Washington, DC: Author.

Bullis, M., Walker, H. M., & Sprague, J. R. (2001). A prom-ise unfulfilled: Social skills training with at-risk and anti-social children and youth. *Exceptionality, 9,* 67.

Charlebois, P., Normandeau, S., Vitaro, F., & Bernache, F. (1999). Skills training for inattentive, overactive, aggres-sive boys: Differential effects of content and delivery of mood. *Behavioral Disorders, 24,* 137–150.

Conroy, M. A., & Brown, W. H. (2002). Preschool children: Putting research into practice. In H. Goldstein, L. Kacz-marek, & K. M. English (Eds.), *Promoting social communi-cation in children and youth with developmental disabilities* (pp. 211–238). Baltimore: Brookes.

Eisenberg, N., & Miller, P. (1987). The relation of empathy to pro-social and related behaviors. *Psychological Bulletin, 101,* 91–119.

Gresham, F. M. (1985). Strategies for enhancing the social outcomes of mainstreaming: A necessary ingredient for success. In J. Meisel (Ed.), *Mainstreaming handicapped children: Outcomes, controversies, and new directions* (pp. 193–218). Hillsdale, NJ: Erlbaum.

Gresham, F. M. (1986). Conceptual and definitional issues in the assessment of children's social skills: Implications for classification and training. *Journal of Clinical Child Psy-chology, 15,* 3–15.

Gresham, F. M. (1998). Social skills training: Should we raze, remodel, or rebuild? *Behavioral Disorders, 24,* 19–25.

Gresham, F. M., & Elliott, S.N. (1990). *Social Skills Rating System.* Circle Pines, MN: American Guidance Service.

Gresham, F. M., & Reshley, D. J. (1986). Social skill deficits and low peer acceptance of mainstreamed learning dis-abled children. *Learning Disability Quarterly, 9,* 23–33.

Grossman, H. J. (Ed.). (1973). *Manual on terminology and classification in mental retardation.* Washington, DC: American Association on Mental Retardation.

Grossman, H. J. (Ed.). (1983). *Classification in mental retar-dation.* Washington, D.C.: American Association on Men-tal Retardation.

Guralnick, M. J. (1992). A hierarchical model for under-standing children's peer-related social competence. In

S. L. Odom, S. R. McConnell, & M. A. McEvoy (Eds.), *Social competence of young children with disabilities: Issues and strategies for intervention* (pp. 37–64). Baltimore: Brookes.

Haring, N. & White, O. (1980). *Exceptional teaching.* Columbus, OH: Merrill.

Heber, R. E. (1959). A manual on terminology and classification in mental retardation. *Monograph Supplement to the American Journal of Mental Deficiency, 62.*

Heber, R. E. (1961). A manual on terminology and classification in mental retardation. *Monograph Supplement to the American Journal of Mental Deficiency, 64.*

Kauffman, J. M. (2005). *Characteristics of emotional and behavioral disorders of children and youth* (8th ed.). Upper Saddle River, NJ: Merrill/Prentice Hall.

Kavale, K. A., Mathur, S. R., & Mostert, M. (2004). Social skills training and teaching social behavior to students with emotional and behavioral disorders. In R. Rutherford, M. M. Quinn, & S. R. Mathur (Eds.), *Handbook of research in emotional and behavioral disorders* (pp. 446–461). New York: Guilford.

Kupersmidt, J. B., & Dodge, K. A. (2004). *Children's peer relations: From development to intervention.* Washington, DC: American Psychological Association.

Ladd, G. W., & Profilet, S. M. (1996). The child behavior scale: A teacher-report measure of young children's aggressive, withdrawn, and prosocial behaviors. *Developmental Psychology, 32,* 1008–1024.

LaFreniere, P. J., & Dumas, J. E. (1995). *Social Competence and Behavior Evaluation—Preschool Edition.* Los Angeles: Western Psychological Services.

LeBlanc, L. A., Sautter, R, A., & Dore, D. J. (2006). Peer relationship problems. In M. Hersen (Ed.)., *Clinical handbook of behavioral assessment* (pp. 377–396). Boston: Elsevier.

Matson, J. L. (1994). *Matson Evaluation of Social Skills with Youngsters* (2nd ed.). Columbus, OH: IDS Publishing.

McDougall, P., Hymel, S., Vaillancourt, T., & Mercer, L. (2001). The consequences of childhood peer rejection. In M. Leary (Ed.), *Interpersonal rejection* (pp. 213–247). London: University Press.

McFall, R. M. (1982). A review and reformulation of the concept of social skills. *Behavioral Assessment, 4,* 1–33.

Merrill, K. W. (2002a). *Preschool and Kindergarten Behavior Scales,* (2nd ed.). Austin, TX: PRO-ED.

Merrill, K. W. (2002b). *School Social Behavior Scales,* (2nd ed.). Austin, TX: PRO-ED.

Odom, S. L., & McConnell, S. R. (1985). A performance-based conceptualization of social competence of handicapped preschool children: Implications for assessment. *Topics in Early Childhood Special Education, 4* (4), 1–19.

Patterson, G. R., Reid, J., & Dishion, T. (1992). *Antisocial boys.* Eugene, OR: Castalia.

Pepler, D. J., & Craig, W. M. (1998). Assessing children's peer relationships. *Child Psychology and Psychiatry Review, 3,* 176–182.

Pepler, D. J., Craig, W. M., & Roberts, W. L. (1998). Observations of aggressive and nonaggressive children on the school playground. *Merrill-Palmer Quarterly, 44,* 55–76.

Stephens, T. M., & Arnold, K. D. (1992). *Social Behavior Assessment Inventory.* Lutz, FL: Par, Inc.

Stichter, J. P., & Conroy, M. A. (2005). *How to teach social skills and plan for peer social interactions with learners with autism spectrum disorders.* Austin, TX: PRO-ED.

Sugai, G., & Lewis, T. J. (1996). Preferred and promising practices for social skills instruction. *Focus on Exceptional Children, 29,* 1–16.

Sugai, G., & Lewis, T. J. (2004). Social skills instruction in the classroom. In C. B. Darch & E. J. Kame'enui (Eds.), *Instructional classroom management: A proactive approach to behavior management* (2nd ed., pp. 152–172). Upper Saddle River, NJ: Merrill/ Prentice Hall.

Valdes, K., Williamson, C., & Wagner, M. (1990a). *The National Longitudinal Transition Study of Special Education Students* (Vol. 1). *Overview.* Palo Alto, CA: SRI International.

Valdes, K., Williamson, C., & Wagner, M. (1990b). *The National Longitudinal Transition Study of Special Education Students* (Vol. 3). *Youth categorized as emotionally disturbed.* Palo Alto, CA: SRI International.

Valdes, K., Williamson, C., & Wagner, M. (1990c). *The National Longitudinal Transition Study of Special Education Students* (Vol. 7). *Youth categorized as learning impaired.* Palo Alto, CA: SRI International.

Wagner, M. (1991). *Dropouts with disabilities: What do we know? What can we do?* Menlo Park, CA: SRI International.

Wagner, M. & Shaver, D. (1989). *Educational programs and achievements of secondary special education students: Findings from the National Longitudinal Transition Study.* Menlo Park, CA: SRI International.

PART IV

Educational Partnerships

Characteristics of Effective General Education Settings for Students with High-Incidence Disabilities

URBAN LEGEND: *The best way to support students with high-incidence disabilities in general education settings is to provide many curriculum modifications and accommodations.*

LEGENDARY THOUGHT: *An effective learning environment includes planned, proactive, and effective instruction.*

Social and political initiatives, as well as interpretations of various laws, have changed general education within the last several decades. Since 1975, when federal law (Public Law 94-142, now the *Individuals with Disabilities Education Improvement Act*, or IDEA) began mandating free and appropriate public education for students with special needs within the **least restrictive environment** (LRE), increasing numbers of special education students have been educated to some degree in general education classrooms. The inclusion movement has resulted in even more students with disabilities being placed in general education for part or all of their instruction (see Chapter 2 for an expanded discussion of inclusion; see also Kauffman & Hallahan, 2005a, 2005b). Today, the majority of students with high-incidence disabilities spend a significant portion of their day integrated into the general education classroom (Lembke & Stormont, 2005; Mercer & Mercer, 2005).

The increased diversity of students now being supported in these general education settings has required shifts in service delivery across general and special education. Both general and special education teachers are finding it increasingly necessary to collaborate across curriculum areas and instructional strategies and to share resources. In doing so, they often find that their responsibilities become rather murky. Which of them should be the lead teacher, and under what conditions should he or she take the leading role in teaching? In an effort to provide guidance and foster collaboration, IDEA aligns ownership of instructional Individualized Education Program (IEP) goals with the place of their delivery. For example, general educators are required to be represented at IEP meetings if the student will be spending *any* of his or her time in that their general education classrooms. If *any* of the IEP goals are to be addressed in that general education, the general education teacher shares responsibility for ensuring that the IEP goals are addressed.

For many special educators certified in high-incidence disability areas, this has changed the nature of their jobs. Some no longer develop and run their own self-contained classroom; instead they have a resource room to which students come only for specific, limited times to receive direct academic instruction or specific behavior support. The rest of the time the special educator might be working with general educators to assist with appropriate instructional strategies, accommodations, and modifications to best meet the needs of the special education student on their caseload who is taught by the general educator.

Chapter 11 highlights the need and importance of effective collaboration and provides a thorough description of many effective research-based models by which educators can accomplish this. Yet many general educators willingly attest that they have very limited, if any, background in educating students with varying disabilities. Similarly, special educators are rarely dually certified and therefore are not experienced with general education curriculum or related teaching formats (e.g., delivering the state math curriculum to 25 fourth graders in large group instruction for 30 minutes).

The goal of the general education setting as one placement on the continuum of options for the delivery of special education services was never to require general educators to become fluent in special education practices. Additionally, with the increased emphasis on student performance outcomes (i.e., the *No Child Left Behind Act*, U.S. Department of Education, 2002), it is as important as ever that both general and special educators employ their skills to emphasize effective practices for all students in these settings. This is especially pertinent considering the increase in numbers of students without identified disabilities who are requiring additional supports to meet basic standards in general education classrooms (Stormont, Espinosa, Knipping, & McCathren, 2003).

This chapter is designed to present many of the variables that have been demonstrated to be characteristics of effective general education settings for students with high-incidence disabilities, including specific strategies identified in the research to promote positive academic and behavior outcomes for these students. It is not a chapter on **inclusion**, nor a chapter on methods of instruction. It is designed to address the fact that for many students with high-incidence disabilities at least some of their educational day is spent in general education settings or accessing the general education curriculum. Therefore, it is imperative to understand how certain instructional and environmental characteristics, as well as accommodations and modifications correctly matched with learning characteristics can optimize student success.

:: THE COMPONENT OF AN EFFECTIVE GENERAL EDUCATION SETTING

A substantial amount of research demonstrates that effective teaching practices, when in effect within a well-designed learning environment, contribute to improved student outcomes (Bateman, 2004; Bos & Vaughn, 2006; Cotton, 1995; Stichter & Lewis, 2006). The research in this area has spanned typically developing students and those with high-incidence disabilities, and it is clear that both groups benefit. Yet from our perspective in focusing on the characteristics of students with high-incidence disabilities, it is important to understand how these core instructional variables must be in place and functionally serve as the foundation for any supplemental curriculum or behavior-specific strategies employed in these settings (Stichter, Lewis, Johnson, & Trussell, 2004).

An example might help us understand how instruction can go wrong and some of what is required for good instruction. Most of us could not imagine trying to put together one of those 1,000-piece, three-dimensional puzzles on our lap while riding a crowded downtown Chicago bus. It really would not matter whether each piece had been color coded by section and we had a simplified set of directions or even a helper sitting next to us telling us what to do. Despite the high level of direct instruction, accommodations, and support, we would be frustrated and probably not succeed. The learning or work environment lacks important characteristics (e.g., flat work space, room to put pieces out flat, physical stability). We would likely be unable to do the task regardless of support. Now take that scenario to a room with a nice flat work space, plenty of room, and physical stability. How well would we do in putting the puzzle together? Probably at least a little bit better. Given that we had no prior experience with this type of task we might naturally approach it the same way we do a two-dimensional puzzle—look for straight edges first, then sort by color and pictorial schemes, and so forth. For a three-dimensional puzzle, this is most likely not the best manner by which to proceed. Yet, if the puzzle maker was now also instructing us, she might determine that a 300-piece puzzle might be a more appropriate first puzzle, and then provide us with an overview of how to do three-dimensional puzzles, accessing our background knowledge of two-dimensional puzzles as well as other three-dimensional items we have previously built, and then providing us with instructional tools to effectively break down the task into manageable parts. We might then be able to access those step-by-step directions and proceed more successfully with the task. So now with the appropriate learning environment, direct instruction, accommodations, and support we are significantly more likely to reach the instructional goal of learning how to create a three-dimensional puzzle than when we started on the Chicago bus. Most if not all of the changes that occurred in this scenario probably seemed intuitive and not particularly individualized. They simply reflect an appropriate learning environment, appropriately matched curriculum, and direct instruction—all elements of a comprehensive approach to instruction referred to as the **Direct Instruction Model** (DI) (Adams & Engelmann, 1996; Stein, Carnine, & Dixon, 1998).

Students with learning and behavioral challenges are highly vulnerable to variations across educational settings and variations in expectations (Bos & Vaughn, 2006). Therefore, it is essential when considering supporting these students within general education settings to assess the degree to which the appropriate combination of environmental and instructional variables is occurring. We discuss these variables in Chapter 12. They can be found within the functional behavior analysis (FBA) prevention model in level 1 and level 2 framework. In this chapter we discuss many components of DI, which is defined as a

> comprehensive system of instruction that integrates effective teaching practices with sophisticated curriculum design, classroom organization and management, and careful monitoring of student progress, as well as extensive staff development. (Stein et al., 1998, p. 228)

Specific discussion of DI as it relates to students with learning disabilities (LD) is found in Chapter 4. A full explanation and examples of DI are best left for a text addressing methods of instruction within curriculum design. The following sections include snapshots of those elements that can be employed by a team across settings, students, and curricula. These elements of DI ensure a foundation of effective instruction and carry with them the potential for needed accommodations and modifications.

:: ESTABLISHING THE LEARNING ENVIRONMENT

Manage the Instructional Process Efficiently

One means by which the educational team can strengthen the setting for students with high-incidence disabilities is to work together to manage instruction efficiently. Johnson (1998) describes a teacher's planful and organized process for determining how all the components of instruction and individuals in the setting are coordinated. For example, the plan of a general education teacher must include the special education student's arrival from and departure to the special education setting as part of the curriculum delivery. The plan is also reflected in the degree to which the student's specific learning characteristics might be incorporated into a lesson or learning unit by design.

For example, does the team anticipate that the oral presentation of a written geography unit summary may not be conducive to the student with learning disabilities or mild mental retardation and, therefore, incorporate a visual mapping component of the lesson as another measure of student performance that can be used to accompany the oral presentation? This preplanning reduces the need for extra strategies or accommodations and maintains the integrity of the lesson for all students. Does the team recognize that the common approach in the afterschool program of picking a partner to rotate through "activity clubs" is problematic for the student with emotional and behavioral disorders (EBD) who has developed a bad reputation among peers or has limited prosocial skills in soliciting a partner? The afterschool program may appreciate the fact that many students could profit from increasing their social and cooperation skills and

The learning environment should reflect a planned and organized process for determining how all the components of instruction and individuals in the setting are coordinated. (Photo credit: Anthony Magnacca/Merrill)

begin a partner rotation system, including specific social skills instruction regarding what to do when you get a partner you are not sure you will like.

In addition to organization and preplanning, effective management of instruction incorporates specific teacher behaviors. The teacher must have core classroom management skills and be able to establish routines, set and maintain expectations, and keep students engaged during instruction.

Periodically, the Northwest Regional Educational Laboratory (NWREL) publishes a research synthesis that addresses curriculum integration and school-based management among other topics. The third edition (Cotton, 1995) identifies a representative list of specific behaviors included in managing instruction effectively. A representative sample of these teacher behaviors is shown in Table 10.1.

Define Diversity as Part of the Setting

Educators are often encouraged to incorporate diversity—to practice multiculturalism in education (Johnson, 1998). The literature strongly supports the assumption that a student's classroom and other educational settings should be a part of his or her culture. Each student's unique characteristics need to be celebrated, and teachers need to

TABLE 10.1 Key variables for managing instruction effectively

- Determine class routines and procedures before school starts.
- Review rules and routines regularly for the first several weeks of school.
- Create and post daily schedules, discuss any changes to the schedule each morning, or beginning of class.
- Review rules and procedures regularly throughout school year.
- Begin class quickly by having materials prepared in advance, so students can be immediately oriented to the task at hand.
- Develop routines and procedures to handle administrative tasks efficiently (i.e., where and when to turn in homework, where to put notes from home or other teachers).
- Establish routines for downtime, such as when students finish seatwork and others are working.
- Develop and follow procedures for obtaining assistance and asking questions during instruction as well as independent seatwork.
- Circulate around the room while students are working to assist with task behaviors and to anticipate potential behavioral or academic difficulties.
- Minimize transition times between activities by planning ahead and organizing students' materials.
- Do not relinquish students' attention until you have given clear instructions for the next activity.
- Orient students to the procedures associated with the next lesson prior to transition.

recognize and address differences among students (Johnson, 1998). This is as important for students with disabilities as it is for those with differing color or ethnicity. For example, teaching respect for language differences and language problems is essential if students are to embrace diversity. Mandatory attendance laws and the expectation of on-time arrival to class do not preclude students from being sensitive to the fact that some cultures have a different perception of time and that the concept of on-timeness to which our schools and work places subscribe may be challenging for some families of various cultures. Similarly, although students are expected to raise their hands, Anne's mother may share with the class how Anne's attention deficit hyperactivity disorder (ADHD) can make it hard for her to remember not to blurt out what she is thinking during large group discussion. Anne's mother may share ways that parents, teachers, and peers can help. At the same time, all students can brainstorm their own quirks (e.g., disorganization) that sometimes gets them into hot water.

By fully defining the idea of diversity, the membership of every student in the class is assured. Defining diversity appropriately means that the characteristics of students with disabilities are better understood by classmates, and peers are better able to assess each student's value as a potential friend. Students are discouraged from defining peers with disabilities solely by their limitations.

Facilitation of Peer Supports and Social Networks

Peers are often an untapped resource in educational settings for students with high-incidence disabilities. This does not mean that typically developing peers should provide all the instruction. Instead, this statement reflects an increasing body of research showing that students with disabilities may be supported in general education settings in two ways with regard to peer interactions. First, we must systematically assess opportunities for typically developing students and those with high-incidence disabilities to interact meaningfully (Bos & Vaughn, 2006; Johnson & Johnson, 1987; King-Sears, 1997). Special education students often have schedules that vary from those of their peers, in the services, accommodations, and modifications that they require.

Even minor adjustments to the schedules of students with disabilities can isolate them from interacting socially with typically developing peers. For example, timeliness is important in getting to a good table at lunch; therefore, a delayed arrival at lunch or other variations can shorten the time students with disabilities can hang out with peers during noninstructional times. In addition, depending on the degree of modifications and accommodations in certain situations (e.g., language arts), typically developing peers may be unsure of how much they share the interests of a student with disabilities. For example, although Sara may not be a strong reader, her peers may not know how proficient she is at basketball during PE. Peer networks often assist students in identifying common interests and establishing predictable times for facilitating friendships. Table 10.2 highlights common features of effective peer network models.

Whether it is through a formal special network approach or simply by systematically creating opportunities, these efforts set the stage for the second part of successful peer interactions—**peer supports.** Peer supports are natural supports in the form of context-based prompts and cues. For example, peer supports operate when a child drops a cookie on the lunch room floor, reaches to get it, and a friend says,

TABLE 10.2   Peer networks

Key Components of Peer Networks

Peer Networks are defined as a group of students who are considered friends. This group introduces a new member. It is important to assist peer networks in understanding how and why they are being asked to include an individual with a disability. Researchers and educators alike have found the following steps as essential for beginning and maintaining this process (Haring & Breen, 1992).

Understanding the value of peer networks	• Increased quality of life for all students involved • Social competency enhanced through peer modeling • Disability awareness
Identifying a peer network	• Who have common interests • Who have common classes • Initially that comprise a group of four or five students
Providing adult support	• Designated adult facilitator • Involvement of primary classroom teacher • Who can provide structure and consistency • Who is comfortable answering questions and training peers on strategies best suited for target student
Attention to set up and monitoring	• Map students' and peers' schedules • Assign formal times to hang out • Ensure opportunities to see one another during normal routines • Complete a set of activities to determine preferences and needs • Assist group in deciding what is essential to teach and best contexts and supports by which to do so • Keep data on interactions and process
Attention to times and contexts for interaction	• Commitment from peers to attend and view as a positive addition to their lives • Commitment from peers to be open and honest • Commitment from adults to: maintain the structure and routines; welcome and support peer feedback; train necessary skills; and incorporate peer comments and suggestions

Adapted from Stichter, J. P., & Conroy, M. A. (2005 Copyright). *How to teach social skills and plan for peer social interactions with learners with autism spectrum disorders.* Austin, TX: PRO-ED.

"Gross, you are not going to eat that are you?" The child who dropped the cookie and was contemplating eating it—barring anything disgusting attached to it—says, "No! I was just getting it so I didn't get yelled at for leaving it!" These same children remind each other to get their backpacks when they are leaving for the bus, or to turn in their work or to stop talking so that everyone does not get in trouble. They even help each other at their desks, generating new ideas during creative writing time. Peer supports extend into adulthood when the neighbor across the hall knocks on your door to tell you that you left your keys in the door or your car windows are down and it's going to rain.

Students with high-incidence disabilities do not have the same teacher or the same accommodations in all school settings. These students often have difficulty learning social cues and prompts, which are so different across varying persons and environments. Peers are typically a natural part of different social environments. Students with high-incidence disabilities need assistance structuring their social conduct and academic learning in environments in which their peers help one another naturally. That is, students with high-incidence disabilities often don't get the social cues that seem natural to their peers.

Fostering Collaboration

At the beginning of this chapter we highlighted the importance of collaboration among educators to support students with high-incidence disabilities across settings. Of equal importance is collaboration with families. Research has consistently indicated that parent and family involvement has a significant impact on the educational outcomes of students (Johnson, 1998; O'Neill, Earley, & Snider, 1991; Turnbull, Turnbull, Erwin, & Soodak, 2006). Parents derive pleasure in their own involvement, leading to feelings of self-enhancement and a better working relationship with the teachers. Teachers view their jobs in a more positive light and experience an enhanced working environment (Flaxman & Inger, 1991). Parental participation is associated with students' improved standardized test scores, attitudes, and behavior, as well as higher grades (Johnson, 1998).

Supporting the involvement of parents of students with high-incidence disabilities is challenging due to the numerous educational settings and school personnel involved with these students. Educators need to encourage home-based and school-based activities. Home-based activities involve students' parents in helping with homework, for example, by reading with students or helping them use learning strategies in novel situations. For example, if Alex is currently working on a measurement unit in class which includes time and distance, his family can ask him to assist them in planning their weekend trip. If the parents have been given information on the specific strategies used to teach Alex these concepts, or learning strategies they could use with him, the family can become an integral part of the generalization of these strategies to other settings and situations. Similarly, if Jamie's family knows what social supports are being used at school to help her manage her temper and settle disputes with peers appropriately, they can support the same process at home when she has disputes with siblings. School-based activities for parents include opportunities to participate directly or indirectly in program delivery. For example, they can serve as afterschool program tutors or extramural activity coaches or they can assist with parties, field trips, and development of materials.

Parental and family participation can occur on many levels and in many settings. However, to accomplish any degree of successful collaboration, communication between home and school must be regular and must occur in varying ways. Informal personal chats and notes are helpful for developing personal relationships, but more formal systems like parent-teacher conferences, report cards, and newsletters ensure consistency (Gestwicki, 1987).

Finally, fostering collaboration is not just for adults. Successful models for peer collaboration have been developed (Johnson, Johnson, & Holubec, 1993; Slavin, 1987, 1991). These are often referred to as cooperative learning models and are designed to teach students how to work and learn together. Collaborative skills are required to participate successfully in cooperative learning groups. The collaboration skills are taught by teachers who assist students in identifying the purpose of these skills, what they look like, and why they are used (Bos & Vaughn 2006; Pressley & Hughes, 2000). Table 10.3 provides an overview of key components of the cooperative learning models. Cooperative learning group types are oriented around goals, which should be matched to the identified social as well as academic outcomes desired.

Cooperative learning groups can be used in a variety of settings as a foundation across a variety of curriculum areas as diverse as academics, ceramics, or social skills instruction as part of team-based sports. As a foundation in key settings for students with high-incidence disabilities, peer collaboration helps develop peer supports as well as expanding key academic and social skills goals.

Integration of Effective Practices

As mentioned earlier, in conjunction with an effectively managed learning environment, another key component of the Direct Instruction Model (DI) is the "integration of effective practices into the curriculum design" (Stein et al., 1998, p. 28). A primary assumption of DI is that effective practices are the same in any published curriculum (Stein et al., 1998). Furthermore, DI assumes that the teacher employs the curriculum to establish essential **background knowledge** to which new knowledge is directly linked. The assumptions underlying DI are, of course, relevant for teaching all students, but are particularly relevant for students with high-incidence disabilities, who often do not have background knowledge or do not link it explicitly to new material and concepts. Stein et al. (1998) refer to five main principles of DI around which instruction in any curriculum area should occur: (a) organize content around big ideas, (b) teach specific and generalizable strategies, (c) **scaffold instruction,** (d) integrate skills and concepts, and (e) provide sufficient review (Stein et al., 1998).

The DI model is not the only instructional framework. However, it is a useful framework for providing an overview of key characteristics of an effective learning environment for students with high-incidence disabilities. Table 10.4 illustrates how the five elements of DI can be interpreted within a typical math curriculum.

Numerous instructional strategies and practices have been identified as effective for supporting curriculum design and effective learning environments for students with high-incidence disabilities (Bos & Vaughn, 2006; Brophy & Good, 1986; Forness, Kavale, Blum, & Lloyd, 1997; Lembke & Stormont, 2005; National Reading

TABLE 10.3   Five types of cooperative learning groups

1. *Positive interdependence/group goal.* Goals are structured to promote accomplishments and success for all group members.

   - Strategies:
     - Structure assignments so the job cannot be completed unless all team members participate.
     - Organize materials and structure responding for group participation (e.g., team members develop group goals collaboratively, one pencil for recorder, one paper submitted by the group).
     - Provide reinforcement to all group members for meeting group goals.

2. *Individual accountability.* Each student's mastery of the assigned content is assessed.

   - Strategies:
     - Provide rewards and bonus points for individual improvement or progress.
     - Conduct random comprehension checks, selecting one group member to respond to questions.
     - Require students to check each others' work and select one paper from the group for review.

3. *Task specialization.* Students become experts on various aspects of the group assignment.

   - Strategies:
     - A group of "experts" may be assigned specific sections of content area texts with the task of preparing a study guide to disseminate to the whole class.
     - Let students select subtopics of a unit to be compiled by the group.
     - Encourage students to select methods of problem solving and responding based on personal strengths (written, oral, demonstration, art project, video, etc.).

4. *Opportunities for success.* The contributions of all team members are valued.

   - Strategies:
     - Team points are awarded based on improvement of past scores.
     - In competitive situations (e.g., tournaments or games), students are placed with peers of similar ability.
     - Required contributions are appropriate to individual's present level, but each contribution is valued equally (e.g., 6 math problems completed correctly for student with disability receives the same points as 12 for a typical peer).

5. *Face-to-face interaction.* Groups are structured to facilitate collaborative efforts.

   - Strategies:
     - Structure the physical arrangement of the classroom to facilitate collaborative efforts.
     - Select instructional methods and cooperative goals that encourage interaction (e.g., reciprocal reading and questioning, elaboration, summarizing).
     - Award points for demonstration of positive collaborative behaviors.

Adapted from Stichter, J. P., & Conroy, M. A. (2005). *How to teach social skills and plan for peer social interactions with learners with autism spectrum disorders.* Austin, TX: PRO-ED.

TABLE 10.4	Examples of curriculum design elements

Organize the curriculum around larger themes or "big ideas" for students. For example, do the students understand that the entire unit on fractions is all about parts of a whole? How can this be done by accessing and developing background knowledge prior to teaching them the actual computational strategies expected in the unit?

1. Teaching strategies to access content that can be used in similar situations or across content areas. For example, has the student been taught specific strategies to read through a word problem, identify the solution question being asked for (e.g., What portion or fraction of the students were wearing shoes with shoelaces in the class?), to find the key elements of the word problem like the denominator (the total number of students with shoes) and then the numerator (students with shoelaces), and how to complete any necessary computations to provide the solution in its appropriate form (e.g., lowest possible denominator)? Teaching consistent word problem strategies that can be generalized across many other curricular areas and situations.

2. Scaffolding instruction refers to aids and supports provided a student while learning strategies. In the word problem scenario above, a student may have a checklist of steps to follow when working through word problems or may be placed in a co-operative learning group with peer support to initially acquire and become fluent with skills associated with that task.

3. Integration of skills and concepts refers to the degree to which skills and concepts in one area are related to those in another for the student and within the curriculum. In the case of the fraction unit, using word problems as part of that unit might support the integration of concepts and skills promoted and taught within language arts and literacy.

4. Review of instruction may be accomplished in many ways, including integration across curricular areas or time.

Panel, 2000; Tarver & DLD/DR, 1999; White, 1998). The following section briefly highlights and reviews many of these practices.

Explicit Instruction

Explicit instruction is defined as a set of procedures that the teacher uses to clearly and overtly teach a student content information (Carnine et al, 2004; Gersten, Carnine, & Woodward, 1987; King-Sears, 1997). Explicit instruction typically employs a three-step process by which the teacher models, leads, and tests students on their understanding and ability to use the new content. For example when learning to write letters, the teacher might model how to make the letter M, then verbally or with visual aids (like a dotted M) have students make their own M's. Next the teacher might ask the students to make their own M without assistance. The structure and rule-based learning of explicit instructional procedures help students with high-incidence disabilities learn successfully. However, as mentioned earlier, meaningful connection to real life (accessing background knowledge) is also important as a final step of explicit instruction. Therefore, associating words representing things and people that the student knows and cares about with the letter M enhances the use and maintenance of the new skill of writing M.

Strategy Instruction

Strategy instruction is functionally designed to reduce the amount of explicit instruction needed for a student above and beyond what the curriculum demands by design. Learning environments oriented toward strategy instruction for all students more successfully support students with high-incidence disabilities by actively engaging them in the learning process (Meichenbaum & Biemiller, 1998) and reducing the need for watered-down curricula and one-on-one supports (King-Sears, 1998). This is because these strategies are designed to provide the student with

---

BOX 10.1 SAMPLE COGNITIVE STRATEGIES

Self-questioning strategies are designed to assist a student to pull main ideas from text and increase comprehension. They generally have five key components:

1. The student is asked to remind himself or herself or is cued regarding the purpose of the material being read. This task is typically to answer specific questions or find specific facts as directed by the teacher or relevant curriculum materials.
2. The student uses a strategy or series of questions to assist her or him in locating the main ideas in the materials and mark them (i.e., underlines, highlights, or rewrites them in a designated spot).
3. For each main idea that the student identified, a question is generated.
4. The student then accesses the content again to answer each question that he or she generated.
5. The student reviews all main ideas, questions, and answers in the passage as they relate to the assigned task.

EXAMPLES OF STRATEGIES

Think Ahead

- What is this section I am reading about?
- What is the main idea and what do I already know about the topic?
- What do I want to know?
- What is my goal?
- What can I do to meet my goal?

Think While Reading

- What have I read about so far?
- Do I understand it?
- If not, what should I do?
- What is the point(s) the author is making, and what did I think about it?

(Continued)

Think Back

- Have I reached my goal?
- How can I use what I read?

SQ3R

Survey—　Survey the chapter
Question—While you are surveying – what do I already know?
Read—　Look for clues when you begin to read, words in bold, under-lined sections, answers to your questions
Recite—　After you have read a section, put in your own words, either orally or in writing
Review—　As an ongoing process, alternate between reviewing notes, and practice with flashcards and summarizing.

K-W-L-Q

Identifying what I **KNOW**
What I **WANT** to know
What I did **LEARN**
More **QUESTIONS** I still have

tools to manage many of the day-to-day social or academic demands within their typical environments (Bos & Vaughn, 2006). Effective use of cognitive strategy instruction has demonstrated increases in social, cognitive, and academic skills in students with learning and behavioral problems (Deschler, Ellis, & Lenz, 1996; Gersten, Schiller, & Vaughn, 2000; Graham, Harris, & Troia, 1998; Mastropieri & Scruggs, 1997; Schumaker & Deshler, 1995). Examples of strategy instruction include teaching students to engage in peer editing when checking each other's work, self-monitor their social behavior, and follow steps in addressing math word problems. Box 10.1 provides a few examples of commonly used strategies in addition to those provided in Chapter 4.

Guidelines for strategy instruction include:

1. Carefully and thoroughly define the specific behavior desired for the student to learn.
2. Pretest or assess the student's current level of the behavior and what strategies the student is currently using, if any. The problem may not only be a lack of effective strategies, but also one of incorrect or ineffective strategy use.
3. Choose strategy steps that reflect those employed by effective problem solvers.
4. Identify the specific strategy steps with the student. This may involve the use of verbal strategies including the use of mnemonics, or visual icons for students who are younger or who have more severe cognitive impairments.

5. Teach any prerequisite skills necessary for performing each step of the strategy.
6. Verbally practice the steps. It is often recommended that students model the steps including some form of self-instruction like self-talk.
7. Use controlled practice, in which students begin with easier steps that they have already demonstrated some proficiency in using and then move to more difficult steps.
8. Teach students to use self-instruction. They may use visual aids such as cue cards to assist them.
9. Teach self-regulation where students reflect on where they are in the process and how well they are doing.
10. Provide explicit feedback throughout training.
11. Teach students strategy generalization, which includes where, when, why, and how they can use the strategy.
12. Ensure opportunities for students to use skills to promote maintenance (Bos & Vaughn, 2006; King-Sears, 1997).

Curriculum-Based Assessment

Using repeated measures taken directly from what is being taught to assess long- and short-term goals over time before, during, and after instruction is called curriculum-based assessment (CBA, sometimes also called curriculum-based measurement or CBM) (Deno, 1985; King-Sears, 1997; Lembke & Stormont, 2005; see Chapter 8 for discussion). Learning environments that support the use of CBA to monitor the progress of their students and use a student's performance data to make instructional decisions lead to higher achieving students. These results have been replicated across grades, subjects, and ability levels (Conte & Hintze, 2000; Deno, 1985; Fuchs & Fuchs, 1986; Fuchs, Fuchs, Hamlet, Phillips, & Benz, 1994). Assessments that are used only for grading purposes or end-of-the-year standards are not considered valid for instructional purposes because they cannot provide specific information to guide instructional decision making or improve learning. State standards of learning expressed as standardized test performance are thus far too infrequent and far too late to be of instructional value (Kauffman, 2002). This is relevant when trying to determine whether, and to what degree, students with high-incidence disabilities may require **differentiated instruction** in relation to the curriculum.

Differentiated Instruction

Students with high-incidence disabilities may require various levels of **differentiated instruction,** depending on the content area and the nature of the disability. For example, if a student has a learning disability in the area of reading, various accommodations or modifications might be required to best support that student in a seventh-grade American history class requiring a great deal of reading. At times, the differences in instruction may be systematic, so that the student always requires more time or someone to read to her during tests; or the differences may be more specifically targeted to a unit or task. Again, this depends on the match between the student's skills, ongoing environmental supports, and curricular demands. For many students, curricular demands include social skill requirements as well as academic skills, and both need to be addressed. The question that often arises for students with high-incidence disabilities is, "How much and what degree of differentiated instruction is appropriate?"

There are four primary categories of **curriculum differentiation,** or changes to curriculum (Giangreco, Cloninger, & Iverson, 1993; King-Sears, 1997).

1. *Accommodations:* These are variations in the delivery of the curriculum or the manner in which the student is asked to perform. These accommodations do not significantly change the content of the curriculum, or change the overall difficulty. Examples might include: having a shorter number of spelling words to know, but from the same list as other students; having more time to take a test; or having fewer math problems to complete.

2. *Modifications:* These are adaptations to the curriculum or expectations regarding student performance related to the curriculum. Whereas the rest of the class may be reading a story to identify the main characters and main points, students with a modified curriculum may be asked to pick out the main character from a list of potential options and then identify the setting from another list to assist in developing a sense of the main idea.

3. *Parallel Instruction:* This type of instruction is provided when significant changes have been made to the conceptual difficulty and/or delivery of the instruction. Thus, the student with higher-incidence disabilities may also be working on math but may be solving fractions on the computer with the use of pictorial representations, while the rest of the class is solving paper-and-pencil algebraic equations. Similarly, the rest of the class might be completing an expository writing assignment on the Civil War, while the instructional aide of the student with higher-incidence disabilities asks her to verbally respond to leading questions about who Abraham Lincoln was and the definition of slavery.

4. *Overlapping Curriculum:* This refers to instances in which the student with high-incidence disabilities is participating in an ongoing curriculum primarily to achieve goals and objectives separate from that curriculum. For example, the student with higher-incidence disabilities might be placed in a cooperative learning group focused on an Earth Day project to work on social skills related to cooperation and appropriate interactions. The small group setting and structured activity may be a perfect setting in which to work on these goals for such a student despite a lack of experience with the Earth Day curriculum. The student is assigned a similar task to other students, but one that does not require many technical skills.

The level and type of curriculum differentiations that are provided depend a great deal on the degree to which the setting employs effective instructional principles, as well as the specific goals and objectives for the student in the environment. Typically, most accommodations and modifications fall within three general categories: (a) modifications of activities and materials, (b) modifications of instruction, and (c) modifications of the environment (Deschenes, Ebeling, & Sprague, 1994; Wagner, 1999; Zentall & Stormont-Spurgin,1995). Table 10.5 provides a representative sample of common modifications for each of the three categories.

TABLE **10.5** Accommodations and modifications

Modifications of activities and materials can include many of the following examples, in which adjustments are made to:

- Level of participation required
- Size of assignment/content
- Difficulty of assignment/content
- Time allotted for assignments
- Level of support provided through cross-age peer tutors or instructional aides
- Manner of presentation, including providing lecture notes, highlighting key points ahead of time, and outlining ahead of time or using taped lectures
- Response required for instruction, such as keyboarding versus handwriting or orally completing the spelling test
- Amount of reading required for nonreading activities
- Amount of writing required for nonwriting activities

Modification of instruction includes altering the way instruction is delivered and may involve various learning strategies and formats. Thus, a teacher might:

- Alter rate of instruction to be responsive to varied attention spans and information processing speeds. This can be done by stopping periodically to assess comprehension, allowing students to work at varied paces, and providing small breaks. A teacher might also shorten directions or provide them one at a time.
- Alter instructional grouping to match a student's strengths. It can be helpful to alternate between whole- and small-group instructions in a single content area like literacy or to break up a new unit in science. For another student it may be appropriate to practice handwriting during individual seat work but optimal to work on math problems in a collaborative peer work group that can support her use of a mnemonic cognitive strategy for adding two-digit problems.
- Match instructional groupings to an appropriate teaching format. Remember that all students benefit from an appropriate combination of direct instruction and practice, hands-on demonstration, and experiential learning. Often these are correlated with curriculum stages related to phases such as **acquisition,** (i.e., direct instruction of new content) and **fluency** (i.e., practice until the skill is well learned or automatic). Students with high-incidence disabilities often experience greater variance across stages of learning as compared to their typically developing counterparts and, therefore, may benefit from variations in the typical teaching formats often associated with the curriculum.
- Alternate forms of curriculum delivery, including oral presentation and visual representation of materials. For example, some students may find that 30 minutes of teacher direct instruction delivered through verbal discussion requires too much **auditory processing.** This is particularly true if these students are expected to translate this information into a written or other permanent product format like lecture notes or math problems. Mixed methods of verbal and visual presentation of materials is an ideal balance for most students. Students with high-incidence disabilities may also benefit from shortened directions, clearer language, and visual checklists or key points to refer to while completing subsequent guided practice.
- Increase opportunities for review relevant to guided and independent practice. Increasing the students' opportunities to become fluent in applying the skills learned correctly and in a relevant manner, as opposed to simply requiring rote memorization helps the student connect key concepts, which can be particularly difficult for some students with high-incidence disabilities.

(Continued)

TABLE 10.5   *(Continued)*

- Provide frequent and concrete feedback. Students learn more clearly and quickly what is expected of them if they are repeatedly provided with information on their performance. This includes academic as well as social skills. Specifically, telling a student, "I like the way you hung in there with that difficult problem and helped your group find a solution," or "That was a great use of the dictionary as a reference for your writing assignment!" are examples of concrete feedback on performance. Building opportunities during direct instruction as well as practice opportunities is essential to assist students in applying and correcting their use of skills. In addition, it can also assist in modeling appropriate components of self-evaluation as part of a self-management program.
- Encourage student summarization of key points. This can be done through student note taking, even if it is just listing key words, or by asking the student to repeat primary themes and/or directions before releasing class or student to complete independent or small group practice.

Modifications of the environment include alterations not only to the physical environment but also to routines, materials, and even behavioral plans that are considered part of the typical classroom structure. These modifications might include:

- Providing preferential seating arrangements. Sometimes these might include seating a student away from doors and windows to reduce visual and auditory distractions.
- Providing a quiet zone or study carrel for some students to work free of distraction.
- Providing easier or more consistent access to the teacher for support than typical routines allow (e.g., during independent seatwork).
- Allowing the student to stand during instruction or take brief walks around the room.
- Allowing some independent work to be done with a partner.
- Providing students with self-management tools such as a daily planner, timer, or checklists to manage their work and assist them with organizational needs.
- Setting up the environment with increased study skills tools such as outlines, written steps, lists, or visual schedules to assist students in following key steps to study more effectively and complete their work.
- Supporting and implementing individualized behavior management plans developed for particular students to ensure consistency and enhanced effectiveness across settings.

SUMMARY

Supporting students with high-incidence disabilities effectively in general education settings means teaching them effectively in such settings. The IEP team should develop a clear picture of which curricular areas should be involved and where the student with high-incidence disabilities should be taught, based on the specific strengths and needs of the student (the present level of performance). As high-lighted throughout this chapter, the instructional emphasis and goals for the participation of a student with high-incidence disabilities in a general education setting may vary greatly. The necessary considerations range from obtaining a clear picture of a student's ability to access the general education curriculum effectively with little or no curriculum variations, to targeting specifically social skills within a particular class in which the student is not expected to perform academically as well as others do.

Irrespective of the level of needs or targeted goals, supporting students with high-incidence disabilities requires a planful and proactive approach to instruction that is not defined by accommodations and modifications.

Characteristics of effective general education settings for students with high-incidence disabilities are the same as effective learning environments for all students. Yet, these settings are rarely sufficient without a well developed plan for students with learning needs that cause them to need special education.

COMPETENT TEACHING BOX   BOX 10.2

Knowing your students . . .

Students with high-incidence disabilities are increasingly supported in general education settings to achieve a variety of academic and social goals. The specific supports needed and characteristics of effective learning environments will vary depending on these goals and most certainly depending on the specific student's learning and behavioral profile. However, the following key considerations will be helpful when developing a plan for educating these students in general education settings.

- Most individuals identified with high-incidence disabilities are vulnerable to inconsistencies in curriculum format and instructional delivery. They are often missing or have difficulty accessing appropriate background knowledge to help them acquire new information. For this reason, students need explicit instruction, including strategy use that is consistently presented and modeled and for which multiple opportunities for practice are provided.
- Students with high-incidence disabilities often have difficulty generalizing information and skills to other settings and across situations. Yet, these students often experience more educational settings and education providers than any other population. Therefore, collaboration among school personnel and with families is essential to provide consistent strategy prompts and opportunities to practice across settings and people.
- Peers are an untapped resource. Peers are present across most settings and can provide natural supports both formally within structured cooperative learning groups or more informally through peer networks. Research indicates peer support models are effective in enhancing direct instruction goals as well as generalization and maintenance outcomes.
- Students with high-incidence disabilities will benefit from different models of curriculum differentiation depending on the setting and the instructional goals associated with the placement decision. One student may need parallel curriculum in one setting and basic accommodations in another. Students' strengths and needs should be assessed for each setting in connection to the curriculum expectations prior to placement.

Competent teachers . . .

- Employ a proactive approach to support students with high-incidence disabilities in general education settings. This includes planning for the unique needs of the student as part of the ongoing curriculum and routines of the setting.
- Employ a system of classroom management, effective curriculum design, and direct instruction strategies to ensure acquisition, maintenance, and generalization of content and skills for students with high-incidence disabilities.
- Design students' instructional outcomes to align with environments and situations that occur before, during, and after instruction. This includes transitions to other settings as well as social and academic expectations.
- Use ongoing progress monitoring systems to ensure that assessment is directly linked to instruction. Data from assessment also support ongoing modifications to ensure that the goals of instruction within general education settings are targeted effectively.
- Provide accommodations and modifications as a supplement to effective curriculum design for students with high-incidence disabilities.

CASE STUDIES

MAC

Mac is an 8-year-old boy identified with mild mental retardation. He spends most of his day with the other second graders in Mrs. Lindsay's class, except for about a half-hour a day when he is with the literacy specialist in her room getting extra help with reading and writing. The rest of the day he follows the same schedule as his peers, but with a parallel curriculum for most of the content areas. During large group instruction, Mac is assisted by a paraprofessional who helps him follow along in his reader while the teacher or a peer reads. He is always given two questions ahead of time that he and his aide answer during free reading time before large group, so that when the teacher calls on him he knows what to expect and is ready with the answer. That way the whole class does not have to wait on him and he does not get too overwhelmed and nervous to answer. When the class moves on to independent seat work to do their mini-writing assignments, Mac goes to the computer and does a program that helps him with decoding and word chunks.

During independent math time, the rest of the class works on word problems involving two-digit subtraction while Mac plays a game with his paraprofessional that works on one-to-one correspondence or does another computer program that helps him with basic addition by using visual icons that he has to drag with his mouse to make his addition piles. For small group math and social studies instruction, Mac is part of a cooperative learning group that is set up to achieve a group goal. This is his favorite part of the day because he gets to spend the most time with his peers, and he is always in charge of handing out all manipulative materials to everyone.

Mac's team has coordinated and planned for his entire day. They have chosen for now to limit his time outside general educational settings and have found that the parallel curriculum is working well to meet his educational goals as well as correspond with the daily curriculum of the second grade class. However, the team is constantly monitoring his progress and realizes this plan may not be a permanent one and will require adjustment as he gets older and his social and academic demands change.

1. How do you think Mac would do in school if he weren't provided individual supports?
2. What specific effective teaching practices do Mac's teachers use to help him learn?
3. What is the long-term outcome for Mac?

CHRISTY

"Well, to be honest, I am not sure how she is going to handle high school next year. Even the other girls were laughing at her this time. She opened her locker to get out her social studies book and the entire contents of the overstuffed locker exploded onto the floor. You might even say there were a few projectiles, given that Mr. McBee, whose room was across the hall, picked up one of her notebooks and walked it back to her. This always happens, the locker mess, the peers snickering, and Christy's subsequent tardiness to class. I am sure that's why she skipped class. This particular time was very disruptive to traffic flow in the hall and probably pretty embarrassing." This was the description by the hall monitor to the rest of the middle school team members during a meeting to discuss Christy's progress and recent succession of missed classes.

"Having her in class is really no different," explains her social studies teacher. "She is always late; never has her homework done, or if it is done it's not with her and is instead back in that notorious locker. She does not keep up with class instruction, is constantly asking what page we are on, has me repeat the instructions... and when I pair her up with her peers they never seem to know how to work together and she gets frustrated and withdraws. They get annoyed that she is not doing her part, and then her parents get concerned that she has too much homework."

Christy's team continued to share notes and recognized patterns in her behavior, including common needs for organization, class preparedness, and curriculum access. They realized that they needed to address all of these issues simultaneously with a series of accommodations and strategies to assist Christy in spending more time on curriculum content and appropriate interactions with her peers then on just trying to get to class. They developed a homework assignment notebook so that each teacher could use the same format and help make sure that Christy had the assignment, date due, and the appropriate times necessary to take home to complete the assignment as well as what needed to come back to school. This way Christy's parents could better assist her in completing her work and supporting her use of self-monitoring strategies using the sheet and the notebook. In addition, a similar notebook was created to assist her in organizing her materials for each class and having a list that specified, for each class, what she needed to bring to class. This was checked by each teacher before leaving class for the next time she would come to class. The middle school learning specialist worked with her and the principal to assign Christy a locker that was more centrally located to her classes. This allowed her more time at her locker to keep it organized. They helped her organization by creating a system for what needed to go in the locker and what needed to go home, go back to class, or be thrown out.

The learning specialist then worked with each teacher to identify instructional routines—a kind of consistency that allowed Christy to focus on the content of instruction and not on variations in the schedule or routines for administrative tasks, such as how homework would or would not be turned in on a specific day. Once these were put in place, the team met again. They had seen noticeable improvement in Christy's ability to come to class prepared, stay on task, and keep organized.

However, there remained a few curricular areas in which Christy was still challenged to keep up. Again there seemed to be some patterns across these areas. This time it seemed that Christy did not understand how to read a passage for content. She was not getting her work done independently or in group activities in which she had to pull out key pieces of information from reading passages. This seemed to occur across curricular areas. In addition, the team identified some key social skills deficits that Christy had in interacting with her peers formally and informally. The learning specialist identified a few self-questioning and story mapping strategies that would be good to assist Christy across subject areas. In addition, teachers were also provided with information on how to maximize the effectiveness of cooperative peer learning groups so that clear roles and goals could be established for the students to assist with enhanced outcomes and reduced frustration.

Christy is still challenged to stay organized and to accomplish certain curricular content tasks. However, the collective efforts to provide her with strategies as well as enhance the consistency of support in her environment have noticeably optimized her ability to concentrate on the cognitive strategies. She is learning to better access the curriculum content and is improving her grades. Her team is constantly monitoring the effectiveness of her plan. They also anticipate beginning a peer network by second semester so that Christy has a group of peers to transition to high school with next fall.

1. What is Christy's biggest challenge in school?
2. Where would Christy be in school if the learning specialist had not intervened?
3. Why didn't anyone help Christy earlier?
4. What does the future hold for Christy?

REFERENCES

Adams, G. L., & Engelmann, S. (1996). *Research on direct instruction: 25 years beyond DISTAR*. Washington, DC: Retrieved September 29, 2006, from http://www.eric.ed.gov/ERICWebPortal/Home.portal.

Bateman, B. D. (2004). *Elements of successful teaching: General and special education students*. Verona, WI: IEP Resources.

Bos, C. S., & Vaughn, S. (2006). Strategies for teaching students with learning and behavior problems (6th ed., p. 412). Boston: Allyn & Bacon.

Brophy, J. H., & Good, T. (1986). Teacher behavior and student achievement. In M. C. Wittrock (Ed.), *Handbook of research in teaching* (3rd ed., pp. 328–375). New York: Macmillian.

Carnine, D. W., Silbert, J., Kame' enui, E. J., & Tarver, S. G. (2004). *Direct instruction reading* (4th ed). Upper Saddle River, NJ: Merrill/Prentice Hall.

Conte, K. L., & Hintze, J. M. (2000). The effects of performance feedback and goal setting on oral reading fluency within curriculum-based assessment. *Diagnostique, 25* (2), 85–98.

Cotton, K. (1995). *Effective schooling practices: A research synthesis*. Portland, OR: Northwest Regional Education Laboratory.

Deno, S. (1985). Curriculum-based measurement: The emerging alternative. *Exceptional Children, 52,* 219–232.

Deschenes, C., Ebeling, D. G., & Sprague, J. (1994). *Adapting curriculum and instruction in inclusive classrooms: A teacher's desk reference*. Bloomington, IN: Institute for the Study of Developmental Disabilities.

Deschler, D. D., Ellis, E. S., & Lenz, B. K. (1996). *Teaching adolescents with learning disabilities: Strategies and methods* (2nd ed.). Denver: Love Publishing.

Flaxman, E., & Inger, M. (1991). Parents and schooling in the 1990s. *The ERIC Review, 1,* 2–6.

Forness, S. R., Kavale, K. A., Blum, I. M., & Lloyd, J. W. (1997). Mega-analysis of meta analyses. *Teaching Exceptional Children, 29*(6) 4–9.

Fuchs, L. S., & Fuchs, D. (1986). Curriculum-based assessment of progress toward long-term and short-term goals. *Journal of Special Education, 21,* 69–82.

Fuchs, L. S., Fuchs, D. Hamlet, C. L., Phillips, N. B., & Benz, J. L. (1994). Classwide curriculum-based measurement: Helping general educators meet the challenge of student diversity. *Exceptional Children, 60,* 518–537.

Gersten, R. Carnine, D., & Woodward, J. (1987). Direct instruction research: The third decade. *Remedial and Special Education, 8*(6), 48–56.

Gersten, R., Schiller, E. P., & Vaughn, S. (2000). *Contemporary special education research: Syntheses of knowledge bases in critical instructional issues*. Mahwah, NJ: Erlbaum.

Gestwicki, G. (1987). *Home, school and community relations: A guide to working with parents.* Albany, NY: Delmar.

Giangreco, M. F., Cloninger, C. J., & Iverson, V. S. (1993). *Choosing options and accommodations for children (COACH): A guide to planning inclusive education.* Baltimore. Paul H. Brookes.

Graham, S., Harris, K. R., & Troia, G. (1998). Writing and self-regulation: Cases from a self-regulated strategy development model. In D. Schunk and B. Zimmerman (Eds.), *Self-regulated learning: From teaching to self-reflective practice* (pp. 20–41). New York: Guilford.

Johnson, D. W., & Johnson, R. T. (1987). *Learning together and alone* (2nd ed.). Upper Saddle River, NJ: Prentice Hall.

Johnson, D., Johnson, R., & Holubec, E. (1993). *Cooperation in the classroom.* Edina, MN: Interaction.

Johnson, G. M. (1998). Principles of instruction for at-risk learners. *Preventing School Failure, 42,* 167–174.

Kame'enui, E., & Darch, C. (1995). *Instructional classroom management: A proactive approach to behavior management.* White Plains, NY: Longman.

Kauffman, J. M. (2002). *Education deform: Bright people sometimes say stupid things about education.* Lanham, MD: Rowman & Littlefield Education.

Kauffman, J. M., & Hallahan, D. P. (2005a). *Special education: What it is and why we need it.* Boston: Allyn & Bacon.

Kauffman, J. M., & Hallahan, D. P. (Eds.). (2005b). *The illusion of full inclusion: A comprehensive critique of a current special education bandwagon* (2nd ed.). Austin, TX: PRO-ED.

King-Sears, M. E. (1997). Best academic practices for inclusive classrooms. *Focus on Exceptional Children, 29,* 1–23.

Lembke, E. S., & Stormont, M. (2005). Using research-based practices to support students with diverse needs in general education settings. *Psychology in the Schools, 42,* 761–763.

Mastropieri, M. A., & Scruggs, T. E. (1997). Best practices in promoting reading comprehension in students with learning disabilities: 1976–1996. *Remedial and Special Education, 18,* 197–213.

Meichenbaum, D., & Biemiller, A. (1998). *Nurturing independent learners: Helping students take charge of their learning.* Cambridge, MA: Brookline.

Mercer, C. D., & Mercer, A. R. (2005). *Teaching students with learning problems,* 7th ed. Upper Saddle River, N J: Merrill.

National Reading Panel (NRP). (2000). Teaching children to read: An evidenced-based assessment of the scientific reproach literature on reading and its implications for reading instruction: Reports of the subgroups (NIH Publication No. 00-4754). Washington, DC: U.S. Government Printing Office.

O'Neal, M., Earley, B., & Snider, M. (1991). Addressing the needs of at-risk students. A local school program that works. In R. C. Morris (Ed.), *Youth at risk,* (pp. 122–125). Lancaster, PA: Technomic.

Pressley, A. J., & Hughes, C. (2000). Peers as teachers of anger management to high school students with behavioral disorders. *Behavioral Disorders, 25*(2), 114–130.

Schumaker, J. B., & Deshler, D. D. (1995). Secondary classes can be inclusive, too. *Educational Leadership, 52*(4), 50–51.

Slavin, R. E. (1987). Cooperative learning: Where behavioral and humanistic approaches to classroom motivation meet. *Elementary School Journal, 88,* 29–37.

Slavin, R. E. (1991). Synthesis of research on cooperative learning. *Educational Leadership, 48*(5), 71–82.

Stein, M., Carnine, D., & Dixon, R. (1998). Direct instruction: Integrating curriculum design and effective teaching practice. *Intervention in School and Clinic, 33* (4), 227–234.

Stichter, J. P., & Lewis, T. J. (2006). Classroom assessment: Targeting variables to improve instruction through a multi-level ecobehavioral model. In Michel Hersen (Ed.), *Clinical Handbook of Child Behavioral Assessment,* (pp. 569–586). Boston: Elsevier.

Stichter, J. P., Lewis, T. J., Johnson, N., & Trussell, R. (2004). Toward a structural assessment: Analyzing the merits of an assessment tool for a student with E/BD. *Assessment of Effective Intervention, 30,* 25–40.

Stormont, M., Espinosa, L., Knipping, N., & McCathren, R. (2003, Fall). Supporting vulnerable learners in the primary grades: Strategies to prevent early school failure. *Early Childhood Research & Practice, 5*(2), 545–548.

Tarver, S. G., in collaboration with the DLD/DR research Alerts Committee, (1999). Focusing on direct instruction. *Current Practices Alerts, 2.* Joint publication of the Council for Exceptional Children's Division for Learning Disabilities and Division for Research.

Turnbull, A. P., Turnbull, H. R., Erwin, E., & Soodak, L. (2006). *Families, professionals, and exceptionality: Positive outcomes through partnerships and trust.* Upper Saddle River, NJ: Merrill/Prentice Hall.

U. S. Department of Education. (2002). *No child left behind executive summary.* Washington, D.C.: Author.

Wagner, S. (1999). *Inclusive programming for elementary students with autism.* Arlington, TX: Future Horizons.

White, W. A. T. (1998). Meta-analysis of the effects of direct instruction in special education. *Education and Treatment of Children, 11,* 364–374.

Zentall, S., & Stormont-Spurgin, M. (1995). Educator preferences of accommodations for students with attention deficit hyperactivity disorder. *Teacher Education and Special Education, 18,* 115–123.

Collaboration, Consultation, and Co-Teaching

URBAN LEGEND: *The Individual Education Plan (IEP) meeting is an example of effective collaboration.*

LEGENDARY THOUGHT: *An IEP meeting does not in and of itself constitute effective collaboration—collaboration is only effective when implemented as a dynamic process, requiring teaming among stakeholders, shared goals, strategic planning and problem solving, time, commitment, resources, and measurement of positive outcomes for students and team members.* ◆

Collaboration, consultation, and co-teaching are terms often used to describe "best practice" for serving students with high-incidence disabilities. Teacher preparation and certification, programs are filled with professional competencies about collaboration, consultation and co-teaching, but what do these terms really mean? How do effective collaboration, consultation, and co-teaching really work? Who should be part of the collaborative process? Who is qualified to be a consultant? Who should co-teach and when should co-teaching occur? Do professionals engage in collaboration, consultation, and co-teaching at the same time or do these three models of service delivery occur separately? These and many more questions are the focus of this chapter.

Collaboration, consultation, and co-teaching are educational service delivery models for providing instruction to students with high-incidence disabilities. The effectiveness of these models is demonstrated by their effects—that is, outcomes for students with high-incidence disabilities and the professionals who work with them. Professionals can judge the successfulness of collaboration by examining questions, such as the following: Do students learn? Did a student's behavior improve? Do teachers improve their instruction with students with high-incidence disabilities? How do you know that collaboration is effective in accomplishing the targeted outcomes? Before answering these questions and others, we begin with a review of terminology and the historical and legislative foundations that have driven a collaborative approach to instruction.

:: WHAT ARE COLLABORATION, CONSULTATION, AND CO-TEACHING?

The overall goal for collaboration, consultation, and co-teaching is to provide the best educational services for students with high-incidence disabilities. However, the techniques that individuals use when implementing each of these approaches may differ depending on the student's needs and instructional situations.

Collaboration is a process that occurs when a group or team of individuals work together to design, implement, and evaluate the outcomes of an educational program for a student or students with high-incidence disabilities. Collaboration is a collective effort, requiring equal respect and value for each person's participation on the collaborative team. In addition, collaboration requires sharing of resources and responsibilities for participation, decision-making, and accountability for outcomes among all members of the team (Friend & Cook, 2003). Voluntary participation on the collaborative team and confidentiality among team members are other important characteristics. However, one of the most important characteristics to remember for effective collaboration is keeping the student(s) the team's priority (Mostert, 1998).

Consultation occurs within the framework of collaboration. During consultation, one educational team member who has more expertise, knowledge, and skills in a particular area of teaching or instruction than the others on the team share this information, instructing the other team members how to master the knowledge and skills (Correa, Jones, Thomas, & Morsink, 2005). As Correa and her colleagues (2005) suggest, consultation occurs in a collaborative way and not in an authoritative manner. Typically, all team members bring different types of expertise to the team; therefore, consultation or reciprocal sharing occurs across all team members. As with collaboration, consultation is a process that involves trusting and equal relationships among team members, open communication, and collaborative approaches to problem identification and problem solving. Typically, consultation involves identification of a problem, pooling team knowledge and resources to address the student's problem, and sharing the responsibility of implementation and evaluation of outcomes among team members (Brown, Wyne, Blackburn, & Powell, 1979). The consultant tries to bring about change through the consultation process (Tharp, 1975); however, consultation is more effective when team members voluntarily enter into the process and the individual being consulted with is actively involved. One distinguishing characteristic of the consultation process is that, typically, the consultant does not work directly with the student(s), but rather through another team member, such as the parents or the classroom teacher. Brown, Pryzwansky, and Schulte (1998) identified five important characteristics of effective consultants: (a) appreciation of other team members' values, (b) problem-solving abilities, (c) self-awareness and reliance on self-generated standards, (d) ability to establish working alliances (including characteristics such as empathy and positive regard), and (e) willingness to take interpersonal risks. The core of effective consultation is building interpersonal relationships, engaging in problem solving, and sharing critical knowledge (Gutkin, 2002).

Co-teaching is a collaborative approach for serving students with high-incidence disabilities in the same classroom. As special education and other related services become more prevalent in general education classrooms, there is a need to expand our co-teaching model of service delivery. Cook and Friend (1995) say that co-teaching occurs when at least two professionals work together to deliver instruction to a student or group of students in the same classroom. Often, these professionals include the special education and general education teachers or a general education teacher and a related services professional (e.g., speech-language pathologist). There are several models for implementing co-teaching, but most often, co-teaching involves the professional team members working together to coordinate, deliver, and evaluate instruction for an individual student or group. The key factor in co-teaching is that both professionals are actively engaged in the delivery of instruction (Cook & Friend, 1995).

Similar to collaboration and consultation, in order for co-teaching to be effective, professionals must work together closely to develop a trusting relationship with one another. Teachers need training and support from the school district prior to developing a co-teaching service delivery model, according to Walther-Thomas and colleagues (1996). School districts should engage in a systematic planning process that includes planning for co-teaching on three levels: (1) district level planning to ensure needed support and resources, (2) school level planning to ensure administrative support, staff development, and adequate planning, and (3) classroom level planning to ensure equal and shared responsibilities and roles. Professionals engaging in co-teaching must be flexible and have a strong desire and commitment to change their teaching styles and engage in shared instruction with another professional within a single classroom. Prior to entering into a co-teaching relationship, teachers may want to ask themselves questions such as: How open am I to experimenting with different teaching activities and styles? How willing am I to share my classroom and instruction of students with another professional? How comfortable am I trusting another professional to instruct students in a quality manner? (Cook & Friend, 1995).

Are Collaboration, Consultation, and Co-Teaching the Same or Different?

Collaboration, consultation, and co-teaching have many similarities; yet they also have distinguishing characteristics. All three terms describe a service delivery approach that includes a group or team of individuals working together to serve students with high-incidence disabilities. In addition, all three terms have the following characteristics in common—

- Trust among team members,
- Open communication,
- A strong commitment to working with others,
- Respect for individual team members,
- Shared decision-making and shared problem solving, and
- Accountability for outcomes.

Collaboration is a more generic term that is often used to describe eclectic services that encompass several different strategies, including consultation and co-teaching. Consultation is most applicable when one team member has a particular area of expertise that can be shared with the rest of the team members to increase their knowledge and skills in a particular area, leading to more effective instruction for the student. Co-teaching is a collaborative process in which two or more teachers make a commitment to deliver instruction to a student or group of students together in the same classroom. Regardless of the specific strategy used, approaching instruction from a collaborative approach is considered best practice for serving students with high-incidence disabilities. Collaboration works most effectively when team members volunteer to enter into collaborative relationships with one another. By volunteering to engage in collaborative relationships (whether they are engaging in co-teaching, consultation, or another form of collaboration) team members have ownership over the process and are more strongly linked to the ultimate outcome—improved services for students with high-incidence disabilities.

Even though a collaborative approach is considered best practice, this approach is also a legal requirement for serving students with all disabilities, including high-incidence disabilities. In the next section of this chapter, we provide a brief overview of the historical and legal foundations for collaboration.

:: WHY COLLABORATE? HISTORICAL AND LEGAL FOUNDATIONS FOR COLLABORATION, CONSULTATION, AND CO-TEACHING

Historical Foundations

As discussed in Chapter 2, a collaborative or consultative service delivery model has been emphasized as a critical educational component of services for students with high-incidence disabilities for many years, Beginning in the 1970s, early leaders in the field of special education proposed various service delivery models to address the needs of all students with disabilities. One aspect of these service delivery models included consultation in general education classrooms for students with high-incidence disabilities. For example, Deno (1970) outlined a **cascade of services** model that included a range of services across all types of educational settings. Within her service delivery model, Deno included consultation by special educators in general education classrooms as one level of service delivery. In the following year, Lilly (1971) suggested that one of the roles for special educators is to provide consultation, training, and support to general education teachers who are serving students with disabilities in their classrooms. Through these models, both Deno (1970) and Lilly (1971) provided the foundational framework for the collaborative approach to serving students with disabilities.

Since Deno (1970), several educational initiatives have increased the need for collaborative relationships. For example, since 1970, several major movements have increased the push for including students with high-incidence disabilities in general education settings. In 1975, the call for special educational services in the least restrictive environment was introduced along with the subsequent school reform movement. These initiatives not only provided further impetus for inclusion of students with disabilities in general education settings, but the application of collaborative strategies became more vital to the success of these students in these settings (see Chapter 2 for a discussion of least restrictive environment, school reform, and inclusion). The 24th Annual Report to Congress on Implementation of IDEA indicated that over half of all students with disabilities are served in general education classrooms at least 80% of the time (U.S. Department of Education, 2002). Therefore, the need for special and general educators to work together, collaboratively, to meet the needs of all these students is imperative. Professional collaboration is not only an expectation of teachers serving students with disabilities, but in order to serve these students in inclusive settings, collaboration across a team of professionals, including parents, is a requirement (Idol, 2002; Pugach & Johnson, 1995, 2002;

Stanovich, 1996). As schools change and adapt to new legal requirements, standards, curriculum, instructional practices, and service delivery models, collaboration becomes even more crucial (O'Shea, O'Shea, & Algozzine, 1998).

Another motivating drive for a collaborative approach stems from professional organizations, such as the **Council for Exceptional Children** (CEC) and the **Interstate New Teacher Assessment and Support Consortium** (INTASC). These professional organizations have placed a heavy emphasis on building collaborative relationships between general and special educators. CEC views collaboration as a critical component of teacher preparation and includes collaboration as a separate content standard for special education teacher preparation programs (see CEC's website at http://www.cec.sped.org/ps/). In addition, the INTASC (2001) responded to the **Individuals with Disabilities Education Act** (IDEA, 1997) by developing standards for general educators serving students with disabilities in their classrooms to increase collaborative relationships with special educators.

Another educational trend providing further momentum for a collaborative approach to serving students with high-incidence disabilities is the emphasis on **effective schools.** Research suggests that schools are more effective when the staff within the entire school work as a team, engaging in collaboration, rather than each teacher working individually. In fact, Purkey and Smith (1985) suggested that two important variables outlined in the effective schools literature are collaborative planning and collegial relationships. A collaborative approach to educating all students across the school may not only increase the effectiveness of the school, but it will likely increase productivity and morale (McLaughin & Schwartz, 1998) and lessen teacher's feelings of isolation (Wadsworth, 1997).

In summary, the collaborative approach to serving students with high-incidence disabilities has a long conceptual history in special education. Even though we have discussed collaboration conceptually as the most effective way to educate students with high-incidence disabilities, we must remember that engaging in collaboration is also part of the legal requirements for serving students with disabilities. With the enactment of PL 94-142, the Education of All Handicapped Children's Act in 1975, using a collaborative approach not only became best practice, it became a legal mandate by implication.

Legal Foundations

PL 94-142: The Education of All Handicapped Childrens Act of 1975

When PL 94-142, Education of All Handicapped Childrens Act (EAHCA) was enacted in 1975, collaboration became a legal mandate for serving students with all disabilities. Although collaboration was not specifically identified as a service delivery model, many components of PL 94-142 (1975) emphasized the need for collaboration and consultation. For example, areas requiring a collaborative approach were implied in the mandates of a multidisciplinary evaluation team, nondiscriminatory evaluation, and preparation of an Individual Education Plan (IEP). The IEP team may include special educators, general education teachers, related service personnel, administrators, nurses, social workers, school counselors, and physicians, who together evaluate students with disabilities and plan their educational programs. Besides the requirement to serve students in the least restrictive environment, another requirement of the law that incorporated a collaborative approach was the focus on providing a free appropriate public education (FAPE) and including parents and students in the educational decision making process. In order to accomplish all of these mandates, collaboration is an essential ingredient. As each reauthorization of PL 94-142 (now IDEA) occurred (in 1990, 1997, and 2004), the need for collaboration and consultation became more and more apparent (Cohen, Thomas, Sattler, & Morsink, 1997).

PL 99-457: Education of All Handicapped Childrens Act Amendment

In 1986, PL 99-457 (an amendment to EAHCA) continued the initial emphasis on collaboration through LRE, FAPE, multidisciplinary teaming, IEP teams, and parental and student participation. However, the mandate to collaborate expanded beyond the level of the school and into collaboration across agencies within a state. This amendment mandated statewide collaboration of the agencies serving infants and toddlers with disabilities. The various agencies were required to work together to develop a comprehensive, statewide service delivery system for infants and toddlers with disabilities. In addition, this amendment mandated service for preschool-aged children with disabilities, increasing the need to collaborate as young children transitioned between early intervention programs and school-based programs.

PL 101-476: Individuals with Disabilities Education Act (IDEA) and PL 105-17 (IDEA Amendments)

PL 101-476 which renamed the Education for All Handicapped Children Act the Individuals with Disabilities Education Act (IDEA) was reauthorized again in 1997. Collaboration was highlighted in many of the components of IDEA, and both the 1990 and the 1997 versions placed increased emphasis on collaboration among special and general educators and related service personnel with the mandate to include more students, particularly students with high-incidence disabilities, in general education classrooms. The inclusion of students with medical concerns, such as **traumatic brain injury** (TBI) and students with complex needs, such as autism, required increased collaboration between the educational and medical communities. Additionally, IDEA (both the 1990 and the 1997 reauthorizations) included an increased emphasis on transition services for students 14 years and older to assist them in moving from school to work, making collaboration between schools, community agencies, and the public even more pronounced. With the 1997 reauthorization, the changes regarding the use of **functional behavioral assessments** (FBA) and **behavioral intervention plans** (BIP) to address the behavioral needs of students also increased the need for collaboration. By legal definition FBA and BIP are procedures designed to comprehensively address students' problem behavior and need to be conducted by a school-based team. Therefore, collaboration is at the center for developing effective FBA and BIPs. Finally, as with previous reauthorizations, IDEA (1990, 1997) emphasized the inclusion of parents and students in the educational process, increasing the need for team members to move beyond collaborative efforts with each other and expanding their collaboration with students' family members to include them as active team members in the provision of educational services.

No Child Left Behind (NCLB) and PL 108-144: Individuals with Disabilities Education Improvement Act Amendment

Two more recent legislative actions, the **No Child Left Behind Act** (NCLB, 2001) and the reauthorization of the **Individuals with Disabilities Education Improvement Act** (IDEA, 2004) continued building on the legal foundation emphasizing collaboration for service provision. Both NCLB and IDEA (2004) required increased collaboration between special and general education teachers through the requirement for highly qualified teachers across core academic subjects, including English, reading or language arts, mathematics, science, foreign languages, civics and government, economics, arts, history, and geography and certification as a special education teacher or passing a state special education licensing exam. With the requirement of highly qualified teachers, both general and special educators need to collaborate more to meet their students' needs. To this end consultation and co-teaching models are increasingly employed.

Another requirement of NCLB and IDEA (2004) is the participation of all children, including children with disabilities, in the state assessments. IDEA now requires that the IEP team determine how the student with a disability will participate in the assessment; therefore, IEP teams need to plan these strategies collaboratively to facilitate the student's success on the state assessment or an alternative assessment.

In addition to these two more recent requirements, NCLB and IDEA (2004) continue to emphasize the collaboration and participation of the parents and student on the IEP team, conducting a FBA, and conducting a **manifestation determination** to address disciplinary problems. For further information on the provisions of NCLB and IDEA (2004), refer to http://www.ed.gov/nclb.

Summary

In summary, collaboration for service to students with high-incidence disabilities has a long history in special education. The emphasis on collaborating among professionals and with family members has been a continuous theme beginning in the early 1970s and running throughout legislative initiatives. Although collaboration is an implied legal mandate, the laws do not clearly outline *what* collaboration is, *how* it should be accomplished, and *when* it should occur in our schools that serve students with high-incidence disabilities. Nor does the law or its regulations state *how to evaluate* the effectiveness of collaboration. The remaining sections in this chapter address these issues.

:: PUTTING CONSULTATION, COLLABORATION, AND CO-TEACHING INTO PRACTICE: HOW DOES IT WORK?

Building collaborative working relationships for serving students with high-incidence disabilities is a process that evolves over time and changes according to the context in which it occurs (Pugach & Johnson, 2002). As suggested by Wangemann, Ingram, and Muse (1989), the "key ingredients" for facilitating collaboration include clarifying the purpose, roles and responsibilities, shared ownership, adequate resources, sufficient time, overlapping interests, leadership from key administrators, and ongoing evaluation. In this section, we discuss how collaboration works across different types of services as well as who is included in the collaborative process.

Who Is Part of the Collaborative Team?

As stated above, collaboration takes on a different form depending on the educational setting and individual student's need and situation. Because of this, the individuals who are a part of collaboration may differ. Collaboration may occur among special educators, general educators, administrators, school psychologists, **English as Second Language** (ESL) teachers, **physical therapists, speech-language therapists, occupational therapists,** paraprofessionals, **adaptive physical education teachers, behavior specialists,** and so forth. In addition,

Collaboration for students with high-incidence disabilities includes persons from the school environment as well as collaborators from outside the school context such as related healthcare professionals, service providers, and family members. (Photo credit: Anthony Magnacca/Merrill)

collaboration may occur among individuals outside the school setting, including health professionals (e.g., nurses or physicians), **juvenile justice workers, vocational educators,** and others who are involved with the student in some manner. Although collaboration includes various professionals, the student and family should always be members of the collaborative team when possible. For example, a collaborative IEP team for a student with learning disabilities (LD) in a general education classroom might include teachers in general education and special education, the student, the school psychologist, and the student's parents. However, a collaborative IEP team for a student with **Fragile X syndrome** included in the same general education classroom might include these same individuals with the addition of a behavior specialist, a speech-language pathologist, a nurse, and an occupational therapist. Finally, a collaborative IEP team for a student with EBD in this same classroom might include the general and special education teachers who are co-teaching in the classroom, the student, the school psychologist, an individual from the community mental health agency, a behavior specialist, and the student's parents. Again, these team members would be a part of the collaborative team based on the student's educational needs. Because each team member brings different expertise to the collaborative process, the number of members and who the members are depends on the nature and complexity of the purpose behind collaboration. Table 11.1 outlines the various professionals and roles they play as teams members that may be involved when serving students with high-incidence disabilities.

How Does Collaboration Work?

Working collaboratively with other professionals or a parent to design and implement effective instruction for students with high-incidence disabilities sounds easy, but it requires commitment and dedication from all individuals involved. Although there is no single strategy or recipe for collaborating, Katzenbach and Smith (1999) have identified key guidelines and strategies that can facilitate the collaborative process.

First, successful collaboration is likely to happen only if collaboration is both respected by and made a priority of the school's administration. The principal and other school administrators must not only view collaboration as an important instructional strategy; they must also provide the resources needed for collaboration (e.g., release time for teachers to plan, supports for adaptation of instructional materials) and be respectful of the collaborative team's efforts and time commitment. The school administration sets the climate for collaboration, which is an essential foundation for success. Next, collaborative teams should have a stated purpose and goals. These goals provide direction for the team's collaborative activities. For example, if a goal of an IEP team for a student with MMR is to increase the student's inclusion in a general education setting, then the team would engage in collaborative planning to meet this goal. Another important guideline is that team members need to be able to fulfill their roles and responsibilities competently. Team members must be willing to dedicate time to the collaborative process, engage in collaborative problem solving with the targeted goal in mind, and gain additional training as needed. As team members engage in effective collaboration, role release between team members often occurs. Role release means that team members teach each other specific skills and competencies. Once team members acquire and become competent in learning these

TABLE 11.1 Roles and responsibilities of professionals serving students with high-incidence disabilities

Personnel	Direct Services Provider	Team Member
Special educator	• Assess educational achievement • Design instructional program • Implement academic-behavioral strategies • Follow-up on skills taught by others	• Serve as a case manager • Interpret assessments • Observe in other settings • Consult on individualizing instructional techniques
General educator	• Implement academic/behavioral strategies • Assist in social integration	• Consult on curriculum • Consult on group management techniques
Parent	• Reinforce academic and behavioral programs at home	• Provide background information • Consult on possible interventions
Administrator	• Reinforce appropriate behavior	• Provide information on services available in school and community • Assist with scheduling and class size
Psychologist	• Assess psychological functioning	• Interpret test results • Collaborate in designing interventions and data collection strategies
Speech-language therapist	• Assess speech-language development	• Interpret test results • Provide follow-up materials for other team members • Consult on strategies to use
Counselor	• Provide counseling on self-concept, getting along with adults and peers, and so forth	• Collaborate with others about emotional or behavioral situations
Physical and occupational therapist	• Assess physical and occupational needs	• Interpret test results • Collaborate with others on ways to enhance physical development or classroom modifications
Hearing and vision specialists	• Assess hearing and vision • Teach strategies such as auditory training, listening skills, orientation, and mobility	• Interpret test results • Teach others how to use special equipment or materials
Adaptive physical educator	• Assess psychomotor skills • Remediate areas of physical fitness	• Collaborate in designing cooperative games and motor development activities • Collaborate in assisting in conducting FBA and developing BIP
Behavior specialist	• Assess problem behaviors • Remediate behavioral concerns	• Teach strategies for dealing with problem behaviors
Adaptive technologist	• Assess instructional and adaptive technology needs • Modify instruction	• Collaborate in adapting instruction through technology • Teach strategies for modifying assignments through technology
Family members	• Work with their child to remediate learning and behavioral difficulties	• Provide critical information to professionals pertaining to their child • Teach professionals strategies that have been found to be successful at home

Correa, V. I., Jones, H. A., Thomas, C. C., & Morsink, C. V. *Interactive Teaming: Enhancing Programs for Students with Special Needs*, 4th ed., 2005, p. 356. Adapted by permission of Pearson Education, Inc., Upper Saddle River, NJ.

skills, they take over instructional implementation with the student. For example, a behavior specialist may collaborate with a general education teacher and provide instruction on how to contingently reinforce on task behavior through the use of a token economy for a student with an EBD in the general education classroom. Once the classroom teacher demonstrates competence in implementing contingent rein-forcement, the teacher independently implements this instructional strategy in the classroom. Role release is most likely to occur if there is good communication as well as mutual respect and trust among collaborative team members. Awareness of the individual roles of team members is another important aspect of collaboration as well as building the collaborative team itself. As stated before, collaborative teaming can be a slow, but worthwhile process.

To illustrate the collaborative process, we examine how a collaborative team* responds to Corey, a student with learning disabilities who is fully included in a fifth-grade class. Corey's general education teacher notices that he is beginning to lag significantly behind his peers, especially in math, and is often disrupting other students. The collaborative team that is responsible for providing educational serv-ices to Corey is made up of his general education teacher, the special education teacher who provides consultative services to his general education teacher, and Corey's parents.

First, the collaborative team meets to identify the specific problems that Corey is demonstrating and the characteristics of his problems. In this particular case, Corey has a learning disability that significantly affects his math skills; however, until recently, Corey has been able to keep up with the rest of his class when as-signments have been modified. Although modification of assignments has been successful, recently, his general education teacher has seen an increase in Corey's disruptive behavior (e.g., getting out of his seat, talking out of turn to his peers, and refusing to complete his tasks) during math instruction and seatwork activi-ties. In addition, Corey is not completing his homework math assignments. His general education teacher calls a team meeting to discuss her concerns. The team meets and identifies Corey's specific learning and behavior problems. Then, the team begins to collaboratively problem solve—discussing reasons why Corey may be engaging in these behaviors and possible solutions. In this situation, the team believes that as the math instruction and assignments increase in difficulty, Corey has a more difficult time understanding and mastering math concepts. In addition, his parents express concern that during homework, Corey is increasingly becoming oppositional, refusing to complete his homework and often not coming out of his room for hours. During this meeting, the team collectively decides to re-evaluate Corey's math abilities and expand the modifications of Corey's math assignments in order to help him become successful. The team believes that if Corey is able to com-plete the math activities, his disruptive behaviors will decrease and his compliance in the school and at home will increase. The special education teacher agrees to assist

---

* Collaborative teams are referred to by a number of different names in the literature including: teacher assistance teams (Chalfant, Pysh, & Moultrie 1979), student assistance teams (Cooley, 1993), child study teams (Moore, Fifield, Bryce, Deborah, & Scarlato, 1979), peer referral teams (Graden, Casey, & Christenson, 1985), instructional support teams (Pavan & Entrekin, 1991, mainstream assistance teams (Fuchs, Fuchs, & Bahr, 1990), and so on (see also Kauffman, Mostert, Trent, & Pullen, 2006).

the classroom teacher in evaluating Corey's math abilities and making modifications to his assignments as needed. Corey's parents agree to provide Corey assistance, as needed, during homework activities. The team members decide to implement these practices, collect data on their effectiveness, and meet again in 2 weeks to evaluate Corey's progress.

This description provides one example of how collaboration can work in a school setting. Again, there is not a single strategy for engaging in collaboration. As the individual situation changes, problems change, and team members change, various collaboration strategies evolve to address these issues.

Collaboration: Models in Practice

The literature offers a number of different models for implementing collaborative team models to serve students with high-incidence disabilities (e.g., Cooley, 1993; Chalfant & Pysh, 1989; Fuchs et al., 1990; Kauffman et al., 2006; Moore et al., 1979; Pugach & Johnson, 1995, 2002). Each of these models outlines strategies for individuals to use when working with learners with instructional needs. Application of these models will depend on the purpose of the team, needs of the student, and the context in which these needs are addressed. The following is a brief description of three types of collaborative teams often seen in schools.

One of the most common types of teams seen in schools is the **Child Study or Child Resource Teams** (Hayek, 1987). Typically, these teams were developed in response to the federal and state mandates to address the need for **preferral, referral, and eligibility** activities in schools. The team members that most often comprise Child Study Teams are the guidance counselor or another school administrator, the school psychologist, the special education teacher, a general education representative, parents, and related service personnel as needed. Most often, referrals to the Child Study Team originate from the general education teacher who is concerned about a particular student. In most schools, Child Study Teams meet regularly to discuss students that have been referred to the team. As mentioned, typically, these teams deal with issues around prereferral, referral, and eligibility into special education.

Another type of team in schools that is most applicable to learners with high-incidence disabilities is the **Individual Education Plan** (IEP) team. Typically, this is a **multidisciplinary team** that includes members who are involved in implementing the goals of the student's IEP. Team members may include, but are not limited to, individuals such as the student's teachers, both general education and special education teachers, as applicable, the student, the student's parents or guardians, and related service personnel (e.g., speech-language pathologist, behavior specialist). The purpose of the IEP team is to design an individual education plan to meet the target student's educational needs. Although some states are exempt, for the most part, legally, the IEP team is required to meet no less than annually to review the student's goals and objectives and develop new goals for the upcoming year. Team members work collaboratively, sharing information and their expertise with each other. Through collaboratively teaming, students are more likely to receive educational services that are coordinated across all aspects of their educational program.

A third type of team that is more informal and may be seen in some schools is called a **Teacher Assistance Team** (TAT; Chalfant, Pysh, & Moultrie, 1979; Chalfant & Pysh, 1989). A TAT is a school-based team designed as a preferral intervention model to address student's problems prior to determining eligibility for special education services. Teacher Assistance Teams are comprised of three elected teachers as well as the teacher who is referring the targeted student. In addition, parents or related service professionals are invited to join the team, when applicable. The purpose of the team is to assist the referring teacher in evaluating the target student's educational concerns and developing modifications and adaptations to address these concerns. The TAT either provides direct assistance to the referring teacher or provides indirect assistance to the teacher by making referrals to a specialist (Friend & Cook, 1996). Although TATs are not seen in all schools, this type of assistance model has been discussed in the literature (e.g., Pugach & Johnson, 1995) and continues to be used as a model for other collaborative teams in schools (e.g., Logan & Stein, 2001).

How Does Consultation Work?

Collaboration and consultation go hand in hand. Consultation is one form of collaboration. It typically involves one person consulting with another rather than several individuals working as a team. As you can imagine, sometimes consultation is best. The type of collaborative consultation that is most useful depends on the particular situation and the student's needs. When implementing collaborative consultation, the target is the student. The consultant is the person that has the expertise required to address the student's needs. Therefore, the consultant works collaboratively with the person needing consultation, sharing this expertise, to address the student's problem. Consultation is different from teaming in that the consultation is indirect—the consultant does not work directly with the student, but provides support to the individual working directly with the student (Idol, Paolicci-Whitcomb, & Nevin, 1995). For example, a TAT team may be used to assist the classroom teacher and school staff members in identification of a student's particular educational needs; therefore, the type of expertise needed on the TAT team would need to uniquely match the student's needs—lending itself to the consultative model.

For consultation to be effective, consultants need to have a collaborative working relationship with the individuals with whom they are consulting. Researchers have suggested that one of the key factors for successful consultation is communication (Pugach & Johnson, 2002). Communication is a "dynamic and ongoing process in which people share ideas, information, and feelings" (Correa et al., 2005, p. 135). Lang, Quick, and Johnson (1981) suggest that effective communication is purposeful. It has clear intent, is planned and personalized, and is open and unambiguous. Friend (1984) surveyed principals, general education teachers, and resource teachers and found that consultation was most effective when there was a climate of trust between the individuals who are the consultants and the persons they are consulting with. In addition, they found that clearly defining problems and immediately resolving conflicts that may occur were other characteristics of successful communication and consultation skills. These many seem like commonsensical ideas, but they are extremely important if collaborative consultation is going to be successful.

The following example provides a more detailed description of how the collaborative consultation model may work in a school.

Ms. Harrell, a first grade teacher, is concerned about one of her students, Garrison, who has been diagnosed with **attention deficit hyperactivity disorder** (ADHD). He has age-appropriate academic abilities but is demonstrating disruptive behaviors during academic instructional activities, such as math and reading. Specifically, Garrison often yells out, gets out of his seat, and talks to the child sitting next to him. In addition, Ms. Harrell is concerned that when she has the students complete individual assignments at their desks, Garrison is not completing his work. Ms. Harrell is concerned that Garrison's behaviors are not only interfering with his learning, but may be impeding the learning of the other students in her class. She has tried to redirect Garrison's behaviors but has not found her strategies to be successful. Ms. Harrell contacts Ms. Lopez, the school's behavior specialist, for assistance. First, Ms. Lopez meets with Ms. Harrell to identify the problem and collect information that Ms. Harrell views may be relating to Garrison's disruptive behaviors. After meeting with Ms. Harrell, Ms. Lopez directly observes Garrison in the classroom and collects behavioral observation data on Garrison's disruptive behaviors across several activities and days. Once Ms. Lopez has collected enough information on Garrison's disruptive behaviors, she meets with Ms. Harrell to share the information and develop strategies for addressing his behaviors. In this case, Ms. Lopez has identified several factors that may be contributing to Garrison's behaviors. Often, children with ADHD have difficulty following verbal directions in a group. Therefore, one strategy Ms. Lopez suggests to address this issue is to provide Garrison with a brief written explanation of the expectations of the task and to have a peer buddy in the classroom review these instructions prior to independent seatwork activities. In addition, to decrease Garrison's disruptive behaviors (i.e., yelling out loud, getting out of his seat, and talking with his neighbor), Ms. Lopez helps Ms. Harrell design a **self-management program.** Ms. Lopez designs the program and works collaboratively with Ms. Harrell on implementation of the program and a method for evaluating the outcome of the interventions. Once these intervention strategies are implemented for several days, Ms. Lopez follows up with Ms. Harrell to evaluate Garrison's progress and the usefulness of the implementation of these two strategies.

Consultation: Models in Practice

Some situations may lend themselves to collaborative consultation rather than the collaborative teaming we described earlier. For example, consultation between general and special educators may occur when the general education teacher needs information and support from the special educator in strategies for addressing the academic and behavioral needs of a particular student (Friend & Cook, 2003; West & Idol, 1987). In this case, the special educator may meet with the general education teacher to identify the particular problem, evaluate the problem (either directly or indirectly), and work collaboratively with the general education teacher to develop strategies to use to address the student's needs.

Consultation may involve two teachers, but it may also occur between a general or special education teacher and a person doing related work (e.g., school psychologist) to address the instructional needs of a particular student (Pugach & Johnson, 2002). For example, the school psychologist may have pertinent information to share with the classroom teacher regarding the student's instructional preferences or academic abilities that could be used to modify instruction or assignments. Again, in this situation, the classroom teacher and the school psychologist would collaborate to develop appropriate instructional strategies to meet the student's needs.

Another common type of consultation is between classroom teachers and behavior specialists (e.g., see Bergan, 1977; Sugai & Tindal, 1993). Using a behavior analytic approach, Sugai and Tindal (1993) outline a collaborative consultation model for addressing problem behaviors. In this model, problem behaviors are identified using observable and measurable terms, evaluated and analyzed within their context, and then behavioral interventions are developed to address the problem behavior. A critical component of the behavioral consultation model is developing interventions that are evaluated according to changes in the target students' behavior.

Finally, Logan and Stein (2001) outline another approach designed to address problem behaviors of students referred to as the **Research Lead Teacher** (RLT). This model combines collaborative teaming and collaborative consultation. Teacher study groups are developed in schools and trained in various evidence-based strategies for intervening on problem behaviors including **Applied Behavior Analysis** (ABA) and **Functional Behavioral Assessment** (FBA), providing the teachers in the school with the basic knowledge and skills in these areas. Then, when they encounter a problem or situation with a student with whom they need assistance, the teachers contact the RLT, who has behavioral expertise. The RLT utilizes peer coaching, modeling, and collaborative consultation strategies to help develop appropriate interventions to address the student's needs. When its effectiveness was evaluated, Logan and Stein (2001) found that teachers reported that 80% of the behavioral interventions developed through this model were effective in ameliorating the student's problem behavior.

An increasingly common type of consultation in schools is **organizational consultation** (e.g., see Sugai & Horner, 1999). This type of consultation occurs when the consultant is hired to serve as a facilitator to help the school promote organizational change. For example, one organizational consultation trend across the nation is **Positive Behavior Support** (PBS). PBS is a federally funded initiative designed to prevent and address problem behaviors in schools. When implementing a PBS model, a consultant who has expertise in PBS is hired to assist the school in making changes in the school's disciplinary strategies. The consultant works collaboratively with the teachers, administrators, and staff in the school to reorganize the structure of the school so that problem behaviors are prevented whenever possible, appropriate behaviors are taught and reinforced, and problem behaviors are decreased. Wallace, Anderson, and Batholomay (2002) found that consultation targeting school-wide approaches and environmental factors within classrooms increased the success of inclusion of students with disabilities across four high schools.

How Does Co-Teaching Work?

Co-teaching is another form of collaboration. However, rather than working as a school-based collaborative team or collaborative-consultative team, co-teaching means that two teachers working in the same classroom share the responsibility for instructing a group of students. One of the strengths of co-teaching in comparison to other collaborative models is that it provides students with direct instruction in the settings in which they are functioning and learning (Salend et al., 1997). However, co-teaching is not for everyone. Similar to other forms of collaboration, co-teaching requires mutual trust and respect for one another as well as good communication. In addition to these skills, co-teaching requires working in close contact in a committed partnership with another professional. As seen in Table 11.2, Cook and Friend (1995) outline questions for creating a collaborative co-teaching relationship. In addition to these areas, Pugach and Johnson (2002) suggested six requirements for successful co-teaching:

- Challenging one's self to improve teaching skills
- Sharing responsibility of student's learning with your teaching partner
- Sharing responsibility for instructing students with your teaching partner
- Communicating regularly with your teaching partner
- Supporting your teaching partner
- Actively working to include all students in the learning process of the classroom.

The following example provides an illustration of how a co-teaching model is implemented.

Tanglewood Elementary School is a school serving elementary-aged children with a variety of needs and abilities, including students with high-incidence disabilities. Ms. Gates teaches a multiaged classroom that serves grades 1–3. In addition, Tanglewood Elementary includes a self-contained special education classroom serving many of the students with high-incidence disabilities in kindergarten through grade 3. The self-contained class is taught by Mr. Marley. Ms. Gates has several students in her classroom who demonstrate learning and behavioral problems, including students with ADHD and one student with a Traumatic Brain Injury (TBI). Ms. Gates is concerned that these children may not be receiving the individualized instruction they need. Mr. Marley's class is fairly small, and as inclusion of students with disabilities in general education classrooms across the district becomes more prevalent the district has discussed relocating Mr. Marley's class to another school that could use a second special education classroom. Mr. Marley and Ms. Gates attend a workshop on co-teaching to facilitate inclusion of students with disabilities. Following the workshop, they approach their principal, requesting the administrative support to pursue the possibility of developing a co-teaching classroom at Tanglewood. What they have

TABLE 11.2	Questions for creating a collaborative working relationship in co-teaching
Topic	**Questions**
Instructional beliefs	• What are overriding philosophies about the roles of teachers and teaching, and students and learning? • How do our instructional beliefs affect our instructional practice?
Planning	• When do we have at least 30 minutes of shared planning time? • How do we divide our responsibilities for planning and teaching? • How much joint planning time do we need? • What records can we keep to facilitate our planning?
Parity signals	• How will we convey to students and others (for example, teachers, parents) that we are equals in the classroom? • How can we ensure a sense of parity during instruction?
Confidentiality	• What information about our teaching do we want to share with others? • What information should not be shared? • Which information about students can be shared with others? • What information should not be shared?
Noise	• What noise level are we comfortable with in the classroom?
Classroom routines	• What are the instructional routines in the classroom? • What are the organizational routines for the classroom?
Discipline	• What is acceptable and unacceptable student behavior? • Who is to intervene at what point in the students' behavior? • What are the rewards and consequences used in the classroom?
Feedback	• What is the best way to give each other feedback? • How will you ensure that both positive and negative issues are raised?
Pet peeves	• What aspects of teaching and classroom life do each of you feel strongly about? • How can we identify our pet peeves so as to avoid them?

Source: From Cook, L., & Friend, M. (1995). Co-teaching: Guidelines for creating effective practices. *Focus on Exceptional Children, 28*(3), pp. 1–16.

in mind is a class that would serve students with and without disabilities, ages kindergarten through grade 3. Ms. Gates and Mr. Marley spend a year planning their co-teaching classroom. They visit other classrooms where co-teaching is being implemented, talk with other teachers who are implementing co-teaching in their district, attend further workshops, and research different co-teaching models. In addition, they get to know each other's teaching styles to make sure they are compatible. They discuss and examine their instructional beliefs about teaching and develop strategies for implementation of a collaborative co-teaching model. They incorporate time for problem solving and communication and confer with each other about discipline techniques, classroom routines, instructional routines, and pet peeves. Once they decide to move forward with co-teaching, they approach their principal, requesting the administrative support they need for successful implementation. Also, they request an additional weekly planning period and reduced teacher-pupil ratios. The following year, Mr. Marley and Ms. Gates implement co-teaching. They are equal partners in the classroom, both of them sharing responsibility for all students in the class. Mr. Marley teaches Ms. Gates strategies for working with the students with disabilities. Ms. Gates teaches Mr. Marley strategies about managing a whole classroom of typical students. They also have recruited community volunteers that assist them in providing individualized instructional support for students.

Models in Practice

Several different co-teaching models have been developed for serving students with high-incidence disabilities. Cook and Friend (1995) outline five of them. The first is called "one-teaching, one supporting." In this model, one teacher has primary responsibility for planning and delivering instruction to students, and the other teacher provides support. The next model is "station teaching." In the station teaching model, the co-teachers divide the responsibilities, each one being in charge of a part of the instructional content. Students move between teachers to receive instruction. The third model is "parallel teaching." In parallel teaching, the teachers collaboratively plan the instruction; however, the students are divided up between the two teachers for instruction. This allows the teachers to lower the teacher-pupil ratio. Alternative teaching is a model in which one teacher provides instruction to the entire class, while the second teacher provides individual or small group instruction to students who need additional assistance in learning the instructional content. This model is also referred to as a classroom within a classroom (Adelman & Taylor, 1998). This model involves cross-age instruction in which a smaller group of students with similar needs are instructed separately from the larger class. Adelman and Taylor (1998) outline strategies for establishing this model in a school and facilitating planning for increasing the effectiveness of the model. Finally, Cook and Friend (1995) discuss team teaching, a model in which both teachers collaboratively plan and provide instruction to all the students in the class at the same time. This is the model illustrated in the example that Ms. Gates and Mr. Marley chose to implement.

:: CURRENT TRENDS AND OPPORTUNITIES FOR COLLABORATION, CONSULTATION, AND CO-TEACHING

Collaborating Within the School

Teachers and staff have many opportunities to engage in collaboration, consultation, and co-teaching. One opportunity that lends itself particularly well to collaboration and consultation is the eligibility and placement process. The school psychologist, guidance counselor, and special education teacher often consult with the general education teacher in completing prereferral activities, suggesting interventions that may ameliorate the student's problem. In fact, researchers have suggested that collaboration on pre-referral may help to reduce general educators' referrals for special education (Adelman & Taylor, 1998; Sindelar, Griffin, Smith, & Watanabe, 1992). **Response to intervention** (RTI) is a newer approach to making eligibility determinations, particularly for students with high-incidence disabilities. It lends itself to collaboration. RTI is based on prereferral practices and allows schools to provide services from an intervention perspective rather than identify students for special education services from a psychometric framework. Simply put, when using RTI to identify students in need of special education services, various evidence-based practices are implemented in order to address the student's learning or behavior problems (Fuchs, Mock, Morgan, & Young, 2003; Gresham, 1999). Eligibility decisions for special education are then made based on the student's academic and behavioral changes following the implementation of the interventions—that is, the student's response to interventions.

Standardized state assessments or high-stakes testing is another current trend or opportunity that lends itself to increased collaboration and consultation between general and special educators. With the legal requirement of NCLB and the reauthorization of IDEA (2004), children with high-incidence disabilities are included more and more often in standardized state assessments to measure district-level progress. As students with disabilities are included in these tests, teachers need to make appropriate modifications and adaptations. Therefore, general and special educators need to work together to make sure that the manner in which the state assessments are administered are nondiscriminatory and appropriate for the student's test taking abilities.

Inclusion of students with high-incidence disabilities in general education classrooms is one current trend that requires collaboration. Collaboration activities add to the success of inclusion (Friend, 1984; Salend, 1994; Wood, 2002). In fact, McLeskey and Waldron (2002) describe collaboration as a "cornerstone" to the success of inclusive education. For inclusion to be successful, teachers must make a number of adaptations and modifications to assignments. In order to implement these adaptations, they need other professionals' assistance and expertise. Collaboration, consultation, and teaming are ways to help support these curricular modifications (Correa et al., 2005) and increase teacher effectiveness (O'Shea, Williams, & Sattler, 1999).

Finally, the implementation of functional behavioral assessment (FBA) and behavioral intervention plans (BIP) are two other trends that require teachers and support staff to collaborate within the school (Jolivette, Barton-Arwood, & Scott, 2000). In order to conduct FBAs and develop BIPs, teachers often need to collaborate with a behavior specialist, school psychologist, or special educator to examine the factors that influence the occurrence of the behavior and identify intervention strategies that decrease the problem behavior and increase appropriate replacement behaviors. The Center for Effective Collaboration and Practice (http://cecp.air.org/) provides a number of strategies that can be used by teams to implement FBA practices and develop BIP.

Collaborating Across Schools

Collaboration of professionals also occurs across school placements. For example, when young children identified as having high-incidence disabilities transition from early childhood programs into elementary schools, a transition team should collaborate to facilitate a smooth transition between educational programs (Hanline & Knowlton, 1988; Lowenthal, 1992; Summers et al., 2001). Collaboration should occur at all levels of transition, including transitions from elementary to middle school, middle school to high school, and finally, high school to a vocational placement or college (Kohler & Field, 2003). At each of these times of transition, teachers, support staff, and parents need to collaborate to assist the student in making a smooth transition from one placement to another. Teachers in both placements working collaboratively to share information, strategies, and ideas, as well as, teachers working collaboratively with the student and the parents, will facilitate the success of these transitions.

Collaborating Outside the School

It is critical that teachers collaborate with the families of the students in their classrooms (Kauffman et al., 2006). Collaboration with families occurs in many different ways. For example, collaboration with families can occur as information exchanges, written notes, and phone calls. Other types of collaboration can occur via legal meetings, such as IEP meetings, placement and eligibility meetings. For some teachers and families, collaboration occurs on a regular basis through parent-teacher conferences and home visiting. Regardless of the type, family members can provide essential information about their child's learning needs and be an integral part of the decision making process regarding their child's educational program. In addition, by involving parents, the degree of conflict between the school and the student's parents can be decreased (Turnbull, Turnbull, Shank, & Leal, 1999).

Finally, collaboration between teachers, school staff, and professionals in the health and mental health field is another critical opportunity for collaboration. Student's who have medical needs (e.g., student's on medication or students with health related impairments, such as TBI, ADHD), often require ongoing consultation with a medical professional to monitor their condition and progress. It is essential for teachers to collaborate with these professionals in order to coordinate instructional services with the medical practices being implemented. For example, if a student who has ADHD or EBD has recently changed medication, the student's teacher should collaborate with the student's physician and parents in order to assist in evaluating the effectiveness of the medication. Often, students with EBD and their families are also involved in a number of wraparound services, such as counseling or other mental health services. Again, collaboration of the teacher and individuals in these wraparound services is another prime opportunity for collaboration to occur.

:: EVALUATING THE EFFECTIVENESS OF CONSULTATION, COLLABORATION, AND CO-TEACHING: DATA SPEAK LOUDER THAN WORDS

Although we know that collaboration is an important strategy in the education of all students with high-incidence disabilities, how do we evaluate the collaborative process and its outcomes? As with all evidence-based strategies, we need to collect assessment data to evaluate effectiveness. Bahr, Whitten, Dieker, Kocarker, and Manson (1999) found that collaborative teams were most effective when they had a plan for implementing collaborative activities and evaluated the outcomes according to their plans. However, when evaluating collaborative activities, assessment data should be collected directly on the collaboration activities, rather than verbal report or other information procedures (Bahr et al., 1999). In fact, the most valid way to measure successful outcomes of collaboration is to measure the student's outcomes directly. For example, if a behavior specialist collaborates with a general education teacher to assist in conducting a FBA and implement a BIP, the direct assessment of the student's problem behaviors following the collaborative development and implementation of the FBA and BIP should be used to evaluate the collaborative activities. As suggested by Witt, Gresham, and Noell (1996), we need to collect data directly on the effectiveness of all instructional activities, including collaboration activities, to know whether our strategies work. We can measure effectiveness and outcomes of the collaboration directly by collecting direct observational data, evaluating students' behaviors prior to and following intervention, comparing pre- and post-test outcomes, and evaluating **permanent products.**

Another important way to evaluate collaboration is to examine the skills gained and outcomes produced by team members. For example, the following components should be evaluated: (a) team practices (including the effectiveness of practices implemented following collaboration); (b) follow-up on collaborative interventions and activities implemented; (c) quality of collaborative services, and (d) solutions to barriers that are encountered through the collaborative process (Bahr et al., 1999). Although direct observation and measurement of the outcomes of collaboration may be preferable, it is often difficult to observe outcomes directly; therefore, **indirect measures** may be helpful in evaluating collaborative activities. For example, rating scales, interviews, and checklists can be used to determine whether the collaborative activities were implemented as planned and were successful in obtaining the targeted outcomes. Teachers can use a rating scale to evaluate the collaborative process itself or to determine if a student's behavior or learning changed after collaboration occurred. Similarly, interviews can be used as an evaluative tool by asking team members questions regarding the effectiveness of the collaboration process or whether there were changes in the students' behavior as a direct outcome of the collaboration process. Finally, checklists can be used to evaluate whether the collaborative process was implemented as planned and if the target students' met their goals.

Regardless of *how* collaboration, consulting, and co-teaching activities are evaluated, assessment of the *outcomes* of the process should be conducted to determine the *effectiveness*. As stated earlier, collaboration is only effective when implemented as a dynamic process, requiring communication among stakeholders, shared goals, strategic planning and problem solving, time, commitment, resources, and measurement of positive outcomes for students and team members.

SUMMARY

The purpose of collaboration is to provide effective intervention services to students with high-incidence disabilities, either through indirect service delivery, such as consultation activities or direct service delivery, such as co-teaching. Although collaboration does not always occur in the form of direct intervention, the importance of the collaborative process is still critical. Collaboration can increase service delivery in the LRE (Givens-Ogle, Christ, & Idol, 1991), and the likelihood of successful inclusive placement (Schloss, 1992). It can reduce the number of referrals to special education (Fuchs et al., 1990) and facilitate post-school outcomes. In fact, collaborative teaming can "make or break" effective service delivery for students with high-incidence disabilities. Many of these students have complex educational needs and require a variety of professionals to work together to meet their needs. If teachers do not collaborate with each other, related service personnel, and families of students, the students are less likely to receive the services they need.

Barriers that teachers, other professionals, and family members encounter when collaborating with one another are mostly practical matters that can be solved through administrative support and resources for the collaborative process. For example, teachers often report a lack of time needed to collaborate (Brownell & Walther-Thomas, 2002). Large case loads has also been suggested as a practical barrier to

collaboration (Johnson, Pugach, & Hammittee, 1988). However, practical barriers can be addressed if collaboration is a priority. Philosophical or conceptual barriers may be somewhat more difficult to address. For example, collaborative efforts are impeded when professionals have meaningful differences in teaching philosophies and training (e.g., one teacher approaches instruction from a **constructivist** viewpoint and another teacher is a **behaviorist**). Collaborative efforts are also impeded when professionals are resistant to change and there is a lack of standardization and clarification of various roles. For example, a veteran teacher may not want to implement practices that a novice teacher has recently been taught. Lilly (1987) suggested that consultation is often discussed more than it is practiced. Different professionals have their own areas of expertise and strength and often view their missions and responsibilities differently from one another. For collaboration to be effective, the administration in schools needs to provide the leadership, technical assistance, training, support, and resources needed.

Students, professionals, and family members all benefit from collaboration. Professionals increase their knowledge, improve interpersonal skills (e.g., problem solving, communication, group interaction), increase their competence (Cross & Villa, 1992), and have higher morale, and lower attrition. Professionals are more likely to be able to attend better to the individual needs of students and are more likely to be open to changes and new ideas.

There is a long history of collaboration in special education, especially in relation to students with high-incidence disabilities. As stated by Idol and West (1991):

- Collaboration is not a new concept.
- Collaboration is not an end unto itself; rather it is a catalytic process used in interactive relationships among individuals working together toward a mutually defined, concrete vision or outcome.
- Collaboration is an interactive relationship first, then a technique or vehicle for change.
- The foci and outcomes of educational collaboration are multiple, with student outcomes being only one important outcome, the others being adult and system/organizational outcomes.

- Educational collaboration as an adult-to-adult interactive process can be expected to have an indirect impact on student outcomes—the process of educational collaboration among adult team members typically yields changes in team member's attitudes, skills, knowledge, and/or behaviors first, followed by changes in student and/or organizational outcomes.
- Educational collaboration may be used as a team process for effective planning and decision making as well as problem solving—thus it can be an effective tool for proactive strategic planning or reactive, but efficient, problem solving in any organizational structure in the school.

However, the most important aspect of collaboration is the benefit to students, teachers, and family members.

COMPETENT TEACHING BOX   BOX 11.1

Knowing your students . . .

Knowing your students and your fellow colleagues helps us to collaborate better. When you collaborate with other professionals, parents of your students, and your students themselves, you might want to remember the following:

- Collaboration is a generic term that is used to describe a strategy for serving students with disabilities.
- The type of collaboration that you engage in will depend on the targeted student's specific needs. In some situations, consultation is more appropriate; whereas, in other situations a co-teaching model may be the most appropriate.
- The overall goal for collaboration, consultation, and co-teaching is to provide the best educational services for targeted students with high-incidence disabilities. Therefore, the student should always be the focus of collaborative activities.
- Effective collaboration requires trust and open communication among team members, a strong commitment to working with others, respect for individual team members, shared decision making and problem solving, and most importantly— accountability for outcomes of the collaborative process.
- Collaboration is a strategy that can be used across many educational services and settings, including inclusion of students with disabilities, manifestation determinations, functional behavioral assessments and behavioral intervention plans,

high-stakes testing, nondiscriminatory assessment, eligibility and placement in special education, and individual educational planning. Collaboration may also occur among individuals outside of the school setting, such as medical professionals.

■ To provide effective services for students with high-incidence disabilities, a number of professionals need to be involved in the collaborative process including administrators, teachers, related service personnel, family members, and the student (as appropriate).

■ Effective collaboration requires a commitment from the professionals themselves as well as administrative supports.

■ Collaboration is appropriate for students of all ages with a variety of needs.

Competent teachers . . .

■ Identify the goals for the student and themselves that can be accomplished through collaboration.

■ Develop a plan and identify the best process for collaborating to meet those goals.

■ Identify the team players that should be involved in the collaborative process.

■ Identify strategies and necessary supports for maintaining a collaborative working relationship and making the relationship successful.

■ Develop a problem solving and communication plan for implementing collaboration.

■ Evaluate the outcomes of their collaborative plans, making modifications as necessary.

⊞ CASE STUDIES

AARON

Aaron is a 7-year-old boy who attends the local elementary school. He has mild cerebral palsy accompanied with mild mental retardation, motor coordination difficulties, and speech and language deficits. Aaron can walk independently, but he has an unstable gait. He is able to speak, but often others have a difficult time understanding his speech. When he first entered elementary school, the Child Study Team evaluated Aaron and recommended placement for special education services in a self-contained classroom that serves children with disabilities, physical therapy services, and speech-language services. Over the past several years, Aaron has been making remarkable progress. He has become more independent, his speech-language skills have improved, and he has begun to make friends at school. At his last IEP meeting, Aaron's parents met with his special education teacher, physical therapist, and speech-language pathologist and requested that Aaron be educated in the general education classroom for part of his day. The IEP team decided that they would begin enrolling Aaron in physical education classes, art classes, and music classes with his same-age peers. In addition, the special education teacher suggested that they might also want to consider including Aaron in the general education class during academic activities, including language arts and math.

The IEP team knows that in order for Aaron to be successful in these educational settings, collaborative teaming and consultation needs to occur. Therefore, the IEP team requested that the school's Technical Assistance Team (TAT) develop a plan and implementation strategies for successfully including Aaron in the general education classroom. First, Aaron's special education teacher met with the TAT team (including the special education, general education, art, physical education, and music teachers) to talk about strategies for including Aaron. Aaron's parents attended the meeting to let the teachers know their goals for Aaron. At this meeting, Aaron's strengths and needs were discussed as well as opportunities for inclusion with same-age peers. Following this meeting, all TAT team members agreed that Aaron had many strengths and agreed to be a part of the collaborative team. Next, the special education teacher on the TAT spent time in each of the other teachers' classrooms, observing routines, expectations, and skills Aaron needed to be successful in those classrooms. The special education teacher consulted with each teacher to identify what types of accommodations and modifications would be needed for Aaron to be successful. Following these consultations, the special education teachers worked independently with each of Aaron's teachers to help implement the modifica-

tions. In addition, she worked with Aaron to teach him specific skills he needed to be successful. Prior to implementing the inclusion plan, the TAT met to discuss concerns, issues, and strategy for problem solving in case difficult situations arose. The TAT decided to meet biweekly for the first several months to compare notes and discuss Aaron's progress. In the meantime, the special education teacher agreed to consult daily with each of Aaron's teachers for the first week to ensure that any problems would be addressed. The TAT outlined targeted goals for Aaron to accomplish over the year including: (a) attend general education classes 80% of the school day; (b) develop friendships with peers in each general education setting; (c) independently complete activities and tasks required for participation in each general education classroom. The TAT collected indirect and direct measurement of Aaron's progress toward accomplishing these goals as well as the general education teacher's acceptance of the collaborative consultation process and Aaron's inclusion into the general education settings. Throughout the year, the TAT worked collaboratively with Aaron's teachers and parents to implement the inclusion plan and monitor Aaron's progress.

1. Would Aaron be able to get the supports he needs without the collaborative efforts of the TAT?
2. What are some of the challenges that professionals who are part of the TAT encounter?
3. Do the efforts of the TAT help Aaron be served in an inclusive setting?

JANICE/KEVIN

Janice is a fifth-grade teacher in a school that serves a number of students who are at high risk for learning and behavior problems. Janice has 22 students in her class, 3 of which have learning disabilities, 2 of which have ADHD, and 1 which has EBD. The school Janice teaches in, Wilson Elementary, has decided to implement a Positive Behavior Support (PBS) model, providing a disciplinary structure across the school to help manage problem behaviors. The school hired a national expert in the field to train the staff in PBS strategies. All teachers and staff members have been involved in the training and have implemented many of the agreed upon schoolwide intervention strategies. Janice, however, is still having difficulty with several of the students in her classroom, particularly those with learning and behavior problems. Often these students do not complete their assignments and act out during instructional time. In fact, one student, Kevin, who has emotional and behavior disorder (EBD), is particularly disruptive to everyone in the classroom. He speaks out during instructional times, is noncompliant, off-task, walks around the room, and is disruptive to the other students in the class. When Janice tries to discipline him, he does not respond. In fact, his disruptive behavior often increases. One day, following a disastrous math lesson, where Kevin constantly disrupted the lesson, Janice asked the behavior specialist, Ms. Rodriguez, for help with Kevin. Ms. Rodriguez observed in Janice's class for several days, across several activities. She collected direct observational data on Kevin's behavior in Janice's class, evaluated Kevin's abilities in relation to his assignments, and how Kevin responded to Janice's instructional strategies. Following these observations, Ms. Rodriguez met with Janice to discuss her findings. During this meeting, she shared with Janice a number of suggestions that may help in addressing Kevin's behavior. First, Ms. Rodriguez suggested that Kevin's behavior may be a result of his inability to complete the math assignments. Although Kevin has an EBD, he also has a learning disability. Therefore, Ms. Rodriguez and Janice decided to adapt Kevin's assignments to make them more appropriate for his ability level and his attention span. Next, since Kevin finds Janice's attention reinforcing, Ms. Rodriguez suggested that Janice ignore Kevin's inappropriate behaviors as much as possible and increase her attention to Kevin when he engages in appropriate behaviors. Finally, Ms. Rodriguez suggested that Janice implement a reward system that includes earning points for appropriate behaviors across her entire classroom to increase all of the students' on-task behavior. Ms. Rodriguez collaboratively consulted with Janice over several weeks to implement these strategies within the class. In addition, Ms. Rodriguez modeled the praise strategy she suggested Janice use with Kevin. In order to evaluate the outcomes of these activities, Ms. Rodriguez and Janice collected periodic observational data on Kevin's behavior. Following the assignment modifications, they determined a significant increase of Kevin's on-task behavior and a decrease of Kevin's off-task and disruptive behaviors. In addition, Kevin's outbursts and out-of-seat behavior declined and the other students' behavior improved following the implementation of the reward system.

1. Why didn't Janice make classroom modifications to address Kevin's needs?
2. What types of supports did Ms. Rodriguez provide that helped Janice meet Kevin's needs?
3. Was PBS an effective intervention for addressing Kevin's needs in this class? Why or why not?

CARRIE

Carrie is a 17-year-old junior in high school with Asperger's syndrome and learning disabilities. Carrie's strengths are in the area of reading, but her needs are in the areas of math,

social skills, and unusual repetitive behaviors. Academically, Carrie excels in her reading classes, but has difficulty staying on grade level with her peers in math class. Socially, Carrie is lonely and has no friends in or outside of school. When Carrie does interact with the other students, her verbal behaviors are often bizarre and inappropriate, resulting in the other students at school teasing and gossiping about her. Carrie's parents are concerned, because Carrie appears to be depressed. She has become more and more reclusive and often refuses to go to school. Carrie's parents talked with the school's guidance counselor; however, the guidance counselor had limited knowledge about the needs of students with Asperger's syndrome. The guidance counselor suggested that the parents contact their physician who recommended a child psychiatrist. Carrie's parents contacted a child psychiatrist who has expertise in working with children with Asperger's syndrome. The child psychiatrist evaluated Carrie and decided to prescribe an antidepressant to address Carrie's reclusive and repetitive behaviors. In addition, the child psychiatrist referred Carrie and her parents to the local Resource Center for Autism (a state agency serving students with autism and related disorders) which employs a behavior specialist that specializes in students with autism. The behavior specialist met Carrie and her parents and evaluated her social behaviors. Following this meeting, the behavior specialist observed Carrie at school. After collecting data, the behavior specialist met with Carrie, her parents, the guidance counselor, and her primary teachers at school to discuss possible strategies for facilitating Carrie's peer interactions. At this meeting, Carrie and her parents shared with school staff that Carrie had begun taking antidepressants to address her depression and repetitive behaviors. In addition, Carrie shared that she wanted to make friends at school. The behavior specialist suggested developing a peer network intervention that could begin at home in Carrie's neighborhood and then transfer into the school setting. Carrie identified a few activities that she would enjoy learning more about, such as horseback riding, dog training, and computer games. The guidance counselor and Carrie's teachers identified several students in the school that have similar interests and would be good candidates for including in Carrie's peer network. The behavior specialist worked with Carrie's parents and the guidance counselor to develop a plan for implementing the peer network activities at home and at school. The peers were identified and trained in strategies to facilitate peer interactions with Carrie. Carrie was taught strategies for engaging in appropriate social behaviors and decreasing her inappropriate behaviors. Carrie's parents provided opportunities at home and in the community to encourage peer interactions. Finally, Carrie's teachers provided opportunities at school to encourage peer interactions. The behavior specialist continued to meet with the group to evaluate Carrie's progress.

1. Was it appropriate for Carrie to receive homebound services after her TBI?
2. Is prescribing an anti-depressant to help Carrie's depression an appropriate strategy?
3. What types of teaming skills are needed to help Carrie receive a free appropriate public education?

REFERENCES

Adelman, H. S., & Taylor, L. (1998). Involving teachers in collaborative efforts to better address the barriers to student learning. *Preventing School Failure, 42*(2), 55–59.

Bahr, M. W., Fuchs, D., & Fuchs, L. S. (1999). Mainstream assistance teams: A consultation-based approach to pre-referral intervention. In S. Graham and K. Harris (Eds.), *Teachers working together: Enhancing the performance of students with special needs* (pp. 87–116). Cambridge, MA: Brookline Books.

Bahr, M. W., Whitten, E., Dieker, L., Kocarker, C. E., & Manson, D. (1999). A comparison of school-based intervention teams: Implications for educational and legal reform. *Exceptional Children, 66*(1), 67–83.

Bergan, J. R. (1977). *Behavioral consultation.* Columbus, OH: Merrill.

Brown, B., Pryzwansky, W. B., & Schulte, A. C. (1998). *Psychological consultation: Introduction to theory and practice.* Needham Heights, MA: Allyn & Bacon.

Brown, D., Wyne, M. D., Blackburn, J. E., & Powell, W. C. (1979). *Consultation: Strategy for improving education.* Boston, MA: Allyn & Bacon.

Brownell, M. T., & Walther-Thomas, C. (2002). An interview with Dr. Marilyn Friend. *Intervention in School and Clinic, 37*(4), 223–228.

Chalfant, J. C., & Pysh, M. V. (1989). Teacher assistance teams: Five descriptive studies on 96 teams. *Remedial and Special Education, 10*(6), 49–58.

Chalfant, J. C., Pysh, M. V., & Moultrie, R. (1979). Teacher assistance teams: A model for within-building problem solving. *Learning Disability Quarterly, 2,* 85–96.

Cohen, S. S., Thomas, C. C., Sattler, R. O., & Morsink, C. V. (1997). Meeting the challenge of consultation and collaboration: Developing interactive teams. *Journal of Learning Disabilities, 30*(4), 427–432.

Correa, V. I., Jones, H. A., Thomas, C. C., & Morsink, C. V. (2005). *Interactive teaming: Enhancing programs for students with special needs* (4th ed.). Upper Saddle River, NJ: Merrill/Prentice Hall.

Cook, L., & Friend, M. (1995). Co-Teaching: Guidelines for creating effective practices. *Focus on Exceptional Children, 28*(3), 1–16.

Cooley, E., & Yovanoff, P. (1996). Supporting professionals at-risk: Evaluating interventions to reduce burnout and improve retention of special educators. *Exceptional Children, 62*(4), 336–355.

Cooley, V. E. (1993). Tips for implementing a student assistance program. *NASSP Bulletin, 76,* 10–20.

Cross, G., & Villa, R. A. (1992). The Winooski School System: An evolutionary perspective of a school restructuring for diversity. In R. A. Villa, J. S. Thousand, W. Stainback, & S. Stainback (Eds.), *Restructuring for caring and effective education* (pp. 219–240). Baltimore: Brookes.

Deno, E. (1970). Special education as developmental capital. *Exceptional Children, 37,* 229–237.

Friend, M. (1984). Consultation skills for resource teachers. *Learning Disability Quarterly, 7*(3), 246–250.

Friend, M., & Cook, L. (2003). *Interactions: Collaboration skills for school professionals* (4th ed.). Boston: Allyn & Bacon.

Fore III, C., Martin, C., & Bender, W. N. (2002). Teacher burnout in special education: The causes and the recommended solutions. *High School Journal, 86*(1), 36–45.

Fuchs, D., Fuchs, L. S., & Bahr, M. W. (1990). Mainstream assistance teams: A scientific basis for the art of consultation. *Exceptional Children, 57*(2), 128–139.

Fuchs, D., Mock, D., Morgan, P. L., & Young, C. L. (2003). Responsiveness-to-intervention: Definitions, evidence, and implications for the learning disabilities construct. *Learning Disabilities Research & Practice, 18*(3), 157–171.

Givens-Ogle, L., Christ, B. A., & Idol, L. (1991). Collaborative consultation: The San Juan Unified School District Project. *Journal of Educational and Psychological Consultation, 2*(3), 267–284.

Graden, J. L., Casey, A., & Christenson, S. L. (1985). Implementing a prereferral intervention system: Part I. The model. *Exceptional Children, 51*(5), 377–384.

Gresham, F. M. (1999). In W. D. Tilly & J. Grimes (Eds.), Special education in transition: Functional analysis assessment as a cornerstone for noncategocal special education (pp. 107–138). Longmont, CO: Sopris West.

Gutkin, T. B. (2002). Training school-based consultants: Some thoughts on grains of sand and building anthills. *Journal of Educational and Psychological Consultation, 13*(1, & 2), 133–146.

Hanline, M. F., & Knowlton, A. (1988). A collaborative model for providing support to parents during their child's transition from infant intervention to preschool special education public school programs. *Journal of the Division of Early Childhood, 12,* 116–125.

Hayek, R. A. (1987). The teacher assistance team: A prereferral support system. *Focus on Exceptional Children, 20*(1), 107.

Idol, L. (2002). *Creating collaborative and inclusive schools.* Austin, TX: PRO-ED.

Idol, L., Paolucci-Whitcomb, P., & Nevin, A. (1995). The collaborative consultation model. *Journal of Educational and Psychological Consultation, 6,* 329–346.

Idol, L., & West, F. (1991). Educational collaboration: A catalyst for effective schooling. *Intervention in School and Clinic, 27,* 70–78.

Individuals with Disabilities Education Act, 20, U.S.C. *et seq.* (1990; 1997; 2004).

Interstate New Teacher Assessment and Support Consortium (2001, May). Model standards for licensing general and special education teachers of students with disabilities: A resource for state dialogue. Washington, DC: Council of Chief State School Officers.

Johnson, L. J., Pugach, M. C., & Hammittee, D. J. (1988). Peer collaboration. *Teaching Exceptional Children, 20*(3), 75–77.

Jolivette, K., Barton-Arwood, S., & Scott, T. M. (2000). Functional behavioral assessment as a collaborative process among professionals. *Education and Treatment of Children, 23*(3), 298–313.

Katzenbach, J. R., & Smith, D. K. (1999). The wisdom of teams: Creating the high-performance organization. New York: Harper Collins Publishers.

Kauffman, J. M., Mostert, M. P., Trent, S. C., & Pullen, P. L. (2006). *Managing classroom behavior: A reflective case-based approach* (4th ed.). Boston: Allyn & Bacon.

Kohler, P., & Field, S. (2003). Transition-focused education: Foundation for the future. *Journal of Special Education, 37,* 174–183.

Lang, D. C., Quick, A. F., & Johnson, J. A. (1981). *A partnership for the supervision of student teachers.* DeKalb, IL: Creative Educational Materials.

Laycock, V. K., Gable, R. A., & Korinek, L. A. (1991). Alternative structures for collaboration in the delivery of special services: *Preventing School Failure, 35*(4), 15–18.

Lilly, M. S. (1971). A training based model for special education. *Exceptional Children, 37,* 745–749.

Lilly, M. S. (1987). Response to "Consultation in Special Education" by Idol and West. *Journal of Learning Disabilities, 20,* 494–495.

Logan, K. R., & Stein, S. S. (2001). The research lead teacher model. *Exceptional Children, 33,* 10–15.

Lowenthal, B. (1992). Collaborative training in the education of early childhood educators. *Teaching Exceptional Children, 24*(4), 25–29.

McLaughlin, M., & Schwartz, R. (1998). *Strategies for fixing public schools.* Cambridge, MA: Pew Forum, Harvard Graduate School of Education.

McLeskey, J., & Waldron, N. L. (2002). Inclusion and school change: Teacher perceptions regarding curricular and instructional adaptations. *Teacher Education and Special Education, 25*(1), 41–54.

Moore, K. J., Fifield, M., Bryce, S., Deborah A., & Scarlato, M. (1979). Child study team decision making in special education: Improving the process. *Remedial and Special Education, 10*(4), 50–58.

Mostert, M. P. (1998). *Interprofessional collaboration in schools.* Needham Heights, MA: Allyn & Bacon.

No Child Left Behind Act (2001). Retrieved Sept. 28, 2006, from http://www.ed.gov/nclb/landing.jhtml.

O'Shea, D. J., Williams, A. L., & Sattler, R. O. (1999). Collaboration across special education and general education: Preservice teacher's views. *Journal of Teacher Education, 50*(2), 147–157.

O'Shea, L. J., O'Shea, D. J., & Algozzine, R. (1998). Collaboration across special education and general education: Preservice teachers' views. *Journal of Teacher Education, 50*(2), 147–157.

Pavan, B. N., & Entrekin, K. M. (1991, April). *Principal change facilitator styles and the implementation of instructional support teams.* Paper presented at the meeting of the American Educational Research Association, Chicago, IL. (ERIC Document Reproduction Service No. ED 425 603.)

Pugach, M. C., & Johnson, L. J. (1995). Unlocking expertise among classroom teachers through structured dialogue: Extending research on peer collaboration. *Exceptional Children, 62,* 101–110.

Pugach, M. C., & Johnson, L. J. (2002). *Collaborative practitioners, collaborative schools* (2nd ed.). Denver, CO: Love Publishing Co.

Purkey, S. C., & Smith, M. S. (1985). School reform: The district policy implications of the effective schools literature. *Elementary School Journal, 85*(3), 353–389.

Salend, S. J. (1994). *Effective mainstreaming: Creating inclusive classrooms* (2nd ed). Upper Saddle River, NJ: Merrill/Prentice Hall.

Salend, S. J., Johansen, M., Mumper, J., Chase, A. S., Pike, K. M., & Sorney, J. A. (1997). Cooperative teaching: The voices of two teachers. *Remedial and Special Education, 18*(1), 3–11.

Schloss, P. J. (1992). Mainstreaming revisited. *Elementary School Journal, 92*(3), 233–244.

Sindelar, P. T., Griffin, C. C., Smith, S. W., & Watanabe, A. K. (1992). Prereferral intervention: Encouraging notes on preliminary findings. *The Elementary School Journal, 92,* 245–259.

Stanovich, P. J. (1996). Collaboration—the key to successful instruction in today's inclusive schools. *Intervention in School and Clinic, 32*(1), 39–42.

Sugai, G., & Horner, R. (1999). Discipline and behavioral support: Practices, pitfalls, and promises. *Effective School Practices, 17,* 10–17.

Sugai, G. M., & Tindal, G. A. (1993). *Effective school consultation: An interactive approach.* Pacific Grove, CA: Brooks/Cole.

Summers, J. A., Steeples, T., Peterson, C., Naig, L., McBride, S., Wall, S., Liebow, H., Swanson, M., & Stowitscheck, J. (2001). Policy and management supports for effective service integration in early Head Start and Part C programs. *Topics in Early Chidhood Special Education, 21*(1), 16–31.

Tharp, R. G., (1975). The triadic model of consultation: Current considerations. In C. A. Parker (Ed.), *Psychological consultation: Helping teachers meet special needs.* Reston, VA: The Council for Exceptional Children.

Turnbull, A., Turnbull, R., Shank, M., & Leal, D. (1999). *Exceptional lives: Special education in today's schools* (2nd ed.). Upper Saddle River, NJ: Merrill/Prentice Hall.

U. S. Department of Education (2002). 24th annual report to Congress on the implementation of the Individuals with Disabilities Education Act. Retrieved November 2003, from strategic and annual reports at http://www.ed.gov/about/reports/annual/osep/2002/index.html.

Wadsworth, D. (1997). *Different drummers: How teachers of teachers view public education. A report from Public Agenda.* New York: Public Agenda.

Wallace, T., Anderson, A. R., & Batholomay, T. (2002). Collaboration: An element associated with the success of four inclusive high schools. *Journal of Educational and Psychological Consultation, 13*(4), 349–382.

Walter-Thomas, C., Bryant, M., & Land, S. (1996). Planning for effective co-teaching: The key to successful inclusion. *Remedial and Special Education, 17*(4), 255–264.

Wangemann, P., Ingram, C. F., & Muse, I. D. (1989). A successful university-pubic school collaboration: The union of theory and practice. *Teacher Education and Special Education, 12,* 61–64.

West, J. F., & Idol, L. (1987). School consultation (Part I): An interdisciplinary perspective on theory, models, and research. *Journal of Learning Disabilities, 20,* 388–408.

Witt, J. C., Gresham, F. M., & Noell, G. H. (1996). What's behavioral about behavioral consultation? *Journal of Educational and Psychological Consultation, 7,* 327–344.

Wood, J. W. (2002). *Adapting instruction for mainstreamed and at-risk students* (4th ed.). Upper Saddle River, NJ: Merrill/Prentice Hall.

Prevention and Early Intervention: Setting the Stage for Effective Learning

URBAN LEGEND: *The primary goal of special education is remediation and maintenance, whereas social programs and medicine are more likely to focus on prevention.*

LEGENDARY THOUGHT: *Effective instruction is prevention.*

Throughout history societies have viewed individuals with disabilities in many ways, sometimes in radically different ways compared to contemporary views. At times children with disabilities were abandoned and left to fend for themselves. At other points they were locked up in a misguided effort to keep society safe from the influence and actions of these "deviants." As our understanding of the nature and causes of disabilities evolved, we began to appreciate that although different, these same individuals could benefit from educational experiences through targeted instruction and related opportunities. We also learned, long ago, that we need to step in as early as possible to prevent disabilities from occurring at all, if we can, or from getting worse than necessary.

History is of little value if we do not learn from it. Despite what we now understand about the dynamic nature of disabilities, the multiple potential causes, and the effects of combining various environmental and biological risk factors, educators have often viewed their role primarily in terms of **remediation** (which is intended to correct something). The assumption, going as far back as the wild boy of Aveyron, is that special educators are given a student with a deficiency and the goal is to correct it to the extent possible. Current views of disabilities as conditions that, although lifelong, vary in severity throughout the course of one's life, limit the validity of these prior assumptions.

Chapter 3 highlights the fact that although we do not fully understand the causes and specific risk factors for *all* disabilities under *all* conditions, we certainly know enough to engage in active **prevention**. In education there is often a perception that prevention is a medical or community initiative and that our job is to educate the children we have been given. Our goal is for increased recognition that by beginning remediation early, utilizing research-based practices, remediation tends to be more successful. This is because when we respond promptly to potential risk factors and related learning concerns for students, as opposed to waiting until they become problematic, we can be very successful in preventing many forms and levels of disabilities, particularly high-incidence disabilities.

The general public tends to make a distinction between prevention and education. This is most clearly evident when a particular problem comes to light, such as school violence or high school graduates who are unable to read. In these cases schools are charged with inadequate control or maintenance of the problem and community leaders are charged with addressing the societal conditions that are assumed to be causing the problem (e.g., absentee parents, increased violence in the media, poverty). Although, at both levels, school and community, the identified concerns and accompanying calls for action may be appropriate, these assumptions underestimate the power of teachers to lessen and prevent difficulties in learning and behavior.

Our belief and that of others is that effective education (including special education) prevents problems and that a prevention perspective provides educators a more comprehensive template for early intervention (Kauffman, 2005a, 2005b; Simeonsson, 1991; Walker, Ramsey, & Gresham, 2004). This has been increasingly evident over the past 25 years as the breadth of federal mandates in special and early childhood have expanded from initially serving ages 6–17 to birth–21 years of age. By using an established system of prevention, targeted to specific groups and specific levels of intervention (Caplan & Grunebaum, 1967; Walker et al., 2004) educators can become a critical part of effective prevention at all levels. There is a great deal of evidence to suggest that the role of education for students with high-incidence disabilities is actually **primary, secondary,** and **tertiary** prevention. The remainder of this chapter is dedicated to defining and exploring these three levels of prevention for students with high-incidence disabilities. We highlight the disorders of emotional and behavioral disorders (EBD), learning disorders (LD), and mild mental retardation (MMR) under the separate prevention headings, but you should remember that many of the same risk factors and prevention strategies are relevant for individuals identified with a variety of high-incidence disabilities.

:: DEFINING PREVENTION

The term *prevention* resonates in unique ways across different disciplines. Everybody seems to like the idea, although it is very hard to get people to put it into practice (Kauffman, 1999, 2003, 2004, 2005b). Most people think preventing disabilities involves medical research on causation (e.g., the human genome project, efforts to stop pregnant mothers from smoking, or ensuring that children are not physically abused or malnourished). However, schools might be also considered a source of prevention because children who stay in school are less likely to get in trouble with the law, are more like to learn to read, and are more likely to be successful adults.

But what about students who already exhibit **risk factors** (e.g., inherited learning difficulties, undesirable home environments)? What about students with identified disabilities (e.g., MMR, EBD, LD)? Aren't we past prevention in these cases? When children are young (0–5 years old) our efforts are typically called **early intervention;** what, then, is the goal for the rest? Only remediation? In this chapter we argue that reducing risk at any time is a part of prevention, and that schools can significantly contribute to reducing the effects of present and potential risk factors.

According to the American Heritage dictionary, the definition of prevention is to "avoid or thwart." Educational prevention involves highly trained professionals assessing and actively engaging in activities that effectively reduce the number of, or lessen the effects of, disabilities. That is, educational prevention avoids or thwarts risk at some level. Teachers are the professionals who need to be trained to identify and intervene at all three levels of prevention—primary, secondary, and tertiary—as part of a multidisciplinary team. The idea of three levels of prevention is not new. Actually, as far back as the middle of the 19th century, psychiatrists were begging those in control of institutions to focus on new cases or to allow what we now call secondary prevention (Stribling, 1842; see Caplan & Grunebaum, 1967 for a more recent model of preventative psychiatry). We have known for a long time that prevention at all levels is important. Putting what we know into practice—well, that is a different matter and very difficult to achieve (Kauffman, 1999; Kauffman & Landrum, 2006; Tankersley, Landrum, & Cook, 2004).

Primary prevention reduces the occurrence of new cases of the identified problem within the general population (Horner, Sugai, Todd, & Lewis-Palmer, 2004). Primary intervention (sometimes also called universal intervention) is what most people think of as prevention: programs of free prenatal care for mothers, drug prevention programs, subsidized housing, immunization programs, and public awareness announcements about the importance of reading to children, to name a few. These programs are designed to promote the overall health of the community and therefore reduce exposure to potential risk factors for disabling conditions. Schools are also considered an essential part of primary prevention. Schools provide free and reduced lunch to ensure that students are not suffering from nourishment-related learning delays, assist in providing health screening for vision, hearing, immunization, or other potential health-related learning and behavioral risks (e.g., mandatory child abuse reporting). Although primary prevention can seem very global in nature, it also can be targeted to a specific group identified as at-risk or as particularly vulnerable, such as students with behavior or learning problems (Simeonsson, 1991). However, by definition primary prevention is never directed at a particular individual (Kauffman, 1999, 2005b).

Secondary prevention is designed to address conditions that have emerged but can be ameliorated. It is designed to restore health or remediate learning if possible, thereby eliminating or minimizing the effects of the risk factors. Secondary prevention capitalizes on **resiliency** (protective factors the individual has against risk status) through programs designed to remove or reduce the effects of existing conditions that put the individual at risk for even more serious problems. Remedial instructional programs and generic behavioral programs are examples of secondary prevention in schools.

Tertiary prevention is designed to lessen the adverse consequences or complications of existing conditions. For example, tertiary prevention may be intended to limit the complications of a mental illness, lessening the likelihood that an individual will need to be institutionalized. Programs designed to help adults cope better with their learning disabilities or to be able to perform in spite of their mental retardation so that they do not lose their jobs, and programs designed to reduce the repeat offending (i.e., **recidivism**) of juvenile delinquents are other examples of tertiary prevention.

By employing a preventive approach to the education of students with high-incidence disabilities we can better address some of the issues that tend to complicate and frustrate educators in their efforts to educate and support these students. By addressing learning and behavioral problems at all three levels, we are better able to collaborate with other disciplines like social work, counseling, and medicine. This **multidisciplinary** approach has been stipulated by federal law to comprehensively address the needs of students at risk for or identified with disabilities.

Here, in a nutshell, is what each level of prevention is designed to do, whatever the problem may be:

1. **Primary**—keep the problem from occurring at all.
2. **Secondary**—correct the problem.
3. **Tertiary**—keep the problem from getting out of control.

All three levels of prevention are important in our judgment, and most people say they agree. In practice, we see public policy putting a lot of emphasis on level 3, a little on level 2, and virtually none on level 1. Kauffman (1999, 2005b) has suggested that there exists varied reasons for this, yet despite acknowledging why, getting people to change the focus to primary prevention is not easy. Primary prevention requires long-term, sustained effort. It is not something that can be achieved easily or quickly (Eddy, Reid, & Curry, 2002; Kauffman, 2003). Keep in mind, as you read further that the boundaries between the three levels are not always distinct. That is, sometimes what we do may be on the borderline between primary and secondary prevention, or it may be hard to categorize what we do as secondary or tertiary prevention because it seems to be a little of both. In addition, the effects of different levels of prevention may be less distinct given various levels of challenges that each may successfully address.

Primary and Secondary Conditions

As you may remember from our discussion in Chapter 3, there is no *single* cause for any high-incidence disability. We discussed the fact that many high-incidence disabilities are not the result of one biological or environmental cause, but result from interaction among multiple factors. At-risk status for learning or academic disability often places an individual at risk for multiple other potential disabling conditions. These *secondary disabilities* or *secondary conditions* are by definition those related to a primary disability and can not occur in the absence of a *primary condition;* (Institute of Medicine, 1991; Pope, 1992). According to the Institute of Medicine, these secondary conditions are highly preventable by addressing the primary condition. This is because secondary conditions do not have to have a biological cause but occur due to a functional limitation or other environmental or social risk factors. Recall the analogy made in Chapter 3 regarding the potential impact of a five-step fall on several different people with varying levels of fitness and youth. If a senior citizen who has not been exercising regularly and watching his or her diet falls down five steps, he or she will tend to have a greater likelihood of sustaining an injury, perhaps a broken ankle. Due to poor overall strength at the time of the fall, his or her recovery time from such an injury may be twice as long as will be the case for an athlete. A broken ankle then may restrict the elderly person's mobility for several weeks, creating poor circulation problems in the person's legs and a subsequent blood clot. The blood clot, which has severe health risks, becomes a secondary condition.

Common primary prevention for senior citizens is to watch their diet and get regular physical activity (among other potential measures) to reduce the likelihood that secondary conditions occur. People with diabetes are also constantly engaged in primary prevention of potential secondary conditions (e.g., heart problems, amputation) by managing their primary condition, diabetes. Similarly, with individuals with MMR or LD effective intervention for these learning problems must include appropriate adaptive behavior and social skills instruction to prevent potential secondary conditions such as EBD. By definition, students with EBD are not experiencing deficits in their *ability* to learn given academic material, but consistently experience high rates of academic failure. For this reason, individualized education plans for these students cannot solely focus on social instruction. For these students prevention includes an emphasis on effective instructional practices to deter the development of learning difficulties and subsequent behavior challenges stemming from academic failure. Prevention efforts must be developed and sustained to recognize not only primary but potential secondary conditions.

Prevention of Secondary Conditions

Several types of risk factors have been identified as relevant to the promotion of secondary conditions (Institute of Medicine, 1991). Although these same categories can be used for primary disabilities, in this section we focus on their relevance to secondary conditions. Biological factors are one potential source for the occurrence of secondary conditions. For example, individuals with Down syndrome experience a high correlation with some degree of mental retardation. This retardation is consistent with the genetic and biological composition of the identified syndrome. However, the degree of mental retardation is also often correlated with environmental risk factors.

Environmental risk factors can be sufficient to promote a primary disability as well as a secondary condition. Environmental risk factors typically associated with secondary conditions can be divided into physical and social-environmental (Pope, 1992). The physical environment refers to those settings in which an individual is expected to function. Therefore, the degree to which the individual is provided adequate shelter, nutrition, as well as stimulation and opportunities to learn determines risk. As highlighted in Chapter 3 a lack of the basic physical needs can affect the degree to which an individual functions. For educational settings this translates into schools and classrooms that have enough appropriate learning materials, sufficient stimulation through effective instruction, hands on learning, and positive interaction with adults and peers (Conroy et al., 2002).

Socio-environmental risk factors are linked to the expectations and opportunities provided by the environment. In the community we recognize disparities in these opportunities when we drive through different neighborhoods, assess different community recreation centers (or the lack of them), and notice varying levels of crime. Schools embody these expectations through schoolwide codes of conduct (Horner et al., 2004) and instructional expectations (Conroy et al., 2002; Cullinen, 2002). Many of these behavioral and classroom management expectations will be further explored in the subsequent sections on PBS and functional behavioral assessment (FBA) prevention models. By expecting that all students will learn to read (Kame'enui, 2002), recognizing that all students benefit from targeted direct instruction, and that a primary disability of LD, MMR, or EBD does not preclude measurable gains in traditional and functional academics, educators can make a marked impact on the prevention of socio-environmental risk factors for secondary conditions for students with high-incidence disabilities. It is also important to note that this type of prevention is necessary throughout a student's educational career.

Research on the ability of individuals with disabilities to engage in self-determination has increased in the last few decades, particularly for those with some form of mental retardation (Gaudet, Pulos, Crethar, & Burger, 2002; Wehmeyer & Palmer, 2003). This emphasis stems from a growing understanding that lifestyles and behavioral factors constitute a unique set of risk factors for secondary conditions. Targeted instruction and tools must be provided for individuals with behavioral and learning problems to develop an understanding of the immediate and long-term effects of their choices. These systematic efforts can help prevent numerous secondary conditions due to drug use, negative peer relations, learned helplessness, and lack of engagement in vocational (work skills) and academic instruction. It is frequently assumed that individuals with MMR will not be able to master skills when they can. For people with LD, some academic subjects will always be hard and undesirable. For those with EBD, deviant behavior is to be expected. However, as discussed in Chapter 2, when we use the term *disability* in conjunction with these people it is meant to highlight areas in which they need instruction, not to establish what they cannot do.

Prevention of EBD

As we pointed out in Chapter 1, most individuals with emotional or behavioral disorders (EBD) get treatment, only after years of delay. Kauffman (1999, 2005a, 2005b) has discussed some of the reasons for this, but others have noted the consequences of failure to take preventive action. For example, Wang et al. (2005) stated:

> Long periods of untreated illness may also be harmful to those with less severe disorders. Preclinical studies suggest that neural "kindling" can cause untreated psychiatric disorders to become more frequent, severe, spontaneous, and treatment refractory. In addition, epidemiological studies suggest that school failure, teenage child-bearing, unstable employment, early marriage, marital violence, and marital instability are associated with early-onset untreated mental disorders... Furthermore, most people with one disorder progress to develop comorbid disorders and such comorbidity is associated with an even more persistent and severe clinical course. (pp. 610–611)

Thus, prevention of EBD presents particular challenges. True, not all studies show that failure or delay in providing special education, mental health services, or other interventions is detrimental in the long run. Nevertheless, if we are to be serious about prevention we must address signs of difficulty as soon as they are detectable.

To prevent EBD we must address risk factors associated with misbehavior. In Chapter 3 we discussed risk factors and resiliency. Risk factors are conditions or precursor behaviors (early stages of misbehavior that have been linked with the development of EBD). **Resiliency** is the degree to which an individual or a system can withstand or resist and not succumb to those risk factors. Resiliency factors are those that buffer an individual against risk.

Risk is not an all-or-nothing proposition. There are different levels of risk—minimum, high, and imminent (Bauer & Shea, 1999). Everyone is at risk for everything at some level. Being at risk means that an individual's risk for a particular outcome is elevated significantly. **Minimal risk** refers to the chance that most children

FIGURE 12.1   The path to long-term negative outcomes for at-risk children and youth

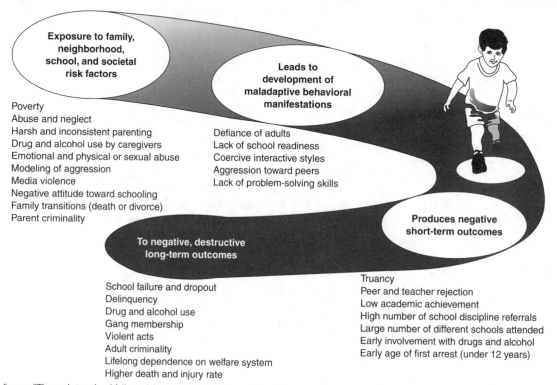

Source: "The path to school failure, delinquency and violence: Causal factors and some potential solutions," by H. M. Walker and J. R. Sprague, *35*, p. 68, in *Intervention in School and Clinic,* 1999, PRO-ED, Inc. Reprinted with permission.

have of developing EBD. These children typically have stable home and community environments, stable temperaments, and are recipients of active and effective parenting. **High risk** refers to children experiencing one or more risk factors including skill deficits, negative social interactions, or numerous environmental stressors (e.g., poverty, inadequate adult supervision), or a combination of these factors. **Imminent risk** typically designates children experiencing several risk factors simultaneously and to a significant degree, such as poverty, absent or abusive parents, difficult temperaments, and academic and behavioral skill deficits. Figure 12.1 depicts risk factors leading to EBD. The more risk factors a child experiences, the more likely he or she is to follow the path to negative, destructive, long-term outcomes.

Primary prevention addresses all three groups—those at minimum, high, and imminent risk—simultaneously. Primary prevention is designed to keep disabilities from emerging (after EBD is apparent, primary prevention is a moot point; primary prevention can't occur for that child). However, primary prevention is put into place for all children, even those who need more, because primary prevention helps reduce the overall impact of the primary disability and helps prevent a secondary condition. The effectiveness of primary prevention is not measured by the response of

FIGURE 12.2   Path to success at school

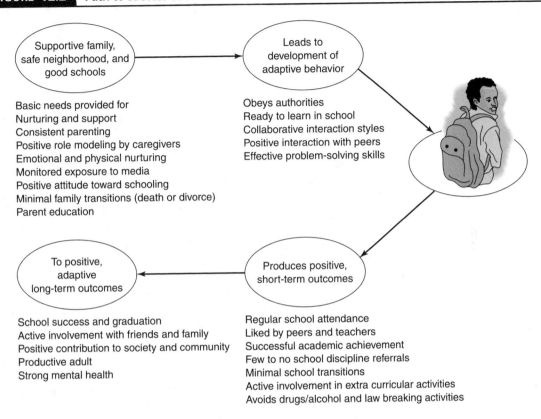

an individual but by overall reduction in the **incidence** (number of identified cases) of EBD in the general population or in a targeted at-risk group (e.g., inner-city children living in poverty) (Cullinan, 2002; Kauffman, 1999, 2005b). Primary prevention is designed to keep new cases from emerging. It helps prevent children from developing negative long-term outcomes (see Figure 12.1).

We want to do all we can to help children stay on the pathway depicted in Figure 12.2, which depicts the resiliency factors that may help counteract the risk factors depicted in Figure 12.1. Some of these resiliency factors are things we cannot change directly as educators but must work toward with other professionals and other agencies (e.g., include poverty, family problems, and community variables). Educators can and must change what happens in school. They must do everything they can to help children develop the skills they need to be successful academically and behaviorally at school. This is part of prevention.

Keep in mind, too, that the development of disabilities is not usually sudden. The onset of disabilities is typically insidious—subtle, gradual, and hard to detect at first. It is usually much more like a car starting to go off the road than like a train derailing. A car going into a ditch and a train derailing have dire consequences, but getting a car back on the road is much easier than putting a train back on the track once it has jumped off. Primary prevention, by analogy, is like catching children who are driving over the line that marks the edge of the road. Once they're on the shoulder, we need secondary prevention. For those in the ditch, we need tertiary prevention.

In education, primary prevention can be applied at many levels, including the school district, a school, or a particular classroom. In EBD, primary prevention has focused primarily on the prevention of behavioral and social problems exhibited by preschool and primary school-aged children. The preschool-primary emphasis is based on the strong link between the early onset of antisocial and violent behavior and chronic EBD (Walker et al., 2004). Given the rise of disruptive and defiant behavior as well as antisocial behavior in schools (Horner et al., 2004) the implications for students at risk are significant. Most children with EBD are at risk not only for emotional and behavioral difficulties but also for academic failure (Kauffman, 2005a, 2005b; Skiba, 2002).

Schools are also the *single* source of mental health support for many students needing such services (i.e., students with attention deficit hyperactivity disorder [ADHD], conduct disorders, and other types of EBD) (Hoagwood, 2001). This emphasizes that schools, classrooms, and educational personnel must be active in prevention efforts. Evidence-based practices in mental health services indicate the need for integrated efforts when addressing the **psychosocial** (emotional and behavioral) needs of students with EBD (Hoagwood, 2001). Evidence also indicates that school-based prevention targeting school, classroom, home, and peer environments reduces the risks of conduct problems (Blueprint for Change, 2001; Rones & Hoagwood, 2000). Comprehensive school-based prevention models are just emerging and this limits our ability to present any one model that has met established criteria of evidenced-based practices. Proposed models have demonstrated promise and are constructed from elements that have demonstrated their effectiveness (see Eddy et al., 2002; Walker et al., 2004). For this reason we feel it is important to describe the components of some of these models as tools for educators when assessing their own prevention efforts.

Positive Behavior Support (PBS)

Schoolwide positive behavior support is an example of a three-tiered model of prevention designed to address antisocial and aggressive behavior at all three levels to prevent, reduce, and lessen the negative impact of behavior problems (Horner et al., 2004). In this model, primary prevention is designed to provide all children in a school or school district a good base of positive behavior management. Researchers in this have identified six systems variables and five practices that are necessary to effectively implement primary prevention (Colvin, Sugai, & Kame'enui, 1994; Sugai & Horner, 2002). The systems variables include: (a) team-based implementation; (b) administrative leadership; (c) documented commitment; (d) adequate personnel and time; (e) budget; and (f) an information system (Horner et al., 2004). This system is predicated on the belief that schools, teachers, and students cannot effectively engage in practices that consistently and over time demonstrate success without systems-level support.

BOX 12.1 EXAMPLE OF SCHOOLWIDE PBS GUIDING PRINCIPLES: PINNACLE PRIDE

Pinnacle Elementary is a community where all members learn, grow, and become good citizens. Using the Pinnacle Pride Expectations everyday and everywhere helps everyone achieve this goal!

Be Kind
Be Safe
Be Responsible
Be Respectful
Be Peaceful
Be Cooperative

Pinnacle Pride Guiding Principles. Pinnacle Pride is designed to create a climate of cooperation, academic excellence, respect, and safety at Pinnacle Elementary. Pinnacle Pride is based on seven guiding principles. We believe that these principles will help create an optimal learning environment for the students, staff, and families at Pinnacle Elementary. The guiding principles are:

1. Clear expectations for student behavior
2. Clear and consistent strategies for teaching appropriate behavior
3. Clear and consistent strategies for encouraging appropriate behavior
4. Clear and consistent consequences that discourage inappropriate behavior
5. A support system and individual behavior programs for students with unique or exceptional needs
6. Clearly designed methods for evaluating and revising the Pinnacle Pride program
7. The characteristics and philosophy of the Pinnacle Pride program will be communicated to students and parents

---

The identified practices for primary prevention within this school-based model include (see Box 12.1 for example):

1. *Defining Behavioral Expectations:* These constitute five or six positively defined behavior expectations that reflect the social value of the school and serve as the framework for the behavior curriculum (not disciplinary policy) of the school.
2. *Teaching Behavioral Expectations:* The school-wide behavioral expectations are repeatedly taught to students in multiple settings through linkage to specific behaviors and reinforcement for appropriate use.
3. *Monitoring and Encouraging Performance of Expected Behaviors:* A plan is created to ensure that classrooms and school settings are constantly reminding students of the values of appropriate behavior through systems of reinforcement (i.e., social, tangible, positive reinforcers are given for meeting expectations).

4. *Preventing and Discouraging Problem Behavior:* A planned approach and description of minor and major problem behavior is defined and consequences are consistently applied. Students and teachers are well informed of the planned consequences for varying levels of problem behavior.

5. *Collecting and Using Data for Decision Making:* Records are kept to indicate how well the plan is working and what might need to be changed (Horner et al., 2004).

We need more data on the success of school-wide positive behavioral support in schools across the country. This model is still in its early stages of development and can be derailed by anti-scientific interpretations of it or by misrepresentations (see Mulick & Butter, 2005). The ability to sustain the model over a long period of time and the ability to replicate this model across the nation are still unknown. We have highlighted positive behavioral support because it demonstrates a growing school-based model for a continuum of prevention. It is important to recognize that this model has not been demonstrated to be universally applicable at the primary level within classrooms and other related school settings. Ongoing research is working to define the applicability of the PBS model for those settings as well as effective levels of secondary prevention within the schoolwide continuum (Horner et al., 2004).

Currently, specifically for students with EBD, secondary levels of prevention have focused on small group social skills interventions and peer coaching for teachers to identify and fine-tune instructional approaches that have proven to be effective for targeted groups of students demonstrating at-risk behavior (Walker & Shinn, 2002; Walker et al., 1996). At the tertiary level, the PBS model includes a large variety of proven practices for individual support of students. This list, which is not exhaustive, can include individual counseling or therapy, direct skill instruction on social skills, and effective behavior strategies including **self-management** strategies (a student learns to monitor and adjust his or her own behavior as the context requires) (Crone, Horner, & Hawken, 2004; Hawken & Horner, 2003). In addition, because many of the core principles of PBS are based on the science of applied behavior analysis (ABA) (Horner et al., 2004), tertiary interventions often rely heavily on the process of functional behavioral assessment (FBA) to identify and develop appropriate function-based (what does the behavior get for the individual) interventions (O'Neill et al., 1997). The process of FBA is more clearly outlined in the following section.

Functional Behavioral Assessment (FBA)

The functional behavioral assessment (FBA) model of prevention presented by Conroy and her colleagues also employs the three-tiered model of primary, secondary, and tertiary prevention for managing the behavior of young children (Conroy, Davis, Fox, & Brown, 2002). However, FBA may be applied regardless of the student's age (O'Neill et al., 1997). FBA is a way of assessing the "function" or purpose of behavior to help teachers and others find better—more effective and less punitive—ways of helping students at risk of or having EBD learn socially acceptable behavior (for further explanation, see Box 12.2).

The FBA model of prevention is based on extensive research in the area of functional behavior assessment and early intervention (Conroy, Brown & Davis, 2001; Chandler, Dahlquist, Repp, & Feltz, 1999; Schill, Kratochwill, & Elliott, 1998).

BOX 12.2 FUNCTIONAL ASSESSMENT

A functional assessment:

- Clearly describes the challenging behaviors, including behaviors that occur together
- Identifies the events, times, and situations that predict when the challenging behaviors *will* and *will not* occur across the range of daily routines
- Identifies the consequences that maintain the challenging behaviors (what the person "gets out" of the behaviors) (e.g., attention, escape, preferred items)
- Develops one or more summary statements or hypotheses that describe specific behaviors, specific types of situations in which they occur, and the reinforcers that maintain the behaviors in that situation
- Collects direct observational data that support these summary statements

A functional assessment can be done in many ways and at different precision levels depending on the behavior severity. A person who has observed undesirable behavior in different situations and concluded that "she does that because. . ." or "he does that in order to. . ." has also developed a summary statement about things that influence behavior.

A complete assessment allows confident prediction of the conditions under which the challenging behavior is likely to occur or not occur and when there is agreement about the consequences that perpetuate the challenging behavior.

Functional assessment methods fall into three general strategies:

Information gathering (interviews and rating scales). This method involves talking to the individual and to those who know the individual best. It also consists of formal interviews, questionnaires, and rating scales to identify which events in an environment are linked to the specific problem behavior. Questions to answer include: What challenging behaviors cause concern? What events or physical conditions occur before the behavior that increase the behavior's predictability? What result appears to motivate or maintain the challenging behavior? What appropriate behaviors could produce the same result? What can be learned from previous behavioral support efforts about strategies that are ineffective, partially effective, or effective for only a short time?

Direct observation. Teachers, direct support staff, and/or family members who already work or live with the person observe the person having challenging behaviors in natural conditions over an extended period. The observations must not interfere with normal daily environments. In most cases, observers record when a problem behavior occurs, what happened just before the behavior, what happened after, and their perception as to

(Continued)

the function of the behavior. When an observer collects 10–15 instances of the behavior, he or she might discover where a pattern exists.

Functional analysis manipulations. Taking the assessment one step further is the functional analysis. In this process, a behavior analyst systematically changes potential controlling factors (consequences, structural variables, e.g., task difficulty or length) to observe effects on a person's behavior. These determinations involve creating situations that will reduce, eliminate, or provoke the challenging behavior to test whether the hypothesis is correct. Functional analysis—expensive in time and energy—may be the only way, in some cases, to ensure an adequate assessment. It is the only approach that clearly demonstrates relations between environmental events and challenging behaviors. To support the functional assessment, also consider measuring activity patterns (the variety and degree of community integration and relationships).

The objective of functional assessment is not just to define and eliminate undesirable behavior but also to understand the structure and function of behavior to teach and promote effective alternatives.

Functional assessment is a process for looking at relationships between behavior and the environment. It is not simply a review of the person with challenging behaviors.

Adapted from the following fact sheet developed by the Beach Center on Families and Disability for the Research and Training Center on PBS, funded by the National Institute on Disability and Rehabilitation Research of the U.S. Department of Education, www.pbis.org, accessed September 29, 2006. Adapted with permission from R. E. O'Neil, R. H. Horner, R. W. Albin, J. R. Sprague, K. Storey, & J. S. Newton (1997). *Functional assessment and program development for problem behavior, a practical handbook* (2nd ed.) Pacific Grove, CA: Brooks/Cole. Reprinted with permission from Wadsworth, a division of Thomson Learning, www.thomsonrights.com.

This model focuses primarily on the classroom and more clearly defines a process for all three levels of prevention within that environment. The suggested areas of emphasis within this model are presented here to highlight how important teachers and good classroom management are to prevention efforts at all levels.

In the FBA prevention model, Level 1 is considered primary intervention and focuses on the physical and instructional environment of the classroom for all students. Changes in the classroom environment include all children regardless of their identified risk status. As was highlighted in Chapter 3, environments that are not supportive or healthy and include multiple stressors for children can contribute to causing EBD. As Kauffman and colleagues suggest, the first thing a teacher who is having behavior management problems should consider is instruction (Kauffman, Mostert, Trent, & Pullen, 2006). Stressors and unhealthy environments for students in the classroom can include poor organization as well as ineffective instructional techniques and conditions likely to produce misbehavior, such as refusal of the teacher to accommodate legitimate individuality, inappropriate teacher expectations, inconsistency in responding to behavior, and so on (Kauffman, 2005a). Key areas identified in FBA include:

- Physical classroom arrangement
  - *Arrangement of classroom space:* Is there enough space for required activities; does it promote traffic flow and smooth transitions?

- **Materials:** Are the number, type, and ease with which students can independently access them age- and activity-appropriate?
- **Classroom schedule:** Are low- and high-intensity activities rotated; is there a schedule posted and reviewed?
- **Staffing patterns:** Is there adequate student to staff ratio and are adults actively aware of the behavior of all students across the room?

- Instructional classroom environmental assessment
  - **Instruction of behavioral expectations:** How are behavioral expectations provided, how often, and are they effective? Assess whether students truly understand and have skills to perform expectations
  - **Consistent, specific, and immediate feedback:** Are students provided information concerning their performance regularly and immediately?
  - **Instructional level:** Are the instructional activities appropriate for the skill level of the students?
  - **Praise:** Is there a high density of positive to negative statements presented to the students?
  - **Instructional strategies:** Are best practice guidelines used in providing instruction (e.g., modeling to practice to independent)? (Conroy et al., 2002)

Level 2 (secondary prevention) focuses on assessment and intervention for high-risk behaviors. The emphasis here is on students and behaviors that were unresponsive to level one (primary) prevention and may require more targeted intervention to restore and develop skills (secondary prevention). At the secondary level, more targeted assessment is done for those students who continue to demonstrate unacceptable or high-risk behavior. The emphasis on students at risk for behavioral problems is a targeted assessment of social, communicative, and behavioral abilities. Although Conroy et al. do not specifically mention it, we would also include targeted academic assessment (Sutherland & Wehby, 2001; Wehby, Symons, Canale, & Go, 1998). Global questions that can be asked or should be incorporated in an assessment of these domains are:

- How does the child communicate with peers and adults to indicate a need or preference?
- Does the child have the necessary social-communicative skills to successfully interact with peers or adults in multiple situations?
- Does the student have the social and communicative skills to resolve conflict with peers in the classroom, or in less structured social settings? (Conroy et al., 2002).

By answering questions like these, specific interventions can be designed that address particular target areas of need for one or more students. Students cannot benefit from the best-designed learning environment or classroom management if they do not possess the skills to effectively interact within those systems.

Level 3 is tertiary prevention, in which individualized interventions are designed to teach alternative behaviors and new skills. The FBA prevention model suggests employing the components of a functional assessment at this point for students who have not responded to level 1 and level 2. Such an assessment strategy further identifies behavioral and academic strengths and needs in various contexts. At this stage for students who have been more formally identified as having EBD, the behavior problems are chronic. The goal at this level is to diminish the direct and indirect effects of these problems on the daily functioning and future opportunities of the student (Kauffman, 1999, 2005b; Short & Brokaw, 1994). In addition, through the process of FBA, the multidisciplinary team of parents and educators work through a process to assess and identify the communicative **function** (what the student gains from the behavior—its purpose) of the problem behavior. Such purposes are typically an attempt to escape (the student yells swear words at the teacher in order to be sent to the office, thereby avoiding the math test) or to acquire something (the student speaks quietly and avoids eye contact so that the teacher will approach and spend more one-on-one time with the student as he or she attempts to compete a writing task). A process of assessment is conducted (see Box 12.2) to identify the **setting events** (what current or previous settings had an effect on the behavior), the **antecedent** (what happened right before the behavior) and the **consequences** (what reinforces the behavior to keep occurring—such as desired attention, or escape from tasks).

Once the purpose of the behavior is determined, the team can assess whether the reason for the inappropriate manner in which the child is communicating a want or need is due to a **skill deficit** or a **performance deficit.** A skill deficit means that the child has not learned the appropriate skill or cues for a skill to be used. For example, the child does not know how to interrupt others appropriately when he or she has a need. A performance deficit means that although the child has the skill, he or she cannot execute it correctly and consistently under the right circumstances. For example, the child may be able to explain to you what to do when he or she has a question or need (i.e., I raise my hand and wait to be called on), but instead he or she regularly executes it incorrectly (i.e., the child blurts out) or inconsistently. Once the purpose of the behavior (function), the nature of the behavior (skill or performance deficit) and the context (settings, antecedents, and consequences) of the behavior are identified, the team is better able to individualize a plan suited to remediate (teach) the use of a new behavior in the appropriate context. The teacher provides attention for appropriate behavior as opposed to inappropriate behavior to achieve the desired effect. This reinforces the new skill and its use (performance) for future generalization to other environments and situations that the student finds undesirable and challenging. This in turn then reduces the risk of failure or negative consequence (loses a job due to poor social skills) in future environments.

Box 12. 3 provides a summary of FBA data and subsequent plan components at the tertiary level for one student, Jill, with EBD who was referred for tertiary level support due to ongoing problems with getting started on her work and high rates of complaining regarding her inability to complete the work correctly. Jill's plans consisted of varying levels of support, including a self-management system (contract) debriefing with a counselor on Monday mornings, self-help skills to assist her with time management in the morning as well as specific skills to gain teacher attention appropriately.

Prevention of LD

As with EBD, prevention efforts for LD are strongly linked to the context in which the academic performance is expected. As we mentioned earlier, although we have divided this chapter into sections for particular disabilities, the risk factors and

Part of the functional behavioral assessment process is to make direct observation of the context of the behavior of interest, including what occurred before and after the behavior. (Photo credit: Patrick White/Merrill)

prevention efforts described are not mutually exclusive. However, the main concern in LD is academic problems, although social or behavioral problems often accompany LD and must be addressed. Here we concentrate on the academic problems of LD. In this section, our emphasis is on prevention related to instruction.

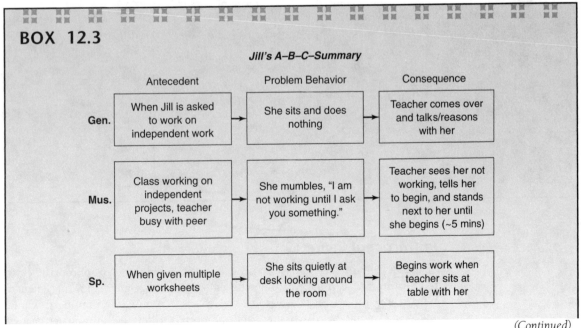

BOX 12.3

Jill's A–B–C–Summary

	Antecedent	Problem Behavior	Consequence
Gen.	When Jill is asked to work on independent work	She sits and does nothing	Teacher comes over and talks/reasons with her
Mus.	Class working on independent projects, teacher busy with peer	She mumbles, "I am not working until I ask you something."	Teacher sees her not working, tells her to begin, and stands next to her until she begins (~5 mins)
Sp.	When given multiple worksheets	She sits quietly at desk looking around the room	Begins work when teacher sits at table with her

(Continued)

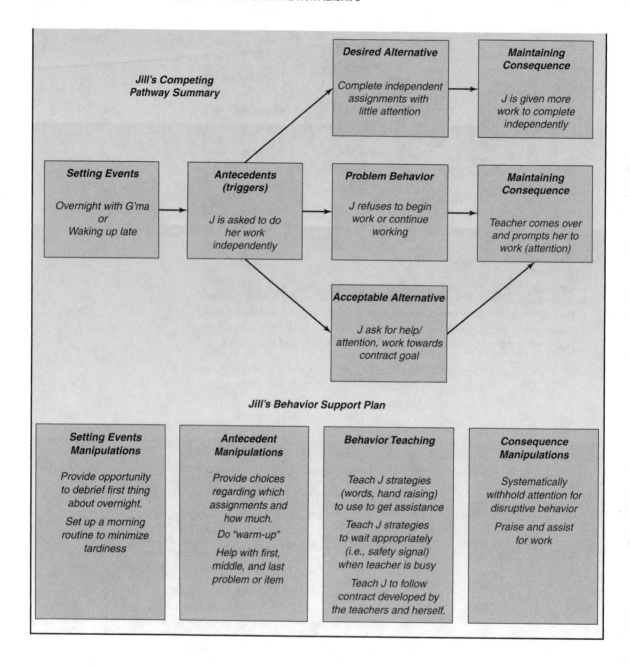

Jill's Competing Pathway Summary

Desired Alternative

Complete independent assignments with little attention

Maintaining Consequence

J is given more work to complete independently

Setting Events

Overnight with G'ma or Waking up late

Antecedents (triggers)

J is asked to do her work independently

Problem Behavior

J refuses to begin work or continue working

Maintaining Consequence

Teacher comes over and prompts her to work (attention)

Acceptable Alternative

J ask for help/attention, work towards contract goal

Jill's Behavior Support Plan

Setting Events Manipulations

Provide opportunity to debrief first thing about overnight.

Set up a morning routine to minimize tardiness

Antecedent Manipulations

Provide choices regarding which assignments and how much.

Do "warm-up"

Help with first, middle, and last problem or item

Behavior Teaching

Teach J strategies (words, hand raising) to use to get assistance

Teach J strategies to wait appropriately (i.e., safety signal) when teacher is busy

Teach J to follow contract developed by the teachers and herself.

Consequence Manipulations

Systematically withhold attention for disruptive behavior

Praise and assist for work

Instructional Context

The context of instruction has been widely discussed in terms of appropriate class-room setup, rich learning environments, and appropriate classroom management to support engaged and active learning. An effective context for learning promotes engaged exploration, discussion, and supports the learner in connecting new information with background knowledge. The composition of an effective learning context has been researched for decades (Brophy & Evertson, 1976; Stichter, Lewis, Johnson, & Trussell, 2004), most often in the context of behavioral or early childhood development. Nevertheless, the large body of research in this area demonstrates that key classroom setting variables are consistently linked with effective learning.

The importance of learning environments for all ages was once again emphasized in a recent review by the Committee on Integrating the Science of Early Childhood Development (2002). This committee constituted a collaborative effort by the Board on Children, Youth and Family, National Research Council (2001), and Institute of Medicine (1991). Among their many findings, this group reported that the *quality* of childcare, constituting the environment, interactions, and instruction of care providers, carries the most significant weight regarding the influence of child care on children's development (Committee on Integrating the Science of Early Childhood Development, 2000). This influence on development extends from social and emotional to cognitive and linguistic development with direct correlations to short- and longer-term outcomes in the areas of academic achievement as well as delinquency (Shonkoff & Meisels, 2000).

Research in elementary and secondary classrooms has shown similar correlations between instructional contexts and academic achievement. Frequently these variables are referred to as curricular variables and include the instructional nature of activities and how tasks are assigned, as well as environmental considerations such as the layout of the room and access to materials (Kern & Dunlap, 1998). Such variables are pivotal for context-based prevention efforts because the research strongly indicates that adjustment in these variables can not only alter academic behaviors but also predict increased positive outcomes for the learner. The following identifies a sampling of frequently cited classroom-based context variables.

- General Environmental—Instructional Variables
  - Effective classroom set-up to reduce noise, increase structure, and ensure that key educational and instructional information is easily visible and accessible
  - Clarity and consistency of classroom procedures
  - Clarity and consistency of classroom expectations
  - Appropriate student-teacher ratios

The manner in which instruction is presented is also critical. Educators have long recognized that there seems to be a very small subgroup of students who are able to learn despite poor instruction. Yet, a greater number, perhaps the majority of students, are deeply affected by a lack of effective instruction, particularly those presenting with various risk factors (Hallahan, Lloyd, Kauffman, Weiss, & Martinez, 2005). It is therefore essential that educators focus on the specific instructional activities that occur throughout the day and consider those very factors in creating their schedules and daily lesson plans (Jones & Jones, 2001). The following list reflects some of those important considerations.

- Specific Instructional Contexts
  - The degree to which large and small group instruction is alternated with independent work

- The degree to which one-on-one instruction as well as peer collaboration opportunities are available
- The amount and length of instructional transitions that occur between activities or academic subjects
- The degree to which materials are organized and ease of accessibility
- The degree to which instructional "downtime" is minimized
- The amount of time that the teacher circulates around the room

Specific features of instructional presentation are prevention activities both at the secondary and tertiary levels. These variables reflect specific teacher behaviors when providing instruction and are considered essential for ensuring that students understand the nature of the work and that academic learning time is increased (Good & Brophy, 1996). The following are key examples of these instructional variables.

- Task Presentation
  - Amount of instruction provided by the teacher
  - Provision of clear instructions
  - Degree of instructional examples/models/guidance provided by the teacher
  - The ability of students to model or paraphrase instructional steps
  - The degree to which the teacher ties background knowledge or references and students' previous experiences to new material
  - The degree to which the teacher previews each task
  - Amount of wait time the teacher provides to allow students to adequately respond
  - Degree and types of feedback and prompts provided to the students by the teacher
  - Effective use of assigned seatwork

Targeting Specific Academic Problems

Despite the unquestionable preventive value of good instruction, we are very aware that specific subject areas must also be the focus of prevention efforts at all three levels. These preventative interventions have been called for by many at the federal and local levels of education to reduce the incidence of students experiencing significant deficits in literacy, arithmetic, and other academic subjects (Finn, Rotherham, & Hokanson, 2001). Currently, numerous programs and strategies exist to provide preventative interventions across many academic and related areas of instruction (Vaughn, Gersten, & Chard, 2000). Key techniques have been highlighted in previous chapters. Here we articulate examples of initiatives and strategies in literacy at the primary, secondary, and tertiary levels.

Large-scale research has repeatedly emphasized the impact and longevity of reading disabilities for school age students as well as adults. According to the National Reading Panel Progress Report (2000) more than 17.5% of the nations' children (about 10 million) will encounter reading problems within the first three years of schooling. Despite our efforts to intervene with these students, 75% of students identified with reading difficulties in the third grade continue to be reading-disabled in the ninth grade (Finn et al., 2001; Francis et al., 1996). This body of research highlights that effective instruction and prevention intervention prior to grade three currently presents the most significant long-term impact for the acquisition of necessary literacy skills.

| TABLE 12.1 | Preventive interventions for reading disabilities |

- *Primary*
  - Early language and literacy experiences from infancy through childhood
  - District/schoolwide reading programs
    - Basal Reading — highly structured and sequential reading programs to teach reading to all children through variations of:
      - Phonics approach
      - Whole language approach
  - Title I Reading
  - Accelerated reader — computer reading program (Samuels, Lewis, Wu, Reininger, & Murphy, 2003)

- *Secondary*
  - Direct instruction techniques — systematic teaching of skills, error correction, guided oral reading, applied reading comprehension techniques
    - Reading mastery
    - Corrective reading
  - Reading recovery — emphasized phonics in meaningful contexts
  - Peer tutoring approaches
    - Classwide peer tutoring (CWPT)
    - Peer-assisted learning strategies (PALS)
  - Teaching early reading skills — emphasizing phonemic awareness, structural analysis, and word recognition

- *Tertiary*
  - Repeated reading
  - Reciprocal teaching — predicting, question generating, summarizing, clarifying
  - Direct instruction techniques (systematic teaching of skills, error correction, guided oral reading, applied reading comprehension techniques)
    - Reading mastery
    - Corrective reading
  - Mnemonic strategies (i.e., keyword method, acronyms)
  - Learning strategies
  - DRTA (Directed Reading Thinking Activity)
  - CSR (Collaborative Strategic Reading)
  - Story maps, semantic mapping — for reading comprehension
  - Activating prior knowledge
  - Edmark—computer program for sight-word practice

Research also indicates that preventative intervention for older students may best occur in more segregated settings supported by specialized instruction from specifically trained educators (Hallahan et al., 2005; Kauffman & Hallahan, 2005a, 2005b). Lyon and colleagues argue that up to 70% of students identified as poor readers receiving specialized services could be reduced by early intervention and prevention programs (Lyon et al., 2001). The table below represents a sample of research-based programs designed to prevent reading problems at the primary, secondary, and tertiary levels across all age levels. Even though we have placed each under certain levels of prevention, it should be noted that these again are not necessarily mutually exclusive categories of prevention. Many of these programs may be implemented as part of one or more levels of prevention activities.

Prevention of MMR

Separating this chapter on prevention of high-incidence disabilities by disability categories is difficult. As you have probably realized, different prevention efforts under EBD are applicable and appropriate for the prevention of LD as well. Similarly, this overlap exists with MMR. Prevention of behavior and learning problems are very relevant to students with MMR. In addition, these students have increased risk of developing secondary conditions affecting overall health, resulting in additional cognitive and physical delays (Pope, 1992). For this reason, our discussion of prevention in MMR takes a more in-depth focus on a comprehensive health program model, specifically as it applies to schools.

The American Association on Mental Retardation developed a model to match risk factors and prevention activities (AAMR, 2002). The model identifies four risk factor categories, *biomedical*, *social*, *behavioral*, and *educational*. For each of these categories primary, secondary, and tertiary prevention activities are identified as they pertain to newborns, children, teenagers, and adults.

The **biomedical category** includes many of the risk factors and preventive interventions discussed in Chapter 3, including screening for potential lead poisoning, nutritional problems, and metabolic disorders (e.g., screening for phynelketonuria [PKU], a metabolic disorder present at birth, and dietary control for prevention of MMR). Tertiary efforts are focused on specific physical and mental health services (e.g., physical therapy).

At the primary and secondary levels, prevention of **social risk** includes activities designed to prevent domestic violence and promote parent-child interaction. Specific activities designed to increase the independence and overall functioning of an identified individual encompass tertiary level activities for this risk category.

Activities in this model designed to reduce **behavioral risk** factors at the primary and secondary levels include promoting healthy behaviors (e.g., avoiding substance abuse, positive interactions with children, avoidance of accidents). Tertiary activities are designed to promote targeted behaviors (e.g., adaptive behavior skills) to maintain or increase physical and mental health.

Educational risk factors are targeted through primary prevention activities such as broad-scale efforts to teach social skills, parenting, and sexuality. Secondary activities include special education early intervention services, with more targeted services at the tertiary level. Activities designed to address all four of the risk categories in the model can and should be conducted across all contexts, particularly in schools.

Approximately one-third of the 1990 Health Objectives for the nation involved schools by targeting school-age children (Allensworth & Wolford, 1988). Since that time, increased efforts have been employed to use public school systems as an essential setting for prevention (Healthy People 2000). Recognizing the importance of a comprehensive program of prevention in which the failure of any single link in the program can negatively impact the outcome is not new (Rutstein, Berenberg, Chalmers, Childs, Fishman, & Perrin 1976, p. 583). Schools and educators are among these essential links. Yet research continues to indicate that education personnel and schools are frequently ill-equipped due to a lack of education and training to adequately and appropriately serve such a link. One area of considerable difficulty, due to a lack of training, is a comprehensive understanding of the potential **trajectory** (expected developmental path) of students with mental retardation, particularly those with milder versions. It is frequently assumed that mental retardation is a static disability for which a predictable path of development is expected. Once the high point or ceiling of this path has been reached, the primary focus shifts to preventing **regression** (loss of previously acquired gains) (Pope, 1992). Therefore, much of the education and treatment model has been designed around providing intervention until a plateau is hit, and then the emphasis shifts to maintenance of these skills. Such a model does not provide much room for proactive prevention efforts.

As mentioned previously, the model of prevention for other high-incidence disabilities will certainly be relevant for many concerns associated with MMR. Yet as was described in Chapter 3, it is essential to recognize the potential for **development retardation** (increasing delays brought on or enhanced by under-stimulating environmental factors) even for those already MMR or at risk for it. In other words it is important to consistently recognize the importance of the educational environment and instructional delivery and content for the prevention of school failure of students with MMR. Therefore, the role of educational settings is to ensure that an appropriate curriculum, level of supports, and instructional strategies are in place to enhance the individual's protective factors (their strengths) in an effort to prevent secondary conditions as well as enhance overall functioning within school, home, and community (Beirne-Smith, Ittenboch, & Patton, 2001).

The AAMR describes this type of prevention as reduction of the discrepancy between the individual's behavior capacity and the performance requirement of the individual's environments (AAMR, 2002). According to the AAMR, many individuals with mild to moderate cognitive disabilities will require **intermittent** to **limited** supports. These are defined by as needed support (intermittent) for some individuals who require increased intervention for only episodic situations. Limited support is typically for those who require more consistent but not intense support through transitional periods (school to work) or for a few key areas like balancing a checkbook (AAMR, 1992).

Given that the level of support as well as the nature of support will be highly individualized depending on the student, some prevention efforts will suffice at the primary level, whereas other efforts will require secondary and tertiary levels of support. For some students, prevention efforts described as PBS or FBA may be sufficient. However, the AAMR has identified key activities and curricular emphases that are essential to reduce or prevent the potential for expanding discrepancies between abilities and environmental expectations. These specific activities are referenced in Table 12.2 and represent two key themes.

First, environments must reflect activities and structures that are designed to enhance and build upon protective factors of the student. These include presenting and breaking down necessary and common social as well as academic tasks into processes that reflect the student's optimal learning style. For example, many of us prefer to learn through visual stimulation. In other words, we ask people to write it down, or indicate that we like to read it first, think about it, and then get back to someone. Others find it difficult to sit and read for a long period of time

TABLE 12.2	Essential activities associated with teaching and educational activities

Students should be provided with:

- Appropriate levels of supervision
- Appropriate levels of individualized instruction and training
- Appropriate feedback based on data
- Appropriately organized learning environments
- Appropriate support within inclusive environments

Students should be engaged in:

- Accessing educational settings
- Ongoing interaction with teachers and peers
- Decision making as part of their educational team
- Acquiring and using problem solving strategies
- Acquiring and accessing functional academics (e.g., reading signs, counting change, using calculators)
- Acquiring and using self-determination skills
- Acquiring and using health and physical education skills
- Accessing technology for learning
- Accessing transitional services for school to adult transitions

Adapted from American Association on Mental Retardation (2002). *Mental retardation: Definitions, classifications, and systems of support* (10th ed.). Washington, DC: Author (pp. 153, 157).

(those reading this book are clearly an exception of course) and count on an engaging professor or lecturer to provide us with key oral explanations of the topic so we can process the information **auditorally** (by listening). When we access information in a way that helps us learn best we are helping to prevent our own school failure or limitation in independent functioning by learning new skills and information.

In addition, people who experience increased frustration and potential failure in certain subject matter (such as greater challenges with math concepts than philosophy) will likely pursue occupational training that increases their chances of being successfully employed (e.g., being a literacy specialist as opposed to an engineer). Typically, K–12 schools employ curricula that reflect beliefs about what students should master as they progress through their educational careers in order to become independently functioning adults. Although these general curricula tend to work for a majority of students, for others it may put them at risk for school failure and lifelong dependence on others. For those students, it is paramount that they pursue a more **functional curriculum.** A functional curriculum has the same goal of ensuring that each student is supported to become an independently functioning adult who can successfully get his or her basic needs and wants met. However, similar to the track many university students pursue when choosing a college major, a functional curriculum emphasizes building on strengths to enhance overall functioning and skill acquisition. Without the opportunity to adjust how some students achieve the desired outcome (e.g., learn to balance their checkbook using a calculator as opposed to requiring the ability to do it with paper and pencil), many more would shift from being at risk for school failure to experiencing school failure in addition to secondary conditions associated with behavior and learning problems.

:: EARLY INTERVENTION

Intense and lifelong emphasis on prevention of primary disabilities and secondary conditions as well as the development of quality **early intervention** programs can significantly alter the path of an individual's ability to function and develop.

National Agenda

Early intervention is a national agenda for many reasons. First, it is the law. The initial special education legislation passed in 1975 (PL 94-142) was designed to assure that all children with disabilities have the right to a free and appropriate public education. This initial law required that all states educate students with disabilities from the ages of 6–17 years. If these states provided services to students without disabilities from the ages of 3–5 or 18–21, then they would also have to provide services for same-age children with disabilities (Heward, 2003). During its subsequent reauthorizations, the federal law, now called the Individuals with Disabilities Education Act (IDEA), has applied to all individuals from 3–21 years of age. Beginning in 1997, the U.S. Congress provided an incentive system in the form of federal monies to all states to develop a comprehensive and multidisciplinary early intervention service system for young children (birth–3 years old) with disabilities and their families. Similar to individualized education programs (IEPs) for students from 3–21 years of age, programs for younger children were encouraged to have **individualized family services plans** (IFSPs) to design and implement individualized early intervention.

Each state has addressed this call for early intervention in varied ways to best reflect resources, regional needs, and fiscal issues. However, there are several guiding principles from which early intervention service delivery is developed. Given the broad range of risk factors and causes of the disabilities described in this text, comprehensive early intervention programs need to be **transdisciplinary** (across different professional disciplines) in their approach. Essentially, they need to adopt a multidisciplinary team approach to supporting the needs of young children. This is designed to ensure that the needs of the whole child as well as their family are assessed and plans can be comprehensively developed. For example, direct intervention to stimulate language development for a child at risk of learning disabilities is only minimally helpful if the child continues to be exposed to peeling lead paint on the walls. Similarly, if the child is experiencing eating difficulties, coordination with medical personnel is necessary to reap the benefits of a corresponding early stimulation program.

Family participation is another essential component of effective early intervention. Within the transdisciplinary approach, family members are considered equal members of the team. Supporting families—especially parents—to implement best practice strategies helps develop positive parent-child interactions and access of families to needed community resources. Moreover, support for the family is highly correlated with positive outcomes for the child (Smith & Fox, 2003). In fact research has repeatedly identified three essential family patterns that highly correlated with a child's development.

- Family's ability to ensure the child's health and safety
- Quality of parent-child interaction
- Extent and diversity of family-provided experiences within their surrounding environments (Guralnick, 1997)

Service coordination is another principle in the development of effective early intervention. The emphasis on service coordination results from the realization that no one person or organization will be able to provide all the potentially necessary services or resources necessary to meet the needs of all children in early intervention programs. Although at times referred to as case management, the individual who serves as the primary service coordinator works most directly with the family and young child. By taking on the coordination of different agencies and requirements, the family can spend time focusing directly on interactions and opportunities with their young child.

The service coordinator is also most specifically charged with understanding the culture, customs, and norms associated with that heritage when working with families. As we discussed in Chapter 3, parenting practices and environmental expectations can vary greatly across cultures. Working closely with families to understand, translate, and coordinate as needed a successful marriage of culture and societal expectations can play an essential role in effective early intervention services.

Transition planning is a lifelong task for all individuals, particularly for those receiving early intervention services. Specific attention to transitions may be needed for students with or at risk for high-incidence disabilities when services change from home-based to center-based (e.g., daycare center or preschool) or from center-based to elementary school (Chandler, 1993). Typically, while planning for transitions, new members of the team are added, some present members may begin to fade, and the type and nature of services and interventions may vary in amount, location, and or delivery.

What Works in Early Intervention

Given the diversity of how states and regions have responded to the incentives and mandates of the federal law to provide early intervention services, it is not surprising that there is a great variety within the written work on what is *effective* early intervention. Recently, a large group of collaborators for the Center for Evidence-Based Practice: Young Children with Challenging Behavior, conducted an extensive review of current early intervention programs designed to address the needs of children at risk for poor academic or social competence (Smith & Fox, 2003). Most notable and humbling was their overall finding.

TABLE 12.3	A systems approach to prevention and early intervention programs: Key features of existing model programs

System components:

- Comprehensiveness and individualization
  - Prenatal counseling to mothers with an emphasis on parenting
  - Use periodic screenings to monitor children's growth and development and parent-child interactions
  - Effective programs are tailored to the community and settings in which they operate
  - Early intervention programs demonstrating outcomes for young children meet Developmentally Appropriate Practice (DAP)
  - Provision of comprehensive services requires collaboration with other agencies and the development of an individualized plan

- Family support
  - The syntheses found that programs providing both child-centered and family support models were more effective than those that simply provided family support
  - Family support program focuses on the entire family
  - Family advocates and service coordinators are assigned to assist families in identifying needs and acquiring services
  - Flexibility in support is important to families
  - Providing culturally competent service is a priority of family support programs
  - Services and supports accessible to families should include case management, parenting education, parenting support groups, child care, respite care, home visiting, access to community services, respite and peer mentors

The science of promotion, prevention, and intervention efforts has not expanded far beyond the development of model demonstration programs. . . , efforts must examine the transportability of evidence-based practice to usual care settings (Smith & Fox, 2003, p.10).

Smith and Fox (2003) highlighted the fact that due to increased research and funding in the area of early intervention, researchers have been able to effectively collaborate with childcare providers and service provider agencies to develop programs that demonstrate positive gains for children receiving the early intervention services. However, these programs have not become mainstream and currently remain the exception rather than the norm. Their review identified several components and key features of these model systems and programs of early intervention. Systems components included:

Comprehensiveness
Individualization
Family support
Collaboration and coordination
Eligibility and access procedures
Insurance policies and work force considerations

Only the first three are expanded in Table 12.3.

TABLE 12.4	Features of effective prevention and early intervention programs

Prevention programs

- Previous prevention efforts have been effective in reducing or minimizing the risk factors associated with low-income families experiencing multiple risks
- Prevention programs are financially advantageous through taxpayer saving generated by more mothers who are able to work and children graduating from high school and entering the work force
- As with effective systems, prevention programs provide services to the child and family
- Prevention programs that included a center-based early education program included well-trained staff working in a low teacher-to-pupil ratio

Early intervention programs

- Early screening efforts were essential in identifying children for whom direct and systemic intervention would be helpful
- Each of the reviewed models included direct instruction to parents and children
- Interventions for children focused on social skills, compliance, academic engagement, and self-regulation
- Educational interventions with parents included behavior management and strategies to encourage their child's development

Prevention and early intervention programs were also analyzed and included data from a longitudinal study of children in existing model demonstration programs. Additionally, the research base was again reviewed for common threads of effective early prevention programs. These are summarized in Table 12.4.

:: EARLY INTERVENTION: THINK AGAIN

As our previous discussion of early intervention programs suggests, the law—and most states and local communities—have responded, albeit not consistently or entirely effectively, to calls for intervening early in children's lives. But early intervention means more than intervening early in a child's life. If we are to practice prevention most effectively, it also means intervening at the first signs of trouble in older children who are not identified as infants or toddlers as having disabilities. Most children with high-incidence disabilities are not identified until they are in school, and then usually only after they have developed very serious problems that are hard to correct. This type of early intervention—stepping in at the first signs of struggle or failure—is the one that meets most resistance. Yet it is the type of early intervention with promise for helping the greatest number of students with high-incidence disabilities, especially those with EBD (see Kauffman, Bantz, & McCullough, 2002). You might think about why, when the chips are down, most people do not really want to do this. Kauffman (1999, 2003, 2005b) offered some speculation about why we seem to want to wait until there is absolutely no doubt that the child is having bad trouble before we respond.

SUMMARY

Active engagement by schools and related personnel in primary, secondary, and tertiary prevention is essential. Effective collaboration within and across disciplines and families is the only way effective prevention can occur. Continued support for research and demonstration projects in these areas will assist administrators and public policy makers to further assess and expect best practice components for within all prevention programs nationwide. Meanwhile, and simultaneously, educators need to continue to work collaboratively within systems of support, seek necessary training, and actively engage in prevention efforts at all three levels.

COMPETENT TEACHING BOX   BOX 12.4

Knowing your students . . .

What we know about our students helps us teach them more effectively. What we know about our students is NOT an automatic prescription for educational strategies or placement.

What you might want to remember about education as prevention of high-incidence disabilities:

- Many students enter school with high risk factors associated with school failure. These risk factors can include: living in poverty, living with neglect or abuse; and developmental disabilities due to genetic inheritance. Prevention of school failure occurs at three levels: primary, secondary, and tertiary. Optimal prevention incorporates all three concurrently.
- Research has demonstrated the preventative effects of quality instructional practices and learning environments.
- Specific academic disabilities (e.g., reading disabilities) can be prevented through intensive evidenced-based instruction (e.g., direct instruction, learning strategies) that reflect age-appropriate context.
- Early intervention programs prevent primary and secondary conditions by providing early screening for potential risk factors. Instruction is provided to families and children through contextually appropriate opportunities to focus on social skills, compliance, academic engagement, and self-regulation. Additionally, these programs provide behavior management strategies as well as comprehensive supports to families.

Competent teachers . . .

- Learn to recognize risk factors as well as protective factors demonstrated for individual students.
- Seek out early screening and baseline assessments for students in an effort to monitor for ongoing and appropriate progress.

- Facilitate school- and community-based resources designed to increase contextually appropriate opportunities to develop social skills and self-regulation strategies with typically developing peers as role models.
- Recognize the need for intensive and individualized instruction for students at risk for specific learning and behavior problems.
- Recognize the important of all levels of prevention and align their practices with evidence-based schoolwide and community-based initiatives toward prevention.
- Actively pursue effective and ongoing collaboration with *all* families and relevant caregivers.

BENTON ELEMENTARY SCHOOL

The Thomas Hart Benton Elementary School is a Midwestern elementary school that has approximately 250 students. It is considered a Title I designated building due to the proportion of students that receive free and reduced lunch. A few years ago the school decided to address multiple needs in the area of behavior and academic progress by engaging in building-wide primary levels of prevention. They decided to employ a school-wide PBS model described previously in this chapter. The following is an overview of the expectations, process for encouraging those expectations, and process for engaging in data-based decision making.

Thomas Hart Benton Elementary

School-wide Expectations
Be Safe
Be Respectful
Be a Learner

Teaching Expectations
The three expectations are taught through the use of social skill lesson plans—a.k.a. Cool Tools. The Cool Tools were developed with assistance from the University of Missouri's Center for Schoolwide Positive Behavior Support. A new social skill lesson plan is taught each week. The school's discipline aide is in charge of distributing the lessons to teachers.

Encouraging Appropriate Behavior
Students earn "bee" tickets for demonstrating safe, respectful, and learning behaviors.

Staff Supports
Several strategies are used to remind students and staff of the weekly Cool Tool and PBS goals. Every day, a student will announce the Cool Tool of the week during the morning announcement. Signs and bulletin boards are posted throughout the building and in the teachers' lounge. The PBS team's "cheerleader" posts regular e-mails that recognize teachers who teach and practice the Cool Tools. Each staff member has a PBS binder that includes all lessons, routines, and procedures. PBS is on every staff meeting agenda.

Celebrations
Each class sets a classroom goal. When the goal is reached, the class celebrates. After 10,000 tickets are earned by the entire school, a schoolwide celebration is planned. Schoolwide celebratory activities have included balloon launchings, tree plantings, popsicles for lunch, trips to the park, lunch in the classroom, and extra recess.

Data
The discipline aide is responsible for entering data on office referrals, in-school suspensions, and out-of-school suspensions into SWIS (i.e., School-wide Information System). Our behavior report form was revised to match SWIS and includes the student's name, problem behavior, location, and time of day. Once a month, the PBS team examines the data and data reports are shared with all staff. Individual student reports are reviewed when conferencing with parents. Annually, staff complete the EBS Survey and results are used to develop the PBS team action plan.

Parent Communication
There are several ways that we communicate with parents about PBS. In every student's Friday take-home folder, teachers include information about PBS, typically on the social skill focused on for the week. A more general article about PBS or a social skill is included in each PTA newsletter. These articles are written by PBS team members. Lessons, pictures, and cafeteria and playground routines are also posted to the school's web site.

1. What evidence of key system variables and practices for School-wide PBS do you see present in Benton's description?
2. Why would these practices be viewed as primary intervention?
3. What type of students needs might not be met solely by these types of primary activities?

CHANDLER

In Chapter 3, you met Chandler, a young boy later identified with a variety of learning disabilities. If you recall Chandler also presented with a series of other risk factors surrounding his health care and home environment. School personnel felt that although the assessment and subsequent diagnosis was helpful in educational planning for Chandler, several of his *outside* needs would have to be met for him to optimally benefit from a well-designed educational plan.

Chandler seemed to be coming to school hungry each morning as well as tired. As you may recall money was tight and the transportation schedule was problematic for Chandler's family. School enrolled him in the free and reduced lunch program which afforded him the opportunity to eat breakfast before school as well. Additionally, with his mother's permission, a neighboring family was identified that could drive Chandler to school with their son, therefore leaving a little later than the bus schedule. The school social worker was also able to take advantage of some state and county programs for health screenings and dental care by enrolling Chandler's family in some medical assistance programs. By doing this, Chandler and his siblings were able to get dental care from the dental bus twice a year when it came to the school as well as routine physicals and vision and hearing screenings from a similar mobile unit. These assessments confirmed that Chandler had some cavities that needed filling, excessive ear wax buildup that had resulted in a temporary mild hearing loss, and seasonal allergies.

By coordinating these services, Chandler's IEP team felt increasingly confident that he was better able to benefit from targeted instructional strategies they had designed for him.

1. Given the definition of primary and secondary prevention, which of the supports provided above are primary?
2. Which are examples of secondary prevention?
3. Could some of them serve as both? Why or why not?

RHIANNON

Recall the case of Rhiannon, the girl identified with EB/D in Chapter 3. Although she had been the recipient of various levels of primary and secondary levels of prevention, the intensity and frequency of her behaviors warranted the IEP team to pursue a more tertiary level of support in the form of a functional assessment (see Box 12.2). Figures 12.1 outlines the identified factors that contributed or set the stage for her problem behavior of a combination, as well as the variables that maintained (reinforced) her behavior of work refusal and extreme verbal outbursts. Figure 12.1 also displays the desired behavior and outcomes by her teacher. As you can see, these were not compatible with Rhiannon's behavior or desired outcomes. Figures 12.2 displays the resulting behavior teaching plan (BTP) that was developed to provide Rhiannon with some classroom modification as well as specific skills to better achieve her function while completing work done in an appropriate manner.

1. Are any of the setting events or antecedent modifications in the BTP, changes that could be made classroom wide?
2. Are any of the individual skills she is being taught potentially appropriate for other students?
3. What is the importance of addressing the setting events that occur out of school?

REFERENCES

Administration for Children, Youth and Families (2001a). *Building their futures: How early head start programs are enhancing the lives of infants and toddlers in low-income families*. Summary report. Washington, DC: Author.

Allensworth, D. D., & Wolford, C. A. (1988). *Achieving the 1990 health objectives for the nation: Agenda for the nation's schools*. Kent, OH: American School Health Association.

American Association on Mental Retardation. (2002). *Mental retardation: Definitions, classifications, and systems of supports* (10th ed). Washington, DC: Author. (pp. 152–159).

Baker, S., Gersten, R., & Scanlon, D. (2002). Procedural facilitators and cognitive strategies: Tools for unraveling the mysteries of comprehension and the writing process, and for providing meaningful access to the general curriculum. *Learning Disabilities Research and Practice, 17*(1), 65–77.

Bakken, J. P., & Whedon, C. K. (2002). Teaching text structure to improve reading comprehension. *Intervention in School and Clinic, 37*(4), 229–233.

Bauer, A. M. & Shea, T. M. (1999). Preventing emotional/behavioral disorders. In A. Bauer & T. Shea (Eds.) *Learners with emotional and behavioral disorders: An introduction* (p. 272). Columbus: Merrill Prentice Hall.

Beirne-Smith, M., Ittenbach, R. F., & Patton, J. R. (2001). *Mental retardation* (6th ed.). Upper Saddle River, NJ: Prentice Hall.

Blueprint for Change: Research on Child and Adolescent Mental Disorders. (2001). A report of the National Advisory Council of the National Institute of Mental Health. Intervention Development and Intervention Deployment. Washington, DC: NIMH.

Brophy, J. E., & Evertson, C. M. (1976). *Texas teacher effectiveness study: Classroom coding manual*. Washington, DC: National Institute of Education (DHEW) [BBB06621].

Caplan, G., & Grunebaum, H. (1967). Perspectives on primary prevention. *Archives of General Psychiatry, 17*, 331–346.

Carr, M. R. (2004, January 4). My son's disability, and my own inability to see it. *The Washington Post*, B5.

Chandler, L. K. (1993). Steps in preparing for transition: Preschool to kindergarten. *Teaching Exceptional Children, 25*, 52–56.

Chandler, L. K., Dahlquist, C. M., Repp, A. C., & Feltz, C. (1999). The effects of team-based functional assessment on the behavior of students in classroom settings. *Exceptional Children, 66*, 101–122.

Chard, D. J., Vaughn, S., and Tyler, B. J. (2002). A synthesis of research on effective interventions for building reading fluency with elementary students with learning disabilities. *Journal of Learning Disabilities, 35*(5), 386–406.

Colvin, G., Sugai, G., & Kame'enui, E. (1994). Curriculum for establishing a proactive school-wide discipline plan. Project PREPARE. Eugene: University of Oregon.

Committee on Integrating the Science of Early Childhood Development. (2000). In J. P. Shonkoff & D. Phillips (Eds.), *From neurons to neighborhoods: The science of early childhood development.* Washington, DC: National Academy Press.

Conroy, M. A., & Brown, W. H. (2001). Promoting peer-related social communicative competence in preschool children with developmental delays: Strategies for use by early childhood practitioners. In H. Goldstein, L. Kaczmarek, & K. M. English (Eds.), *Promoting social communication in children and youth with developmental disabilities* (pp. 211–236). Baltimore: Paul H. Brookes.

Conroy, M. A., Davis, C. A., Fox, J. J., & Brown, W. H. (2002). Functional assessment of behavior and effective supports for young children with challenging behaviors. *Assessment for Effective Intervention, 27*(4), 35–47.

Crone, D. A., Horner, R. H., & Hawken, L. S. (2004). *Responding to problem behavior in schools: The behavior education program.* New York: Guilford.

Cullinen, D. (2002). *Students with emotional and behavioral disorders: An introduction for teachers and other helping professionals* (p. 399–400). Columbus, OH: Merril/Prentice Hall.

Daro, D. A., & Harding, K. A. (1999). Healthy families America: Using research to enhance practice. *The Future of Children, 9*(1), 152–176.

Eckert, T. L., Ardoin, S. P., Daisey, D. M., & Scarola, M. D. (2000). Empirically evaluating the effectiveness of reading interventions: The use of brief experimental analysis and single case designs. *Psychology in the Schools, 37*(5), 463–473.

Eddy, J. M., Reid, J. B., & Curry, V. (2002). The etiology of youth antisocial behavior, delinquency, and violence and a public health approach to prevention. In M. R. Shinn, H. M. Walker, & G. Stoner (Eds.), *Interventions for academic and behavior problems II: Preventive and remedial approaches* (pp. 27–52). Bethesda, MD: National Association of School Psychologists.

Finn, C., Rotherham, A., & Hokanson, C. (Eds.) (2001). *Rethinking special education for a new century.* Washington, DC: Thomas B. Fordham Foundation and the Progressive Policy Institute.

Forness, S. R., Kavale, K. A., Blum, I. M., & Lloyd, J. W. (1997). Mega-analysis of meta-analyses. *Teaching Exceptional Children, 29*(6), 4–9.

Forness, S. R., Serna, L. A., Nielsen, E., Lambors, K., Hale, M. J., & Kavale, K. A. (2000). A model for early detection and primary prevention of emotional or behavioral disorders. *Education and Treatment of Children, 23*, 325–345.

Francis, D. J., Shaywitz, S. E., Stuebing, K. K., Shaywitz, B. A., & Fletcher, J. M. (1996). Developmental lag versus deficit models of reading disability: A longitudinal, individual growth curves analysis. *Journal of Educational Psychology, 88*(1), 3–17.

Fuchs, D., Fuchs, L. S., Mathes, P. G., and Simmons, D. C. (1997). Peer-assisted learning strategies: Making classrooms more responsive to diversity. *American Educational Research Journal, 34*(1), 174–206.

Fuchs, L. S., Fuchs, D., & Bishop, N. (1992). Teacher planning for students with learning disabilities: Differences between general and special educators. *Learning Disabilities Research & Practice, 7*, 120–128.

Gaudet, L., Pulos, S., Crethar, H., & Burger, S. (2002). Psychosocial concerns of adults with developmental disabilities: Perspectives of the self, family member, and provider. *Education and Training in Mental Retardation and Developmental Disabilities, 37*, 23–26.

Good, T., & Brophy, J. (1996). *Looking in classrooms* (7th ed.) New York: Harper & Row.

Gunn, B., Biglan, A., Smolkowski, K., Ary, D. (2000). The efficacy of supplemental instruction in decoding skills for Hispanic and non-Hispanic students in early elementary school. *The Journal of Special Education, 34*(2), 90–103.

Guralnick, M. J. (1997). Second generation research in the field of early intervention. In M. J. Guralnick (Ed.), *The effectiveness of early intervention.* Baltimore: Paul H. Brookes.

Hallahan, D. P., Lloyd, J. W., Kauffman, J. M., Weiss, M., & Martinez, E. (2005). *Introduction to learning disabilities* (3rd ed.). Boston: Allyn & Bacon.

Harrington, M., Perez-Johnson, I., Meckstroth, A., Bellotti, J., & Love, J.M. (2000). *Protecting children from substance abuse: Lessons learned from Free to Grow Head Start partnerships.* Princeton, NJ: Mathematical Policy Research, Inc.

Hawken, L. S., & Horner, R. H. (2003). Evaluation of a targeted intervention within a school-wide system of behavior support. *Journal of Behavioral Education, 12,* 225–240.

Healthy People 2000: National health promotion and disease prevention objectives. (1991). Washington, DC: Public Health Service, U.S. Department of Health and Human Services.

Heward, W. L. (2003). Ten faulty notions about teaching and learning that hinder the effectiveness of special education. *Journal of Special Education, 36,* 186–205.

Hoagwood, K. (2001). Emotional and behavioral disorders in youth. *Washington Watch,* Fall 2001, 84–87, 90.

Horner, R. H. Sugai, G., Todd, A. W., & Lewis-Palmer, T. (2004). School-wide positive behavior support: An alternative approach to discipline in schools. In L. Bambara & L. Kern (Eds.), *Individualized supports for students with problem behaviors: Designing positive behavior support plans* (pp. 359–90). New York: Guilford.

Institute of Medicine. (1991). Pope, A. M., & Tarlov, A. R. (Eds.). *Disability America: Toward a national agenda for prevention.* Washington, DC: National Academy Press.

Jones, V., & Jones, L. (2001). *Comprehensive classroom management: Creating communities of support and solving problems* (6th ed). Boston: Allyn & Bacon.

Kame'enui, E. J. (2002). *An exploded view of five essential steps to preventing reading difficulties in young children.* Presentation at the Lake Tahoe Institute, Lake Tahoe, NV.

Kauffman, J. M. (1999). How we prevent the prevention of emotional and behavioral disorders. *Exceptional Children, 65,* 448–468.

Kauffman, J. M. (2003). Appearances, stigma, and prevention. *Remedial and Special Education, 24,* 195–198.

Kauffman, J. M. (2004). Foreword. In H. M. Walker, E. Ramsey, & F. H. Gresham (Eds.), *Antisocial behavior in school: Strategies and best practices* (2nd ed.) (pp. xix–xxi). Belmont, CA: Wadsworth.

Kauffman, J. M. (2005a). *Characteristics of emotional and behavioral disorders of children and youth* (8th ed.). Upper Saddle River, NJ: Prentice Hall.

Kauffman, J. M. (2005b). How we prevent the prevention of emotional and behavioural difficulties in education. In P. Clough, P. Garner, J. T. Pardeck, & F. K. O. Yuen (Eds.), *Handbook of emotional and behavioural difficulties* (pp. 429–440). London: Sage.

Kauffman, J. M., Bantz, J., & McCullough, J. (2002). Separate and better: A special public school class for students with emotional and behavioral disorders. *Exceptionality, 10,* 149–170.

Kauffman, J. M., & Hallahan, D. P. (2005a). *The illusion of full inclusion: A comprehensive critique of a current special education bandwagon* (2nd ed.). Austin, TX: PRO-ED.

Kauffman, J. M., & Hallahan, D. P. (2005b). *What special education is and why we need it.* Boston: Allyn & Bacon.

Kauffman, J. M., & Landrum, T. J. (2006). *Children and youth with emotional and behavioral disorders: A history of their education.* Austin, TX: PRO-ED.

Kauffman, J. M., Mostert, M. P., Trent, S. C., & Pullen, P. L. (2006). *Managing classroom behavior: A reflective case-based approach* (4th ed.). Boston: Allyn & Bacon.

Kern, L., & Dunlap, G. (1998). Curricular modifications to promote desirable classroom behavior. In J.K. Luiselli & M. J. Cameron (Eds), *Antecedent control: Innovative approaches to behavioral support.* Baltimore: Paul H. Brookes.

Levine-Coley, R., Chase-Lansdale, P. L., & Li-Grining, P. (2001). Child care in the era of welfare reform: Quality, choices and preferences. *Welfare, Children & Families, Policy Brief 01–4.*

Love, J. M., Kisker, E. E., Ross, C. M., Schochet, P. Z., Brooks-Gunn, J., Paulsell, D., et al. (2002). *Making a difference in the lives of infants and toddlers and their families: The impacts of Head Start, executive summary.* Washington, DC: U.S. Department of Health and Human Services, Aadministration for Children and Families.

Lyon, R., Fletcher, J. M., Shaywitz, S. E., Shaywitz, B. A., Torgeson, J. K., Wood, F. B., Schulte, A., & Olson, R. (2001). Rethinking learning disabilities. In C. Finn, A. Rotherham, & C. Hokanson (Eds.), *Rethinking special education for a new century.* Washington, DC: Thomas B. Fordham Foundation and the Progressive Policy Institute.

Mathes, P. G., Torgesen, J. K., & Allor, J. H. (2001). The effects of peer-assisted literacy strategies for first-grade readers with and without additional computer-assisted instruction in phonological awareness. *American Educational Research Journal, 38*(2), 371–410.

Mercer, C. D., & Mercer, N. A. (2001). *Teaching students with learning problems.* New York: Merrill Prentice Hall.

Meyer, M. S., and Felton, R. H. (1999). Repeated reading to enhance fluency: Old approaches and new directions. *Annals of Dyslexia, 49,* 283–306.

Miller-Heyl, J., MacPhee, D., & Fritz, J. (1998). DARE to be you: A family support, early prevention program. *Journal of Primary Prevention, 18,* 257–285.

Mulick, J. A., & Butter, E. M. (2005). Positive behavior support: A paternalistic utopian delusion. In J. W. Jacobson, R. M. Foxx, & J. A. Mulick (Eds.), *Controversial therapies for developmental disabilities: Fad, fashion, and science in professional practice* (pp. 385–404). Mahwah, NJ: Erlbaum.

National Reading Panel. (2000). *Teaching children to read: An evidence-based assessment of the scientific research literature on reading and its implications for reading instruction.* Washington, DC: National Institute of Child Health and Human Development.

National Research Council. (2001). *Eager to learn: Educating our preschoolers.* Committee on Early Childhood Pedagogy, Commission on Behavioral and Social Sciences and Education. Bowman, B. T., Donovan, M. S., & Burns, M. S. (Eds.). Washington, DC: National Academy Press.

Olds, D., Eckenrode, J., Henderson, C., Kitzman, H., Powers, J., Cole, R., et al. (1997). Long-term effects of home visitation on maternal life course, child-abuse and neglect, and children's arrests: Fifteen-year follow-up of a randomized trial. *Journal of the American Medical Association, 278,* 637–643.

O'Neill, R. E., Horner, R. H., Albin, R. W., Sprague, J. R., Storey, K., & Newton, J. S. (1997). *Functional assessment and program development for problem behavior.* Pacific Grove, CA: Brooks/Cole.

Pope, A. (1992). Preventing secondary conditions. *Mental Retardation, 30,* 347–354.

Reynolds, A. (1994). Effects of preschool plus follow-on intervention for children at-risk. *Developmental Psychology, 30*(6), 787–804.

Rones, M., & Hoagwood, K. (2000). School-based mental health services: A research review. *Clinical and Family Psychology Review, 3,* 223–1241.

Rutstein, D., Berenberg, W., Chalmers, T., Childs, C., Fishman, A., & Perrin, E. (1976). Measuring the quality of medical care. *New England Journal of Medicine, 294*(11), 582–588.

Samuels, S. J., Lewis, M., Wu, Y., Reininger, J., & Murphy, A. (2003). Accelerated reader vs. non-accelerated reader: How students using the accelerated reader outperformed the control condition in a tightly controlled experimental study. Technical Report. Minneapolis: University of Minnesota.

Sandall, S., McLean, M. E., & Smith, B. J. (2000). *DEC recommended practices in early intervention/childhood special education.* Longmont, CO: Sopris West.

Schill, M. T., Kratochwill, T. R., & Elliott, S. N. (1998). Functional assessment in behavioral consultation: A treatment utility study. *School Psychology Quarterly, 13,* 116–140.

Shonkoff, J. P., & Meisels, S. J. (Eds.). (2000). *Handbook of early childhood intervention* (2nd ed.) New York: Cambridge University Press.

Short, R. J., & Brokaw, R. (1994). Externalizing behavior disorders. In R. J. Simeonsson (Ed.), *Risk and prevention: Promoting the well-being of all children.* Baltimore: Paul H. Brookes.

Simeonsson, R. (1991). Primary, secondary, and tertiary prevention in early intervention. *Journal of Early Intervention, 15,* 124–134.

Simmons, D. C., Fuchs, L. S., Fuchs, D., Mathes, P., & Hodge, J. P. (1995). Effects of explicit teaching and peer tutoring on the reading achievement of learning-disabled and low-performing students in regular classrooms. *The Elementary School Journal, 95*(5), 387–408.

Simpson, J., Jivanjee, P., Koroloff, N., Doerfler, A., & Garcia, M. (2001). *Promising practices in early childhood mental health.* Systems of care: Promising practices in children's mental health, 2001 series (Vol. III). Washington, DC: Center for Effective Collaboration and Practice, American Institutes for Research.

Skiba, R. J. (2002). Special education and school discipline: A precarious balance. *Behavioral Disorders, 27*(2), 81–97.

Smith, B. J., & Fox, L. (2003). Systems of service delivery: A synthesis of evidence related to young children at risk or who have challenging behavior. *Center for Evidence-Based Practice: Young children with Challenging Behavior.* Tampa, FL: University of South Florida, Center for Evidence-Based Practices: Young Children with Challenging Behavior.

Snow, C. E., Burns, M. S., & Griffin, P. (Eds.), (1998). *Preventing reading difficulties in young children.* Washington, DC: National Academy Press.

Strain, P. S., & Timm, M. A. (2001). Remediation and prevention of aggression: An evaluation of the Regional Intervention Program over a quarter of a century. *Behavioral Disorders, 26*(4), 297–313.

Stichter, J. P., Lewis, T. J., Johnson, N., & Trussell, R. (2004). Toward a structural assessment: Analyzing the merits of an assessment tool for a student with E/BD. *Assessment for Effective Intervention, 30,* 25–40.

Stribling, F. T. (1842). Physician and superintendent's report. In *Annual Reports to the Court of Directors of the Western Lunatic Asylum to the Legislature of Virginia* (pp. 1–70). Richmond, VA: Shepherd & Conlin.

Sugai, G., & Horner, R. (2002). The evolution of discipline practices: School-wide positive behavior supports. *Child & Family Behavior Therapy, 24*(1/2), 23–50.

Sutherland, K. S. & Wehby, J. H. (2001). The effect of self-evaluation on teaching behavior in classrooms for students with emotional and behavioral disorders. *Journal of Special Education, 35,* 161–71.

Tankersley, M., Landrum, T. J., & Cook, B. G. (2004). How research informs practice in the field of emotional and behavioral disorders. In R. B. Rutherford, M. M. Quinn, & S. R. Mathur (Eds.), *Handbook of research in behavior disorders.* New York: Guilford.

Vaughn, S., Gersten, R., & Chard, D. (2000). The underlying message in LD intervention research: Finding from research synthesis. *Exceptional Children, 67,* 99–114.

Vaughn, S., & Klingner, J.K. (1999). Teaching reading comprehension through collaborative strategic reading. *Intervention in School and Clinic, 34,* 284–292.

Walker, H. M., Horner, R. H., Sugai, G., Bullis, M., Sprague, J. R., Bricker, D., & Kauffman, M. J. (1996). Integrated approaches to preventing antisocial behavior patterns among school-age children and youth. *Journal of Emotional and Behavioral Disorders, 4,* 193–256.

Walker, H. M., Ramsey, E., & Gresham, F. M. (2004). *Antisocial behavior in school: Strategies and best practices* (2nd ed.). Pacific Grove, CA: Brooks/Cole.

Walker, H. M., & Shinn, M. R. (2002). Structuring school-based interventions to achieve integrated primary, secondary, and tertiary prevention goals for safe and effective schools. In M. R. Shinn, G. Stoner, & H. M. Walker

(Eds.), *Interventions for academic and behavior problems: Preventive and remedial approaches.* Silver Spring, MD: National Association of School Psychologists.

Wang, P. S., Berglund, P., Olfson, M., Pincus, H. A., Wells, K. B., & Kessler, R. C. (2005). Failure and delay in initial treatment contact after first onset of mental disorders in the national comorbidity survey replication. *Archives of General Psychiatry, 62,* 603–613.

Webster-Stratton, C., Reid, M. J., & Hammond, M. (2001). Preventing conduct problems, promoting social competence: A parent and teacher training partnership in Head Start. *Journal of Clinical Child Psychology, 30*(3), 283–302.

Wehby, J., Symons, F., Canale, J., & Go, F. (1998). Teaching practices in classrooms for students with emotional and behavioral disorders: Discrepancies between recommendations and observations. *Behavioral Disorders, 24,* 51–56.

Wehmeyer, M., & Palmer, S. B. (2003). Adult outcomes for students with cognitive disabilities three–years after high school: The impact of self-determination. *Education and Training in Mental Retardation and Developmental Disabilities, 38,* 131–144.

Glossary

ABC procedure   A procedure designed to determine what affects the behavior of a particular student. The ABC components are the antecedent (what triggers the behavior), the behavior, and the consequence (what immediately follows the behavior).

Aberrant behavior   Specific behavior or actions that are judged inappropriate in a given social context.

Abstract   The highest level of mathematical understanding by which the student can compute without the support of manipulative objects or any pictorial representations. The student uses only numbers. The student at this level can explain the specific operation.

Academic achievement test   A test designed to measure the knowledge or proficiency of an individual in something that has been learned or taught. Typically, these tests measure individual academic achievement in reading, mathematics, written language, and general knowledge.

Accommodation   A variation in the delivery of instruction or in the manner in which the student is expected to perform. These accommodations do not significantly alter the content of the curriculum or change the overall difficulty of the course work. With respect to individuals with disabilities, any modification or adjustment that will enable such individuals to participate in regular education classrooms or employment in order to perform essential functions. For example, a wheelchair-accessible table allows a student with a physical disability to attend and participate in a general education classroom.

Accuracy   Reading the word correctly, whether by decoding or by recognition of high-frequency sight words.

Acquisition   The initial phase of learning when the student is learning how to perform a new skill or how to use new knowledge; feedback should focus on the accuracy and topography of the student's response.

Adaptive behavior   The collection of conceptual, social, and practical skills that individuals have learned in order to help them function, such as basic skills in reading and writing, as well as personal hygiene, socialization, and communication. The typical performance of individuals without disabilities in meeting environmental expectations. Adaptive behavior changes according to a person's age, culture, and environmental demands.

Adaptive physical education   An aspect of physical education in which instruction is specifically altered and adapted to be compatible with a student's physical abilities.

Alphabetic principle   The process of how letters and combinations of letters represent the small segments of speech called phonemes.

American Association on Intellectual and Developmental Disabilities (AAIDD)   Until 2006, known as the American Association on Mental Retardation (AAMR).

American Association on Mental Retardation (AAMR)   A professional organization whose mission is to promote progressive policies, sound research, effective practices, and universal human rights for all people with intellectual disabilities. Founded in 1876, the AAMR was formerly known as the American Association on Mental Deficiency. The AAMR is also responsible for creating definitions of MR that are based on the level of accommodations needed and on the adaptive skills of individuals, rather than on the level of IQ. The AAMR suggests intervention and prevention strategies for working with individuals with mental retardation. The organization also advocates the civil rights of individuals with mental retardation, particularly the right of self-determination.

Analytical trait scoring   A method of using preestablished criteria to judge student writing—including idea expression, language usage, organization, word choice, and style.

Anecdotal record   Narrative data written to provide information about various aspects of a student's academic, social, behavioral, and/or emotional status. Events contained in the record are usually sequenced, identifying each behavior, its antecedent, and its consequence.

Antecedent   An event, occurrence, or stimulus that precedes a particular behavior.

Anxiety disorder   A psychological disorder characterized by abnormal apprehension or fear, often accompanied by physical symptoms.

Aphasia   Problems with speaking or total loss of speech following traumatic brain injury or stroke.

Applied behavior analysis (ABA)   A scientifically based approach of observing, analyzing, and modifying behavior through arrangement of antecedents and consequences. ABA uses behavioral strategies, such as positive reinforcement, shaping, and chaining, that have been found to be successful for teaching individuals with disabilities.

ARC Formerly known as the Association for Retarded Citizens. An organization originally formed by parents and friends who are advocates of civil rights for individuals with developmental disabilities.

Articulation disorder A disorder of speech that involves errors in pronunciation. An individual with an articulation disorder may omit or distort word sounds. For example, a lisp is usually considered an articulation disorder.

Asperger's syndrome (AS) A developmental disorder on the autism spectrum. Individuals with AS are considered "high functioning" because they do not have delays in cognition or language. However, they may have social impairments and engage in restricted behaviors.

Assistive technology (AT) Any device or mechanical aid that substitutes for or enhances the function of some physical or mental ability that is impaired. Assistive technology includes pencil grips, voice synthesizers, wheelchairs, and so on.

Asymmetry Lopsidedness; not symmetrical. With respect to learning abilities, research shows an association between individuals with asymmetrical brains—for example, larger right planum temporale and deficits in neurolinguistic processing, receptive language, and reading comprehension; or smaller planum temporale in people with dyslexia.

Attention deficit hyperactivity disorder (ADHD) A disability characterized by symptoms of inattention, hyperactivity, and/or impulsivity that are developmentally inappropriate and are not the result of other conditions. Symptoms must have occurred prior to age 7 and must exist in two or more settings. There are three categories of ADHD: predominantly inattentive, predominantly hyperactive-impulsive, or combined.

Attribution Belief in the causes of success and failure.

Attribution training Giving students feedback that the source of their accomplishments is hard work and perseverance.

Auditory processing The ability to process information by listening.

Autism A spectrum of pervasive developmental disorders that are characterized by language delay, cognitive deficits, extreme withdrawal, ritualistic behaviors, and self-stimulation.

Autism spectrum disorder (ASD) An umbrella term used to refer to individuals who display characteristics commonly associated with autism. ASD includes the following disorders: autism, Asperger's syndrome (AS), Rett syndrome (RS), childhood disintegrative disorder (CDD), and pervasive developmental disorder not otherwise specified (PDD-NOS). Most of the disorders in ASD are characterized by idiosyncratic behaviors related to verbal and nonverbal communication and social interactions, and are generally, but not always, evident before age 2 years.

Automatization Learning a skill so well that it can be performed automatically, without having to think through the steps in doing it.

Background knowledge Knowledge that is brought to the classroom by the student prior to learning. This knowledge comes from previous instruction, development, history, and culture. Background knowledge is the base level from which new learning occurs.

Behavior The manner in which a student acts or comports himself or herself in various situations.

Behavior intervention plan (BIP) A plan designed specifically for individuals with problem behaviors. As part of a functional behavioral assessment, a BIP should include instruction for teaching appropriate behavior, as well as strategies for decreasing inappropriate behavior.

Behavioral earthquake Inappropriate behavior that is low in rate (infrequent), but high in intensity (very serious).

Behavioral inhibition The ability to stall or stop a response, to interrupt a behavior, or to refrain from responding immediately. Behavioral inhibition is the ability to allow executive functions to occur, and is generally delayed or impaired in individuals with autism, attention deficit hyperactivity disorder (ADHD), or emotional or behavioral disorder (EBD).

Behaviorally impaired Behaving in a way that does not meet environmental expectations and so causes social distress. Adaptive behavior changes according to a person's age, culture, and environmental demands.

Behavioral neurogenetics The scientific study of how genetic factors influence brain development and how those factors are linked to behavioral and cognitive disabilities. In addition, one's behavior can create neurological pathways, especially with the plasticity of the brains in children. For example, when children learn music at an early age, their temporal lobes are larger than those of their nonmusical peers.

Behavioral risk factor   Any factor that places a person at elevated risk of developing disabilities.

Behaviorist   An educator who relies on the notion that all behavior is made up of observable and measurable incidents that can be quantified.

Behavior modification   Analyzing and modifying behavior by using a series of strategies and techniques developed by B. F. Skinner and adapted and modified by other behavioral and developmental psychologists.

Behavior specialist   A consultant whose primary focus is on determining the function of inappropriate behaviors in students and creating intervention plans to replace the inappropriate behaviors with different, appropriate behaviors that serve the same function as the inappropriate behaviors.

Biomedical causes   Causes that can be attributed to specific organic medical conditions such as genetic abnormalities.

Bipolar disorder   Any of several psychological disorders characterized by alternating episodes of depression and mania (sadness and happiness).

Blend   The ability to connect sounds of individual phonemes into syllables and words.

Braille   A language/code that enables blind people to read and write through the use of a system of embossed characters formed by using a "Braille cell," which is a combination of six dots consisting of two vertical columns of three dots each.

Cascade of services   A model of service alternatives ranging from regular classroom to residential placement.

Categorical provision   As related to special education, the illegal placement of exceptional children in educational services on the basis of their categorical label. An example would be having all students with autism contained in the same classroom simply due to their category.

Central cortex (parietal lobe)   The small area at the top of the hindbrain that serves primarily as a reflex center for orienting the eyes and ears. It lies behind the forebrain and is a relatively narrow, short top of the bulging stalk of nerve fibers and nuclei called the brainstem. A relay station for sensory impulses, among other things it adjusts the size and movement of the pupils.

Central nervous system   The body's messenger system that allows electrical synapses to travel between the brain and the nerves via the spinal cord in order to send or receive stimuli.

Central nervous system dysfunction (CNSD)   The result of neuronal death or injury. Various factors are capable of influencing the vulnerability of the developing brain and its response to injury—including infectious agents, drugs, immune status, and neuroendocrine status. The nature, degree, length, frequency, and reversibility of these influences, as well as genetic vulnerability of the fetus, may determine the relative importance of the mechanisms and the location and severity of the deficits. CNSD is often a presumed cause of learning disabilities; however, many individuals with CNSD, such as those with cerebral palsy, do not necessarily evidence learning disabilities.

Chaining   Procedures used to teach an individual a skill by engaging in a series of behaviors, usually beginning with the least difficult part of the skill and working toward the most difficult. Types of chaining procedures include backward chaining, forward chaining, self-instruction, picture prompts, and written task analysis.

Checklist   A teacher-made or standardized instrument used to record observations of student performance while demonstrating a particular skill or skill set.

Child find   A component of the Individuals with Disabilities Education Act (IDEA) that requires states to identify, locate, and evaluate all children with disabilities, ages birth to 21, who are in need of early intervention or special education services.

Child find specialist   A developmental child specialist who is qualified to administer assessments, screenings, and evaluations of children between the ages of birth and 21 to determine if they may have disabilities.

Childhood disintegrative disorder (CDD)   A developmental disorder on the autism spectrum that is characterized by typical development up to the age of 2 years, followed by loss of speech and other skills. CDD differs from autism, is usually associated with mental retardation, and affects social behavior and communication as well as including repetitive or stereotypical behaviors.

Child study movement   An integration of education and psychology pertaining to child development and learning, developed by G. Stanley Hall during the early half of the 20th century.

Child study team   Team consisting of staff from the school—including the principal or assistant principal, a team coordinator, the child's teacher, at least one other staff member knowledgeable about the particular child's grade, a school psychologist, and a guidance counselor. The school social worker may also attend, depending on the needs of the child and his or her family. The purpose of the child study team is to assess the child's needs in order to help determine specific types of services and interventions.

Chromosome Within a cell, the structure that carries the genetic information in the form of DNA. Each chromosome is composed of a single long molecule of DNA made up of a combination of specific proteins (ATGC). Typically, developing humans have 22 pairs of autosomes and 2 sex chromosomes. One member of each pair of chromosomes is inherited from the father and the other from the mother. *Note:* Individuals with Down syndrome have an extra chromosome (therefore, the condition is sometimes called trisomy 21).

Cloze procedure An alternative form of assessing reading comprehension in which the teacher removes words from a passage and asks the student to fill in the blanks.

Cognitive therapy A method of counseling and teaching students who have specific disabilities to overcome deficits in adaptive behavior, social adjustment, and passive learning. Cognitive therapy alters the student's thinking process and concept of self.

Cognitive training An instructional method of teaching students with specific learning disabilities to overcome deficits in motivation and problems of learned helplessness and passive learning. Cognitive training alters the student's thinking process and concept of self.

Collaboration The process that occurs when a group or team of individuals work together to design, implement, and evaluate the outcome of an educational program for a student or students with high-incidence disabilities. The collective effort requires equal participation and respect for each member's participation, with each individual working toward the goal of providing the best practices for the student(s) in question.

Comorbidity Two or more disorders or diseases occurring simultaneously within the same individual. For example, children with autism can also have obsessive-compulsive disorder (OCD).

Compulsory education Schooling that is mandated by law.

Concrete Early understanding of computation concepts. At this level, the student can demonstrate math facts by moving objects.

Conduct disorder A specific emotional and behavioral disorder in which the child exhibits inappropriate acting out and/or aggressive behavior that is out of the context and, persistently violates the rights of others.

Conflict resolution strategy A learned behavior or response that allows students to resolve disagreements or to ameliorate defiant behaviors through self-management strategy.

Consequence An event, occurrence, or stimulus that follows immediately after a target behavior.

Constructivist An educational philosophy rooted in the notion that all meaning is relative to each person's experiences and how he or she views the world. There is no objective truth.

Consultation A process in which team members provide information and expertise to one another. Consultation is typically considered a unidirectional process, with the expert imparting his or her skill, knowledge, and experience to the others on the team.

Content enhancement Modifications that allow students with specific learning disabilities to organize, comprehend, and retain information more effectively by using graphic organizers, guided notes, advance organizers, and visual displays.

Contingent reinforcement The positive reinforcement of behavior of either a specific student or a group.

Contract A written agreement in which there is an opportunity for an individual to self-monitor and self-manage behavior as part of a behavioral modification plan. Contracts can be motivating for individuals with disabilities because it is possible to visually monitor the progress made and to see how close one is to obtaining a reward.

Cooperative homework team (CHT) A team designed to help students correctly complete homework and maximize instructional time as well as benefit from well-designed homework assignments. A CHT uses peer teams to grade and cooperatively make corrections to individualized homework assignments.

Co-teaching A collaborative approach to serving students in the same classroom. Most commonly, a special educator works in a regular classroom.

Council for Exceptional Children (CEC) An international professional organization dedicated to improving educational outcomes for children with exceptionalities, including those with disabilities and those who are gifted.

Criterion-referenced assessment An appraisal that compares an individual score to a specific benchmark or criterion. The assessment is given in terms of how close a student's score is to the established benchmark.

Curriculum-based assessment (CBA) An approach that determines a student's instructional needs by assessing the performance of the student. This is in contrast to curriculum-based measurement, which refers to a systematic set of measurement procedures to gather data for instructional decision making.

Curriculum-based measurement (CBM) A method of measuring a student's progress in academic instruction by monitoring the effectiveness of instruction using frequent assessment measures to determine appropriate instruction.

Cystic fibrosis (CF) A genetic disorder (occurring on chromosome 7) that affects the mucus lining of the lungs and digestive system, causing breathing and other problems. CF is a relatively rare inherited genetic disorder that affects the lungs and digestive system. The earlier the disease is diagnosed, the more effective the treatment. Most children diagnosed with CF now reach early adulthood due to improvements in nutrition, physiotherapy, and antibiotic treatment; some reach their 40s and 50s.

Decode An individual's ability to use the alphabetic code in order to form words accurately and automatically. There are four phases of decoding: pre-alphabetic, partial alphabetic, full alphabetic, and automatic. Also, interpreting a social context so that one can make an appropriate response.

Deinstitutionalization A social movement of the 1960s and 1970s intended to obtain improved, humanistic, and less expensive care for chronically mentally ill persons and/or people with mental retardation by moving them from large, centralized mental hospitals into smaller group homes in their own communities.

Delayed echolalia (DE) One of two types of echolalia (the other is immediate echolalia) engaged in by individuals with autism. In delayed echolalia, the individual vocally echoes a phrase (for example, the complete script of a TV commercial or a favorite movie script) after some lapse of time.

Depression A psychological disorder marked by sadness, inactivity, difficulty in thinking and concentrating, and feelings of dejection.

Developmental evaluation An in-depth assessment of a child's skills, administered by a trained professional such as a licensed psychologist. Evaluation tests are used to create a profile of a child's strengths and weaknesses in all developmental areas. The results of a developmental evaluation are used to determine whether the child is in need of early intervention services and/or a treatment plan.

Developmental history Data on a child's early developmental history, usually obtained by interviewing parents, caregivers, or other informants.

Developmentally appropriate practice A method that emphasizes child-initiated learning, exploratory play, and the child's interests.

Developmental retardation (DR) A delay in development. DR can result in school and postschool failure. Two of the main causes of DR are poverty and substandard educational environments.

Developmental screening A quick and general measurement of skills intended to identify children who are in need of further evaluation. A screening test can be in one of two formats—either a questionnaire, completed by a parent or child-care provider, that asks about developmental milestones or a test that is given to a child by a health or educational professional.

Developmental milestone A developmental skill that children acquire within a specific time frame. For example, one developmental milestone is learning to walk. Most children learn this skill or developmental milestone between the ages of 9 and 15 months. Milestones develop in a sequential fashion. Each skill that a child acquires builds on the previous one. These milestones occur across all areas of development, including motor, cognition, communication, and self-help.

Diagnostic prescriptive model An intervention model in which psychological and/or basic skill deficits are revealed by standardized testing, resulting in remediation programs.

Differentiated instruction An educational strategy in which opportunities/environments and instructional practices are tailored to create appropriately different learning experiences for students with differing needs in learning. Examples include acceleration and enrichment, as well as task analyses and mediated scaffolding.

Direct instruction (DI) A method of instruction that is teacher led and that provides students with specific instructions on a task as well as teacher-led practice, independent practice, and immediate corrective feedback.

Direct observation Seeing a behavior as it is exhibited within the environment of the child being observed.

Disability Functional limitations that hinder typical development. Limitations can often be attributed to a physical or sensory impairment, difficulty in learning, or failure of social adaptation.

Discrepancy formula A standard definition used in the identification of individuals with learning disabilities; specifically describes the difference between an individual's IQ and his or her achievement scores. The resulting "discrepancy" between expected aptitude and achievement gives a traditionalist approach to identification of learning disabilities.

Double deficit rapid theory A combination deficit in naming speed and phonological processing that inhibits automatization.

Down syndrome A genetic disorder that results in a newborn baby with 3 rather than 2 copies of the 21st chromosome when cells start dividing, making 47 instead of the normal 46 chromosomes. Down syndrome, sometimes called trisomy 21, is the most common form of mental retardation recognizable at birth. The cognitive disability associated with this syndrome can range from mild to severe.

Due process A right possessed by parents and/or legal guardians of students with disabilities. Due process allows the parents and/or legal guardians a legal hearing if they dispute the identification, evaluation, educational placement, or any other matter related to their child's free and appropriate public education.

Dyscalculia A deficit in the ability to perform mathematical functions.

Dysgraphia The partial inability to remember how to make certain alphabet or arithmetic symbols in handwriting.

Dyslexia A specific reading disorder characterized by difficulties in single-word decoding, usually reflecting insufficient phonological processing. This disorder is often unexpected in relation to age and other cognitive and academic abilities and can severely impair the individual's ability to read.

Dysthymia A psychological disorder that is similar to depression but is marked by a longer duration and a milder form than seen in clinical depression. Dysthymia is less disabling than a major depression; sufferers are usually able to go on working and they rarely require hospitalization.

Early intervention The process of teaching/training young children (0 to 5 years old) who have symptoms of or risk factors for specific disabilities.

Early interventionist A member of a team of professionals, such as doctors, nurses, psychologists, educators, and therapists, who work together to assess the needs of a young child with established disabilities. The early intervention team also assesses the needs of the family and offers support and opportunities to improve the quality of life for the child.

Early intervention service A service, such as speech therapy or physical therapy, provided to an infant or child under the age of 5 who has been diagnosed with a developmental delay or other disability. Under the Individuals with Disabilities Act (IDEA), the child and family are entitled to request whatever early intervention services are needed as part of an individualized family service plan (IFSP).

Echolalia (immediate echolalia) In individuals with autism, a vocal behavior that involves the repetition or echoing of verbal utterances made by another person. It is believed that immediate echolalia may serve many functions for a person with autism, such as a verbal exchange used to indicate affirmation of a prior utterance and/or to request an object or actions.

Educable mentally retarded (EMR) An outdated term indicating individual who can achieve academically on a third- to sixth-grade level and usually has an IQ that falls between 50 and 75.

Educational risk factor A factor in the educational environment (classroom or school) that puts the student at risk for school difficulty.

Education for All Handicapped Children Act (EAHCA) Public Law 94-142; a 1975 act mandating the right to a public education for all students with identified disabilities. EAHCA was the first in a series of laws that now govern special education.

Effective design Instructional design tailored to the specific learning needs of students.

Effective school An educational belief that a school in which the staff works as a team, engaging in collaboration, focusing on evidence-based teaching strategies to tailor instruction to meet the needs of a diverse learning community, is considered to be an effective school; a school in which most or all students reach an expected level of achievement.

Eligibility The determination that a child has met the criteria (prereferral, nondiscriminatory multifactored assessment) for identification as having a disability covered under IDEA.

Embryo An organism in its early stages of development prior to birth. In humans, the embryo is the developing child from conception to the end of the second month of pregnancy.

Emotional and behavioral disorder (EBD) A chronic condition characterized by behavioral or emotional responses that are different from age, cultural norms, or ethnic norms to such a degree that educational performance and social adaptations are adversely affected.

Emotional disturbance (ED) In IDEA, a student shows one or more characteristics over an extended period of time and to such a degree that his or her educational performance is adversely affected. These characteristics include an inability to learn that cannot be explained by intellectual, sensory, or health factors; an inability to build or maintain satisfactory interpersonal relationships with peers and/or teachers; inappropriate types of behavior or feelings under normal circumstances; a general pervasive mood of unhappiness or depression; and a tendency to develop physical symptoms or fears associated with personal or school problems.

Emotional handicap   Emotional and behavioral disorder or emotional disturbance; an emotional or behavioral disability.

English as second language (ESL) teacher   An instructor who teaches English to learners whose native language is other than English.

Error analysis   The technique of analyzing patterns of errors in mathematical computations so that the teacher can make determinations on the nature of any math difficulties that the student may be experiencing.

Establishing operation   An antecedent behavior that is typically present in the behavior of students with emotional and behavioral disorder.

Eugenics   A social philosophy and pseudoscience popular in the early 20th century that advocated the purported "improvement" of the human race by selective breeding, birth control, genetic engineering, and even extermination of those considered not "genetically pure." Proponents stated that eugenics would lessen human suffering, lessen the incidence of genetically caused medical conditions, save society money, and even create a more intelligent human race.

Executive control   Functions of internalizing behavior in order to plan for changes in the future. Included are nonverbal working memory, internalization of speech, self-regulation, and motivation.

Executive functioning   Skills needed for organization and planning. Individuals with Asperger's syndrome, although considered high functioning, have executive functioning deficits and thus struggle with organizational skills. Fortunately, executive functioning skills can be developed with the help of relatively simple strategies such as the use of homework logs, assignment checklists, or day planners.

Explicit instruction   A teaching method that uses carefully designed materials and activities to provide structures and supports that aid students with special needs in organizing and assimilating new information.

Expressive vocabulary   The level of comprehension of the syntax of written and spoken language by the speaker or writer.

Externalizing   Problem behaviors that are exhibited outward toward other individuals; acting out.

Fetal alcohol effects (FAE)   A pattern of delayed development associated primarily with hyperactivity and difficulties with learning. Many developmental problems are consistent with prenatal exposure to alcohol, yet do not meet all of the diagnostic criteria for fetal alcohol syndrome. Often children with FAE are later diagnosed with a learning disability or attention deficit hyperactivity disorder.

Fetal alcohol syndrome (FAS)   A pattern of delayed growth and development, both mental and physical, with cranial, facial, limb, and cardiovascular defects, found in some children of mothers who drank alcohol during pregnancy. There is some controversy over the amount of alcohol a pregnant woman must drink to cause her child to have FAS. The most common abnormalities associated with FAS are prenatal and postnatal inability to thrive, microcephaly, developmental delay or mental retardation, a short upturned nose with sunken nasal bridge, a thin upper lip, and cardiac defects.

Fetus   A term used to refer to a baby in utero during the period of gestation between eight weeks and birth.

Fluency   A combination of accuracy and high rate. Often used in reading but may be used to designate fast, accurate performance of any skill.

Fragile X syndrome   A genetic abnormality in the X chromosome—specifically, a broken part at the bottom of the 23rd pair of chromosomes. It is considered part of the autism spectrum. Fragile X syndrome is considered the single most common inherited cause of neurodevelopmental neuropsychiatric dysfunction known that can be diagnosed with a DNA test. The syndrome occurs in 1 out of 300 to 400 children. Individuals with fragile X tend to have strengths in verbal tasks but tend to be particularly weak in the area of visual-spatial functioning, particularly math. They also have problems with perseveration, hyperarousal, echolalia, gaze aversion, stereotypical movements such as hand flapping, and qualitative abnormalities of communication such as repetitive speech.

Free appropriate public education (FAPE)   For students with special needs, the special education and related services provided in conformity with an individual education plan (IEP). FAPE requires that a school district provide special education and related services free for all students with disabilities.

Frontal cortex   The portion of the brain involved with executive reasoning, planning, abstract thought, and other complex cognitive functions in addition to motor function. Frontal regions of the cerebral cortex, which mediate executive functions, are targets of natural and drug rewards as well as of stressful situations.

Full inclusion   Placing all students, regardless of their special needs, in their neighborhood school's general education classrooms for the entire school day.

Functional academic skills   Basic reading, writing, mathematics, and learning readiness skills. These skills are commonly taught in elementary school to individuals with mild mental retardation. The emphasis at this age is on identifying the skills needed to develop a sense of independence and the ability to make successful transitions into adulthood. For example, students are taught how to read phone books, newspapers, and labels on foods and medications, as well as how to make change and fill out job applications.

Functional behavioral assessment (FBA)   An assessment model based on direct observation of a student's behavior and used to figure out the function of behavior (i.e., why the student behaves in a certain way). The practice of determining the consequences (purpose of behavior), antecedents (what triggers the behavior), and setting events (in what contexts the behavior occurs) of inappropriate behavior.

Functional curriculum   A type of instruction whose focus is on teaching individuals material that is relevant to participation in activities of daily life.

General education curriculum   The curriculum provided to students in general education classes, usually designed to assist in the development of academic skills that prepare a student to continue in school and graduate after completing the 12th grade.

Generalization   The ability for an individual to learn a new behavior or skill in one setting and then transfer the behavior or skill to other settings.

Gene   The hereditary material that determines how an organism will look and behave. Coded in a cell, a gene is a single unit located on a chromosome and passed from one generation to the next. Genes are responsible for hair and eye color, for example.

Genetics   Inherited qualities having to do with information that is passed from parents to offspring through genes in sperm and egg cells.

Gifted   A student who exhibits high performance capability in intellectual, creative, and/or artistic areas. A gifted individual may possess an unusual leadership capacity or may excel in a specific academic field.

Handicap   The problems that a person with a disability or impairment faces during interaction with the environment. A disability may pose a handicap in one environment but not in the context of a different environment.

Hemisphere of the brain   One of two halves into which the human brain is divided—right and left. Each hemisphere of the brain is dominant for certain behaviors. For example, it is theorized that the right hemisphere is dominant in spatial abilities, face recognition, visual imagery, and music, whereas the left hemisphere may be more adept at calculations, math, and logical abilities.

Heritability   The tendency for a particular disorder to be passed from a parent to a child via genes.

Heterogeneous grouping   The practice of creating a diverse group of students for instruction.

High-functioning autism (HFA)   Description of children with certain types of autism based on age of onset, level of intellectual functioning, and the presence of spoken language. Children diagnosed with Asperger's syndrome and/or pervasive developmental disorder not otherwise specified are considered to have high-functioning autism because they can communicate verbally. However, such individuals may be unable to relate in a socially appropriate manner to others. Furthermore, they may exhibit stereotypical traits such as repetitive or ritualistic behaviors, perseveration, and idiosyncratic eating practices.

High risk   A level of risk indicating that a student may have one or more factors that in combination predict likelihood of development of a particular disability.

Holistic trait scoring   An assessment tool for judging samples of writing. In holistic trait scoring, the scorer makes an overall judgment of the writing sample by using samples of the group, establishing a range from best to worst, and any other sample values deemed appropriate. The scorer will then assign a value according to a predetermined scale.

Homogeneous grouping   The practice of placing students within classes according to one or more selected criteria such as age, ability, disability, achievement, and interests.

Human Genome Project   A government-funded international multi-site project designed to create a gene directory that can be used to answer questions such as what specific genes do and how they work. The Human Genome Project has produced a complete map of human DNA. Furthermore, maps of the gene sequence of many species have now been made. The map of human genes will allow scientists to identify variations within genetic makeup and potentially to identify the genetic basis of abnormal characteristics.

Hyperactivity   Behaviors such as constant talking, excessive movement, and fidgeting. Individuals who demonstrate hyperactivity can also have difficulty controlling impulsiveness and inattentiveness, as well as difficulty engaging in leisure activities quietly. Hyperactivity commonly occurs in individuals with attention deficit hyperactivity disorder and emotional and behavioral disorder.

Imminent risk   A level of risk indicating that development of a particular disability is likely in the near future.

Impulsivity   Characterized by impulsive behaviors such as often blurting out answers before questions have been completed, having difficulty waiting to take one's turn, and interrupting or intruding on someone else's conversations. Impulsivity commonly occurs in individuals with attention deficit hyperactivity disorder.

Inattentiveness Examples include often forgetting important details and becoming easily distracted by environmental sights and sounds. Inattentiveness commonly occurs in individuals with attention deficit hyperactivity disorder.

Incidence The number of new cases of a specific condition.

Inclusion Placing students with disabilities in regular education classrooms.

Inclusive early childhood program A preschool in which curriculum is designed to serve diverse groups of learners, including children with and without disabilities.

Independent living skill A skill needed by individuals with mild mental retardation in order to become independent and live on their own when they transition into adulthood. For example, for an individual to live alone, he or she needs to be able to work, rent an apartment, manage a bank account, pay bills, clean house, clean clothes, and so on.

Indirect measure An assessment technique that involves rating scales, interviews, and checklists instead of direct observation measurements to determine targeted outcomes.

Individual education plan (IEP) A plan mandated by the Individuals with Disabilities Education Act (IDEA). IDEA requires that all children with disabilities have an IEP developed by an educational team. The plan must include a statement of present level of academic performance, instructional goals, educational services to be provided, and criteria and procedures for assessing whether the goals have been met.

Individualized family service plan (IFSP) A plan similar to the individual education plan except that it is for families with young children (birth to age 3) with disabilities. An IFSP is drawn up by an early intervention team to ensure that young children and their families receive the services they need.

Individuals with Disabilities Education Act (IDEA) A federal law that states that in order to receive funding, public schools must provide a free and appropriate education to all children regardless of the severity of their disabilities. This legislation was first enacted in 1975 and in 2004 was called the Individuals with Disabilities Education Improvement Act.

Informal reading inventory (IRI) Test that provides in-depth information about a student's reading comprehension. An IRI can be teacher constructed, but many inventories are commercially available. Students read passages and teachers ask questions regarding comprehension of the material that was read.

Interim alternative education setting (IAES) A separate educational setting in which students with emotional or behavioral disorders are placed due to their inability to thrive in a regular school setting. The goal for these alternative settings is to teach students how to self-manage their behavioral deficits and to learn appropriate behavior in order to be reintegrated into the regular school environment.

Intermittent support For individuals with mental retardation, support considered to be on an "as needed" basis. The student will not always need this level of support. The support may be transitional in nature and may last throughout the life span of the individual.

Internalizing An individual's problem behaviors that are self-contained, without any apparent outward expression.

Interstate New Teacher Assessment and Support Consortium (INTASC) An assembly of national and state education agencies created in 1987 to focus on the preparation, licensing, and ongoing professional development of teachers.

In utero A term used in biology to refer to events that occur in the womb before birth.

Invented spelling In early spelling development, the student begins to notice initial letter-sound correspondences and is able to represent these in his or her spellings, most often with the first letter of the word. Soon afterward, students are able to represent all the sounds in the word with letters that make those sounds. For example, "speleng" might be invented for spelling.

Itinerant service Specialized services provided by a person who is not always present, as might be the case in which a psychologist visits a classroom on a schedule or a social worker travels from school to school.

Job coach A person who assists disabled adults in their place of employment, providing vocational assessment, instruction, appropriate workplace behavior training, planning, organization, and other important skills needed for successful employment.

Juvenile delinquency Criminal or illegal acts performed by juveniles. During the 1800s, juvenile delinquency was considered a mental disorder that required institutionalization.

Juvenile justice worker Within a criminal justice agency, an individual who works with youthful offenders.

Labeling A sometimes pejorative term used to refer to the identification or diagnosis of children with disabilities. Labeling can cause social stigma. However, labels are important because they ensure that children with disabilities get the special services they need.

Learned helplessness A student's belief, prior to attempting to solve a problem, that his or her efforts will result in a negative outcome; the belief that "I can't do it" before even trying to complete the problem.

Learning disability (LD) A disorder that results in substantial difficulties in speaking, listening, reading, written expression, or in mathematics. Other conditions may occur along with a learning disability, but are not the primary cause of the learning deficit. Any of a number of different cognitive impairments. People with LD can sometimes have emotional difficulties as a result of their disability.

Least restrictive environment (LRE) A principle of federal law (IDEA) requiring public agencies to establish procedures to ensure that children with disabilities are educated with children who are not disabled to the greatest extent feasible and according to the special needs of the child. The law states that children with disabilities should not be in separate or special classes or schools unless the general education environment cannot effectively serve the needs of the child with disabilities. A LRE may include some supplementary aids and services that cannot be offered in a general education class.

Licensed psychologist A professional licensed to provide psychological services including testing and the evaluation or assessment of personal characteristics such as intelligence, personality, abilities, interests, and aptitudes; counseling or psychotherapy; and other forms of treatment of psychological or behavioral problems.

Likert scale An assessment instrument that asks respondents to answer a series of statements by choosing from an array of options; for example, by indicating whether they strongly agree (SA), agree (A), are undecided (U), disagree (D), or strongly disagree (SD) with each statement.

Limited supports An intensity of support that is consistent over time but not intermittent in nature.

Local education agency (LEA) The education authority that is responsible for curricular details, school budgetary matters, hiring and training of educators and staff, and ensuring that the timely completion of all required interventions and assessments is achieved in relation to federal and state statutes.

Locus of control Belief that control of one's behavior is internal or external.

Long-term memory Memory that is effectively unlimited; remembering something for days or longer.

Maintenance The ability to maintain a new, learned behavior or skill over time after the initial training has ended.

Maladaptive behavior The inability to perform the typical behaviors within environmental expectations; behaving in ways that interfere with normal social development.

Maldevelopment A being or an organ that did not develop in a typical way; for example, brain maldevelopment of a fetus. The term was introduced in France in the 1990s to replace the term *underdevelopment*. Maldevelopment can occur only during a specific time in development of the brain—namely, the fifth and the seventh month of pregnancy.

Manifestation determination The determination of the cause of a student's behavior when the school is considering suspension of that student from school. A decision must be made as to whether the inappropriate behavior is being caused by (is a manifestation of) the student's disability. By law, schools must make this determination prior to imposing a suspension.

Mastery motivation The intrinsic motivation that an individual has in interacting with his or her environment in order to learn about that environment. It appears early in life and is regarded by many researchers as a key motivator for development. Some researchers believe that young children with mental retardation show lowered mastery motivation compared to their typically developing peers.

Maze procedure Similar to a cloze procedure, in which the teacher gauges a student's reading comprehension by removing words from a reading passage. The maze differs from the cloze in that the maze procedure provides choices for the student to insert into the blank spaces of the reading passage.

Mean The arithmetic average of a group of scores contained within a distribution.

Mean length of utterance (MLU) A numerical computation given by collecting a sample of a child's spoken language, counting the number of utterances, and then dividing by the total number of morphemes in the sample. The MLU is thought to represent the morphological complexity of language use in young children.

Mental retardation (MR) Characterized by impaired or incomplete mental development, a low IQ, and significant functional limitations in adaptive behavior originating during the developmental period (i.e., before age 18).

Metabolic A term used to describe the chemical and physical changes that occur in the body when molecules are either broken down or built up in cells and tissues.

Metacomprehension The ability to plan and arrange comprehension into various structures to suit particular needs at a specified moment.

Metamemory   The ability to think about and organize one's memory in a substantive manner.

Mild mental retardation (MMR)   Characterized by a significant subaverage intellectual functioning that exists concurrently with deficits in adaptive behavior, manifests itself during the development period, and adversely affects a child's educational performance. Children with mild forms of mental retardation are often identified by measurements of an IQ test with a score at or about 70 (AAMR, 2002); evidenced by significant functional limitations in at least two of the following skills: communication, self-care, home living, social/interpersonal skills, use of community resources, self-direction, functional academic skills, work, leisure, health, and safety; also defined as needing intermittent supports.

Minimal risk   A level of risk that is considered low to negligible for developing a particular disability.

Mnemonic strategy   A memory-enhancing skill that is taught to aid students in retention of information. Methods include letter strategies, keyword, pegword, and reconstructive elaborations.

Modification   Adaptation to the curriculum or to expectations regarding student performance.

Mood disorder   A psychological disorder in which the emotion exhibited is inappropriate for the circumstance.

Morpheme   A meaningful word part such as a root, prefix, or plural ending.

Morphological awareness   The knowledge of morphological structures of language. Can be assessed informally through observation of a student's language use.

Morphology   How words are formed and understanding the meanings of word parts.

Motivation   A student's ability to activate, guide, and maintain behavior.

Multidisciplinary team (MDT)   A group of professionals from diverse disciplines who come together to provide comprehensive assessment and consultation in the special needs of individuals with disabilities. MDTs can determine eligibility for special education services and can develop individual education plans for students with disabilities.

National Mental Health and Special Education Coalition   A comprehensive national initiative that partners educators, primary care providers, mental health providers, related mental health professionals, and families in order to increase their understanding that children's mental health disorders are real, common, and treatable.

Negative punishment   The removal of a reinforcing stimulus in order to decrease the occurrence of a behavior.

Negative reinforcement   The removal of an aversive stimulus in order to increase the occurrence of a behavior.

Neurobiological   A term referring to the biological study of the nervous system. Research on the origins of learning disabilities has been linked to neurobiology.

Neuropsychological assessment   An assessment model that links psychological characteristics to appropriate brain-site functioning.

Neurotransmitter   A naturally occurring brain chemical that communicates between nerve cells. Neurotransmitters are thought to be largely responsible for a person's feelings, emotions, actions, and behavior. Some of the most commonly studied neurotransmitters are dopamine, acetylcholine, serotonin, glutamate and norepinephrine.

No Child Left Behind (NCLB)   A federal law with the goal of improving performance standards of all of America's primary and secondary schools by increasing teacher and student accountability through standardized testing and an increased focus on reading. The No Child Left Behind Act of 2001 (Public Law 107-110) is a reauthorization of the Elementary and Secondary Education Act of 1965 (ESEA).

Nondiscriminatory evaluation   An IDEA requirement that assessments be free of bias. This could mean an assessment written in the native language of an individual or an assessment that is sensitive to diverse cultural norms.

Normalization   Belief that students with disabilities should be educated in environments close to those of their typically developing age peers.

Norm-referenced assessment   A standardized assessment instrument that compares a student's performance to a normative group of the same age or grade level.

Number sense   A fundamental aspect of developing math skills. The awareness of numbers in everyday life and how they can be compared and manipulated.

Occupational therapy (OT)   A therapy that has the primary purpose of assisting individuals with disabilities to achieve or maintain capacity to function in daily living activities at a level that allows as much independence as possible; helps individuals develop adaptive skills, such as dressing, bathing, and toileting, that will aid in daily living and improve interactions with the physical and social world; focuses on developing functional skills related to sensory-motor integration, coordination of movement, fine motor skills, and self-help skills.

Occupational therapist A licensed therapist whose primary focus is on teaching individuals functional physical skills required in daily living. The need for instruction could be due to developmental delays, cognitive deficits, or injury.

Oppositional-defiant disorder (ODD) Confrontational responses to authority figures. A child with ODD exhibits noncompliant (disobedient) behavior without provocation.

Organizational consultation An outside consultant whose primary focus lies in promoting organizational change within a school.

Orthographic patterns The ability to spell words based upon conventional spelling rules.

Orthographic processing The ability to establish representations of letter sequencing (spelling) in memory.

Overlapping curriculum An ongoing curriculum for students with high-incidence disabilities, primarily to achieve goals and objectives separate from the specific curriculum goals (e.g., using group work in order to teach social skills to a student with special needs).

Parallel instruction Significant changes to the conceptual difficulty and/or delivery of the instruction in order to meet the specific needs of the learner.

Peer support A strategy using the peer group to change a student's behavior. Some examples of peer support are peer monitoring, positive peer reporting, peer tutoring, and peer group mentoring.

Performance assessment A systematic observation of student performance conducted at any time while the student is performing a specified task.

Performance deficit A student who lacks fluency in a particular skill.

Perinatal The time span shortly before and after the birth of a baby.

Permanent product Something that can be saved for later assessment, such as writing. Permanent products are often used to determine educational outcomes.

Pervasive developmental disorder not otherwise specified (PDD-NOS) A developmental disorder also referred to as atypical autism. PDD-NOS fails to meet the autism onset criteria. It may or may not be associated with developmental delays and can affect social, communicative, and repetitive behaviors.

Phenylketonuria (PKU) A genetic metabolic disorder that can cause mental retardation in babies who have difficulty breaking down and using the amino acid phenylalanine. If PKU is diagnosed immediately after birth, various forms of mental retardation can be avoided by a diet restricting foods that contain phenylalanine.

Phonological awareness The foundational reading skill in which a student recognizes sound segments in words that are presented orally.

Phonology The sound system of language, how a word sounds to an individual.

Physical therapist A licensed therapist whose primary focus is on improving/rehabilitating an individual's physical strength, agility, endurance, and gross and fine motor functioning.

Physical therapy (PT) A therapy that addresses sensory and gross motor functions. Physical therapists can assist students by helping them learn optimal positions for various tasks, by teaching them how to move in the classroom and around the school, and by helping them overcome their physical limitations by developing strength and coordination.

Planum temporale The posterior (back) superior (upper) surface of the superior temporal gyrus in the cerebrum of the human brain. It is the structure in the brain believed to be involved with language.

Portfolio assessment Collecting and analyzing samples of student work as a form of assessment. Portfolio assessment offers a holistic option for evaluating student performance, but it is difficult to use for daily instructional decision making due to limits of expressing growth over a short period of time.

Positive behavior support (PBS) A federally funded initiative designed to prevent and address problem behaviors in schools.

Positive punishment The introduction of an aversive stimulus to decrease the occurrence of a behavior.

Positive reinforcement Presenting a reward or a desired event immediately following a behavior, making that behavior more likely to occur.

Postnatal The period beginning immediately after the birth of a child and extending for about 6 weeks.

Pragmatics Using language in social situations; the study of how language is used to influence others.

Prefrontal lobe The anterior (front) part of the frontal lobe portion of the brain responsible for behavior, learning, judgment, personality, and other executive functions.

Prenatal The time before birth when a baby is developing in utero; specifically the time between conception and birth of an infant.

Prereferral Trials of an intervention or problem-solving sessions before a student is referred for evaluation for special education.

President's Committee on Mental Retardation (PCMR) A federal advisory committee established in the 1960s by presidential executive order to advise the president of the

United States and the Secretary of Health and Human Services on issues concerning people with mental retardation. The PCMR coordinates activities among federal agencies and assesses the impact of government policies on the lives of mentally retarded people and their families.

Prevalence   The number or percentage of people who have a particular disorder at any given time.

Prevention   Keeping something from happening; precluding a disability or keeping it from getting worse.

Prevocational preparation skill   A skill for adults with impaired cognitive functioning. Prevocational preparation includes basic work routine orientation, communication skills, job ability assessment, and self-management skills.

Primary condition   The cause of a person's disability; the foundational cause from which other disabilities can develop.

Primary identification   An assessment and identification process designed to identify children having or at risk of having a particular disorder.

Primary intervention, primary prevention   An intervention that is designed to eliminate or counteract certain risk factors so that a disability is never acquired. Intervention that seeks to reduce the occurrence of new instances of a specific problem within the general population.

Primary trait scoring   An assessment tool in which all writing is deemed to be purposeful and directed toward a specific theme and/or audience. The focus of the scoring centers on the audience and the purpose of the writing activity. First, the trait must be identified, and then a scale is developed to measure the sample.

Proactive behavior plan   A classroom strategy used particularly with students who demonstrate challenging behavior, but also considered effective for all students. Proactive behavior plans include, but are not limited to, environmental arrangement conducive to promoting appropriate behavior in students, techniques such as "catching" students being good, concise and consistent rules, teacher–student contracts for behavioral expectations, teacher's realistic expectations of students with challenging behaviors, and group management plans.

Probe   An instructional activity in which a teacher seeks to ascertain the rate or fluency of a student's performance in reading or mathematics. A probe is usually short in duration and in number of problems or length of passage.

Profoundly mentally retarded (PMR)   The category for individuals who have IQs of 25 and below. According to the American Association on Mental Retardation (AAMR), the categories for mental retardation should be based on level of support needed; consequently, an individual considered profoundly mentally retarded would require pervasive supports.

Prosody   The way oral reading sounds, including expression and inflection of the reader's voice and placing of pauses between phrases.

Psychosocial   A term referring to the emotional and behavioral needs of a student.

Psychodynamic   Based on psychoanalytic theory, a term that focuses on mental and emotional processes, especially those experienced and developed in early childhood, and their effects on past and current behavior, feelings, and relationships.

Psychological processing disorder   A disorder characterized by the inability to appropriately process sensory, emotional, and/or cognitive stimuli within the receptive centers of an individual's brain.

Psychopathology   Mental illness.

Psychotic disorder   A psychological disorder in which one loses the understanding of reality shared by most people.

Rapid naming speed   The ability to quickly retrieve the spoken referent for visual stimuli.

Rate   A numerical representation of the number of tasks accomplished within a given period of time; can be considered on two reading levels: word-reading automaticity and text-reading rate.

Receptive vocabulary   The comprehension of the written and spoken word by the listener or reader.

Recidivism   Recurrence; the repeating of problem behavior over time.

Referral   The next step after a student has been through a prereferral assessment to determine the need for additional analysis and assessment in order to decide whether the individual has a specific disability.

Regression   The loss of previously acquired gains in skill or performance levels of behaviors.

Regular education initiative (REI)   Mid-1980s concept that gave more responsibility to general education teachers and staff in the education of students with disabilities. The expectation was that students would receive special education services but would still participate in the general education classroom, where the general education teacher would assume responsibility for at least part of the students' education.

Reliability   The degree of consistency of measurement, or how consistently a specific instrument measures the same construct over time, individuals, or parts of the test.

Remediation   A specific educational program that is designed to teach a person to overcome a discrepancy through intensive teaching or reteaching.

Repetitive behavior One of the diagnostic criteria for autism. Repetitive behaviors include motor mannerisms such as rocking back and forth and/or hand or finger flapping.

Representational A level of comprehension of math operations by which the student can demonstrate understanding with pictures or tally marks on paper; differs from concrete understanding in that there is no use of manipulatives.

Research lead teacher (RLT) In a teacher study group, the primary teacher who has expertise in behavior intervention strategies. The RLT utilizes peer coaching, modeling, and collaborative consultation strategies to devise appropriate interventions that address the student's needs.

Resiliency The ability of an individual to combat or to be protected from risk of specific conditions.

Resiliency factor Something that decreases the likelihood of an individual's having negative outcomes in different areas of life. For example, in the education of a child, resiliency factors might include good parenting skills, an attentive teacher, and genetic factors.

Resource room A classroom in which students with qualifying special education needs spend at least part of their day receiving individualized special education services.

Response to intervention (RTI) An alternative method of identifying students with specific learning disabilities; identification based on a student's response to effective instruction rather than on the basis of test scores.

Restricted interests One of the diagnostic criteria for autism. Restricted interests can include persistent preoccupation with body parts or objects, restricted patterns of interest, and abnormal intensity of focus on one particular thing.

Rett syndrome (RS) A developmental delay, related to the autism spectrum, characterized by physical and motor difficulties. Individuals with Rett syndrome do not necessarily have communication or social interaction difficulties. In this way, RS differs from other disorders on the autism spectrum.

Rhyme The practice of finding words that sound similar.

Risk factor A condition or event to which an individual may be exposed that increases the chance that the person will develop a disability.

Rubric A scoring instrument used to evaluate the quality of a student's work and to record his or her degree of mastery.

Running record A method of assessing the accuracy of oral reading in which the teacher listens to a student's oral reading and then records marks on a page to indicate how the student read each word. The teacher also notes error types, including substitutions, omissions, insertions, repetitions, and hesitations. Analysis of the type of errors and the patterns of errors can guide future instruction.

Scaffolded instruction A variety of procedures that give the learner response cues and other supports. The supports are then gradually withdrawn so the student can respond independently to naturally occurring stimuli.

Schizophrenia A mental illness that is characterized by a distorted view of the real world; by a greatly reduced ability to carry out one's daily tasks; and by abnormal ways of thinking, feeling, perceiving, and behaving.

School psychologist A professional trained to assess the intellectual, behavioral, developmental, and educational level of a student. Often the school psychologist is part of the child study team.

School reform movement In special education, the shift in U.S. public schools away from separating students with disabilities from other students in the school and toward mainstreaming disabled students into the regular classroom. Beginning in the late 20th century, this movement sought to bring the rights of those with disabilities to the forefront of educational reform.

Screening Using a variety of formal and informal assessments and observations to identify students who might have specific disabilities.

Secondary disability A concomitant disability that is related to a primary disability and that does not occur in the absence of a primary condition.

Secondary intervention An intervention designed to reduce or eliminate the effects of existing risk factors.

Secondary prevention An intervention designed to address various conditions that have occurred but can be improved or kept from getting worse.

Section 504 plan A plan authorized by the Rehabilitation Act of 1973. Section 504 of the Rehabilitation Act states that no individuals shall be excluded from a public education on the basis of having a disability. The laws related to Section 504 focus mainly on accommodations for individuals with disabilities and can sometimes offer services to individuals with disabilities who do not qualify under the regulations of IDEA.

Segment The ability to divide words into their individual phonemes (sounds).

Self-advocacy The ability of students with specific learning disabilities to demonstrate an understanding of their disability, an awareness of their legal rights, and the ability to communicate understanding of their needs and rights to those in a position of authority.

Self-contained classroom A special classroom, usually located within a regular public school building, that includes only students with qualifying exceptional needs.

Self-determination The ability to make one's own decisions about the various aspects of importance in one's life; acting autonomously, having self-regulated behavior, and responding in a psychologically empowered and self-realizing manner.

Self-instruction The method of instruction in which the steps in a particular task are verbalized at first by both the teacher and the student, eventually by the student alone.

Self-management program A behavior program designed to allow the student to have the skills necessary to recognize, control, and adapt or alter his or her behavior to a more appropriate behavior via preestablished and practiced routines.

Self-monitoring A form of observational data collection in which target individuals observe and collect data on themselves. Commonly used with individuals with mental retardation or emotional and behavioral disorder for monitoring their own classroom behaviors.

Semantics The meaning system of language, including both word meaning and sentence meaning.

Setting event The current or previous setting that has an effect on a specific behavior.

Severe mental retardation The category for individuals with mental retardation who have IQs between 25 and 40. According to the AAMR, the categories for mental retardation should be based on the level of support needed. For example, a person with severe mental retardation would require extensive supports, as opposed to individuals with mild mental retardation, who may require only intermittent support.

Shaping The reinforcement of successive approximations of the target behaviors.

Short-term memory The mental ability to recall information that has been stored for a relatively short time period ranging from a few seconds to a few hours.

Sight word A high-frequency word—such as *was* and *said* and *because*—that does not closely follow decodable patterns. These are words that a proficient reader reads on sight without stopping to decode.

Situational analysis A situation in which the student interprets the context of an interaction to determine the appropriate response.

Skill deficit A deficiency in the acquisition of a particular skill.

Social competence A student's ability to perform a set of contextually appropriate behaviors that elicit desirable and socially valid outcomes that span adaptive behaviors and specific social skills.

Socially valid A response outcome that can be interpreted as forming a correct answer in terms of expectations elicited from a specific social interaction.

Social maladjustment A student's pervasive and consistent inability to perform a set of contextually appropriate behaviors that elicit desirable and socially valid outcomes spanning adaptive behaviors and specific social skills.

Social skill A specific behavior that when successfully executed within an appropriate context can lead to socially valid outcomes.

Social skills instruction Teaching specific behaviors that, when performed successfully within an appropriate context, can lead to socially valid outcomes.

Social skills training Training that includes teaching manners and positive interactions with others—such as approaching others in socially acceptable ways, asking for permission, making and keeping friends, sharing, developing academic survival skills, listening, following directions, finding better ways to handle frustration and anger, learning an internal dialogue to cool oneself down and reflect upon the best course of action, finding acceptable ways to resolve conflict with others, using words instead of physical contact, and seeking assistance for conflict resolution.

Sociometrics Measurement of social affiliation.

Speech and language impairment A disorder characterized by speech that deviates from the speech of other people so much that it (1) calls attention to itself, (2) interferes with communication, or (3) provokes distress in the speaker or listener.

Speech-language service A service provided by a speech-language therapist or pathologist for an individual with a communication disorder. These services can include assistance in such areas as oral-motor therapy, articulation, expressive and receptive language, semantics, pragmatics, and syntax.

Speech-language therapist or pathologist (SLP) A licensed therapist whose primary focus is on teaching individuals with deficits in spoken language.

Stage of learning One of a hierarchy of steps in which the act of learning is acquired by each learner, with acquisition being the first and most superficial stage, followed by fluency, generalization, maintenance, and adaptation.

Standard deviation (SD) The arithmetic computation that represents the variability that accompanies the mean in describing a distribution. This statistical representation allows the user to know the distance of a particular score from the mean in terms of a standard score that represents an equal increment for each SD. A unit of variance.

State education agency (SEA) The regulatory agency responsible for oversight of school districts within the state. Many of the requirements mandated by federal statute are initiated and monitored by the SEA. The SEA is also responsible for apportionment of federal and state funds earmarked for general education and specific educational programs. The SEA is also responsible for establishing and reporting the achievement standards that are required in order to receive federal funding.

Stereotypical behavior One of a variety of repetitive or restrictive behaviors found in individuals with EBD, MR, or ASD. These behaviors can include hand flapping, rocking, echolalia, perseveration, and obsessive-compulsive behaviors.

Stimulus cuing A stimulus that provides information about what to do by suggesting the next words of something forgotten or imperfectly learned, such as a prompt to do a desired task.

Strategy instruction Instruction in *how* to do a task. An educational strategy designed to reduce the level of explicit instruction necessary to complete instruction by teaching students the necessary tools to maximize learning opportunities through organizational skill development, academic skills, and social skills, while providing ample instruction and subsequent practice to master these skills.

Symmetry Having two parts that correspond equally with each other in terms of size, form, and arrangement. For example, the symmetry of brains can affect brain functions that distinguish individuals with learning disabilities from those without learning disabilities.

Syndrome The association of several clinically recognizable features, signs, symptoms, phenomena, or characteristics that often occur together so that the presence of one feature alerts the physician to the presence of the others.

Syntax The linguistic rules for forming phrases and sentences.

Task analysis A strategy for teaching a complex behavior or task by breaking it down into a sequence of manageable components.

Task persistence Sticktoitiveness. The ability to concentrate on projects and to stick with an activity even when it is somewhat difficult. Many individuals with mental retardation lack the skill of task persistence at first, but with practice and patience it can be developed.

Teacher assistance team (TAT) A school-based team designed as a prereferral intervention model to address a student's problems prior to determining eligibility for special education services.

Temperament Distinct genetically based sets of psychological tendencies or dispositions with which all individuals are born. These tendencies affect and shape every aspect of the individual's personality development. Temperament begins with a multitude of genetic instructions that guide the development of the brain and then are affected by prenatal management. A child's temperament is present at birth and remains relatively stable throughout life but can be modified somewhat.

Teratogen A substance that can cause birth defects or malformations in a fetus. Examples of teratogens that can affect a fetus include infections, X-rays, and high and consistent levels of mercury or lead. Infections contracted by the mother during the first trimester of pregnancy (e.g., measles, AIDS, venereal diseases) have been directly linked with central nervous system damage in the developing fetus. The incompatibility between the blood type (e.g., Rh factor) of the mother and the fetus can also be a teratogen. Teratogens are highly correlated with various forms of mental retardation and other disabilities.

Tertiary prevention An intervention designed to lessen the negative consequences or the increasing complications of existing conditions; a third level of prevention.

Timing An instructional activity in which a short time duration (e.g., 1 minute) is given for a student to complete a written passage or mathematical problems. The goal is to see how many words or problems can be read or solved within the time period.

Title I program Program made possible by federally designated funds provided to improve the academic achievement of children from low-income families. More than half of all public schools receive Title I funds. A school must have at least 40 percent of its student population from low-income families to qualify for this money. The proportion of low-income families is most frequently measured by the percentage of students receiving free and reduced-price lunches.

Trainable mentally retarded (TMR) Now an outdated term indicating an individual who has an IQ of between 30 and 50 and can achieve academically up to second-grade level work. Such individuals are also able to learn practical skills that will help them find employment.

Trajectory   The path and rate of development of a child. Despite the tremendous variations in normal development, most children fall within the bounds of typical development.

Transdisciplinary team   An intervention team designed to assess an individual's specific needs; the team members span different professional disciplines. This allows varied approaches to best serve the student.

Transition plan   Under federal law (IDEA), a plan that must be included in a student's individual education plan by the time he or she is 14 years of age. IDEA defines transition services as a coordinated set of activities that promote a student's movement from school to postschool activities, including postsecondary education, vocational training, integrated employment (including supported employment), continuing and adult education, adult services, independent living, and community participation. The plan must be based on the individual student's needs. Some states require transition planning to begin before the child is 14 years of age. Ideally, transition planning includes the student's participation in developing his or her own plan.

Traumatic brain injury (TBI)   Damage to brain tissue caused by an external mechanical force, such as in an accident or fall. Symptoms can include, but are not limited to, loss of consciousness and posttraumatic amnesia. TBI can also affect an individual's cognitive abilities as well as personality and social skills.

Trimester   The 3-month periods that make up the human gestation period of approximately 40 weeks. The first trimester of pregnancy is a crucial time of fetal development because during this time the fetus is particularly susceptible to central nervous system damage.

Trisomy 18   Also known as Edwards syndrome; a chromosomal abnormality that is more severe and less common than Down syndrome. Symptoms include severe learning disabilities and often numerous physical defects, such as cleft lip and palate, clubfoot, and malformation of internal organs. Individuals with trisomy 18 have an extra chromosome 18.

T-unit   A phrase that can stand alone, such as an independent clause with several dependent clauses attached to it. T-unit length is calculated by counting the total number of words written and dividing by the number of T-units.

Type-token ratio   The proportion of unique words in a writing sample. To calculate the type-token ratio, first count the number of words written, and then count the number of words that are written only once in the passage (unique words). Divide the number of unique words by the total number of words to arrive at the type-token ratio for the sample.

Validity   In measurement, measuring what you think you are measuring. Validity answers the question "Does this test measure what it is supposed to measure?"

Vocational   Instruction within a specific occupational category. Vocational areas usually are considered to include such things as skilled labor in construction, computer work, automotive, nursing, drafting and graphic design, and electrical trades.

Vocational educator   A teacher who provides instruction within a specific occupational category.

Vocational training   Training offered for a specific vocation in industry, agriculture, or trade, and/or courses in which a learner studies a specific trade for occupation.

Working memory   The ability to retain information while performing a mental operation.

Wraparound service   Multiple services provided as a package to maintain children with emotional and behavioral disorder in their neighborhood schools and communities; multiple services "wrapped around" a student.

Writing prompt   An assessment of writing that includes only a topic sentence or story starter designed to elicit ideas from students.

Zone of proximal development   Vygotsky's theory in which the difficulty level of learning is created by presenting material that is neither too hard nor too easy for students to comprehend.

Name Index